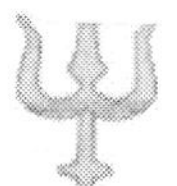

ANCIENT HISTORY OF ARATTA-UKRAINE
20,000 BCE – 1,000 CE

Yuri Shilov

ISBN-13 : 978-1505241624

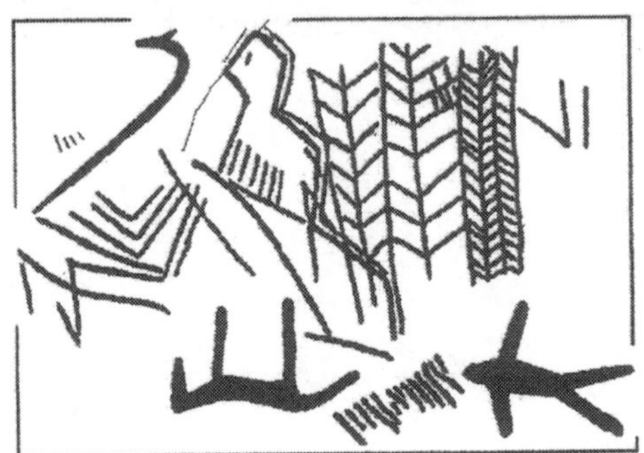

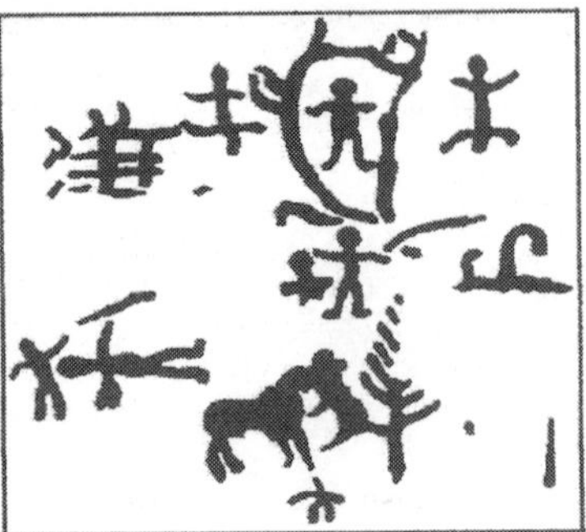

Fig. 1.
Top: Ukrainian folk icon Cossack Mamai, soul of the righteous, with his horse.
Bottom: Aryan sacrificial images of 3rd – 2nd millennia BCE from Stone Grave in the Zaporizhia Region (lower left) and Tash-Air cave in Crimea (lower right), Ukraine. The image from Stone Grave, showing both a horse and a man lying, cruciform, together with that of Cossack Mamai, emphasise the direct continuity of the traditional importance of the horse since the time of Aratta to that of Cossack Ukraine

Cover: Ukrainian ethnography:
Top: 'Cossack Steppe, warning signals' (detail) by Serhii Vasylkivsky (1854-1917).
Bottom left: Contemporary painted Easter eggs and embroidery (both showing traditionally maintained Arattan designs) and a 5th mill. BCE figurine of the Trypillian archaeological culture.
Bottom right: Trypillian pot, c.3,500 BCE, "Ancient Aratta-Ukraine" Museum, Trypillia, Kyiv Region.

ANCIENT HISTORY OF ARATTA-UKRAINE
20,000 BCE – 1,000 CE

Page

Frontispiece 2
Contents 3
Prefaces from the Translators 6
Review 14

Introduction
Ancient History of Aratta-Ukraine : The urgent need for clarification 18
1. History began in Aratta. 19
2. Is the "all-powerful doctrine" of historical-materialism correct? 22
3. The Trinity paradigm – the latest methodology of a world view. 26

Chapter 1
The Chronicle of Shu-Nun 29
1. The beginning of the Great Neolithic Revolution. 30
2. The Circum-Pontic zone. 32
3. The problem of the Indo-European language community. 34

Chapter 2
The Origin of Civilisation 39
1. The beginning of the Great Neolithic Revolution on Ukrainian Territory. 39
2. Buh-Dniester and Sursk-Dnipro archaeological cultures. 40
3. Ethno-historical interpretation of memorials. 42

Chapter 3
Aratta : the most ancient state in the world 47
1. The appearance of the State of Aratta. 48
2. Aratta of the Danube and Dnipro interfluve. 50
3. Persian and Indian Aratta. 61

***Chapter* 4**
Arián : the country of Aryans 66
1. The problem of Aryans in historiography. 67
2. Discovery of the Lower Dnipro ancestral homeland of Aryans. 69
3. Aryans: a historical sketch from Aratta to Bharatta. 72

Chapter 5
The Dark Ages of Europe 81
1. Atlantis, Pelasgia and Hyperborea. 82
2. "Super Northern" Apollo and his followers. 88
3. From Hyperborea to Troy and Delos. 92

Chapter 6
The "Veles book" and its place in ancient literature 97
1. The origin of the Vedas. 98
2. The general root of the Indo-European epos. 104
3. Sources and research problems of the origin of Rus. 109

4. ***Chapter 7***
The Eternal depths of Slavdom 118
1. The times of mammoths. 118
2. The Middle Stone Age. 122
3. The foundation of Aratta. 125

Chapter 8
From Aratta to Hyperborea 130
1. The Arattan stratum of pre-Slavic culture. 131
2. Pre-Slavs and the appearance of Sumer and Oriana. 134
3. The common source of Slavs and Pelasgians. 139

Chapter 9
The Origin of Ukraine and Rus 149
1. Leleges – Lida – Ruthenians. 150
2. Eneti – Veneti. 154
3. What then is Rus? 158

Chapter 10
"The Veles Book" on the origins of Slavs and Rus 163
1. Orissa and Borusia as the general Slo(a)vian homeland. 163
2. The Veles Book on the origin of Rus. 168
3. Social traditions and faith of pre-Kyivan Rus. 172

Chapter 11
Ancient Times 181
1. The Pre-Scythian population of the Northern Black Sea area. 181
2. Were the Cimmerians expelled by Scythians? 191
3. Rus and Bosphorus. 199

Chapter 12
The Emergence of Kyivan[1] Rus 211
1. The Venedi, Ants and Sklavins. 211
2. The establishment of Kyiv, capital of Rus. 220
3. "Great land of ours..." 224

Epilogue
Kyani : Indo-European dynasty 232
1. Kyani, Indo-European dynasty of Oriana-Dandaria. 233
2. The precepts of the Volhvs [Magus-priests]. 241
3. The divine essence of *The Veles Book.* 245

Conclusion & Outlooks
The Origins, Status & Future of Slavic studies 249
1. Upper Palaeolithic (19th – 10th millennium BCE). 252
2. Mesolithic (9th – 7th millennium BCE). 253
3. Neolithic (7th – 4th millennium BCE). 257
4. Eneolithic or Copper-Stone Age (5,400 – 2,200). 260
5. Bronze Age (2,200 – 1,020 BCE). 268
6. Ancient times. 272
7. Early Middle Ages. 277
8. Conclusions and outlooks. 282
References (cited in the Conclusion). 287

References 293

Tables 297
I - XI : Maps and archaeological findings. 298
XII - XIV : Appearance of writing. 320
XV - XVI : Calendars and Sanctuary-observatories. 326
XVII - XIX : Abodes, settlements and kurhans. 330
XX - XXIII : Anthropomorphous kurhans, idols, figurines and masks. 336

XXIV - XXVII : Image of the Foremother. Origin of the ethnic group. 344
XXVIII - XXXI : Weapons, means of transport and ploughs. 345
XXXII - XXXIII : Human sacrifices. The image of the Saviour-Rider. 360
XXXIV - XXXVII : Symbols. 364
XXXVIII - XL : Serpentine archetypes of conception and revival. 372
XLI - XLII : Geo-cosmic connections of the bio-field. 380

Photos 384

Glossary 416

Back Image 469

[1] *The traditional and most commonly used English name for Ukraine's capital city is Kiev, but in 1995 the Ukrainian government adopted Kyiv as the mandatory romanisation for use in legislative and official acts. (Ref. "Resolution of the Ukrainian Commission for Legal Terminology No. 5").

TRANSLATOR'S PREFACES

(1) by Dr. Tim and Lee Hooker (Trishula Translations).

What was Aratta? Where was it and why is that most ancient and obscure civilisation important to us today? This English language translation of Dr. Shilov's masterly study of the "Ancient History of Aratta-Ukraine[1]" will fully answer these questions …

It is often said that history has a habit of repeating itself and that the study of history helps us avoid the mistakes of our past. Perhaps a more positive view would be to say that it ensures we remember the fortunes and glories that our ancestors successfully cultivated and that we should strive to emulate them. Similarly, there seems to be a common misunderstanding that, perhaps due to some natural law, there is an overall tendency for all things to progressively evolve and improve over time. Certainly, in terms of culture and civilisation, the past is commonly considered to have been more basic and primitive compared with what we enjoy today. So when we come across an ancient culture that by many criteria can be deemed to have been more 'civilised' than our present society, we should be humbled and take notice. Such was the ancient civilisation of Aratta. The fact that this was the world's oldest known culture, predating even fabulous Sumer, is especially surprising and worthy of attention, not only by historians, but by everyone who cares about the sustained fortunes of mankind and our environment.

Historical civilisations have always held a fascination for us. One cannot help but admire the skill and building technology inherent in the ancient Egyptians pyramids, or how the Incas and Aztecs were able to fit together colossal, irregular, stone blocks with a precision that we cannot duplicate today. Even the constructions of Neolithic man bear testimony that our ancient ancestors not only had impressive technological skills but also the mathematical understanding to be able to build their megalithic astronomical observatories with exquisite geometric precision – yet there is little, if any, mention of these marvels in British schooling.

It is therefore astonishing to discover that the Sumerian civilisation (4th – 3rd millennium BCE) is not included in the British school curriculum even though historians often specify it to have been the earliest (known) civilisation. All the more strange to find that in 1927 that Master of many ancient languages, Professor L.A. Waddell[2], recorded that "*the whole family of Aryan languages with their written letters is derived from the Phoenician language and script and its parent the Sumerian, and that about fifty per cent of the commonest words in use in the English language today are discovered to be Sumerian in origin with the same word-form, sound and meaning.*"

We had been impressed by the long list of significant achievements that originated in Sumer: metallurgical, ceramic and textile industries; irrigation, navigation and seafaring trade; medical treatments and surgical techniques; music, literature and law codes. All this is known from their mastery of writing and the archaeological discovery of their extensive libraries. We know about their pantheon of gods and mythologies, their extraordinarily detailed astronomy, precision mathematics and even their school curricula. Yet here was a civilisation that seemed to burst 'ready-made' into the world according to archaeologists. Even more surprising is to read that their king lists refer back to the time of the Flood and that the Sumerians had their own historians trying to discover their origins and association with the fabulous land of Aratta from which they believed their civilisation derived. What was Aratta, we wondered?

Several locations across Iran have been tentatively suggested as probable identifications of Aratta. However, when we learned that there was firm evidence of it having been on the territory of modern-day Ukraine we immediately accepted an invitation from Dr. Volodymyr Krasnoholovets to meet Dr. Yuri Shilov (his close friend and author of this book) and to join a small party that they would conduct to various significant Arattan sites across Ukraine. Whilst we recognised that this was one of those 'once-in-a-lifetime' opportunities that you have to seize with both hands, we didn't fully realise how much this would change our lives, nor that we would be devoting much of our time in the following years to translating Shilov's books.

Although we had embarked upon translating Dr. Shilov's works for our own learning about Aratta, it soon became apparent that this knowledge was of such importance that it should be published for accessibility by the wider English-speaking world. To achieve this, we have been assisted by Dr. Krasnoholovets who, line by line, has checked and refined our translations, particularly with regard to ensuring correct spelling of the many Ukrainian place names; historical and mythological characters; ancient cultures and traditional customs – Neolithic, Slavic and Vedic. Although Dr. Krasnoholovets is one of Ukraine's leading Fundamental Physicists, internationally recognised for pioneering a completely new understanding of space and mass, it is his extensive knowledge of ancient cultures, particularly Vedic mythology and customs and his impressive mastery of the English language that have ultimately guided our translation of Dr. Shilov's book to fruition.

Throughout our tour across Ukraine we were on a steep learning curve and roller-coaster of experience. Driving 440km south from Kyiv alongside the mighty Dnipro river, we were plunged into the colourful world of Cossack customs by attending the International Festival of Cossack martial and traditional arts. This annual event always takes place on their sacred island of Khortytsia, in the Dnipro river opposite the city of Zaporizhia. Set in the riverbank woodland, the clamour and colour of their vigorous martial competitive contests, interspersed with political orations, was only matched by a deep recognition of their vibrant reverence for maintaining their ancient Slavic customs that originated in Aratta.

We travelled south another 90km to meet again with the Cossacks at the enormous kurhan of Kuliaba-Mohyla[3]. This unexcavated mound, built in Aryan times about 4,000 - 6,000 years ago, stands well preserved high on the plateau overlooking the Azov lowlands. Whilst Dr. Shilov explained to the assembled Cossacks the historical significance of this man-made hill set amongst the waving steppe grasses, a kobzarist played folk tunes, illustrative of the verse written by the famous 19th century Ukrainian poet, Taras Shevchenko^:-

Wind whiffs blow,
Along the field walks.
On a kurhan sits a kobza-player,
On and on the kobza plays ...

Years later, as we progressed in translating "Ancient History of Aratta-Ukraine", we came to appreciate more deeply the significance of this gathering and the wealth of Vedic and Arattan history that was contained in the many hundreds of kurhans (steppe pyramids) across Ukraine. What Dr. Shilov discovered at the base of Aryan kurhans and has disclosed to mankind were stylised scenes from the ancient *Rigveda* that had been assembled in stone... Our gathering on Kuliaba kurhan ended with Dr. Shilov explaining "Now I will take you to the hill of Stone Grave and show you the engraving of Enlil" [a Sumerian deity].

The State Historical-Antiquarian Museum-Reserve of Stone Grave was located 15km further south, close to Melitopol. This is Ukraine's most significant site of antiquity. According to the Reserve's Director at that time, B. Mykhailov ("Petroglyphs of Stone Grave", 1999) it ranks in international and historical importance beside the Lascaux cave paintings in France, Karpov's cave in Russia, the Nazca lines in the Peruvian desert, Easter Island's giant statues and Britain's Stonehenge, to mention just a few. The massive sandstone slabs making up the hill of Stone Grave contain over 60 grottos, richly inscribed with petroglyphic proto-Sumerian texts that date back at least to 12,000 BCE. Although these grottos are filled with sand to preserve the petroglyphs, many of the texts have been deciphered by Sumerologist Anatoly Kifishin[4]. Amongst the many panels of texts, Kifishin deciphered the names of familiar 'Sumerian deities' such as Enlil, Inanna, Gatumdug, Ninlil and Dumuzi. Here too is the record of the astonishing association between the ancient priest-rulers of Aratta and those of Çatal Höyük, Anatolia, in the times before Sumer and even before the Flood. As we explored Stone Grave we could not help but be awed that this was the sacred sanctuary of the world's earliest state and civilisation whose hidden texts had survived for millennia, since the Golden Era. To have been conducted around Stone Grave by Dr. Shilov himself and to then join Cossacks on top of Stone Grave for their ceremonial

Druidic blessing and closure of their annual Festival was an enormous privilege. At the Museum we bought a copy of Mykhailov's book on Stone Grave[5] for our further enlightenment.

En route back to Kyiv, we detoured to the ancient Dnipro river crossing at Keleberda, near Komsomolsk, Dr. Shilov explained that this remarkable site was the historic location where Arattan and Aryan cultures first faced each other across the expanse of river. A special moment for reflection. We visited Dr. Shilov's own museum at Kremenchuk where we were to bid him farewell with sincere thanks for generously sharing with us his time and prodigious knowledge. The next day, Dr. Krasnoholovets took us to the impressive Aratta-Trypillia Museum at Trypillia, 40km south of Kyiv. Magnificently displayed there were the awesome ceramics of the Trypillian archaeological culture [which so impressed and inspired Picasso] – richly decorated vases and plates that appeared as fresh and intact as though they'd been made yesterday but which were undoubtedly many thousands of years old.

Back in Kyiv, with its bustle of modernity, we were immediately struck by the observation that street market traders were deeply aware of the extraordinary antiquity of their nation's history. Browsing amongst books and maps laid on the trestle tables of street market stalls we noticed a remarkable abundance of Shilov's books. If nothing else, this clearly reflected the value and importance that Ukrainians place upon Dr. Shilov's research and the preservation of their ancient heritage and yet, as far as we were aware, the importance of this history is virtually unknown to the Western public. That was about to dramatically change…

In 2008 the world's first International Exhibition of the Cucuteni-Trypillia Civilisation was hosted by the Vatican; the fact that it was jointly opened by the Presidents of Ukraine, Romania and the Republic of Moldova impressively underlined the importance of this culture in the history of civilisation. This unprecedented display of ceramics, ranging from huge, magnificent, elegantly beautiful vases, richly decorated and brightly coloured, to exquisitely small and delicate figurines, brought a sense of awe and wonder to the thousands of visitors who came from every corner of the globe. The over-riding response from all those who attended was (1) "Why have I not heard anything about this civilisation before now" and (2) "Where can I learn more about it?"

The answer to the first question sadly lies in the nature of the politics which steered study in the direction of historical materialism in 20th century USSR, as eloquently expressed by M. W. Thompson in his Foreword to "Archaeology in the USSR" by A. L. Mongait (1961)[6]. "*It became clear at an early stage after the Revolution that it was difficult, if not impossible, to transform a society, industrialize it, and collectivize its agriculture if the universities, schools, museums etc. were disseminating views that indirectly questioned the necessity for such a transformation. During the first ten years after the Revolution there was relatively little ideological interference with archaeology. [...] With the First Five-year Plan and the general social upheaval of the period after 1928 all that changed. All the forces of Russian society were marshalled to support the new industrial and agricultural transformations. In archaeology recriminations, denunciations, and arrests followed in quick succession. A substantial but uncertain number of museum assistants, university lecturers, and other holders of archaeological posts were arrested. [...] The whole period of the 1930s was marked by attempts to replace the existing terms for periods and divisions into terms corresponding to those of Marx and Engels*"..

Stalin's regime purged Soviet archaeology of the notion that Russian nationalism was not entirely autochthonous even though it had actually experienced historical cultural input from the migrations of a variety of nations and tribes. As Neal Acherson explained[7]: "... *between 1930 and 1934 some 85 per cent of the profession fell victim to the purge. Most of them were deported to Siberian or Asian labour camps or exile. Some were shot or committed suicide when the NKVD came to arrest them. But most ... died in the GULAG. [...] Today migration theory is securely back in Russian and Ukrainian archaeology but it has returned with the tatters of nineteenth century nationalist historiography still flapping around it. [...] Unpopular to this day remain those who argue that the whole balance of Russian history-writing about 'civilisation' and 'barbarism' is skewed, who ask why the steppe nomads and non-Slav cultures encountered by Kievan Rus... must still be dismissed as backward and 'barbaric'".* Indeed, in "*Ancient History of Aratta-Ukraine*" Dr. Shilov freely gives illuminating examples of such political accusations and censorship imposed upon several researchers, himself included.

Fortunately, since the collapse of the USSR in 1991, these studies have received renewed interest, especially within Ukraine. Consequently, answers to the second of the above questions are to be found here in "*Ancient History of Aratta-Ukraine*" where Dr. Shilov addresses the migration of ancient tribes and nations and the effect such cultural interchange has had on the development of civilisation from its archaic inception on the Steppes of Aratta.

It is necessary to recognise, however, that for new ideas or discoveries to gain acceptance it is helpful for the author to present them initially within the recognised framework of the foregoing doctrine and that this is especially important when raised against the politically controlled framework of the old Soviet dogma. Thus, it may help the reader understand the author's structure of "*Ancient History of Aratta-Ukraine*" if we summarise a description by M. W. Thompson (see above) of the Marxist view of archaeology. There, the most important object of study in history was the 'means of production' for it was upon those means that the 'social system' depended. Five systems were characterised which followed one another consecutively: (a) primitive social, (b) slave-holding, (c) feudal, (d) capitalist and (e) socialist systems. Thus, the 'periodisation' of known history into these five stages was one of the main preoccupations of Soviet historians. The first and last systems were classless while classes were the main feature of those in the middle. For the first three stages the words 'prehistoric', 'ancient' and 'medieval' can be substituted for the Marxist 'primitive', 'slave-holding' and 'feudal' without much loss of meaning. The view that primitive society was communal/classless thus gave archaeology a special interest in Soviet eyes. In the 1930s, Engels devised a system of periodisation based on Marx's publication in 1884 of *The Origin of the Family, Private Property, and the State.* He presented five stages: (a) the primitive herd (lower Palaeolithic), (b) primitive community (upper Palaeolithic), (c) matriarchal clan society (Neolithic), (d) patriarchal clan society (Bronze Age), (e) the break-up of tribal society (Iron Age)". Accordingly, in "*Ancient History of Aratta-Ukraine*", Dr. Shilov presents his concluding chapter (in the style of a scientific monograph) sub-divided into sections based on Engel's recognisable systems of Upper Palaeolithic, Mesolithic, Neolithic, Eneolithic, Bronze Age, Ancient times and Early Middle Ages.

In conclusion, this book has been translated in a way which best preserves the timbre of the author's writing style and his cultural milieu. In other words, whilst communicating the vital content in an intelligible fashion to an English-speaking reader, the translation respects the tonal framework of the Russian language which may at times seem somewhat forthright or even brusque but is always unambiguous and sincere. There is a reason for this tone; unlike English, which has become a relatively analytic language over time, losing many of its 'cases', Russian nouns inflect for at least six cases which means the translator into English must instead use prepositions, syntax, diathesis (active/passive verbal voice) to convey meaning. The largely synthetic structure of Slavic language, succeeds, just like Sanskrit, in preserving the integrity of its forms of synthesis. Despite our languages sharing a common linguistic root, it is therefore all the more wonderful that the glorious character and individuality of this Slavic language has been so cherished and preserved.

Finally, Dr. Shilov provided a comprehensive Glossary for the Russian edition of this book. However, for this revised translated edition in the English language, we felt that additional notes would benefit readers, especially many unfamiliar historical, geographical, cultural or folkloric terms, accordingly, with Dr. Shilov's approval, we have enlarged the Glossary, indicating our supplementary terms and notes with an asterisk. Furthermore, where we have felt that a name or term could be explained succinctly, such notes have either been enclosed in square brackets within the main text or provided as endnotes at the end of each chapter. Larger bodies of text within square brackets are the work of the author.

Translators notes.

1. * Notes added by the translators.
2. ^ Glossary term.

3. [ ] Explanatory terms added by the translators.
4. All references to the enumerated boards of *The Veles Book* have been appropriately corrected from the Cyrillic alphabetic order to that of the Latin alphabetic order. Thus, (following Yatsenko B. I., *The Veles Book.* Translation and comments. – Kyiv, 1995; 2001), the order of the Cyrillic lettered boards 'а, б, в, г, д, е, є, ж, з' have been given in the equivalent Latin sequence of 'a, b, c, d, e, f, g, h, i'.

(2) by Dr. Volodymyr Krasnoholovets (Department of Theoretical Physics, National Academy of Sciences, Kyiv).

The study of human society from ancient to contemporary times allows one to distinguish two types of culture. The first type is the culture of communal primary Aratta – a developed country of pre-slavery, pre-capitalist and pre-totalitarian civilisation. This type of culture, even to this day, is still preserved in folk traditions - at least we try to preserve these traditions. Such commune culture rests on a **figurative-intuitive perception of the world**, which, through world archetypes, subconsciously brings culture to an energetic-information field (i.e. the all-powerful, all-seeing god of the Slavic, Indian and Persian Vedas). This culture functions in the mode of "autonomic consciousness". Community efforts strive for connection to this "autonomic consciousness", learning the harmonic behaviour in space with its available subtle laws; the laws of this connection then automatically lead a person through life.

The second type of culture is characterised by secondary, totalitarian civilisations (slave-holding, feudal, capitalist and present day socialist societies); it is a culture that is based on a **logical-analytic world outlook**, which, through the means of rationalism, leads culture towards material manifestations of the real world. Initially humanity gets huge benefits, taking (material) form, but these are not essential. This type of culture has changed over to "voluntary/conscious control", which gradually turned off the mode of "autonomic consciousness". In the end it led to the deadly events of the 20th century: wars, environmental disasters and so on, and whether mankind wants it or not, the movement has begun once more of reverting to the mode of "autonomic consciousness" but this time at the level of up-to-date technology and with a modern outlook.

Thus, the overall development of civilisation can be compared to a 'seasonal' progression through a spiral chain of years. Civilisation (such as Aratta) began in the 'springtime' and after passing through 'seasons' of totalitarianism it cycles on to begin a new 'springtime'. The place of Ukraine in this process, and of Slavic peoples in general, is the completion of those eras (uniting the first and the second turns of civilisation), which initiated the Italian Renaissance, continued through the German Reformation, raised the French [and West European] Enlightenment and strengthened the Anglo-American scientific and technological revolution. Now the neo-Slavic **Pravoslavia**^ begins – an era of a new springtime for humanity, a new "autonomic consciousness", and we call it the process of democratisation, self-administration and so on. From the Slavs, a rebirth of harmonious community has to begin, just as happened during the times of ancient Aratta.

The ancestors of modern Slavs noted the need to honour Prava, because they were *Pravo Slavni*. However, the term *Pravoslavni* was oversimplified in translation to Western languages; the term was tied up with Christianity and reduced to meaning "Orthodox Christianity". But actually the literal translation of *Pravo Slavni* is "those who glorify the law (or that which is right)" (in ancient Ukrainian *slavni* means glory and *pravo* means law, or right). This law, or right, means the laws of Space, which are omnipotent and rule over all on the Earth.

So, now we must ask, 'What is the greatest relevance to us of the ancient Vedic heritage of Aratta?'

Firstly, they had a structured society composed of four varnas: Brahmans (priests who were strategists), Kshatriya (the host of administrators and elders), Vysya (citizens) and

Shudra (those who in their physical and mental development could only be subservient). These four varnas were not hereditary. The Brahmans and Kshatriya selected talented young people and taught them, according to their ability, for service to the community. An important feature of their civilisation was the upbringing of children and adolescents, which concerned not only families but also the entire community.

Secondly, the Brahman-priests of Aratta and Oriana recognised the reality of life in the netherworld – the immortality of the soul: here the soul of the deceased merges with a united field of comprehensive space (a pervasive field), which we now call the bio-field, or the information field. An important, but lost, part of the ancient Arattan society was the practice of cultivating field sensitivity or, as we would say today, extrasensory sensitivity. The whole community was simply a harmonic ensemble. Everyone knew what to do and what not to do in any given case, since deviation from the rules of harmony led to loss for the individual and for society as a whole. People did not sing mournful songs [because the 'negative' concept of mourning did not exist]. In Arattan society everything was subordinated to this pervasive field, they felt the field and tried to perform their actions in harmony with it. After the death of the material body, its soul passed into the pervasive field. This was not a fancy, it was a deep scientific knowledge based on their figurative and intuitive perception of the environment. In particular, they always chose places for sanctuaries which had a strong earth energy. The Arattans developed a cult of the Sun, Moon and other heavenly bodies, as they felt and understood that the behaviour of those bodies significantly affects the course of earthly life. They invented 80% of the symbols we use today. Amongst those symbols, the swastika was important because it characterised the vortex movement of celestial bodies and their consequent effect on the behaviour of biological bodies on the earth (see Figure overleaf).

Thirdly, the culture of Aratta remained practically unchanged for 3000 years! Can we name even one society which existed, for example, for even 10 years, without internal conflicts, wars and quarrels? It was the Arattan community which the Vedas called the Golden Age of mankind.

The siting of their sanctuaries in places with strong earth energy has become particularly meaningful. Geologists point out the presence of terrestrial mantle channels where physical devices behave abnormally. Until recently such phenomena were associated with electromagnetic fields. However, there have been studies by independent researchers which show the existence of fields that are not related to electromagnetism. In this context, probably the most consistent studies of the structure of real space and the physical processes occurring within it, and hence the origin of fundamental physics, have been conducted by the author of this preface, which led to an understanding of the pervasive energy-information field, or bio-field (Figure A).

Mathematical studies by the late mathematician Prof. Michel Bounias and by this author, have shown that the constituent of real physical space is a mosaic cellular structure, from which Mass appears as a deformation of an elementary cell. The motion of any object (from a particle to a macroscopic body) through such a structure of space generates a cloud of excitations, which accompany the object. In quantum mechanics these excitations of space represent a substructure of the so-called particle's wave ψ-function. In macroscopic physics these excitations result in the gravitational potential of the object in question, i.e. Newton's law of universal gravitation. These excitations are carriers of the force of inertia. They carry not only mass but also the fractal properties of the object radiating them. These excitations may overlap and hence create inerton waves. This signifies that everyone emits his or her own inerton waves, and since these waves accompany each individual they may superimpose with those of other individuals. Consequently, we may conclude that the inertons influence our mind, consciousness, activity and life in general. Thoughts and feelings are full components of the universe but whilst 'emotions' receive little scientific attention[8] they may have a physical impact in terms of inerton waves, which are a particular kind of space fractal deformation accompanying the motion of any object. Thus, inertons are real carriers of the pervasive energy-information field, or Bio-field. [In dowsing, for example, it is the inertons emanating from regions within the ground of different mass that influence the consciousness and perception of the dowser.]

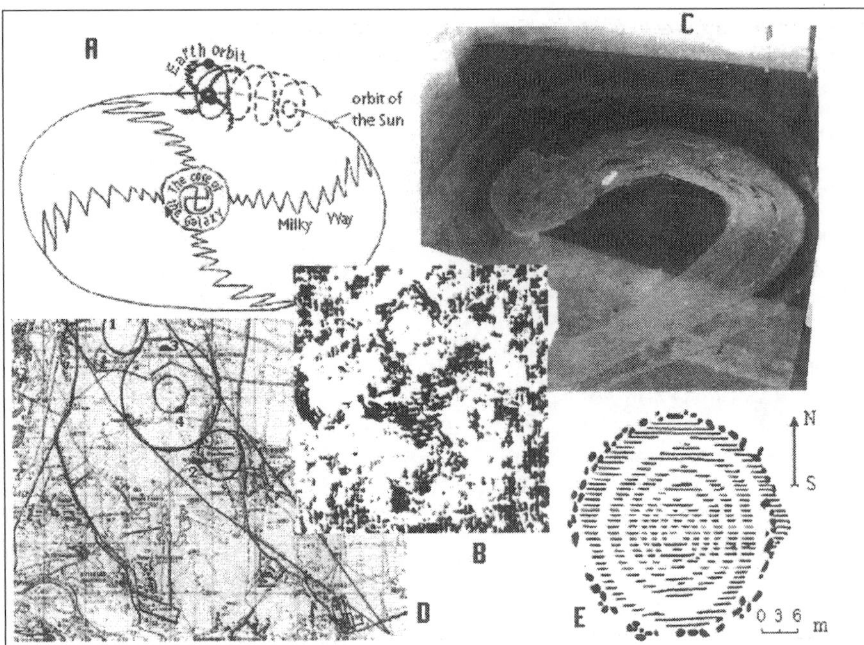

Figure. A: The Earth within energetic flows of the Sun and the Galaxy; B: Photograph of a human embryo in an initial stage of development; C: The pattern (of dust on the still surface of water) reflecting the energetic structure of space over a submerged tomb at the Palazzo Della Cancelleria, Vatican (photo by Yu. Shilov); D: Map of the location of Aratta-Aryan kurhans at Tsehelnia (1), Kormylytsia (2), Stovbuvata (3) and Yerystivska Mohyla (4) between fractures of the Earth's crust and the energetic circles of mantle channels; E: Diagram of magnetic variation at the Rollright Stones (England); at the centre of the circle, the Earth's magnetic field is weakened i.e. the average intensity of the magnetic field of each of the seven turns of the spiral is significantly lower than that occurring outside the stones.

Our community is gradually ripening, being led towards an understanding of the existence of this pervasive information field. In its turn, it seems space [as fundamental consciousness] also tries to help people comprehend the necessity for deviation from a purely logical-analytic world view: in recent years we may observe the appearance of an increasing number of children who relate more closely to the figurative-intuitive world outlook; for them, purely material benefits are secondary.

Thus, it is our challenge: to create a new type of human society in which intellectual and spiritual wealth will coexist in equal rights, and all people will live together in harmony with both the universal material laws and the field laws of Nature. It is the heritage of Aratta that is able to help us approach a new flourishing era of mankind.

References

V. Krasnoholovets, *Inerton fields: Very new ideas on fundamental physics*, American Inst. Phys. Conf. Proc. - December 22, 2010 - Volume **1316**, pp. 244-268. SEARCH FOR FUNDAMENTAL THEORY: The VII International Symposium Honouring French Mathematical Physicist Jean-Pierre Vigier (12-14 July 2010, Imperial College, London), Eds.: R. L. Amoroso, P. Rowlands and S. Jeffers; 10.1063/1.3536437 (Issue Date: 22 December 2010).

M.C. Bounias & V.Krasnoholovets. *Scanning the poorly-known structure of space*: *Part 2.*

Principles of Construction of Physical Space. Kybernetes: The International Journal of Systems & Cybernetics. Volume 32. No7/8, pp. 796-1004 (2003).

---

[1] Previously published as "Основы славянской цивилизации" (*Foundations of Slavic Civilisation*), Part I, *Prehistory of Rus'*, published by Осознание, Москва (Awareness, Moscow). 2008. ISBN: 978-5-98967-006-0.

[2] *A Sumer Aryan Dictionary* (1927) by L.A. Waddell, LL.D, CB, CIE, Fellow of the Royal Anthropological Institute, Fellow of the Linnaean Society, Honorary Correspondent of the Indian Archaeological Survey, Professor of Tibetan (London University).

[3] Near the village of Staro-Bohdanivka in the Melitopol district of the Zaporizhia region.

[4] A. G. Kifishin, *Ancient Sanctuary of Stone Grave. The experience of the decipherment of the Proto-Sumerian archive of XII-III millennia BCE*, Aratta, Kyiv, 2001; 846 pages (in Russian).

[5] B. D. Mykhailov, *The Petroglyphs of Stone Grave*, Dikoe Pole, Zaporizhia & Institut obshchegumanitarnykh issledovanii, 1999; 238 pages (in Russian).

[6] M. W. Thompson, translator's Foreword in *Archaeology in the USSR* by A. L. Mongait (1961), Penguin books, originally published (in 1955) as *Arkheologiya v SSSR*).

[7] *Black Sea* by Neal Acherson (1995), pub. Jonathan Cape, London. ISBN 0-224-04102-9.
Notes : The translator's have added many supplementary, explanatory notes to the author's text. These are provided in the form of asterisked footnotes, but where a name or term could be explained using just one or two words alone, such notes have been enclosed in square brackets within the main text. Where larger bodies of text are encountered in square brackets, they are the work of the author.

[8] Since this preface was written, the academic study of Emotions has received scientific attention e.g. at Oxford Centre for Emotions and Affective Neuroscience and a number of other university departments in the UK now engage in scientific, scholarly research, as well as other academic institutions worldwide.

ANCIENT HISTORY OF ARATTA-UKRAINE
20,000 BCE – 1000 CE

REVIEW

Since the times of Ancient Greece, when Herodotus^ wrote *The Histories,* (484-425 BCE), the population of Eastern Europe was regarded as uncivilised and barbarous, as a consequence of "not having statehood" and "muttering a language, which was not clear to the Hellenic Greeks". This bias was strengthened by Byzantium – the successor of Greece and Rome – which adopted Christian religion and the Bible in 330 CE. The ideology of the slave-holding system was therefore bolstered by means of Church oppression towards *God's servants and Pagans*. Paganism, when translated from Ancient *Rusian* into modern terminology, has a meaning closer to a concept of "unmediated communal belief" and the Christian church, from its very origin, opposed this on the grounds that it was 'not organised, as a religion'. However, because Eastern Slavs (nowadays Ukrainians, Belarusians^ and Russians) accepted Christianity rather later than other European nations (in the period between 988-1386 CE), the religious-political law-makers of its historiography allocated to them the very last place in the hierarchy of civilisation. This is the foundation of the semi-official *Tale of Bygone Years^* written by the Chronicler Nestor, an orthodox monk, in the 12th century.

Until now this has in the main been considered the truth, being endorsed and promoted by the authority of science, based on the above-stated works, rendering service to the political doctrines blessed by the Church. It would still be considered so, had not the revolutions and world wars of the 19th - 20th centuries compelled mankind to seek the true origins and foundations of civilisation - without which its modem status and prospects cannot be understood and, thus, prevent new disasters. Whether it was wanted or not by politicians and church authorities, scholars exceeded the limits of the fatally erroneous doctrines to go more deeply into facts that were older than the times of slave-holding. Nevertheless, by the end of the 2nd millennium CE it transpired that even the doctrine of historical materialism^, «almighty, because it was true» was, in fact, just a continuation of the biblical policy towards "the Apocalypse" (i.e. "the world revolution, in which the Slavic peoples must burn") – and by no means was this the future promised by Marxist-Leninists in their "bright future for all mankind". Alongside this, the reality of a past Golden Age was starting to become apparent – the 'springtime' of a civilisation that had preceded the slave-owning system and which is now returning as a new 'springtime' for this civilisation, precisely in accord with the predictions of Holy Writs that were recorded long before the Bible.

Those writs, together with the pagan priests, were ruthlessly destroyed by the Churches in Europe and the Middle East, and in due course, in America; whilst in India, China, Japan, "the organised world religions" of Semitic origin proved powerless because the "paganism" in those lands tightly preserved its 'springtime' integrity in terms of the harmony of culture, the indivisible syncretism of its social, economic, scientific, philosophical, religious, artistic, political and other defining characteristics. The Colonisers failed to dismember, de-harmonise or revolutionise the cultures of Indo-China, and it will be necessary to study the reason for this.

The Indian Vedas^ became the key source for the study of the problem of pagan, pre-Christian cultural stability. According to the calendars that are recorded in them, (from the middle of the 5th millennium to the end of the 2nd millennium BCE), Brahman^-priests founded this Veda [Knowledge] before the Bible was composed (1st millennium BCE to the beginning of the 1st millennium CE), and those calendars show that, far from the world coming into being around the middle of the 4th millennium BCE, (according to Judaic chronology), the self-creation of the universe, according to Vedic doctrines, took place around 4,320 million years ago – corresponding with modem scientific concepts regarding the genesis of the Solar system and the Earth. This miracle captivated scientists in the UK, France, Germany and Russia from the end of the 18th century. The remarkable closeness of the pre-Christian cultures of Europe and India also came to light, as a result of the migrations of Aryan tribes somewhere around the middle of the 2nd millennium BCE.

Researchers of linguistics, archaeology, ethnography and other experts of historical science, began to search for the source, for the ancestral homeland of the Aryans, and thus of the Vedic culture they had created. In the open spaces of the Eurasian continent from India to Britain, from Scandinavia to Palestine^ there remained no ethno-historical zone that had not been surveyed with reference to the Vedas. The scientists were led by mankind's aspiration for a Saviour doctrine based on the cyclic recurrence of the Golden Age but they were pressured by the political ambitions of national interests involved in religious competition. Even in the circumstances of 20th century catastrophes, the latter two factors remained pre-eminent, and (after the collapse of Marxism-Leninism and the repentance of the Papacy for the sins of the church before mankind) their subsequent agony is rather dangerous. Against the backdrop of those circumstances, the circle of searches gradually narrowed around the Ukrainian Dnipro^ area.

The notorious problem of the Aryans is now speculated by the ideologists of fascism. It is only specialists who are aware that the above-mentioned narrowing of searches for the ancestral homeland of the Aryans was initiated in 1820 by the German geographer K. Ritter who had raised questions regarding the similarity between Indo-Aryans and the (S)indics, or (S)indus [Hindus] of the Kuban area in ancient times. In 1942 the same observation was put forward by the Austrian linguist P. Krechmer who also pointed out that the location of Old Sindic^ (after Herodotus) is in the lower reaches of the Boristhen^. Between these dates there were some additional corresponding publications by British and Polish archaeologists, namely, G. Childe and T. Sulimirski, respectively. In the 1950-70s solving the problem of the location of the Aryan ancestral homeland was approached in works by the Bulgarian V. Georgiev, Ukrainian V. Danylenko^, American M. Gimbutas and Russian O. N. Trubachev. At the end of the 20th century the following monographs appeared: V. Danylenko *Stone Grave* (Kyiv, 1986); V. A. Safronov *Aryan pre-homelands* (Gorkii, 1989); I. F. Kovalev *The social and spiritual culture of the tribes of the Bronze Age (from materials of Left Bank Ukraine)* (Dnipropetrovsk, 1989); Yu. Shilov *Pre-homeland of Aryans* (Kyiv, 1995), *Prehistory of Rus–Ukraine* (Kyiv – Khmelnytsky, 1998); O. N. Trubachev *Indoarica in the Northern Black Sea Area* (Moscow, 1999); B. D. Mykhailov *The petroglyphs of Stone Grave* (Moscow – Zaporizhia, 1999); S. I. Nalyvayko *Secrets of Sanskrit Revealed* (Kyiv, 2000); A. G. Kifishin^ *Ancient sanctuary Stone Grave. The experience of the decipherment of proto-Sumerian archive from XII-III thousand BCE.* (Kyiv, 2001). These books finally solved the question of the ancestral homeland of Aryans in favour of the Ukrainian Dnipro area. A more informed understanding of other Vedic doctrines needs to be tackled, namely those that describe immortality and the reincarnation of the soul, the cyclic nature of life and social foundations, yogic^ teachings etc. In the above monographs and in the present book *Ancient History of Aratta-Ukraine*, a clearer picture emerges of the origin and primary (pre-Indian) formation of Vedantic culture.

During the era between the 20th – 17th millennium BCE, marked by a very cold glaciated period in Europe, there emerged the country of Aratta^, a land well organised by priests [*n.b.* Vedic priests did not intercede in man's natural communion with god], located between the Carpathians and the Caucasus, the Volga region and the Danube area. More than any other country, Aratta developed the practice of mammoth-hunting. The subsequent extinction of those colossal animals and the natural changes that ensued contributed to the demise of Aratta. In the 12th millennium BCE the last keepers of its wisdom deposited their collective knowledge in the caves of Stone Grave (near the present city of Melitopol, in southern Ukraine). A second outstanding cultural zone, created by the successors of Aratta, formed between the Carpathians and the Baltic region in the 9th millennium BCE, from where the resettlement of Eurasians began ("Svidertians" according to the provisional names given by modern linguists and archaeologists) with movements to the Urals and along the north and south coasts of the Black Sea. The last stream of hunter-gatherers turned for the first time to cattle-raising and in due course acquired the most ancient agricultural techniques of the "Afro-Asians", or "Natufians^" of the Middle East. The largest settlement of "pre-Indo-Europeans", or "Tukhunians" (the direct descendants of the "Euroasian-Svidertians") resided near the modern town of Çatal Höyük (in Turkey). The ecological-demographic catastrophe of the mid 7th millennium BCE compelled them to drift closer together, towards their kin, their relatives, the keepers at Stone Grave, who had invented a written language and embarked upon writing the most ancient sacred texts of that time. In 6200±97 BCE, they recorded a written agreement concerning mutual aid, the first such document known to the world. This marked the beginning of the Statehood of Aratta, and – along with it – the beginning of world civilisation.

The State of Aratta was the very embodiment of the "Golden Age" and the foundation of the "Indo-Europeans". The apotheosis of Aratta is presently and principally known under the provisional title of "Trypillian archaeological culture"[1] (named after the village of Trypillia^, below Kyiv[2], from where it was first identified). The people of Sumer^ considered themselves derived from this Aratta, their ancestral homeland from which they had become separated as a direct consequence of "the Flood" – the breakthrough of the Mediterranean Sea into the Black Sea, which had been separate seas up until the mid 4th millennium BCE, just as the Caspian and Aral Seas are still separate today. The well-trodden path of the priest-rulers between Aratta of the Dnipro area and Mesopotamian Sumer became the "Azov-Black Sea line of development of the steppe Eneolithic" (according to V. Danylenko), around which the community of Aryan tribes began to coalesce. The centre of Arián^, (located between the lower reaches of the Dnipro and Kuban until 2nd – 4th centuries CE, known as Dandaka and Dandariya, which means 'Mace-bearing Aria^') was concentrated along the steppe borders of Aratta (that existed there as Art-Arsania until 9th – 11th centuries CE). Its Brahmans founded the Vedic culture, comprising those two branches – Aratta and Arián - which constituted the core of the "Indo-European language community^".

The formation of the Vedas was principally connected with *kurhans* (burial mounds), the prototype of which was the *Kur-gal* or *Kur-an* of Stone Grave (meaning, respectively, 'Large Mountain' and 'Mountain to the sky'). This descriptive name of Kur-gal for Stone Grave is also a metonym of the creator god Enlil^ who was known here, according to its inscriptions, since the 8th – 7th millennium BCE. From him arose the Slavic *Lel^* and Indo-Aryan *Lilith*, as well as the Jewish *Eloi* (separately from the Enlil of Sumerian-Babylonian^-Assyrian^ archives). The most ancient kurhans appeared in the Ukrainian Dnipro area on the expanses of Arián and Oriana^, the coastal arms of Aratta. Oriana (Orissa^, Odissa) of the mid 3rd – 2nd millennium BCE was a permanent centre of considerable migrations eastward and westward: to Bharata (modern India) and to Asia Minor (Paphlagonia^, Troad^ etc.). From Asia Minor's Troad this movement continued into Italian Etruria and the Adriatic, and from there to the Carpathians, the Baltic and Pannonia^.

It was with the reverse movement of a number of migrants, those who began to return to the Dnipro area between the 2nd – 1st millennium BCE, that ethnonyms "Rusy"^ (*Ruses*) and "Slaviane" (*Slavs)* became known for the first time. Nevertheless, their origins go back to at least 2300-1700 BCE for it is only in this period, when the Solar zodiac was headed by the constellation of Taurus, that there could have been a divine pair, Svaroh^ and Dazhboh^-Svarozhych^. Because the historical memory of *The Veles Book* and others extends back 20,000-21,000 years, one has to seek the ethnogenesis of Slavdom in the remote depths of Aratta's formation, not only of its State but also its previous presence as a formation of mammoth hunters. We hope that appropriate republications of the *Veda Slovena^* (viz. the Oryan forerunner of the Indo-Aryan Vedas found in the Rodope mountains during the second half of the 19th century), the above-mentioned *Veles Book^* and *The Hand/ Law of the Empress (of the World)*, i.e. Shu-Nun (as Stone Grave was called in ancient time), will supplement additional data on Slavic history.

Thus, according to the latest scientific studies, [i.e. studies which are not limited by political and religious ideas], the Slavic people (eastern in particular) turn out to be the core of the Aryan and Indo-European people as well as being common to, i.e. the root of, all human civilisation. The latter circumstance draws the problem away from questions of national ambitions and gives it a global importance. It turns out that the "Barbarians" are the ethnocultural genetic fund of the Earth.

Further annihilation of Slavdom, according to Biblical and Semitic scripts, will result in an Apocalypse affecting all humanity. This must not be allowed! Therefore, this book is mapping the core of planetary civilisation, a civilisation which needs to know and protect its greatest sanctuary. The main cultural-chronological range of the work is described above: it corresponds to *The Veles Book* and covers the period from the 20th millennium BCE up to its termination in CE 879 on the eve of the baptism of Rus^. Nevertheless, this book also includes digressions to the present and even forecasts on the future.

For the basis of this book, Yu. Shilov took his widely approved publications of 1990-2002, integrated in the latest (sixth) edition of his *Sources of Slavic Civilisation*[3]. In that book, the 1st part – *Pre-history of Rus* – is a historical summary, based principally on the written memorials of the foundation of Indo-European civilisation leading up to the history of Rus. [The present volume, *Ancient History of Aratta-Ukraine,* is a further revision of that Part I, including this Review, which the author specifically prepared for the present translated edition]. The objectives of the first part of the book are supported by the two ensuing sections, of which Part II – the "*Vedantic Heritage of Ukraine*" – considers the ethnographic reflections of that study, and third part – "*Cosmic Secrets of Kurhans*" – analyses the archaeological evidence from kurhans. At the same time, the materials of the final section allow the reader to penetrate the astrophysical, geophysical and biophysical foundations of the Vedic doctrines (in accordance with the definitions of contemporary science) and this distinctly shows the extreme importance of consulting the Vedas for achieving the transition from our contemporary culture into a future age. In this way a cyclic repetition is revealed towards a Golden Age for humanity in the not so distant future, the pathway to which is presently blocked by "Doomsday" decrees derived from biblical and semitic doctrines. The position of the above-mentioned details of Indo-European doctrines clarifies the "Doomsday" limitations of the slaveholding ideology, and totalitarian ideology derived from it, in the circumstances of which appeared the Bible, *The Communist Party Manifesto*, *State and Revolution* and others, which still continue to function.

This book, as described above, has a wonderfully reliable scientific structure. The *Ancient History of Aratta-Ukraine* is directed to all members of society, not only to scientists, but also artists, churchmen and politicians and to anyone who is concerned for the fate of global civilisation. The author, Dr. Yu. Shilov, has tried to remove all educational, ageist, religious, political and ethnic limitations to the understanding of this book, which has been artistically and copiously illustrated. Amongst those who prepared the book for publication the author particularly wishes to mention A. S. Poleshchuk (design concept) and P. L. Korniyenko (illustrations).

We hope that *Ancient History of Aratta-Ukraine* will worthily serve the grand ideal of the reconciliation of nations for the transition of universal civilisation to a new cycle in its endless development.

M. I. SENCHENKO
Professor of the United Nations,
International Academy of Information

---

[1] This same culture was also found in Romania where it became known as the Cucuteni culture. These cultures are now designated collectively as the Cucuteni-Trypillian culture.

[2] In 1995 the Ukrainian government adopted Kyiv as the mandatory city name for use in legislative and official acts. (Ref. "Resolution of the Ukrainian Commission for Legal Terminology No. 5").

[3] *Sources of Slavic Civilisation* by Yuri Shilov, 2008, Moscow; ISBN: 978-5-98967-006-0. Part I, *Pre-history of Rus,* is presented here, with minor additions and revisions, under the title of *Ancient History of Aratta-Ukraine*. Parts II, *The Vedantic Heritage of Ukraine,* & III, *Cosmic Secrets of Kurhans,* are currently available only in Russian but are in the process of being translated to English.

ANCIENT HISTORY OF ARATTA-UKRAINE: THE URGENT NEED FOR CLARIFICATION

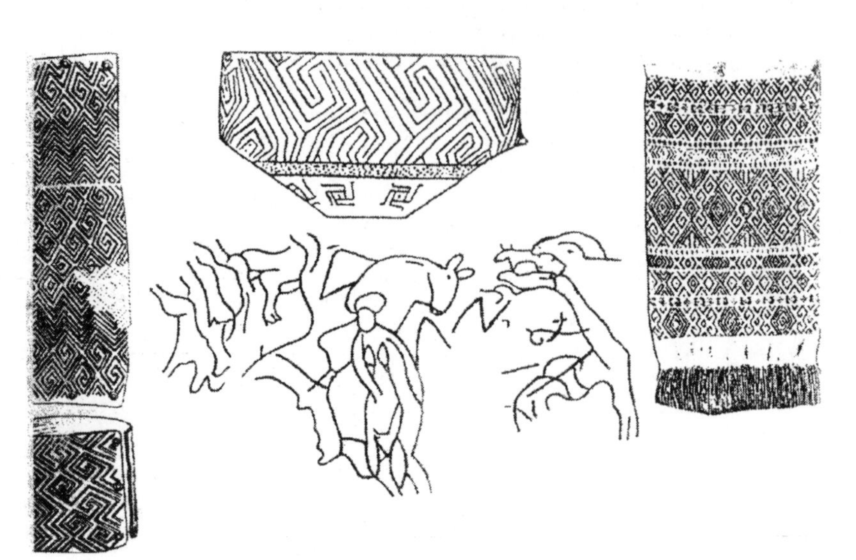

Fig. 2 : **Aboriginal ornaments of the Indo-Europeans**. A bracelet of mammoth hunters (left) from sites at Mizyn (Ukraine), compared to a modern towel (right). Upper centre – a bowl, 6th millennium BCE, from Can Hasan (Anatolia) and (below) an image, 12th – 10th millennium BCE ,from Stone Grave (Dnipro area).

INTRODUCTION

History, the teacher of life, is also the teacher of our ancestry. History consists of a corpus of facts derived from sources which remain as just 'sources' to science since facts are simply *de facto* expressions of historical standpoints/opinions. The chronologies and inter-relationships between these facts form the foundations of scientific theories and political ideologies. The challenge of theories developed from these facts and sources is to produce a true understanding of the origins, principles, motivating forces and perspectives of the historical process. This places an enormous responsibility on the shoulders of historians towards mankind – for both the scientific reliability of the sources and for their factual interpretation. The grandiose ideologies of the twentieth century and preceding centuries grew from precisely this foundation.

This book synthesises sources and hypotheses from the mid-19th century which began to uncover a fundamentally new quality of scientific comprehension, not only of native history but of civilisation in general; not only of Ukrainians and Slavs but also of Indo-Europeans and the whole of humanity. The broader community would remain unaware that the smooth development of this national and international comprehension was periodically disrupted because its development required unique specialists, historians with a wide range of interests and a precise world outlook, together with honest and courageous people who were freely able to conduct their research without hindrance.

It is from this perspective that *Ancient History of Aratta-Ukraine* has been created – it is intended not only for scientists but also for a more general readership. In this book, the mystery of the origin of civilisation is revealed in the greatest depth possible for these times and the disclosures offer a framework for the latest theories concerning the foundations, movements and perspectives of historical evolution.

1. **History began in Aratta.**

Expert historians understand history as the written past of mankind i.e. the pre-literate past comes before the historical period. It is also believed that the emergence of writing is one of the most obvious manifestations of 'civilisation', namely, statehood.

The 1930's saw the beginning of large-scale archaeological excavations in Mesopotamia with the finding of "clay tablets" that pre-dated the Bible. There is a saying that "History began in Sumer" with this history dating to the end of the 4th millennium BCE, or less than two and a half millennia after the formation of the World, according to the Bible...

Fig. 3: **Ornaments** from burials at the settlement of Sunhir (near Vladimir), 30th–24th millennia BCE, a symbolism which persists in Orthodoxy today.

However, these same clay tablets disclose that the Sumerians deduced themselves from a certain Aratta... and since 1963, clay tablets with pre-Sumerian letters began to be found in Romania, in Bulgaria and then in Ukraine^. The content of these inscriptions, together with the remains of the first cities found on Earth, revealed evidence that the State of Aratta was already in existence in the Danube valley by the 7th millennium BCE.

Between the middle of the 6th - 5th millennium BCE, the centre of Aratta was displaced to the region between the Danube and Dnipro rivers where it is now known by the conditional scientific title of the "Cucuteni-Trypillian^ archaeological culture". Here, mainly in the territory of the modern Cherkasy region, the traditions of Aratta lasted until the time of Kyivan Rus^ whose structure, as verified by Arabian travellers of the 9th – 11th centuries, included the princedom of Arsania with its capital Arta. Its predecessor (i.e. Aratta) was probably regarded by Old Persians as their earthly paradise of Arta and by Hindus as their state of Bharata^, so-named in its honour. (There was also a province named Aratta in India). This occurred around mid-2nd millennium BCE when tribes of so-called Indo-Iranians (although they were, more correctly, Aryans by autonym) settled on the banks of the Sind^ river (which over time became named as it is still named, the Dnipro river).

The basic inscriptions of Aratta (from the 12th – 8th – 3rd millennium BCE) were preserved in the numerous grotto-sanctuaries of Stone Grave, the most ancient mytho-historical chronicle in existence in the world, situated beside the Molochna^ river (River Milk), which flows through the Zaporozhye region along the left bank of the Dnipro river. Between the 1930's and 1980's, these illustrative inscriptions were discovered by the archaeologists O. N. Bader, M. I. Rudynsky, V. M. Danylenko and B. D. Mykhailov. According to the definitions of A. G. Kifishin (linguist-Sumerologist) and Yu. A. Shilov, (historian, archaeologist and Vedic scholar), this unique chronicle recorded numerous expeditions by pagan priests travelling between Mesopotamian Sumer and Aratta in the Dniester-Dnipro area.

It is therefore already possible to consider the claim, "History began in Aratta", that is, it began on the present territory of Ukraine. The five thousand year era from its start in the Dnipro area until Cimmerian^-Scythian^ times, as described by Herodotus the Ancient Greek historian, has to be given worthwhile consideration as the pre-history of Ukraine.

In the meantime, academic science is in no rush to consider either these historical sources or their conclusions. In the early 1960's, the Romanian archaeologist N. Vlassa was stripped of his academic rank for discovering that the 6th millennium BCE Tartaria tablets bore written script: that discovery contradicted to a considerable degree the directives of "historical materialism" - with regard to the occurrence of writing in the slaveholding states of Mesopotamia at the end of the 4th millennium BCE - which dictated that it certainly could be no older than the pre-class societies of the Danube area. Besides depriving academician N. Vlassa of his rank, top level historical-materialist functionaries also chose to ignore a 1965 publication by the outstanding Sumerologist, A. Falkenstein, who confirmed the Tartaria script as writing and moreover defined it as proto-Sumerian. During 1995-1996, statements by M. Yu. Videyko (in the journal *Archaeology*, No. 2, Institute of Archaeology, National

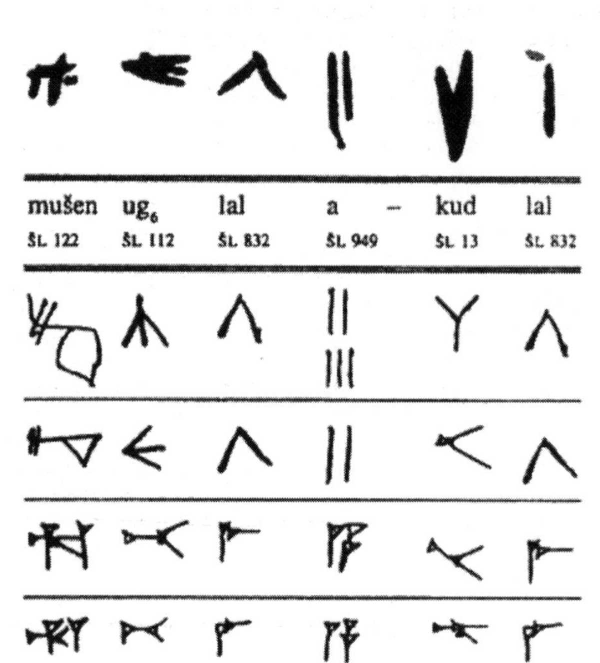

Fig. 4: **Proto-Sumerian writing at Stone Grave** (top). A sample of their decipherment by A. G. Kifishin, by means of comparison with Sumerian script.

Academy of Sciences of Ukraine), completely ignored the above incident and labelled the ingenious Sumerologist A. G. Kifishin, a 'falsifier' for his initial reading of inscriptions from the Danube and Dnipro area as proto-Sumerian. In another example, V. Ya. Pervukhin, in the encyclopaedic book, *Slavs* (1997), argued that "the first evidence of Slavs comes from foreign authors of the 6th century". The author evidently clings to the same unshakeable position as the monk Nestor, the Rusy chronicler. The researches of "heretical" Slavists of the 12th – 17th centuries are completely ignored as are the sacred books of the Slavs with their historical memories of pre-Sumerian and even pre-Arattan times [i.e. prior to the Statehood of Aratta].

It just so happens that new facts emerging during 19th – 20th centuries, concerning the origins and foundations of civilisation (i.e. statehood), were principally compiled by archaeologists and rather less so by linguists, ethnologists etc. so archaeology increasingly began to take responsibility for this sector of history. Nevertheless, this discipline of historical science has no right to impose its conclusions on society as final. My own archaeological conclusions are no more than its workshop. Public confidence in the stature of archaeology (gained through the disclosure of events, phenomena and laws of history) should not be so great that it sets itself apart, it should merge with ethnography, anthropology, linguistics and other historical disciplines. This is how it is in the West. However, in the countries of the former USSR where the reigning ideology was one of "historical materialism", the archaeologists received a monopoly from the Party and totalitarian government for the interpretation of sources of history and civilisation in exchange for the commitment of scholars to adjust their findings in line with the "all powerful, because it is true" Marxist-Leninist doctrine… Did historians then cease to work and to think as before in the circumstances of independent Ukraine? Do we have a qualitative basis to depict a historical portrait of the state to which scientists, politicians and artists must align and work accordingly? No! We don't.

The Institute of Archaeology of the Ukrainian SSR (re-named since 1992 as the

Institute of Archaeology of National Academy of Sciences of Ukraine), not only concealed but also destroyed facts, developments and researches over the decades. The reasons for this and the ways in which it happened were outlined in detail in the documentary novel *Sanctuaries* by Yuri Shilov (Kyiv, 2001). The matter cannot simply be ascribed to "Soviet domination by Russia". The Slovenian historian J. Rugel remarks (in the epilogue to the book *The Veneti: Slavic Ancestors* by P. V. Tulaev, Moscow, 2000), that in his country "the practice of 'buying souls', especially those of academics, has become an effective tool of an inherently totalitarian state policy... which formed back in the 19th century... Therefore, a corrupt view on the origin and history of Slavs took root in education... Until recently, German explanations satisfied the West, which willingly fights for human rights but not for the rights of nations… A breakthrough in a new understanding of Central European history in the cultural environment of the West is slow, but inevitable. In Eastern Europe this breakthrough is faster, aided in particular by the idea of Slavic reciprocity" and, I would add, in particular by historians of Ukraine and Russia - although not all of them!

Let us look, for example, at an interview by P. P. Tolochko for the Ukrainian newspaper *Day* on 11th August 1998; the interview went under the expressive title: *It is impossible to depart from the truth of history for the sake of politics and political lobbying.* Prof. Tolochko, Director of the Institute of Archaeology, National Academy of Sciences Ukraine, emphasises: "Despite the active myth-making of our time (assertions made by only some authors on the subject of Ukrainian Aryans), I think that as a way to end the 20th century, this has no future. With these myths we will only encourage an attitude of ironic-condescension towards us from the world. We need to grow up". At the end of 2000, when the Institute of Archaeology published *The Ethnic History of Ancient Ukraine* and the third volume of the *Ancient History of Ukraine*, Professor Tolochko also said (in the newspaper *The Weekly Mirror*, 27th January 2001): "After Ukraine gained independence, we moved away from the hateful indoctrination of social, ideological Party disciplines but we have run into the no less dangerous extreme of raking up everything that is bad and instantly declaring it as Ukrainian history. Even the Trypillian culture has become part of it already…"

This attitude [of exclusion] may be seen as acceptable to some people but not to an educated person, especially not an academician. Firstly, as with the case of V. Pervukhin, there is a tendency to specify a 'cut-off' date for the history of Slavs and Slavic studies. Secondly, if some mathematicians and physicists since the 1930's began to notice the impossibility of furthering the development of natural sciences by continuing to exclude a dialectical return to an intuitive-mythological perception of the ancestors in the Humanities, then the historian P. Tolochko must be aware of that.

In defence of the "scientific approach" of P. Tolochko, it can only be said that "from a position of common sense" (i.e. at an elementary level), he imputes that myth creation is identified with nonsense. For the specialist, this is unacceptable because myth creation is a function of the visual intuitive perception of the world, inherent to primary culture (in time, folk culture) and also, over time, for all world arts... common sense ought to tell the academician that no flags, emblems, anthems nor states can exist without myths and not only now "at the end of the 20th century" but also when considering the next millennium as well.

However, let us deviate from the cultural educational programmes to look at what actually motivates the aspirations of the best Ukrainian historians and archaeologists to understand the latest discoveries about the ancestral roots of our nation and statehood.

Here is the position of the world famous expert in Slavic archaeology and history – the Russian academician B. A. Rybakov, whom P. Tolochko regards as his teacher: "The ancestors of the Aryans lived in the Dnipro area... There is every reason to suppose that the *Rigveda*^ arose on the banks of the Dnipro river. In Rusy chronicles the word "*ostantsy*" is mentioned, which means '*those who remained*' [still lived along the banks of the Dnipro river], i.e. the 'remainders' of those whose tribes had gone to India. My call to Ukrainians is this: start learning Sanskrit [the language of the Indo-Aryan *Rigveda*], for its language signs were found amongst your tribes and they will restore the connection between times". These thoughts by B. A. Rybakov, quoted from his foreword to a book *The Appeal to Slavs* (Moscow, 1998) by N. I. Kikeshev, are based on the research of the academicians O. N.

Trubachev and Yu. A. Shilov; they particularly reflect the positive review by the linguist Trubachev, on the works of the archaeologist Shilov in the journal *Questions of Linguistics*, No. 3 (1996, Moscow).

The All-Slavic Council read out its Programme at the International Tribune of the VII All-Slavic Congress (Prague, 2-5 May 1998). It was published in an almanac of the same name (Moscow, 1998). The document begins with these words: "The Slavic world has an ancient history. The ancestral period goes back to pre-Aratta – the most ancient state on Earth... Having been affirmed at 6200 BCE, it became the primary core of the Indo-European peoples... There is evidence for this: beginning in the 7th millennium BCE, the chronicle of our civilisation was traced on the walls at Stone Grave, located near the city of Melitopol in present day south-eastern Ukraine".

Despite the apprehensions of academician P. Tolochko, a mood of ironic-condescension did not arise amongst listeners from either Ukrainian or Russian delegations who had joined forces to create such a document. Instead there was close attention and concerned hope for an in-depth review of not only Slavic but also of all human civilisation worldwide and a review of its foundations with the aim of understanding its status and identifying its prospects. There was a similar reaction by the delegates at the international conference concerning research on the subject of Troy^ which took place in Moscow in March, 1997. There, A. G. Kifishin, B. D. Mykhailov and Yu. A. Shilov presented lectures on Arattan-Sumerian connections, the chronicle of Stone Grave and the concordance of finds in kurhans^ of the Ukrainian Dnipro area with the Aryan-Indian *Rigveda*.

Meanwhile, the journal *Archaeology* (The Institute of Archaeology, Nat. Acad. Sci. of Ukraine), No. 4 (1992), No. 2 (1995) and No. 2 (1996) has done everything possible to discredit the researchers mentioned above. In the documentary story *Victory!* by Yu. Shilov, there is a scene describing a departmental meeting at the Institute in which a scientist condemns the publications *Ancestral Homeland of the Aryans* and *The Vedic Heritage of Ukraine...* calling B. Rybakov and O. Trubachev "chauvinists"... It has to be asked: Why is it that Russian academicians can dignify the history of Ukraine but the Institute of Archaeology of National Academy of Science of Ukraine, headed by academician P. Tolochko, humiliates it? From what we have been told, only one answer suggests itself: the professional, moral and intellectual level of those named "chauvinists" significantly exceeds that of those "sincere Ukrainians" from the Institute of Archaeology of the National Academy of Sciences of Ukraine.

This state of affairs must change, fast, starting with their attitude to historical sources and primarily, to the issue of Aratta.

2. Is the "all-powerful doctrine" of historical materialism correct?

Fig. 5 : **Cross-shaped decorations from Cimmerian burials** at the village of Zolne (Crimea).

The reason behind the backlog of the latest discoveries made in academic science from historical sources (which continued, despite the official line of the Institute of Archaeology, National Academy of Sciences of Ukraine, as shown above) lies in the evil perpetuation of the traditional methodology of "historical materialism". In the meantime, the popular expression "the doctrine of historical materialism is all powerful, because it is true" is no less erroneous than "history began in Sumer". Both are wrong because they do not know [or show] the true onset of history nor, significantly, the origins of civilisation. Most importantly, Historical Materialism fails to grasp the essence of history and is confused in its content.

Any phenomena – including doctrines of the historical development of mankind – have form, content and substance. Formal theory states: "Over all, there is Divine will, as the king has so agreed it, so the heroes have carried it out". Historical materialism has disclosed the contents of history in terms of its social and economic pillars, the presence of classes, contradictions between them etc. According to the Marxist-Leninist doctrine of historical materialism, the pre-historic period (i.e. the pre-literate period) was characterised by a pre-class structure, i.e. it was primitive-communist ('-communal' or '-public', in the Russian sense as opposed to the French sense). When the systems of ancient *Homo sapiens* started to collapse, that heralded a period of military democracy complete with dissensions and wars. Mankind then found a way out of this bloody chaos via state order (civilisation), primarily in slaveholding – an exploitative system. Since then, all class formations are marked by struggle and tension, which are replaced by social and economic harmony in a new communistic, already classless society... Because this scheme only considers the person as a manufacturer and a social being without taking into account his birth, death and spiritual world (which is a function of the fundamental field principle of the material world, reduced by Marxist-Leninism to its material manifestations), it does not fulfil the essentials of history.

The essential theory of the historical development of mankind, as well as the necessary amendments to historical materialist doctrine, is disclosed for the first time in this book.

It is wonderful that works by Karamzin, Kostomarov, Hrushevsky and other classics of historical science of past centuries are now being re-issued even though, in many respects, their researches have become outdated especially in terms of the study of sources as well as in understanding the origins, foundations and outlook of the historical process.

The ancestral written languages of Sumer and particularly of Aratta, were discovered by scientists many years after the death of the fore-mentioned researchers and their contemporaries [who cannot be blamed for their failure to include such information]. For the same reason, Marx, Engels and Lenin – the founders of historical materialism – were not so much guilty as ignorant. However, the historical materialist ideology of totalitarianism is guilty because of its distortion and concealment of facts and for the persecution of progressive scientists.

Tragedy was to shape the destiny of the outstandingly creative Ukrainian archaeologist V. M. Danylenko (1913-1982), a member of the Institute of Archaeology of the Academy of Sciences of USSR. This honoured leading intelligence officer, doctor of historical sciences, was not permitted to publish his monograph completed in 1965 entitled *The Cosmogony of Primitive Society*. The book was devoted to a consideration of the

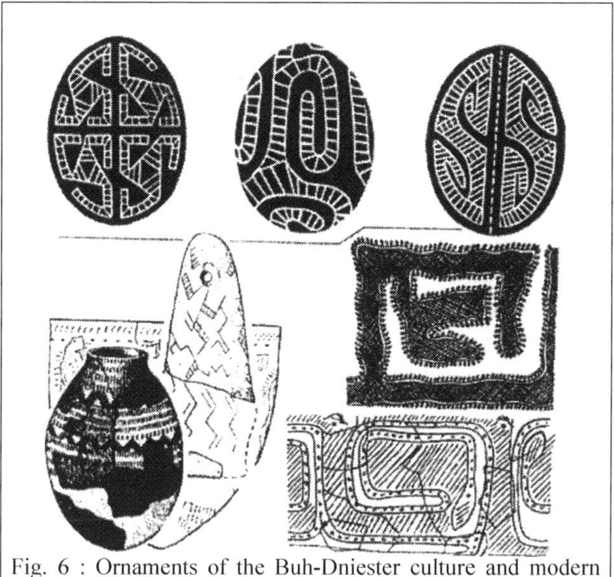

Fig. 6 : Ornaments of the Buh-Dniester culture and modern hand-painted eggs of Ukraine.

spiritual world of the Buh^-Dniester^ culture^, which preceded the Trypillian culture. It was only possible to publish this book in 1997-1999... Danylenko was also unable to publish invaluable details of the Sumerian clay tablets from the Volyn region of Ukraine, nor the autobiographies of the first princes of Rus, written in mysterious "symbols and cuts" from pre-Christian times; these historical finds and their photographs were stolen (possibly even destroyed) after the death of the researcher.

Colleagues of V. N. Danylenko, despite knowing of the inscriptions of the 7th – 3rd millennium BCE from Stone Grave and other locations, refused to recognise them as writing on the grounds that, according to Marxist 'logic', a written language cannot precede statehood and statehood was not introduced to the Ukrainian territory (according to Marxism) until the time of the slaveholding Greeks in 700-500 BCE and subsequent centuries. On the basis of such politicised thinking, there was no acknowledgement of the cities of the Trypillian archaeological culture (Aratta) that were revealed in the 1960's by pilot-surveyor K. V. Shishkin and archaeologist M. M. Shmahly, a pupil of Danylenko...

In view of the above, it is easy to see why the study of ancestral written language and the pre-history of Ukraine in general (in the 1960's -1980's) was not initially the work of experts but of amateurs (amongst whom there were of course talented, though unqualified, researchers such as M. Z. Susloparov and A. P. Znoyko)...

It is hard to overcome traditions and attitudes, to understand truths...

It should be reiterated and clearly understood that the authors of the *Bible* and, particularly, *The Histories* of Herodotus or the *Tale of Bygone Years* by Nestor^ the Chronicler do not reach back any further than to the times of slaveholding. Aratta however, is the apotheosis of pre-class (communal) times. Historical materialism, which until now for good reason is regarded as the most fundamental doctrine of historical science, does not have the scope to recognise (so unknown to its founders and incomprehensible to its apologists) the Arattan type of states, even though they operated with such concepts as "primitive communism" and a "communal system". We will keep returning to this problem.

Let us consider the modern state of academic historical science, which allegedly disowns Marxist-Leninist methodology. Did it produce a new science?

Not for the first time, a new scientific concept which aimed to reach the standard of a monograph was promulgated by a doctor of historic sciences, L. L. Zaliznyak, in *Essays on the Ancient History of Ukraine* (Kyiv, 1994), a member of the Institute of Archaeology, Nat. Acad. Sci. of Ukraine, and the Institute of Ukrainian Studies at the Taras Shevchenko Kyiv National University. In this work, just as during Soviet times, the history of Ukrainians is said to start after the time of the old state of Kyivan Rus, and the history of Slavs is said to start after late Roman times; the author's "novelty" resides in the cursing of Moscals [i.e. Muscovites (or Moscowians), known in the modern West as Russians] along with Marxist-Leninism and in addition, (after juggling certain historiographic facts) the author presents the archaeological Trypillian culture, (the most famous apotheosis of the state of Aratta) as pre-Semitic... Having suffered withering criticism in the press and scholarly literature from Shilov, Zaliznyak's next publications concerning Trypillian culture attempted to conceal his ideological position but in fact, he did not change his position at all. Was he fulfilling someone's political directive?

For objectivity and thoroughness, the greatest such claim comes from collective editions of this same Institute of Archaeology, Nat. Acad. Sci. Ukraine: *The Ancient History of Ukraine* published in two volumes (Kyiv, 1994-1995) and *General History of the State*, volume 1 (Kyiv, 1997), which are, respectively, textbooks for senior schools and academics. Here, the "patriotism" of the type discussed above is reduced but with regard to the origin of the Slavs (Ukrainians, in particular) and the formation of their state being not earlier than Kyivan Rus of the 9th century, the books say practically the same. They say that the Trypillian culture has "no clear ethnographic features" but as to which ethnic group, nation, or at least pre-nation they belonged, no words can be found; nevertheless, they claim they were not Indo-Europeans (so, this means they were Semites?). The social order of Trypillia, with its "proto-cities" covering an area up to 450 hectares, with thousands of sophisticated two-storied houses etc., has been determined as being primitive-communal where "conditions were ripe for a material segregation and the isolation of a clan elite, in particular chiefs". It is hard to see precisely how, from these and similar definitions, these archaeologists of modern Ukraine wished to overcome the "settled methodological and historiographic schemes" of historical materialism.

At the same time, the Institute of Archaeology of Nat. Acad. Sci. of Ukraine is more active in holding back, or holding up to shame, "the latest enthusiasm of the public" [for Trypillian facts]. Separate specialists who, in their studies, direct themselves to public demand and enthusiasm are accused of "constructing this or that concept whilst not always strictly adhering to the facts of their science". But this is very good indeed! As already shown, archaeologists must be guided not only by the needs of their branch of science but by the whole of historic science in general.

Let us look at the literature recommended to students for the study of the ancient history of Ukraine. There is a prevailing impression that this is the monopoly of archaeologists alone since in the list of literature there are no publications by ethnographers, linguists and experts in fine art. Moreover, not all archaeologists are presented there. One can afford to be indulgent to the first textbooks produced by a newly-independent Ukraine in 1994-1995 but the first volume of the academic compendium of Ukrainian history published in 1997 did not even refer to the fundamental monographs (which disclose the place of Ukraine amongst other countries in the remote past), such as *Cosmology of Primitive Society* by V. M. Danylenko (Kyiv, 1965; Kyiv, Moscow, 1997), *Petroglyphs of Stone Grave in Ukraine* by B. D. Mykhailov (Zaporozhye, 1994) and *Pre-Homeland of the Aryans* by Yu. A. Shilov (Kyiv, 1995); there is no mention of the extremely important articles of 1990-1996 by Sumerologist A. G. Kifishin nor by S. I. Nalyvayko et al, a specialist in Indian culture. In the light of what has already been said, it is hardly surprising that the innovative hypotheses of these authors were disregarded, however, it is unforgivable to silently pass over the principal historiographic facts they present such as the Proto-Sumerian writings of Stone Grave; the calendars and observatories of steppe kurhans and other sanctuaries; the appearance of myths and rituals related to the Sumerians, Greeks, Hindus and Slavs; testimonies to the origin of the "Trypillians" as the oldest state in the world and, moreover, the Indo-European state of Aratta; the key value of kurhans of the Ukrainian Dnipro area to the solution of the problem of locating the ancestral homeland of Aryan tribes and the formation of the Vedas... It is important that all of these rigorous studies were carried out on the basis of comparing archaeological data with that of ethnography, linguistics and also the comparison of works of our own historians with the works of foreign colleagues. For Czechs, Italians, French, British and other European nations the presence, for example, of calendar observatories and figurative structures in kurhans has been irrefutable for at least a century and has been recorded in encyclopaedias. So why are these facts ignored in Ukraine? Why are the 27-year long efforts of Shilov in the halls of the Institute of Archaeology of the Nat. Acad. Sci. of Ukraine to remove this discrepancy, by conducting a proper examination of native kurhans in the named volume, only mentioned in passing and without any reference to the author's works? How was it possible to pass this over in silence and even more so in the textbook *The Archaeological Researches of Kurhans* by M. A. Chmykhov, Yu. A. Shilov, and P. L. Kornienko (Kyiv, 1986, 1989)? All of this, together with the fact that kurhans were "the pyramids of the Ukrainian steppes", the national sanctuaries of Ukraine!..

So, here is a nation waiting impatiently for qualitative studies by scientists. Unfortunately, owing to the absence of such studies, people began to reconstruct their history for themselves, unprofessionally (via the heads and hands of amateurs). That is the real reason behind a desecration of reality! The main fault lies with the above-mentioned specialists and other humanity faculties of the Academy of Science of Ukraine. These institutions have not yet overcome, as indicated earlier, the methodology of historical materialism aimed at igniting world revolution, the doomed fuel of which must become the Slavic nations (according to Marx, Engels, Trotsky, Lenin and so on). The Slovenian scholar, Just Rugel, directly criticised the Marxist regime with the observation that: "The cultivation of an inferiority complex about their supposedly poor history, especially by means of schooling for the younger generation, exposed the intention [of the regime] to lead the Slovenes into self-destruction".

The matter, therefore, is extremely urgent and serious! Throughout the 20th

century there has been a growing urgency to reconsider the scientific, philosophical, religious and political concepts underpinning the origin, foundation and prospect of worldwide civilisation. Unprejudiced specialists are needed for such a revision, ones who could investigate a vast quantity of sources which, although known, are but poorly understood by researchers with historical materialist training. Therefore, the principal purpose of this book is to offer assistance to the formation of an understanding of history within the society from which a new generation of scientists and historians has to grow.

3. The Trinity^ paradigm – the latest methodology of a world view.

Fig. 7 : **A pagan cross of the time of the baptism of Rus** (according to B.A.Rybakov).

If historical science seems to be thoroughly armed with the methodology of historical materialism but is still unequal to an adequate disclosure of the development of mankind, would it be any better to trust religious doctrines? According to biblical publications, the Almighty created the Universe with the Earth and mankind sometime between 5509-3760 BCE (from various calculations) but what then should be done with the indisputable data derived from astronomy, geology and archaeology? The tendency is to ignore them (see, for example, studies by the famous Ukrainian authors, the political scientists Yu. Kanygin and Z. Tkachuk, in *The Ukrainian Dream* (Kyiv, 1996), who are honoured in its laudatory foreword by the country's ex-President L. Kravchuk supported by V. Medvedchuk, H. Surkis [1], by doctors of science and others).

The well-known modern thinker, P. A. Kharchenko, founder of the Ukrainian International Academy of Original Ideas, has proposed an effective solution: a return to the ideology inherent to pre-class societies and which has until now been preserved in the Brahmanic doctrines of India (albeit a return at a new level of the spiral of development, in a new quality of theory and practice). The Trinity is typical of such ideology, a tri-unity of science, philosophy and religion (instead of being dualist, in dual contention, as in historical materialism).

Let us dwell on the concept of TRI-UNITY as recorded in *The Veles Book* (cited here, as later, in the translation from ancient Russian by B. I. Yatsenko (Kyiv, 1995, 2001)).

According to that concept, the creator of TRI-UNITY is recognised as Dazhboh (the zodiacal constellation of Taurus), who is the son of God Svaroh (the solar zodiac). This concept was developed during 2300-1700 BCE, the time when a corresponding calendar-celestial situation co-existed. This is also the time when insights arose into the co-relationships between the Celestial, Earthly and Nether worlds – Prava^, Yava^ and Nava^, respectively (*The Veles Book*, board 1):

In vain we recalled our valiant old times,
Since where we go – it is unknown.
And so look back and speak
That we feel ashamed to know Nava, Prava and Yava
And also wholeheartedly know and think...
Prava was secretly encoded by Dazhboh,
And along it, like yarn, Yava is flowing
That created our life.
And then when it will move away, death sets in.
Yava is flowing and is creating in Prava.
And Nava is after them.
Till now exists Nava and after that is Nava
And in Prava is Yava ...
Those are the souls of our ancestors looking at us from Paradise
And there from pity cry and evoke to us

That we did not save Prava, Nava and Yava;
Did not take care of them but still sneered.
It is true, that we are not worthy to be Dazhboh's grandsons.

Close to the conclusion of *The Veles Book* (before its last entry, 879 BCE) a more simplified understanding of Tri-unity existed, as opposed to that from the "*valiant old times*" (2300-1700 BCE). It was based on a 12-month calendar personified in a hierarchy of gods and seasons of the year. There is far more dualistic imagery (*The Veles Book*, board 11a):

Thus, when we pray, we must first of all worship Trihlav [*Three-Headed*]
We praise Svaroh, grandfather of God,
who is the beginning of that divine generation
and to every family is the well-drawn prophetic...
And to God Perun^, the Thunderer, and to the god of fight and fighting
we will say do not stop to twirl the living phenomena...
And to God Svitovyd^ we proclaim glory –
He is the god of Prava and Yava, and we sing songs to him
when a holiday comes.
And through him we know how to see the world and to exist in Yava.
And he will safeguard us from Nava, and we praise him...
And this is a great secret, just like Svaroh.
Perun and Svitovyd – those both are detained in the sky.
And from both sides of them Biloboh [White God] *and*
Chornoboh [Black God] *fight –*
And they hold the sky in order that
The world will not be thrown down.
And beyond both of those are Khors, Veles^, Stryboh^ holding
And behind them – Vishen, Lelo, Lityts.

The TRINITY is really an approximation of our three-dimensional world. To comprehend any phenomena we need to process/detect it, in terms of form, content and feeling/spirit, constantly referring it back to our human consciousness ("the sub-cortex of the brain"), consciousness ("cerebral cortex...") and super-consciousness ("the bio-field aura"). Deeply religious scientists and philosophers, such as Newton, Hegel and Florensky, embodied their understanding of Trinitarity in the dialectics of a thesis: N – antithesis – synthesis (= thesis N +1, as historical materialism and other scientific areas are understood); one now has to understand it as follows:

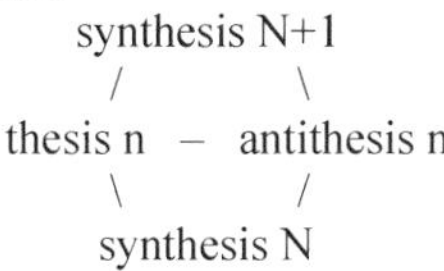

By choosing to regard religion as the antithesis of science (and philosophy, which has vainly tried to reconcile those two poles, as the failing synthesis), Marxists and historical materialists proclaimed them irreconcilable, overlooking the leading function of religion (from the Latin *religare* 'to bind'). They also failed to understand the significance of the narrow role awarded to materiality within classical Heraclitean-Newtonian science, and being ignorant of the philosophical relationship with the ("spiritual") field, they misunderstood the fundamental principle of the material world...

Until recently, philosophy struggled over the problem of prioritising matter and consciousness, ultimately reducing them to a substance and an idea (not even a field!) and struggling with the problem of 'was there a Universe in itself or was it created by an intelligent God?' Since the mid-1970's, similar questions, such as, "which came first, the chicken or the egg" concede their irrelevance to matter: is consciousness a product of the brain in a skull or is a skeleton with a 'brain-filling' playing the role of a peculiar "television tube" for the perception of an omnipervasive Information Field (i.e. Divine Will, as adherents of unscientific but religious understanding believe)? Such questions grew out of the studies of physicians (e.g. surgeons N. I. Pirogov, V. F. Voino-Yasenetsky, W. Penfield; psychic investigators R. Moudi and M. Stabon; psychiatrists E. Keubler-Ross; psychoanalysts S. Freud, C. Jung, S. Grof; biophysicists C. Castaneda, G. N. Petrakovich, N. P. Adamenko and others). These investigations began from a vain endeavour to locate the centre of thinking in the cerebral cortex and continued by probing into subconsciousness, resulting in the discovery of an "intellectual bio-field" (the immortal soul). Such discoveries have been made by R. Moudi, M. Stabon, E. Keubler-Ross, S. Grof and other scientists by means of generalised experiments involving those who transcended clinical death or who experienced reincarnation ("the migration of the soul" from deceased people or other creatures), as well as those having extra-sensory capabilities.

Parallel research revealed that Indo-Aryan Brahmans and other sages of pre-ancient peoples were perfectly expert in the Trinitarity of form, content and spirit; subconscious, conscious and superconscious; scientific, philosophical and religious; for millennia they skilfully used their figurative-intuitive knowledge which in some respects, often surpassed that of logical-analytical knowledge inherent to the most recent culture.

These discoveries showed the inestimable value not only of the philosophical-religious legacy but also the corresponding scientific-practical heritage of such texts as the Egyptian *Book of the Dead*, Indo-Tibetan culture (Yogic, Vedic literature, etc.), the Rusy *Veles Book* and its rarer analogues in the traditional ("pagan") cultures of Aryans and other nations. The synthesis of ancient doctrines and the latest scientific achievements unveiled semi-intuitively that - originating even at the end of the 19th century with Vivekananda and Blavatsky, Roerich^ and Prabhupada, and formulated after 1980's by P. A. Kharchenko - the Trinitary paradigm had become the primary methodology of this objective process (and evidently the most successful and well-chosen). It is quite evident that the Vedic culture (partially retained and changed over time in Arsania and Dandaria or with the "Royal Scythians", as well as in ancient Rus, Persian Iran and Indian Bharata) originated in Aratta and Arián. This provides a grandiose body of factual material for the development and examination of the above-stated synthesis. It would be a sin not to take advantage of this treasure of world-wide significance.

It is hoped that the triumphant initiative demonstrated by the glorious Ukrainians Danylenko, Kharchenko and others will find support and development in the work of subsequent post-historical-materialist generations of scientists.

Suggested Reading

1. Yatsenko B. I., *The Veles Book*. Translation and comments. – Kyiv, 1995; 2001.
2. Danylenko V., *The Cosmogony of Barbaric Society / The Beginnings of Civilisation*. – Moscow, 1999.
3. Shilov Yu., *Prarodina Aryans*. – Kyiv 1995; *The Beginnings of Civilisation*. –
4. Moscow, 1999; *The Truth of "The Veles book*". – Kyiv, 2000.
5. Grof S., Moudi R. et al., *Life After Death*. – Moscow, 1991.
6. Kharchenko P. A., *From Individual to God-man*. – Kyiv, 1993; *Trignozis*. – Kyiv, 1998.
7. Adamenko N. P., *Tripleness of the Absolute. The Tripleness of the Soul* / The Reports of International Convention Trinitar Knowledge. Kyiv, 1997-1998, No. 1.

---

[1] Viktor Medvedchuk and Hryhoriy Surkis are Ukrainian politicians and businessmen.

CHAPTER 1

Fig. 8 : **Deer hunters in the Mesolithic Age**. An artistic reconstruction by P. L. Kornienko.

THE CHRONICLE OF SHU-NUN^

Historians understand civilisation to be synonymous with statehood. Broader interpretations of the first of these two concepts exist, however, as exemplified in the archaeological cultures which preceded the formation of states in the Ancient East. According to the precepts of historical materialism, the necessary complex of traits for a culture to achieve civilisation-statehood are undoubtedly considered to be the separation of agriculture and crafts, trade, written language, class differentiation of society – and cities.

Archaeologists have now traced the embryonic existence of the first three of these attributes – agriculture and crafts, trade and written language – from the upper Palaeolithic era (i.e. from the end of the 'Old Stone Age', about 40 – 15 millennia ago). A particularly striking discovery, made by the linguist A. G. Kifishin, was the presence of proto-writing, which was first manifested at the celebrated cave site of Arcy-sur-Cure in France – dated to the 35th millennium BCE. This expressed the highest achievement of the European culture of mammoth-hunters – the most advanced culture of that world.

The latest research by anthropologists and geneticists shows that about 80% of Europeans today are descended from a generic group of Palaeolithic ancestors. According to P. A. Underhill, three large communities developed in Europe about 24 millennia ago, where they lived on the territory of future Spain, the Balkans and Ukraine; their descendants now dominate the northwest, central and eastern parts of Europe.

Around the 13th – 12th millennium BCE, the intense melting of glaciers and the extinction of mammoths, triggered the transition from the Palaeolithic to the Mesolithic i.e. middle Stone Age, way of life. In the Ukrainian, or Eastern-European centre some outstanding settlements already existed, such as at Mezhyrich^ and Myzino, which were saturated with unsurpassed examples of ornamentation, calendars and also proto-writing. It is little wonder that on this territory – in the numerous caves and grottoes of Kamyana Mohyla^ [Stone Grave^] situated in the valley of the River Molochna [Milk] near the present-day city of Melitopol – a clan of oracle-priests and keepers of ancient wisdom was formed.

Developing this further, by the turn of the 8th and 7th millennium BCE, they had already created the world's first system of symbols, proto-writing – which (according to A. G. Kifishin) allowed names, events, and dates, etc., to be read.

As we can see, the embryo of history and of civilisation – the very concepts which experts unfailingly connect with written language – are precisely detected in Ukraine, in the lower reaches of the Dnipro... What place did this circumstance later hold in the formation of a global civilisation?

1. The Beginning of the "Great Neolithic Revolution"

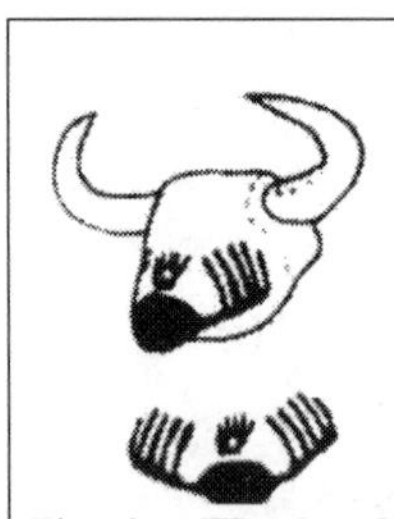

Fig. 9 : **The head of the bull-Taurus** from the temple at Çatal Höyük.

The Mesolithic era was followed by the Neolithic era, the 'New Stone Age'. It is within this era that researchers find the origins of civilisation – either being unaware of, or else ignoring, the discoveries made by the Russian linguist A.G. Kifishin at the end of the 20th century. It was Kifishin who further developed the discoveries that had been made by the British archaeologist G. Childe.
In the mid-twentieth century, Gordon Childe detected evidence of pre-civilisation during the so-called "Great Neolithic Revolution". With this knowledge he then built on the foundations of historical-materialism, synthesising the latest data from archaeological excavations in the Near East covering the period of the 9th – 5th millennium BCE. He also took into account existing developments offered by linguists, ethnographers and representatives of other historical disciplines. The most authoritative amongst them were the linguists.

In 1903, the linguist H. Pedersen proposed a hypothesis concerning Nostratic^, the parent language of a primitive community that seems to have arisen in the Near East after the Flood, i.e. from the times of the Biblical Noah, and which was carried around the world by his sons Ham, Shem and Japheth. From the eldest son came the Semitic people (Jews, Arabs, etc.) and from the youngest, Japheth, came the Indo-Europeans (Hindus, Persians, Greeks, Germans, Balts and Slavs, etc.). L. L. Zaliznyak tried to modernise this obsolete concept in his *Studies of the Ancient History of Ukraine* (Kyiv, 1994) and *The Ancient History of Ukraine of X-V thousand BCE* (Kyiv, 1998). Nevertheless, starting from the 1950s, V. N. Danylenko and N. D. Andreev, and since the 1980s, V. A. Safronov, began to form another fundamental concept that was favourably announced in the last treatise of N. A. Nikolaeva, *Beginnings of Slavic and Eurasian Mythologies* (Moscow, 1999).

According to Andreev and Safronov's theory, the pre-history of the Indo-Europeans and the Semites began independently from one another around the 10th – 9th millennium BCE from the Eurasian (or Boreal, according to Andreev) and Afro-Asian communities. Amongst these Eurasians, ***pre-Indo-European*** communities were preceded by a culture of plant-gatherers and, prior to that, by mammoth-hunters during the Palaeolithic era. However, the last three glacial periods led to the extinction of the mammoths leading to an alteration of culture, of which the most advanced became the Mesolithic culture of deer-hunters. These were the "Eurasians" (as called by the linguists), or "Svidertians"^ (by archaeologists) who arose in the glacial-adjacent areas between the Carpathians and the Baltic. Advancing further south, a western branch of the "Eurasian-Svidertians" appeared in Asia Minor where they tamed goats and were the first community of cattle-breeders; they built rectangular dwellings that became one of the ethno-cultural signs of the embryonic proto-Indo-Europeans. A second branch of them joined the "Palaeo-Europeans" (more conservative relatives) on the lower reaches of the Dnipro and in Crimea, and a third (still Eurasian) branch went east and became the ancestors of the Ural-Altai people...

During that time, from Asia Minor up to Sinai, there lived a linguistic community of African tribes, creators of the so-called Natufian archaeological culture. They did not know of the bow and hunted with the sling, living mainly by collecting edible plants and accordingly, they developed into the first farmers. Whether the hunting was successful or not,

Fig. 10 : **The appearance of the Eurasian language community** (of the Svidertian archaeological culture). Maps drawn up by A. A. Bilousko and Yu. Shilov.

their skill in farming cereals yielded up to 800 kg/hectare and a family of four workers could collect a ton of grain per week. They protected their round dwellings by building community walls, thus creating the first fortress or even proto-city with an area of up to 3 hectares; modern researchers name this community "Jericho A"^.

Towards the end of the 8th millennium BCE, the Svidertians of Asia Minor were aware that proto-cities and other "Natufian" settlements extended up to Sinai. "Jericho B" reflected the formation of a new, somewhat mixed ***proto-Indo-European*** culture, which became the carriers of the "Takhuny" archaeological culture. The centre of "Takhuny", with an area of 14 hectares, became a proto-city in Anatolia near the modern-day settlement of Çatal Höyük^ (southern Asia Minor). Its population, probably not for the first time, combined agriculture with cattle breeding, and preserved their faithful reverence for the real Foremother – who was still, and had been, inherent to the Eurasian mammoth-hunters...

The "Great Neolithic Revolution" may be described as the transition from a gathering economy (collecting and hunting) to a reproductive one (agriculture and cattle breeding). This revolution, according to G. Childe, "transformed the human economy offering people control over their provisions", etc., thus creating the conditions necessary for the emergence of civilisation (statehood). Ever since then, Man started to drift away from Mother Nature, turning into its not-so-clever host. Thus began the original chain reaction of escalating contradictions in ecology, interbreeding, property, social structure, class, governance, internationalism...

The introduction into the economy of even primitive levels of agriculture and cattle breeding led, as early as the 1st millennium of the "Neolithic Revolution", to a 16-fold increase in the population of the Near East; average density increased to 5 people per 1 km^2 (compared to 1-7 people per 100 km^2 during the Palaeolithic and Mesolithic eras, when the entire population of the world was only about 5 million). It swelled into a population explosion, triggering the distant migrations of people and the spread of new forms of economy.

2. The "Circum-Pontic zone" ^

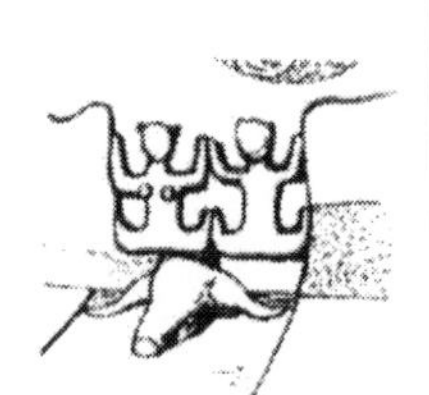

Fig. 11 : Reliefs from one of the temples of Çatal Höyük.

In the 7th millennium BCE, almost from the beginning of the "Great Neolithic Revolution" (which ended in only the 3rd millennium BCE in northern Eurasia, even later in other places), Anatolia in the south of modern Turkey became the most developed centre of proto-civilisation. This discovery was made at the beginning of the 1960s by means of the scientific-cultural methods introduced by the British archaeologist James Mellaart.

In Southern Anatolia, Mellaart excavated two extremely important settlements, dated from 6500-5650 and 5700-5000 BCE, which had existed in the vicinity of two modern villages, Çatal Höyük and Khajilar. These were embryonic, pre-Indo-European sites.

Prehistoric Çatal Höyük (or "Shu-eden-na Ki-dug^", as it was then called in the scholarly opinion of A. G. Kifishin) covered an area of 14 hectares and was, in its time, the greatest settlement in the world. For the 900 years of its existence it was re-built 12 times. Its houses were constructed from essentially the same type of mud-brick as houses that are being built in the Middle East today; a temple centre was identified, where, perhaps, priest-rulers lived and worked. The interiors of all 40 excavated temples were decorated with magical scenes – mostly of a calendar-zodiac^ type e.g. drawn and relief images of deer, bulls and rams, as well as a human-like Mother Goddess and Twins. For these images, the skulls of sacrificial victims and animals had been used. The dead were often buried in the area beneath a stove bench or fire place although later, the dead were buried in the streets. This seems to suggest that any culturally-generated polarisation between life-and-death was insignificant.

The economic basis included agriculture and cattle-breeding, although even settled farmers continued to hunt. Everything was based on the exchange of goods (in particular, local obsidian - used for manufacturing instruments - was exchanged for imported cockleshells, used for adornment). Significant development was achieved with netting and weaving, pottery and the first metal products (copper, lead).

There is evidence that the intensification of irrigated agriculture led, on the one hand, to a sharp growth of the population, and on the other – to increasingly saline soil. In addition to these stresses there was an increase in the eruptions of surrounding volcanoes and other natural catastrophes, as well as an increase in military skirmishes: Çatal Höyük, situated 320 km from Khajilar, was later repeatedly burned. All this led to a population explosion that compelled the priest-rulers to search out new lands for resettling their people.

Çatal Höyük communicated and traded goods with Syria, Cyprus and other areas of the Mediterranean. With the onset of the problems outlined earlier, a removal expedition was conducted to the borders of the Circum-Pontic zone (i.e. around the Black Sea). This expedition took place about 6200 BCE, reaching at least as far as the lower reaches of the Dnipro river if not passing through all the Black Sea coastal areas. This discovery was made only recently by the outstanding linguist A.G. Kifishin who compared the specific complexes of proto-writings from Stone Grave with those at Çatal Höyük. (Figs. 1, 4, 12)

The first reasoned assumptions about the writing at Stone Grave were promulgated in publications by V. Danylenko and B. Mykhailov in 1986 and 1992.

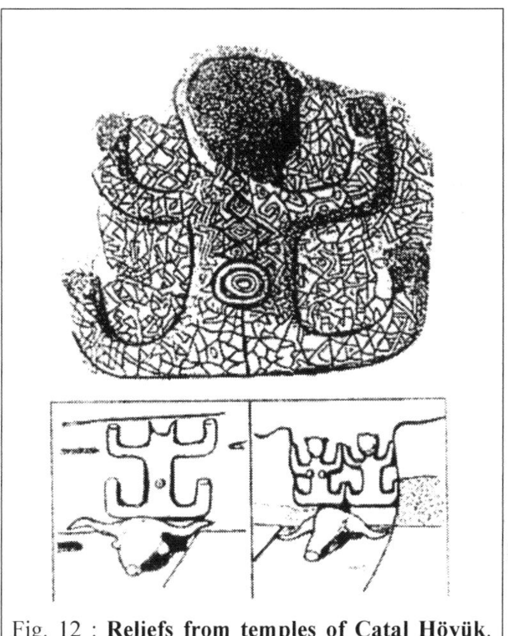

Fig. 12 : **Reliefs from temples of Çatal Höyük.** Above – the Foremother from temple 23/VII.

Danylenko had, even earlier, discovered traces of direct communications between the priests of the sanctuary of Stone Grave and those of the settlement near Çatal Höyük. He connected the origin of Indo-Europeans with the eastern contacts of the carriers of the Svidertian archaeological culture of the 8th millennium BCE. At Stone Grave (Shu-Nun, or 'Hand/Law of the Empress', featuring texts begun there in 6137-5702 BCE), A. G. Kifishin traced the transference of a copied text that matched the beginning of a chronicle, the earliest known on Earth, in the specially built temple 23/VII at Çatal Höyük (Shu-eden-na Ki-Dug, 'Hand/Law of the Blessed Steppeland') decorated by a bas-relief of that Empress – the Foremother of the world.

According to J. Mellaart, temple 23/VII can be dated to 6200 ± 97 BCE. In my opinion, this copied text is the very first written agreement showing the co-existence of two previously related but different peoples – (the "Svidertians" who dispersed from Eastern Carpathia to Anatolia and the Northern Black Sea Coast) – whose union started the *pre-Indo-European* community, and, along with it – world civilisation.

This discovery by the linguist A. G. Kifishin accords with earlier conclusions from the archaeologist V. N. Danylenko, the anthropologist S. I. Kruts, the zoologist V. I. Bibikova and others, that at a settlement near Stone Grave, in the cultural strata from the 7th to 6th millennium BCE, vessels suddenly appear that are specific to Çatal Höyük along with the bones of domestic cattle of a Near-Eastern origin and that in the lower reaches of the Dnipro river, burial grounds of the same time period contain human remains of an East-Mediterranean type. At one time, this type of people, just like the local population, were related to the Svidertian archaeological culture – but in the 9th millennium BCE their ways had diverged. Now, after 2–3 millennia, representatives of the Takhuny culture (see above) had already returned to the Dnipro area.

So, we have grounds for presenting a precise conclusion: at about 6200 BCE, Çatal Höyük – at that time the centre of the most developed culture in the known world – established direct communication with the Ukrainian Dnipro area. Whilst in contrast, the sanctuary of Stone Grave had begun to function long before that – it was known in the world since at least 11,582 BCE. This date is designated here (near to images of mammoths, etc.,) with the aid of comparisons between the cycles of the Moon and of Sirius; such dating was retained in the Near East and during Sumerian times.

3. The Problem of the "Indo-European Language Community"

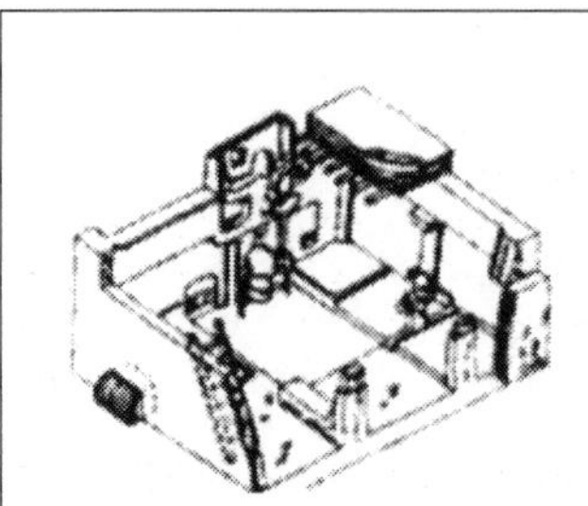

Fig. 13 : Interior of a temple at Çatal Höyük.

The modern understanding of the appearance of proto- and pre-Indo-European communities of people has already been stated by scientists (V. N. Danylenko, M. D. Andreev, V. A. Safronov, Yu. A. Shilov and others). A conditional definition of the "Indo-European language community" was formulated by linguists between the 18th – 19th centuries.

Whilst exploring the most ancient literature of India – which was written in the archaic, 'synthetic' Sanskrit^ language – the British scientists (Jones, Wilkins and others) and in due course French (J. I. N. Baudouin de Courtenay), German (Bopp, Schleicher et al.), Ukrainian and Russian scientists (Potebnia^, Fortunatov) found surprising similarities with the classical languages of Europe. Using lexicons and grammars of Sanskrit and the old Persian (Iranian), Greek, Italian, German, Slavic and Lithuanian^ languages – A. Schleicher, utilising Darwinian theory, considered the specified languages to be branches of a parent language tentatively called "Indo-European". At the same time, O. O. Potebnia proposed the concept of a "language system", [of comparative analysis] which allowed for an origin based on interactions between both related and different peoples.

There was initially an idea (F. von Schlegel, 1806) that the site of the ancestral homeland of the Indo-Europeans was in India but that idea disappeared with the discovery that the [linguistic] provenance of the indigenous population was Dravidian^, whilst the Indo-European languages had spread amongst them only after the arrival of the Aryans towards the middle of the 2nd millennium BCE. Further searches for an ancestral homeland then started to move ahead in the West.

At the same time, in 1820, the German scientist K. Ritter noticed the similarity of the names of India and (S)Indiki – the ancient name of the Taman^ peninsula. Thereby, Ritter had begun to discover the formation of an Indo-European community in the Northern Black Sea region, – the largest (at least between the 5th – 2nd millennium BCE) in the region of the Circum-Pontic zone. Later on, fruitful work was carried out by the British scholars G. Childe, G. Clark and S. Piggot, the Polish T. Sulimirski, Austrian P. Krechmer, Bulgarian V. Georgiev, Ukrainian V. M. Danylenko, American M. Gimbutas, Russian N. Ya. Merpert, S. A. Safronov, and others.

Until recently, the search for the ancestral homeland of the Indo-Europeans and for their early history was principally conducted by using linguistics; the peak of this achievement is found in the outstanding monograph by T. V. Gamkrelidze and V. V. Ivanov *Indo-European language and the Indo-Europeans* (Tbilisi, 1984). They identified the primary ancestral homeland in the Armenian highlands, settled in the 5th – 4th millennium BCE by the carriers of the archaeological cultures of the Kura-Araxes^ circle. A secondary ancestral homeland was also identified which accorded with the position of the above authorities, i.e. in the steppe kurhans of Eastern Europe. However, these conclusions cannot be considered reliable without analysis of the archaeological sites: the settlements, sanctuaries and burial grounds, etc. Therefore, from the end of the 19th century, archaeologists, anthropologists and ethnographers had already started to run into problems with tracking the development of the Indo-Europeans. Then new experts appeared – V. N. Danylenko, B. A. Rybakov, V. A. Safronov and Yu. Shilov, – who had the qualifications and ability to correlate the data of all these sciences and to build important conclusions.

As early as the 1950's, V. Danylenko proved that the kurhans (i.e. mounds) and Corded Ware ceramics – attributes which German archaeologists, at the beginning of the 20th century, defined as inherent to the early Indo-Europeans – appeared for the first time in the most ancient Pit Grave (Yamna^) Culture of the Ukrainian Dnipro area. Thus V. N. Danylenko confirmed and concretised the assumptions by G. Childe and T. Sulimirski who believed that the major features associated with early Indo-Europeans, were present under the kurhan burials of the same Pit Grave Culture of flexed bodies strewn with red ochre.

Subsequently, in the monographs *Cosmology of a Primitive Society* (Kyiv, 1965; 1997; 1997; 1999), *Neolithic Ukraine* and *Eneolithic Ukraine* (Kyiv, 1969; 1974) V. N. Danylenko connected the archaeological, mythological and linguistic aspects of the Indo-European problems and presented a deeply reasoned picture of the Indo-Europeans forming into a community in the Circum-Pontic zone (especially in the Ukrainian Dnipro area), as well as beyond its frontiers – from the Altai over to Britain. Within the ambit of the Indo-European nations were the communities of Buh-Dniester, Trypillian and related archaeological cultures. The developments of V. N. Danylenko were picked up by N. Ya. Merpert and M. Gimbutas (although without extending any appropriate acknowledgments to the original trailblazer, Danylenko). The researcher who advanced the reputation of Danylenko to a significant degree was V. A. Safronov.

In his monograph *Pre-Homelands of the Indo-Europeans* (Gorky, 1989), V. A. Safronov corrected not only the archaeological aspects but also, in particular, the linguistic aspects of the above-mentioned work by Gamkrelidze and Ivanov. The spouses of V. A. Safronov and N. A. Nikolaeva also made a significant contribution to solving problems concerning the origin of the Indo-Europeans as stated above. We shall now outline the conclusions of S. A. Safronov concerning the subsequent developmental steps of this community.

Acknowledging the Balkan Vinca^ culture as the direct successor of Asia Minor's Çatal Höyük, the researcher identifies the latter of these two archaeological cultures with the very first civilisation in the world, that is, one which possessed statehood – with cities, writing and sanctuary-observatories. There were some setbacks for the first ***Indo-European*** tribes (not their ancient predecessors, the proto- and pre- tribes) around the boundary

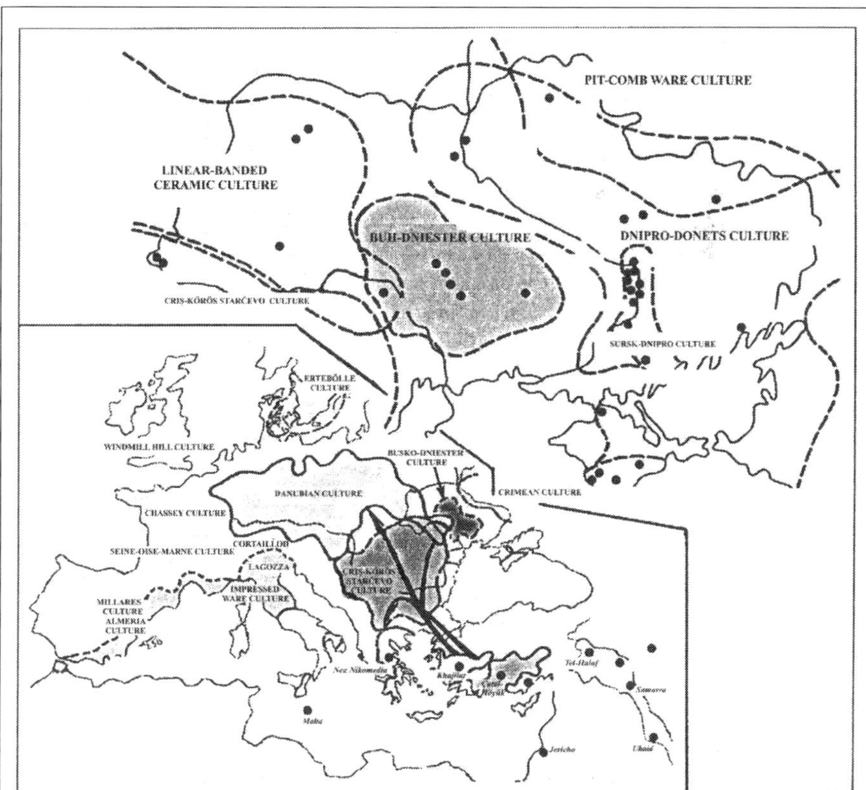

Fig. 14 : **The origin of the state of Aratta** (Kerech, Buh-Dniester and other archaeological cultures of the 7th–5th millennium BCE). Maps composed by A. A. Bilousko.

between the 4th – 3rd millennium BCE, a period when the cultures of Sumer and Egypt were ascendent. S. A. Safronov explains that a change in climate was responsible for a slump in Çatal Höyük's cultural achievements – as for Vinca, it was hampered by occupying an environment amongst the less-developed Eurasian aboriginal peoples and there were also shifting priorities in agriculture and animal husbandry (however the later is less representative because with the new climatic conditions historically, it appeared to have been more productive).

Safronov went further than Danylenko in discrediting 20th century orthodox ideas with regard to the origin of civilisation being 'the light from the East', but then shrank back from historiography – silently by-passing Trypillia and the previous European archaeological cultures. Meanwhile, the culture of Çatal Höyük had ceased to exist by 5650-5000 BCE and the Vinca culture was to emerge almost a millennium later. In this 500-1000 year time gap, many of the pre-Indo-European tribes moved from Asia Minor to the Balkans, and further, on to the Dnipro; they were considered by archaeologists to be carriers of the Keresh, Boyan^, Cucuteni and Trypillian cultures, etc. V. N. Danylenko also analysed those cultures and proved in particular, in his *Cosmology of a Primitive Society* (Kyiv, 1965; Moscow, 1999), that the mythology of the Indo-Europeans (though it would be more logical to say pre-Indo-Europeans, *Yu. Shilov*), belonged to the Trypillian culture.

B. A. Rybakov adheres to the same position in his monograph *Paganism of Ancient Slavs* (Moscow, 1981), tracing the traditions of the Trypillian archaeological culture down to the time of Kyivan Rus and modern Muscovite (Moscowian) Russia. At the same time in modern Ukrainian studies, there has been a tendency to connect Trypillia, along with all other agricultural cultures of a Near-Eastern origin, with pre-Semites. The research works undertaken by Danylenko, Safronov, Rybakov, Trubachev and Kifishin, were deemed pseudo-scientific and ignored as being "chauvinistic"; at the same time the idea of "inter-ethnic values" was proposed, allegedly with progressive capitalist overtones, which was nothing more than the modernisation of the notorious "inter-nationalism" – though no longer carrying communist credentials.

Ideas are only useful when they are based on a set of historiographic, scientific sources and honest research. Caught up in the fraudulent "pre-Semitic" nature of Trypillia (owing to the suppression of the studies and treatises already outlined above that resulted in a distorted sequence of events in the evolution and direction of the mutual interaction of cattle-breeders and farmers, etc.), L. L. Zaliznyak, in his subsequent monographs (after *Studies of Ancient History of Ukraine* (Kyiv, 1994), hides his speculative idea concerning the obscurity of an ethno-linguistic provenance for Sumer and so forth, but continues to exclude "Trypillians" and most other ancient farmers from the circle of Indo-European nations, considering them less developed when compared with Semitic culture-bearers. Despite being an archaeologist – in fact, being the recognised specialist in the Svidertian culture mentioned above – Zaliznyak investigated its archaeological finds more superficially and more narrowly in time and space, than did Safronov and Nikolayeva in their *Sources of Slavic and Eurasian Mythology*. However, he plunged into the depths of linguistics that were difficult for him to understand and from which he obtained his doubtful arguments.

V. M. Illich-Svitych's little article, "*The Most Ancient Indo-European-Semitic language contacts*" (in *Problems in Indo-European Linguistics*, Moscow, 1964) was perceived in its time as discovering the influence of Semitic farmers on the contemporary Indo-European cattlemen. Zaliznyak had also stood by this view. But, after the publication of S. A. Starostin's considerably weightier study "*Indo-European-North Caucasian Isogloss^*" (in *Ancient East. Ethno-cultural Communications*, Vol. XXX, Moscow, 1988) the situation became better understood, which Zaliznyak himself recognised, in his *Backgrounds of Ukraine X-V thousand BCE* (Kyiv, 1998), that what had been attributed to pre-Semites by Illich-Svitych was in reality Hattian-Hurrian^. According to ethno-linguistics, Hattian and Hurrian gravitate towards pre-Indo-European which, according to G. A. Klimov and M. V. Alexeev (*Typology of the Caucasian Languages*, Moscow, 1980), differed significantly from the following Indo-European language; Zaliznyak also admitted that in the 7th – 5th millennium BCE (when the Indo-Europeans started to form from the pre-Indo-Europeans) and when "Afro-Asians" were in existence (see above), that there were as yet no Semites.

Nonetheless, he brushed over that. Of the few facts collected by Illich-Svitych, the overwhelming majority do not (according to I. M. Diakonov and V. A. Safronov) go back further than the middle of the 3rd millennium BCE. Since that time, the western Semites, ancestors of the Arabs, had begun to leave the dying lands of Arabia to take over Mesopotamia, which had been rendered habitable by Sumer, establishing there Akkad's supremacy under Sargon I (2371-2316 BCE). And just a thousand years after them – travelling through Egypt according to the Bible – the Eastern Semites, Israelites or Hebrews, appeared on the historical arena; yet, "the presence of those same tribes in Palestine was only recorded from the 13th century BCE" (Yu. Zablotska, *History of the Near East in an Antiquity*, Moscow, 1989). Consequently, L. L. Zaliznyak's attempts to manipulate the data of historical linguistics to describe the ethnogenesis of the 8th – 4th millennium BCE (when non-existent Semites, or unknown pre-Semites, allegedly dominated the very developed pre- and Indo-Europeans) met neither the requirements of science nor of common sense.

On the other hand, G. Clark and S. Piggott, in their monograph *Pre-Historic Societies* (London, 1965) gravitated in the other direction owing to their unfamiliarity with Ukrainian archaeological, linguistic and ethnographical sources. Recognising an Indo-European ancestral home in the steppes between the Carpathians and the Caucasus and also recognising this community as the highest culture for its time, the authors rather exaggerated their role in the formation of agriculture and significantly so in the formation of Eastern civilisations: "Those steppe inhabitants over 5,500 years ago colonised Mesopotamia, Iran, India and other countries of the Ancient East. They brought there the horse, cart and agriculture. When we now address the principal areas of the most ancient agricultural population it is found to have more in common with Trypillia than with the Ancient East". It is possible to agree with this last finding as it is in accordance with the appearance of the 'Indo-Europeans' (to be precise, its Aryan branch) in the environment with the first horses, carts and chariots.

Before concluding the topic of "The Neolithic Revolution", which generated the most ancient "Indo-European community", it is necessary to pause once again at its major achievement – writing.

Safronov proposed that it should be deduced from Vinca of around the 5th – 4th millennium BCE. However it is necessary to recognise the superiority of the reasoned findings of A. G. Kifishin which have been outlined above; the key fact is the similarity between proto-Sumerian inscriptions from 6200 BCE at Çatal Höyük and at Stone Grave. In due course, this writing matured in Keresh, Vinca and other cultures; a particular position was held by the priest-keepers of the very first archive in the world at Stone Grave. For this position, V. N. Danylenko isolated the Buh-Dniester culture – interpreted by him as the forerunner of the Trypillian archaeological culture – which was, according to the assumption of Kifishin, the main creator keeper of the most ancient writing. Here, in the Dnipro-Danube area, amongst archaeological sites located in modern Ukraine, Bulgaria and Romania, were the first writings about Aratta, the pre-Sumerian state. Aratta undoubtedly became the forerunner of the Indo-European powers: the Bharata of the Indo-Aryans, the Artan of the Etruscans, the Arsania with Arta of the Slavs and Persians, the Ortopolis of Greece, as well as the Artaplot and Orativ of the Ukrainians.

Suggested Reading

1. Childe G., *The Ancient East in the Light of new Excavations* (Moscow, 1956).
2. Mellaart J., *The Most Ancient Civilisations of the Middle East*. – Moscow, 1982.
3. Danylenko V. M., *Neolithic Ukraine* (Kyiv, 1969); *Eneolithic Ukraine* (Kyiv, 1974); *Cosmology of Primitive Societies / The Beginnings of Civilisation* (Moscow, 1999).
4. Safronov V. A., *Aryan Indo-European Fore-motherlands* (Gorky, 1989).
5. Nikolayeva N. A. and Safronov V. A., *Beginnings of Slavic and Euro-Indian Mythology*. – Moscow, 1999.
6. Rybakov B. A., *Paganism of Ancient Slavs* (Moscow, 1981).
7. Gamkrelidze T. V. and Ivanov V. V., *Indo-European Language and Indo-Europeans*

(Tbilisi, 1984).

8. Kifishin A. G., *Geno-structure of pre-Greek and Ancient Greek Myth/Image-Sense in Antique Culture* (Moscow, 1990); *Proto-Writing of the Palaeolithic. The Most Ancient Inscriptions of Stone Grave and their West European Analogues/Features of Development of Upper Palaeolithic in East Europe* (St. Petersburg, 1999).

CHAPTER 2

Fig.15 : **Neolithic people of the Buh-Dniester culture.**
Artistic reconstruction by P. L. Kornienko.

THE ORIGIN OF CIVILISATION

In the preceding chapter it was shown that the start of world civilisation and the origin of the Indo-European peoples exhibited a similar course of development, during the period of the 12th – 8th millennium BCE along the northern and southern coasts of the Black Sea and along the eastern coast of the Mediterranean. It was said that this process developed into Aratta, the very first state in the world, which reached its apotheosis in the 'Trypillian archaeological culture'...

We shall pause to consider the pre-conditions for this apotheosis in the region of the Danube-Dnipro river interfluve.

1. The beginning of the Great Neolithic Revolution on Ukrainian Territory.

We have already discovered that the so-called "Great Neolithic Revolution" (GNR) was initially characterised by the transition from hunting/gathering to cattle breeding and agriculture. It has also been said that in the Danube-Dnipro region – on the territory of future Ukraine – the beginning of this transition was marked by expeditions of priests about 6200 BCE.

Fig.16 : **Tablet from Stone Grave**. 8–7 millennia BCE, the boundary between the Mesolithic and Neolithic.

It was from that time, in the late Mesolithic burial grounds in the area above the Dnipro rapids^ that remains of people of an East-Mediterranean type are found, along with remains of the local Palaeo-European population - often with flint weapon tips embedded in their bones (nevertheless, representatives of each ethnic type were still buried within the same burial grounds). Thus, if the priest-rulers of Stone Grave and Çatal Höyük had agreed to the co-existence of their people, their real synthesis into a common (but by no means uniform!) ***pre-Indo-European*** community did not proceed without a few dark clouds... However, there are examples of peaceful co-existence: the well-known settlement and burial ground at Lepenski Vir^ (near the Danube Iron Gates gorge), where the triumphal progression of the pre-Indo-Europeans began and also the productive economy that typified them in the Dnipro area.

Distinctive sites and cemeteries of subsequent gatherers, fishermen and hunters, of the late Mesolithic era exist in the area of the Dnipro rapids. The remains of five rectangular semi dug-outs, located in a circle, were excavated near the modern village of Osokorivka. In the middle of the settlement, in their communal courtyard which covers an area up to 6 x $5m^2$, there were camp-fire remnants. Near the settlement of Vasylivka, archaeologists and anthropologists investigated two burial grounds, one with 24 and the other with 44 burials of local Palaeo-European people which also contained foreign, East Mediterranean types. The predominant burial ceremony (according to D. Ya. Telegin and others) that had prevailed in the Near East was as follows: the dead were buried in a flexed position (a foetal position), lying on their side, with hands folded together [as in prayer], towards the face; there were also burials with the body fully extended, which accorded with the local customs. The burials in each of them were mostly of males and moreover they bore evidence of death from skirmishes: there were broken skulls and flint arrow tips and spears embedded in the bones. Thus began the relationship between the aboriginal dwellers and the first immigrant settlers from overseas (i.e. from the "Fertile Crescent" along the length of the south-eastern coast of the Mediterranean, the Black Sea coast and Caspian Sea). Later, these tribes got along together, not just here, but also in the Dnipro rapids area, where they formed the Sursk-Dnipro archaeological culture of cattle-breeders – not only the most ancient pastoralists in Ukraine, but also in the whole of Eastern Europe.

By the end of the Neolithic period – which in Ukraine encompassed the period from the end of the 7th millennium BCE to the early 4th millennium BCE, and up to the 3rd millennium BCE in the north – the Mesolithic appropriating economies only prevailed in the forest areas. The farming economies became dominant from the very beginning of the Neolithic in the Buh-Dniester, and in due course in the Sursk-Dnipro cultures. It is from there that the pan-European Corded Ware Culture^, agriculture and cattle breeding practices were borrowed by some settlements in the Transcarpathian region and Crimea...

Neolithic settlements were characterised not only by long semi-dug-outs with fires, but also cult places and sanctuaries/shrines of the most ancient type; the first ceramic pottery and weaving, polished stone axes, etc., varied fishing instruments, and also agricultural hoes; the first copper adornments, all appeared towards the end of this era. Typical burials were just like those in the ancestral homeland of Asia Minor, being flexed and single, but in due course – and under the influence of the original population – there were collective burials of the extended type within long semi dug-outs, which mimic the shape of the communal meeting houses. The Neolithic period also witnessed the formation of the tribal way of life, based on a matriarchal family structure. Elements of material and spiritual culture, tools, ornaments and so on offer grounds for reaching conclusions concerning the ethno-historical features of the individual tribes and their relationships.

Let us now consider the first agricultural-cattle breeding culture in Ukraine, together with the whole of Eastern Europe.

Fig. 17 : A vessel of the Buh-Dniester culture.

2. Buh-Dniester and Sursk-Dnipro Archaeological Cultures

These cultures were first distinguished by V. N. Danylenko in the 1950-1960s. The key archaeological finds – settlements with single inexpressive burials – are concentrated in settlements along the middle reaches of the Dniester and Southern Buh rivers as well as in the Dnipro area above the rapids. These cultures existed for two to two and a half millennia, that is, not less than the universally known cultures of Sumer, Egypt or Greece; in their development, each of them went through several stages. The development of the **Buh-Dniester** archaeological culture was marked by three distinctive stages.

The first stage covered, approximately, the period between 6200-5000 BCE, that is, from the time when priests from Çatal Höyük made their Circum-Pontic expedition to Stone Grave (according to V. N. Danylenko and A. G. Kifishin); and then continued up until the end of the settlements of Çatal Höyük and Hacilar^ types on the ancestral homeland of the Indo-Europeans in Asia Minor (according to J. Mellaart and others). This phase features the most ancient ceramic utensils found in Eastern Europe from the Buh-Dniester culture and they are similar to the most ancient ceramics of the Balkans (i.e. the settlement of Nea-Nicomedeia in Greece and in the Hungarian Keresh culture). The similarity extends not only to their shape and decoration but also to the mythology reflected in them (according to Danylenko). In due course, ceramics similar to the Buh-Dniester type spread beyond the steppes of the Ukrainian Dnipro steppe area up to Caspian Turkmen. According to these examples and to other data (flint implements, anthropological remains, etc.), scientists were able to trace the origins and mutual relationships of local and immigrant tribes, charting the formation and spread of the Indo-Europeans and other tribes.

Early settlements of the "Buh-Dniester" type kept to the river flood-plains. Their elongated ground dwellings and semi dug-outs typically occupied an area up to 35m^2; they had indoor fires on a stone base as well as pits for garbage. The settlement of the rocky island of Bazkov on the Southern Buh occupied an area of 0.04 hectares, bordered by a field on the muddy riverside site. Agricultural hoes fashioned from antlers, knife-sickles made from wild boar fangs and bones with flint inserts were found at this settlement along with hunting implements such as the tips of darts and arrows. Near to the animal bones was a cluster of shells – evidence that a significant proportion of their economy was devoted to fishing and gathering. Amongst the ceramic housewares there was a preponderance of pointed-bottom pots, and bowls... A settlement near the village of Sokoltsi, on the flood-plain terrace of the same river, occupied an area of 0.1 hectares and consisted of at least five dwellings, each of which was probably intended for a family group.

The second stage, dated to the 5th millennium BCE (revised to the 6th millennium BCE from the most recent data), carried similarities to the Keresh, Corded Ware and other archaeological cultures of the Balkan-Danube area. Despite the similar ethno-historical connections and influences, the Buh-Dniester culture at this time became entirely original and acquired an autochthonous form.

The type of settlements remained practically unchanged, although by the end of this stage, separate (public?) buildings and stone walls appeared. There is evidence of improvements in their hoes, sickles, and ceramics. Amongst the latter are flat-bottomed pots and bowls; vases, cups and flasks also appear. The ornamental decoration remained mainly in the form of incised wavy bands and zig-zags. Ceramics were also produced with a partly-polished surface, sparingly ornamented with knobs and indents.

The third stage began around the 4th (or 5th) millennium BCE. This stage shares the same temporal boundary as that separating the Neolithic and Eneolithic eras, that is, the late Stone Age and the early Copper Age. It shows influences from the concurrent Balkan cultures of Vinča^ and Hamangia^ and also the early stages of the Danube-Dnipro culture of Trypillia (or Cucuteni as it is named after its earliest discovery in Romania and Moldova). The date given for this stage, just like the previous stage, can be lengthened in the context of a corresponding, modern trend to re-date Trypillian and other archaeological cultures of the Neolithic – Bronze Age eras. Accordingly, it will be necessary to change and re-present the state of the relationship between Aratta of the Dnipro area and its off-shoot, Mesopotamian Sumer....

The most recent settlements of the Buh-Dniester culture continued to develop the tradition of the previous settlements, though at the same time they were close to early-Trypillia. So, the settlement near the village of Savran on the Southern Buh had an area of about 0.3 hectares and was drawn out along a terrace above the flood-plain, being limited in its extent by the proximity of the river, granite cliffs and high shore. The dwellings were either constructed directly on the ground surface or slightly set into it. The largest house was rectangular in shape, with an area of 6 x 5m^2; the corners were lined with stone and reinforced by pillars, and the walls were covered by plastered wattle. In the south-western part of the building, the fireplace was constructed from stone and next to that – a store of bone fragments, utensils, hoes and other tools. The latter are identical to early Trypillian tools.

In the context of the development of the rather large Buh-Dniester culture, the **Sursk-Dnipro** archaeological culture, whose tribes lived mostly in the area of the Dnipro rapids, may be acknowledged as its eastern advance post. It is possible that its priests specifically supervised the sanctuaries of Stone Grave, which had been established no later than the 12th millennium BCE.

The Sursk-Dnipro culture was formed at the end of the first stage of the Buh-Dniester culture and it disappeared either at the same time as the end of the last phase or a little later. At the mouth of the River Samara and on the islands of Sursky, Shulaev and Strilcha Rock, archaeologists have excavated nine corresponding settlements, and several more plain monuments are known.

The area of the settlements reached 0.03 hectares. On Sursky, three half-dugouts were revealed, grouped around a general courtyard with a fire in the centre. Multi-generation family groups probably lived in each dwelling and all the residents of the settlement were kin or else closely related. An important detail of this and other settlements are pear-shaped pits with traces of basket-ware in the bottom which contained food stocks. Sharply ground ceramic dishes preserved the traditions of early Buh-Dniester culture and vessels made of stone demonstrated the influence of Near-Eastern cultures of Çatal Höyük. Amongst the tools were the most distinctive fishing hooks, hunting arrows, and adzes for chopping trees; there were grub-hoes made of deer antlers and bone sickles with flint inserts peculiar to the agricultural and cattle breeding cultures of Buh-Dniester and Trypillia.

The later change from coastal to inland settlements probably owed much to the need to seek protection from predators and enemies, as well as for seeking better environmental and economic conditions. This probably brought them, just like the emigrants from the Eastern Mediterranean in the previous Mesolithic era, into the same place – above the Dnipro river rapids – where they developed practices that suited an appropriating economy rather better than a performing economy. Nevertheless, even without taking into account the pressure of the local Dnipro-Donets culture of fishermen and hunters, the Sursk-Dnipro culture at the end of its existence had achieved considerable success in the breeding of cattle and small livestock. It is significant that Indo-Europeans in the ancestral homeland of Asia Minor cultivated goats and sheep, whereas domestic cows, bulls and bullocks, perhaps the first in the world, appeared on the settlement near Stone Grave by the 6th millennium BCE – it is highly likely that such pastoral priority remained for some time in the Sursk-Dnipro culture.

3. Ethno-Historical Interpretation of Memorials.

Fig.18 : **Ukrainian pysanky** [painted egg] **with an image of Berehynia*.**

When summing up all the foregoing points and expanding their historical interpretation, it must be remembered, first and foremost, as identified by V. N. Danylenko, that the isolated Buh-Dniester and Sursk-Dnipro archaeological cultures were the first agricultural and cattle-breeding cultures not only in the territory of Ukraine, but in the whole of Eastern Europe. They appeared about 6200 BCE and were a direct consequence of the Circum-Pontic^ expedition of the priest-rulers from Çatal Höyük, whose remaining northern outpost was preserved here in the pre-Indo-European community (and those cultures derived from it) just before the 4th millennium BCE. According to a hypothesis by A. G. Kifishin, it was specifically the priests of the Buh-Dniester culture (or its Sursk-Dnipro off-shoot) who became the guardians and chroniclers of the Stone Grave sanctuary – *Shu-Nun,* on the River Molochna – *Nun-Birdu* ('the Hand/Law of the Empress' and

'Empress of the Steppe', as attested by the type of pre-Sumerian engravings that prevailed at that time). According to this same hypothesis, it was this culture – together with its pre-Danubian 'sister' culture of Keresh, that was directly related to Çatal Höyük in Asia Minor – and was the very same Aratta, from which proceeded the foundation of Sumer in Mesopotamia.

The hypothesis is based on a comparison (by Danylenko) of the products, lifestyles and mythology of the tribes of Çatal Höyük, Keresh, Buh-Dniester, Sumer, Greece and other cultures, as well as a comparison (by Kifishin) of developments in their writing and historical-mythical texts. The position of Aratta as a 'state' was first specified on the plates of Stone Grave and on the clay tablets of Keresh, providing information about its canals, fortresses, ceremonies and sacrifices, pagan priests and warriors, as well as its gods. It was there, and in the following cultures of the Danube area, that the names of the highest deities of the future culture of Sumer are there to read: the sky god, Anu, and the creator god and culture-bearer, Enlil (to some extent, they became forerunners of the Slavic *Lel* and *Divana*). The images of these and other gods, and their accompanying inscriptions, have now been recorded and deciphered at Stone Grave. It was found that the texts on its repositories No. 5, No. 7 and No. 37/4 were copied by the pagan priest-librarians of the most ancient Sumerian city of *Shu-Nun* (as it was called at that time, after Stone Grave); these copies are now known by scientists as the tablets, PI-32 and PI-128, from the Sumerian *Shu-Nun* (which is modern Jemdet-Nasr^). In particular, in each of the cited texts, the names of semi-mythical yet pre-Sumerian rulers were presented: Mu-gi, Ki-Sal, Sali-Tush and others who ruled in the Dnipro area between 4303-4217 BCE (dated from Kifishin's decipherment, which he considered "surprisingly exact").

Such inscriptions from the Second Stage of the "Buh-Dniester people" (proto-Daci-Mizians, according to Danylenko; proto-Sumerian or Arattans according to Kifishin), along with numerous archaeological findings, suggest the preservation of ties between the related carriers of the Balkan-Danube cultures of Keresh-Boian and the Corded Ware ceramic culture – which derived from them – that spread into the territories of future France and

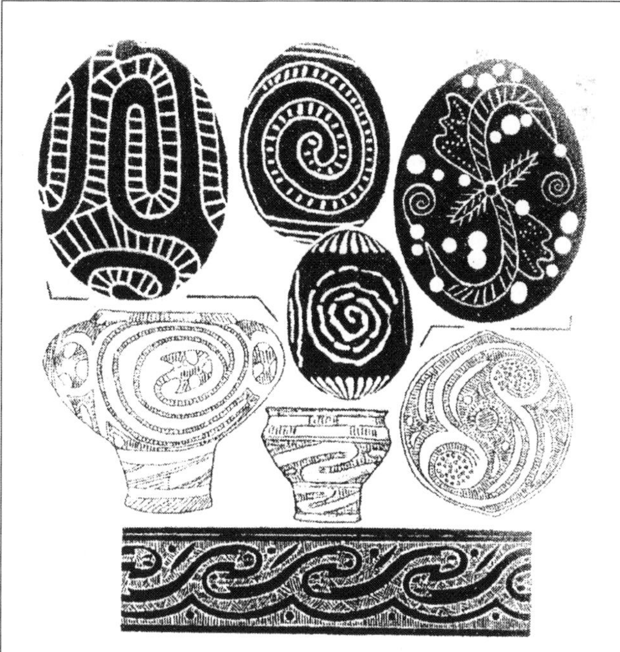

Fig. 19 : **Ornaments of Aratta and Ukraine**. Housewares of the earliest Trypillian archaeological culture of the 6th–5th millennium BCE and modern pysanky (hand-painted eggs).

Ukraine (the upper Dniester river and west of the Volyn region). It was from these relationships that the embryonic conditions for the appearance of the majestic Cucuteni-Trypillian culture were formed. On the other hand, the "Buh-Dniester people" were in contact with the local population represented by the Dnipro-Donets^ and other cultures of the Palaeo-European type – who were descendants of the eastern branch of the carriers of Svidertian culture (see above). The synthesis of these two lines and other ethno-cultural developments gave rise to the onset of the "Indo-Europeanisation" of Europe. In India the same process probably started with the appearance of Sumer and similar cultures in Arattan

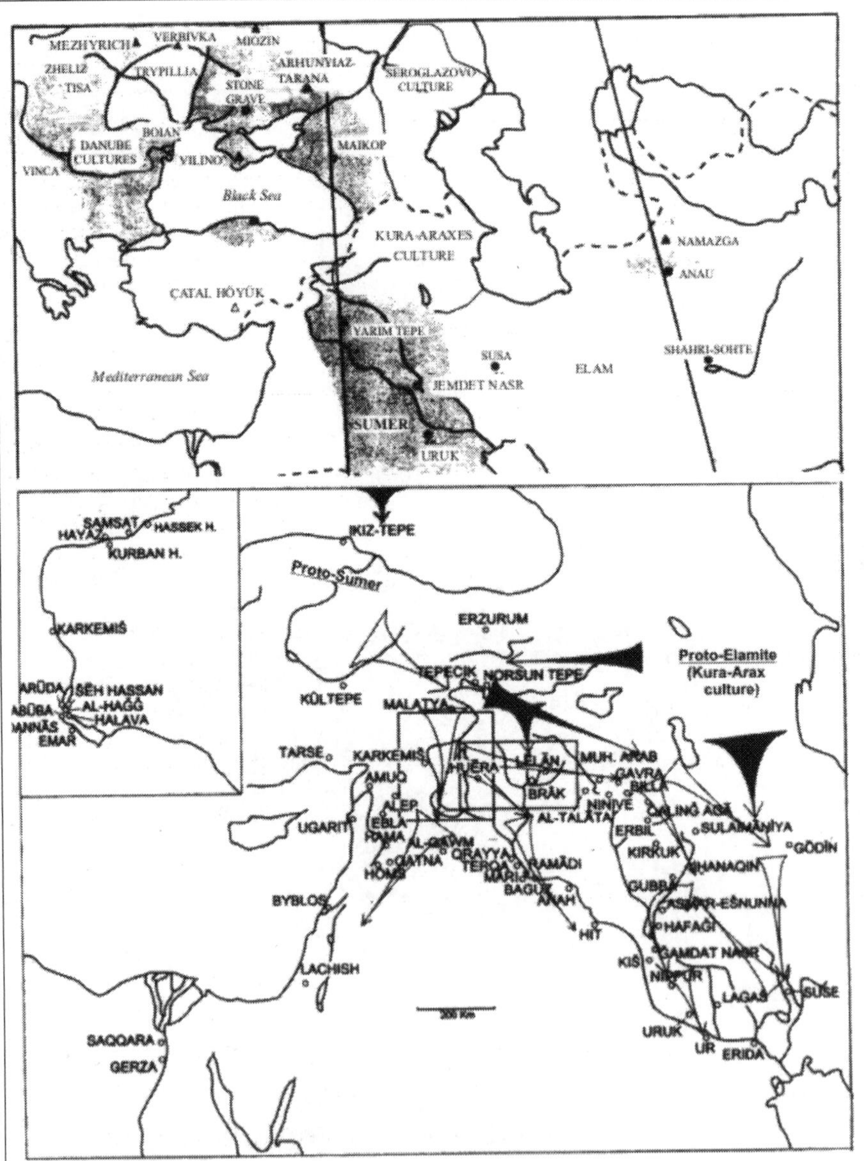

Fig. 20 : **Resettlement of Proto-Sumerians from the Northern Black Sea original homeland** in the 6th–4th millennium BCE; according to M. Lebeau (at the bottom) and A. G. Kifishin (*The ancient sanctuary of Stone Grave. The experience of deciphering the Proto-Sumerian archive of XII – III millennia BCE* – Aratta, Kyiv, 2001, p. 56, 560).

Punjab^ – known to archaeologists from the ruins of cities near Mohenjo-daro and Harappa.

Over time, the European Danube area and for a long time the Dnipro area, would become the greatest Indo-European centre in the world, until the partial Aryan migration into India around the middle of the 2nd millennium BCE, but during the 6th millennium BCE, this centre remained in its Anatolian ancestral homeland with its proto-towns near modern Çatal Höyük and Hacilar. It's possible that the end of the first of these, Çatal Höyük, and the appearance of the second, Hacilar, in 5650-5700 BCE (according to J. Mellaart), was a consequence of the geological catastrophes which caused the Mediterranean Sea to flood into, and connect with, the previously isolated Black Sea. In R. Ballard's opinion, this occurred about 5600 BCE.

In its third and final stage, the Buh-Dniester culture partly merged with the Dnipro-Donets culture, and partly with the early Trypillian culture – and may have partially moved into the Caucasus and Mesopotamia, taking a role in the formation of Sumer. There is no doubt that the latter culture wasn't only composed of carriers of the Buh-Dniester culture, but also, of early Arattan culture. However, it becomes increasingly evident that the main impulse behind the appearance of Sumer in the marshy interfluve between the Tigris and Euphrates, included those [leaders of the migrations and, probably, their kin and tribes] who went out from the lower reaches of the rivers of the Danube, Dniester, Buh, Dnipro and Molochna. Those were the most fertile areas of the Circum-Pontic zone of the (then) pre-Indo-European community of tribes and it was specifically here that the foundations of civilisation (of statehood) were laid.

The uncertain relationship between Sumer and the Indo-European community and other peoples, is a consequence of the formation of the first, Sumer, on the basis of the second, which was still a modest pre-Indo-European nucleus, as outlined above. There are two root causes for the appearance of pre-Sumer in Aratta. The first, and most obvious cause, is a population explosion amongst the farmer-cattle-breeders of the Black Sea coast. Secondly, a more direct reason, which we will consider shortly, is the "World Flood^" caused by the breakthrough of the waters of the Mediterranean Sea into the Black Sea. It will be expedient to base further consideration of this reason on the most recent geological datings of the Flood (compared to those proposed by R. Ballard), although this raises the problem that Sumer did not appear at a date as early as the Buh-Dniester and Trypillian archaeological cultures.

The pre-Danubian cultures of Keresh-Boian and Buh-Dniester in the East, as well as the Corded Ware ceramics culture of Western Europe, were the result of the first big ethno-cultural migration from Anatolian Çatal Höyük, Hacilar and other pre-Indo-European settlements during the 7th – 6th millennium BCE. In the 5th millennium BCE a second, greater, migration began, which initiated the Vinča archaeological culture in the Danube area. It is specifically from this culture that V. A. Safronov begins the history of the ***Indo-European*** ancestral homeland – from the second migration in time and territory (after the first, centred on Çatal Höyük in Asia Minor). One can agree with this in the sense that the Danube area, both at the turn of the 7th and 6th millennium BCE (which is not considered by Safronov, but is taken into account by Danylenko) and again in the 5th millennium BCE, received the

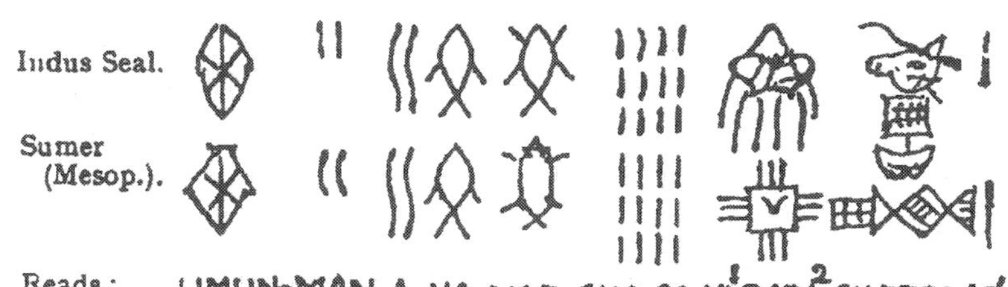
Indus Seal.
Sumer (Mesop.).
Reads : UMUN-MAN A-HA MAR SHA-GA-NI BARA GU-EDIN-AS
Transl. : Lord-Companion AHA, the son of SHAGANI, The *Pharaoh* in Edin Land.

Fig. 21 : **The similarity of the earliest Indus Valley writing** (Mohenjo-daro) **and Sumerian** (Mesopotamian). By Prof. L. A. Waddell; U.K.

vanguard migrants from Asia Minor and that the Vinčan wave marked the quite emphatic beginning of the term, "Indo-European" (whereas the first, Keresh wave, together with Aratta and Sumer that were generated by it, was still "pre-Indo-European"). This ethno-history of the second wave is akin to the first, but yet another migration broke the two thousand years of cultural evolution of the Keresh-Boian and Buh-Dniester types; their carriers were regrouped and this moved the centre for further development of the Danube area close to Dnipro, where archaeological finds of this renewed centre are now known under the conditional names of Cucuteni (in the territories of Romania and Moldova) and Trypillia (on the right-bank of Dnipro river in Ukraine). It then retained pre-Indo-European traditions, whilst the final Indo-Europeanisation of Europe began with the Vinča culture.

The Sursk-Dnipro culture, which owed its existence to the Buh-Dniester culture, was significantly influenced by the aboriginal Palaeo-European population and was further destined to connect with the Dnipro-Donets and other cultures of the Volga-Don area, forming the basis of the Seredny-Stoh^ archaeological culture in the same Dnipro area above the rapids. The ethno-historical identity of the "Buh-Dniester people" and their amalgamation with the "Trypillians" has been mentioned above. Relating to the Sursk-Dnipro, Dnipro-Donets and Seredny-Stoh cultures, we can say that V. N. Danylenko linked them to the proto-Tocharian^ ethno-historical community which in due course produced the Tocharians – carriers of the Afanasievo^ and other archaeological cultures of the Ural-Yenisey steppes. In an ethno-linguistic respect, they were related to the fore-mentioned proto-Indo-Europeans, who also came from the "Svidertians" of the Mesolithic era. However, it was not their western but their eastern half which formed the basis of the Ural-Altaic peoples (Finno-Ugric and Turkic peoples). The Tocharians somewhat isolated themselves from this general direction but their roots were, obviously, established in some western or central (Dnipro-Crimean) "Svidertian" branch.

The role of the terms proto-, pre- and -Slav in the process of forming the "Indo-Europeans" will be discussed below.

Suggested reading

1. Danylenko V. M., *Neolithic Ukraine*, Kyiv, 1969.
2. *Archaeology of Ukraine SSR,* Vol. 1, Kyiv, 197

CHAPTER 3

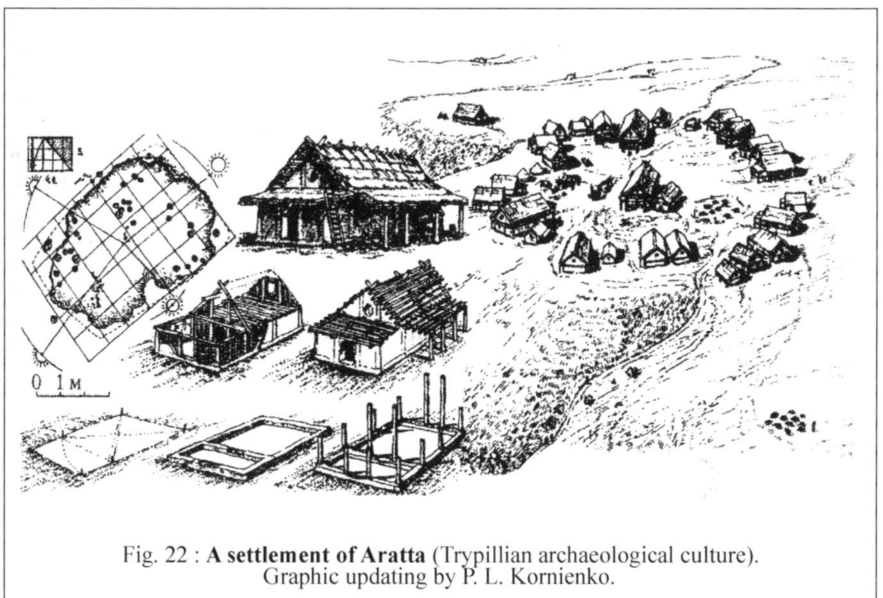

Fig. 22 : **A settlement of Aratta** (Trypillian archaeological culture).
Graphic updating by P. L. Kornienko.

ARATTA – THE MOST ANCIENT STATE IN THE WORLD

When considering the origin of the formation of Aratta it will be helpful to examine the existence of an earlier prototype stage in the development of that State, which is dated, according to a hypothesis by A. G. Kifishin, towards the end of the Palaeolithic era. Kifishin had deciphered an inscription of the name *'Aratta'* on a mammoth skull found at a settlement dating from the 18th – 12th millennium BCE near the village of Mezhyrich (between the rivers Ros^ and Rosava).

When the mammoth fauna eventually started to die out, the burgeoning problems presented by the changing ecological-demographic conditions required a radical decision from the established priest-rulers of the hunting society. The priests decided to solve the problem by dividing the centre of the area inhabited by the mammoth hunters of that time (located between the valleys of the Danube and the Volga, and the Carpathian and Caucasus mountains) into four sectors, thus periodically varying the combined exploitation and preservation of those places.

These regulations successfully maintained the habitat over several millennia at a level sufficient to permit the continuation of the *Palaeolithic cultures* until the climatic catastrophes and last glaciations of the 13th – 11th millennium BCE which led to their replacement by *Mesolithic cultures*. Nevertheless, the traditions of pre-Aratta – '*The Country lit by the Sun'* – were maintained (at least, in the archives of Stone Grave, whose inscribed chronicles began with images of mammoths and calendar marks from 11,582 BCE; perhaps over time, even earlier marks will be found and deciphered). Then there arose a new need for further regulations, this time to ensure the viability of the Indo-European people whose community had been forming, since the end of the 7th millennium BCE, along the western half of the Black Sea (which at that time was not yet connected to the Mediterranean). The priest-rulers of Shu-Nun (Stone Grave) renewed the ancient schema that was to become the foundation for the formation of the state of Aratta – distinguished by its early cities and writing, etc.

Clearly, the hypothesis by Kifishin that was briefly outlined at the start of this chapter, now requires further development and not just from the efforts of one generation of experts in the various disciplines of historical science. Undoubtedly, the translations of texts and dates recorded in our work will be specified (by this author) in the future. For the moment we accept the hypothesis of A. G. Kifishin's work, which accords well with various scientific sources and which does not contradict empirical generalisations of historiographic facts... Let us consider them.

1. Appearance of the State of Aratta.

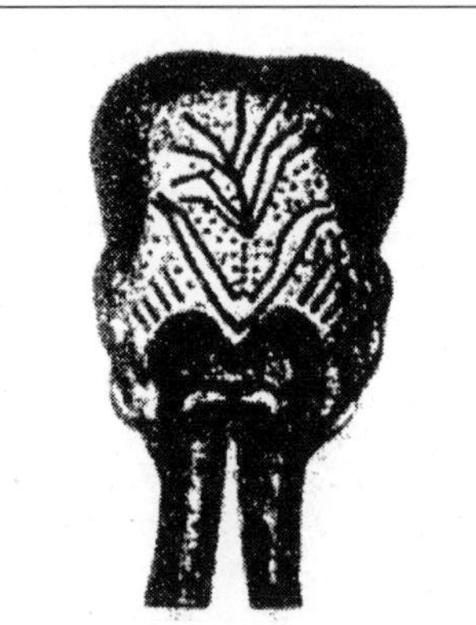

Fig. 23 : **The earliest ideogram of Aratta**. Ancient inscriptions on the skull of a mammoth from the site of Mezhyrich, 18th–12th millennium BCE.

At around 6200 BCE an expedition of priest-rulers from Shu-eden-na Ki-dug (*'Hand-Law of the Blessed Steppeland'*, as the settlement near the modern Turkish settlement of Çatal Höyük was then called) reached the sanctuary at Stone Grave (Shu-Nun, that is, *'Hand/Law of the Empress'*) on the left bank of the River Dnipro. They copied inscriptions from plates 4, 39, 9/6, 10, 29, 25/A, 25/B, 37/4, 34/A (according to the provisional numbering of the Rudynsky-Mykhailov archive[1]) in the following particular sequence. The linguist, A. G. Kifishin, who discovered this, deciphered these lines (given here in abridged form) based on subsequent Sumerian analogues, as follows:

No. 4 : *Goddess Gatumdug^, the Empress of the Steppe, condemned to death Anu, the Lord (of the sky).*

No. 39 : *On the lot of Goddess Inanna^, Great-Mother of the Blessed Steppe-land, the hero Sukhur^-Alal, ruled for 224 years.*

No. 9/6 : *Shining Anu^ judged the Seed of Mind by water and affirmed celebration in the City. Nindara and Utu^* [goddess of the Underworld and god of the Sun] *judged the seed tied by the Court of Water. Meslampaea struck the Big Bird* [death] *who judged Taurus who was defeated.*

No. 10 : *Ishkur^* [the Thunder-god, heir of the Mammoth] *in Righteous years was a greater judge of Ashnan^* [the goddess of grain].

No. 29 : *Bear (or She-bear) with Lyra judges.*

The first calendar-mythical subject set out in this manner is seen to be very concisely outlined; the relationships between the various fragments of this subject are almost comprehensible to us.... however, a list of the legendary-historical rulers of the Blessed Steppe-land (from the area above the Dnipro rapids as far as the coastal mouth of the River Molochna) is presented further on and the terms and main business of their panels are specified:

No. 25/A : *Meen-alal (water/seed connected) – 440 years, Pub-alal (he connected water 20 times) Sal-thuja (the settled woman, who found the decision) – 5 year old, Banzi* ('the Bow of souls') *– 60 years and at the lady-ruler Ki-sal* ('the Earth women') *– 83 years, Adamgi* ('mankind' and 'the Seed of marriage') *83 times righteously judged by water over in the 50th sanctuary. He passed 270 years, then in the time of Dumuzi^ – 23 years. Enlil-pail ruled 34 and 109 years and 182 more. And before that Mugi ruled 32 years and 690 more and 181. Before him for 92 years Sukhur-asal* (antediluvian 'Carp of Water Woman'*) was ruling. This information is in accordance with the tablet of Kas-Kisim together with him 132 more and 50 years, when during 21 years "fastened water" flowed in the time of the god Dumuzi, who ruled for 123 years.*

This chronicle continues in similar spirit on plates No. 25/B, 48/A, 37/4, 34/A. (in which the narrative and the facts interlace with strange calendar-astronomical-mythological calculations, etc., whose significance is elusive to us). Amongst the most interesting references in the archived tablets or other chronicles of the priests, are names such as the Icy Bog (Glacier?) and the Water of Depths (Deluge?); and references to cities (which in that time were probably more akin to settlements) and gods who would become, in due course, inherent to Sumer; the narrative covered the same mythological subjects which, through four millennia, would form the basis of Sumerian poems; there are descriptions of "a serpent in the team of two bulls" etc., which relates directly to images from Stone Grave; such images are also found on the cliffs of the Caucasus and on Mesopotamian seals (Tables XXXI, XXXII).

A replica of these very ancient world chronicles, from the 7th millennium BCE, was reproduced on a bas-relief at the Çatal Höyük Foremother temple No. 23/VII, built in 6200 ± 97 BCE, probably in honour of the expedition that returned to their native Shu-eden-na Ki-dug [from Stone Grave, 'Shu-Nun']. According to Kifishin, the differences in these copies from the original records (i.e. those at Shu-Nun) are insignificant; the most essential difference being a missing inscription on No. 48/A and a variation in 34/A (at the end of the copy) with regard to the details of Çatal Höyük.

Both this original and its copy of the most ancient chronicles in the world, mark the beginning of the history of world civilisation and at the same time, the final composition of the Indo-European community and the onset of its development in the Circum-Pontic zone. This began with the pre-Danubian archaeological culture of Keresh which became the second synthesising centre of the indicated community (after Asia Minor's Çatal Höyük); a third centre (that reached its zenith in due course in Trypillia) was cradled in the bosom of the Buh-Dniester culture and its Sursk-Dnipro off-shoot. The latter probably controlled the district of Stone Grave – an embryonic "pre-Indo-European" community, no less significant than that of Çatal Höyük. Indeed if the second of these centres produced not only an agricultural-cattle breeding economy but also the city-state (with pre-statehood) system of public relations, then the first not only invented written language but also the first domesticated large horned cattle and the practice of ploughed agriculture. In addition to their animal bone remains at the settlement near Red Mountain, this is also indicated in calendar imagery at "The Grotto of the Bull", the central sanctuary adjoining the settlement at Stone Grave. The most ancient image of this animal, the bull, still retaining attributes of the mammoth, is dated to the 7th millennium BCE (by A.G. Kifishin and other researchers). From a later period (both typologically and chronologically, from the 6th – 4th millennium BCE), is a second image of a bull – which is still associated with that first proboscidiform^ image, with water pouring from its mouth, and at the same time being the embodiment of Taurus – which is placed adjacent to the image of a plough of the 'Sumer-Elamite type'. But because neither of those countries existed at that time, and because the image of the plough was connected with a harnessed bull team – the oldest such image in the world – it is necessary to connect this invention with the priests of Shu-Nun (Stone Grave).

By the 6th millennium BCE, the world's first-ever state – Aratta – had already formed within the depths of the Keresh culture. Along with the remains of cities on the territories of what are now Hungary and Bulgaria, this is certified in numerous forerunners of the clay tablets associated with future Sumer; these antecedents, in turn, originate from Shu-Nun (the inscriptions from Stone Grave and then from Çatal Höyük already mentioned). However, amongst the inscriptions at Shu-Nun (Stone Grave), references to Aratta appear no earlier than the Danube references which describe Aratta as a foreign country (relative to the left bank of the lower reaches of the Dnipro – which, indeed, was not in the area of Trypillia, nor in her preceding archaeological culture of Aratta): *"On the hill of Duku demons-utuhs of Aratta judged people"* etc.

To researchers of the Keresh culture, the best known of these texts is: *the (sacrificial) lamb, grasped by a priest of Aratta; Urash (Sky god) channel priest, the (magic) brick of definition 40; a (sacrificial) kid (goat) of the Wall of Warriors.*

So, this ancient Aratta already had channels and fortresses, professional clerics and lawyers, a social hierarchy, certain rituals and cults, and gods. The population density at this stage of the most ancient state in the world is about 50 times higher than the density of the surrounding population. It is evident that this '*Country (of farmers) lit up by the Sun*' not only considered itself to be the successor of Asia Minor's Shu-eden-na Ki-dug but also the more ancient, pre-Dnipro Shu-Nun whose archive they continued to use and through which passed, as we shall see, the distant relations of Aratta (Fig.20, Table V).

2. Aratta of the Danube and Dnipro interfluve.

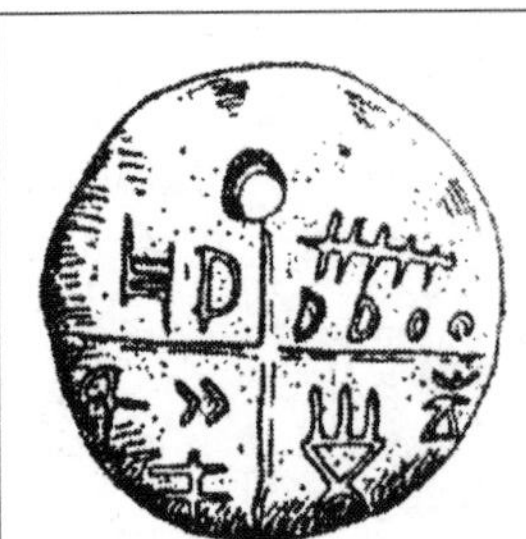

Fig. 24 : **Proto-Sumerian tablet from the Danube area** (according to N. Vlassa and A. Falkenstein). Tartaria (Romania), 6th millennium BCE.

This culture has become known to the modern scientific community as the "Cucuteni-Trypillia archaeological culture" to give it its conditional name. It has already been stated that it originated from the Keresh, Corded Ware, Boian and Buh-Dniester cultures. Let us remember that it consisted of their regrouping of the first, pre-Indo-European wave of migrants from Asia Minor, who settled (mixing with the local Palaeo-European population) along the banks of the Danube up to the Dnipro and Molochna. This regrouping was brought about by the ecological-demographic changes that occurred around mid-5th to 6th millennium BCE, which led to a second great wave of migration from Asia Minor's ancestral homeland, which formed the Vinča culture of the Balkans.

Throughout the twentieth century, a huge body of literature was published about the Cucuteni-Trypillia culture. Nevertheless, it was almost exclusively archaeological in nature with few researchers offering any historical interpretations. The matter would be improved if researchers started to actively explore appropriate written records.

From clay tablets found in the Danube area (translated by A. G. Kifishin) we learn that somewhere in mid-5th (or 6th) millennium BCE, a god of the Netherworld, Kulla^, and the goddess of the Steppes, Gatumdug, put aside their quarrels and united against an invasion of warriors sent by the goddess Ishkhar[2] from the south-east (possibly forerunners of the Hurrian Uzhhars and Aryan Ushas^?), threatening the lands of Aratta. As already mentioned, it's perhaps in response to the second migration from Asia Minor, the ancestral homeland (and the founder of the Indo-European community), that there was local resistance on the part of the population from the previous wave of pre-Indo-Europeans who had taken root in Europe and already created Aratta at some time in their past.

Some inscriptions from the Cucuteni culture on the territory of modern Romania also deserve particular attention, such as this example:

...a descendant of the Lord of the Country of fields, the Sun god judges the slain in the garden, this is the second sanctuary of the twins of Inanna; 2 hoes (ritually) established in 5 fields....

This text bears comparison in some of its details with the inscription found on a pre-Sumerian tablet from the Volyn region of Ukraine, deciphered by V. N. Danylenko; he interpreted its characters thus:

Send in (help) to the settlement of {....place-name} *5 teams of bulls with ploughs by* {...calendar number}.

These inscriptions, together with archaeological and other supporting data, indicate the high level of cultural achievement in the second Dnipro-Danube Aratta (in terms of that era and that territory). The basis of this Arattan economy was a developed form of agriculture – not only using the hoe but also the plough. The main crop was a double-grain variety of wheat but single-grain einkorn and spelt, two varieties of barley, millet and beans were also cultivated. There were gardens, orchards, vegetable plots, and at the Dniester-Prut interfluves they had vineyards. They reared large and small horned cattle, pigs and in due course they trained horses though they didn't cease hunting, fishing and gathering. They practised the noble crafts: the working of wood and stone, pottery making, metallurgy and weaving. The cities and regions of the different areas of Aratta were perfectly adapted to prevailing local conditions so they offered a variety of economic models (not only producing, but even appropriating economies!). They had already reached a fairly well-established level of development during earlier times so there was little necessity to change or vary their structure – just a need to rearrange some aspects, most notably in the development of the related skills of pottery and metallurgy. The historical background to their social relationships, everyday life and ideology will be considered in due course.

Like the preceding Buh-Dniester culture, the **Trypillian** culture also lasted for about two millennia and passed through three distinct stages.

The **First Stage** refers to the most ancient settlements of the Cucuteni-Trypillian culture which appeared in the second half of the 5th millennium BCE (a date since revised, in accordance with the most recent data, to 5400-4600 BCE) in the territory of south-eastern Transylvania, the Moldavian pre-Carpathians and the valleys of the left-bank tributaries of

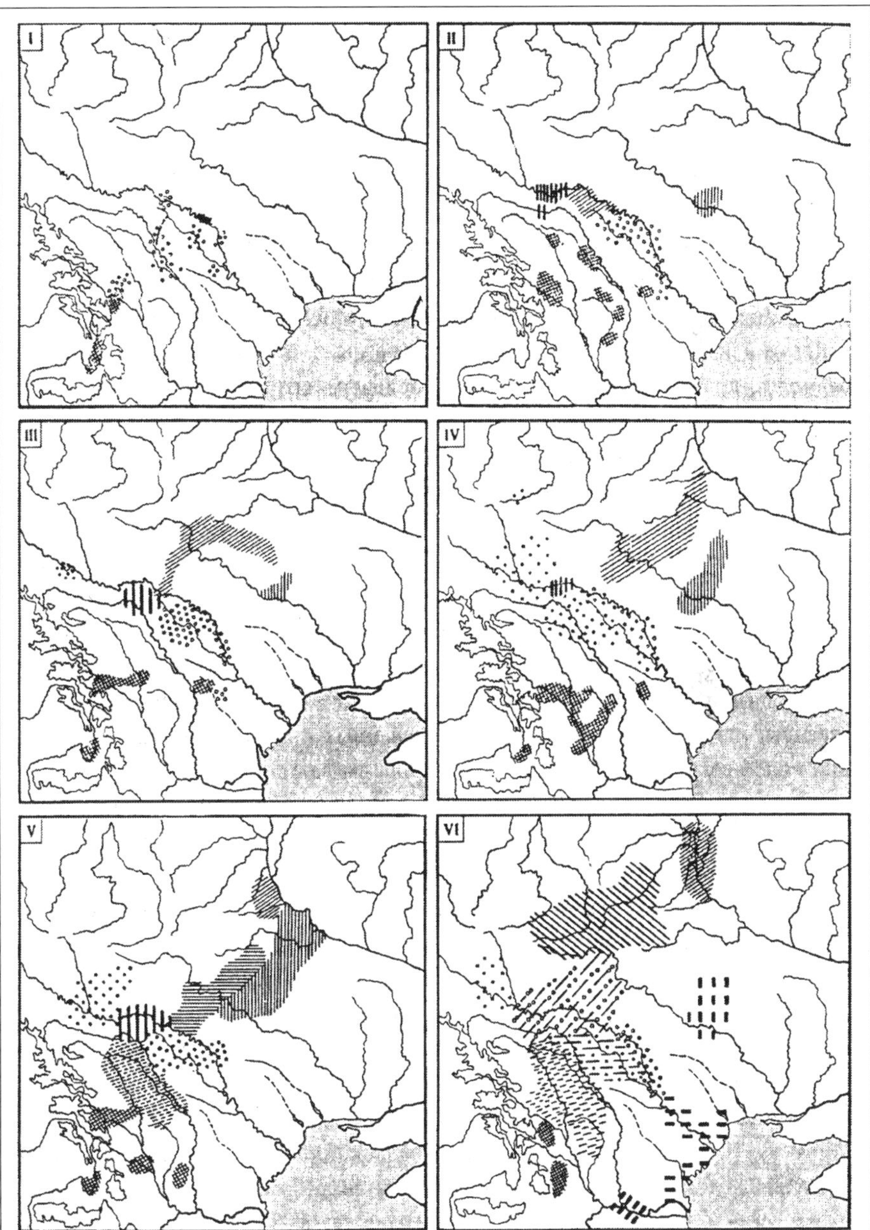

Fig. 25 : **Growth of Aratta between the 6th–3rd millennium BCE**. The territory of the Cucuteni-Trypillia archaeological culture from the Stage I (5400-4600 BCE) to the end of Stage III (2750-2250 BCE). According to E. K. Chernysh.

the Danube. Even at that date, rectangular ground dwellings that occupied an area of up to $50m^2$ already prevailed: they consisted of a wooden framework, wickerwork walls, a solid ceiling with an attic area above; gable roofs covered by straw, reed or turf; the interior and exterior of the houses were coated with clay and chaff which were then bleached, dyed, painted and decorated in the same designs as their ceramics. Even now, similar dwellings can still be found in the more remote villages of Ukraine and Moldova (Photos 21-25, Fig. 22).

Typical dwellings featured residential 'pits' (dug foundations) and open fires on stone hearths; homes were two-storied, with passages between neighbouring houses, having circular window openings (possibly closed with tightly stretched bladders of bulls or other animals). Ditches surrounded the perimeter of each settlement. Each irregularly built settlement usually did not exceed 1 hectare in area and the number of houses it supported was about 20. A more thoroughly investigated settlement (by S. N. Bibikov) was situated above the Middle Dniester, near Luka-Vrublevetscka which stretched along the riverbank and was naturally protected by a steep slope. The largest houses, with an area of $130m^2$, were probably intended for communal needs. There are no signs of definite property or class hierarchy having been present in Arattan "Trypillia".

It is particularly important to note the emergence of a new type of sanctuary-observatory which replaced the temples that had once been inherent to Çatal Höyük. These new observatories, which were for calendar purposes, were set out in an open area in the form of circular earth banks enclosing an internal ring ditch within which, lunar and solar risings and settings were recorded 1- 4 times. They appeared towards the end of the 5th millennium BCE and continued until the middle of the 2nd millennium BCE, set out along what, at that time, constituted the northern boundary of agriculture; observatory structures like this reached as far as Stonehenge^ in Britain and Arkaim in the Trans-Urals and offer to posterity the clearest possible evidence of the state structure of Aratta and of the high intellect of her rulers (Table XVI).

Aratta is mentioned on one of the clay tablets found at the settlement of Gorbunovsk (in the south-eastern Urals):

"*When Utu* [the Sun god] *possessed Lyre^ in Aratta – Dumuzi* [then the ruler or God], *sent seeds to Ninazu^ in the abyss*".

The inscription corresponds to the text on plate No. 9/6 at Stone Grave which was also copied into temple 23/V11 at Çatal Höyük although the text on the copied plate seems more arbitrary:

"*Lord Anu caused a shining celebration to brighten the City. Meslamtaea^ Bird, struck Nindara^ and Utu has staged a 'Water Court'*".

Each of the plates had been thrown into water during a calendar-conditional ritual – and in some way, they were connected with the penetration of the priests of Aratta into that distant country and had spread here, along with the same sanctuary-observatories mentioned already, as well as productive economies, (agriculture in particular – in which L. R. Kyzlasov found a reference to the Tazminsk culture of Southern Siberia having been influenced by Sumer). Archaeologists date the Gorbunovsk settlement to the 3rd millennium BCE, but the tablets can be dated to a much earlier time of the 6th – 4th millennium BCE (when the chronicle of Shu-Nun was well established and when Aratta had developed the pre-Indo-European community, and also when the Tocharians, amongst others, had began to move beyond the Urals).

At the end of this early stage, the population of Aratta left Transylvania and extended their territory to the Southern Buh river. The number of settlements increased ten-fold, reaching 200 or more. Two-storied houses appeared containing furnaces, kitchens and bakeries, barns and cellars; driers for grain were developed in the form of circular semi-dugouts with a deep fire-hearth in the centre. Wooden furniture has not yet been traced by archaeologists but there is evidence of raised earthen benches for stoves and altars with fire places, remnants of human and animal bones, utensils, figurines. "These monumental, multi-purpose constructions – social-housing complexes, were seen in Trypillian culture at an early stage of its development" and these buildings were in no way inferior to the architecture of later stages – notes M. Yu. Videyko, ("*Old settlements of Ukraine*" in *The Album of*

Archaeological Sources and Reconstruction, Kyiv, 2000). Further changes in the layout of villages and cities were not so much defined by developments in their architecture, as by variations in demographic and social change within the state (Table XVIII).

Almost all of the figurines from this First Stage represent a seated woman – the Foremother. Her head and ornamentation were turtle-like. Possibly, these features represent Gatumdug, as the features of Inanna were more realistic in the figurines of the following stage. The stomach and breast area of the Foremother were generally decorated, with rhomboid, diamond-shaped symbols representing the fertile field. (In addition, researchers found imitations of grains made from a mix of various flours inside the stomach of these statues.). On the breast was a serpentine symbol representing the origin of man (the god Kull?). The same symbols were inherent to the preceding Buh-Dniester culture; their figurines showed an emergent outline at this stage.

The incised and linear-banded principle of ornamentation was still maintained. However, it became significantly more varied, as also did the vessels: large earthenware pots for preservation of grain and other supplies, large and small kitchen clay pots and vases, ladles and spoons, bowls and strainers. In some, anthropomorphic forms began to appear – an embodiment of the image of the Foremother, etc. (Table XXIV: 17-21).

Burial grounds from the early and middle stage of Trypillia have not yet been found; only separate burials of offerings in the home are known. The dead were probably cremated and their ashes carried away by water. There are ethnographic parallels for this practice (particularly in India) – it was widespread amongst Indo-European people whose word '*naus*' not only meant 'a vessel/boat', but also 'deceased' and 'death'. Evidence from ancient Aratta testifies to the use of cremation (not of the common dead, but of sacrificial victims), and it's even seen in pre-Trypillian inscriptions:

40th reign. On the order of god Shaue the elder is ritually burnt. This is 10th (sacrifice);

The Woman Warrior has glorified [has burnt as victims] warriors of the sanctuary of Fire, not giving (them) leave of (burning) sanctuaries;

The Woman Warrior glorified (them) in the Steppe.

Burning was thought to resurrect the person; the practise of voluntary or compulsory self-sacrifice was a widespread civic duty. Whilst the priestesses and priests governed society, the warriors, except for their direct duties, served in temples and were sacrificed as elders. In any event, the role of the priest was similar to that of the Indo-Aryan ruler of the Ramayana^, who ploughed the ('Furrow') known as Sita, the breast-fed infant

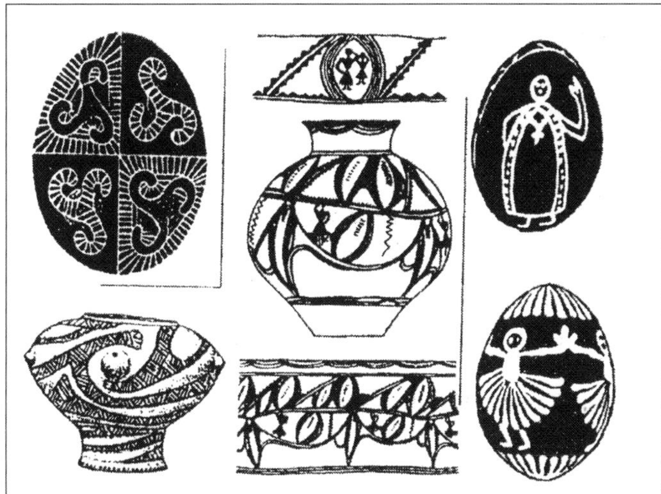

Fig. 26 : **Ornaments of Aratta and Ukraine**. Housewares from the 6th–4th millennium BCE and modern pysanky (hand-painted eggs).

who appeared during the ruler's ritual ploughing of the land. The word 'slave' is mentioned only once – *"a slave of the Country's plough"*. But is the term, translated by A. G. Kifishin based on the archives of Sumer, understood correctly? No slaves were kings of Egypt, nor were the first rulers of Muscovy, yet each of them oversaw the ploughing of the first furrow in Spring....

In relation to the chronicle of Stone Grave (which the priests of the Sursk-Dnipro culture, probably an off-shoot of Buh-Dniester culture, continued up to the beginning of the next stage of Trypillia), there is recorded on plate No. 25 which is already familiar to us, a continued list of rulers who headed the inhabitants of the Dnipro area after 6200 BCE, (translated as above, by A. G. Kifishin and featuring some "surprisingly precise dates", explained below).

The Second Dynasty began with the patriarch A-Enzu, who conducted some reforms in 5852 BCE (during the time of Utu-Me-Akud) and again in 5702 BCE (during the time of A-Kilime). According to the latter, a partial migration was undertaken to the site where the city of Ur would be built in Mesopotamia. The migrants united around the priests of the Moon God Sina^ in Ur and established the dynasty of *"The House of Baragesi"* in 5662-5622 BCE. And in 5069 BCE, during the time of the 18th ruler of the 2nd dynasty, A-Imdugud appeared – founding the alternative *"House of Imdugud^"* in the ancestral home of Aratta, namely in the Ukrainian Dnipro area.

These and other dates in the history of Aratta and Sumer are constantly being refined by historians and archaeologists. According to scientific data from the second half of the 20th century, the recorded dates of 5702-5069 BCE (which are probably legendary, just like the dates of the Biblical patriarchs for example), would have to be 'rejuvenated' by 2,500 years to bring them closer to the formation of Mesopotamian Sumer towards the end of the 4th millennium BCE[3]. However, during the last decade, experts have narrowed the date of the Trypillian culture to approximately 5400 BC E (extending earlier dating by approximately one millennium), which comes closer to the end of Çatal Höyük (5650 BCE) and according to the latest dating, (5600-5500 BCE) accords with the breach of the Mediterranean Sea into the Black Sea – which was the principal reason for Sumer becoming isolated from Aratta. So, perhaps the 'surprisingly precise dates' on Plate No. 25 as deciphered by A. G. Kifishin, are not so far from the truth.

The **Second Stage** of development of "Trypillian" Aratta began about 3600 BCE (4600 BCE according to M.Yu.Videyko). The economy, everyday life, and territory had changed little but the number of settlements and their area had increased significantly; some tribes or kin had reached the Dnipro area above the River Ros (Fig. 25, III-IV).

Small settlements had disappeared and the area of this phase of settlement now averaged 3-40 hectares. Settlement plans changed to being concentric with a central public area; embankment fortifications, etc., were replaced by walls interconnecting the external ring of houses. Perhaps they were protective in function, not so much from enemies, but from predators such as wolves, bears and lions (which thrived along the Northern Black Sea Coast at that time, and also during Scythian times). Houses became larger and were mainly two-storied (Fig. 22). They were occupied by family groups spanning three generations. Dwellings were grouped with economic outbuildings at the edges of the settlement (as had been the case earlier and would remain so in the future) according to ancestral-family and economic ties. Many cult models of houses and sanctuaries survive, amongst them were temples that resembled the older designs from Çatal Höyük and Hacilar.

The greatest development within crafts was the fashioning of stone and metal – the forging and welding of copper-wares, together with elementary casting of bronze – and pottery making. Potters already used the kiln but did not know the potter's wheel. Besides the traditional simply ornamented kitchen vessels however, the use of "ceremonial" ceramic ware was further developed, being painted before kilning using multi-coloured paints: white, yellow, red and various shades of brown. Female and other figurines were considerably more varied. The majority no longer featured a stylised 'turtle' [or beaked-type] head, but featured human heads (with the traditional form of nose), sometimes even portraying individual people; their ornamentation frequently featured details of clothing. Although they were mainly cultic figurines, they nevertheless provided an opportunity to represent the

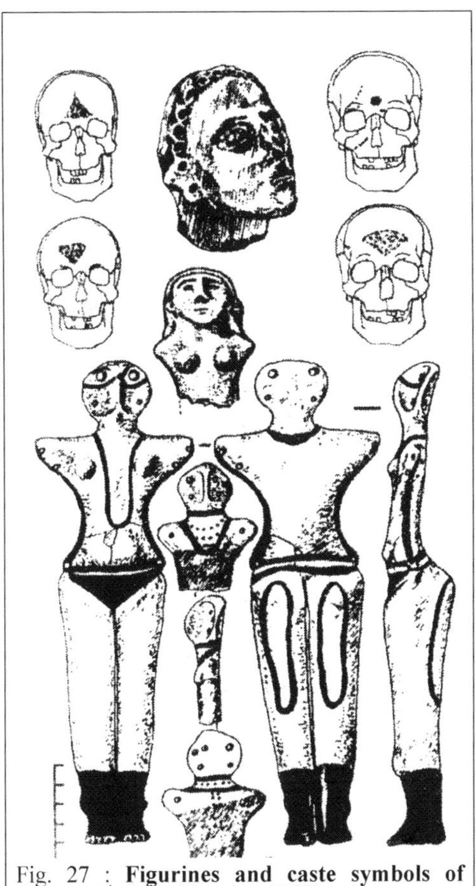

Fig. 27 : **Figurines and caste symbols of Aratta,** 4th–3rd millennium BCE.

appearance of the Arattans.

Women evidently braided their hair, but during the rituals at least, they favoured a long hairstyle with a central parting; at the back of the head, the length of hair was variously concealed in either a decorative net or continuous covering. Caps were worn on the head, sometimes mushroom-shaped hats. Around the neck were necklaces, ingots and pieces akin to pectorals^ that were sometimes supplemented by pendants or ribbons trailing at the back. Tunics were of different lengths and with varied cuts, as well as jackets. Underwear consisted of bands wrapped around the hip area. Kilted by belts, they wore cross-belts slung over one or both shoulders. They wore shoes, sandals, boots and knee-boots, frequently with fur cuffs. Yes, they were typical Ukrainian women!

Nevertheless, the faces of people were painted, perhaps tattooed. They used red and other coloured paints just the same as on skulls from the "Usativ^ variant of late Trypillian culture". This indicates that these people retained symbolic traces of caste and kin on their bodies, evident on their foreheads and in their hairstyles; the equivalent practice still occurs in Bharatta^ (India). Here and there, men are represented with '*oseledets*' [a long narrow lock of hair hanging from the top of the head], hitherto characteristic of Ukrainian Cossacks^. In India this style is worn by the descendants of Vasistha^, one of the authors of the *Rigveda*. It is believed that the father of this Brahman was Varuna^ himself; the oldest spelling of his name in Mitannian was – Uruvanash. Was he not a descendant of the Arattan Urash and Pelasgian^ Uran?

Traditional statues of standing women predominate but now they are not only of mothers but also depict maidens. On altars and on anthropomorphic vessels they are quite often combined, such as the Aryan Aditi^ and Ushas or (in the opinion of V. N. Danylenko) the Greek Demeter^ and Persephone^. However, the figurine of a woman seated on a Bull-horned throne is also widespread. M. A. Chmykhov regarded such combinations as the origin for the Greek myth of Europa and Zeus^; however, it's also helpful to closely connect them with the 'Indo-European'-Aryan Prithvi^ and Dyaus^': the mother-'Earth' and father-'Sky' who were represented in the form of people or long-horned cattle. S. I. Nalyvayko very strongly connects the myth of the abduction of Europa with the origin of the foremother of cows, Surabhi^ (like Europa) – 'the Super Earth goddess' – who according to the *Mahabharata*^, gave birth to Nandini, the favourite cow of the fore-mentioned sage Vasistha. Surabhi arose at the creation of the world and gave milk to the world to drink, living in Rasatale – the seventh, lowest sphere of the Earth; four cows borne by her support the cardinal points. Illustrations of all of these representations can be seen in bowls of the Usativ culture, which are shaped in a way similar to the udder (though this occurs in the third stage of Trypillian culture; Table XVIII:3. We have run forward a little here).

The appearance of the Dyaus-Prithvi image was probably connected to the spreading influence of the pre-Danubian Lendel^ culture (which replaced the Vinča culture) and with the emergence of the fundamentally new sanctuary-observatories that were mentioned earlier. However, having inherited a circular layout for settlements, these were now situated, not near small rivers but on "bald mountains^" i.e. treeless hills that were far more suitable for calendar-astronomical observation. Probably ever since the times of matriarchal rule, such hills started to be called "Dievychy" (meaning "Maiden/Maidan^-like" in English) and they were considered to be gathering places for sorceresses. However the resulting name was derived from both the female, and male hypostasis of Daeva-Dyaus (later – Devi and Deva).

The writing on some of the Cucuteni-Trypillia tablets recorded the fore-mentioned references to sanctuaries and some knowledge of the twins of Inanna. Images of these, or of similar twins/pairs, were presented in temples at Çatal Höyük. There are good reasons to believe that with the spread of these sanctuary-observatories they began to be transformed into Apollo^ and Artemis (as the personification of the main constellations of the zodiac and zenith, i.e. as Taurus with the Pleiades and as Ursa Major with the Pole star) – the children of Zeus (Dzeus → Dyaus) or Diya and Latona^ (Lato^ → Rato), 'Sky'-father and 'the 'Circle' with the meaning of the Zodiac, or 'Law' (the Rita of Aryan tribes). A. G. Kifishin considers that the Greek Apollo and Helios are analogous with the proto-Sumerian (i.e. Arattan) Urash.

By the end of the Second Stage in the development of "Trypillian" Aratta, one can incorporate the above-mentioned lines from the proto-Sumerian chronicles of Shu-Nun – Stone Grave on the Molochna River. We can also attach some evidence of the Indo-Aryan *Ramayana* and *Mahabharata*. The main events of the second of these epic traditions relates to the period between 3138-3102 BCE. S. I. Nalyvayko reasonably compares Aratta of this grand epic with the archaeological culture of Mohenjo-daro^ of Punjab. On the other hand, he compares those two cultures with Aratta and the Trypillian culture of the right-bank of Dnipro river in Ukraine. He then compares adjacent Dandara and Odra (Odisa, Orisa) – with Dandaria and Odissa, or Orissa (Oriana of *The Veles Book*). The last two territories were in the lower reaches of the Dnipro and Dniester. Dandaka^ of the *Ramayana* corresponds to the ancient name of the area that is now the modern Kamyshova Bay in Crimea. Later on we will provide more details about this subject.

The Odessa^ region of Ukraine is located along the coastal section where the above mentioned Usativ archaeological culture began to arise (near the modern village of Usativ) between the 4th – 3rd millennium BCE. It formed with a strong synthesis of Aratto-Aryan traditions, which can be considered as being reflected in historic Oriana-Orisa (from 'Hor(d)esy', according to S. I. Nalyvayko, meaning 'Country of the Bull') (Tables XXXVII).

The **Third Stage** of development covers approximately the period between 3000-2250 BCE (3500-2750[4]) which correlated with the history of Sumer (or with its past history and roots). At the beginning of this stage, the centre of this 'Country of Farmers' was firmly established in an area almost surrounded by river waters of the Southern Buh, Sob, Ros and Syniukha, and here the greatest development in the entire history of Aratta was reached. It is quite probable that the banks of the Ros were at some time both a border and lively trade point between Aratta and Arián. S. I. Nalyvayko believes that the Ros at that time was identified with the Vedic river Race, from which developed the near-mythical tale (in the *Rigveda*) about the theft of cows belonging to serpent-warrior Indra^ by the 'merchant' Pani. It is perhaps at that time that the village of Panikarcha arose in the modern Cherkasy region of Ukraine; also the surnames Panikar amongst Cossacks and Hindus, and the town of Roden' near the mouth of the Ros – named in honour of Rudra^, son of the fore-mentioned Surabhi.

In the early 1960's, in the Cherkasy region, the pilot K. V. Shishkin and archaeologist M. M. Shmahly discovered aerial evidence of Trypillian cities (i. e. Arattan) with areas spanning 300-450 hectares. Having a concentric lay-out, the cities were surrounded by much smaller villages with irregular buildings, as well as sanctuary-observatories of the Lendel type. It seems likely that each of these large complexes already represented an autonomous state, akin to the contemporaneous city state of Ur in Sumer though that only reached 45 hectares, and to the future 'polis' or city states of Greece. The largest city (near the village of Talianky^) had the outline of a right foot – probably the foot of Vishnu^. Numerous images of "the three steps of Vishnu", as described in the *Rigveda*, are widely represented on steles and in the graves of Aryan burial kurhans in the Dnipro area, and several "plates [stone slabs] with footprints" are featured at Stone Grave. The earthly incarnations of Vishnu are considered to be the two principal heroes of the above-mentioned epic poem – Rama^ and Krishna^.

The second largest city in size has been studied in far better detail; it is adjacent to Talianky in the neighbouring village of Maydanets^ (in the Talne district of the Cherkasy region). In outline plan the city had an egg-shaped appearance with the pointed end facing south. From this end there were four concentric rows of two-storied houses and opposite them – three rows. Inside the central ellipse, with dimensions of 800 x 1200m, were located several areas of 1-3 hectares and 500 houses; the ellipse itself was made up of 225 houses.

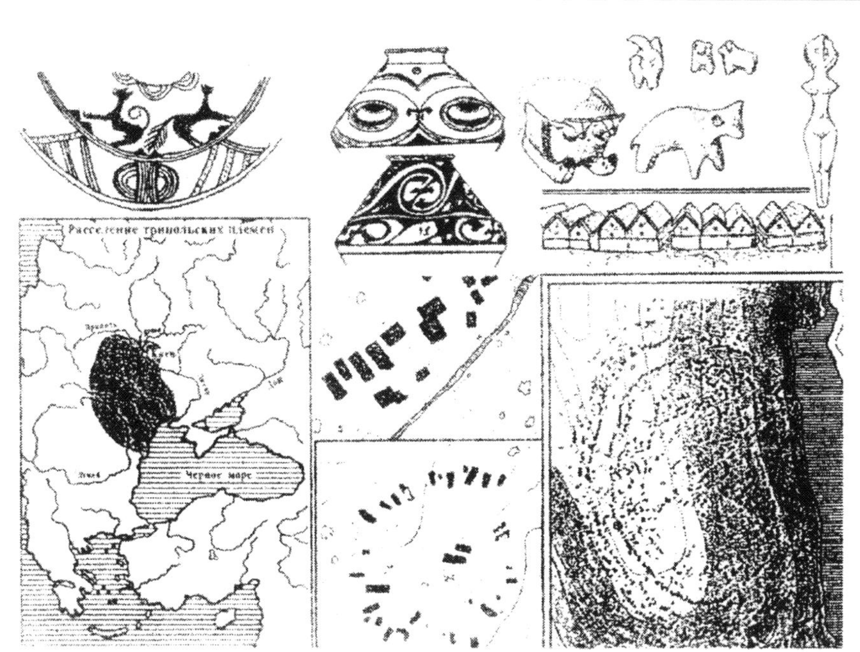

Fig. 28 : **Village, settlement and city of Aratta**. [Decorated ceramics]. On the right – the plan of one of the largest cities of Aratta (at the modern village of Maydanets in the Cherkasy region). According to K. V. Shishkin, V. P. Dudkin et al.

The second ellipse was composed of 350 buildings, and the third one of more than 115; the fourth, outermost (now destroyed in places), reached 1300 x 1900m average ground space. The average floor area of a house (for the two floors together) was about 60-120m^2, but some were 300m^2. Heating and the preparation of food in the home were achieved in dome-like furnaces and open fires with openings in the ceiling (on a garret) above them.

Researchers started to draw attention to the dating and similarity of socio-economic processes in the Trypillian archaeological culture compared to the civilisations of the Near East (in particular of Sumer), and clearly needed to unravel this mystery. The first steps were taken by the linguists. Although they ignored Trypillia, T. V. Gamkrelidze and V. V. Ivanov nevertheless distinguished an Indo-European language with Sumerian and Elamite^ borrowings. Professor L. Waddell, in the *Sumer-Aryan Dictionary* complete with English commentary, came to the eloquent conclusion: "Sumerians – these are the early Aryans". (This is too definitive; it's necessary to say "Arattan" instead of "Aryan"). Relevant archaeological data started to accumulate so that, as early as the 1950s, V. N. Danylenko was able to distinguish, near these sources, the "Azov-Black Sea line of development of the steppe Eneolithic", which was connected to the Trypillian culture at the time of the Mesopotamian civilisations. Winter-dwellings, burials and separate Trypillian findings have been identified, anticipating those in Crimea and Sumer – and even in Volyn, i.e. the Volyn region (where Danylenko received two clay tablets from local historians). Similar journeys extended the "Azov-Black Sea line" of the Circum-Pontic zone, a trail already blazed by representatives of the Buh-Dniester, Dnipro-Donets and Novo-Danylivka cultures in the direction of Asia Minor and Mesopotamia. The most obvious manifestation of Arattan-Sumerian communications at the beginning of the 3rd stage of Trypillia, was found beneath the Velyko-Olexandrivsk^ kurhan (in the same regional centre of the Kherson region) between the 4th – 3rd millennium BCE, where two priests from Sumer and Aratta had been buried. The end of this stage was marked by with the isolation of "Usativ people" (named after a village near Odessa) who had mastered a sea route through to Asia Minor and were provided with metal from there, having abandoned the traditional Arattan life in Transylvania-Carpathia.

The primary reason for the relationship between Sumer and Aratta – indeed, perhaps even more than the Sumerian veneration for Aratta as its ancestral homeland – is to be found in the aftermath of the geo-cosmic catastrophe that led to the breakthrough of the waters of the Mediterranean Sea into the Black Sea (which before the catastrophe had been separated, rather like the relationship between the Aral Sea and the Caspian Sea). Prior to Sumer, Mesopotamia had been sparsely populated by Dravidian tribes, carriers of the native Ubaid^ archaeological culture. From archaeological evidence as well as written data from Stone Grave, Sumer, Babylonian-Assyrian libraries and, based on their data, the Hebrew Bible, it's now known that "The Flood" must have taken place, according to different interpretations of the latter sources, between the years 6984-5509-3483 BCE, and according to geological data – it must have occurred between the same 7th – 4th millennium BCE (see an earlier reference to the 5600-5550 BCE range). At the time of the catastrophe, the level of the Black sea rose by no less than 100 m and this caused flooding downstream of the rivers – particularly from the Danube up to Kuban – consequently forming the Sea of Azov. This led, on the one hand, to the consolidation of the local population and to the sudden growth mentioned earlier of the *cities* of the Buh-Dnipro centre of Aratta, and on the other hand, to the formation of the second wave of displaced people at Ur in Sumer (Tables I, V).

At the end of this late stage of "Trypillian" Aratta the large cities with several thousand two-storied houses and with 10-40 thousand inhabitants, the greatest cities in the world at that time, just disappear. Their collapse was probably due to Ur (i.e. as a result of their policies and hierarchical "castle/village" disparity). Many of the settlements were moved to the northern forests, up as far as the lower reaches of the right-bank of the Prypiat and the left-bank of the Desna. At the same time, Aratta went down to the Dniester valley on the coast of the Black Sea, forming there the fore-mentioned Usativ culture (Oriana, Orissa). They developed metal working (down to tempering and casting in moulds), practiced cattle farming traditions, bartering and even commerce, seafaring and fishery, as well as forming close relationships with the adjacent semi-nomadic cattle-breeders – the most ancient Aryans.

A consequence of this way of life was the destruction of traditional matriarchal traditions and the rise of patriarchy. All of these changes were manifested most glaringly in the replacement of female figurines with male imagery, the spread of burials with metal weapons, as well as an increase in the number of kurhans – which feature characteristics that reflect the principal myths of the Aryan *Rigveda* (Table XXXVIII).

Along with these kurhans found in Usativ there are also cemeteries similar to those that existed in contemporary cultures, which are also found in other areas of Trypillian culture. Whilst the practice of corpse inhumation was prevalent amongst Aryans in the south, cremation prevailed in the north, a practice which probably exclusively represented the early tradition of Aratta.

A connection is traced between the custom of breaking figurines – and in due course the breaking of anthropomorphic stele – with the dismemberment of the corpse in human sacrifices. These corpses cannot possibly be considered as slaves, even if sacrifice together [paired] was made with the usual burial. It is more likely that these were a paired couple who were simultaneously intended for the gods of heaven and the netherworld: destined, for example, for father-Dyaus and mother-Prithvi. Their combined image corresponds to the appearance of Vedic Dyave who is represented on a stele from kurhan No.

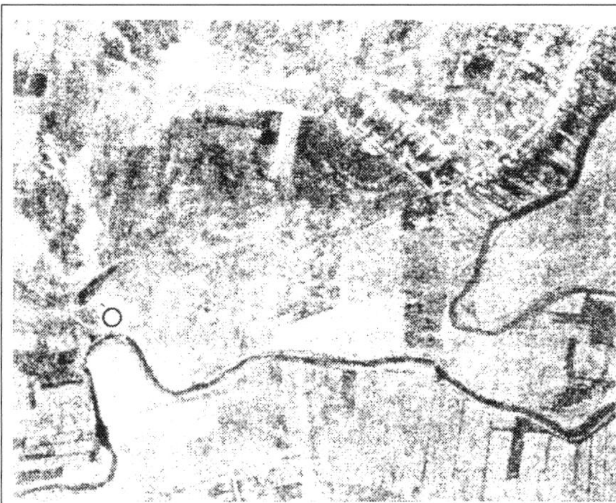

Fig. 29 : **Stone Grave**. Above: An early 1940s aerial photo of the site (circle in left centre) between the ancient and modern river beds of the River Molochna. Below: The ancient river bed is more clearly seen in the 2008 satellite image below (courtesy of Google Earth). In both images, West is uppermost.

3-1 near Usativ, and shown surrounded by large and small deer (a very archaic zodiac indeed!), along with three horses – symbolic of the three-season year of the early Indo-Europeans. Amongst other memorials are traced likenesses with the pre-Indo-European Gatumdug (her kurhans are in the form of a turtle or frog) and even Inanna (on some figurines and anthropomorphic vessels), along with pre-Hittite and other Indo-European deities: Telepin, Tark-Targely, Apolinus-Apollo, Vishnu, and also the Aryan deities: Vale and Vritra^, Parjani and Aditi, Pelasgian-Greek Artemis and Priapus, etc. These determinations made by Yu. Shilov (*Ancestral Homeland of the Aryans*, Kyiv, 1995) concur very well with the conclusion of A. G. Kifishin (*Ancient Sanctuary of Stone Grave*, Kyiv, 2001) concerning the appearance of writing at Troy II (2600-2450 BCE) in Asia Minor and to the proto-Sumerian writing that connected their own myths and calendars with those of the Greeks. On the other hand, the conclusions reached by V. N. Danylenko, B. A. Rybakov, K. Rendiu and other researchers are supported with regard to the Indo-European lineage of Trypillia (but meaning – Aratta).

As already mentioned, the attention of researchers was increasingly drawn towards making comparisons between similar historical processes occurring in late Trypillia and in Mesopotamia at the same time. Just when the cities appear and start to flourish, so do clay tablets with inscriptions. By the demise of the independent existence of Sumer and the beginning of the accession of Akkadian dynasties (the western Semites) which are simultaneously unified, the culture of "Trypillian" Aratta moves into decline. There may have been an attempt to move towards irrigated agriculture, a practice inherent to the slave-holding states of the East. Ancient authors have documented the existence of some old channels in the lower reaches of the Danube, the estuary of the Dnipro-Buh, and Kuban; some of which are still evident today. Scientists tend to explain away such parallels in cultural developments with global climate fluctuations, preferring not to consider economic and other factors. Those factors, as the latest discoveries of A. G. Kifishin and others show, were far more substantial triggers.

Records at Stone Grave show that this site was visited in 2782 BCE by a delegation from their 'sister' city of Shu-Nun which took away copies of inscriptions from plates Nos. 2-7 for their ancient Sumerian library. It is likely that there is a precise connection between this historic visit and the development of a famous Sumerian cycle of five poems called "Secret Sanctuaries", in which the foremother Inanna and the hero-god Ningirsu^ (one of the sons of the creator-God Enlil) are guardians of the seven most ancient kudurru^ – temple steles. Kifishin believes that these steles, covered in pictures and notations of mammoths, depict exactly the same Sumerian pictograms as those found by Danylenko in the "Grotto of the Churinga" at Stone Grave.

In 2535 BCE (on plate No. 25), a complete chronicle of descendants of the "*House of Imdugud*" was recorded, ten years before they were at war with their kindred Sumerian "*House of Baragesi*", whom they conquered (see above). In 2530 BCE, a new Sumerian delegation left numerous inscriptions on plates No. 1 and No. 52/A and renewed some old connections. Amongst them the "*Lord Eshnunna^*" is signified – whose city, from precisely that year, was at war for 30 years against Kish^ (together with Ur, Uruk and Lagash^). There was another visit in 2517 BCE, during which an inscription was made on plate No. 7: "*Shara^, Lord of the Country* (Sumer) *and Sem/Seven* (a reference to the number of kudurru in the "Secret Sanctuary" – see above). Shara was the name of one of the lunar gods whose lower body was human and mortal. Probably, this delegation not only had a tradition of regulating the sanctuary, comparing their respective chronicles but also left a sacrificial burial (a grave with the legs and pelvis of a man, covered with an anthropomorphous stele with the inscription of "*Shara"*) near the modern town of Nadezhdino at the mouth of the River Molochna.

There is late evidence of direct communication with Sumer – when it was already Akkadian or early Babylonian – in the local image of a central episode from the "Epic of Gilgamesh^" recorded on two vessels in catacomb burials of the 22nd millennium BCE which were found in kurhans between the Molochna and Dnipro. This was the time when several long-term campaigns were completed by a few tribes from the Dnipro area and others against the northern expansion of the Sumero-Akkadian rulers Sargon I and Naramsin, whose armies reached the Caucasus. It is possible that some of the Aratto-Aryan participants of this campaign did not return to the Dnipro river area but moved to the Indus. If this is not what had happened, even at the end of the existence of the cultures of Trypillia and Mohenjo-daro, then how could the name of Aratta have been transferred from the right bank of the Dnipro to the Punjab? How were cities filled by "Mahabharata" artefacts, not inherent to Aryans? We shall return to these complex questions.

The rebuff to Akkad^ by the "Five Nations of the North" coincided with the final disappearance of the Trypillian culture (in particular, the Usativ culture), although its traditions are traced in the following related Ingul^ mid-Dnipro and other archaeological cultures. In the environment of these successors of Aratta, researchers find the first manifestations of Slavic and Greek cultures (actually these displays are considerably more ancient, as has already been pointed out with references to monographs of Danylenko and Rybakov – and will be further shown below.)

If there were skirmishes at some outposts of Aratta and Sumer, they could not claim a significant role in the fate of those states. However, a significant role could be played by their differing ideologies – being primitive-communistic in Aratta and slave-holding in Sumer. The sharp demarkation between these states was caused, foremost, by their respective traditions of shifting agriculture and of fixed irrigation systems: Aratta could traditionally solve its internal discord by the method of re-settlement, whereas Sumer adhered to its tied system of irrigation channels that had developed from a policy of totalitarianism. When Aratta was directed to choose a path in the face of burgeoning Ur-policies, its priest-rulers probably decided that it was better to return to the old Foremother traditions. The future *Arta-Arsania* (which existed on the territory that had been *Aratta* down to the times of the birth of Rus i.e. old Kyivan Rus), seems to have succeeded better than Oriana – the successor to the "Usativ variant of Trypillia" – which failed.

The echo of historical clashes in post-Arattan times is found in *The Veles Book*, about which more will be said.

3. Persian and Indian Aratta.

These clashes between Aratta and Sumer weren't just scientific hypotheses but a matter of historical fact, as confirmed in a written record, *Enmerkar^ and the Lord/High priest of Aratta*, a Sumerian poem. However, this source wasn't referring to the 'The Country of Farmers' in the Danube and later in the Dnipro area, as outlined above but to an outpost of the Dnipro culture located somewhere in the mountains (probably beyond Ararat) to the east of the Sumerian city-state of Uruk. As a south-eastern outpost from the 'second' flowering of Aratta already discussed, this other city-state of Aratta which will be considered shortly, perhaps marked the beginning of the future Arta of the Persians, and possibly even the Indian Aratta. We will consider the arguments of this hypothesis.

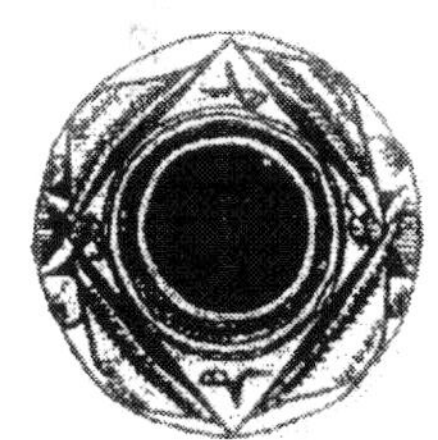

Fig. 30 : A vessel of the Samarra archaeological culture, Northern Mesopotamia.

The poem is written on several surviving clay tablets and consists of 30 sections. Enmerkar is the name of "the principal and strongest serpent of Sumer", High Priest of the temple of the god Enlil in Uruk. This priest-ruler, in late 2800 BCE, was the second in line of that dynasty which had removed itself from northern Aratta; the fifth in line was Gilgamesh (around 2615 BCE), with whom we shall shortly become acquainted. The poem regards the goddess Inanna as the foundress of Eastern Aratta; she is the main temple goddess, attended by the hero-shepherd Dumuzi; this couple are already known to us from earlier texts. Enmerkar seeks to subordinate Aratta, and in order to achieve this he requires the goodwill of Inanna. As a token of submission, Aratta is directed to send metal, stone, timber and also masters for decorating the temples of Uruk. In the event of refusal, Enmerkar threatens the population of Aratta with slavery, destruction of the city and with the death of its High Priest. The latter gives this answer:

I, High Priest appointed by the pure hand (of Inanna).
Sceptre of the heavenly king (Anu), mistress of the Universe,
"Innin[5]" of all laws, bright Inanna
In Aratta, country of pure ceremonies truly brought me,
In the mountains before Her, put me as the gate –
So, how then can Aratta submit to Uruk?
The mountain (Aratta) – is a hero, saturated with wisdom,
It is like a dawn[6] in the evening, going to the house
and driving away the darkness before his face.
It is like the Moon rising in the sky,
whose face is filled with brilliance.
It is like the trees, surrounding the mountains.

(Note the coincidence of the description "pure hand" used for the goddess Inanna and the description "Hand of the Empress", used by Aratta and Sumer for the ancient name of Stone Grave (Shu-Nun)).

Having seduced Enmerkar, the goddess left Aratta and ceased to patronise it. The Messenger of the High Priest of Uruk repeatedly carried his threatening orders to Aratta, though returned with vague answers. Messages consisted of threats, magical riddles and reminders about the times when not just in Sumer but in other countries, "all pious humanity, the whole universe spoke with one sincere voice in praise of Enlil", whose main temple was now in Uruk (although, hadn't Enlil's main temple formerly been in the ancestral homeland of Danube-Dnipro Aratta?). The answers from Aratta also recalled past times of historical truth (see above), giving them cause to complain about current "Aratta being similar to a flock, which has dispersed; – its ways now hostile to the earth"; and instead of sending tribute from Aratta, which Enmerkar had demanded, his enemy begs him to send grain to the hungry Arattans. This entreaty was granted – although not immediately. Interestingly, the grain from Uruk was brought on donkeys – whilst for returning the reciprocal gifts which Enmerkar demanded, the inhabitants of Aratta decided to send them instead on horses (first domesticated by the Black Sea Aryans, neighbours of the Dnipro area's Aratta). However, before the Arattans had time to gather everything, here was the messenger from Uruk back again – with a new riddle about a sceptre that should be brought to the temple of Enlil. To this, the High Priest of Aratta replied with a similar riddle.

Diplomatic communications such as this became so complicated over time that the poor messenger became unable to remember the messages. It was supposedly then that Enmerkar specifically 'invented' and set down the first letters on a clay tablet. Nevertheless, this priest of Aratta by some miracle, was easily able to read the text. (Remember that written language first appeared amongst the magical images of Stone Grave and was taken from there, through Çatal Höyük, by priests of the Danube-Dnipro Aratta and from here had been passed to Ur, Uruk and other areas of Sumer, as well as to the synchronous cultures of future Persia and Central Asia.) And while he thought over his next answer – Inanna, relenting on her decision about her home city – filled its fields with long-awaited rains.

Now the 'Sacred Country' was saved from famine and protected by its overflowing rivers! In addition, the goddess of Aratta arranged a celebration in honour of Dumuzi. Inanna ordered an old woman to bring a virgin for her beloved (note what was said earlier concerning interrelations between Maiden and Mother in the culture of Aratta in the Dnipro area). After weighing up these changes, Enmerkar decided to bring a peaceful end to the dispute and he sent to Aratta a new batch of grain and also cattle on the festival of Dumuzi. In response, Aratta finally sent the gifts for the temples of Uruk. Despite the end of this poem being poorly preserved, it is nevertheless, explicit, that on this holiday someone taught Enmerkar that it was better to settle matters not by war, but by peace. The sympathies of the Sumerian author are on the side of peaceful Aratta.

A problem arose around the 4th – 3rd millennium BCE concerning the migration of Arattans from south-eastern Europe to the East which, accordingly, affected their relationship with the Aratta of the Dniester-Dnipro interfluve (Ukrainian Trypillia), and downstream of the Hilmend river (Persian Shahri-sothe) and of the Indus river (Indian

Fig.31 : **Mapping the cultural relationship between Ukrainian Trypillian BII-CII and Indian Mohenjo-daro** in vessels from the "PLATAR" collection, (on the left), from settlements at Nemyrivske village in the Balta district of the Odessa region and Konivka village in Kelments district of the Chernivtsi region (upper projections on the bowls-casings), also a vessel from Changu Daru (on the right).
Depicted on the first vessel (SII) "the palm-like plant has archetypes in the iconographic tradition of the Ancient East", and "crescent moons belong to a canon which, probably, arises from a territory far beyond the original Trypillian culture" [M . Yu. Videyko, Encyclopaedia of Trypillian civilisation, PLATAR, Kyiv, 2004; Vol. II, p. 184]. Drawing of housewares (BII) by T. M. Tkachuk, Decorative Systems of the Trypillian-Cucuteni cultural-historic community (Painted dishes), Vinnytsa, 2005; Chapter I, pp. 156, 186].

Mohenjo-daro).

Formal-typological methodology does not provide archaeologists with much opportunity to solve or even to outline this problem (see: M. Yu. Videyko, "*In Search of the Power of Aratta*", *Archaeology* (Kyiv), No. 2, 1995) – and it can scarcely be resolved now, archaeologically, without studying the remains of sites that were flooded by the Azov and Black Sea inundation that resulted from the "Great Flood". Other, more investigative methods were developed by V. N. Danylenko (*Cosmology of a Primitive Society*, Kyiv, 1997; Moscow, 1999) and A. G. Kifishin (*The Ancient Sanctuary of Stone Grave. Experience of deciphering the proto-Sumerian archives, XII-III millennia BCE* – Kyiv, 2001). When he deciphered this archive at Stone Grave, Kifishin was able to conclude that this location was the precise source of the writing system that was eventually taken out as a framework, in the 4th – 3rd millennium BCE, by the migrating "proto-Elamite, Namazgian, proto-Sumerian and 'Srubna' cultures" (the latter to be understand as 'Trypillian': *Yu. Shilov*) into Persia, Central Asia, Mesopotamia (and, as shown in Chapter II of Kifishin's book, it also became the writing system of India and China). Clearly, this was more of a linguistic methodology than the innovative archaeological methods which were advanced by Danylenko.

When tracing the development of the spiritual culture of Eurasia from the Palaeolithic through to the Bronze Age, V. N. Danylenko discovered a partly-common source for Egyptian, Aryan, Pelasgian, Slavic, Finno-Ugric, and Greek mythologies in the mythologies of Sumer. Consistent clues for the researcher were the images of the Earth-Mother and Sky-Father – primarily manifested as representations of women and bulls. Apart from this generic similarity, he also compared their specific design and noted any instances of primordial serpents, turtles and birds connected with them. He found other primordial images, beyond the possibilities of sheer chance, of spontaneous or archetypal-stage manifestations of ethno-cultures who were not in contact (or so we must assume!), reminiscent of the "palaeolithic Venus" of the European mammoth-hunters, also found amongst the cattle-breeders of Southeast Europe who, for the first time, domesticated large horned cattle and it was through these pastoralists that arable agriculture was passed on. The pastoral-agricultural way, such a feature of the most ancient lifestyle, was traditionally characterised in Ukrainian Aratta (in the Sursk-Dnipro and Buh-Dniester cultures, and from the latter to the Trypillian culture, according to Danylenko). From there, it had also already extended to the West – in the cultures of Corded Ware ceramics and Tell Halaf – and to the East – including the "genetically related" Mohenjo-daro proto-Indus culture and other Asian cultures which had 'borrowed', together with their painted ceramics, other corresponding social acquisitions including the image of the "celestial bull"). In these new regions, Arattan centres could arise, not necessarily with different names but with a culture analogous to the Trypillian model. Such metamorphoses are well-known to historians from the subsequent Roma, in city-states and provinces like Romania, Rusy, in the Adriatic, Carpathians, Baltic, Black Sea, Kyivan and then Muscovy (Moscowia, i.e. modern Russia) and Bulgaria, both the Volga region and the Danube area.

Let us recall that in Russia [old Kyivan Rus], the tradition of Aratta existed before the Tatar-Mongolian invasion (as a princedom of Arsania with its capital Arta), and in Ukraine it still smoulders in Oratovo in the Vinnytsia region up to the present time. The Indo-Aryan *Mahabharata* placed Aratta in the Punjab, where it may be compared with the archaeological culture of Mohenjo-daro. Modern Hindus name their country Bharata, which can be understood as 'Divine Aratta'. In Iran/Persia, the memory of Aratta was embodied in the image of sacred Arta – the ideal country of ancient times whose name remained the by-word for the highest conduct and order. The Etruscans had their city-state of Artana. Arta survives in the name of a modern town in Romania. In each of its instances, Aratta and its off-shoots were connected with the Indo-European people, which testifies to the corresponding attributes of Sumer and the "Trypillian archaeological culture".

Thus, the traditions of the most ancient Indo-European state of Aratta live on! It remains to this day (at least, in Ukraine and India) as it always had been, the competent root of universal civilisation. The Arattan Aryan tradition is alive and still connected to that community of tribes of nomadic cattlemen, which arose in the 4th millennium BCE in the country between the Dniester and Dnipro, along the steppe borders of Aratta.

Suggested reading

1. Kifishin A. G., *Pre-Greek Genostructure and Ancient Greek Myth,* in Image and Meaning in Ancient Culture, Moscow, 1990 (in Russian);
   Sumer and Proto-Sumerian Inscriptions of Stone Grave, in Ukrainian World, Kyiv, 1995, p.1-3 (in Russian);
   Priests of Çatal Höyük at Stone Grave in 6200 B. C., Kyiv, 1996, pp. 4-6 (in Russian);
   *The Terrible Wrath of Gods and Exodus of the Peopl*e. On the Reconstruction of one Ritual Sacrifice in Myth, Moscow, 2000 (in Russian);
   Ancient Sanctuary of Stone Grave. Experience of Proto-Sumerian Decipherment of the Archive XII-III Millennia BCE, Kyiv, 2001 (in Russian).
2. Kosarev M. F., Kifishin A. G., *Clay Tablets of Gorbunovsk Peat-bog*, in Sacrifice, Moscow, 2000 (in Russian).
3. Nalyvayko S. I., *Secrets of Sanskrit Revealed.* – Kyiv, 2000.
4. Poleshchuk V. V., Shepa V. V., *Historical Bio-geography of the Danube,* Kyiv, 1998 (in Russian).
5. *Archaeology of the Ukrainian S.S.R.*, Kyiv, 1972, Vol. 1 (in Russian).
6. *Eneolithic USSR,* Moscow, 1982 (in Russian).

---

[1] The classification of the plates or petroglyphic stone slabs within the 65 grottoes of Stone Grave. (Mykhailov, B. D. '*The Petroglyphs of Stone Grave'*. – Zaporizhia - Moscow, 1999.)

[2] In the original Russian text, she is 'Ишхары' which transliterates as 'Ishkhary'. She was the goddess of grain and love, and was often identified with Ishtar. (Black, Jeremy and Anthony Green. 2003 (1992). *Gods, Demons, and Symbols of Ancient Mesopotamia.* Austin, TX: University of Texas Press).

[3] Note the paragraph above which refers to the king list having been continued after 6200 BCE.

[4] These dates are perhaps attributed to M. Videyko? (see page 77 : The Second Stage).

[5] An alternative Sumerian name for Inanna.

[6] Dusk or, perhaps, moonrise?

CHAPTER 4

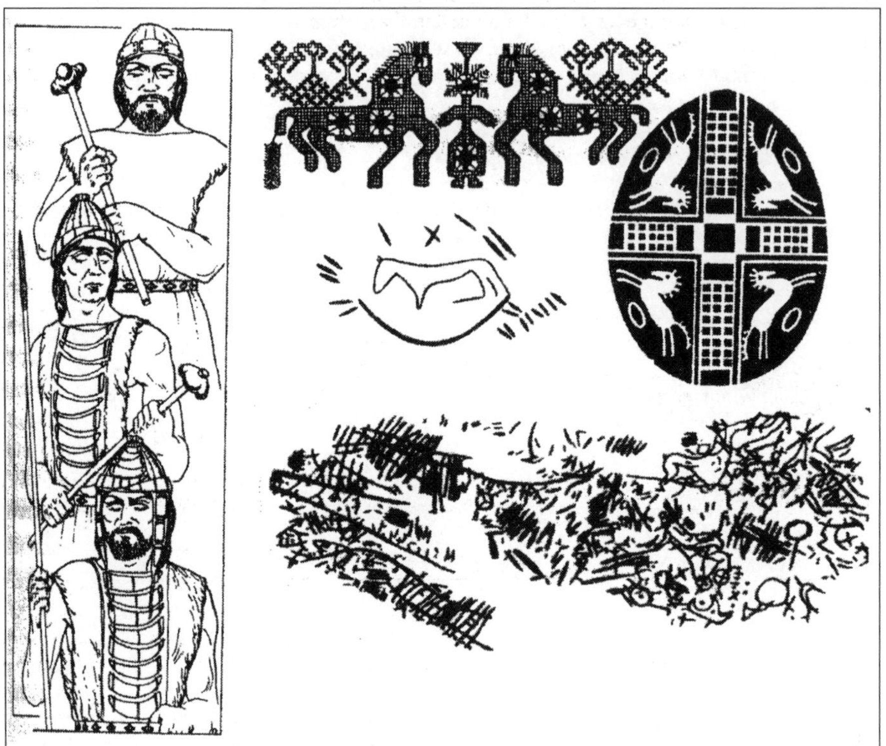

Fig. 32 : **Aryan characteristics in Slavic culture** (top and right). **Horses and chariots at Stone Grave (**images centre and lower). **Reconstruction of weapons from Mariupol burial ground**, by P. L. Kornienko (left)

ARIÁN^ – THE COUNTRY OF ARYANS

Aryans! Today, this word is negatively associated with the ideology of the Second World War – the most terrible in the history of mankind. Fascist ideologists of the "Third Reich" who embraced racialist thoughts, appropriated the term to describe the German people as Aryans. Their ideology was based on worse than a lie, it was based on half-truths about what they thought the term *Aryan* signified, [a master race ideology].

At an early stage in the development of India, European merchants and missionaries, and in due course the colonialists and scientists of the 15th – 18th centuries, began to notice with some surprise that the sacred books of this land of Bharata were written in the 'synthetic' Sanskrit^ language. For Europeans that fact should not have been such a surprise, given the familiarity of the grammar, the vocabulary and the names of pre-Christian gods. For example, the name of the well-known deity Zeus, whom the ancient Greeks also called *Dzeus* and *Diey,* which meant 'Sky (Shining Light)' or 'Day', carried precisely the same meaning as the name of the Celtic god *Dis*, the Slavic *Div*, the Persian *Dev* and also the Indian *Dyaus* and *Dyave.*

In the late 18th century the study of Indology began, having been initiated by British linguists and subsequently developed by French, German and Russian scientists. Fairly quickly it became apparent that the most ancient book of India (and evidently of the world) was the *Rigveda* – a title that meant 'Wise Speech', or 'Sacred knowledge' – which described tribes who called themselves *Arias* (meaning 'ardent', 'ploughmen', 'nobles' etc.)

who had come to India from a place in the west, where birch trees grew, where amber could be found and where snow fell in winter – namely, from Europe. This marked the start of a scientific quest to find the ancestral home of the five Aryan tribes who had reached India in the middle of the 2nd millennium BCE; their arrival was recorded not only in the sacred hymns of the *Rigveda*, but also in the epic poems of the *Ramayana* and *Mahabharata*.

1. Problems of Aryans in historiography.

At the outset (and sometimes even now when outmoded usage survives amongst non-specialists), the conventional term "Indo-European" and the autonym of "Aryan" were thought to be synonymous. Gradually, though, it became clear that the latter term had arisen after the first term and it only accounted for some of the nations who comprised the "Indo-European language community" – like the Slavs, Germans and other related nations.

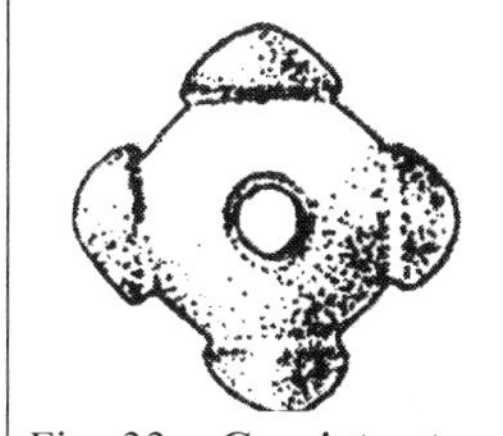

Fig. 33 : **Cruciate stone topped indian club**, similar to those found in a Mariupol burial ground, 6th–4th millennium BCE.

The initial research was dominated for a considerable time by the German researcher R. Rot, later joined by A. Ludwig, who carried out the classic translation of the *Rigveda.* R. Rot and O. N. Bohtlingk published a comparative seven-language "Dictionary of Sanskrit" (1855-1875) at the Petersburg Academy of Sciences. During the same period, F. Bopp published "Comparative Grammars of Sanskrit, Zend, Greek, Latin, Lithuanian, Old Slavic, Gothic and German languages" to which Armenian, Old Prussian, etc., were soon added. Thus can be summarised the 100-year study of the problem of the Indo-European community (or Indo-German/German-Aryan, as it was then described) which laid the general foundation for further research.

For A. Shleiker, the descendants of the Aryans could be found amongst some of the tribes of India and Persia/Iran, as well as amongst the Ancient Greeks, Italians, Celts and Goths (ancestors of the French, Germans, and Britons), Slavs and Lithuanians. Between the 19th and 20th centuries the majority of researchers gravitated towards the theory of "cultural waves", a supposed periodic migration from a few highly-developed centres, as proposed by J. Schmidt. Favouring this theory, but using dubious archaeological and anthropological data, the Austrian scientists K. Penka and K. Paape, and in due course the German archaeologist G. Kossina, situated the "Indo-German" (pre-Aryan) centre on the territory of Scandinavia and Germany. It is this theory that subsequently provided the armoury for the ideologists of German fascism.

By the early 19th century, other hypotheses were proposed for locating the ancestral home of the Indo-Europeans and Aryans. Hence, the German geographer K. Ritter focused attention on the similarity of *India* with *(S)Indika* – the name of the Taman peninsula during ancient Scythian times. Herodotus and his contemporaries had frequently named the *Sinds* as *Inds*, and Hesychius^ even emphasised: "*Sinds are ethnically Indians*". However, K. Ritter adhered to the reigning hypothesis of the time (1820) concerning an Aryan migration from India. During the Second World War, the Austrian linguist P. Krechmer came to similar conclusions but also paid particular attention to the "Scythian Sindic" (Pliny, IV: 84) who, after this name was transferred to Kuban, remained in the lower reaches of the rivers Buh and Dnipro. It is worth questioning whether, long before the Scythians, the migration of the Aryans might have taken place from there? Furthermore, the linguists O. N. Trubachev and S. I. Nalyvayko pointed out that the Dandarians subsequently existed there – these were the 'Mace-bearing Aryans', who, prior to the Middle Ages, maintained the tradition of an Aryan ancestral home in the Northern Black Sea area (Table X, Fig.84).

During the 1950's, the Bulgarian linguist V. Georgiev narrowed the options for the ancestral home of the Aryans ("Indo-Iranians") to the lower reaches of the Dnipro. This was acknowledged in a series of articles by the Russian linguist O. N. Trubachev in *Indo-Aryans in the Northern Black Sea region* (1975-1981), subsequently published as a separate book (1999). However, another tendency then prevailed: M. Meierhofer, I. M. Diakonov and E. A. Grantovsky were absorbed in locating the mid-Asian centre of the Aryans prior to their campaign into India; this pushed the problem of an ancestral home into the background. T. Ya. Elizarenkova, the well-known translator and commentator on the *Rigveda* (Moscow, 1989, 1999), maintains this position.

A powerful contribution to O. N. Trubachev's hypothesis was made by V. A. Safronov in the 1989 publication, *Ancestral Homelands of the Indo-Europeans*. In his book, having compared the archaeological and linguistic data, this researcher defined the Yamna archaeological culture as the Persian branch of the Aryans, but the Dnipro-Kuban culture (Hurrians, according to Shilov) – as Indian; (the Yamna were Indo-European, according to G. Childe, T. Sulimirsky and M. Gimbutas; Indo-Iranian or Aryan, according to V. Georgiev; Proto-Tocharian according to V. M. Danylenko, and after the Seredny Stoh – basically an Aryan substratum, according to Yu. Shilov). Danylenko (*Eneolithic Ukraine*, Kyiv, 1974) proved to be nearer the truth than Safronov. Separating the historically attested Aryans from the Trypillian archaeological culture (as they were termed by their discoverer, V. Khvoyka) and from the Yamna archaeological culture (as considered by G. Childe et. al.), Danylenko purported an Aryan connection to the "Azov-Black Sea line of development of the steppe Eneolithic", which, despite passing through "Yamna" territory, still served as a conduit between Trypillia (Aratta) and the civilisations of the Near East (Sumer). Within the borders of this "line", the researcher assumed the Proto-Aryans belonged to the Lower-Mykhaylivka^, Kemi Oba^, and other cultures. Subsequently, (after the 1995 publication of *Ancestral Homeland of the Aryans* by Yu. Shilov) it became clear that the "Azov-Black Sea line" turned out to have been the catalyst, the axis for the formation of the Aryan community

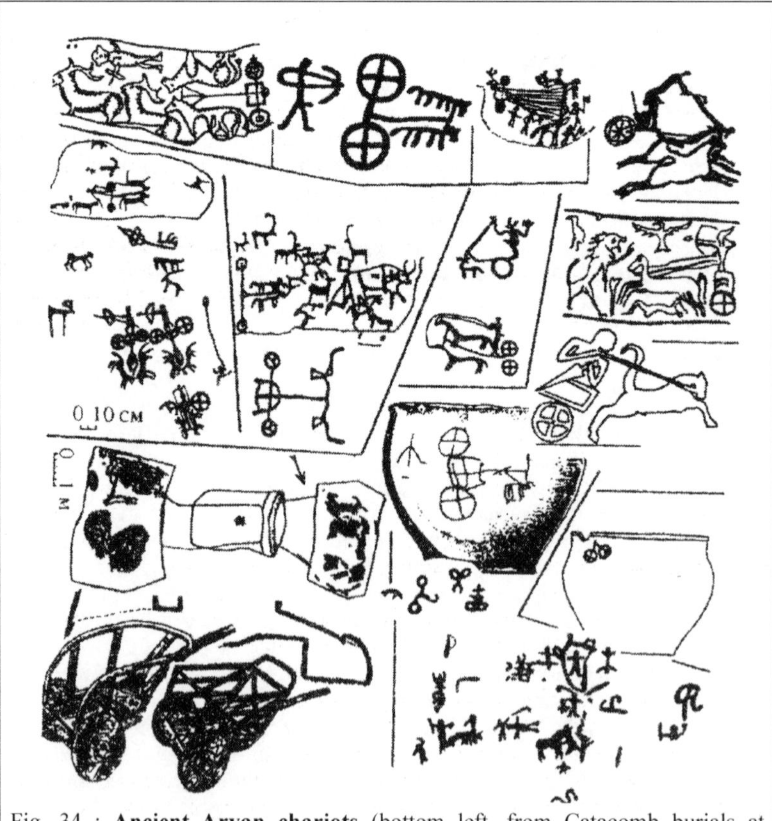

Fig. 34 : **Ancient Aryan chariots** (bottom left, from Catacomb burials at Tyahunov Grave in the Dnipro area of Ukraine,) and their images in Eurasian steppes, 2nd millennium BCE.

of tribes – which initially included representatives of the Lower-Mykhaylivka, Kemi Oba, Seredny Stoh, Yamna and other old-rural cultures of the Dnipro area.

In the last few decades there have been other, less successful, attempts by archaeologists to solve the problem of the origin of the Aryans. E. E. Kuzmina (1974), following G. Clark and S. Piggot, tried to connect the *Rigveda* with the Aryans after finding wagons buried beneath kurhans of the Yamna culture. When V. F. Gening first published (1977) findings from his excavation of the burial ground of Sintashta (in the Arkaim Valley, Southeast Trans-Ural), he listed a chariot, offerings and cremations from the beginning of the Srubna^ cultural-historical community and compared these elements to a funeral rite described in some hymns from the *Rigveda.* Kuzmina tried to take the initiative with the book *Origin of Indo-Aryans in the Light of the Latest Archaeological Discoveries* (Moscow, 1977; co-authored with K. F. Smirnov), where she published similar, but extremely plain materials. L. S. Klein, in articles from 1979 onwards, tried to connect the Aryans, not with the Yamna or Srubna cultures but with the intermediate Catacomb^ culture from between the 3rd – 2nd millennium BCE. It was in precisely the steppe Dnipro area (burial No. 27 of the Tiagunov grave near the village of Maianivka) that M. M. Cherednychenko and S. Zh. Pustovalov found the most ancient battle chariot which was dated to the boundary of the 3rd and 2nd millennium BCE, the first such images of which, were perhaps to be found at Tash-Air cave in Crimea. By the mid-2nd millennium BCE, images synchronous with those of the Sintashta^ culture were found on pots of the Srubna culture in the Dnipro area and Trans-Volga region. At that time, the immense migrations of Aryan tribes had begun and this process was reflected in numerous depictions of battle chariots in the cultures of pre-Grecian Mycenae, Scandinavia, the Near East, North Africa, Altai, Tuva^, China, Pakistan and India (Fig. 34, Table VI).

Whenever any one of the three fore-mentioned lines of research was selected (after Kuzmina, Klein and Gening), subsequent archaeologists tended to refer to the *Rigveda* even more frequently. At the forefront were those researchers who had continued the work in Arkaim^. Here there were good, though relatively late monuments dating from the 2nd millennium BCE, which were declared as clear evidence of the Aryan ancestral homeland. However, no-one troubled to mention similar findings from another equally expressive centre of the same period, near Lake Sevan^ in Transcaucasia, which had been investigated in the 1950s. What is more, they tried to suppress the evidence presented in '*The Original Home Land of the Aryans* (Kyiv, 1995) in which Yu. Shilov analysed the archaeological finds of the Ukrainian Dnipro area which were 1500-2000 years older than those in Arkaim and Sevan. In recent years the position began to be corrected: the researchers at Arkaim have already acknowledged that the Aryans arrived at Arkaim from the steppes of Ukraine – from the borders of Aratta.

2. Discovery of the Lower Dnipro Ancestral Homeland of the Aryans.

Since the late 1980's, the work of the linguists P. Krechmer, V. Georgiev, O. N. Trubachev, and also the archaeologists V. M. Danylenko and V. A. Safronov substantiated the hypothesis concerning the ancestral homeland of the Aryans – an early branch of the "Indo-European community" – in the steppe Dnipro area up until Scythian times. But in order for this or any other hypothesis (e.g. Nordic-Germanic) to become a theory, i.e. in order to produce the most reliable scientific picture, it was necessary to reliably connect and align the linguistics, archaeology, ethnography, and history, etc.

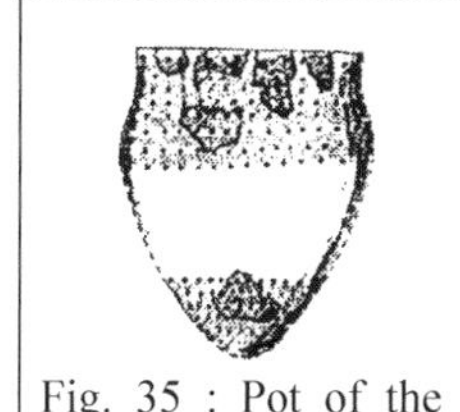

Fig. 35 : Pot of the Seredny Stoh culture.

How can the ancient remains of settlements and burials be "compelled to talk"; how can we possibly know the names of early tribes without there being any inscriptions? V. N. Danylenko, followed by B. A. Rybakov and other supporters of the semiotic method of deciphering the past, offered a way out: a reconstruction of the myths, as reflected in the mute archaeological facts and then a comparison of those reconstructions with the recorded myths of various peoples. After pursuing this course, Danylenko, in the monograph *Cosmology of a Primitive Society,* discovered an Indo-European affiliation to the Buh-Dniester and Trypillian archaeological cultures, and Rybakov emphasised, with regard to the latter, consistencies with Slavic ethnography.

The semiotic (sign) analysis of archaeological findings from the Black Sea-Caspian steppe was carried out by Yu. Shilov in 1975-1995. In his book, *Ancestral Homeland of the Aryans,* he summarised the achievements of his predecessors and colleagues. In the reconstructions of the myths of various steppe tribes from the period of the 4th – 2nd millenium BCE, this researcher relied on the calendar-astronomical markers and their reference points; on the sequence of ritual actions; on the figured constructions and various images, offerings etc., although the principal objects of analysis were the burial kurhans (mounds).

From previous excavations, it was evident that the most important kurhans were those from the late Trypillian cultures close to Usativ near Odessa. Using archival documents from E. F. Lagodovska and others, and also using his own work, the archaeologist V. G. Petrenko discovered within these kurhans, stone constructions and ditches in the forms of a turtle and a frog, a serpent around an egg, astral symbols, and zoo-anthropomorphic deities. Shilov interpreted these images as corresponding to the myths featuring the serpent Vritra and the embryo of the new-year universe, Vala^, also Dyaus and Prithvi – the Sky-Father and Earth-Mother. These myths form the basis of the Indo-Aryan *Rigveda*; their archaeological similarity specifies the place, time and ethno-historical conditions of the origin of the Vedic Aryans.

It was later found that priests from 'Trypillia-Aratta' in the middle of the 4th millennium BCE, had imparted to their neighbouring steppe inhabitants, mythical tales about Vala and Vritra, making their mytho-ritual (of the New Year, etc.) the principal feature of the future *Rigveda* and also the instrument for influencing the young Aryan community (which V. Khvoika incorrectly identified with Trypillia). Their expressive conformity with this mytho-ritual is shown in the following archaeological finds between the middle of the 4th – 2nd millennium BCE: the base of kurhans at Tsehelnia^ and Kormylytsia^ (at the mouth of the River Psel; Seredny-Stoh, Dnipro-Donets, Trypillia or Lower-Mykhaylivka, post-Mariupol^ archaeological cultures); kurhan No. 1 near the village of Starohorozheno^ (River Inhul; Novo-Danylivka or Early-Yamna and Kemi Oba cultures); kurhan No. 2 near Kremenchuk (River Southern Buh; Yamna and Early-Catacomb cultures); grotto No. 55 of Stone Grave (at the River Molochna, Ingul Late-Catacomb culture); and behind the Chaplynsk kurhan (near the town of Perekop; Srubna culture). In burial ground No. 12-1 near the village of Kairy, in the vicinity of Kakhovka, a preservation of the main Aryan mytho-rituals can be traced via their descendants, the Cimmerians^; the Scythians^ (kurhans Nos.4-1, 3-1, 2-1) who later utilised this ancient tradition for developing a mytho-ritual honoring their ancestors – Herakles^ and the serpent-leg goddess Borysthena (the old Greek name for the River Dnipro). (Tables XXXVIII, XXXIX, XL).

In these and other specified kurhans, quite a few of the subjects and images were identified with Vedic mythology and they will be given further consideration later in this book. It is necessary to emphasise that although Aryan correspondences were the most numerous and profound, other correspondences were also discovered. Amongst them, evidence of the pre-Greeks, whose roots lay in Aratta, were fairly widespread. Judging from materials found at High Grave^ and other kurhans near the village of Starosillia^, the Vedic images of Suri and Pushan^, Rudra and the Maruts^ (they are connected with the sun, chariots, weapons and battles) suggest they were the progenitors of the Hurrians.

In parallel with deconstructing the mythologies, Shilov paints a picture of the formation of the Aryan community co-existing with different, even ethnically different tribes; besides the Aryans there were pre-Greek, Hurrian, Slavic and Cimmerian tribes. Thus, the Aryans were not a "racially pure nation" but they did have a specific ethno-cultural core (from the Sursk-Dnipro, and in due course from the Seredny-Stoh, Yamna and Srubna cultures) and together they made up an ethnically varied commonwealth; the same may be said of every nation, (the large ones at least). The mytho-rituals that united this community (the myths being akin to a national idea or religious doctrine), were formed long before them

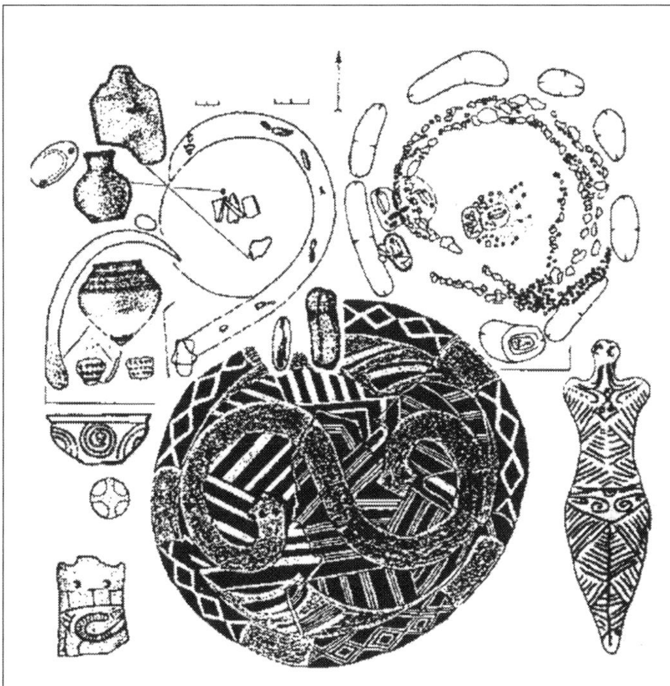

Fig. 36 : Serpent-images on ceramics and in the structure of Arattan and Aryan kurhans, 5th–3rd millennium BCE.

– in other (Arattan) ethno-historical environments – being preserved within the Aryan tribal environment that relocated to India and survived to serve those who inherited the Aryan ancestral homeland (i.e. the Dandari or 'Mace-bearing Aryans', the Cimmerians, Scythians and Slavs).

How have scientists perceived the publications of Yu. A. Shilov?

His colleagues from the Institute of Archaeology at the National Academy of Sciences of Ukraine tried to disparage them, substituting academic discussion with unreasoned charges and political speculations on the theme of 'Russian chauvinism' etc. (Journal of *Archaeology*, No. 2, Kyiv, 1996). In contrast, N. R. Guseva detected "a convergence of the ideas of Yu. Shilov with a burgeoning Ukrainian national-chauvinism" (Journal, *Heritage of Ancestors*, No. 4, Moscow, 1998).

The author was well-qualified to analyse the matter (in *Homo Sovieticus; Victory!*, Kyiv, 1995, 2000), having arrived at the following conclusions: the principal cause of the artificial glorification of the Trans-Ural centre and the intentional under-estimation of the role of the Dnipro area as an ancestral home of the Aryans, was not founded on scientific rationale but on a political bias. It is like two sides of a coin that brackets Zionism not only with Ukraine and Russia, but also with all Indo-European people. This same Guseva (*Antiquity: Aryans. Slavs*, Moscow, 1996; and others), put forward an "Arctic theory" for their ancestral home having been located, if not at the Polar region, then in the Northern Ural Mountains, which appeased Russian patriotism and removed its origins from Kyivan Rus. Ms. Natalia Romanova relied on theories that were already out-dated at the turn of the 19th – 20th centuries – the books *Paradise Found, or The Cradle of Mankind at the Arctic Pole* by F. Warren; *Arctic Motherland of the Vedas* by B. G. Tilak. Arkaim, in the Urals – associated with the North – is far from the Black Sea coast which was declared by L. L. Zaliznyak and others, to have been eternally Semitic (*"and you, Slavs, touched by your closeness to the Aryans are looking for a common ancestral homeland in the Tundra!"*), and so the Trans-Ural archaeological finds became the historical basis for sources of speculative pro-Zionist history, all for the sake of politics.

In scientific, artistic and popular non-fiction books, Shilov confirmed his theory about the Dnipro area being the ancestral home of the Aryans and for the first time, outlined this world as being very distant from the representations of the Communists (i.e. Historical Materialist), Fascists and Zionists.

A positive, though qualified review of *Ancestral Homeland of the Aryans*, was published by O. N. Trubachev in the journal *Problems of Linguistics* (No. 3, 1996, Moscow), and B. A. Rybakov supported both authors in the preface to N. I. Kikeshev's book *Appeal to the Slavs* (Moscow, 1998).

3. Aryans: a historical sketch from Aratta to Bharata.

Fig. 37 : Pot of the Yamna archaeological culture.

So, the Aryan community of tribes emerged as a specific phenomenon within the borders of an older and larger, 'Indo-European language community'. Their ethno-historical nucleus in the Circum-Pontic zone at around the 7th – 5th millennium BCE, formed part of the oldest state in the world, Aratta; the Aryans were also mobile within the environment of this nucleus. Around the middle of the 5th (or even 6th) millennium BCE, the state of Aratta moved from the Danube nearer to the Dnipro river area; here, a need arose for a new route to the Asian homeland of the 'pre-Indo-Europeans'. The Arattan priest-rulers of the Dnipro area (currently known as the Trypillian archaeological culture) paved the way for this path along the northern shores of the Black and Azov Seas. The development of the so-called 'Azov-Black Sea line of development of the Steppe Eneolithic' had been laid through the element of semi-nomadic aborigines who were also Indo-European but nevertheless of foreign ethnicity. To ensure the success of this 'way of Aratta', it was implemented with the assurance that foreign missionaries, when in a strange environment, would not use force but would protect the sanctity of the small groups of mineral explorers, breeders, etc., who, from time to time, were sent out from the Dnipro area to the Caucasus, Anatolia and Mesopotamia. In this way, those missionaries also became the axis around which the Aryan community of tribes began to form.

This background history of the Aryans along with the catalysing influence of Aratta on the formation of their community was lost somewhere in the Sursk-Dnipro culture that probably controlled the proto-Sumerian sanctuary of Stone Grave. The carriers of this, the most ancient cattle breeding culture in Eastern Europe, were possibly the first to tame horses and to meet the Transylvanian metallurgical centre and, as a consequence of these innovations around middle of the 4th millennium BCE, the 'Sursk-Dnipro' people grew into the 'Novo Danylivka' people and thence into the 'Seredny Stoh' people – for whom the horse and metal became customary.

The 'Seredny Stoh' people and their forebears inter-married with the aborigines of the Dnipro-Donets culture and began a period of distant campaigns using the first detachments of cavalry of the Novo-Danylivka type. At that time, they were the most mobile and insuperable force. The activities of the Arattan missionaries evidently began with these daunting Novo-Danylivka people from whom arose the carriers of the Lower-Mykhaylivka and then the Kemi Oba archaeological cultures. The evidence for contact between all of these cultures is traced in settlement materials at Stone Grave and also the fore-mentioned kurhans at the rivers Psel, Inhul, Inhulitsa and Dniester. It was probably at this time (second half of the 4th millennium BCE, when Sumer emerged as a result of the 'World Flood') when paths were laid towards the Volga and to the south of Mesopotamia. Inscriptions attest to the latter on plate No. 25/B at Stone Grave (referenced above), at a Novo-Danylivka type burial near Uruk, on stone maces of Susiana type in Novo-Danylivka or Dnipro-Donets burials near the city of Mariupol and in the village of Mykolske on the Dnipro river, etc. (see Tables XXXII: 14, XXXIII: 13; Fig.77).

The most expressive Aryan memorials at Stone Grave are those known as the 'Horse Plate' and the 'Footprints Plate' (in honour of the nomad-god, Vishnu); the 'Dragon Grotto' (which has images of the main attributes of the core mythology of the *Rigveda*: i.e. 'the Home' of the new-year embryo Vala and serpent Vritra, defeated by the foot of Vishnu and the arrows of Indra); and an image of the self-sacrificing horseman (Gandkharva^, the Saviour^ of the Aryans) near the central altar on the summit of Stone Grave.

The start of the Aryan community and its isolation from the Indo-European corpus was reflected most obviously in the kurhans of Velyko-Olexandrivsk near the village of Starosillia, in the modern Kherson region, also in kurhans at the mouth of the Psel (near Komsomolsk in the Poltava region). At the heart of the Velyko-Olexandrivsk kurhan were burials of two priests, one from Aratta and one from Sumer. The graves were surrounded by

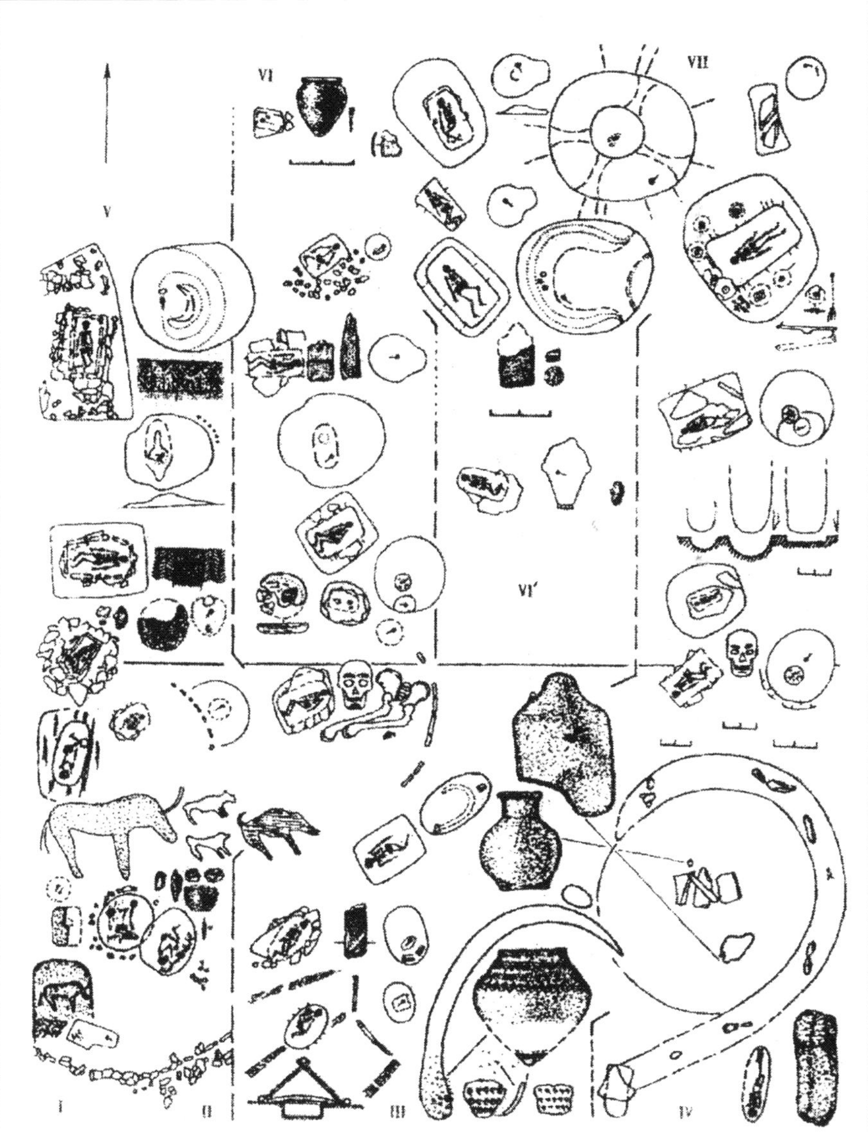

Fig. 38 : **Aryan Formations** - reflected in ancient burial kurhans of the Ukrainian Dnipro area, 5th–3rd millennium BCE.

a simple cromlech^ (a ring of stones) with two plaques on which a zodiacal scene was depicted: *Taurus* – as a red bull, passing behind *Sagittarius* – as a black wild boar. It is possible that these constellations also represented their respective countries. Thus the Sumerian totem of the Wild boar (the Vedic Varaha^) would be transferred in due course to Vara^ – '*the Aryan open expanse*' [the concept of sacred geography]. After the specified graves of these priests came the burial of one of the most ancient Aryan Brahmans, whose burial rite needs to be considered as a synthesis of the previous two. Further development of this ritual is traced in the kurhan of High Grave near the village of Starosillia, which also revealed the beginning of the composition of the Aryan *Rigveda*. Additionally, formations under the kurhans of Tsehelnia and Kormylytsia near Komsomolsk, were influenced by the main mytho-ritual of the *Rigveda*, namely the serpent Vritra (embodied here in the contours of ditches) who guarded Vala – the embryonic New-Year of the universe – and Vritra who was slain by the serpent-warrior Indra (personified in a granite stele of a man and an outline similar to a club).

The final expression of the state of Arián came forward around 2800 BCE, a time when the Seredny-Stoh culture developed into the Yamna culture, when strong links had been established between Aratta and Sumer and when missionary work on the routes between the Dnipro area and Mesopotamia was concentrated in the hands of Brahman-"Kemi-Obans". From kurhans at the mouth of the River Psel, strong evidence for an Aryan influence was traced in their outlines of the Vala mytho-ritual for the New Year; from kurhans near the village of Starohorozheno – there were formations detailing the main Aryan myth which featured serpent-warriors and liberators of the embryo, i.e. Indra and Vishnu, and at High Grave and the neighbouring Veliko-Olexandrivska's kurhan – the boundary between the Indo-European Dyaus-Prithivi^ and the purely Aryan Adityas is traced.

In the lower reaches of the Dniester and Dnipro rivers, particularly in the coastal region of the future Odessa, a contact zone of Aratta and Arián was formed; this area was named Oriana, or Orissa (according to S. Nalyvayko and Yu. Shilov). This became the hub for future migrations both westward, into Troad, Etruria etc., and eastward, towards India. Between this region and Aratta, located to the north, the settlement of Borustenia or Borysthenes began to develop (according to *The Veles Book*), although, according to ancient literature, it's better known as Borisfenida.

Thus, developed Arián and its apotheosis can be identified with Oriana – which had an Arattan foundation connected with significant Aryan influences. The 'essence' of the Orianian-Aryans resided not in any ethnic, racial purity but in their preference for Statehood (orientated towards Aratta as their supreme model). Painted skulls from burial grounds near the villages of Usativ and Mayaky^ retained symbols of their *varnas*^ (identified from character signs on the bones of the forehead and face, as well as from the traces of hairstyles), indicating the development of an advanced hierarchy synonymous with the concept of "Aryanism". This concept was permeated with the imperatives of high knowledge and observance of its precepts – i.e. the requirement for self-regulation (or "democracy", as it is considered within the European tradition), based on societal adherence to objective laws.

In the *Artkhashastra*, or *Science Policy* (Moscow, 1993), written in India during the 1st millennium BCE, it states: "***The Law for Brahmanic stage*** – *is studying, teaching others,* [varnas and the general populace], *sacrifice for themselves and for others, distribution of gifts and their receipt* [for the accommodation and activities of the Brahman]. ***The Law for Kshatriya***^ – *studying, sacrifices, dispensing of gifts, competing for funds to facilitate a life of military science and the protection of living beings.* ***The Law for Vaishya***^ – *studying, sacrifices, distribution of gifts, arable farming, animal husbandry and trade.* ***The Law for Shudra***^ – *obedience and domestic management, obedience to the twice-born* [who were drawn from the first three varnas], *crafts and acting*". The "Twice-Born" were those who passed the course of instruction that best matched their natural abilities, who acquired the necessary knowledge and skills relevant to the corresponding Varna and obtained, as a consequence, initiation into a valuable role in public life as a Brahman-'priest', a Kshatriya-'warrior' or a Vaishya-'commoner'. The ancient Shudras were not slaves nor servants but those who didn't pass the initiation owing to immaturity, intellectual inferiority and so forth. But as it was for the Shudra of those times, so it was for the Aryans (it was mainly a case of their potential ability)... Subsequently, as has happened already in India, this Aratto-Orianian-Aryan schema of social structure started to become formalised and to acquire caste differences and eventually, class distinctions.

The harmonious union between the 'Kemi Oba' and the 'Yamna' cultures (i.e. the most ancient Aryans), was short-lived: it resulted in the uprooting of the Usativ (i.e. Orianian) variant of the late Trypillian (i.e. Arattan) culture – along with its sea route to the ancestral homeland in Asia Minor – prior to the arrival of the Starosillia-type Alazan-Bedensk culture from Transcaucasia. These newcomers were probably one of the Hurrian clans or tribes who, at the turn of 2400-2300 BCE, began to suffer from the northern expansions of Sargon I and Naramsin, the founders of the Semitic dynasty of Akkad in Sumer. Possessing the first carts and tented-wagons[1] in the Steppe, as well as having access to Transcaucasian metal, these 'Starosillia' resettlers became more desirable allies for the local 'Yamna' culture. Excavation materials from the village near Starosillia show that on the eve of the creation of a new alliance of tribes, the 'Starosillia' resettlers occupied an unrepresentative burial mound near to the outstanding High Grave, whereas the 'Kemi Oba' used High Grave itself (burials No. 3 and No. 4), the most grandiose sanctuary in the region. In due course, the Kemi Oba departed, either of their own volition or by enforcement, and the prestigious Grave was occupied by the 'Starosillia' resettlers who constructed an incredibly labour-intensive mytho-ritual burial (No. 8). Inside that grave was the earliest cart ever found (the most ancient known to science) along with 12 roads (revealed by aerial photographs of the environment around High Grave), which spread out to the steppe horizon and served as the orientation points of a solar-zodiacal type of calendar observatory. This was an outstanding symbol of both the calendar and of a symbolic blessing for the beginning of the campaign march made by the allies into Mesopotamia. It probably also served to repel the expansion policies of Sargon I and Naramsin.

On their return from this campaign – which, like the 28-year campaign of the Scythians to the Near East, lasted a very long time – the allies resumed their burials in High Grave. During this time and throughout the period to 2300 BCE, the 'Yamna' and 'Starosillia' cultures had substantially merged, generating the necessary prerequisites for the future Aryan-Hurrian state of Mitanni^. The first specific embryonic evidence for this merger

Fig.39 : **Reflection of the contact between two tribes of Aryans and Hurrians** (carriers of Yamna and Starosillia cultures) in burials between 2400-2300 BCE near the village of Starosillia in the Velyko-Olexandrivsk district, Kherson region.

can be detected in a stone fortress in Eastern Europe, situated above one of the ferries across the lower reaches of the Dnipro (near the modern village of Mykhaylivka^ in the Novo-Vorontsovky district of the Kherson region).

In the meantime, despite a significant rapprochement with the aboriginal population, the late 'Starosillia-Hurrian' settlers became the foundation of the new, Catacomb archaeological culture. Catacombs were employed as reusable, family crypts instead of pits (remember that the 'Yamna culture' is also known as the 'Pit Grave culture'[2]). Specifically, in such kurhan graves as those near the villages of Voskresenka and Vasylivka (in the Molochna and Utliuk river valleys), local pots were found bearing images representing the central episode from the Sumerian-Akkadian *Epic of Gilgamesh.*

The Catacomb culture, which was formed under circumstances significantly shaped by the slaveholding influence of Mesopotamia, finally fixed patriarchal attitudes within the Aryan tribes. The Kemi Oba culture remained the keeper of matriarchal Arattan traditions (which by this time had already lost its "Trypillian" image). Their most recent archaeological traces are concentrated in Crimea, where during ancient times the mountain inhabitants, i.e. the Tauri, honoured Devi-'The Maiden' by offering her human sacrifices. It is possible that it was precisely from Taurida (Crimea) that a group of 'Kemi Oba' arrived, 600 years later, to make one of the last burials (No. 1) in a kurhan (No. 4), near the Grave, prior to sealing up the entire complex…

The consolidation of patriarchy was accompanied by a considerable alteration in their world outlook: instead of a belief in resurrection, the idea developed of an afterlife in the realm of the ancestors and with Yama^. A significant innovation was the spread of militant cults centred on Rudra (the name means 'The Roarer' but also 'Kind') and his sons the Maruts ('Storm' gods, etc.). The first of them [Rudra] became famous for a victory over the old gods (in particular over Daksha^ of the 'Kemi Oba' and over Pusana of the 'Yamna' cultures), and the latter [the Maruts] eventually became a detachment of the ancient serpent-warrior Indra. It is possible that carriers of the Catacomb culture entered cultural history as

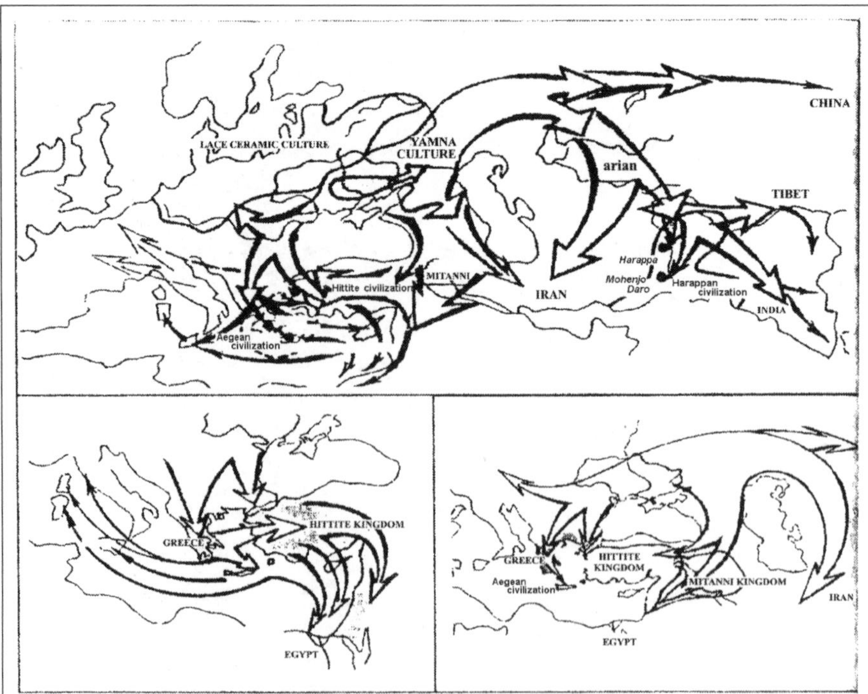

Fig. 40 : **Migration of Indo-Europeans** (Aratta, Arián etc.) in the 3rd–2nd millennia BCE. Maps composed by A. A. Bilousko.

the Kshatriya Vratiya – who were recorded in the Indo-Aryan Upanishads^ and the Laws of Manu (Manusmriti^).

The descendants of primitive-communal Aratta responded to the fore-mentioned strengthening of slaveholding tendencies by creating their own Catacomb culture. Archaeologists have conditionally named it 'Ingul' (after the River Inhul[3], a left-bank tributary of the Southern Buh). It was particularly characterised by the proliferation of axes and other weapons as well as by images of the "foot of Vishnu" etc.; there was often a combination of both of these, plus other attributes, in burial chambers. These symbols were consistent with the Vedic doctrine concerning the incarnations of Vishnu, the sixth of which was called Parashurama^ (meaning 'Rama with an axe'). According to the Upanishads, Vishnu-Parashurama destroyed the fore-mentioned Kshatriya Vratiya, but the Law of Manu traced the following people from them: the Shaka, (better known as the Scythians who are related to the Saki) and even the Yavana and Achiana people (who were Greeks: Dorians^ and Achaeans^). Such evidence corresponds with archaeological data with reference to the replacement of the first, the Saki, by the second, the Greeks and of some mixing of the carriers of the Catacomb and Ingul cultures, also the gravitation of the latter towards the Pelasgian-Greek ethnoculture.

Patriarchal attitudes, as detected from the funeral rites of the "Ingulers", were less obvious than those of the "Catacombers", even their main theme seemed to be a return to resurrection, though no longer a blessing to Mother-Earth, owing to the personal victory of the deceased over netherworldly forces. For this purpose they were armed with a magic weapon: in 'Ingul' burials, arrows, maces and axes are found but also playing-bones (i.e. dice) and sextant-bowls (which, although they were also weapons, were more subtly intellectual). Predominantly, they featured an image of the Titan^-godfighter Apollo, and in due course – the sacrifice of his brother, Dionysus^, the suffering victim of the supernatural Titans. A change in the priorities of these deities took place between 1800-1700 BCE, a period when the New Year's Taurus was superseded by the age of Aries and geo-cosmic

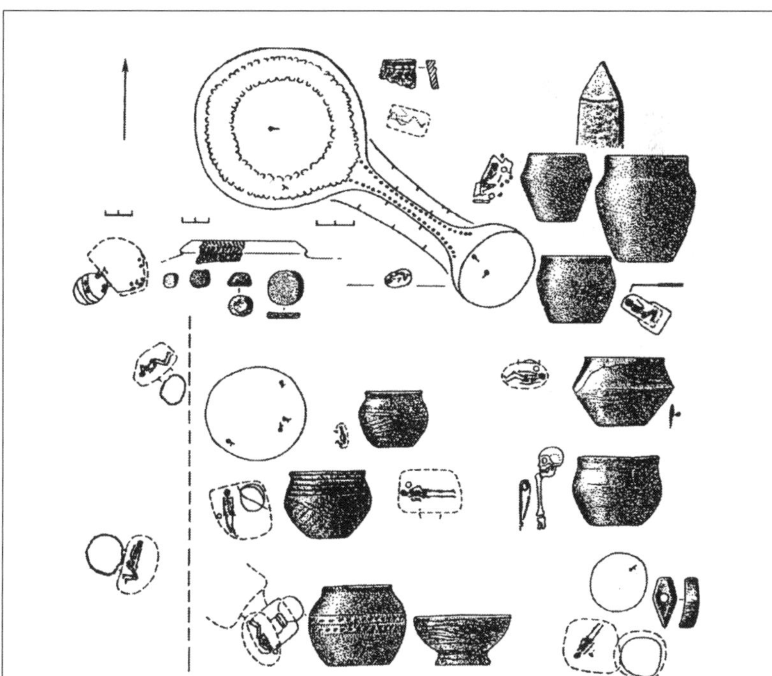

Fig.41 : **Aryans and Pelasgians of the Ukrainian Dnipro area** on the eve of the migration of mid-2nd millennium BCE. The reflection of the historic process in subsequent burials at High Grave (at Starosillia) and nearby kurhans.

catastrophes destroyed the Cretan civilisation. Distant connections to the subsequent "Ingulers" who reached Crete and Egypt are traced in these perturbations. It should be noted that during 2000-1700 BCE, the dominance of "Ingulers" in the Ukrainian Dnipro area and of "Catacombers" between the lower reaches of Don, Volga and Kuban at those times, possibly corresponded well with the traditional opposition between Aryan Asuras and Devas: demons of netherworldly 'life-giving forces' and 'shining' heavenly gods. The spread of playing-bones (i.e. dice) was a compelling reminder of the role they played in the *Mahabharata*: the main events of the 'Great Bharata' (the wars of descendants) began when Pandav lost his kingdom to his brother Kaurav.

The demise of the Ingul culture, laid by distantly connected carriers, was perhaps related to the beginning of the most ancient Aryan state of Mitanni. It appeared between 2800-2600 BCE in the north of Mesopotamia but the name (according to the authoritative definition of O. N. Trubachev) was connected with the Meotians and Meotida^ – which was the name of the Sea of Azov at that time – indicating contact between the Indo-Aryan and Hurrian tribes (which also accords with data found by other researchers). Trubachev's linguistic conclusion is that the separation of the Aryan or "Indo-Iranian" community into two branches had already taken place on the Northern Black Sea coast, prior to the expansive migrations to Persia and India. This agrees with archaeological and ethnographical data but demands a significant correction.

At this point it is necessary to repeat and emphasise what has already been stated: this separation [into two branches] was already in existence, because this is how it had been originally! The Aryan community had not emerged from pre-ethnic cultures (even though it had a partial basis in the carriers of the Sursk-Dnipro, Seredny Stoh cultures etc.), it had emerged as a result of contact with the pilgrims of Aratta and Sumer. Eventually, this community sustained two corresponding poles which always existed (until the Middle Ages), and which were focused – in accord with its founding traditions – towards Asia Minor and Mesopotamia. It is only possible to talk about periods of greater or lesser consolidation of these polarisations along the shores of the Northern Black Sea. A notable section of O. N. Trubachev's research relates to the central period in the history of the Aryan community which dates to the end of the 3rd millennium BCE (i.e. after the demise of Aratta), when it had adopted for itself the role of "heart of the Indo-European world" (known as Dandaria – meaning 'Mace-bearing Aria' – which lasted until the establishment of Rus [i.e. old Kyivan Rus]. However at its core (in terms of peace and heart) were Slavs, the direct successors of Aratta. The events of 2800-2500 BCE may be considered as comparable with the tradition of the Laws of Manu about Vena: "*The chief of the royal Rishi^, once owned the entire land, but his thinking, undone by passion, created a confusion of Varnas.*" This Brahman *Vena,* being Aryan, could be the ancestor of the Venedi^ i.e. the western branch of the Slavs...

The catastrophes and migrations of 2700 BCE, which have already been mentioned, led to the replacement of the Catacomb culture by the Srubna culture (or, more precisely, by the Ingul – or 'Multi-bead' culture which may be considered as the beginning of "Srubna time"). The virtual disappearance of the Catacomb graves, family burials, etc., as well as the construction of new kurhans, indicated an aspiration (primarily of the priest-rulers) for a return to the harmonious ways of "Yamna time". The distribution of elongated kurhans with numerous examples featuring obvious approximations of "*Moody's tunnel of immortality*" (to use a very 20th century example[4]) suggests that 'Srubna' people could still resurrect ancient traditions and invest them with their positive achievements from "Catacomb time"... However, the pressure of geo-climatic and socio-economic shifts proved to be stronger than the will of the priests ("the primitive intelligentsia"), a fact which triggered the activation of a very old doctrine, dating back to the times of Aratta, which foretold the end of the blessed 'Day of Brahma'^. In Aratta, this infinite cycle of decline and renewal (renaissance) in the Universe was reflected in the ritual burnings of old settlements as a consequence of the land having become exhausted from many years of cultivation and moving on to new land with virgin soil, and to new pre-built settlements. They probably still moved around in this way until around 1700 BCE; however, they now began to spread the rite of cremation into the kurhans.

The presence of late "Ingul" and "Kemi Oba" cultures (genetically related to Aratta and therefore with the Indian branch of the Aryan community) are traced in the pre-Grecian Mycenaeans and in the Aryan-Hurrian state of Mitanni to the north of Mesopotamia, and also in Indo-Aryan Arkaim beyond the Southern Urals. In the middle of the 2nd millennium BCE they paved the way for subsequent migrations, from which grew the basic territories that would become Persia/Iran and India. By the definitions of O. N. Trubachev, S. I. Nalyvayko and some other linguists, the names of these countries, and also many of their numerous place-names and hydronyms, originated from the Azov-Black Sea steppes, particularly from the shores of the Sind-Dnipro (in both cases 'Rivers', in the languages of the Aratto-Indian and Aryan-Iranian populations). Amongst the abundant archaeological evidence from this area was the key to the so-called Borodino treasure – a unique complex of 17 high-quality articles found in 1912 by peasants from the village of Borodino (in the present Odessa region) during the destruction of the kurhan of "a mighty chieftain who lived during the period 1550-1450 BCE" (T. B. Popov, *Borodino Treasure*, Moscow, 1985). Silver spears, pins and a dagger resembled, in terms of their shape and ornamentation, materials from the Creto-Mycenaean culture but their raw material originated in the pre-Urals. Even closer to India, in the East Sayan mountains [east of the Altai mountains] – three stone axes were produced from Jade/Nephrite, and a fourth had its counterpart only in Kuban. In both of these regions, three white-topped clubs were found to be made of talc stone, common to the area. It is noticeable in this case that at least some of these items were made by local master craftsmen of the Northern Black Sea region.

Those who did not join the migrations from this region remained and created the Sabatynivka culture^, (first excavated at the village of Sabatynivka in the Odessa region), of the earliest Cimmerians. The carriers of this archaeological culture all but ceased the building of kurhans and returned to the construction of the once-inherent agricultural and pastoral settlements of Trypillian times (i.e. Aratta), though with less ambitious, single-storied constructions built predominantly of stone rather than wood.

It was people of the Sabatynivka culture who constructed the closing fill at High Grave. Yu. Shilov traced within it several very important points that make this memorial one of the key archaeological sources for recovering the history of the Aryans. Firstly, the tomb at High Grave embodied the symbolism of the Sun whilst its neighbouring kurhan symbolised the Moon, and the bank that connected them symbolised the Celestial (Milky) Way. An analogy [for this inter-connection] is found in the "Wedding Hymn" of the *Rigveda*, in which the marriage of the Sun and Moon is personified by the bride Surya (the Sun) riding to her bridegroom Soma^ (the Moon) along the Celestial highway. Secondly, these constructions at High Grave relate to the neighbouring kurhan No. 4 which corresponds to a complex of altars to Shruti^ ('that which is heard') of a type still being built in India for the performance of Vedic hymns. Thirdly, the construction of High Grave in the middle of the 4th millennium BCE began with the burning of huts over the dead and two millennia later it was completed with a cremation of the last corpse on top of the kurhan. This matches the doctrine of the "Day of Brahma" that begins with the fiery nucleus of the Universe and ends with the burning-renewal of the worldwide fire. It also reflects the accumulation of local traditions by the community of Brahman-priests, which can be treated as the primary codification of the hymns of the *Rigveda*, which were completed in India.

The testimony of *The Veles Book* concerning Aryan-Slavic relationships will be considered in due course, but for the moment it is sufficient to identify the authors of this 'Book of the Slavs' with the Cimmerians. It is necessary though to include the presence of the principal theme from the Vedic mytho-rituals beneath a Cimmerian burial ground, No. 12-1, near the village of Kairy. Underneath the burials was a composition of three sacrificial pits in the form of a serpent (Vritra), an embryonic flexed person (Indra), between whom was a ring (Vala). The shapes and ornamentation of the ceramic vessels, metals and other ornaments revealed the influence of Carpathian cultures, this was confirmed by the anthropological evidence of the bodies... In the neighbouring burial mound of a 5th century BCE Scythian chieftain, it was possible to trace the synthesis of Aryan-Cimmerian traditions through a legend concerning the origin of the ancestor of the local Scythian serpent-legged goddess and the foreign Herakles^.

Down through the centuries the traditions of Aratta and Arián, Oriana and Dandaria continued to exist in the Dnipro area, long after the demise of the Trypillian and then the Sabatynivka archaeological cultures. Those traditions existed there until at least the 11th century, at Arsania-Arta, an old Rus country, and traditional reminders also survived in modern, autochthonous Ukrainian ethnoculture. The native traditions could have come, in particular, from the inhabitants of the 'Sabatynivka'-Cimmerian settlements near High Grave which were built simultaneously with the construction of the final closing fill at High Grave. Judging from the evidence of domestic fragments, the Scythians, Sarmatians^ and Slavs lived on there until later times, into the 4th – 10th centuries.

On the territory of modern Odessa, stood ancient Oriana (Orissa, or Odissa), co-existing with a crucial part of Dandaria (around the modern Tendrovska spit opposite the mouth of the Dniester river), and even into the first century CE the culture continued to honour the god Shiva^ (perhaps Sivash^, and also Siva^ of *The Veles Book,* may be derived from him?). This is evidenced by late antique inscriptions carrying the names of Shiva which had been commonly used in India: Butanath and Mahadevi^. A version of the last name – Deva or the Divine – is linked to the main sanctuary of the Tauri of Taurida, also associated with numerous Divych-mountains ("Maidan-like mountains") of Ukraine and across Europe. There is such a mountain, overlooking the Dnipro; and from Trypillia, three "Serpent walls"^ stretched for hundreds of kilometres. Maybe these were the origin of the Trishula-trident of Siva-Mahadevi?! Such shrines are still revered by people up to the present day.

Suggested reading

1. Elizarenkova T. I., *The Rigveda*, Russian translation, comments and notes, Vols. 1 to 3, Moscow, 1989, 1999.
2. Elmanovich S. D., *Laws of Manu*, Russian translation, comments and notes, Moscow, 1992.
3. Shilov Yu., *Ancestral Homeland of Aryans*, Kyiv, 1995.
4. Trubachev O. N., *Indoarica in the Northern Black Sea Coast,* Moscow, 1999.
5. Nalyvayko S. I., *Secrets of Sanskrit Revealed*, Kyiv, 2000.
6. Safronov V. A., *Indo-European Ancestral Homelands*, Gorki, 1989.
7. Lagodovskaya E. F., Shaposhnikova O. G., *Mikhailov Settlement*, Kyiv, 1962.
8. Sharafutdinova I. N., *The Steppe Dnipro Area in the Bronze Age*, Kyiv, 1982.
9. Zdanovich G. B., *Arkaim: Research. Searches. Discoveries*, Scientific Ed. Cheliabinsk, 1995.

[1] The Russian word used here is 'кибитки' (Kibitki) which has two meanings: (1) a tent, like a Yurt, and (2) a covered vehicle, either a snow-sleigh or wheeled gypsy-wagon.

[2] The word for 'pit' in Russian and Ukrainian is 'яма' (yama) (which is also the name of a deity of the netherworld in the Aryan Vedas and *The Veles Book* of Slavs).

[3] It is appropriate here to mention again that the Ukrainian River 'Ингул' is pronounced 'Inhul' in Ukraine but as 'Ingul' in Russia. Accordingly, from Soviet times, the homonymic archaeological culture has been more commonly called 'Ingul'.

[4] Moody coined the term *near-death experience.* (Raymond Moody, *Life After Life: the investigation of a phenomenon – survival of bodily death*, San Francisco, CA: Harpers San Fran, 2001. ISBN 0-06251739-2).

CHAPTER 5

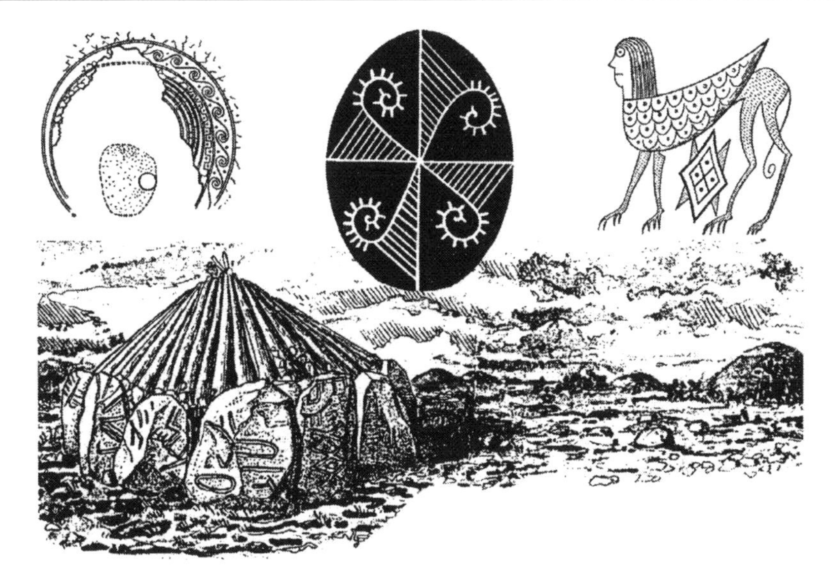

Fig. 42 : **From Pelasgians of Aratta up to Ukraine**. A kurhan of the 4th millennium BCE at the village of Verbivka in the Cherkasy region (reconstruction by A. A. Bobrinsky, A. S. Trofimova, P. L. Kornienko) and subsequent memorials of Pelasgian type, traditions that are traced (centre) on Ukrainian Pysanky [hand-painted eggs].

THE 'DARK AGES' OF EUROPE

The 'Dark Ages' of European history began around the 2nd millennium BCE, a time when archaeological and linguistic sources became very confused by geo-cosmic catastrophes, population explosions, and the migration of tribes and nations. Therefore historians generally bypass this period, their sources being limited to the quotations of Homer^ and Herodotus.

The epithets, 'History began in Sumer', and 'Father of history' can ostensibly be attributed to the ancient Greek traveller Herodotus (484-430 BCE). Both of these descriptions (along with many others) are inexact cultural-scientific stereotypes which, over time, became the prevailing doctrine but which now hamper our understanding of the true state of affairs.

We have already had the opportunity to be assured that history actually began about 6200 BCE in Aratta – from which Sumer, in particular, proceeded. As for the role of the 'Father of history', perhaps that title can be better claimed by the pre-Arattan chronicler, Kaskisim, whose plate is mentioned in inscription Nos.17, 19/D, 25/A, 26, 34/A at Shu-Nun (Stone Grave).

For about two thousand years, Europeans believed that their history began in Greece – or more precisely, with the Greek siege and fall of Troy in Asia Minor around the 13th - 11th centuries BCE. Nevertheless, don't forget that the victors themselves (see *The Histories* of Herodotus: II, 56; VI, 137; VIII, 44, etc.), together with their state and culture, were products of the ruins of Pelasgia and Atlantis^. It was believed that no-one in the ancient world was wiser than the Greeks. As a matter of fact, not only did they understand their own pre-history poorly but they did not even know about the origin of Zeus, Apollo and their other gods, inclining to the idea that they originated in Egypt, Pelasgia, 'Super-northern' Hyperborea or, with the Pelasgic-Trojans (whose dates, birthplaces and deaths also remained unknown), or in the imagination of Homer. Is it possible to rely on such unsteady authority for gleaning information pertinent to the origin of Slavs and other nations? Is it possible to say: "because the 'Father of History' didn't mention anything about Slavs and Germans, etc. – that means that they didn't actually exist?" No, it is impossible to say that, especially since the names of nations (even the names they called themselves!) changed over time and ancient authors noticed barbarians only when they got in the way of the vital interests of their states.

So, there is no compunction to trust authorities such as these, instead, it is preferable to re-piece an accurate picture of the threshold of historical antiquity from fragments which were left not only by Greco-Roman historians, but also by the authors of *The Veles Book* and other legends. Thus an attempt will be made to trace the appropriate migrations from Aratta and Arián.

1. Atlantis, Pelasgia and Hyperborea^

Fig.43 : Ukrainian painted egg with ornamentation of "Creto-Minoan style".

Admirers of the mysteries of Atlantis only know, as a rule, the evidence left by Plato (427-347 BCE). However, experts also know that this famous ancient Greek author was a philosopher and politician rather than an historian. Facts interested him only as raw materials for developing his own ideas. Using the legends of Atlantis (whose location he specified rather uncertainly), Plato made an example of a theocratic society, as opposed to Athenian democracy, and used that example as a warning, in his opinion, about its destructive tendencies. When recording details of the pre-Athenean war with Atlantis, and the extinction of the latter, the philosopher predicted the same fate would befall Athens if it failed to cease angering the gods. The chronology, as recorded by Plato, does not stand up to scrutiny considering the demise of Atlantis is said to have occurred 10 millennia before Solon, [who apparently shared the story of Atlantis with the great-grandfather of Plato's 'Critias'] representing 12 generations since the times of the Titan Atlant^. Allowing for three generations to a century (as demographers do), this amounts to just 400 years. Even permitting 1200 years, to make allowance for incomplete genealogical knowledge by the philosopher, a date of around 10,000 years is evidently mythical.

There are records by other Greek authors who, although they lived after Plato, nevertheless still truly preserved folk legends of Atlantis. Diodorus Siculus (1st century BCE), referring to testimonies from inhabitants of the island of Samothrace, informs us that the Pontis Euxine (Black Sea) "*used to be a lake before the Deluge but the rivers which flowed into it disturbed it so significantly that it overflowed its banks, bursting out into the Hellespont^, inundating the best part of the shores of Asia ... This would explain why fishermen had pulled the tops of [stone] columns out of the sea with their sweep-nets; testifying to the fact that even the cities were flooded*". The Atlanteans, together with Phrygians, lived around Lake Triton (which, following an earthquake and the Flood, had been converted into the Sea of Marmara^), which the author of the *Historical Library* placed in Africa, because he conflated legends describing ancient Lycia and Luwia of Asia Minor with those of modern day Libya. The same mistake was repeated by Herodotus, who traditionally placed the mountains and country of Atlantis near this Lake Triton, which no longer existed.

What is the best way of separating this and similar evidence, where it has already been so entangled by the Greeks? *The Encyclopaedia of Classical Ancient History* by Pauli-Vissova covered the sweep of modern research in its many volumes which appeared in Germany between 1893-1980. Here, the best experts on antiquity collected and processed Greek Mythology, which not only allowed them to track the lineage of tribes and heroes over two millennia but also of the preceding millennia BCE. Stepping onto this same path, A. G. Kifishin (in *Genostructure of pre-Greek and Ancient Greek Myths, 1990*) went to the generic root of the mythologies of Greece, Sumer, and Egypt and put forward the problem of Aratta, existing in the 7th – 4th millennium BCE, as an historical reality expressed in the Keresh archaeological culture – as Trypillia.

According to a schema outlined by Kifishin based on the *Encyclopedia* of Pauli-Vissova, the **Titan Atlas,** or Atlant, was the grandson of the sky-god Uranus^ and earth-goddess Gaia, the brother of Prometheus^ and the son of Iapetus (whose name was probably borrowed by the authors of the Bible for the name of Japheth. This assumption is especially likely since amongst the nearest descendants of Atlas we see Shem, the name of the second son of Noah the flood-survivor). Furthermore, because Atlant was also the nephew of Pelasg, the geographic territory of Pelasgia has to be somewhat older than Atlantis. Myths sometimes name the ancestors of both countries as 'super-northern', or Hyperborean. This indicates that their common ancestral home – the legendary Hyperborea – lay somewhere to the north of Pelasgia and Atlantis, but where exactly?

If historical Atlantis (rather than the place imagined by Plato and others) was situated on the coast of the future Sea of Marmara, and the most ancient place known to ancient authors was Pelasgia, in Arcadia, then it is logical to search for the ancestral homeland beyond the Black Sea, which at that time was called the Pontis Euxine. Its alternative name of 'Hospitable Sea' is a product of the "popular etymology" of ancient Greek times, when its aboriginal Aratto-Aryan name was changed from the way it was pronounced in Sanskrit as Panta Ukshan, meaning 'The way of the Bull' (i.e. Taurus) (according to S. I. Nalyvayko). Two other names corresponded to this calendrically and ritually conditional, primordial name: 'the Bull passage' of the Bosphorus[1] and 'the Solar way' of the Hellespont. So the Pelasgian and Greek straits between the Black, Marmara and Mediterranean Seas already existed after the Dardan flood when the name for the Hellespont was fixed as the Dardanelles. Yet, even earlier, before the Hellespont, it was called the Dnipro; it was also named Euxi, 'the Bull'. On the other hand, the *Borysf*en (or Borysthenes, as the Greeks generally named the Dnipro in ancient times) was sometimes called the Dardanelles. There were also two Bosphoruses: the Thracian Bosphorus^ (as it is now) and the Cimmerian (the modern Kerch^ strait).

The most ancient manifestations of *borysthen* are found amongst the Atlanteans, the descendants of Atlant. Amongst them, *borysthen*^ was the name of their titanic storehouse of vital powers. Don't the Dnipro rapids stand at the heart of this mythology? Hasn't a granite sanctuary-observatory dated to the end of the 3rd millennium BCE been excavated by archaeologists on a summit of the island of Khortytsia^ (just below the Dnipro rapids)? This character is akin to the bull-man of Achelous^ of the tribes of Kranaos and Eleusin, the family of Atlant. He is a forerunner of the Trojan War hero *Achilles* (or originally Achelous?) in honour of whom the present Tendrovska spit was named (opposite the mouth of the Tiras-Dniester), whose name preserves the memory of Dandaria. According to the evidence of Aryan and other authors, Achilles came from the banks of the Meotida (Azov area), and his soul found refuge on the island of Levkada^ (the modern Snake Island, near the mouth of the Danube)...

As we see, the vitality of the first-ever state in the world, Aratta, did not disappear at the end of the 3rd millennium BCE, but spread with the migrations of people from the Indo-European community. Herodotus (IV: 49) list the name Artanes, an inflow of the Danube; another river of Thrace was named Artesk, like the known area of Taurida. Thus the extent of influences between the 3rd – 2nd millennium BCE went from the Northern Black Sea coast towards the future Hellas^. Connected with this movement is the spread of legends describing about the Floods of Ogyges, Deucalion and Dardan and legends describing the end of Atlantis. We will consider these legends as a way of clarifying the time and circumstances of the re-settlement of the "Hyperboreans".

A close descendant of Atlant was **King Ogyges**, ancestor of the women called "Avengers" (Amazons?^) and founder of agricultural mystery plays. An island of the same name, Ogygia, belonging to him is where Odysseus was kept for seven years by Calypso, the daughter of Atlant. In due course this island was named Lefkada (see above) – the 'White Cliff', located before the entrance to Hades^, the realm of the dead. It was considered that it was precisely here that the souls of the distinguished Trojan War heroes burned eternally – Achilles, Patroclus, and also Helen [of Sparta]. Nevertheless, Hades, which was visited by

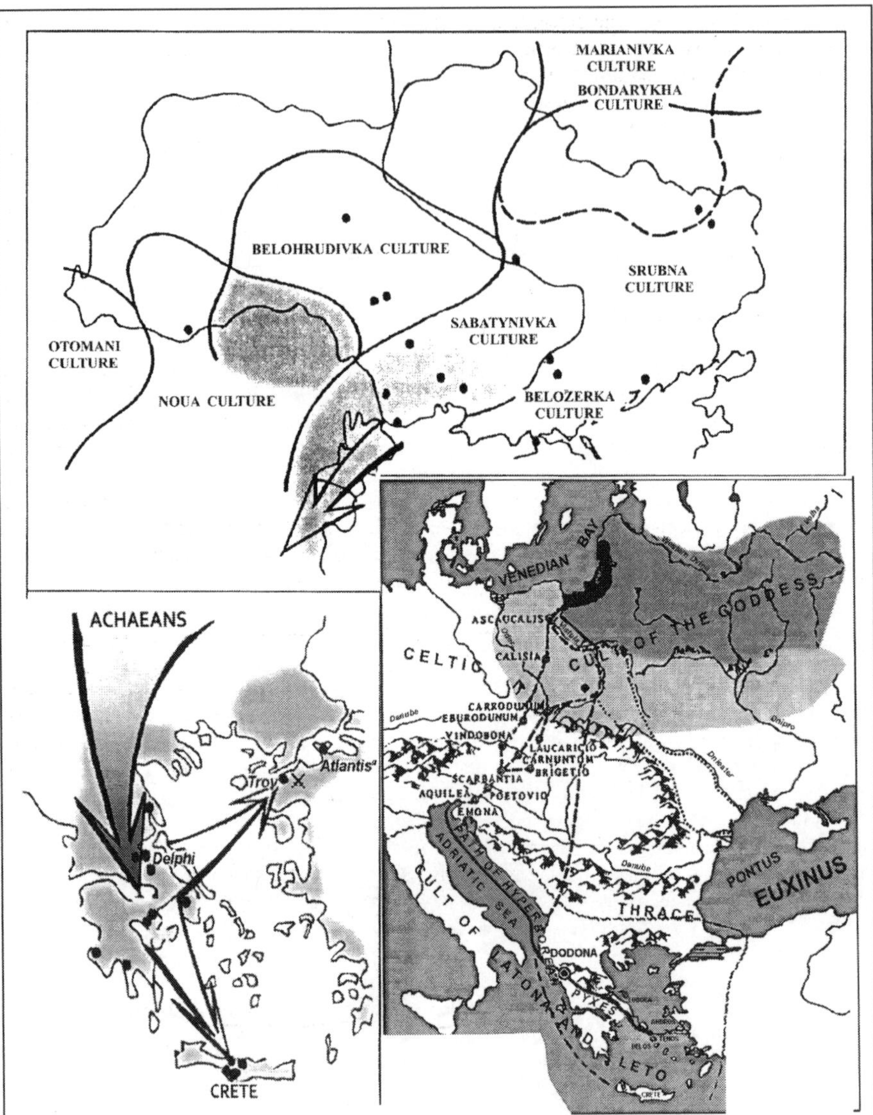

Fig.44 : **The migration of Aryan nationalities** in the second half of the 2nd millennium BCE (according to A. A. Bilousko) and the travels of the Hyperboreans (bottom right; acc. to B. A. Rybakov).

Odysseus during his wanderings immediately after the Trojan War, was situated in the homeland of Achilles – beyond the Cimmerian Bosphorus, on the coast of Meotida (the Sea of Azov), (apparently, amongst the mud volcanoes of Sindiki – i.e. modern Taman).

There was a catastrophic flood in Ogygia (either in 2450 BCE, when an earthquake destroyed Troy-II, or in 2136 BCE, according to the Roman historian Varro) which was caused by "a change in the colour, size, form and course" of Hesper (the planet Venus) who was one of the Hesperides – daughters of the Titan Atlant. When Atlas/Atlant went to the aid of Kronos, who was killed by his son Zeus, Atlas/Atlant was condemned by Zeus to hold up the sky/earth on his shoulders. The Pelasgians' later appeared in Greece, with their beliefs that accord with the mythological canon of Diya-Dzeus-Zeus which included Zeus' lover Leto and their children, Apollo and Artemis, who had run away from

Hyperborea. It is in this same place, in Hyperborea, that images of Zeus himself appeared for the first time, as well as his son Apollo (in burials of 1800 BCE in kurhan No. I-II near the village of Kairy, between the town of Kakhovka and the village of Hornostaevka). It is little wonder that being Hyperboreans (as were Pelasg and Atlant, if we recall), these gods were not immediately given precedence over the local gods of the future Greece. It is possible, that the Ogygian and other flood legends of the Greeks, were derived from even more ancient flood legends, from the time when Sumer was separated from the coastal part of Aratta.

Pelasg was considered to be a Hyperborean but he was also the patriarch of the pre-Greek tribes of the Morey/Athens peninsula of Greece. According to his involvement in the Ogygian flood, this patriarch brought some Orianian or Arattan tribes to dry land in a new homeland, when other tribes of Oriana had migrated by sea away from the mouth of the Dniester River, into Asia Minor. According to legend, having then partially resettled in Troy, they took away from Greece a Pelasgian meteorite which was an embodiment of Rhea, Foremother of the gods, who was the younger daughter of Uranus (according to Thracian and Greek myths). These migrations correspond with the arrival, at the end of the 3rd millennium BCE, of the Indo-European *Hittites* (probably, the ancestors of the *Getae*, of future Thrace) on the land of the *Hattians* of Asia Minor, who were, perhaps, their conservative, yet pre-Indo-European ancestors. However, this wave of migrants belonged more to the Illyrian community which, through the Dominy archaeological culture then in Thessaly, was connected with the Usativ culture (i.e. Oriana). These assumptions are supported by elements of the Hittite language at Tauris which is related with those tribes of the Northern Black Sea, as well as some kinship of the Illyrians with the Cimmerians (and Slavs).

The other name of Rhea of the Thracians was Pandora. She was the mother of Pyrrha, the wife of **King Deucalion,** who also experienced a terrible flood that was sent down to the Titans by Hellenic Zeus for murdering his son Dionysus (whose cult began to squeeze out the cult of Apollo after 1700 BCE, i.e. when Aries took ascendancy in the zodiac at the change over from the former supremacy of Taurus). Humanity perished because of the Deucalion flood, generated by Gaia – the 'Earth Goddess', the wife of Uranus. Deucalion

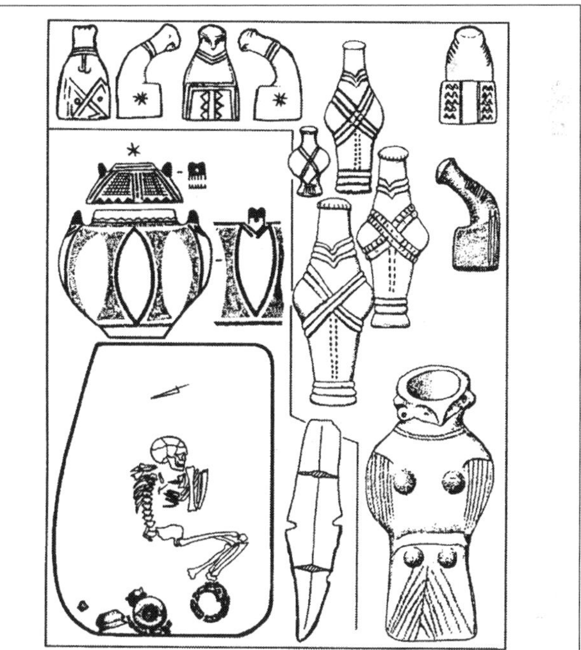

Fig.45 : **Memorials of Oriana**. Entombment, dagger, vessel and figurines of the Usativ culture (one of the variants of late Trypillian culture) between the 4th–3rd millennium BCE.

and Pyrrha produced a son, Hellen, founder of the Hellenic-Greeks (Athenians, and others). He produced a son Dora, patriarch of the Dorian-Greeks, amongst whom the best known were the inhabitants of the city-state of Sparta. Incidentally, after the flood, a new population was formed by Deucalion and Pyrrha from spartos–'stones', who seemed to be secondary, or accessory to the Hellenes. However, the even more numerous "lower-people" were considered to be Pelasgian. According to Herodotus (I : 56), the Asia Minor Greek-Achaeans or Ionians "*were in the first instance Pelasgic in origin; their tribe never left their own land* (perhaps because it was close to the Illyrians, Hittites and Hatti); *the Hellenes were not numerous before coming together with the Pelasgians*", but because of their bellicosity, and the acceptance of their language and customs by other tribes, they overgrew and assimilated other related, subordinate tribes, such as the Pelasgians, Ionians and others.

Deucalion's flood was caused by the next great line up of planets. These cyclical-astronomical events altered gravitational relationships within the Solar System, triggering geological catastrophes (in particular, earthquakes and volcanic eruptions). This is what occurred around 1700 BCE, resulting in Crete being abandoned by its population for a long period of time. It is clear that people connected the onset of the catastrophe which took place at precisely that time (which also accorded with astronomical laws), with the change of supremacies in the zodiacal constellations, already alluded to above. Thus 'Our God', Dionysus (whose cult origins can be traced in kurhans in the area of Stone Grave in the Molochna valley) became the embodiment of the "dying and rising Taurus", whose deification until the beginning of 17th century BCE, was as the apotheosis of Apollo, the elder 'brother' of Dionysus. The most ancient appearance of the family of Zeus is traced amongst the corresponding sub-kurhan burials from 2000-1700 BCE of the Ingul archaeological culture in the Buh-Don region. It was definitely to this place, (in Tartarus, in the mountains of Taurida), that the Titans were exiled by Zeus - their famous descendant Prometheus then appeared in the Caucasus.

According to ancient authors, Deucalion's flood happened when the Pelasgian King Cecrops^ reigned in pre-Grecian Athens. At the same time there was a partial migration of these Pelasgians to Italy where they became neighbours to their own kin who had started to move there from the Troad during the 18th century BCE. The most ancient of the known migrations of the Trojans to Italy took place under the leadership of the brothers Oenotrus^ and Peucetius who regarded themselves as great-great-grandsons of Zeus and Neba (Niobe?), great-grandsons of Enoch and grandsons of Pelasg.

The flood which destroyed Atlantis occurred during the lifetime of **King Dardanus**^ – though some authors identify that flood with Deucalion or with a time before him. This confusion had existed even in the accounts from ancient times and seems to have arisen from efforts to connect and reconcile the various Pelasgian-Greek legends and myths with those of other tribes.

After the murder of his grandfather Uranus, Atlant had suffered the punishment of Zeus for wanting to help Kronos. He was either turned into a pillar of stone, a range of mountains [Atlas Mountains] or forced to hold upon his shoulders either the sphere of the Earth, or the Sky. This is how he appeared to Herakles and the Argonauts, who also witnessed the Dardan Flood.

In calculating the date of this flood, A. I. Asov drew attention to the fact that the crew of the "Argo"^ had seen the land of Atlantis on their outward journey, but Odysseus, who travelled back along this route, was no longer able to see it. Thus the flood which swallowed Atlantis must have occurred within the space of time between these journeys. After the flood, Dardanus (the grandson of Atlant), migrated from Samothrace into Asia, where his descendants became the Kings of Troy. Because Laertes^, the father of Odysseus, was amongst the Argonauts when the latter sailed on the Black Sea immediately after the Trojan War (which took place, as currently accepted, in the middle of the 13th century BCE), A. I. Asov considered that the end of Atlant's reign could not possibly be further back than the boundary between the 15th - 14th centuries BCE. During that period, Egypt was ruled by Akhenaten, whose reforms were triggered, in large measure, in response to the catastrophic eruption of the volcanic island of Santorini (near Crete). There are hints of this in the *Argonautica* by Apollonius of Rhodes, the main keeper of the Library of Alexandria (3rd century BCE).

The first author to describe the epic voyage of the "Argo" is believed to have been the semi-mythical poet and singer, Orpheus, one of its crew members. He lived in Thrace and Taurida, where, beyond the Cimmerian Bosphorus, lay the main entrance to the land of the dead – Hades, where Orpheus went in search of his love, Eurydice. The Argonauts had sailed from their native Peloponnese in the same direction, to Colchis. Having passed the straits of the Dardanelles and the Thracian Bosphorus (which had existed since the time when the Mediterranean had become joined to the Black Sea), the travellers guided their ship towards the mouth of the River Acheron (perhaps the Kuban) near the entrance to Hades. There they landed at the city of Aiaia/Aeaea/Eya, which lay on the island of the same name, native home to the Medes^, but during the times of Odysseus, its name was known as Tsertse or Kirke/Circe (whose name is consonant with the later name of Korchev, and then of modern Kerch). Based on these and other indications, O. N. Trubachev and A. I. Asov (and prior to them, the classical philologist, V. V. Latyshev) reasonably transferred the main events of the ancient Argonauts from Colchis to Taman – in those days Sindica and Cimmeria – whose existence here during the journeys of the Argonauts and Odysseus, is questionable (unless the time of the Trojan War is acknowledged to have taken place at 1030-1020 BCE – further details to follow).

The Argonauts returned by an alternative route, across the Danube (the Ister/ Istros). According to geological and palaeo-zoological data, at the beginning of the 3rd millennium BCE the Danube drained into the Adriatic Sea but it also had a second arm that drained into the Black Sea. The first arm was closed off during the Dardan flood in accordance with a curse by the king [Aeëtes] of Aea (in Colchis), from whom the Argonauts had stolen the 'golden fleece', causing the "Argo" to became stranded in the silt of this or another tributary. The Argonauts were compelled to turn for help to Atlant who then lived near Lake Triton. (Here the author of the poem uses old information, from times earlier than the flood of Ogyges). Herakles had either got there earlier or had not sailed to Aiaia at all. The Argonauts found the Hesperides, the daughters of Atlant, in tears because the hero had already plucked the apples of eternal life in their garden and in doing so had killed their guard, the dragon Ladon^. According to another version, Herakles brought the apples to Atlant/Atlas, having offered to take on the firmament for the hero [who bore it on his shoulders]... The Argonauts offered a sacrifice to Triton the River god, who opened a way to the Dardanelles for them, enabling them to leave. (Before that, the way was temporarily closed again – according to the legends of Orpheus and Apollonius, it was closed even before the time of "the Flood" that separated Sumer from Aratta).

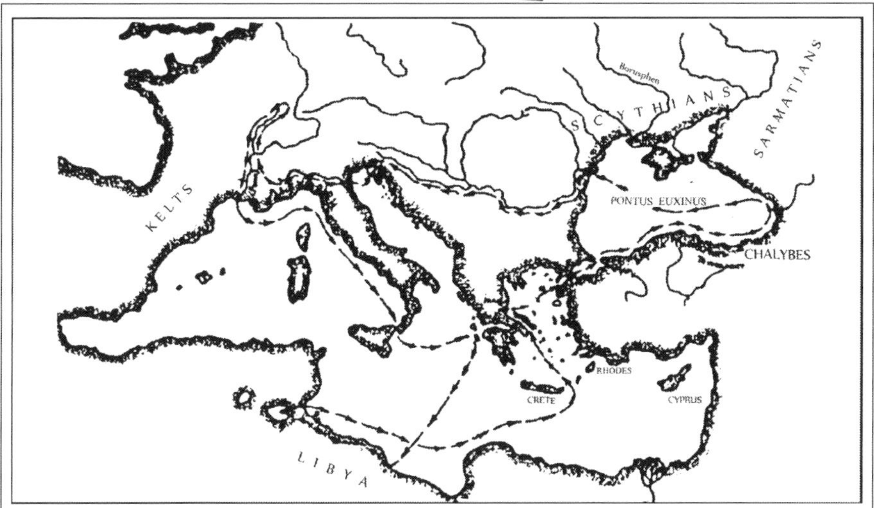

Fig.46 : **The journeys of the Argonauts and Odysseus**. According to Apollonius Rhodian and A. B. Snisarenko.

Unfortunately, we cannot hope to connect the chronology of the actual and mythical events; each time the myth recorders composed a description of the Flood (etc.) they were recorded as happening at varying times i.e. they were timeless events. According to astrophysical, geological, archaeological and written data, the Dardan flood occurred around 1250-1178 BCE, but if it didn't take place during those years, then it took place at the same time as the Trojan Wars [i.e. their dates were synonymous whatever the actual dates]. At this time, tectonic activity led to an appreciable increase in different kinds of radiation which undoubtedly affected the activity of migrations, the cruelty of wars, and the occurrence of human mutations…

According to Diodorus Siculus, who preserved for us the most realistic legends about the loss of Atlantis, King Dardanus – the grandson of Atlant – escaped from the flood to the island of Samothrace, then on to Mount Ida where he founded a city; his descendant Ilus would later found Ilion near this city. According to the archaeological data of H. Schliemann and his followers, this could be Troy-VI which flourished in 1700-1250 BCE and perished, as it now transpires, due to a terrible earthquake (L. I. Akimova, *Troy and Schliemann*, Moscow-Milan, 1996). "Homeric Troy" should now be considered to be the 7th city that Schliemann excavated at a hill in Hissarlik; Troy-VII was re-built on the ruins of the fore-mentioned earthquake and it existed throughout 1250-1020 BCE, when it was twice burned by enemy invasions.

Thus, even the legend of the *Argonauts* should be perceived as the synthesis of centuries-old wanderings between Oriana (or even Aratta) of the Northern Black Sea and overseas, the southern regions of the settling 'Indo-Europeans'. One of them, on the territory of future Greece, was the region of *Argolid* with its capital at *Argos* on the River Inachus (redolent of Enoch, the father of Pelasg). The founder of that city was considered to be the son of Zeus and Niobe, and it was from there that the mythical Io departed (Ionia in Asia Minor derives from her name), persecuted by the jealous wife of Zeus, through Cimmeria down to Egypt (Herodotus, I:1). And travelling with the Hyperboreans in the opposite direction, through those lands to Delos^, was the legendary *Arga^* – possibly the priestess *Agrimpasa,* whom Scythians called "Aphrodite Urania" (Herodotus, IV; 59, etc.), possibly coming from Argokena or Argoda, which may have been cities of Taurida with Indo-Aryan names?

L. I. Akimova was right to point out the impossibility of finding an unequivocally scientific connection between the legendary history of Troy and its archaeological ruins. At the same time, the researcher made a significant discovery: the *Iliad* of Homer is based on the assumed mytho-ritual struggle between maternal and paternal lineages with the latter succeeding in being implemented. Relative to the historical evidence, there was more interest in the predecessors of Plato than in the real history of Atlantis.

2. "Super-Northern" Apollo and his followers.

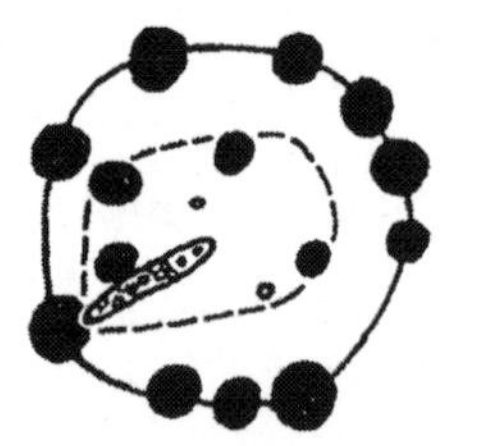

Fig.47 : **Sanctuary-observatory of ancient Slavs**. Tshinets archaeological culture, settlement of Pustynka (central Dnipro area) from the second half of the 2nd millennium BCE. Excavations by S. S. Berezanska, interpretation by Yu. Shilov.

The Greco-Roman historian Plutarch, who belonged to the highly intellectual clan of the highest attendants of Apollo, tells an interesting story about the dispute amongst those servants over the significance and meaning of the Y-shaped sign above the entrance to Apollo's main temple (at Delphi^, under Mount Parnassus). Note that this is the beginning of the expression 'Unified Whole'[2] which allegedly interprets the enigmatic name A-POLLO (meaning 'not multiple', an indivisible 'singularity', according to the logic of such interpretation). This disputed meaning is one more example of the ignorance of the "wise Greeks", even about the basis of their own civilisation.

The mystery is, in fact, revealed from a different perspective. The 'horizontal Y' is the astral sign of the constellation Aries, which headed the zodiac (i.e. its upper culmination began to coincide with the vernal equinox) in about 1700 BCE (see above). Some time later the well-known legend of Apollo's protection and patronage of the ship "Argo" developed – on which Jason^, Orpheus, Herakles, Laertes and some other outstanding heroes of Hellas had sailed to Colchis in search of the Golden Fleece, supposedly the hide of Aries – the Ram, as a sacrifice to Zeus. Prior to 1720-1700 BCE, the primary constellation of the zodiac had been Taurus which had specifically epitomised the earliest known rival-son of Zeus since Apollo, Paion[3] (namesake of the Aratto-Aryan Parjani, the Aryan-Slavic Perun etc.). As for the many interpretations of the name of *Apollo*, the two that are most scientific are: the namesake of the Aryan *Krishna Gopal(on)* and the Slavic *I(Yu)vana Kupala^*, with whom is associated the name 'Ne-horod' (non-city) [conceptually perhaps, A-Polis/Apollo, as in 'non-Polis'].

Indeed, there were once ***cities*** in the river valleys and '***non-cities***' [i.e. empty spaces] on high bald mountains which were better suited to astronomical-calendar observations. Complexes of settlements and sanctuaries precisely like this were typical of Aratta from the 5th – 3rd millennium BCE. Specific "rotunda"-sanctuaries (consisting of ring ditches and embankments with 1-4 openings positioned in accordance with the directions of the risings and settings of the Moon and Sun at the equinoxes and solstices) – which could also be utilised secondarily as cattle enclosures. These "rotunda"-sanctuaries emerged in the **Danube** area and from there spread to Britain (Stonehenge and other rotunda-sanctuaries) and to the Altai (Arkaim and others). With these sanctuary-observatories the Arattan rulers had created a unified system of calendar-economic-ceremonial services, which extended along the northern boundary of agriculture of that time [c. latitude 58 degree N.] (Table XVI).

The authenticity of this reconstructed mythological canon of the Arattan system of sanctuary-observatories is supported by specific correspondences between the names of Aratto-Sumerian *Nidaba*, Pelasgian-Greek *Niobe* and Trojan-Rusenian^ *Nebo*, as first pointed out by A. G. Kifishin and Yu. Shilov.

The "Steppe Queen/Goddess" Nidaba was mother to the goddess Ninlil – wife of the Aratto-Sumerian creator-God Enlil, forerunner of the Slavic 'Lel'. Niobe was Queen of one of the Pelasgian tribes; in one myth, Niobe gave birth to Argus the King of Argos, from Zeus himself. In another myth, Artemis, with Apollo, shot the children of Niobe [the Theban Queen] with arrows because the queen did not properly esteem their mother Leto. It's likely that this legend arose from squabbles between aboriginal peoples and the Arattan priests (the creators and protectors of these important sanctuary-observatories, necessary for calendar-astronomical observations in harsh environments). Even more probable is the ritual of human sacrifice. Indeed, at the centre of an early rotunda near Fribritz^ (in southern Austria) dating to the 4th millennium BCE, skeletons were found of young men and women, barely covered with earth, who had been slain, just like Niobe's children, by an arrow in the back. This monument is the earliest evidence for the origin of Apollo and Artemis but they were probably occluded by images of their predecessors at that time. These could have been the pre-Indo-European Lada^ and Iasion^ (who perhaps resembles Jason the Argonaut) – the 'Mother, wife' and 'Jason'[4] who had more expressive calendar clarity and connection with agriculture than the previous Divanna^ and Ivan/Yuval. The name Ivan is derived from the Slavic word 'Iva', (meaning Willow, world tree of the "Indo-Europeans"), and the name Yuval, in Sanskrit, means 'youthful', equating to the "Young god" identified with Krishna, and is also one of the epithets of Apollo. He appears, primarily, as the 'Protector (of cows)' – as Gopala(n) Krishna and Kupala I(Yu)Van. The latter, however, could also be Protector of the 'Kola ("rotundas")', 'Koleno (kin)' and 'Earth (territories)'.

Divanna (Iva) and Ivan were still deities of the lunar calendar. The active introduction of a solar-zodiacal calendar began at the end of the 3rd millennium BCE in the environment of the so-called Starosillian type of Alazan-Bedensk culture (which Safronov attributes to the Dnipro-Kuban culture) – a kin or tribe of Hurrians who were newcomers to the Dnipro-Danube area (according to Yu. Shilov). This Sino-Caucasian or pre-Indo-European ethnic group is known to have closely communicated with both the Aryans and the pre-Greeks; the start of such inter-relations has been found in the Ukrainian Dnipro area from 2400-2000 BCE. It is probable, that the pre-Hittite name of Apollinus was specifically spread through the Hurrian tribes, the female version of which – Apollonia – was known amongst the descendants of the Pelasgians. Formerly, this solar deity could have been called Iloen, as he was endowed with the name Apollo by the Rusenians (or Etruscans), later being also honoured as Apla. Apollo inherited the epithet 'Radiant' – *Phoebus* – from his grandmother, the Moon goddess, from a time when she was of more importance in sanctuary-observatories than the Sun (until about 2300 BCE).

If pre-Apollo embodied the greatest importance in the zodiac during 4440-1700 BCE, as the constellation of Taurus, his twin sister pre-Artemis embodied the Pole Star together with the Bear, that is, "the space-axis of the universe". His twin could also be in Taurus, where she was esteemed, until Apollo, as Tauropola 'the protectress of the bull (large-horned cattle)'. Logically their parents were considered to be the 'Sky' and the 'Zodiac'. In the Indo-European world (Arattan, Pelasgian, Aryan, Greek, Slavic, etc.) 'Father-Sky' was referred to as Dyaus, Dii-Dzeus-Zeus, Divas, (Di(e)v(a)^, etc., and 'Mother-Zodiac' as referred to as *Rhato* ('Circle'), *Leto-Latona, Lada*, etc. The Indo-European *Rato* is close to the Aryan *Rita*, and to the Slavic and Persian *Arta*. These are, in a helpful way, related to Apollo, Gopalan and Kupala (see above). In Greek mythology this heavenly family was headed by the Pelasgian (in origin) Zeus who sometimes prophesied from a high oak (Homer: Odyssey XIV: 328, etc.). This associates him with Div, who called from the top of a tree in the *Tale of the Campaign of Ihor Svyatoslavlich.* Moreover the Slavic words *Klikat* and *Kikat* are related to the Greek *Kikon* – 'Cygnus' – who was Apollo's Hyperborean companion and a constellation in the Celestial (Milky) Way. The son of *Kikon* (according to Virgil) was the Etruscan *Kupavon* (comparable to the Slavic *Kupaloy*), ally of the Trojan Aeneas.

Data retrieved from aerial photography (by K. V. Shishkin), revealed that sanctuary-observatories of this "rotunda" type, accompanied all the large settlements and cities of the 'Trypillian archaeological culture', that is, of Aratta of the Dnipro area. Amongst them is a half excavated circular sanctuary at the village of Kozarovychi^ near Kyiv and a rectangular one near the village of Mayaky in the Odessa region. The latter is connected with the "Usativ variant of Late Trypillia", with Orissa or Oriana (part of Aratta at the end of its prime) which during the 3rd millennium BCE advanced to the Black Sea coast and established a navigable connection with the ancestral home of Asia Minor.

It was perhaps during the Orianian times of Troy I-III (2930-2220 BCE) that the ideas referred to earlier concerning Borysthenes and Achilles, and also Ogyges, who fought with Achilles, emerged. This battle and the Ogygian Flood occurred, perhaps, about 2450 BCE, and since Asia Minor Troy-II lay in ruins for a long time from the earthquake, the

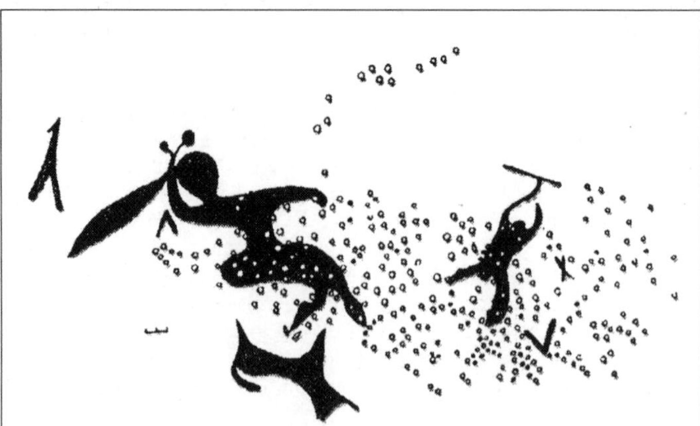

Fig.48 : **The struggle of gods for the soul of Zeus**, embodied in the constellation of Canis [Major?]. Image from 3rd millennium BCE from the "Grotto of the Bison" of Stone Grave.

Orianian settlers could have taken part in its reconstruction. In support of this, an illustration [Fig.48] in the "Grotto of the Bison"[5] at Stone Grave is identified with a specific Trojan myth describing the struggle of a goddess (Opis, Artemis or another) with a god (Orion? [cf. Orian?]) for the soul of Zeus himself (then still weak) and, furthermore, in the necropolis of the rebuilt Troy III-IV, steles have been found that are typical of the Usativ and Yamna burial mounds of that time in the Northern Black Sea area.

In some myths the ancestors of the Trojans were named as Tros, Electra, the latter being a daughter of Atlant. Troy-I was said to have been built at a place where Zeus had cast a palladium^ of Electra – a phallus fetish made from the bones of Pallant (in some traditions, the mortal father of Pallas-Athena). This occurred on the hill of Ata in whose name the memory of Aratta is probably concealed, but in general, all these features are inherent to Oriana, where patriarchy became entrenched. There was a sudden onset of cultic transformation from Arattan figurines of goddesses to immanently phallic representations. Suppression of matriarchal traditions was reflected in the myth of the Titan Iasion, murdered by Zeus; Iasion was the son of Electra and the beloved of Demeter, the 'Mother Goddess'.

This mythological event was, perhaps, consistent with the period of Deucalion's flood and was dated in agreement with the celestial-calendar system headed by Zeus and his family; later, in the period of the Dardan flood, this system was claimed by the legendary Jason and the Argonauts. This calendar system was directly preceded by the personage whom the Greeks considered to be Atlant. In the opinion of Pliny the Elder, "*he knew of the celestial sphere long before Anaximander the Milesian began* [his map of the world]." And in the words of Diodorus Siculus, "*Atlant was associated with astronomy and showed the first form of the sphere; from that originated the legend that he supports the whole Earth on his shoulders. By this it is implied that Atlant determined and described the terrestrial sphere.*" Afterwards this calendar-geographical mythological tradition was continued by legendary travellers: the Hyperborean Abaris, the Greek Aristaeus and other sanctuary-observatory attendants who were no longer professing Atlant, but Apollo.

The ancient (not less than 100 years before Crete) embodiment of the dual pairing of Zeus Taleisky and Apollo Targelia is detected in two Ingul culture burials of c. 1800 BCE from kurhan No.1-II near Kairy. Small casting moulds with "Zeus" from burial No. 11 point to liaisons with Asia Minor and Crete. Actually, this was the time of Deucalion's flood, a time of tribal migrations and changes in their pantheon, and probably at the same time, the Lelegi-Pelasgian array was first isolated from the Hellenes (in the Lower Dnipro area, as we've seen). It is considered that before these cataclysms, the head of Olympus^ was married – in his first marriage – to *Metida* [Metis[6]], the daughter of Oceanus^ (the primogenitor of all Hellenic-Greek gods). Her name is related to *Meotida*, the name of Sea of Azov, which was pre-ancient in its origin and formed because of the breakthrough into the Pontus (the Black Sea) of the waters of the Mediterranean Sea and Atlantic Ocean. Metis had manufactured a potion, through which Kronos, the grandson of Oceanus, vomited out the children he had swallowed – the sisters and brothers of Zeus. Zeus, having learned that his future son would usurp the throne of Zeus, swallowed pregnant Metis by trickery; however, Metis was pregnant with a girl, not a boy, and she grew and grew, splitting his head open and out came fully-formed Athena. This last tale corresponds very particularly to the spread of skull-trepanation, specifically in the Ingul culture.

In this kurhan near Kairy, and still more expressively in the upper reaches of the Molochna river, are reflected the beginnings of the cult of Dionysus – the younger step-brother of Apollo. The separation of these deities arose, as already noted, about 1700 BCE due to the fact that the New Year of Taurus was superseded by Aries and the tragic cult of the 'god' Dionysus was introduced for the mourning of "perished" Taurus. Such calendar-mythological innovation is clearly traced in the shapes and decoration of sextant-bowls of the Ingul culture to which M. A. Chmykhov devoted much energetic study. And again the same: the cult of Dionysus appeared later in Greece than in its Hyperborean homeland – the Dnipro area.

The mythical escape of Leto – the mistress of Zeus – from Hyperborea to Delos with young Artemis and Apollo, occurred after the death of Metis and before the birth of Dionysus. It is closer to the reality of the legend which details the divine twins arrival there along with Hyperborean pilgrims, than it is about the abduction of the idol of Artemis from Taurida by her Greek maid-servant, Iphigeneia, who helped her brother Orestes. The similarity of his name with the fore-mentioned Aristaeus leads to the supposition that both were attendants of the observatories of Apollo.

When he was adopted in Greece, Apollo did not forget his ancestral home and returned to it again and again for half of each year. Hyperborea became "the other world" of this unique, dying and rising 13th Titan, who was introduced to Olympus to fight annually, with variable success, with his father-rival Zeus. The mythology of this particular struggle was embodied in a dual pair of sub-kurhan burials, No. 11 and No. 13, of priests of ancient Hellenic Zeus and Apollo; we will return to this complex from kurhan No. 1-II near Kairy time and again.

3. From Hyperborea to Troy and Delos.

Fig.49 : **Dionysus mystery plays**. Image of 5th century BCE on a Greek vessel.

S. I. Nalyvayko and other researchers have highlighted an association between the names Troy-Ilion [Ilium[7]] of Asia Minor and with Trypillia and Gelon of the Ukrainian Dnipro area. Let us leave for the moment any consideration of the 'solar' semantics of Ilion and Gelon, and instead emphasise the more obvious association of Trypillia (the provisional title of the archaeological culture whose name came from the nearby ancient settlement where excavations reflected the apotheosis of the state of Aratta) with the city of Tripura of the Vedic Asur people, and also with Tripoli which arose at the beginning of the 2nd millennium BCE in the eastern Mediterranean. These coincidences are bolstered by evidence of a relationship between particular names of their neighbouring populated areas: Homeric Alube ('Silver' (city) located somewhere in the Taman peninsula); Ukrainian Khalepie (village); Haluppi or Harappa of former Punjabic Aratta; and the Syrian Haleb or Aleppo. The same may be said, from the 4th millennium BCE, for the known coastal city of Tyre in the Mediterranean and another at the mouth of the River Tiras (i.e. the Dniester). The latter is, in truth and with regard to those times, known by its modern provisory title of "Mayaky settlement of the Usativ variant of Late Trypillian culture", and the name of the city as Tyre was only evident in ancient times. However, Greek-colonists could have restored the ancient name from the legends which remained in their midst, such as the legend (according to Herodotus) of the Scythians originating from wandering Herakles and a local goddess. Furthermore, the lower reaches of the River Tiras flowed over former Oriana (Orissa-Odissa, according to S. I. Nalyvayko), which was the coastal part of Aratta.

In Tyre, as well as in Odissa (presently Belhorod-Dniesterovsky and Odessa, respectively) steles dating to the late antique period were found with epithets of the Indo-Aryan God Shiva – one of the three highest gods of the Indian pantheon – was identified, by Greek authors, with Dionysus. According to Herodotus (IV: 109), the latter was specifically esteemed in Gelon – the greatest city-state in Europe of that time – between the Tanais and Borysthenes rivers (at the intersection of the borders between present-day Poltava and Kharkiv regions). However, indications of the Dionysian cult celebrations in Gelon every three years are more characteristic of the cult of Shiva celebrations, also held once every three years. Shiva could also have participated in the destruction or construction of a city near modern Trypillia (perhaps legendary Tripura?) – judging by the three multi-kilometre long earth-walls that extend from there, reminiscent of the same Trio and corresponding to the trishula (the trident of Shiva). In addition, earth-walls extend from the Divych-mountain over the Dnipro. Its name, 'Divych/Maiden' as we already know, not only complies with the name of a Tauridan maiden (Artemis or Iphigeneia), whose sanctuary also stood on a mountain over a precipice, but also with those of numerous similar sanctuaries of the Indo-European world that arose for the veneration of Dev or Devi ('God', 'Goddesses', (Dev(as)^, i.e. 'Heaven' in all cases). Sometimes they are hidden away inside such names as 'Sivyi[8] (ox-bull-Taurus)' Shiva and 'our God' Dionys[us], who belong to the same constellation which emerges most obviously in the Roman form of the name – Bacchus or Bakhs.

At the beginning of the 2nd millennium BCE, the Aratto-Aryan or Orianian migrants to the eastern Mediterranean Sea created at that place the country of Palestine – the 'Country of Pelasg'. Its later population were known to Egypt as one of the tribes of "Sea Peoples", and to the authors of the Bible as Philistines. In the 18th – 16th centuries BCE the Aryans of the Azov region, along with the Hurrians, founded the first state of Mitanni (if Oriana is discounted) in the north of Mesopotamia. During the times of Greek colonisation, in the 7th – 6th centuries BCE, or even as early as the time of the pilgrimages of Odysseus and the Argonauts to the Pontus Euxine, a movement began in the opposite direction, which according to the testimony of Herodotus, even then retained a long-ancient Hyperborean tradition to send, and even to bring gifts to the temples of Artemis and Apollo on the island of Delos in the Aegean Sea.

What did the Greeks and Romans have to say about the Hyperboreans, not knowing their origins and not even believing in their existence (as Herodotus confessed)?

"*About the Hyperboreans nothing is known neither by Scythians, nor other people of this part of world, except Issedonians*", with whom contemporary researchers identify the Massagetae^ or some even more ancient population east of the Urals and Altai. In Hyperborea "*there cannot be anything to see and it is impossible to penetrate there due to flying feathers*", namely snow. This is profoundly wise information! However, that is nullified by reports that the Hyperboreans gave sacrificial gifts to the Scythians. These gifts were wrapped in wheat-straw and they brought those gifts "*to the boundary of their possessions and passed them on to their neighbours requesting they deliver them to other nations*" up to Greek Delos. So, how are we to understand this? Did the Scythians know of the Hyperboreans? Specifically, whether they lived beyond the Polar circle, or whether they could grow wheat? We have a dubious mixture of geographic information, memories from the "Golden Age" of Aratta of the Northern Black Sea and speculation about a utopian-coveted country.

However there it was, the Delos-Greeks communicated with delegations of Hyperboreans who preserved the tradition of Aratto-Sumerian pilgrimages in the Circum-Pontic zone and elsewhere. Herodotus tells us that the first nomads from Hyperborea to Delos were the young women Arga and Opis (the names of whom, along with others, we find amongst the offspring of Pelasg and Atlant), who arrived to thank Artemis-Ilithyia/Eileithyia for an easy act of delivery. However, they didn't arrive alone but came with the Hyperborean gods (perhaps in the form of idols) Apollo and Artemis, which were then buried near the sanctuaries. At the same place, though a later time, were buried the Hyperborean damsels Hyperoche and Laodice (and these were very well-known names to the Pelasgians!), along with five attendants who formed the last delegation, which allegedly was the first and last

Fig.50 : **Lato rescuing the twins Apollo and Artemis from the serpent Python**. Image of 4th century BCE on a Greek vessel.

time that gifts were personally brought to Delos covered in [wheat] straw. Perhaps the damsels were offered in sacrifice to the gods but such an act of self-abasement was already so incomprehensible to the Greeks that their authors did not leave us evidence. Herodotus only specified that such delegations had long ceased but in memory of those pilgrimages, Greek girls and boys brought wreaths and branches with locks of their own hair to the graves of those Hyperboreans. The 'father of history' notes that, just as in his own time, Thracian women still brought gifts to queen Artemis, wrapped in wheat-straw.

On the island of Lemnos, centuries after Herodotus, there lived the Pelasgi-Sintili^, whose second name accords with their Sindic ancestral homeland, perhaps still in the lower reaches of the Dnipro rather than the Kuban. There were also Sinds amongst the migrant-tribes of Punjabic Aratta, from whom, perhaps, proceeded the names of Indus [Sindus] and India [Sindia]; these precise names were also encountered in the Kuban area.

So, we have some robust data concerning ethnic, territorial and chronological definitions of the mysterious Hyperboreans. The divine maiden Artemis, who together with her twin-brother Apollo, was born in Hyperborea, was inherent to Thrace and Taurida (i.e. modern Bulgaria, Romania, Moldova and Crimea). Iphigeneia was apparently snatched by Artemis and brought to Taurida when Iphigeneia's father Agamemnon decided to bring the girl in sacrifice to the gods, all in exchange for a favourable wind to sail his ships to doomed Troy. The Tauris esteemed the Maiden (much like Artemis and Iphigeneia) from ancient times. These two countries, Taurida and Thrace, can be regarded as the successors of Aratta, owing to the Thracians preservation of the traditional culture of Cucuteni-Trypillia, and by the Tauris of the Kemi-Oba culture.

The origin of the name Aratta-Arta is possibly bound up with the name Arte-m(other)-Ida. Ida^ 'was held in esteem' by Aryans, Pelasgians, and in time by the Greeks, as the goddess of sacrifices. At first this goddess was considered to be the daughter of the first-ancestor, Manu, and mother, Kubera, – brother of Ravan (the enemy of Rama) and the friend of Shiva. Her attendant-brahman, Vasistha, transformed Ida-Ilus into a boy but Shiva turned Ida into a girl again. Therefore it is not surprising that Ilus established Troy-Ilion near Ida's mountain. The name of this goddess was also used for sacred mountains in Hellas and Crete; it could also be the same in Taurida (Taur-Ida). In Ilion the Pelasgian-Trojans adored Rhea, the mother of mankind and of the gods, also naming her Mother Ida. Consequently, she could be '*Arta's Mother Ida*'. The custom of wrapping gifts to *Artemis* (and to Apollo) in wheat-straw, along with the names of the goddess and state of *Aratta,* are connected with the name Artos-'bread', which the Greeks exported in the time of Herodotus and later in large quantities from farmers of the Northern Black Sea area.

This reference drew the 'father of history' to the people of Hyperborea. It indicated that they had cities! According to the testimony in *History of Antiquity* (II: 47) by Diodorus, who was guided by ancient Greek sources, Hyperborea was situated on a large island (which modern researchers are inclined to see as Britain, however, it could be the Arattan interfluve of the Buh, Syniukha and Ros rivers) which had a city, dedicated to Apollo. His sanctuary was located there as a "circular temple", which was patronised by its priests – the *Boreades*. Their ancestral name is connected not only with the 'North' but also with *Borysthenes* (the Dnipro). Despite their 'far-north' position, the Hyperboreans allegedly gathered crops twice a year. In addition, they not only reached Delos, but also "*some Greeks visited Hyperborea*". Not therefore such an unknown, distant and cold country!

Meanwhile many modern supporters of the "arctic theory" (actually, the version that claimed a North European ancestral homeland for the Indo-Europeans, mentioned earlier) are guided by a description of the Hyperboreans from the Roman geographer, Pliny the Elder: "*For up to six months they have continuous day and the same for night ... In this land favoured by agreeable climate, their homes are situated in forests and groves ... They never die, but if old people feel that they lived sufficiently long, they joyfully rub their bodies with fragrant ointments and leap into the sea from cliffs. At night they hide away in caves ...*" As we can see, this is a collection of incompatible phrases about a polar year and an agreeable climate, about woods and groves of more southerly latitudes, etc. Even so, at least this medley is more realistic than descriptions of one-eyed people owning golden gryphons as described in the writings of 'the father of history'.

Fig.51 : Ceremonial figurines of Solar carts and chariots of the 2nd–1st millennium BCE. Central Europe.

So, we are confident that the legends of Hyperborea and its derivatives, Pelasgia and Atlantis, originate from the Northern Black Sea Aratta. The Greeks originated there and it was the origin of at least some Pelasgians, as well as some of their tribes, heroes and gods.

The eve of the Trojan War in the 13th or 11th centuries BCE (according to chronologically uncoordinated legends, myths and archaeological remains) was marked by the following: Herakles and Omphale, the 'Navel of the Earth', generated (without a female-mother, since in that time Troy was already an established patriarchy) the successor of Ilus; he was Laomedon^ – 'Lord of the stone people'. Those "people" are linked by researchers with numerous anthropomorphous stelae in the cemetery behind the south gates of Troy-IV 2200-2000 BCE. The same Laomedon, – was father of Priam, in whose reign the siege and loss of Troy took place – is attributed with organising the construction of its fortress walls. They were mainly built by Poseidon aided by Apollo and the final gate was completed by the mortal Aeacus, [whose mortality made the walls violable] part of which was subsequently attacked by three serpents [symbolic of later attacks by the lineage of Aeacus]. In the competition for championship between the gods, Apollo conquered it and thus became the city patron.

Herakles, having been tricked by Laomedon, started to gather together the Greeks for a campaign on Troy. This took place just before the procreation (by the hero, Herakles, and the serpent-legged goddess, Hyla, in the lower reaches of the Borysthenes-Dnipro) of the ancestors of the Geloni, Agathyrsi and Scythians. Herodotus began his narrative history with reference to those legendary times of Cimmeria and Scythia. We began from considerably more ancient times. Against that background, already described, it is possible to move on to clarify the prehistory of Slavdom and Rus. Furthermore, to show that their sacred texts – *The Veles Book* and *The Veda Slovena*^ – go back earlier than all the previously mentioned works of the Greeks, Hindus, and Sumerians, reaching to the remote 21st millennium BCE for their basis in the world's earliest record of Shu-Nun (at Stone Grave in the modern Zaporizhia region), with its historical-mythological memory that also reaches back to the same time: the 19th millennium BCE.

Suggested reading

1. Herodotus, *The Histories*, Leningrad, 1972.
2. Kifishin A. G., *Genostructure of pre-Greek and ancient-Greek myth*, in: The Meaning of Ancient Culture, Moscow, 1990.

3. Akimova L. I., *Troy and Schliemann*, Moscow-Milan, 1996.
4. Chmykhov M. A., *The Beginnings of Paganism in Rus*, Kyiv, 1990.
5. Shilov Yu., *Mythical "Cosmic wanderers" and calendar work in Europe of V-I millennia BCE*, in: Knowledge of the Universe. Historico-astronomical studies, vol. XXIII, Moscow, 1992.
6. Asov A. I., *Atlantians, Aryans, Slavs: History and Belief*, Moscow, 2000.
7. Mykhailov B. D., *The petroglyphs of Stone Grave*. – Zaporizhia-Moscow, 1999.

---

[1] 'Bull crossing', (the modern Kerch strait), which in Cimmeria reflected the settling of the Aratto-Aryan or Indo-European tribes from the Northern Black Sea area.

[2] Unified whole – conveys the complex meaning of a constant, indivisible singular whole, an immutable elementary or fundamental state.

[3] Hymns sung to Apollo were called paeans.

[4] Ukrainian 'Yasen', which is an ash-tree.

[5] The "Grotto of the Bison" (No. 36b of the 62 identified grottoes at Stone Grave) contains drawings of a buck and horse (in black and brown dyes) that overlap thin drawings of a mammoth, bison, bird, and serpent. It also has a scene (see Fig. 48) of a woman (in black dye), possibly seated, with her arm extended and head held back a little, a dog (in dark-brown dye) with raised tail, and a man (in black dye) in an active pose with a club [or spear] in his raised right hand. (B. D. Mykhailov, *Petroglyphs of Stone Grave*, Zaporizhia-Moscow, 1999). The scene is set against a background of stars, suggestive that the two figures are deities. The pose of the man, with his weapon raised in his right hand, together with a dog, is reminiscent of Orion and Canis Major. Yu. Shilov (*Prehistoric Rus*, Kyiv-Moscow, 1997-1999) contrasted similar images in Grotto 54, the "Grotto of Artemis", with the specifically Trojan myth of the struggle between goddesses and gods for the soul of Zeus, personified in the Golden Hound (that lies with feet uppermost below the warriors, as also seen in Fig.48). B. D. Mykhailov dated the petroglyphs in the "Grotto of the Bison" to the Early Neolithic period, based on the finding of flints, shells and a rhombus tile in the grotto that is similar to two rhombic objects found at the Semenivka settlement in the Odessa Region. (B. D. Mykhailov, 1999).

[6] In Russian, she is called Метида (Metida).

[7] The Russian word for Ilium is Илиона, viz. Ilion.

[8] 'Sivyi' is a transliteration from the original Russian 'Сивый', obviously consonant with Siva (the Sanskrit form of the popular Hindu deity, Shiva).

CHAPTER 6

Fig.52 : **Board 16 of *The Veles Book*** seen behind the scribe. Its 'title' arises from the dedication at the start of the text [*We dedicate this book to our god Veles...*].

THE *VELES BOOK* AND ITS PLACE IN ANCIENT LITERATURE

The Veles Book^, completed in 879 CE, records the pre-history of Rus^ passed down over the course of time since its 20,000-year old origins, with recollections from the Stone Age and of old Rusy^ chronicles, Ukrainian myths and fairy tales... In the 18th century, the scientist M. V. Lomonosov, whilst still unaware of these ancient sources, argued with German politicians about Slavic national history and formulated its sources in the following way: "The Slavic language originated neither from Greek, nor from Latin, nor from any other language; therefore, it must have already been in existence since the most ancient times, with Slavic people speaking their Slavic language even before the birth of Christ". The concepts of this founding father of the Russian Academy of Sciences and the University of Moscow, were supported by Catherine the Great, the German-born Empress of all the Russias, who said: "Long before the birth of Christ, Slavs had a written language", but its characters were either "lost, or have yet to be discovered, and that is why they have not been passed down to us".

These lost characters were indeed eventually found! Russian, Ukrainian and Belarusian scientists worked hard to disclose the origins of Rus but when, at the end of the 20th century, the USSR embarked upon 'Perestroika' (restructuring) it brought about a new shutdown in research, the rationale for which was encapsulated in these words – "At the start of the 1st century CE, Eastern Slavdom did not yet exist – the Slavic people were not yet organised into a united nation... But if one speaks about a provisional date for the onset of Russian culture, then according to my understanding, I would consider the year 988 CE to be the most substantiated. Basically, the Slavic people entered world culture during the last millennium. Anything else is merely assumption". It cannot be said that the author of these words is foolish , on the contrary, the academic D. S. Likhachev is a clever man (consult the epilogue to *The Myths of Ancient Slavdom,* Saratov, 1993). He fully understood what he was doing when he turned his adherents against *The Veles Book*, which had just been discovered for science and culture... Similarly, P. P. Tolochko, the vice president of The National Academy of Sciences of Ukraine, also belongs to the same group of people who tried to sever the root of Slavdom to the 'middle of the crown' (i.e. a little before the odious 1st century CE). The intellect of such practitioners of science is not directed towards an apprehension of truth, but towards a profitable subservience to the new "Germans": on the one hand these modern subscribers support "theories of an Arctic ancestral homeland for the Indo-Europeans" and on the other hand, they support the theory of a "pre-Semitic population" on the Black Sea coasts, where the Aryan nations (really were!) formed.

We have already considered how the formation of the Aryan nations arose – from pre-conditions laid down somewhere in the 20th millennium BCE, which then germinated in 12th – 8th millennium BCE, reaching formation in the 7th – 4th millennium BCE and eventually began branching into the ancestors of modern nations in 3rd – 2nd millennium BCE. The next link to track down in this chain of development will be the formation of the Slavic ethnos. The principal compass for this scientific-methodological search will be sourced in **cultural folk memory** (according to B. A. Rybakov).

This process will begin by attempting to find the historical (i.e. written) tradition of the pre-Slavs and of Slavdom in the collection of writings which eventually became known as, *The Veles Book.*

1. The Origin of the Vedas^.

Fig. 53 : **Vehicle-cart with a pair of harnessed oxen.** Image from Stone Grave, 3rd millennium BCE.

The Veles Book is a collection of sacred texts, the oldest of which is considered to be the very earliest form of the Indo-Aryan *Rigveda*. However, it now seems evident that a text known as the *Veda Slovena,* which was unknown to the world and even to specialist scientists until its discovery in the Rhodope mountains in the second half of the 19th century, is even more ancient than the *Rigveda*. Its Aryan origins may be deduced, not only from its Old Slavonic (Veneti?^) language which is close to Sanskrit language (according to S. I. Verkovich, author of a book analysing this text), but also because of the presence of Ima^ the first-ancestor who came even before Yama, the ruler who reigned over the netherworld in the *Rigveda*. Acting with Ima, the god Vlas can be regarded as an intermediary presence between Vala (representing the embryonic world of the New-Year in the *Rigveda*) and Veles, one of the main deities of *The Veles Book*. Here is an extract from the *Veda Slovena* (as published in the journal *Science and Religion*, Moscow, 2001, No. 2; its original publication and translation into Russian was undertaken by A. I. Asov):

Lord Ima ascended from the Earth to the sky.
And there celebrated sacred service to God.
And Vlasii, after thinking it over, said thus to Ima:
"Oh, Lord! Ima-Lord! You now descend from the sky,
Go, good husband, rather unto the valley,
To the sacred White Garden, where you will put a fence.
And there, bullocks, oxen and cows exist.
Ima, you take just nine of the cows there,
Select the best nine cows,
Suitable for holy sacrifice!..."

The history recorded in *The Veles Book* reached back 21 millennia, into the remote depths of pre-Indo-European history, thus, its historic memory is far more ancient than Vedic history. This offers the first clue in our search. The second clue would be that it should harmonise in some way not only with the Vedas but also with the *Ramayana* and the *Mahabharata* since they were both based, as has long been accepted by world science, on the main mytho-ritual of the *Rigveda* – the struggle of the hero Indra against the serpent[1] Vritra for possession of Vala. Thirdly, *The Veles Book* would be expected to reflect some crossover between Indo-Aryan sacred matters with the texts in Ancient Greek, *The Iliad and The Odyssey*, mentioned earlier, particularly since researchers also noticed their curious similarity to the epic poems of India.

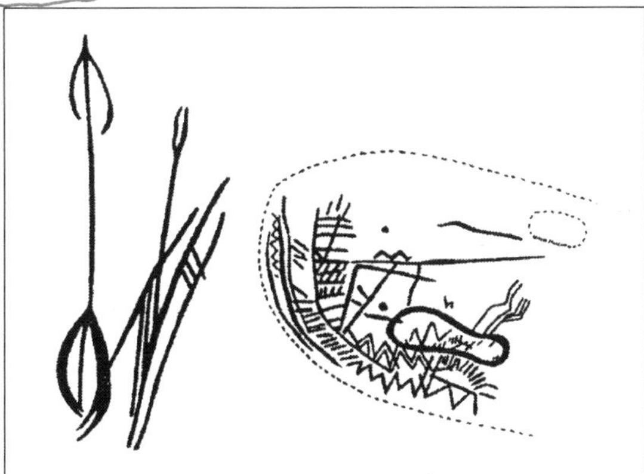

Fig. 54 : **Head of Vritra, crushed by the foot of Vishnu, alongside the destructive arrows of Indra.** Images from "The Grotto of the Dragon" at Stone Grave, early 2nd millennium BCE.

The core data for this exploratory search can be found in the following sources: the annals of Stone Grave, as this is the earliest archive in the world; the cities and sanctuary-observatories of Aratta; its canals/channels in the lower reaches of the Danube, Buh, Dnipro and Kuban rivers which were already described as "old" even in ancient times (Strabo XI: 2.11); and in the kurhans of Oriana and Arián that contain evidence for the origin of the Vedas. This scheme provides a way of opening out the "spatial picture" held within a verbal-written work such as *The Veles Book*. And now we, the researchers, must start work!

We won't repeat here everything that has been said already about Stone Grave in the preceding chapters but will bear in mind the deep knowledge and the high authority of its oracle-priests over the extended formation of the pre-Indo-European and then Indo-European community between the 7th – 3rd millennium BCE. There is a correspondence here with the main mytho-ritual of the Vedas (which, as already emphasised, formed the foundation of the Indo-European epic): the serpent Vritra, who guarded Vala, is struck by the destructive arrows of Indra and then crushed by the foot of Vishnu (Fig.54, Table XLI).

To begin our search for the origin of *The Veles Book*, we'll first outline those instances of state order and writing which formed the features of our sacred texts, distinguishing them from the holy books of slaveholding countries.

The slaveholding regimes of the south-eastern countries were founded as a direct consequence of their particular system of irrigation. Those irrigation systems anchored people to the land, forcing them to accept totalitarian statehood and the accompanying bureaucracy that developed through the instrument of what became written documents: at the start these were economic, legal, religious, and eventually they became literary documents. As already stated, that was the way it used to be on the Northern Black Sea coast but with the difference that these [written documents] were formal cultural expressions which remained marginal, not affecting its core nor its essence. *Communal Aratta,* preceding slaveholding Sumer and Egypt, *was based on the system of sanctuary-observatories* (known as "rotundas" in India and before that, in Ukraine, retaining the aboriginal title of "maidans"), *whose economy, in this northern farming state, could not exist without calendars,* just as the south-eastern countries could not exist without a system of irrigation. The land of Hyperborea, as described by ancient writers, didn't seem to be represented as a state but it was, nevertheless, created under the direction and guidance of the Arattan system which, between the 5th–2nd millennium BCE, developed (from the Danube-Dnipro region) along the forest-steppe zone, to the Trans-Urals and as far as the British Isles.

The Arattan system was maintained through the use of specific elements such as precise maps and calendars, selective programmes [of breeding, etc.] and technologies, social order, festivals, ceremonies, and through the use of Sanskrit – the ('synthetic') language of international communication. Although this system provided a structure for the far-wandering Hyperborean oracle-priests to follow, such systems had become completely incomprehensible by the time of the ancient Greeks. Even the Greek intellectuals, politicians and clerics like Plutarch or Herodotus, knew nothing about the sources and so could not make sense of this tradition which originated around 6200 years BCE with the creators of the state of Aratta – the very core of the Indo-European community of nations. This system of "maidans"-"rotundas" was deployed along the northern agricultural border between 3rd – 4th millennium BCE and extended, together with the practice of agriculture, as far as Mesopotamia and Scandinavia creating, over millennia, the framework of those ties that retained the unity of the Indo-Europeans. This broad framework was much stronger, grander and more mysterious than the ziggurats of Sumer and Babylon, the pyramids of Egypt and Peru, and the temples of Hellas and Rome. The distinguished researcher Gerald Hawkins calculated that the construction of Stonehenge alone, required more effort from the population of Britain of that time than the implementation of the USA Space Programme in the 1960s... Nevertheless, the sacred words of Aratta (as hitherto in Bharata, the former name of India), were only oral. As a rule, texts were memorised and if written down at all, then they were recorded concisely and far less frequently than in the east and not on clay, nor stone, but on wood since it was more portable for transporting over long distances. Accordingly, there are far fewer preserved records of Aratta, Hyperborea and the followers of their traditions than the more durable records of Mesopotamia, Egypt and Greece.

As with the maidans for Aratta, kurhans also became the unifying basis for Aratta's neighbour Arián (Table XXXVIII). A prototype for these kurhans, to be considered shortly, was the natural hill of Stone Grave, known in ancient times as *Shu-Nun,* 'The Hand/ Law of the Empress'. Earlier kurhans extended, perhaps, to Oriana – the Black Sea area that synthesised the two main Arattan and Aryan groups. There, in archaeological finds near the villages of Usativ, Zhovty Yar and others (in the Odessa region) there were traces of the transition from Arattan-"Indo-European" to Aryan representations. This transition was reflected most obviously in the dolmen^ under the kurhan in the settlement of Velyko-Olexandrivsk, in the Kherson region. The first definitively Aryan kurhans (but also bearing traces of Arattan influences) are identified in the mouth of the River Psel: opposite the Dereivka^ settlement of the first Aryan-horse-breeders in the Dnipro area (and probably – of the whole Eurasian steppe), near the crossing in the headstream of the Dnipro rapids.

The first cromlech of the Velyko-Olexandrivsk kurhan was erected around the burials of two emigrants from Sumer and Aratta. At the same time, a human sacrifice, which accompanied them, displayed specific similarities not only with Dumuzi, the Aratto-Sumerian hero, but also with Ima(ru) – first ancestor of the Indo-European peoples, described, in particular, in the *Veda Slovena*. A. I. Asov (see above) justifiably indicates the kinship of Ima with the antecedent of Bohomyr^ from *The Veles Book.* It is known that Ima preceded Yama, the god of the netherworld ("the assembler of ancestors" from the Aryan *Rigveda*). Closely related to them are Vlas and Vala; the first of whom is a forerunner of Veles (Volokh, Vola), and the second – the embryonic New-Year universe. Corresponding functions of Vlas appear through his command for Ima to make an enclosure for 300 bullocks and 300 cows and to perform sacrifice on "Lichen[2]-Day, Vlas'-Day". This precise day was probably depicted in the image featured on the cromlech (a circular perimeter made from stone slabs) in the calendar-zodiac combination headed by the bull-Taurus.

Like many Aryan kurhans of the Northern Black Sea area, the practise of constructing kurhans at Tsehelnia and Kormylytsia in the River Psel area continued over a period of two millennia: between the mid 4th – 2nd millennium BCE. In their foundations, archaeologists traced the germination of the core mythology of the *Rigveda*: serpentine ditches (representing Vritra) around earthen and stone constructions with the symbolism of the embryonic New-Year (Vala), as well as granite idols with indications of serpent-warriors

(Indra and Vishnu). In due course, as will be considered later, the kurhans were shaped in such a way that they symbolised Mother-Earth; several new memorials were placed near them which maintained the symbolism of Vala up until the brink of the partial Aryan migration into India (Figs.38 - 41)

Amongst the hundreds of kurhans excavated by archaeologists some were considerably more expressive than others – like the ruins of Troy or the Tower of Babel – which reflected significant historical phenomena that were also inherent in other monuments, namely: **the initial formation of the *Rigveda*.** The most important of them all is High Grave (near the village of Starosillia in the Velyko-Olexandrivsk district). Although this has already been touched upon and will be mentioned again periodically, this sacred object will be subjected to further examination.

High Grave appeared here around the middle of the 4th millennium BCE (and was refilled up to 10 times over the following two millennia) near the Velyko Olexandrivsk kurhan, behind which were traces of direct contact between the priests of Aratta and Sumer. The primary mound of High Grave was constructed over the grave of a local Aryan, one of the earliest. This mound and its first fillings epitomised Vedic images of the House, Universe, Foremother, Moon, Taurus and Sun. The latter symbol was even repeated three times in upper re-fillings by Brahmans and builders, maintaining just this state over the millennia until the end of the operation of the kurhan.

The primary embankment of the kurhan overlay the residues of a hut that had been burned over the entombment of the ancient man. A second significant fire was laid in the funnel, which represented the womb of the Foremother. A third outstanding fire is connected with the first embodiment of the Sun. The first was laid on the base of an X-shaped sepulchral pit and then moved to the apex of a +-shaped filling. This paired symbolism of the netherworldly and celestial sun (Savitr^ and Suria^ of the Aryans) was

Fig. 55 : **The entombment of the "Oracle Suria (Syria)"** from High Grave at Starosillia (above), together with images from Stone Grave and on a Sumerian seal (below).

reinforced by the presence of a magic 7-wheeled cart in the first symbol and 12 ray-like highways in the second one. The mythological complex also served for calendar-celestial observations, forming the basis of one of the first solar zodiacs. Was this the first glimmering of an insight into the "solar (way) lying in the (zodiacal) sky" – of the Aryan *Svarga*, forerunner to the Slavic *Svaroh*?^ Whatever the case may be, the filling was built up in 2300 BCE, when the cult of this god arose. This kurhan became, indeed, a memorial to Suvar (Satya) Yuga^ – the 'golden age', or 'the generation illuminated by the Sun'. A kurhan with a similar name stands in Zaporizhia above the valley of the River Konka^; situated near the River Don. A fourth, and final fire at High Grave seems to have repeated the primary one. However, if the first fire was set at the bottom of the mound, the last fire was set at the peak of the mound; the first one was connected with the hearth of the Eternal Home, and the last one with the core of the Sun; the first blazed above the deceased, but in the last case the deceased was put into the fire that gravitated towards the after-life, and then – to joyful rebirth. The reason for assigning this interpretation to the final fire was prompted by the connection of the Grave with a neighbouring mound. Together the pair embodied the mythical marriage between the Sun-bride and the Moon-bridegroom riding along the Celestial (Milky) Way, one towards the other. This myth is presented in the Bridal Anthem of the *Rigveda*, which accords with the 'Vesnianky'[3] (ancient spring holiday) of Slavic and other Aryan nations.

As we see, High Grave presented four distinct 'large generations' of Mahayuga^ (the Eternal Home ... Foremother ... Sun ... World Wedding), which represents the principal sign of the Day of Brahma: the beginning and the end of the Universe in a worldwide fire. The beginning of the first and last Mahayugas coincide here with the appearance of the Aryan community of tribes in the 4th millennium BCE, and with their partial migration into India in the 2nd millennium BCE. At the same time, the reciprocal locations, configuration and rituals of the three upper parts of the complex construction of the Grave, correspond to the Brahmanic complex of three Shruta altars ('to hear'), from which even now, Vedic anthems are proclaimed in India.

So, we have valid grounds for forming conclusions with regard to the initial collection of the *Rigveda* anthems being in the Dnipro homeland area of the Aryans, also the separation of the Indian and Persian groups of the Aryan community, and about their first partial migration.

Addressing the problem of the origin of the *Rigveda* in the ancestral home of the Aryans and then linking it with *The Veles Book* of Slavs, has an important significance for the first inscriptions in the 'synthetic' language of Sanskrit. Such inscriptions are actually accessible in Ukraine; their sources are derived from Stone Grave, the earliest chronicle in the world. Data already exists concerning the manifestations within Stone Grave, as well as in its surrounding kurhans and in subsequent written languages such as: Dardan, Creto-Minoan and Runic (according to B. D. Mykhailov, S. Zh. Pustovalov and Yu. A. Shilov). There are grounds for supposing that the Dardan language, with its first written alphabet in the world, was invented by the oracle-priests of Stone Grave[4]. This occurred at the beginning of the 2nd millennium BCE. Around the middle of the same millennium, these shores were visited by the heroes of the ship "Argo". It may be presumed that the main reason why the legendary Argonauts strove to reach Eya^ (the modern Taman peninsula) was not in search of the mythical Golden Fleece *per se*, but in search of what it represented, sacred texts[5] written on lambskin (according to Palephant, 4th century BCE). Amongst them, were there not the notes of the future *Veles Book*? Perhaps, this meant that the Babylonian historian Berossus was referring to the ancient writings of the Scythians?

At Stone Grave, nothing other than Proto-Sumerian images and symbols are acknowledged by the linguist-Sumerologist, A. G. Kifishin, who nevertheless determined, in the monograph *Ancient Sanctuary of Stone Grave* (Kyiv, 2001) that: "Troy II-I formed its own culture, which was differentiated from pre-Slavic culture, full-grown from her communal roots (*from Oriana, the coastal part of Aratta, as shown earlier. – Yu. Shilov*)..., but still used ancient proto-Sumerian letters, as, obviously, pre-Slavic".

In conclusion it is necessary to say that between the 1960-80s V. N. Danylenko (in the manuscript for his monograph *Ethnogenesis of Slavdom*, which vanished in dubious

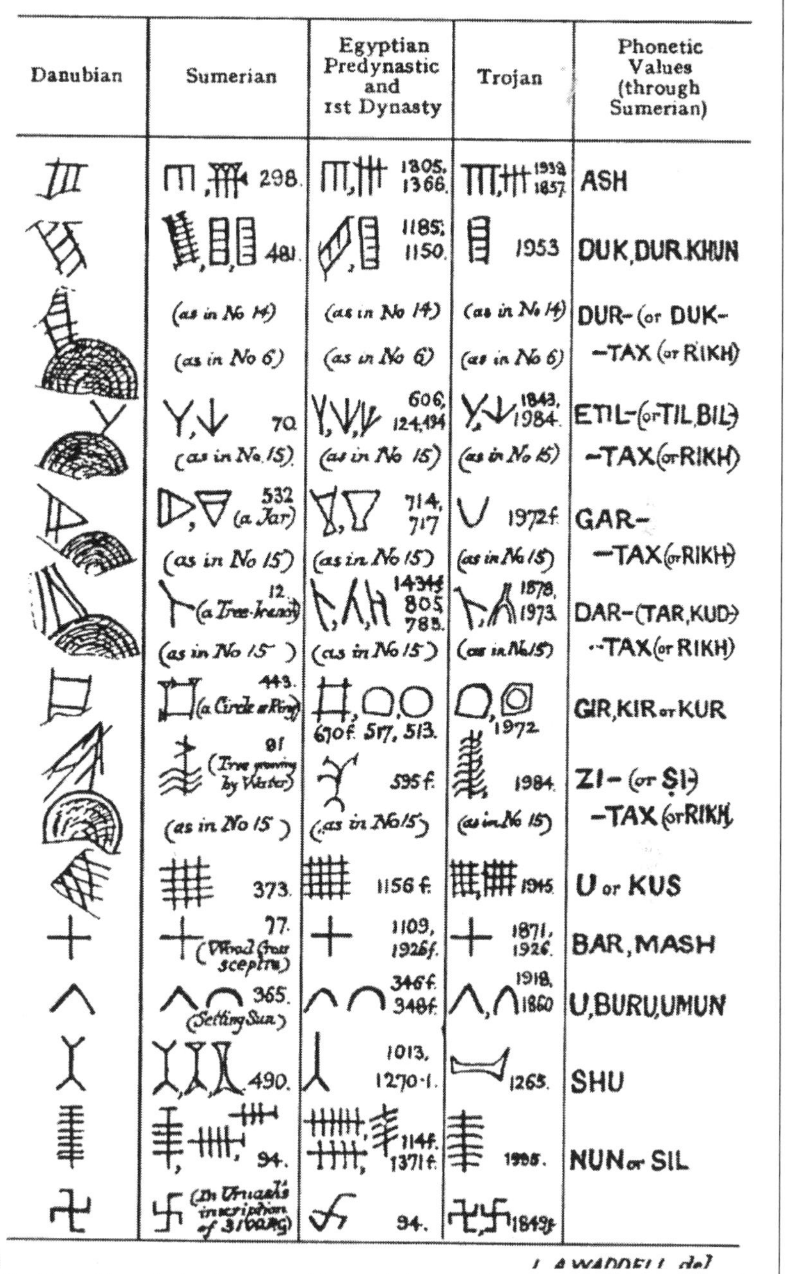

Danubian	Sumerian	Egyptian Predynastic and 1st Dynasty	Trojan	Phonetic Values (through Sumerian)
	298.	1805, 1366.	1939, 1857.	ASH
	481.	1185, 1150.	1953	DUK, DUR, KHUN
	(as in No 14)	(as in No 14)	(as in No 14)	DUR- (or DUK-
	(as in No 6)	(as in No 6)	(as in No 6)	-TAX (or RIKH)
	70	606, 124, 494	1843, 1984.	ETIL- (or TIL, BIL)
	(as in No. 15)	(as in No 15)	(as in No 15)	-TAX (or RIKH)
	532 (a Jar)	714, 717	1972f.	GAR-
	(as in No 15)	(as in No 15)	(as in No 15)	-TAX (or RIKH)
	12. (a Tree-branch)	1434f, 805, 785.	1878, 1973.	DAR- (TAR, KUD)
	(as in No 15)	(as in No 15)	(as in No 15)	-TAX (or RIKH)
	443. (a Circle or Ring)	690f. 517, 513.	1972	GIR, KIR or KUR
	91 (Tree growing by Water)	595f.	1984.	ZI- (or SI)
	(as in No 15)	(as in No 15)	(as in No 15)	-TAX (or RIKH)
	373.	1156 f.	1945.	U or KUS
	77. (Wood from sceptre)	1109, 1926f.	1871, 1926.	BAR, MASH
	365. (Setting Sun)	346f. 348f.	1918, 1860	U, BURU, UMUN
	490.	1013, 1270-1.	1265.	SHU
	94.	1144f. 1371f.	1905.	NUN or SIL
	(In Urnash's inscription of 3100 BC)	94.	1849f.	

L. A. WADDELL del.

Fig.56 : **The similarity of writing of Sumer, Egypt, and Troad,** 4th – 2nd millennium BCE. By Professor L. A. Waddell.

circumstances after his death in 1982), N. Z. Susloparov and O. P. Znoyko (*Myths and Ancient Events of the Kyiv Land*, - Kyiv, 1989) tried to settle the question of writing amongst the carriers who lived in the Northern Black Sea area (those archaeological cultures from Trypillian to Srubna). No more successful, even with a considerably larger volume of actual data, was G. S. Grinevich's attempt to resolve the problem in an amateurish but vibrant book, *Pre-Slavic Written Language. The Results of Decipherment* (Moscow, 1993). Recently, V.

Kulbaka and V. Kachur (*Bronze Age Somatic Cults of South East Europe*, Mariupol, 1998) carried out the first highly-skilled interpretations. On a Srubna culture vessel excavated from a kurhan near the city of Artemivsk in the Donetsk region, they were able to read: "*Turn* (*drink-in-vessel*) *your precious protection to those who hurry* (*into the world beyond*)". This is the earliest, written example of proto-Indian Sanskrit which can be considered here (in conjunction with Trojan-Etruscan letters) to be related to the writing of *The Veles Book*. The *Novhorod Psalter*, recently found by archaeologists and dating from the turn of the 10th – 11th centuries, is written, just like *The Veles book*, on waxed tablets.

2. The general root of the Indo-European epos^.

Fig. 57 : A petroglyph ('portrayed on stone') from Stone Grave.

We will now consider the grounds for arriving at conclusions concerning the origin of events described in the most ancient Aryan epos/epics as having occurred in the Ukrainian Dnipro area. The initial raw data for such a hypothesis was stumbled upon by the linguists O. N. Trubachev, S. I. Nalyvayko and A. G. Kifishin, the historian-art critic L. I. Akimova, and the archaeologists V. N. Danylenko, B. D. Mykhailov and Yu. Shilov. We shall attempt to formulate and debate the hypothesis: to determine the fundamental places – times – events, which inspired the narrators, both in India as well as in Greece. From that creative nexus of a truly Indo-European culture, we will be able to reach a proper conclusion regarding the origin of *The Veles Book*.

World science has long acknowledged the surprising convergence between the myths of the Hindus and the Ancient Greeks and of their respective epic narrative poems the *Mahabharata* and the *Iliad*. Towards the end of the 'Golden Age' a battle took place between, respectively, the Kauravas and Pandavas^ & the Achaeans and Danaoi; it was fought for the return of a kingdom and the sun-like woman. The respective victors were patronised by Krishna Gopala and Apollo Targelia; their totems were cranes and swans (for the first) and swans and cranes (for the second)... It is clear, that the basis of each ethno-historical event lies in a much older age, one in which the ancestors of both nations participated. As already mentioned, their foundation resides in the serpent-god [or serpent-goddess] mythology of the Indo-Aryan *Rigveda*. But how had it happened?

When sources of Vedic culture were discerned in the kurhans of Ukraine – from the Dniester up to the Psel – (Yu. Shilov. *Pre-homeland of Arians* (Kyiv, 1995) it prompted this question: was the Indo-Aryan epic perhaps also conceived on this territory? Having analysed this question, S. I. Nalyvayko (*Secrets of Sanskrit Revealed* (Kyiv, 2000, 2001)) arrived at the conclusion that the "the story of the *Ramayana* shares a clear correspondence with a story in Ukrainian folklore, that of a wonderful golden male-deer, seen by the mistress-sun from a window, who was ordered to capture her.....also, the names of gods, rulers and mighty soldiers which feature in the *Mahabharata* are names which still exist as Ukrainian surnames today.... This leads us to suppose that the ancestors of modern Ukrainians assisted in events described in the *Mahabharata*, and that the events themselves, or at least some of them, could have originated entirely on the territories of Ukraine".

Links to Ukrainian territory were also pointed out by L. I. Akimova (*Troy and Schliemann*, Moscow-Milan, 1996) when considering specific instances from the *Iliad*, its beginnings and the strange discrepancy between the archaeological finds and the history of the Troad of Asia Minor. In contrast to A. G. Kifishin, Akimova does not limit the beginnings of Trojan-Slavic links to Asia Minor but also notes them in the region of Stone Grave.

Contrary to established opinion held by ancient and later traditions that Troy-Ilium was founded by the earliest Athenians, Etruscans or Cretans, L. I. Akimova reached a source-based conclusion concerning three northern tribes that came into the Troad, and then settled there. The researcher reveals the roots of these tribes, and also the Trojan legends, as coming from "the Caucasus, where Prometheus was punished; the island of Leuke[6] located in the Black Sea, where the souls of Achilles, Patroclus and Helen found refuge; and from

Taurida where Artemis had taken Iphigeneia; and then the eastern borders of mythical Hyperborea – the place where Leto conceived Apollo and Artemis.... Stone Grave could be the sacred centre of those nations who over time, passed through Troy, creating such centres of world civilisation as Sumer, Egypt, Greece, Etruria and Italy". As if continuing this idea, B. D. Mykhailov (*The Petroglyphs of Stone Grave*, Zaporizhia-Moscow, 1999) noticed that the description of the sanctuary of Troy closely resembled the composition of the apex of Stone Grave; that there was a "surprising consistency of topography" of its sanctuaries with those of the Ancient-Greek temples of Demeter and Aphrodite; in addition, there were similarities between images of the Azov shrine and the double-bladed axe of Zeus, and of the "God tree" of Dionysus. These conclusions concur with initial manifestations of the mytho-rituals of Apollo, Zeus, Dionysus and their divine-celestial surroundings, traced by Yu. Shilov in the Azov Sea region.

At Stone Grave, Mykhailov also found images of ships of Egyptian and Creto-Minoan types of 3000-1400 BCE and possible corresponding inscriptions. When he discovered "The Grotto of Artemis" at Stone Grave, he dated it to the end of the Stone Age (a time prior to the traditional instance of the mythic goddess), but Yu. Shilov (*Prehistoric Rus*, Kyiv-Moscow, 1997-1999) contrasted images from this grotto with the specifically Trojan myth that centred on the struggle between gods and goddesses for the soul of Zeus, personified in the Golden Hound (who lies with feet uppermost below the warriors. See Fig. 48, page 135). Stelas found in the surrounding kurhans were similar to those found in Troy III-IV of 2390-2000 BCE, which also are mentioned in the *Iliad* of Homer (XVII: 434-436; VII: 87-89):

Like a pillar that is fixed, which stands on a kurhan,
A monument of a deceased husband or eminent wife...
Timeless, seeing it, somebody from later descendants
will say, after sailing in a multi-oared ship along the Black Pontus:
"Here is the grave of a warrior, who died in ancient ages".

Words such as these could have been spoken by Odysseus, as Homer devoted a significant part of the poem to a description of the Black Sea coast between the mouths of the Danube and Kuban, (where Odysseus wandered). *The Odyssey* – this epic is one of the earliest works about our country[7]! Besides the images of ships, inscriptions and stelas that currently remain obscure, relationships between Oriana and Troad can even be traced in the

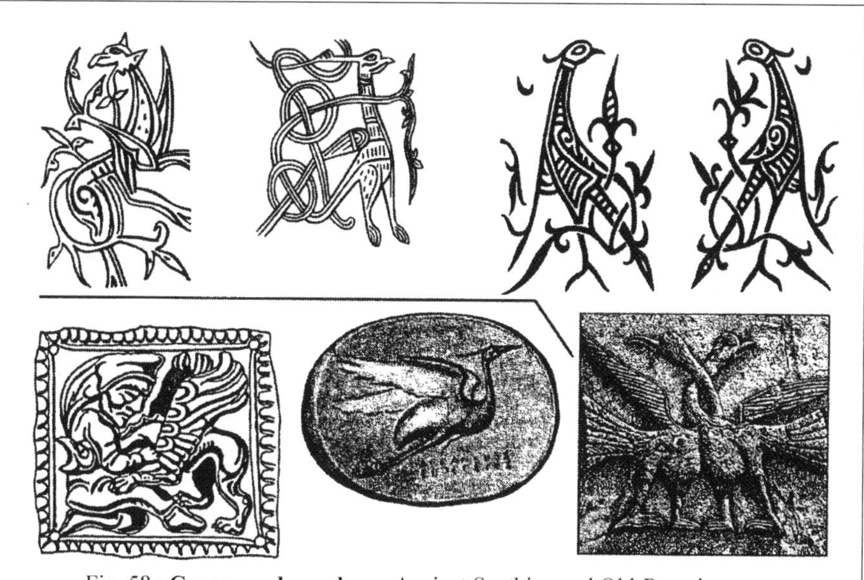

Fig. 58 : **Cranes and gryphons**. Ancient Scythian and Old-Rusy images.

chemical composition, the technologies and the shapes of metal implements (especially of daggers), also in some ceramic products, and in decorations made from amber and shells. By and large we have sufficiently strong grounds for offering a hypothesis about the involvement of the oracle-priests of Stone Grave in the origin of this Pelasgian-Greek epic.

And what about the Aryan-Indian epic? Here the conclusions previously outlined by Yu. Shilov and S. I. Nalyvayko are significantly reinforced by the researches of O. N. Trubachev who studied the origins of the *"Geranomachia"*, which was considered to be a parody on the *Iliad* and is attributed, even from ancient times, to the same author, Homer. However, many factors make it essential to examine 'The battle of the Cranes and Pygmies' far more closely.

Let us start with the fact that in ancient Greece, as indeed up to the present day in Ukraine, there were ceremonial "crane dances". In Russian, we have the common expression *baklushi* (in Ukrainian *bahlai*) which means '*to beat*', which, when expressed in Sanskrit, as *bakah*, or *bahla*, means '*a crane*'. (Incidentally, the name of the eldest brother of Krishna, *Balvir*, or *Balarama,* could be derived from '*bahla*'; see below). In the *"Geranomachia"*, in contrast to the heroes and gods of the *Iliad*, it is the pygmies and cranes that do battle. Also, this text was not a parody – rather, it was evidence for a common narrative, as found in the mythologies of India, Iran, Pelasgia and Greece, Rome, Armenia and Ukraine, having diverged from its source in some ultimate centre. In searching for this centre, O. N. Trubachev (*Indoarica in the Northern Black Sea coast*, Moscow, 1999), came to the conclusion that the theme in the *"Geranomachia"* concerned the war between two Aryan tribes, and that the native land of the mysterious narrative, from those Indo-European countries listed, appeared to be the latter (i.e. Ukraine), more specifically – it was centred in the valley of the River Konka. This district, named in the Olvian Decree of the 3rd – 2nd centuries BCE, is called Kankit: '*Crane-Persecutors*'.

The broad, low country between the Dnipro and its left bank tributary, the Konka, was named the 'Velyky Luh' (i.e. the Great Meadow), or Pletensky estuary by the Zaporozhian Cossacks; the latter name retained the Aryan title 'pleteno', which means 'wide'. The River Konka was fairly recently modified to 'Konsky Wody' (which means 'horse water', commemorating the first battle between the Rusy and Tatar-Mongolians that took place here – on the River Kalka, but over several centuries the conquerors then named it as the Kalkan-su). However, this [modification] is not correct because the original name arose from the Aryan word 'kanka' meaning '*crane*' or '*heron*'. This is justified by the name of the city, above the river, as well as by the testimony of the Roman author Solinus, commentator for the renowned geographer Pliny:

"*That part (of Scythia) which the Scythian-ploughers possessed, is sometimes remembered as the city of Gerania (which barbarians called Kakiton), from where, they say, the pygmies were banished by cranes*". The Greek name of this bird is 'geranos', and the more mythical name is 'gryphon', as mentioned for the first time in *The Iliad*, which arose (according to J. Greppin) from the Vedic 'Garuda'^, descendant of Aryan 'ger', i.e. 'crane'. O. N. Trubachev seemed doubtful about some aspects of such a derivation but he had noted the similar relationship between the mythical Garuda and the Indo-European 'devourer (of serpents)'. The latter, however does not contradict the primary image of the crane; the name 'kanka' can be acknowledged as secondary – which, still being Aryan – had spread after these events, forming the basis for the *Mahabharata*, the *Iliad* and other epics related to them.

The first of the two texts (i.e. the *Mahabharata*) took shape at the time when Garuda was changing to Kanka: the name, '*venerated/respected crane*' was the name given in exile to the elder of the Pandav-brothers patronised by Krishna. Special veneration for the crane in Ukraine is evident from the abundant use of the name in place-names and hydronyms, etc., and the variety of diverse "crane" names. The oldest, and until now the main (Ukrainian) name of 'zhuravel' for this migratory bird, is close to the Persian 'Harahvaite' – 'Crane river', which occupies the mid-point between the Indian Sarasvati and Greek Gerros. The Sanskrit 'saras' at the same time not only means 'crane' or 'heron' but also 'swan'. It turns out that this was a very ancient Palaeolithic name for water fowl – which rarely flew into glaciated areas and which were of no interest to hunters. This could have

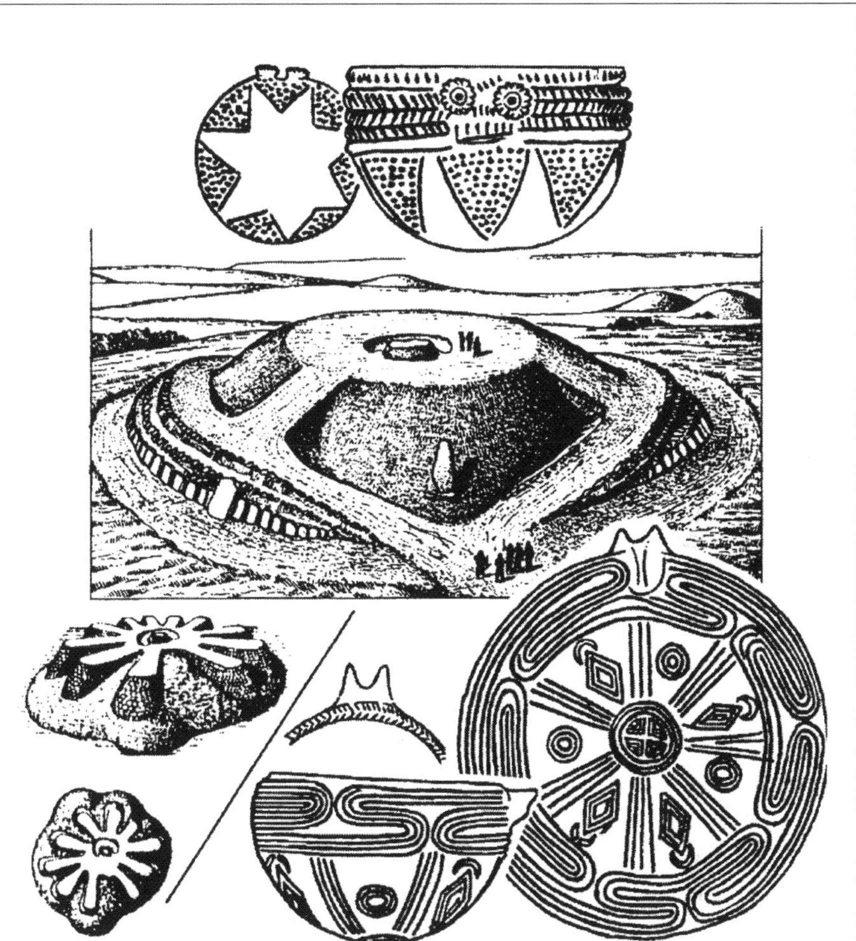

Fig. 59 : **Bowl-sextants and sanctuary-observatory of the Ingul culture** from the beginning of the 2nd millennium BCE. The upper fill of the kurhan at the town of Molochansk (Melitopol district of the Zaporizhia region); excavations by S. Zh. Pustovalov, reconstruction graphic by P. L. Kornienko. Calendric ornamentation of vessels from burials at Snihyrivka (regional centre of Mykolaiv region; above) and Bohachevki (Perekop district of Crimea).

occurred on the territories of future Ukraine but not on the expanses of Greece, Persia, India and other countries lying south of the glaciers (Table I).

Perhaps the cities of Gerania and Ka(n)kiton recorded by Roman authors were not different but neighbouring cities? Or perhaps they were not neighbours but localities with the names Kankit and Ger(ros)? Herodotus (IV: 19-20 et al.) described a territory and a river with the second name and modern researchers identify these with the rivers Konka or Molochna, as well as the area from Nikopol to Melitopol. O. N. Trubachev believes Gerros is a Cimmerian name, with Thracian and Albanian influences noted; Kankiton is absolutely an Indo-Aryan name. The city of Kakiton could be the Horodysche fortification near Savur-Grave^ (between the villages of Hrihorivka and Yulivka in the Zaporizhia region) or the settlement of Zmievske, in the lower part of the river; it seems names of other settlements along the River Konka were not from those times.

In the upper reaches of the River Molochna (Gerros^), archaeologists excavated a Sanctuary to Dionysus with the most ancient manifestation of the cult of the god the Greeks still called Geros – whom they identified as close to both Herakles as well as Krishna. Doesn't the semantic knot of all these gods testify to the direct and common origin of the Indo-Aryan and Pelasgian-Greek epic of creation?

In the *Mahabharata* the Sarasvati [river] is not only a "daughter"-tributary of the Sindh-Indus (as Aryans called the Dnipro, into which flowed the Konka) but also the crane-like, or swan-like wife of Brahma; she is the wise empress of horses and golden chariots whose legend is inherent in Konka... So, it is impossible to rule out the possibility that the Pandavas (or their ancestors) knew the shores of both 'Crane' waters – not only the Sarasvati but also the Kanki-Konka. This clan could have headed the tribe of "cranes" (and perhaps also the tribe of Leleges^, since the Ukrainian word 'lelek' means 'stork') who moved to this wonderful valley, crowding the aboriginal Kauravas-"Pygmies". The name of the latter agrees with the Savuryuga. Would the customs of the mysterious Pygmies have originated from their veneration of the caves of Stone Grave above the Molochna-Gerros river, the valley adjacent to the Konka-Kank? Due to the neighbouring farmers and cattle breeders (expelled from Kakiton, according to the testimony of Solinus; just like the Pygmies), such a confrontation could have arisen (according to the *Mahabharata*) between the Kauravas led by Balvir and the Pandavas headed by Balvir's younger brother Krishna.

The valleys of Gerros and Kankit had citadels, which were named Gerania and Kakiton..... so, could the battle have taken place between those archaeological cultures and ethnic groups, the battle which was represented in an Indo-European myth about cranes and pygmies which was then utilised by the authors of the *Mahabharata* and the *Iliad*? (Table VI).

We can also point to comparable events that took place in the latter part of 3rd millennium BCE in the Dnipro area. During that period, the alliance of tribes comprising local Aryans and foreign Hurrians, well-known to archaeologists as carriers of the Yamna (Pit-grave) and Starosillia cultures, organised a march into Mesopotamia and back. The greater part of the superior population of Aryans remained at home but some of its tribe (perhaps several) could have become the "Pygmies" to those "migratory birds" who later returned from the march. Around 2200 BCE, the latter constructed the first stone fortress in Eastern Europe above the Dnipro crossing, adjacent to the present village of Mykhaylivka in the Novo-Vorontsovsky district of Kherson region; that was the basis of the future Aryan-Hurrian power of Mitanni, which appeared to the north of Mesopotamia. Then those returning from the Mitanni kingdom brought to Shu-Nun (Stone Grave) knowledge of the Sumerian *Epic of Gilgamesh* (according to Yu. Shilov). However, (according to A. G. Kifishin), the creation of the *Epic of Gilgamesh* started here in the Dnipro area even as early as the 6th – 4th millennium BCE.

This epic poem, and the even more historic conditions of its appearance in the Dnipro area, could have become the catalyst for the creation of the later epic describing the tribal relationships between "pygmies and cranes" (drawn from the interrelationship of the Annunaki (i.e. guards) Huvava (or Humbaba) and the hero Gilgamesh), from which the *Mahabharata* later grew, as well as the *Iliad*.

The Mahabharata was closely connected with the main mytho-ritual of the *Rigveda*, from which the *Ramayana* could have sprung. This could have occurred in the environment of the carriers of the Yamna and Kemi Oba cultures and the archaeological cultures of indigenous local "pygmies" nearest to them.

In the *Iliad*, and even more so in the *Odyssey* that followed, the Vedic root is scarcely noticeable, which directs our search for source data for the epics (aside from the *"Geranomachia"*) within the environment of the new incoming carriers of Starosillia and subsequent "cranes" cultures. The most probable founders of the epic songs of Ilium seem to be the carriers of the Ingul archaeological culture from the beginning of the 2nd millennium BCE – not only were they cattle breeding-farmers but also sailors, which reveals connections with the Pelasgians, the Hyksos^ and the Hyperboreans.

Prof. O. N. Trubachev, in his book *Indoarica on the Northern Black Sea Coast*, takes into consideration the fore-mentioned and other sources in his search for Slavic beginnings at this location (just as Kifishin and Akimova had sought for it on the cross roads of the history of Troy). In particular, he focused attention on the ancient veneration for

'Beloberezhie'^ ['White Shore'] along the mouth of the Dnipro – veneration which reached Aryan times, survived antiquity and is traced over the long existence of Kyivan Rus. At the root of the name Beloberezhie, which was well-known to Pliny, Ptolemy and their followers, lies the sanctuary of Scythian-ploughmen on the Kanke. The sanctuary was called 'Rots(k)obe' etc., that is: 'Emitter of light', "from where the cranes descended" (from Stephanus of Byzantium). The Pindar Scholia^ provided evidence for the White Shore located on the Pontis Euxine, where a great multitude of herons could be seen on the shore, visible to seafarers. O. N. Trubachev proposes this hypothesis: "The White Shore, Beloberezhie, Ros – hat is how it was designated in the different languages of the inter-tribal associations of this area. It is here, apparently, that the name Rus – 'White Side' – was conceived, with its original significance now forgotten".

A. I. Asov and other Russian patriots are now searching in other places for 'Belovodie' [White Water], particularly in the Urals and Altai, hoping to find there the sources of *The Veles Book*. Meanwhile to search for that holy reservoir and country it is necessary to turn to eternal 'Beloberezhie', where until the end of antiquity, the state of 'the Mace-bearing Aria' (Dandaria), or Old Scythia persisted. Having participated in the earliest beginnings, of the Indo-European epic, could it not have created its own epic? Is it not possible that it started a sacred book known as *The Saster*^ – the Aryan '*Code of Ritual Practices*', which mentions "The oath of the citizens of Chersonese" of the 3rd century BCE? Is it not possible that it drew evidence from the "Scythian books" concerning the sources of history referred to by Berossos, the Chaldean sage? And wasn't one of those books – *The Veles Book*? Whatever the case, this thread of further searches is entirely real and, as we can see, provided enough facts. More related topics are considered below.

3. Sources and research problems in the origin of Rus.

Fig. 60 : **Goddess surrounded by birds**. Eastern-Slavic embroidery.

In the introduction to this chapter, reference was made to the conflict between the status of Ukraine's youthful national science (following national independence in 1991) and the existing, well-established status of Germany in the 18th century with regard to the problem of researching the origins of Rus [old Kyivan Rus],. The debate was given momentum by Tsar Peter I who commanded the history of the State of Russia to be written but deferred the matter to German scholarship. But those assembled forces, beginning with V. M. Tatishchev writing *Russian History from the Earliest Times,* had the power to destroy and falsify records and other documents, as well as national research.

However, not all foreigners downplayed the status of the Slavs. Thus, a work which was compiled at the beginning 17th century by the Dalmatian Mavro Orbin^, *A book on the historiography of the origin of the name, glory and expansions of the Slav people and their tsars and rulers under many names and with many reigns, kingdoms and provinces*, was re-issued in 1722 in Petersburg. For the first time he posited such tribes as the Veneti and Vandals^ into the Slavic ethnic group (and also the non-Slavic Illyrians, Getae, Goths^ and Sarmatians … nevertheless, it will be seen that Orbin was not altogether mistaken here).

The Frenchman P-C. Levesque (*Histoire de Russie*, 1782) embarked on a research project which was eventually taken up by the patriots of Russia. Levesque proved the relationship between Slavs and Latins (ancestors of the Romans) from even before the Trojan War, after which the latter borrowed from the former many words and concepts... It is therefore not accidental that the next rise of interest in this particular topic was triggered by the French Revolution and further, by the victory of Russia over Napoleon's army. A significant development from that period resulted in the publication of *The History of the Russian State* by N. M. Karamzin, and in rapid succession, in the year 1837, the great Slovak educator P. J. Safarik had published *Slav Antiquity* in Prague and Moscow. He derived the

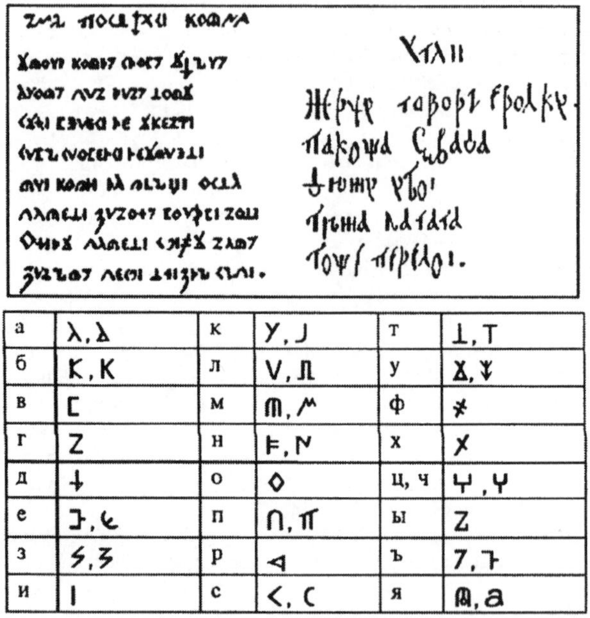

а	λ, λ	к	У, J	т	⊥, T
б	K, K	л	V, Л	у	Ẋ, ¥
в	[	м	m, ʌʌ	ф	≭
г	Z	н	F, N	х	X
д	⸸	о	◇	ц, ч	Ч, Ч
е	Э, ც	п	Π, π	ы	Z
з	ϟ, ȝ	р	◁	ъ	7, 7
и	I	с	<, C	я	Ɑ, a

Fig. 61 : **Traditional pre-Cyrillic writing** in lists from the beginning of 19th century According to A. I. Asov.

Slavs from the Venedi, Nevri^, Budini^, Borysthenes and Stavan of ancient times, considering their ancestral home to have been in Pannonia^ and Illyria…

But the most forward-looking – in the context of world science, politics and religion even of our time – were to be the books by A. D. Chertkov, E. Klassen and F. Volanskii who continued the researches of Orbin, Tatishchev, Levesque and Safarik. We shall focus on these works shortly, here we will just mention that the works were stimulated to a significant degree by a collection of ancient manuscripts – at the time still only partially deciphered, and corrupted with forgeries.

At the beginning of the 19th century the Petersburg collector A. I. Sulakadzev gathered more than 300 rare manuscripts amongst which were *Boyan's^ Anthem to Slavs* (4th century), *The Traveller* (also 4th century), *Kolednik by Dunaets Yalovets* (5th century), *Announcements of Perun and Veles'* (5th – 6th century), *Volkhovnik District, Methods of Order* (6th century), *The Prayer book of Prince Volodymyr* (10th century) and many others.

The only one of these to be preserved – recently found and published – was a copy of the *Boyan Anthem* ^. Perhaps *The Veles Book* had been amongst them but in the known list of Sulakadzev's rarities it was, of course, not registered under this provisional name (which came from its opening words on one of its wooden-plaques) by which it is known to 20th century researchers. The book could have been recorded, in the opinion of A. I. Asov, as *The Patriarchy*: *the whole book carved on 45 beech board-plaques*. Underneath these words is the partially intelligible subscript: "Yagipa Hana smerd [peasant farmer], in Ladoga IX century, about Varangian^ migrants and oracle-priests and writings/characters, taken/driven away to Moravia". Perhaps the description refers to the last copyist of Czech origin, to his place and time of work and to the country of the contractor's copy.

This could even be the copy recorded as follows in this list: "Krynitsa, 9th century, Cherdynia, Olekha (visherts), concerning the re-settlement/migrations of the old inhabitants and the first faith". Here, scribes are also mentioned (one of the named people could also be the contractor), who are, moreover, of Belarusian or Ukrainian origin. This specific copy could have been the one which reached us as *The Veles Book*. Such an assumption accords with the most authoritative conclusions of B. I. Yatsenko, the translator of *The Veles Book* at the end of the 20th century. In his opinion, the plaque texts of the last transcript "*were finally rewritten in the 16th – 17th centuries and in this form they reached our time. Together with the phonetic peculiarities of 9th – 10th century Old-Rusy and Old-Czech languages, they also preserved the dialectical characteristics of the Ukrainian language*".

The Veles Book could have come to us from the collection of P. P. Dubrovski, a fellow collector and friend of Sulakadzev. He was an officer at the Russian embassy in Paris during the French Revolution and, taking advantage of the opportunity, acquired books from the library of the French Queen Anna, which she had received in dowry from her father, Kyivan Prince Yaroslav the Wise^; in France the books were probably stored in the monastery at the abbey founded by Queen Anna in the town of Sanlis ... In any case, the book arrived at the estate of the Donets-Zaharzhevsky Cossack family located in the village of Velyky Burliuk in the Kharkiv region of Ukraine. The book could have been acquired by M. V. Nekliudov, the grandfather of bibliophile K. V. Zadonska who was the last mistress of the estate. Nekliudov was the contemporary of the two collectors mentioned above, he also lived at some time in Petersburg and was a member of a Biblical society... In 1919, revolutionary rebels killed the landowner and ransacked the estate and library; as the heap of plaques with incomprehensible characters were of no use for making hand-rolled cigarettes (i.e. not made of paper), they were saved by the white guard, Colonel F. A. Izenbek.

Fig.62 : **Yaroslav Mudry and his daughter Anna**, Queen of France. Iconic reconstruction according to the skull and medieval statue.

The modern researcher A. I. Asov (*Slavonic Runes and the "Boyan Anthem"*, Moscow, 2000; etc.) who publicised the above information, also relates the dramatic history of the discovery of *The Slavic Veda* (*Veda Slovena^*) and its publication by the Serbian ethnographer-linguist S. I. Verkovich – with its language even related to the Indo-Aryan Vedas. The medieval church burnt this "wooden book", but the Rodopean Bulgarian-Pomaks^ had orally preserved its text. After publication of *The Slavic Veda* in Belgrade, its presence in the Rodope mountains was carefully verified – by a government expedition! – and confirmed by authoritative specialists from France (where the *Mahabharata* had been published during those years). After that, Verkovich was invited to Petersburg by the Tsar, where, under the personal guardianship of Alexander II he issued in 1881 – a tragic year for him – Volume I of the Veda, in the language of the original. The translation of that volume into the Russian language was not published because scientists at the 9th Slavic Congress in Kazan, voted for non-recognition of the authenticity of *The Slavic Veda*. This congress took place shortly after the assassination of the Tsar, (indeed, the ideology of the forthcoming revolution was already brewing…) Since that time, academic science has completely ignored this matter, just as it has ignored information about the collections of A. I. Sulakadzev, P. P. Dubrovski and others.

Amongst those collections, as previously mentioned, there were also forgeries. Nevertheless researchers, by means of their indisputable analysis of the inherent linguistic data in particular, were able to arrive at the same conclusions. According to M. Krasuski (*Antiquity of the Language of Little Russia*^^ [i.e. Ukrainian], Odessa, 1880), during the second half of the 19th century, "foreign scientists became more convinced that the homeland of Aryan tribes was not in Central Asia, but in the so-called Sarmat, or Slavic valley. Consequently, 'Little-Rus' lived on this plain right up to the present time as did the northern settlers that derived from them – the Novhorodians^ and 'Great Russia' in general. It is well known that the adverb 'Novhorodian' is most applicable to "Little Russia". Even this researcher himself arrived at the conviction that the language of Little Russia is not only older than Slavic, not excluding so-called Old-Slavonic, but also older than Sanskrit, Greek, Latin and other Aryan languages.

Coming up in Chapter 8 is an image from the Sumerian-Aryan-Ukrainian dictionary compiled by Professor L. A. Waddell and L. Sylenko; at the end of the 20th century the latter brilliantly confirmed the earlier conclusions of the linguist M. Krasuski (although L. Sylenko did not know him), and in turn M. Krasuski did not know about the works of A. I. Sulakadzev and A. I. Verkovich. Thus, we have several independent historiographic searches which achieve consensus in their facts and conclusions; this circumstance alone offers sufficient grounds for asserting the authenticity of a pre-Christian Slavic literature as well as revealing its historical foundation.

Krasuski did not receive recognition in his time. In addition, the scientific explorations of Chertkov, Volanski and Klassen also failed to find support in official Russian circles because their evidence greatly undermined the traditional stance which regarded the Slavs as savages prior to the birth of Rus [i.e. old Kyivan Rus] and later, this entrenched stance was blessed by the church and endorsed by international diplomacy. Scientific establishments also followed this tradition (and continue to do so even today), they were not interested in the Truth, presuming (as do such high level modern Russian and Ukrainian scientists, as Likhachev, Tolochko and Zaliznyak, etc.) that the matter was limited to conflicts of prestige – ethno-historical, cultural etc. However the 20th century has already shown that scientific distortion of the historical picture led to the formation of fatal ideologies which resulted in millions of victims of terror, revolutions, Holodomors^ and wars – the responsibility for which, along with military servicemen, politicians and churchmen, must also be borne by scientists.

Liberal dalliance with the revolutionaries on the cusp of the 19th – 20th century did not benefit historians. The somewhat mediocre *Lectures on Slavic Antiquity* (Kharkiv, 1910) and *Earliest Fate of Russian Tribes* (St. Petersburg, 1919) by A. L. Pogodin did not help to halt the "infection", which morphed into the offensive not only in fascist Germany but also in Bolshevik USSR. The NKVD^ manufactured "The Case of Slavists", according to which even academicians of world renown – V. Vernadsky, M. Hrushevsky, M. Derzhavin et al. – were condemned by "judges" for having invented the so-called underground organisation, "The National Party of Russia". The pioneering research conducted in the pre-war years, headed by linguist-historian N. Ya. Marr^, still remains largely unknown and the monograph signed by Stalin, *Marxism and the Questions of Linguistics,* has to this day deterred the Academy of Sciences from studying the research problem that the "Etruscans are Rusy" (a quip from those horrendous times). There are also deeper reasons that go back to the Old Testament.

Meanwhile world science did not stand still. Though the direction of any research that would have endangered the nobility was artificially delayed, others developed successfully. The greatest Slavists of the 20th century were rightfully considered to be the Czech historian L. Niderle and the Russian archaeologist B. A. Rybakov. In his *Slavic Antiquity* and *Life of Ancient Slavs*, Ljubomir Niderle begins our history between the Oder and Wisla rivers at the boundary of the 2nd and 1st millennium BCE. Boris Rybakov extended this date and displaced the ancestral home to the Pripyat^; at the same time he specified the first evidence, in symbols and Slavic folklore, of references to mammoths and raised a challenge to the origins of (any!) human history from those times, which were reached by human historical memory... Nevertheless, both researchers confined themselves to using only those sources that were recognised by academic science (a science which frowned upon any attempts by the authorities to search for the origin of Slavs earlier than the beginning of the Christian era); neither utilised the range of sources from *The Veles Book.*

The conspiracy of silence surrounding the true place of the Slavic peoples in the foundations of universal civilisation was breached around the middle of the 20th century. Since 1952 in USA, Canada and France, and since 1960 in USSR, *The Veles Book* began to be published, having been saved from destruction in 1919 by F. A. Izenbek, copied into his collection and then thrust into the light by Yu. P. Miroliubov. The original or ancient copy of the book which was written on oak plaques (in accord with Rusian-Etruscan tradition), apparently disappeared during a fire in the Second World War – although, according to rumour, it is presently safely stored in the Vatican City.

In the wake of the first publications of *The Veles Book* in Canada and USA there was a tremendous boost in studies concerning the beginnings of Slavic ethno-history, supported by Volodymyr Shayan and his disciple and adherent Lev Sylenko. Their essential books *The Faith of our Ancestors* and *Magian Faith* became sacred works for Ukrainians; the second of them especially because the direct meaning of its title forms the root of RUNVIRA[8] (meaning Native Ukrainian National Faith). Whilst the first compendium primarily considered correspondences between Vedic and Ukrainian ethno-culture, the second was a sequential account of human history from the earliest times. For this, they utilised scientific data, principally sourced from West European and American researchers, sources little-known to homegrown science; the majestic roots of our history were now represented from the positive position of foreign scientific authorities. On the other hand, the main deficiency of both immense books was the authors weak knowledge of domestic historiography [the study of sources which affect the way history is written] and the archaeology of the Soviet period; and within historiography (and, what is considerably worse – in conceptual developments), significant discoveries were made.

In Ukraine, Russia and on the expanses of what was then the USSR, the breakthrough in foreign comprehension of Slavic origins began in the 1960-80s from the Kyivans, N. Z. Susloparov and A. P. Znoyko (*Myths of Kyivan territory and Ancient Events*, Kyiv, 1989). They were guided by the old publications of Chertkov, Klassen and Marr, which had languished in library special archives and therefore had not been used by official science. At the end of 20th century this direction was, in effect, completed – in an amateur capacity but still worthwhile for having retained historiographic principles – by the Moscow amateur antiquarian, G. S. Grinevich (*Pre-Slavic written language*, Moscow, 1994).

The most divisive matter for All-Soviet Union historical faculties and the National Academies of Sciences of that time arose from the publication of *Codes of Old-Rusy Chronicles* and so forth, as well as archaeological, ethnographic, linguistic and anthropological sources. However even the outstanding, two-volume *Code of the Earliest Written Information about Slavs* (Moscow, 1994) began with evidence no earlier than the first centuries CE. Academic science continues to ignore *The Veles Book.* Nevertheless, enough scholarly publications have already been produced – in 1994 in the subsequent improved editions by A. I. Asov and B. I. Yatsenko, in 1995 and 2001 in Moscow and Kyiv respectively. The latter publication is still the best. They were extensively used in writing the present *Ancient History of Aratta-Ukraine*. In 1993-1995 V. Ilya and D. Shably in the Kyiv journal *Osnova* ['Foundation'] published a Ukrainian translation of the fundamental monograph of A. D. Chertkov, *Pelasgian-Thracian Tribes who Colonised Italy*. Books awaiting re-publication from this outstanding historian include such titles as *Essay on the Ancient History of Proto-Sloven*; *Migration of Thracian Tribes over the Danube and further North to the Baltic Sea and Rus*, they were published in 1851 but were immediately dropped into special (closed) archives. The monograph, *New Materials for the Earliest History of Slavs (...)* and an accessible essay on the *History of Rusy B.C.* by E. Klassen and F. Volanski, first published in Moscow in 1854, were reissued in St. Petersburg in 1995. The value of these works did not become obsolete; indeed, now is precisely when they have reached their finest hour!

Fig. 63 : **Alphabet of *The Veles Book***. By Yu. P. Miroliubov.

If the political and religious motives mentioned earlier are to be rejected, then what does the essence of the books named here consist of? The hieroglyphic and cuneiform characters of Sumer and the previous written language of Aratta and Shu-Nun (Stone Grave), unknown to the authors of those books, are still only tentatively understood by modern researchers. Only in a few cases is it possible to be sufficiently confident to speak of the relationship between the pronunciation of the names of Enlil and Ninlil with Lel' and Lialia, and of Inanna – with Nanny, etc. After the Ogygian flood in the Troad or in neighbouring and related Lydia (according to the testimonies of ancient historians), the alphabet was devised. Letters began to take on sounds and it was suddenly discovered that Slavic language (but at the same time pre-Greek, pre-Indian and "Indo-European" languages generally) belonged to Pelasgian and to its related [carrier] tribes. Around the middle of the 19th century the Russian researchers Chertkov, Klassen and Volanski began to specifically study this Indo-European matter alongside the beginnings of the ethnogenesis of Slavs.

Academic science still ignores this direction of research which is extremely urgent for all humanity, for the reasons indicated above. An example of the impossibility of solving the problem of the ethnogenesis of Slavs by means of such science is evident in the books of Yu. V. Pavlenko *Prehistory of Old Rus in a World Context* (Kyiv, 1994) and *Pre-Slavs and Aryans* (Kyiv, 2000). They are written professionally and even inspirationally, yet they are hampered by consulting the limited circle of officially authorised sources which ignore *The Veles Book* and the monographs of the researchers specified above, etc. Though the significance of similar researches is small, the considerable harm they do is attributable to the blocking of so-called key scientific sources and developments; blocking only supports an objective which refuses to admit any reconsideration of the historic picture, a picture which has been distorted by interference from science in the interests of politics and religion.

We have discussed the consequences of such distortions and non-admissions. The crux of the problem lies in the fact that without continual addition, reconsideration and refinement of the reality of the past, it is impossible to understand the course of historic process and to develop scientific predictions such that, in their turn, they would not generate inaccuracy of studies, ideological doctrines, political courses – and hence genocides, wars, ecological catastrophes, epidemics and so forth. The ‘volcano’ of errors amassed by Christian (and Anti-Christian) Europe, which took place in the first half of the 20th century, is preparing for a new eruption. As A. I. Asov observes, “nothing has changed in national Slavistics (Slavic science) at this time, since there has been a preserved succession of academics within the Russian schools of science. None of the songs of Veta, recorded by Stefan Verkovich, were ever included in the collections of songs of southern Slavs translated into the Russian language. Those books, which he published in Belgrade, and the fate of his unpublished manuscripts, are still unknown to researchers of ancient faith and the history of Slavs. Neither has there been, until now, a single expedition into the Rodope mountains” (apart from the one organised, over a hundred years ago, by the French government). This is the situation in the field of research into foundations, into sources, into their current state and prospects, not merely for the sake of Slavs – but for the sake of world civilisation.

Characterising Slavistics and Slavic philology in general, A. I. Asov brought to light some of the fundamentally significant breakthroughs achieved by its authoritative representatives. L. N. Gumilev in his books *Ancient Rus and the Great Steppe* (Moscow, 1992), *The Rhythms of Eurasia. Ages and Civilisation* (Moscow, 1993), etc., attempted, rather successfully, to radically alter the paradigm of historical science (by relying less on humanitarian data than on astrophysical and geophysical data). This direction was defined, in some sense, by M. O. Chmykhov in *The Beginnings of Rus Paganism* (Kyiv, 1990); the second edition of this book in 2001 – a somewhat modified overview – was speculatively titled *From the Cosmic Egg to the Idea of the Saviour*. As for the *insignificant, formal and substantial* researches of Slavists, we can still claim some very notable achievements; they are by the acknowledged authorities: B. A. Rybakov with his articles and monographs from the 1960-80s on the ancient paganism of Slavs and Rus, V. V. Mavrodin with a course of lectures on *The Origin of the Russian Nation* (Leningrad, 1978), O. N. Trubachev and V. V. Sedov with their monographs *Ethnogenesis and Culture of the Earliest Slavs* (Moscow, 1991) and *Slavs in Antiquity* (Moscow, 1994), et al. Amongst recent West European Slavicists, the most remarkable are M. Bor, J. Šavli, and other Slovenian researchers of the Veneti.

We can say without exaggeration that the most important breakthrough was made by one of the leaders of the Institute of Russian Language at the Russian Academy of Science, academician Professor O. N. Trubachev. He opened a new field of studies in his monograph *Indoarica in the Northern Black Sea Coast* (Moscow, 1999) and remarked: “the absence of a Slavic relationship with the Bosphorus empire is often remarked upon; the theory with regard to the absence of Slavs themselves in the ancient Northern Black Sea

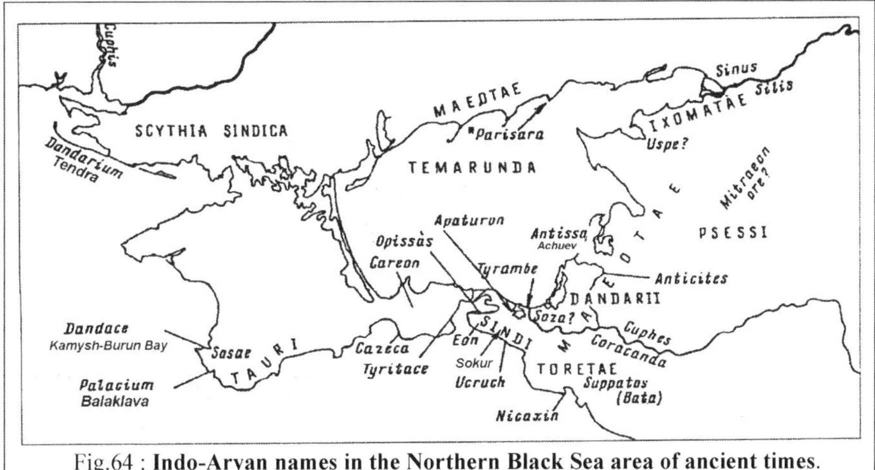

Fig.64 : **Indo-Aryan names in the Northern Black Sea area of ancient times.**
By O. N. Trubachev.

coast is also well-known. These old views need revision in the sense that there were connections between the earliest places of Slavic inhabitation (we deliberately avoid the less apposite term "ancestral homeland") and the ancient cultural region of the Northern Black Sea area and traces of these connections persisted. Furthermore, the named connections, at least in part, relate to the Indo-Aryan component of the northern-Pontic population".

Until Trubachev, the earliest traces of Slavs in the Northern Black Sea coast were sought (with minimal success) through the Irano-Scythian off-shoot of the Aryan community (conventionally termed "Indo-Iranian"); Trubachev discovered the sources of the Slavs through the Indo-Cimmerian off-shoot of the Aryans. This discovery is in remarkable agreement with the testimonies of *The Veles Book* and with the evidence presented by V. N. Danylenko and B. A. Rybakov regarding the relationship of Trypillia with the ethnogenesis of Slavs, which also accord with the theory of Yu. Shilov with regard to the Slavic inheritance of the most ancient world state of Aratta ("Trypillia") – the genetic core of the Aryan community of nations.

The drawback in Trubachev's position is that he ignores *The Veles Book* (where Slav-Indo-Aryan links in particular are expounded), as well as these entirely evident sources that were mentioned earlier: the ancient written monuments of Stone Grave etc., the cities and observatories of Aratta, the semantics of kurhans and other facts, through which the organisational wisdom of ancient priests was made apparent. Not only were they working on technologies, artificial selection, calendars and ceremonies – but also on terminology and languages, on ethnogenesis in general. Not to take account of such information at this moment does not suit researchers. These are no longer the times to be limited by the commonplace attitude that: "A nation is the author of its culture". It is already necessary to clearly understand that there are different levels within a nation and each level creates in its own manner.[9] Whilst investigating the depths of the 'Indo-European language community' and the words extant from that time, of 'synthetic' Sanskrit and its texts, we must not forget the brahmans, or the context and condition of their work, of control by people, including migrations and inter-tribal ties – of which the most communicational tool was language. We shall try to compensate for the deficiencies outlined in the researches of respected O. N. Trubachev in the further development of our description of ancient Rus. This will rest, in particular, on *Secrets of Sanskrit Revealed* by S. I. Nalyvayko (Kyiv, 2000, 2001) which complemented and further developed the above named works of Prof. Trubachev to a significant degree.

From the facts now known, rather than from Herodotus and Nestor with their ordinary followers, we shall begin an examination of the formation of Slavic ethnoculture.

Suggested reading

1. *The Veles Book.* Translation and Comments, Yatsenko B. I., Kyiv, 1995, 2001.
2. Nalyvayko S. I., *Secrets of Sanskrit Revealed*, Kyiv, 2000, 2001.
3. Shayan V., *The Faith of our Ancestors*, Hamilton, 1987.
4. L. Sylenko, *Magian Faith*, New York and et al., 1979.
5. Chertkov A. D., *Pelasgian-Thracian tribes who colonised Italy*, in: *Foundation*, Kyiv, 1993-1995, No. 24 (2) - No. 28 (6).
6. Klassen E., *New Materials for the Ancient History of Slavs...* Moscow, 1854; St. Petersburg, 1995.
7. Asov A. I., *Slavonic Runes and the "Boyan Anthem"*, Moscow, 2000.
8. Tulaev P. V., *The Veneti: Ancestors of Slavs*, Moscow, 2000.
9. Shilov Yu., *"The Veles book" and the Urgency of Ancient Doctrines*, Kyiv, 2001.

[1] Translated from the Russian word 'змием' (zmiyem), which can mean either serpent or dragon.

[2] "Lichen" originated from Ukrainian '*to lichyty*', which means *to calculate*. (V. Krasnoholovets).

[3] The Slavic word 'vesna' means 'spring' and is probably associated with the coming of Vishnu, or Visnu, to people after the long winter. This festival takes place over the days of the solar equinox, when day wins the battle over night. (V. Krasnoholovets).

[4] Archaeological finds from the Troad dating back to the Chalcolithic period show striking affinity with archaeological finds known from the same era in Muntenia and Moldavia, and there are other traces which suggest close ties between the Troad and the Carpatho-Balkan region of Europe. Archaeologists have in fact stated that the styles of certain ceramic objects and bone figurines show that these objects were brought into the Troad by Carpatho-Danubian colonists; for example, certain ceramic objects have been shown to have Cucuteni origins. (Hoddinott, Ralph F., The Thracians, Thomas & Hudson Inc., 1981. pp. 35–38).

[5] Translated from the Russian word 'руно' (runo) meaning 'Fleece'. Since runes are ancient letters, the legend of the Golden Fleece was perhaps a quest for 'valuable writings' [Sacred writing on skins has a very ancient history.]

[6] In modern times known as Snake Island.

[7] The author's Ukraine.

[8] The title of the book *Magian Faith* is the translation from the Russian МАГА ВЕРА (transliterated as MAGA VERA). Hence it provides the root of РУНВІРИ (transliterated as RUNVIRA, meaning the Native Ukrainian National Faith which is the faith in the One God Dazhbog).

[9] According to Vedic decree there must be 4 different levels/castes: from Brahmans to Shudra.

CHAPTER 7

:«Vels-bg»
«Велес-бог»
:«Zehmu... taz Vels bg»: «Земун также и Велес-бог...»

Fig. 65 : Figurine of Veles with Slavonic runes from the temple in Retra in times of late antiquity – early Middle Ages, and a **Rusy ceremonial table cloth** of the 19th century, from the Arkhangel region, reflecting the synthesis of calendars esteeming Heavenly Deer (from the 9th millennium BCE) and the constellation of Taurus (from the 5th millennium BCE).

THE ETERNAL DEPTHS OF SLAVDOM

At the beginning of the previous chapter we became acquainted with the methodology and viewpoint of B. A. Rybakov: the history of a nation begins not from the moment when someone recorded its name nor from the interpretation of such records by scientists – but from those ancient depths in which most of the nation's own ethnoculture had resided. Reaching back 21 millennia (21,123 years – conventionally counting from 2002 CE [present day] and basing the completion of *The Veles Book* in 879 CE, where a 20-thousand year memory of Slavdom is spoken of) – our 'Book' is the most ancient in the world, and along with it, so are we Slavs.

Is it possible to trust this? How can it be verified? The simplest verification is to trace at least the main components of Slavic ethnogenesis from that time, such as references in folklore, inscriptions recording the mammoths and glaciers, and mentions of Aratta and Arián, Cimmeria and Scythia... and we shall do this!

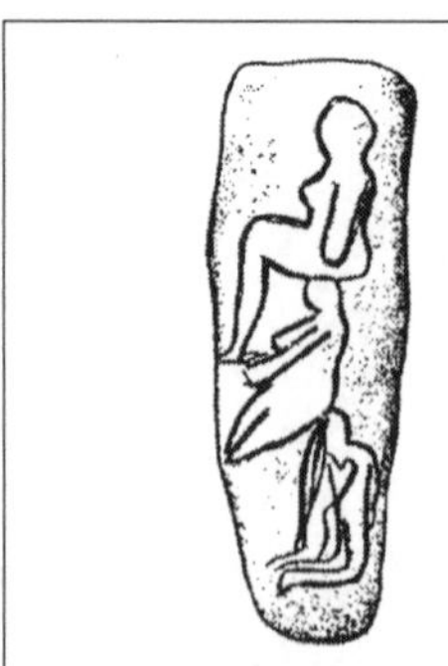

Fig. 66 : **Tablet with images of three Progenitresses**. From Stone Grave, 12th–10th millennium BCE, at the end of the Palaeolithic – the 'Old Stone Age'.

1. The Time of Mammoths.

The first scientific explanation for the improbably ancient designs found on Ukrainian ceremonial towels and hand-painted eggs (Pysanky^) was expressed by V. N. Danylenko in 1965 towards the end of his monograph, *The Cosmogony of Primitive Society*. In due course, Professor B. A. Rybakov became the first to collate the cultural elements of those Slavs (**proto-Slavs**, would be more accurate) of the upper Palaeolithic – i.e. from the 'old Stone Age', the time when modern Cro-Magnon man had emerged and the time of deglaciations of the last Ice Age. According to Rybakov's reasoned hypothesis the most expressive elements from those times are these:

~ ornamentation in the form of rhombuses and their derivative parallel zigzags and meanders which reproduce (according to researches by V. I. Bibikova) the natural saw-cut patterns of mammoth teeth;

~ references in the folklore motifs to those strange animals, to hunting them and to the fight with the fiery serpent-lizard (Yashcher, Yasha^) at the guelder rose bridge^, and such like.

Yashcher sits in a corner,
holding in hand a wreath...

It is entirely probable that the initial form of 'Yashcher-Yasha' was Ishkur. The earliest indications of the name 'Ishkur' were deciphered by A. G. Kifishin amongst the proto-writings of cave sanctuaries in Western Europe (see the collection, *Developmental Features of the Upper Palaeolithic of Eastern Europe*, St. Petersburg, 1999); from there, that name, as well as references to the Mammoth, was transferred into the archive of Stone Grave, and later, into Sumerian libraries. The linguist showed that Ishkur, the thunder-god of Sumer, arose from magical images and expressions of mammoth hunters, the ideogram of whom was passed into cuneiform writing over time.

The next period of development of this mythological image was traced by V. A. Safronov and N. A. Nikolaeva (*Sources of Slavic and Eurasian Mythology*, Moscow, 1999). When they referenced *Paganism of Ancient Slavs* by B. A. Rybakov (Moscow, 1981), the authors forgot that the folkloric Yashcher-Yasha had been traced back to the time of mammoths and this was a testament to the beginnings of proto-Slavic ethnogenesis amongst the "proto-Eurasians" (according to their terminology). But Safronov and Nikolaeva concentrated their attention on Iasion and Attis – men of Pelasgian Ancient Greece and the goddesses Demeter and Cybele of Asia Minor. The researchers derive this 'Mother of the Gods' and 'Earth-Baba (Old Woman)' from the Foremother of the Çatal Höyük sanctuaries, where the appearance of this Foremother is traced from "palaeolithic Venuses" from the tusks of mammoths. Later, Iasion-Attis, through to the Polish Iasi (Jacze), is identified by these authors with the Eastern Slavic Yashcher (Yasha). Between the first two pairs it is necessary to consider Jason, leader of the Argonauts who conquered the serpent guarding the Golden Fleece. The legendary wanderings of the crew of the 'Argo' revived the ancient

Fig. 67 : **Jason and the Serpent-Yasha at the Golden Fleece.**
Ancient image.

relationships between the Indo-European Peloponnese, Asia Minor and the Northern Black Sea area. The most recent manifestation of the canon of this calendar pair, Lada and Iasi ('Wife' and 'Yasen'), are fixed in ecclesiastical curses of the 15th century. The mammoth could be transformed by the Thunder God into the Tree owing to the burgeoning calendar-celestial functions of this male image, eternally related to the image of the Foremother. The Yasen-Tree ['Yasen' in Ukrainian means 'Ash Tree'] represents the world-axis and is a vital feature of sanctuary-observatories which proliferated from the end of the 5th millennium BCE.

Popular recollections about the times of 'Ancient Stone' (the Palaeolithic) are most evidently concentrated in the Ukrainian fairy-tale *The hero Dymko and his brother-in-law Andrushka*. The fairy-tale begins like this:

Long ago, when people still had neither fire, nor basins, nor spoons, they settled on the banks of creeks ... And there, look, when they gathered more and more people, they began to make earthen huts. Then one robust man was found among them called Dymko. He was also a strong man who guarded the village and the creek. He would take a club-staff [sceptre or mace] *and whatever dashing beast would come upon the village he would then swipe it with his club-staff, and kill it right away...*

And among them was an old woman Maria, who lived by herself in the forest and the beasts did not touch her... She came to them, that old woman Maria, and gave as a gift a piece of flint, a pebble and a sponge. Giving these she said:

"You have no fire and I give it to you. Beat the pebble with the flint and the sponge will light up."...

As Dymko and his friends reached the stream, where the people live, they lay out a fire ... They took the water-buffaloes and elephants and moved there, where Dymko's people lived, and settled down with them, and released their cattle to them ...

Suddenly one day a dragon flew above the village... As it stopped, it began to hiss, and the people and cattle were entirely scared. Then Dymko summoned his warriors, took clubs in their hands and made advances to the dragon ... They buried it behind old woman Maria's hut...

With this fairy-tale one is reminded of another original myth written down in Kyiv territory in the 19th century (see: V. Huziy, *A Golden Reed*, Brovary, 1997): *The Earth is a platter that stands on four elephants and they stand on a cloud. The Earth is 196 centuries old.* The latter date corresponds to the beginning of the chronology of *The Veles Book* (boards 4b, 2b, 2a – according to B. I. Yatsenko):

We are great orphans, the divine arm turned away from us.
And so for up to twenty thousand years we could not be created until Rus,
and then Varangians came and took it...
So we live, having learned to catch beasts and to catch fish, from fear having dodged.
Thus we stayed one t'ma[1] *and began to set up castles, laying fire-sites out everywhere.*
In another t'ma (10,000 years x2) *there was great coldness...*
So we moved here and settled down by local fires on Russian earth.
And all that happened two t'ma to the present.
And after those two t'ma the Varangians came ...

Evidence about the onset of constructing "castles[2]" should not be understood in a modern or even Old-Russian sense; instead it speaks of the replacement of cave dwellings by dwellings that were built in alignment. Near the modern village of Mizyn, in the River Desna area, such buildings were found in a settlement (dated by archaeologists to the 25th – 20th millennium BCE). Another settlement (18th – 15th millennium BCE), near the village of Kostenky close to the city of Voronezh, had a social "meeting house" with an area of about 600m². This accommodation was warmed by 9 fires and contained within it a sanctuary, a workshop, stores of weapons and produce... The *elephants* mentioned in the fairy-tale above,

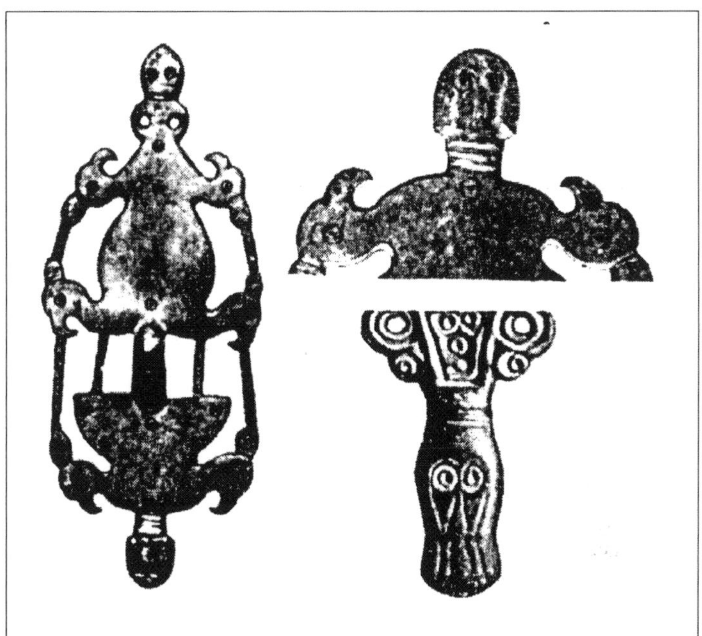

Fig.68 : Old-Rusy images of Yashcher on fastening-fibulas [buckles].

were not driven to the ancestral home of the Slavs; surely, the migrants from the Eastern Mediterranean brought the name with them, where elephants were encountered until the mid-2nd millennium BCE. But perhaps mammoths also had this name? Even long ago the elk [red deer] in Rus was called the "Elephant with branching antlers", [Latin: *Cervus elaphus*]. Yashcher, with tusks, has been portrayed even until recent times (on fastenings and other decorations), frequently together with Foremother Berehynia^ [whose name means Guardian Lady].

As we see, the testimony of *The Veles Book* (which academician D. S. Likhachev with his followers tried to discredit by declaring it fake, and even Professor B. A. Rybakov was implicated in this unscrupulous matter) does not in any way contradict either the popular tradition or its scientific research. The overall conclusion considered from the above sources and their developments is thus: Slavic prehistory reaches back 198-211 centuries ago into antiquity (i.e. to the beginning of our 3rd millennium). This is already ***doctrine*** rather than a version or conjecture. Furthermore, M. V. Lomonosov's idea that the old language of Slavic peoples is too remote for Ancient Greek to have been derived from it and the like should now be understood in terms of this language belonging to the deepest root, to the first sprout, from which the general 'Indo-European language' came. Thus, here is the Greek language but it came from the Pelasgians, and the Pelasgians were from Aratta... The Slavs came from the Palaeolithic, even pre-Aratta (which we remember being associated with the onset of writing). Conventionally, that remoteness can be called *pre*-Slavic because, as has been considered above, it was *pre*-Indo-European.

It is additionally evident that the earliest layers of the Karelian-Finnish *Kalevala* are also reflected in that indicated remoteness – when there was still a 'Eurasian community' before it cleaved into the Indo-European and the Ural-Altai peoples (from which came the Ugro-Finnish and Turkish peoples). Following A. Abrashkin, P. Tulaev is attracted to comparing some of the main heroes of this immense epic to those of Slavic ethnoculture. "*Ilmatar, the daughter of the aerial expanse*", can be 'Matyr Il(ma)'[3]; the wise singer Vajnemejnen born to her can be the 'Husband of Veneti'; and the adept of runes and invocations, Antero, can belong to the Antes, being similar to the Pelasgian Antaeus, and (at least by name) to the Trojan Antenor, who became one of the leaders of the Veneti.

A. G. Kifishin found mythological references to the mammoth, Ishkur, in the archive of Stone Grave, supposedly begun around 11,582 BCE, and to the same legendary times of the 19th – 17th millennium BCE. The question arises: what caused self-awareness amongst the Slavs (even 'pre-Slavs') during this specific chronological range? The most probable answer is found in the book by M. A. Chmykhov *The Beginnings of Rus Paganism* (Kyiv, 1990). Developing his astrophysical calculations, it can be assumed that in 17,035 BCE there must have been a great alignment of the planets, which coincided with an immense peak of Solar activity that cyclically happens once every 9576 years. It is possible that this date was shifted somewhat by the catastrophe of Phaethon^, Venus or Mars – which is recorded in the legends of various peoples on Earth. It is evident that these celestial collisions were accompanied by incredible geocosmic shocks, leading to the subsequent shift of glaciers – which, according to geological data, were at their greatest extent precisely between the 18th – 15th millennium BCE. Beginning from that period, the oracle-priests began to closely monitor the sky and calendar, laying the foundation of a chronology which was retained by the earliest chroniclers of Stone Grave; this then entered into the ethnogenesis of Aratta and the Slavs, who were the direct successors of old Aratta.

From the end of the 3rd millennium BCE the archive of Stone Grave was continuously supplemented by new records, drawings and such like; perhaps it is here that the creation of the Indo-European epic began (see earlier section). Later, whilst there were interruptions [in the records], the priestly tradition of this memorial was interrupted only during 7th – 10th centuries CE (B. D. Mykhailov, *The Petroglyphs of Stone Grave*, Zaporizhia-Moscow, 1999). This was the time when *The Veles Book* was last edited. It now appears, in the light of the above, to be perhaps the principal chronicle (after Shu-Nun, or Stone Grave) of the Indo-European community – the period of its final dissolution into the presently known nations.

2. The Middle Stone Age/Mesolithic era

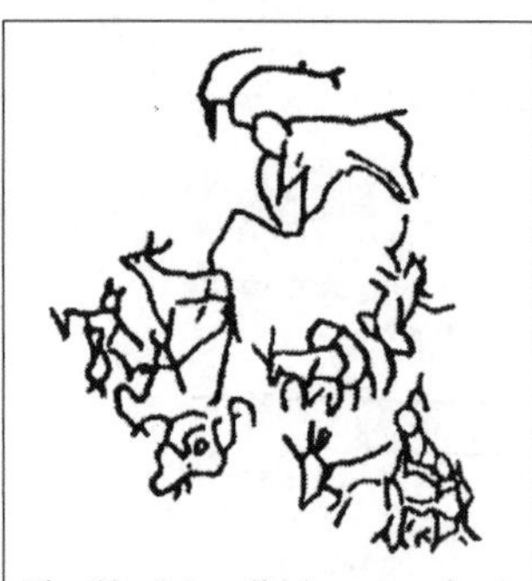

Fig.69 : Mesolithic petroglyph from Stone Grave.

The Palaeolithic was superseded by the Mesolithic, the epoch of the 'Middle Stone Age' in the 12th – 9th millennium BCE, when three branches of 'Eurasian-Svidertians' (according to Safronov and Nikolaeva) diverged from the Carpathians to the Urals, Crimea and even as far as Sinai. What traces did this leave in the folk memory of Slavs (at that time still ***proto-Slavs***)?

Although there is no clear chronology of existing evidence for the culture of the nomadic hunter-archers, the celestial deer, the world tree and the Pre-egg (which V. A. Safronov and N. A. Nikolayeva trace from the 'early Stone Age'), researchers do point out unmistakable bench-marks. We shall take the start of the chronicle of Stone Grave, deciphered by A. G. Kifishin, and try to compare it with Slavic folklore. The example just examined of Ishkur-Iasi-Yashcher-Yasha testified to the prospect and reliability of this course.

There is a noticeable dominance of female names amongst the deities revealed at Shu-Nun (Stone Grave) but masculine names amongst the rulers. So it was also in the sanctuaries of Çatal Höyük, where around 6,200 BCE the priests transferred a copy of the beginning of the chronicle of *The Law of the Empress*. One of the most effective goddesses was Inanna. She "throws the lot of fate" of Enlil, in particular, when he intemperately married Ninlil and was condemned by the gods to pass with his wife through the netherworld. These images and mythological subjects would later acquire more polish and development in Aratta and Sumer (as we have already touched upon). Amongst the Slavs, their tradition is connected with Divanna, Dana^ and others, as well as with the masculine names of Lel' and Lial'. We shall dwell here on the first, the most archaic of them.

Ya. F. Holovatsky considered Divanna the synonym of Dana – the bright goddess of waters – identifying her with the Greek Diana (though, to be more accurate, that should be with the Pelasgian Diana, and in time Etruscan and Roman Diana), reminding us in this case of the 'Scythian' origin of the latter. In reality the origin of D(iv)an(n)a reaches back to proto-Indo-European times, when the earliest cattle breeders of Transcarpathian^-Asia Minor origin occupied 'Jericho A' and gave – probably, at the same time – the name Io(Ia)r-dana, meaning 'Ardent river'. However, if we consider Divanna as Div-Anna or Div-(In)anna – 'Heavenly Sky (day)' or 'Venus of the (night) Sky', then those exceedingly archaic features, which are inherent to this mysterious goddess, become clear. She is an older goddess of heaven than her male hypostasis Anu who (according to the beginning of the chronicles of Stone Grave and Çatal Höyük) was convicted to penalty of death by Foremother Gatumdug.

The Polish Dziewana, being a goddess of forests and hunting, explicitly resembles Diana (with respect to Iasi and Iasion considered above); in this case the deer of

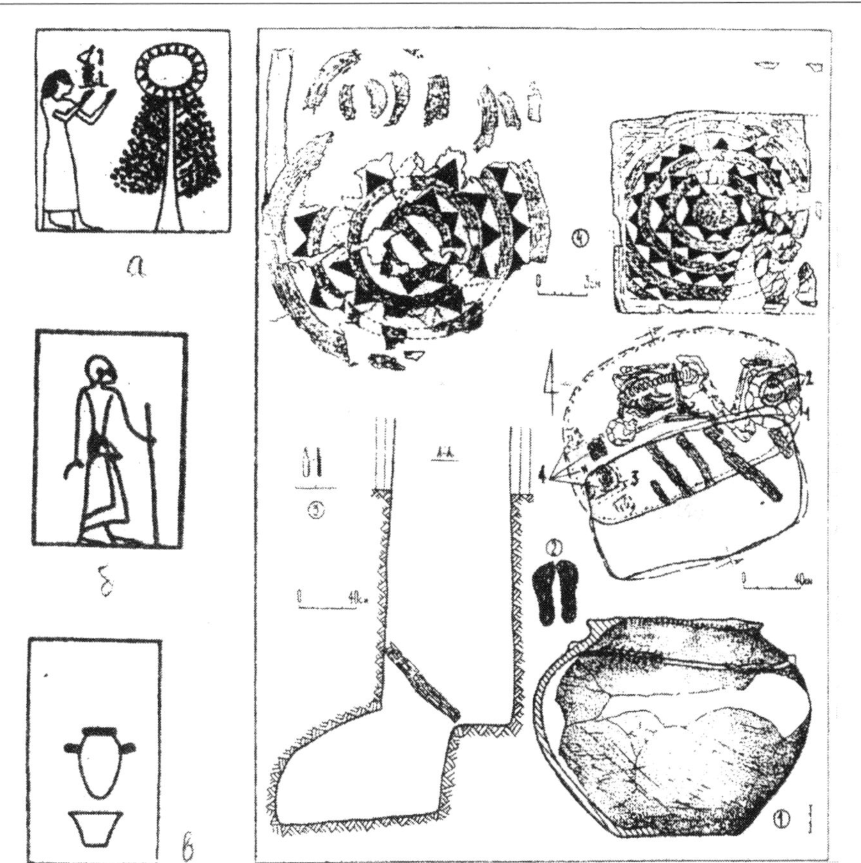

Fig. 70 : **Entombment of Catacomb culture** (burial No. 2 of kurhan No. 1 at the village of Berestove in the Mariupol district of the Donetsk region) **with symbolic triple-stage convergences '(O)Zhivitelya'-Savitar** (Life Creator of netherworldly Sun) and correspondences to the ceremony in the Egyptian *Book of Two Paths* (E. A. Wallis Budge, *The Egyptian book of the Dead*, EKSMO, Moscow, 2004; pp. 454, 463, 414): a(*a*) – chapter LXIV "About ascension to the light in the netherworldly kingdom" which contains the image of the deceased before the Tree of Life, over which the Sun rises; b(*Б*) – chapter LXV-b "About ascension to the light and gaining power over enemies" is decorated by an image of the deceased with a staff; c(*B*) – chapter XXX-A "About how to defend the heart of the keeper of the house of the keeper of seal all right and victorious, from kidnap in the netherworldly kingdom" contains the image of the heart above the vase.

the latter exists as a sign not only of hunting in pre-cattle-raising times but also of the Mesolithic Zodiac (i.e. the 'procession of the animals' of the constellations), the memory of which was preserved in corresponding images of Slavic ornamentation. This should involve the traditional images of one or a pair of deer, together with symbols of a woman, a tree and a river. According to the opinion of M. Yankovich, the researcher of the most ancient zodiacal calendar, such figures signified "Deer near River" (known to us as the constellations of Ursa [Major], Cassiopeia and others, as well as the Milky Way) and "Doe with Fawn" (portrayed, in particular, in a cosmological composition found on a stela of Orianian times from kurhan I-3 near the village of Usativ, in the vicinity of Odessa), who were frequently pursued by "Hunters with Dogs" (i.e. Twins [Gemini], Orion and Dogs [Canis])...

This data is consistent with the thesis of Ya. F. Holovatsky that Divanna was "the most important of the female-water beings of the Slavs", though their origin was not aqueous, but celestial (the Milky Way and other bodies of the night sky which was, just like water, associated with the netherworld). She was, probably the principal heiress of 'palaeolithic Venus', and then of 'hunting pre-Artemis', or Diana whom V. M. Danylenko discovered on the above-mentioned stela. Considering ancient Greek and Aryan mythology in general, their close relationship with Sumer and Egypt was highlighted by Danylenko, Kifishin, Safronov and Nikolayeva; such a close relationship could have been formed during the 9th – 7th millennium BCE in the environment of the tribes of 'Eurasians' and 'Afrasians' who made contact at that time in the Middle East and together created a productive, stock-raising agricultural economy. In the same sense we should consider A. G. Kifishin's attention (*Ancient Sanctuary of Stone Grave*, Kyiv, 2001) being drawn to the profound similarity of the early Slavic calendar with the "subsequent Ancient Egyptian and Greek calendar systems", which passed through the calendar of Troy of Asia Minor in 2,600-2,000 BCE.

Irrespective of the evidence from the above researchers, M. I. Chumarna put forward a hypothesis for the presence of Egyptian parallels in the fairy-tale *The grandfather, grandmother and hen Riaba*". In this case, particular terms which referred to beliefs of Egyptians were emphasised: 'dee-dee' was human blood, which was considered an immortal substance, flowing from ancestors to descendants; 'ba' was the name of the eternal soul, and 'ra-ba' was the sun soul. To this, Chumarna even adds the Egyptian name of the pre-bird Gogotun, a water-fowl (which just like ducks, let out a cry, i.e. 'gogotat' in Slavic languages), but in laying the pre-egg-sun, it could precede 'Hen Riaba' in folklore.

No matter how we react to such an unusual fundamental understanding of this well-known fairy tale, deep parallels are indeed traced between the Egyptian and Ukrainian cultures. Take, for example, our pysanky [hand painted eggs] with their symbolism of solar arms ("rake", "swallows", etc.) or of club-staffs ("hatchets", "finches", etc.) and compare them with the similar symbols of Ra^('Sun')-bearer on the known image of the family of pharaoh Akhenaton. Moreover we have a calendar basis in both examples. It also exists in the mentioned fairy tale. Indeed, apart from the children's version, which ends with the promise of a hen laying "not a golden egg, but an ordinary one" (instead of being broken by a mouse), there still exist two complete versions. The Russian version (in collections by A. N. Afanasiev) tells us about "hen-*Tatary*", who laid an egg that was "colourful, sharp, bony and odd" – indicating the bad condition of its fundamental function. But there are also here, besides the four above-mentioned features, a stove, a house, a granddaughter, a woman making communion bread, a sexton, a bell-tower, a padre and a book – altogether 12 objects, dealing with the breaking of and the mourning for, the golden egg. There are nearly as many in the Ukrainian version, where their calendar-zodiacal content is more understandable: a thatched door, a green oak, a ram heading to water, a bloody creek, a wench with dishes, a priest's wife with a tub, and a priest with a long lock of hair. It is possible that in the Ukrainian version, veneration of the now forgotten 11-month calendar was preserved, which reached the Greeks of Attica, inherited from the Pelasgians, and is traced in archaeological memorials of Ukraine between the 3rd – 2nd millennium BCE. In any case, the cleaving of the golden egg is connected with the summer solstice[4] after which the days become shorter and the nights lengthen.

This fairy-tale is considered to share affinities with the Ukrainian custom to split three Great-Day (Easter) eggs on a cross at the 'seeing-off'[5] (of ancestors); in doing so, the host proclaims: "Pray, great-father, for the deceased persons of father, mother..." and so forth. The reference in the fairy-tale to the priest's haircut, in the form of the plait, which he sliced off with grief, is not a detail associated with Christian clergymen but very similar ti their pagan predecessors. Thus, Ya. F. Holovatsky notes, the social status of Slav priests was "designated by white clothes, with long hair, braided into a plait, etc."

3. The foundation of Aratta.

The state of Aratta was founded in 6,200 BCE when a relationship was established between the sanctuaries of Stone Grave and Çatal Höyük (which in those days, according to A. G. Kifishin, were called Shu-Nun and Shu-eden-na-Ki-dug respectively), and thus began the formation of the pre-Indo-European community and its nucleus, **pre-Slavdom**. That year also marked the boundary between the Mesolithic and Neolithic epochs. The 'New Stone Age' turned out to be short-lived and it flowed rather smoothly into the Eneolithic or 'Copper Age'. In Eastern Europe it began around the mid-6th or 5th millennium BCE, together with the so-called 'Trypillian archaeological culture' and in Central and Western Europe with the predecessors related to this apotheosis of Aratta. References to its earliest times, in the Danube area, are evidenced by veneration of the Danube as the river of the ancestors. Veneration of Divanna continued though her subsequent manifestation hides away behind names like (H)Anna, Panna ('Sovereign'), Iva and others – as sung in the song *Hanna's mummy gathered the community*:

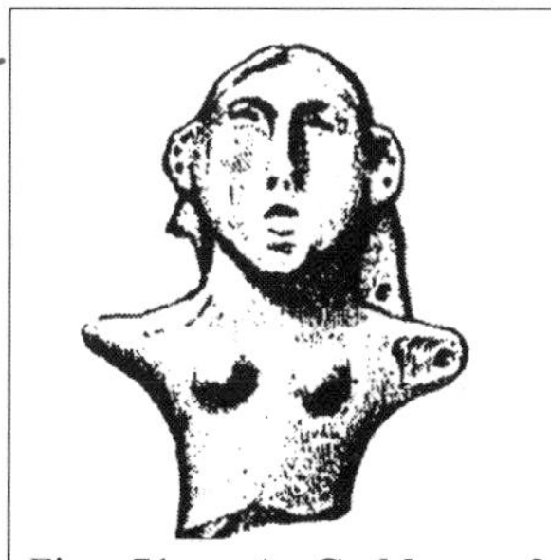

Fig. 71 : **A Goddess of Aratta**. Fragment of a female figurine of late Trypillian culture.

... Do not catch, people, fish in the Danube
That fish in the Danube – that is Hanna's body;
Do not mow, people, on the meadows of grass,
That [grass] *on the meadows – that is Hanna's plait...,*

Prof. A. A. Potebnia mentioned this song as an example of the unity of man connected with nature, in this case, not only with a 'drowned girl' but also with the annual-calendar sinking of Kupala Morana^ (the opposite of Zhivana< Divanna).

From the Song of Hanna, Hanna-Panna is connected with a Ukrainian version of the fairy-tale of the *Golden Slipper*:

Mother was dying. And in dying she called to her daughter and said: Take this, daughter, this grain/seed and tell no-one that you have it. And as misfortune comes to you, plant it... So, she took it, planted it on a meadow, watered it and then she sat down and cried again. She cried, cried and fell asleep. When she awoke, a beautiful willow had already grown from that grain/seed; under the willow was a well, and the water in it was cold and clean, like a tear. The maiden approached the willow and said: Willow light, be opened! Hanna-panna comes...

The companion of the Pelasgian-Greek Diana was known as Verbio who was connected, unquestionably, with the Ukrainian 'verba' (meaning 'white willow'). Amongst the Indo-Europeans this tree was called iva [willow] (likewise named by the Hittites, and even now the Russians call it 'iva') and it was the most widespread embodiment of the World Tree of Life. The virgin Iva[6] in the fairy-tale *Lame Duck* is called the virgin-duck, linking together the forest, water, nest and home, with spindle and heaven. Flying overhead to paradise, the flocks of ducks call:

Over there is our Diva[7] [Divine],
Over there is our Iva [Willow] ...
Let us throw down a feather,
Let it fly with us!

M. Chumarna justly supposes that *Ivan* of Slavic folklore is the masculine hypostasis of *iva*-willow (willow-white), and in our opinion, its wider meaning is a more diverse form of Verbio of the Orianians and Pelasgians. These deities of the summer (or spring, because summer did not exist in the calendar of early Indo-Europeans), may have been solsticial, and could give meaning to the Sanskrit *Yuvan*, or later *Yuval* ('Youthful', being the essence and epithets of both Krishna-Gopala and Apollo Targelia). In any case, the relationship of Ivan Kupala^ and Morana with trees is entirely evident. "The tree of Kupala" was burnt at dawn and the "branches of Morena" were cast in the river... The relationship of Ivan with the Tree of Life also appears in fairy-tales, for example, in the *Tree up to the sky*:

Once a ruler dozed off in the garden and dreamed to himself, that in that day, when a terrible storm passed, there was a seven-headed serpent in a cloud. It grasped his daughter and carried her to the top of a high tree... Ivan examined the tree and drove in an axe, then drew it out and drove it in again above his head. Thus he rose higher and higher...

In general, ethnologists know that the image of the Tree is more ancient than that of the Mountain. And in the culture of eastern Slavs, who preserved early traditions better than other Indo-Europeans, the time and circumstances of this replacement is well fixed. An initial bench-mark for this can be the basis of the well-known Ukrainian kolyada^. The next bench-mark is the chronicle of Shu-Nun. Thus:

When there was no light from anything,
Then there was neither sky, nor Earth,
There was only blue sea,
And amid the sea a green sycamore.
In this sycamore were three pigeons,
Three pigeons council confer,
Council confer, how to establish the world:
– Let us go down to the bottom of the sea,
And we shall reach fine sand,
Fine sand we shall sow:
And to us this will become black earth.
And let us get there the golden stone,
Golden stone we shall sow:
And this will give us the clear sky,
Clear sky, bright sun,
Bright sun, clear moon,
Clear moon, clear summer lightning,
Clear summer lightning, fine stars.

According to the mytho-historical chronicle of Shu-Nun of the Dnipro area, and to the pre-Sumerian tablets of the Danube area of Aratta, one should look to a time somewhere in 7th millennium BCE for the origins of the Red Hill^ spring festival inherent to Slavdom (and even some other European nations) with its Lel', Lial' and 'Polel' who are inter-related with En-lil Kur-gal[8], his wife Ninlil and son Nanna. *The Veles Book* (board 7a) makes no mention of this and links the appearance of the festival with Carpathian Ruskolan [Rusy land] in the 1st millennium BCE.

Red Hill is celebrated at the beginning of May, on the eve of Rahman Great Day^ and Yuri Day^. The first of them is connected with veneration of the wise ancestors and the netherworld but the second is connected with agriculture and cattle breeding. When celebrating Red Hill (where memories of the world Tree of Life are apparent) a "Burial"-kurhan, artificial mound, was usually selected as the site for festivities. It was considered that the male spirits of the mountains gathered on such mounds, whereas on the Bald mountains they were principally female. This division happened after the appearance of Enlil Kur-gal in Oriana (the coastal part of advanced Aratta) in the 3rd millennium BCE. Kurhans with patriarchal burials arose but the maidans (sanctuary-observatories), inherent to matriarchal Aratta, still existed.

The principals taking part in the celebration of Red Hill[9] are pairs of boys and girls who are called 'Red maiden' and 'Grief-Grief mound' or Vorotar [The Gatekeeper of

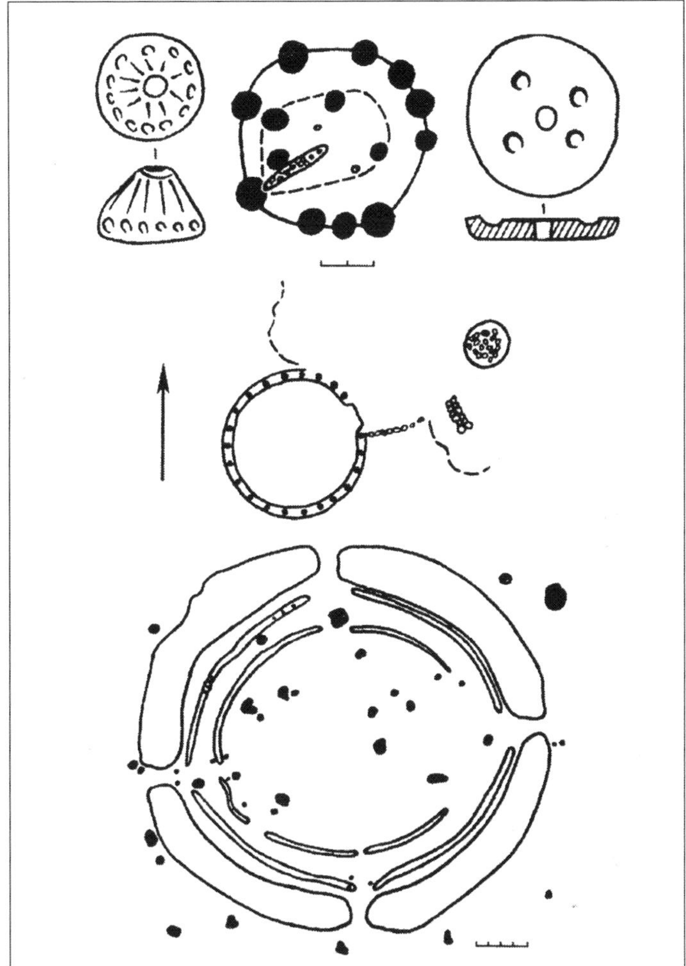

Fig. 72 : **Sanctuary-observatories of the Indo-Europeans from the 4th–2nd millennium BCE.** From top to bottom: archaeological cultures of Tshinets (near Pustynka in the middle Dnipro), north-Caucasian (near Stepanokert), and Lendel (Fribritz, southern Austria).

waters]. A girl who personifies Lel' (Lial') is seated on a stump/mound or other elevation, she is decorated with flowers and endowed with wreaths, Easter eggs and dairy treats. The players give themselves communion by consuming this food in memory of the ancient cattle breeders and the maidens take the wreaths and carry the branches and flowers to the river.

Researchers – in particular, Ukrainian I. Nechuy-Levytsky – long ago came to the conclusion that Slavic Vratar (or Vorotar, Vorot, Vyrva) signified the "alternative name of the ancient evil god Vritra from the Veda" [who held back the waters of the earth]. The ceremony of Red Hill not only reveals many correspondences with the main mythological ritual of the *Rigveda* but also that it is based on the Indo-Aryan *Ramayana* with the cult of Krishna Gopala and others (see the analysis of the fairy-tale of *Princess Olenka and her brother Ivan*). Furthermore, this Slavic festival (known in other nations of Europe, as disclosed by J. Fraser and O. Voropay), turns out to be even more ancient and may actually be the starting point for the two named epics/epos of Indo-Aryan culture [i.e. the *Rigveda* and *Ramayama*], which are reputed to be the earliest in Hinduism. Thus, as already stated, at the core of the mound at Red Hill celebration is revealed the prototype mound at Shu-Nun, Stone Grave, with its Enlil of the 7th – 4th millennium BCE.

It is necessary here to understand Lel' of the Red Hill-mound as a descendant of Aratta and later of the Sumerian Enlil *Kur-gal* – 'The wavering wind of the large Mountain'. The name of this creator-God appeared for the first time in Shu-Nun, just like the myths describing the wandering of Enlil in the netherworld in search of his consort Ninlil. According to subsequent Sumerian myths, the mountain Kian [Earth-Sky] was raised up from the first waters of Akiana (eventually became Oceana/Okeanos of the Pelasgians and Greeks). Enlil, who was conceived within it, divided it into mother-'Earth' Ki and father-'Sky' Anu. Later, Enlil sailed on a ship to the netherworld from where he carried away a hoe or plough for the people. An echo of this mythology is widely presented in Slavic folklore and even in the ornamentations of the Moon and Sun (or World Tree) there are similarities to the cross formed by a boat with a mast – even up to the crosses on crescents that are placed above [Orthodox] church domes.

In order to better understand the role of Enlil, it is necessary to read the conclusions of V. Schmidt, in his *Lectures on Semitic Religion* (Cambridge, 1927), in which he indicated the artificial origin of the name of biblical creator-God Eloya or Elohim (also related, apparently, to Illoen or Ill-as of the Pelasgians-Trojans-Etruscans) whose name was actually derived from Sumerian-Babylonian Enlil. A. G. Kifishin, in the works *"The Terrible Wrath of Gods"* and the *"Exodus of people"* (in the collection: *Zhertvoprinoshenie* [Sacrifice], Moscow, 2000), has essentially taken this back even further following his analysis of some texts at Shu-Nun (Stone Grave), indicating it as the primary source of that data in the libraries of Sumer, Babylon and Assyria which (or rather, the latter of which) was taken advantage of by the compilers of the Bible [i.e. in captivity in Assyria, they first learned of this history which they later used to compile The Bible].

Kifishin considers that corresponding inscriptions and images at Stone Grave from the 7th – 5th millennium BCE relate to the Buh-Dniester archaeological culture, which V. M. Danylenko and others considered to be the forerunner of the Trypillian culture. From the very beginning, this apotheosis of Aratta was inherent to the veneration of images of the goddess-foremother and the bull Taurus. The latter could be called (T)Uras(h) – the name of this celestial god appears amongst inscriptions of the pre-Danubian Keresh culture from as early as the 6th millennium BCE.

In the northern regions of modern Russia there was still a practise, a memory of the calendar-zodiacal change from the Mesolithic Deer to the Neolithic Bull, which occurred about 4,400 BCE. Thus, after the summer solstice and Petrovka'^ festivals, large bulls were slaughtered near churches, with the story reading... "in the past two deer came to our church and it was said that only one should be taken for slaughter and the second to be released". This episode was immortalised in detailed embroidered motifs on old table linen where the following symbols were arranged within a 'calendar' border: the rhombus (symbol of fertility), below which is a gravid-goddess was surrounded by two fawns, above which are a pair of deer either side of a sacrificial altar that has a cross and a bull. When the Church forbade this profane celebration in the 17th century, hundreds of similar table cloths had been used by painters for priming the under-side of icons – where they were fortuitously preserved for science.

Suggested reading

1. *The Veles Book*, Translation and comments by Yatsenko B. A., Kyiv, 1995, 2001.
2. *Ukrainian Popular Fairy-Tales*, Kyiv-Irpin, 1996.
3. *Zolotoslov. Poetic Cosmos of Ancient Rus*. Original introduction and translation by Moskalenko M., Kyiv, 1988.
4. *The Descriptions of Ancient-Slav Legends or Mythology*, Originator Holovatsky I. F., Kyiv, 1991.
5. Chumarna M. A., *From the Beginning of the World*, Lviv, 1996.
6. Rybakov B. A., *Paganism of Ancient Slavs*, Moscow, 1981.
7. Nikolayev N. A. and Safronov V. A., *Beginnings of Slav and Eurasian Mythology*, Moscow, 1999.

8. Mykhailov B. D., *The Petroglyphs of Stone Grave*, Zaporizhye-Moscow, 1999.
9. Kifishin A. G., *Ancient Sanctuary of Stone Grave. The expertise of the decipherment of the Proto-Sumerian archive of XII-III thousand BCE*, Kyiv, 2001.

---

[1] The ancient Slavic word "t'ma" means 10,000 years.

[2] The Russian word 'градиев' (gradiev) translates as 'castles', i.e. a fortified enclosure (cf. Stalin*grad* and Lenin*grad*) but the Slavic word 'град' (grad/hrad) refers to somewhere that is fenced and thus different from the surrounding environment, i.e. in ancient times it was a defensive settlement.

[3] This phrase in Ukrainian means 'mother Il(ma)'.

[4] In the original Russian text the literal meaning of solstice [сонцеворотом] is 'sun gets back'.

[5] Velykden eggs are also put on the graves of parents during "Babski Velykden", in symbolism of revival which, with consent of the church, is called the 'Seeing-off' (of the souls of the departed). (Ref. Shilov, 2008, *Sources of Slavic Civilisation, Part II: The Vedantic Heritage of Ukraine.*

[6] The Russian word here, 'Ивою', translates as 'Willow' which is the same as/meaning of the forename 'Iva'.

[7] Di(e)v(a) – 'Day', 'Sky' (explicitly) in male and female guises; the supreme Indo-European deity, epithet of Shiva and some other gods. It forms the root of the name for Devich-mountains and such like.

[8] 'Kur-gal' was an epithet of Enlil which, in Sumerian, means 'great mountain' and from which the word 'kurhan/kurgan' was probably derived.

[9] Red Hill festival is held outdoors in early Spring. Originally the purpose of the performances was to persuade the mysterious forces of nature to provide a bountiful harvest and happy life but the magical connection behind the songs was eventually forgotten to become merely entertainment. The *vesnianky* [Spring songs] season opened as a rule with a farewell to winter, often marked by the first sighting of migratory birds, and the hope of spring rains. A straw or wooden image of winter was put into/drowned in the water to the singing of *vesnianky.* Then spring, personified by a girl, a Red Maid wearing a flower and verbiage wreath, was welcomed with ritual ['crane' ring- circle] dances. The oldest *vesnianky* are those associated with ritual plant growth and farm work and behaviour of birds with bird-shaped bread tossed into the air to represent birds in flight.. [Some *vesnianky* such as Dunai, Vorotar and Mosty are said to have originated in Western Europe and were brought to Ukraine]. This festival also included/honoured the dead who were believed to return to participate - hence the reason for siting this festival on a burial mound etc. It is conjectured that this is may explain the ancient name of the young men which translates as 'Grief-grief mound' - personifying the grief for souls of ancestors in the kurhan. Wreaths and flowers are taken to the water afterwards - water is an important motif and the end of the season includes a celebration of Mermaids, perhaps in the sense of water spirits or 'spirit of the water'?].

CHAPTER 8

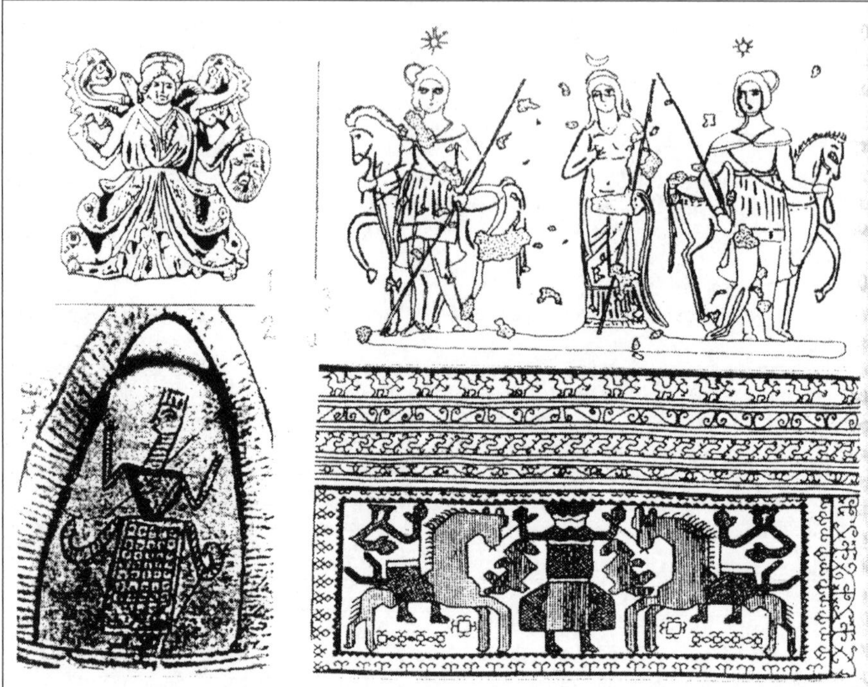

Fig. 73 : **Images of the Foremother in mythologies of the Aryan peoples of Aratto-"Hyperborean" origin**. 1 – Golden platelet from a Kul-Oba kurhan, 4th century BCE: Scythian Goddess Api, "serpent-legged virgin" – Progenitress of the Scythians, of Gelon, Agathirs, Scythe (according to Herodotus); 2 – a similar. image on an ancient Greek vessel from early 1st millennium BCE; 3 – Etruscan-Roman Dana[1] and Dioscuri; 4 – Rusy embroidery: Makosh and equestrian women with ploughs greeting arrival of spring (according to B. A. Rybakov)

FROM ARATTA TO HYPERBOREA

Immediately after the "Trypillian archaeological culture" was discovered in 1893 by V. V. Khvoika, [a Czech national], at the village of Trypillia near Kyiv, an idea took shape (and not only from Khvoika) concerning the relationship between this culture, the Aryans and the origins of Ukrainians. At the same time, similarities were noticed between the bright, dynamic decor of Trypillian ceramics with similar ornamentation on Ukrainian bowls, on traditional decorated eggs [i.e. pysanky eggs decorated with special designs for Easter] and even embroidered motifs on traditional tunics!

In the century that followed, the conditional name of this Trypillian archaeological culture began to be replaced with the autonym *Aratta*, discovered in 1990-1992 by A. G. Kifishin and Yu. Shilov. References to this discovery were included in the recently published monographs *Slavic Runes and the "Boyan Hymn"* (Moscow, 2000) by A. I. Asov and in *Veneti, Ancestors of the Slavs* (Moscow, 2000) by P. V. Tulaev. Here it should be borne in mind that the pre-Indo-Europeans, in addition to the immigrants from Asia Minor and the autochthonous north-western Black Sea area, also shared the social status of Aratta.

Throughout the period of the 7th – 5th millennium BCE, Aratta was, in a similar manner, the common ancestor not only of the Slavs but also of all other Indo-European people. However, with the proliferation of immigrants from the ancestral home of Asia

Minor into Europe, the second wave of immigrants (of the Vinca and Lendel archaeological cultures and those who followed them), developed an Indo-European community of more discrete character. This second wave of migrants was more closely associated with the wider genealogy of Italic, Celtic, and German tribes, whereas the carriers of the first wave (of Aratta), having concentrated on settling the right bank of the Dnipro, generated the ancestors of Slavs, Sumerians, Aryans, and Pelasgians. The descendants of both waves were initially separated then subsequently united – and not only at the borders of the Indo-European world. Indeed, along the Circum-Pontic zone there were other wandering groups – Ugrians^, Hurrians, Kartvelians^ and Semites; groups of Indo-Europeans also migrated into their zones. So, the world of tribes seethed, rather like a chemical reaction.

Comparing data gleaned from archaeology, linguistics and ethnology, it is now possible to trace that late Aratta – its territory extending to northern Borusia and southern Oriana – was predominantly 'owned' by the Slavs and Pelasgians.

Supporters of the work of B. A. Rybakov and O. N. Trubachev now put an origin date for the Slavs (proto-Slavs) at the 3rd millennium BCE. Even though the pre-Slavic Tshinets archaeological culture is considered to be 1500-1200 BCE, the fact that the culture appeared from the Mid-Dnipro area and the latter appeared from the northern part of Trypillia, is not developed by academic science. The problem of the origin of the Pelasgians from (the southern part of) Trypillia was neither investigated nor touched upon by A. I. Sobolevski and N. Y. Marr (S*elected Works*, Moscow-Leningrad, 1935). The latter territory, from between the 3rd – 2nd millennium BCE, clearly began to be divided between the ancestors of the Thracians, Veneti, Etruscans, and Greeks and this process began in the Northern Black Sea area, in interactions with the Slavs from the northern part of Trypillia (namely Aratta).

At the same time, a significant role in the ethnogenesis of Slavs was played by the neighbours of Arattans and Pelasgians – the Aryans. This issue is considered in the following sections.

1. The Arattan stratum of Pre-Slavic culture.

The materials which can be connected with the Trypillian archaeological culture are summarised in monographs by B. A. Rybakov *Paganism of Ancient Slavs* (Moscow, 1981), G. S. Lozko *Ukrainian Paganism* (Kyiv, 1994), and M. I. Chumarna *From the Beginning of Light* (Lviv, 1996). In fact, these sources contain much more – even including a list of the range of agricultural plants and animals, language, traditional industries and work implements, arrangements of dwellings and way of life, etc. – but such clarification of ethno-historical connections requires long and laborious work by many scientific specialists.

Fig. 74 : **Arattan cross.** The cross connection of the cultic "binocular" vessel of Trypillian archaeological culture.

We shall pause at Professor Rybakov's idea that the Trypillian heritage in Slavic culture is, primarily, based on "an ancient matriarchal faith concerning two women/maidens, one a birth-mother; two female [goddess] custodians of the world (who appeared at a time when society was based on hunting, lasting until the times when an agricultural society was developed)". When he wrote those words, this researcher didn't yet know about the pre-Sumerian inscriptions from the Danube and Dnipro areas (i.e. he was unaware of the pre-Trypillian origin of Gatumdug and Inanna [later Ishtar, Babylonian goddess of love]) which is why he inserted the names of Creto-Mycenaean (i.e. Pelasgian) goddesses, Ma-Divia, Hera, Rato (Lato, Latona, Leta), Artemis, Erinia, Hestia, Eleusia[1] (Demeter?) between the unfamiliar names of 'Trypillian' goddesses and the more familiar names of goddesses of the Slavic pantheon. In this case, after A. F. Losev et al., they distinguished Leta and Artemis as the earliest mother and daughter pair after comparing them with the birth-mothers listed above. Rybakov identified Rato–Leta–Latona with Slavic Lada, and Artemis with Tauridian

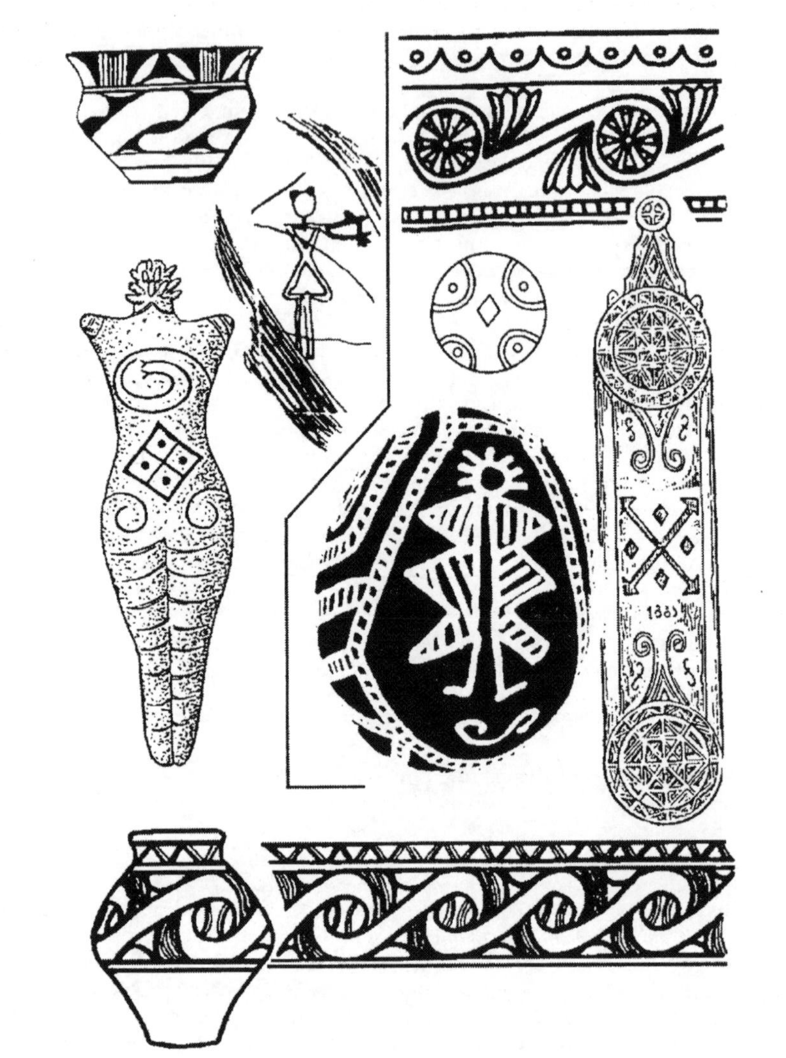

Fig.75 : Ornaments of Aratta, as well as of Ukraine and modern Russia (upper right).

Virgo, connecting this pair after reading an account by Herodotus, describing the self-sacrifice of two pairings of Hyperborean^ women and girls, at the temple of Artemis on the isle of Delos. Instead of regarding this latter goddess, Artemis, as the earliest, we find she has an Aratto-Pelasgian name, an even earlier forerunner, in Divanna-Diana, who frequently appears in Slavic folklore as "Panna".

Correspondence between figurines and housewares associated with Trypillian culture and within Ukrainian ethnography, is not confined solely to ornamentation; there are also examples of specific relationships within folklore traditions. Thus, serpent-like images on the female figurines and other such embodiments of the Arattan Mother-Goddess [Serpent Goddess] find a correspondence in the lyrics of this maidenly song:

Guelder rose-raspberry, a berry dark red!
Oh, I take a flower, serpent takes a hand...
Darling[2] came, and took off the serpent from me.

Guelder rose-raspberry, a berry dark red!

It is possible that Trypillian figurines were specifically used as sacrifices in funereal and other ceremonies, as were the cultic "binocular vessels" that are mentioned in an incantation from the fairy-tale *Princess Olenka and her brother Ivanko*, whose names carry a hint of Divanna-Diana with deer and the Willow tree [Iva].

When hiding after her sinful marriage with Ivanko, the girl thrice applies to Mother-Earth:

You, bells, begin to ring,
you, dolls, begin to sing,
you, Earth, open –
Let me enter into you!

Having found there, in the netherworld, her 'double' in matrimony to Ivanko, Olenka comes out from under the Earth with these words: "... *open – and release me into white light*"...

M. I. Chumarna correctly points out the relationship between Olenka and Ivanko with the considerably older characters, Lialia and Lel', as well as with the Indo-Aryan Sita and Rama. But unlike Olenka, who, conquers the serpent of the netherworld with the aid of a female friend, Sita is taken by the Mother-'Earth' Prithvi who, in that instant, had risen from the netherworld upon a throne of serpents. The correspondence with other such composites – a figurine of the mother-goddess on a throne entwined by a serpent-husband (perhaps connected to the fairy-tale in which Olenka is named "Princess"?) – is also present in the Trypillian culture, as well as in folklore:

Sit, sit, Yashcher,
Lado, Lado!
On a golden chair,
gnaw, gnaw, Yashcher,
a nut grain,
even that is small,
it's too small, it's not enough!
Catch, catch, Yashcher,
A beautiful girl,
the best from the best!

Here is the explicit motive for the sacrifice of the girl to the serpent (in this instance from reminiscences of Mammoth–Yashcher-Yasha), that characterises tales from almost all Indo-European nations. With reference to the previously stated observations of M. I. Chumarna concerning the necessity for the hero-fighter of the serpent to take a wife – it is enlightening to refer to an article by F. B. J. Kuiper "Cosmogony and Conception: A Query" (in *History of Religions* 10, 99 (1970)), in which archetypes connected with "pre-natal memories" such as the moment of conception and formation of an embryo, are considered to be founded on similar mythologies. This article will be considered below.

Parallels with Indo-Aryan *Ramayana* not only draw on a common Indo-European archetype but also equate to a specific historical character. S. I. Nalyvayko, (*Secrets of Sanskrit Revealed*, Kyiv, 2000), devoted two articles to parallels between this epic poem and a Ukrainian folk tale. One article examined the Indian concept of *Svayamvara*^ and the archaic Ukrainian concept of *Svayba*, each connoted the concept of 'choice' during matriarchal times, when a girl herself carried out the selection of a husband. Accordingly, she also did the wooing. The second article closely examined events which occurred in the forest of Dandaka, where Rama and Sita lived in exile. The malicious Ravan, who owned the country of Lanka ('Leukomorie'^, *meadows at the seashore*), despatched a fine deer towards their hut, [seen through the window by Sita] which Rama then rushed to follow into the forest [leaving Sita unguarded] – which gave an opportunity to Ravan to abduct Sita[3].

The researcher points out consistencies with the practises of Vesnianky^ (in which the Sun-Mistress determines to catch the Winter-Deer) and with the ancient names of

Kamyshovy[4] Bay on the coast of south-west Crimea, as well as the north-west coast of the Sea of Azov (Dandaka and Lukomorie). It is also necessary to point out the 'calm and happy' Ramos tribe of antiquity and Ra(o)man-Kosh – the highest mountain of Crimea, through which the caravan route passed in the direction of Dandaka and Lukomorie and under which stood a Taurian sanctuary of the Maiden-Artemis (connected as already noted, with the Indo-Aryan cult of Siva). Sita's name meant '*furrow*', and '*plough-land*'. The sacrifice of bulls, possibly devoted to her, were found in a wide bed in the altar area near the sanctuaries excavated by archaeologists (N. G. and V. I. Novichenkov). Continuing the significance of tales concerning magic deer, A. A. Shchepynsky excavated two kurhans in the valley of the Salhyr river, dating from the cusp of 4th and 3rd millennium BCE, where unique sacrifices of deer dedicated to the Sun were revealed... Many coincidences, and moreover their complexity, flags up questions concerning the origin of the *Ramayana* in the Taurida region, precisely as outlined by S. I. Nalyvayko.

So, not only are the fore-mentioned materials of Slavic ethnography very old and rather complex, they are pre-Slavic. Together with Aratta, they were probably formed not later than, and in connection with, the Indo-Aryan *Ramayana* whose typology and subject precedes events in the *Mahabharata* (which according to Indian tradition was at the end of the 4th millennium BCE but according to the conclusions of the previous part of our book – took place a thousand years later).

2. Pre-Slavs and the appearance of Sumer and Oriana.

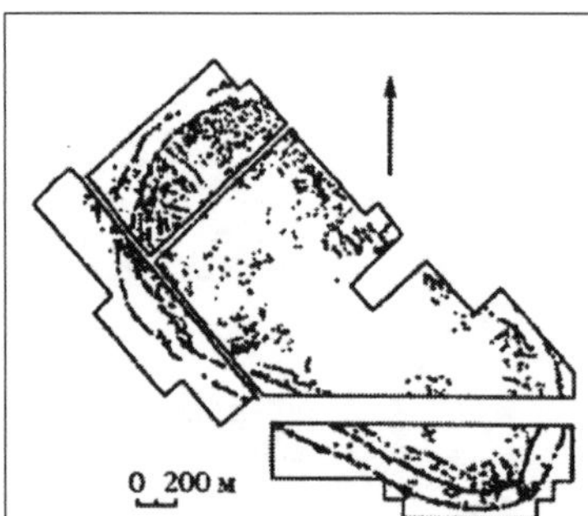

Fig. 76 : **'Talianky'- Capital of Buh-Dnipro Aratta** . Plan (print of the geophysical plan by V. P. Dudkin, from an aerial photo by K. V. Shishkin,) of the greatest city of Aratta-"Trypillia" between the 4th – 3rd millennium BCE situated on the site of the modern village of Talianky in the Talne district of Cherkasy region.

Aratta is recorded in the libraries of Sumer as their northern ancestral homeland. Despite the record of this name, those English and American researchers who speculated on the origin of the Sumerians from the Black Sea steppes, or even from the local Aryans, failed to mention the name of that mysterious country. The first conjecture was expressed by Kifishin, in a footnote to his article "*The Genostructure of Pre-Greek and Ancient-Greek Myth*" (in collected papers entitled *A Sense of Image in Ancient Art*, Moscow, 1990). When summarising proto-Sumerian inscriptions from the Danube area in established European scientific publications, the researcher's own translations of those inscriptions cited Aratta, suggesting that: "the Proto-Sumerian written language reappears in pre-Cucuteni and Trypillia (thereby linking Sumer with Aratta), and from there through Transcaucasia (Maikop^), it reached Sumer in the Uruk IV-III period". When these results reached Yu. Shilov – who had already published several articles (in 1988-1990) on the similarity between Sumerian myths and some images at Stone Grave and its surrounding kurhans – he met the Sumerologist A. G. Kifishin in Moscow in 1993, who pointed out that it was Stone Grave that had inspired his interpretation of its writing. (The honour of this discovery by Kifishin and Shilov was also shared with V. M. Danylenko and his student, B. D. Mykhailov).

The problem of identifying the primary cause of Mesopotamian Sumer becoming separated from the Dnipro area of Aratta during the second half of the 4th millennium BCE (with the possible extension of this date to mid-5th and even 6th milleniia BCE), was solved by Yu. Shilov who identified their [physical] separation – as a catastrophic consequence of the "World Flood" – causing the the Black Sea to become connected with the Mediterranean Sea thus flooding the connecting landmass. This solution accords with evidence from linguistic convergences in the Sumerian, Aryan and Slavic languages (according to the *Sumero–Aryan Dictionary* by L. A. Waddell, augmented by Ukrainian translations in *Maga Vira* by L. Silenko; it may be possible to achieve similar success with Russian and other Slavic translations). English and other Indo-European language examples go far beyond these three. Thus:-

Sumerian	Aryan (Sanskrit)	Ukrainian	English
ag	*agni*	*vohon*	*fire*
abba	*bap, tata*	*batko, otets*	*father*
ama, nana	*amba, matar*	*matir, mama, nenya*	*mother*
ara	*ara*	*ore, ralo*	*plough*
assa	*ashva*	*kin, losha*	*horse*
babi	*bgu*	*buty*	*to be*
bud	*bud*	*bida*	*trouble*
bal	*val*	*val*	*wall(earthen)*
bar 1	*vara*	*vorota*	*gate*
bar 2	*bratr*	*brat*	*brother*
bara	*vira*	*vira*	*faith*
barti	*bgarati*	*boyarynia*	*boyar's wife*
bi	*bis*	*biy, byty(sia)*	*fight*
bid	*vid, ved*	*vyd(ity)*	*to see*
bul	*bgal*	*bil*	*pain*
gari	*aria*	*harny*	*beautiful*
dara	*daru*	*dorohy*	*dear, expensive*
das	*dasa*	*dasy*	*give*
dimma	*tama*	*temno*	*dark*
dug	*dish*	*duma*	*thought*
dur	*drona*	*dur*	*bond*
dym	*dhama*	*dim*	*house, home*
egi, ikh	*ikh, iti*	*ity*	*to go*
khshati	*kshatri*	*koshevy*	*commander*
lil	*lel*	*liubov*	*love*
pad	*pitu*	*obid*	*lunch*
pi	*pa*	*pyty*	*to drink*
pur	*prohi*	*pravyi*	*right*

As this list suggests, in some instances the Ukrainian word-concepts turn out to be even closer to Sumerian than to Aryan-Sanskrit. Over the course of two millennia some of the Aryans moved to India, however, the Ukrainian ethnoculture remained autochthonous from pre-Aryan times, preceding the appearance of Sumer, and even Aratta. The Ukrainian-Sumerian convergences are therefore no fewer than the Sumerian-Aryan. It is also necessary to attribute number, linear measures and weights to the former; thus, the Sumerian '*tuzin*' (number 12) and '*kopa*' (60) are mirrored in the Ukrainian words and concepts of '*dozen*' and '*kopa*' (which is a measure of 60 sheaves of harvested grain); a '*mina*' (forerunner of a the silver Pelasgian-Greek coin) and '*mina*' (in Ukrainian '*minyaty, obmin*', which means 'exchange'); '*hin*' (length of 'elbow') and '*z-hyn*' (which in Ukrainian means the '*bend*' at the elbow); '*sah*' (the distance of separated hands) and '*sazhen*' (in Ukrainian); '*han* and *hon*' (60 or 120 sazhens)… **Such a fundamental relationship could only have arisen in the Dnipro area of Aratta–"Trypillia", at the start of the first formation of the Aryan community of tribes, close to its border, around the mid-4th millennium BCE, until it became separated from Sumer.** According to L. Silenko, **the name 'Sumer' would have originated from** Ukrainian 'Sumirny' (meaning to co-exist peacefully), though it could also derive from, the Vedic word Meru[5].

This hypothesis matches one of the Indo-Aryan myths which describes the origin of the Earth (according to L. N. Sternberg – V. M. Danylenko, *The Cosmogony of Primitive Society*, Kyiv, 1997; Moscow, 1999): "After the Great Flood, the Cosmic Ocean was formed, it was entirely covered by hardened marine foam. Stretched under the entire length of the Ocean was the Golden Toad, whose lively and animating soul was the Creator himself. When the moment arrived for the creation of the Earth, the Creator came from the bowels of a Turtle, adopted its own appearance, rose up and shot an arrow which pierced it right through. After this, the slain monster sank to the Ocean floor, forming the pedestal of the Earth and from its centre grew Mount Sumeru, containing all earthly riches." Danylenko quite justifiably compares the Creator with Vishnu – known in both Aratta and Arián (as evidenced in the footprint outline configuration of the settlement near the modern town of Talianky, as well as in kurhans at the village of Skvortsovka^ and others). In the first settlement – near the modern village of Usativ, in the territories of ancient Oriana – kurhans were also found with the forms of toads and turtles (according to V. G. Petrenko). However, considering the nature of that post-flood "hardened marine foam", it seems to be directly comparable to ice as in the winter freezing of the Azov and the northern coast of the Black Sea.

The names of some cities were probably transferred from Aratta to Sumer: Kyan, (the chronicled name of the "mother of cities of the Rusy" – subsequently Kyiv, the modern capital of Ukraine along with other comparable Slavic towns); Uma (city of Uman'); Kish (from 'Kosh' of Zaporizhia etc.) and Kutu (in Ukrainian 'khata' and 'kut', respectively meaning 'house/home' and 'corner'). Arattan-Aryan-Ukrainian convergences also appear in the social structure of Sumer. Its city-state of Ur was governed by a Council of Elders called the 'duma-Ur' (compare this to the Ukrainian '*dumny derzhavna rada*' and the Russian 'State Duma', '*Gosudarstvennaya Duma*') equipped with a 'lugal' (compare with Ukrainian 'nalygach' - 'whip'); they were all elected by a popular national assembly, called a Veche^.

Amongst the greatest cities in the world studied by archaeologists of that "post-flood" time of Aratta, the largest is located near the village of Talianky in the Talne district

Fig. 77 : **"Foot of Vishnu"** apparent in the small plan of the Arattan city near modern Talianky [right] and amongst the petroglyphs of Stone Grave.

of the Cherkasy^ region. According to data compiled from aerial photography and geomagnetic surveys, the city at Talianky bore the outline of a foot (Fig. 77) – perhaps that of Vishnu, the wandering-god. At Stone Grave [in Grotto 34] similar symbols [foot-shaped petroglyphs] saturate the stone slab called the "Footprints Plate", as well as symbols found on anthropomorphic stelas and graves from Aryan kurhans of the Northern Black Sea area.

The mythology behind "*The Steps of Vishnu*" is widely represented both in the Indo-Aryan *Rigveda*, and in *The Veles Book* of the Slavs (revealing a relationship between the Indian 'vis(sh)i-grammi' and the Old Rusy 'Vesi' with the meaning of 'hromada', i.e. community[6]) in Ukrainian. Vishnu is present within the Slavic custom of kolyadky^ with an undoubtedly Aratto-Aryan root:

From arising,
God Vishnu was born
He has walked the Earth
(and) produced us from the light.

Behind this Vedic myth stands the tale of the God Vishnu in which he annually creates or renews the world in three steps[7], with his third step being into the sacrificial fire. The origin of such myths lies in the periodic self-burning of the cities and villages of Aratta (the burning of the old site followed the construction of a new settlement on freshly-ploughed virgin soil); this custom was dictated by soil exhaustion (over three generations?) from over-working the fields and by the system of rotational (fallow) agriculture. This has already been commented upon. Here are the words from *The Veles Book* (board 19, 24c), which probably recorded that ancient tradition:

We pray to Patar Dyai that he will bring down fire,
*which Mother-Sva-Slava^* [Supreme Bird] *brought on her wings to our fore-fathers...*
They had in those times a state,
and in antiquity they had our Keloune ['General Meeting'],
and cities, and villages, old fire sites,
that created the earth...

It should be emphasised, as previously indicated, that Slavic-Indian correspondences precede the known migration of Aryans from the Dnipro area into Punjab in the middle of the 2nd millennium BCE, i.e. when the cultures of Mohenjo-daro and Harappa existed in the north-west of India, and which in fact related to Arattan ("Trypillian") realities from at least the 3rd (and even 4th – 5th millennium) BCE. The cultures of those Ukrainian and Indian tribes could be connected through the South-Siberian Okunev culture and North Chinese Yangshao^ culture. The possibility of this connection is noted by both Ukrainian and Indian archaeologists, based on telling insights concerning migrations of large groups of people, rather than small groups of priests such as the 'Hyperboreans' (see above). T. S. Passek in *Periodisation of Trypillian Settlements* (Moscow-Leningrad, 1949), for example, writes that amongst the ruins of the city of Harappa located in a province of Punjab, the platforms located there for processing grain are similar to those of Trypillia.

The flood at the time of the Sumerian patriarch Utnapishtim (whom the Akkadian-Babylonians renamed Ziusudra, and the Hebrews as Noah) also led to the appearance of Oriana (Orissa, Odissa, according to S. I. Nalyvayko) – a synthesis of the coastal parts of Aratta and Arián. The Orianian fleet became the first in the world, stimulating the development of astronomical knowledge[8] which was reflected in the development of many examples of Slavic ethnoculture. The ships also appear in the development of the image of the ancient Divanna-Panna in the kolyadka [carol] below:

Behind gates, behind grounds beyond the gates,
A pine tree stands there, clear from the silver,
fine from the gold.
And in that pine tree a ship is floating,
And in that ship is the well behaved Panna...

This motif agrees with another legend that is widespread in the Kyivan region concerning a Golden reed that grew from a seven-year old boy who fell into the water from the hands of a "princess on a golden boat". Other legends corresponding to this exist in the *Atharvaveda* (X: 7, 41). V. N. Guzi cites relevant geological data from the time of the appearance of the specified legend (5th millennium BCE) and attributes it to Trypillia.

It is not difficult to understand that in each of these folk tales, the images of the World Tree of Life and the Moon-ship are present (see the earlier mention of Enlil). This suggests that the kolyadky and the legend appeared during the times of lunar calendar supremacy – which, in the system of Maidans-"rotundas" (the sanctuary-observatories of Aratta) considered above, abruptly changed to a solar calendar at about 2300 BCE. At that time, the 'Sky'-Father of Indo-Europeans was personified as Dyaus-Pitar (Patar Dyai of *The Veles Book*), Mother-'Earth' as Mother Prithvi (Matyr-Sva-Slava, see earlier), and Telets/ Taurus as Urash (Yar-Tur). The parents of Lato/Leto (Lady/Lada) were at first considered to be the Titan Koios/Koeus/Coeus ('Kol' was the Pole Star) and the goddess Phoebe^ (Moon), whose sister was Asteria (the Ukrainian Haister or Pelasgian Hesperia was the planet 'Venus'). This calendar-celestial canon could have arisen at the same time as the appearance of the Arattan Maidans at the turn of the 5th – 4th millennium BCE. It is quite evident that the list of pre-Slavic and pre-Pelasgian gods mentioned above, are related. It is even possible to point to the ancient veneration of Uranus by both nations, a derivative of the more ancient Urash [sky god], also venerated by the Thracians,

Ha! Uran calls mother [Earth]:
Give, mother, the keys,
To unlock the sky –
To release Spring,
Girlish beauty!

The above refrain is sung in the Volyn area [north-western Ukraine] to accompany a circle dance called "*The Crooked Dance*". This Pre-Greek veneration of Uran(us) as the sky god and the primary lord of the Universe and Death certifies the Old-

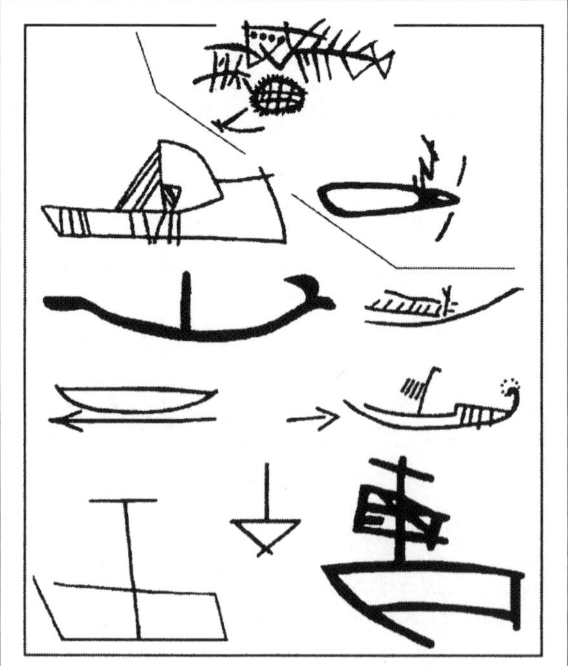

Fig. 78 : **Boats, arks and ships of 7th – 4th millennium BCE** portrayed at Stone Grave. By B. D. Mykhailov.

Rusy *Legend of the Mamai Slaughter* which begins with the words: "Tell this, Uran, how a battle happened on the Don". In those times, Lada was already regarded as the daughter of Perun (Varuna; Uran) and Lititsa, as well as the mother of Lel and Lelia.

The presence of images at Stone Grave, depicting Creto-Minoan-type ships from about 3000-1400 BCE (according to B. D. Mykhailov) has already been noted; a "solar barque", of a type inherent to Egypt, also exists there, as well as several images of arks (perhaps connected with the Deluge?). Furthermore, models of boats and rafts occur in the burial grounds of post-Mariupol culture, in the Yamna culture followed by burials in Aryan kurhans. Perhaps this is where their identification with the dead came from in Slavic 'Nava'^ (which were 'boats', the same meaning as other Indo-European languages). Ukrainians still mark the celebration of Navski^, or Mretski Great Day (from '*mrets*' which means 'deceased') in the Kherson region, they are sometimes identified with the Rahman Holiday [Rahmanski Velykden] (according to O. Voropay). However, these two events are consistently celebrated by most people, before and after the usual Great Day (Velykden^), a festival which the Church attached to the Judaic-Christian Easter. On Great Day everyone makes krashanky^ and pysanky^ eggs ("Easter eggs").

Amongst the hundreds of symbolic images painted onto Ukrainian Great Day pysanky (eggs) several (Navski, Rahmanski and others[9]) specifically stand out: i) the ornaments of the Buh-Dniester culture, even the Çatal Höyük Foremother (known as 'Berehynia'^ from the Kherson region and others) from temple 23/VII, that had been decorated with a duplicate chronicle from Stone Grave, dating to about 6200 years BCE; ii) Arattan motif of Mother-Daughter etc.; iii) motif's inherent to Orianian, Pelasgian, Creto-Mycenaean cultures (the 'waves of the Black Sea' and others); iv) Aryan designs (to which we shall return later). The presence of the first two types accord with the Sumerian commemoration of Great Day, during which eggs would be exchanged – probably, painted and decorated. We can assume their Arattan and Ukrainian relationship from the similarities in ceramic ornamentation etc.

3. The Common source/root of Slavs and Pelasgians.

The "World Flood" resulted in the growth of Sumer [now isolated as a discrete nation], occasioned by the influx of migrants stranded along the flooded coasts of the Pontic Region (i.e. the Black Sea). The flood stimulated migration from that area into all available habitable regions. In fact, in addition to that eastward migration [into Sumer], a movement to the West is also traced. The most obvious connections in this direction are Slavic-Pelasgian (which, in the magazine *Perekhod-IV* ['Transition'], Kyiv, No. 2(4) 2000, I. Kahanets, reasonably considers were directed towards Babylonia and Palestine). According to data from archaeology, linguistics and ethnology, the westward migration could have moved overland through the lower reaches of the Dniester and Danube to the Balkans and beyond – as well as by sea from ports of the Northern Black Sea coast. The most evident locations for investigation by researchers now are generally the ports at the mouths of the Dnipro and Buh, as well as the Kerch Strait.

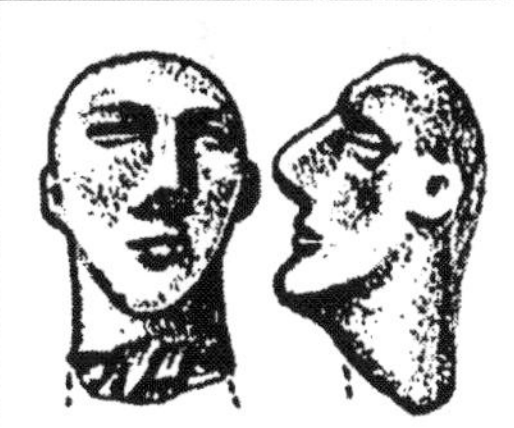

Fig. 79 : Fragment of a Trypillian figurine. Deity or inhabitant of Aratta?

We have already discussed the attraction of the closest descendants of the "Hyperborean Pelasgians" to the first of these areas: the rivers Borysthenous and Achelous, which subsequently became Borisfen and Achilles/Achillea, (these were Greek names for the rivers, they are now the Dnipro river and the Tendrov(ska) spit against the mouth of the Dniester river), which were well-known to mariners of antiquity. Ancient Greek settlements appeared there at the turn of the 8th – 7th centuries BCE and offer some of the earliest known archaeology of the Northern Black Sea coast. According to O. N. Trubachev, the names of Borysthenes [the old Greek name for the Dnipro] and Berezan^ island (a land spit at that time) opposite its mouth, arise from the Indo-Aryan name for 'High place' – Boru-stan

['stan' means 'camp']. In exploring the relationship of the Aryan community with the earliest Slavs, the researcher must pay attention to the similarity of this term with the mid-Dnipro concentration of Berestenoks. In the Middle Ages, the land of Berestei(ska) existed in the berest-tree forests ['*berest*' means 'birch'] – which was indeed, "high" [i.e. northerly] relative to to the earliest Slavs situated to the south of it.

It is necessary to thank O. N. Trubachev for his *Ethnogenesis and culture of earliest Slavs. Linguistic research* (Moscow, 1991) and for his derivation of the pre-Slavic language of the 3rd – 2nd millennium BCE directly from Indo-European, rather than from the intermediary Balto-Slavic stage of the breakup of Aryan unity. Such directness confirms our conclusion that the Slavs were identified with the Indo-European nucleus which was the state of Aratta. However, it isn't necessary to dwell here on research by representatives of academic science, which concerns Oriana and the beginnings of Pelasgia in the Northern Black Sea coast.

Evidence of Greek colonists on the shores of the Cimmerian Bosphorus (Kerch strait) have now been traced to no earlier than the turn of the 6th – 5th centuries BCE. If that is the case, why do Greek legends relating to this country reach back, as a minimum, to mid-2nd millennium BCE: the times of Atlantis and the Argonauts, of the Trojans Achilles and Odysseus? The fact that behind the strait – somewhere in Temarunda or Meotida [the Indo-Aryan name for the Sea of Azov: the 'foster-mother of the Black Sea' and the 'mother sea', according to Trubachev] – lay Aidas/Hades, the 'Unseen' astral light of the dead, with its hints of Pelasgian and Greek legends describing the "World Flood", from which most of the population of the flooded Meotida basin (i.e. Azov) had suffered. Perhaps, up until the time of the Flood, it was called Sumer ('Sumirny', according to L. Silenko), and over the 20 centuries following the relocation of Sumerians into Mesopotamia this name became

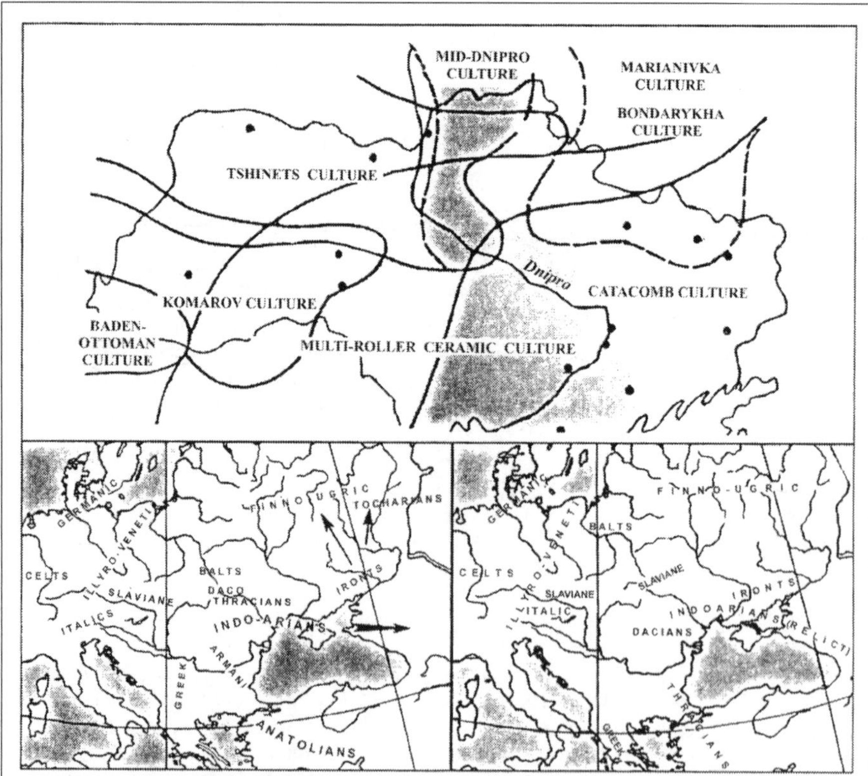

Fig. 80 : European **archaeological cultures** (according to A. A. Bilousko) **and ethnic groups** (according to O. N. Trubachev) **of 3rd – 2nd millennium BCE**, adjacent to the inner seas: Black, Azov, Baltic, Adriatic and Aegean.

Cimmeria (Sauvira, according to S. Nalyvayko) [i.e. Cimmer instead of Sumer], on the shores of the Bosphorus. It is indisputable that before the Flood, and then afterwards – modern Taman was called 'River' Sindic (Indic) and for a number of reasons was allied to the Scythian (S)Indic of the lower reaches of the Borysthenes/Borusthen [the old Greek name for the Dnipro river]. The first of these two, Sindic or Indic, was considered in Rus at that time as the ancestral birthplace of the Siver area (in the modern Chernihiv region). S. I. Nalyvayko showed their relationship with Aratta (seemingly the Punjabian Aratta, not the Aratta of the Dnipro area) - with the country of Sindhu-S(a)uvira of the *Mahabharata*. The Greeks pronounced the second name differently; in the *Iliad* it is called – Cimmeria [hard 's' sound i.e. Simmeria]... Thus, we have another sufficiently reliable site of ethno-historical connections, reaching the cusp of pre- and Indo-European communities.

Having a general basis in Aratta, the ancestors of the Slavs and the Pelasgians consistently gravitated to its northern and southern areas, to Borysthenia and Oriana; there were zones of overlap – these occurred in the Dnipro area and in the old Sindic, Kuban area. We are now interested in the allied relationship between these two Aryan ethnic groups, which came to nothing over the course of three 'post-flood' millennia in migrations and separations, and are now only notable to specialists and to the amateurs of ancient times. This thesis can be justified by the Pelasgian-Ukrainian dictionary, compiled by A. Popravko:

Pelasgian	**Ukrainian**	**English**
dvar	*dveri*	*door*
diviana	*divchina*	*girl*
domus	*dym*	*smoke*
gure	*hora* [10]	*mountain*
harazd	*harazd*	*all right* (good)
hnitus	*hnuty*	*bent*
italya (Italiya)	*telya*	*calf (cattle)*
khata,	*kut*	*house, corner*
kos	*kosyna*	*kerchief*
lib	*khlib*	*bread*
ostie	*ustia*	*estuary*
pagani	*pohany*	*pagan*
pan	*pan*	*gentleman* (Rus. mister)
pelanors	*palianytsia*	*loaf*
purni	*parubok*	*boy, lad, youth*
sankus	*sontse*	*sun*
sventinesa	*svitlonosnyi*	*plea/appeal*
sventinesa pan	*svitlonosny pan*	*appeal to the sun*
sestra	*sestra*	*sister*
skomrakh	*skomorokh* (musician)	*musician*
talan	*talan*	*talent*
tamas	*vtoma*	*tiredness*
teremnon	*terem*	*tower*
tulus	*tulub*	*trunk, torso*
turs	*tur*	*bull* (a type of auroch)
vlok	*vovk*	*wolf*
vraha	*voroh*	*enemy*
zautsas	*zayets*	*hare*
zheuna	*zhona*	*wife*
zhupanos	*zhupan*	(a type of jerkin worn in Ukraine and Poland)

The Pelasgian language is regarded as the earliest historic (written & attested) language of Europe. Meanwhile, Ukrainian and Russian[11], as we see (especially taking into account the above Sumero-Aryan-Ukrainian dictionary), are far from being in any way inferior to ancient Pelasgian – and indeed, still continue to thrive!

Let us now remember what happened in the second half of the 3rd millennium BCE, about a thousand years after the "World Flood", when new geo-cosmic catastrophes occurred, caused by a different planetary alignment, a change in solar activity and by climatic variations, etc. (according to M. Chmykhov et al.)

Until approximately 2300 BCE, the pre-Slavs, who formed the ethnocultural basis of Aratta, esteemed Diya, Mother of the world, the common ancestor for all Indo-Europeans (boards 19, 30 of *The Veles Book*, according to B. Yatsenko). However, after this date the lunar alignments of Arattan sanctuary-observatories [i.e. maidans] of the type at Kazarovychi (near Kyiv) and at Stonehenge (England) were replaced [altered] by solar alignments. In Arattan-Aryan mythology it is claimed of the zodiac deity Svarha/Svarga: '*He is going in the sky, the solar (path or way)*'. He corresponds to the Slavic Svaroh. Having noted their affinity, O. N. Trubachev neglected to take advantage of the unique opportunity to date not only the emergence of the Aryan-Slavic connections but also of Slavdom itself. This possibility is greatly strengthened by enlisting the material in the *The Veles Book*, as well as the fore-mentioned conclusions of A. G. Kifishin concerning the relationship of the Slavic calendar with the Egyptian, Trojan and Greek calendars.

So, Svaroh was the solar deity and zodiac who established a firm position in Indo-European cultures around 2300 BCE. His son Dazhboh has to be understood as the embodiment of Taurus – he fertilised the cow Zemuni-'Earth' and also fathered the 'bull-like' (Tau)Rus, thus creating the bloodline of the Kraventsy-'Korovychi', a term which means 'descended from a cow'[12]. Taurian admirers inter-related Svaroh and Dazhboh [as Sky and Sun deities, respectively] (*The Veles Book* 7f, 36b et al.) because Telets/Taurus headed the solar Zodiac between 4400-1700 years BCE, and the period between **2300-1700 BCE was the time of appearance of the Slavs.** *The Veles Book*, following other Indo-European deities, has Patar Dyai [Father] and Matar-Sva [Mother] (VB: 19, 29, 30) and maybe also the Aratto-Aryan Vishnu and Indra (VB: 30, 31), naming them, [and thus Svaroh and Dazhboh], as creators of both the Universe and their Slavic issue (VB: 15a, 1 et al.):

Fig. 81 : **The similarity of amulets with written symbols** from Sumer and Troy (at the bottom). By L. A. Waddell.

Svaroh who created light [this word also means world or Universe] –
this god of light and god of Prava, Yava and Nava ...
Because this Dazhbo created for us the egg, that is the light-star, radiant to us.
And in that abyss Dazhbo hung our Earth,
in order that it should be held...

The extremely archaic three-season calendar of *The Veles Book* (board 11 and 37a) was formed no later than during this period; it was also inherent to the earliest Indo-Europeans, making references to the calendric peculiarities of their maidans (sanctuary-observatories) which were mentioned earlier with regard to Aratta and Hyperborea:

So here we must defend ourselves from enemies who go from three ends of light, when celebrations approach us.
And those celebrations: first – Kolyada^, and second – Yar and Red Hill, and Ovsiena large and small.
Those celebrations proceed, as the husband goes from the city into the village of fire-keeping.
And by those lands the world goes from us to another and from another to us.

The proposal tendered is that this period, the period of adoption of Svaroh and Dazhboh, should to be regarded as marking the time for the full emergence of Slavic ethnoculture (rather than its sub-divisions of proto-, pre-); this is wholly confirmed by such lines from *The Veles Book* (board 36b, 24c,d):

There we are Sl(a)viany, because we sl(a)vim [i.e. glorify] *gods.*
And surely we are the grandsons of our gods Svaroh and Dazhboh.

We shall shortly specify the circumstances, time and place of the final confirmation of the ethnonym Sla(a)viane (i.e. Slavs).

L. I. Akimova also noticed that during Pelasgian times, the autonym of Slavs corresponded to the sense of "essence of glorious[13] maternal and paternal kin", and it was for their sake that Zeus contrived the Trojan War; "evidently, the Slavs had their ancestral home in that northern territory which would became the centre of creation for future 'Trojan history'". It's possible that precisely in the course of this tradition, medieval authors identified the Greek Apollo (patron of Troy) with Dazhboh and Khors of the Slavs. Furthermore, in the 14th century work, *The Word of St. Gregory concerning the first pagans who worshipped idols and placed religious rites for them,* there is a reference to 'Artemis' being associated with families and with women in childbirth and this association was retained by corresponding Ukrainian representations of the Pole star in Ursa Major, which associated Artemis with the ancient sanctuary-observatories.

Pagan-'nationalistic' self-consciousness is not only expressed in *The Veles Book* but also in the more recent (11th century) *Tale of Bygone Years^*; the latter stated that "in the time of the reign of Svaroh, tongs fell from heaven and people began to forge weapons. Before that clubs and stones had been used for fighting. Then Feosta^ [Egyptian Hephaestus of that time] established the law for wives: she was to restrain herself to marry a single husband... but if she broke the law, she had to be plunged in the stove of fire (because of this he [i.e. Feosta] is named Svaroh)". Dating the beginning of "the time of Svaroh" from here, the end of the Neolithic era, is debatable (except in the thickets of Polissia, north-west of modern Ukraine), nevertheless M. Chmykhov is nearer to the truth here than B. A. Rybakov. Chmykhov connected the appearance of Svaroh in this chronicle with the onset of the Copper Age (which really replaced the Neolithic era in 2300 BCE), and Rybakov connected him with the Iron Age. To a greater extent, the ecclesiastical author Nestor [*Tale of Bygone Years*] is closer to reality by stating that "the son of Svaroh, Sun Caesar, is Dazhboh", and he arose at the threshold of society, when "people began to pay tribute to leaders". It is appropriate to mention here the fairly well-reasoned idea by Yu. Petukhov and I. Kahanets (in *Transition-IV*, No. 2, Kyiv, 2000) that the biblical God S(a)baoth was derived from Slavic-Aryan Svaroh, and substituted for Semitic Yahweh in the reign of King David who was of Indo-European origin.

The period of "Pelasg^, the Hyperborean progenitor" has already been examined with reference to his nearest descendants: to Atlant, to the daughter of Hesperia^ who owned the island Ogygia opposite the mouth of the Danube, and also to King Ogyges – in whose era, at the end of the 3rd millennium BCE, the terrible deluge occurred. However, Atlant was the nephew of Pelasg, the grandson of Uranus[14] and the protector of Cronos (for which Zeus made him suffer when he released the Deucalion deluge around 1700 BCE). Some of these names, as well as their context, are familiar to Slavs: the female name Palazhka (Pelazgia), the god Uran, the calendar star Haister [Venus], as well as Plenka who is the mythical wife of Sviatohor. Sviatohor corresponds to Atlant (who was married to Pleiona); and both Sviatohor and Atlant are Svitovyd [the Slavic four-faced god] of *The Veles Book* (board 11a): "That god Prava [Heaven] and Yava [real life] will safeguard us from Nava [the world of death]";

he is holding earth and sun, and, our handsome stars.
And the strong world creates glory to great Svitovyd.

A. I. Asov records the tale of a blacksmith who predicted that Sviatohor – son of the 'Dark god', hero-Altyn – would wed the serpent-woman from the overseas kingdom of Altyn; which did indeed, came to pass. There is something notable here in common with the Pelasgian-Greek myths of Atlant and Herakles, except that instead of the apples of eternal life from the garden of Hesperides, guarded by the serpent Ladon, we find miraculous golden altyns [coins] and a serpent, who becomes Lado, 'wife' of the hero. It is possible to agree with Asov that "the hero Ilya Muromets^ came to replace the ancient Titan Sviatohor, as a giant-mountain, giant-element". Such replacement here, as we shall see now, is not essential. A similar change arises in the Finnish *Kalevala* (according to P. V. Tulaev) with Antero (mentioned in the previous chapter) who conquered the heroes Vainamoinen^ and Ilmarinen^.

It is worth comparing Ilya Muromets, and some aspects of the blacksmith Ilmarinen, not so much with Perun, the god of war and storm, as with the Pelasgian-Trojan-Etruscan-Rusy counterpart of Apollo – Illoen, or Illo-as. He was the forerunner, or even the embodiment of the sun god Helios – the patron of 'Solar' Ilium^-Troy with its Elena^ and invading Hellenes, as well as the city-state of Gelon/Holun^ in the area between the Dnipro and Don. A Trojan-Etruscan (namely Pelasgian) dedication such as "this was given to the god Illo" is entirely comprehensible even to contemporary Slavs. However, the consonance of the name of the hero Ilya Muromets (i.e. Aryan 'radiant hill' which, according to Trubachev, is comparable with Sviatohor,) [which means 'shining hill'] may be equated with mythical and biblical names: Il(o)ia(s)-thunderer was primordially Slavic, and the name of the Christian prophet Ilya [Elijah] was borrowed by Jews from the same environment as Atlant (son of Iapetus, one of whose descendants was Sim), as mentioned above as Japheth and Sim. The first, full name of the Slavic-Pelasgian deity of thunder could be Illoyas-Paion, or Ilyas-Paion (as Illoyas-Apollo was called in early Crete). Apollo was later included in the Slavic pantheon (VB: 38a), initially in a martial image as Kupalo. This agrees with *The Veles Book* (21):

That was Kupalo who came to us and spoke to us,
that we should become proud and clean by our bodies and souls.
And dropped to his feet,
so that he came to us and guarded us [when] *leading us to brutal battle,*
and so that there we turned faces to the heavens.

The *Altynska Land* and others, which A. I. Asov connected too closely with Atlantis and located between the Bosphorus and Dardanelles, requires clarification. Meanwhile it is necessary to consider the fluidity of the "popular etymology" (the changing sound and significance of words) resting not on an overseas Atlantis, but on coastal Biloberizhia beside the mouth of the native Buh-Dnipro estuary. There, in ancient times, (according to Dion Chrysostom of 1st – 2nd century) lay the fortress "Alektor which... belonged to the wife of the Sauromats king". O. N. Trubachev noticed a reference to this 'Amber' fortress on the islands of Tendra, or Berezan, in the *Golubina* [i.e. Pigeon] *book* (it relates to the *Ptnitsa*, according to Asov – a central part of the Slavic Veda):

To stones, stone is the mother
Karmaus' stone is Ilitor;
And it lies at the Warm sea,
*On the eastern mouth of the **Volhsky**;*
And if some fish from the sea will go,
And will rub itself against the stone,
*Then fishers in **Rus** will not catch that fish...*

The "Warm Sea" is the Black Sea; the spits of **Voloshska** and **Ruska** exist in that particular sea. The origins of the lines quoted above reach back to the time when the Veda was formed; a time when amber reached Troy from the sands of Borusthen, and when Rus esteemed the ***Volhvs-priests***^ and welcomed the ***Volokhy*** (Celts-Gauls, who were partly assimilated over time with the ethnogenies of Halychans, Moldavians and Romanians).

A. I. Asov even focused attention on the similarity between Sviatohor and Atlant in the tale of Prince Ivan, who took rejuvenating apples from a foreign giantess; and also on the closeness of Kashchey^ Tripetovich (from the bylina [heroic poem] about his struggle with Ivan Godinovich) to Triptolemos^ of the Hellenic(?) legend which relates how Triptolemos, together with Demeter, taught the Scythians agriculture. The researcher's doubt is caused only by the fact that this god arrived in Scythia on a chariot with winged serpents from the Greek city Eleusis; it follows, it seems, that it should have been from somewhere like Pelasgia or Hyperborea. But here it is necessary to know that the Pelasgian tribe of Elevsins - in agreement with Kifishin's commentary on Pauli-Vissova's *Encyclopaedia* - was very closely related to Atlant, giving issue to the the same Achilles and Ogygos connected with the mouths of the Dniester and Danube, as well as with the Ogygian Deluge in the second half of the 3rd millennium BCE, indicated above. Perhaps their autochthonous part did not enter into the ethnogenesis from Borysthenes and other "Scythian-Hellenics" (according to Herodotus)? And perhaps these Elevsins were reflected in the name Alector-Alatir-Ilitor (see earlier) who, in *The Agreement of Prince Ihor with the Byzantians*, was called Eleuferia? It is also necessary to note the conclusion by B. A. Rybakov concerning a relationship between old stories of Prince Ivan, Vasilisa-Wonderful and Immortal Kashchey – with Persephone, the daughter of Demeter, kidnapped by the god of the netherworld, Aides/Hades. (The location of Hades was, as we already know, situated

Fig. 82 : **Triptolemos, God of agriculture**, on a chariot with winged serpents. Image on an ancient vessel, 4th century BCE.

on the northern coast of the Black Sea or Sea of Azov). And very much in accord with Eleusinian Triptolemos [and] Rusy Kashchey Tripetovich who say to their horse: "It is possible to sow wheat, wait for the harvest, to make bread and eat until full – then ride in pursuit, and still manage to catch them" (to overtake runaways). In these words, according to Asov, the key to the fairy-tale hinges on the "ancient agricultural legend describing the dying and reviving grain", which personifies Immortal Kashchey; here, Vasilisa symbolises the transition of grain from sowing, to sprouting then ageing. We shall even add here: aren't these recollections a reflection of the banishment of the mythical "Pygmy people" and the real Scythian-ploughmen from the valley of the 'Crane of the (river) Kank'?

Russian folklore, rather than Ukrainian, indicates a greater closeness to the circle of Atlant: the second branch of Eastern Slavs was drawn much further into the western migration than the first.

In contrast, the Eastern Slavs – despite participation in the migrational movements of the 3rd –2nd millennium BCE and later times – had previously reserved for themselves the Arattan ancestral home of Indo-European nations. The Pelasgians, and then the Greco-Roman nations derived from them, replaced the primary pantheon connected with the sanctuary-observatories. In place of the generations familiar with 'Oceanus and Uranus', came Cronos, and then Zeus – a belated modification of the Aryan Divine-Dyaus (still preserved by Slavs in the form of Did, Didukh – alongside the later-affirmed Svaroh).

In the context of the family of Zeus and Lato recorded on maidans, already touched upon, certain changes will test the Slav-Pelasgian Divanna-Diana connection. It is possible that they correspond and were closer to Ma-Divia, '*Mother of Heaven* (i.e. of the Gods)', who was foremost in the Creto-Mycenaean pantheon of Pelasgians in the mid-2nd millennium BCE.

B. A. Rybakov considers Ma-Divia as being identical to the Slavic goddess Divia (the female hypostasis of Diva-Diya-Deda), who was still esteemed a long time after the Christendom of Rus. There is no contradiction of our position here, since Divia is a derivative of the more archaic Divanni. Much the same (taking into account Dyaus) can be said about the Baltic creator-God, Devas Kureias and his wife Deiva Motina.

The Poles know Dziewona^, Dziwana or Dziwa, as their Slavic Diana. The name of this goddess of summer and life is particularly expressive in comparison with the goddess of winter and death, Morana (Marzanna/Morena^) or Mara^. Moreover, in one of the Polish chronicles is written:

To the deity Dziwa, a kapishche [pagan temple] *was sited on the mountain named Dziwec* [meaning 'alive'], *where in the first days of May numerous people reverentially congregate to ask, from that which they consider to be the source of life, for*

Fig.83 : **Tree of Life**, whose symbolism emanates from the canon of the orante* woman in childbirth (Foremother; see Fig. 74, 142-143), and serves as the basis of letter **Ж [Zh]**.
***Oranta** - The Praying Virgin of Eastern Orthodoxy.

lasting and satisfying health. In particular, sacrifices were brought to her by those who heard the first singing of the cuckoo, whose portent conveyed to them how many years of life remained, according to the number of times its voice recurred. They thought that the highest lord of the universe turned himself into the cuckoo and prophesied the continuation of life.

According to the beliefs of the Greeks, Zeus himself came in the image of the cuckoo (cf. the '*zu*'bird of Aratto-Sumerian times; the '*zozulya*' of Ukrainians, is derived from this); it could also be the Divas who call from the top of the tree in *Tale of the Campaign of Ihor Svyatoslavlich*^. The cuckoo and 'Hanna-Panna' are connected with Ukrainian songs, such as this:-

A small river flows,
If I wish – I will leap over.
Give me, my mother, in marriage,
To whom I shall want ...
One year passed, the second flashed,
On the third one I missed –
I turned into a grey cuckoo,
I flew to visit...

Slavs of the Laba area [Elbe] honoured 'Divana'-Dziwana-Dziwa under the name of Siva. She was imagined by them as a naked girl with long hair, a wreath on her head, with an apple in her right hand and a grape in the left hand; the main temple of this Venus-like goddess (we may recall 'Venus'-Inanna) resided in Ratzeburg (Ratnik's [i.e. warriors'] city). In the Polish town of Prilwitc its idol was dressed, though with the name of Zizie, or Sisie, in accord with the name of the mother's breast. In relation to Siva, may we suggest that this name and image could be reflected in the female hypostasis of Aryan Siva. Perhaps *The Veles Book* knows its male hypostasis – the ancestor Si(e)va.

Suggested reading

1. *The Veles Book*. Translation and comments by B. Yatsenko, Kyiv, 1995, 2001.
2. I. Nechuy–Levitsky, *World outlook of Ukrainian nation. A sketch of Ukrainian mythology*, Lviv, 1876; Kyiv, 1992.
3. L. Silenko, *Maha Faith*, – New York and et al., 1979.
4. B. A. Rybakov, *Paganism of ancient Slavs*, Moscow, 1981.
5. A. I. Asov, *Atlanteans, Aryans, Slavs: History and Faith*, Moscow, 2000.
6. O. N. Trubachev, *Indoarica in Northern Black Sea area*, Moscow, 1999.
7. S. I. Nalyvayko, *Secrets of Sanskrit Revealed*, Kyiv, 2000.
8. M. Chmykhov, *The Sources of Paganism in Rus*, Kyiv, 1990.
9. E. Dobzhansky, *Great Day. Drawn and Painted eggs*, Kyiv, 2001.
10. V. Huzy, *A Golden Reed*, Kyiv-Brovary, 1997.
11. A. V. Popravko, *Beginnings of Rus*; in *Ukrainian Karma*, eds. V. Moskovchenko and A. Popravko, Kyiv, 1997.
12. I. Kahanets, Aryan standard. *The Ukrainian idea of the epoch of Great Transition*, in Transition-IV, 2(4) Kyiv, 2000.

---

[1] Eleusia (Eleusis) was the home of Demeter.

[2] The Russian word here is '*Миленький*' (Milen'kyi) which means 'pretty' but it is often used poetically to mean 'dear' or 'darling'.

[3] A similar tale exists in *The Edda* about the heroine Sif.

[4] The word 'Kamyshovy' means *reed*.

[5] Meru, Sanskrit term for 'spine' as in 'axis' which may carry the same harmonious meaning.

[6] The association between 'hromada' and 'vishni-grammi' is more readily understood if the Cyrillic 'h' in 'hromada' is given the Russian pronunciation of 'g' i.e. 'gromada'.

[7] In the *Rigveda*, in hymns 1.22.17, 1.154.3, 1.154.4 he strides across the earth with three steps, in 6.49.13 , 7.100.3 he strides across the earth three times and in 1.154.1, 1.155.5,7.29.7 he strides vertically, with the final step in the heavens. The same *Veda* also says he strode wide and created space in the cosmos for Indra to fight Vritra. By his stride he is said to have made dwelling for men possible, the three being a symbolic representation of its all-encompassing nature. This all-enveloping nature and benevolence to men were to remain the enduring attributes of Vishnu. As the triple-strider he is known as Tri-vikrama and as Uru-krama for the strides were wide.

[8] The primordial astronomical knowledge of Oriana pre-dated by millennia that of the Babylonians. Whilst Babylonian astronomy is better-known for being recent, in fact it is derived from knowledge which originated in Oriana and then passed to Sumer.

[9] In Ukraine there are several different forms of Velykden (Great Day). Babski is one of these but there is also a Rahmanski Velykden. This is not as widespread as the conventional Velykden but both involve baking cakes and decorating eggs "which are consecrated in the church (though not without complaints from some priests about paganism)". The essential difference from the conventional Velykden is the specific imitation of the allied Red Hill celebration. (Ref. Shilov, *Origins of Slavic Civilisation*, Part II: *The Vedantic Heritage of Ukraine*. 2008. Moscow. ISBN 978-98967-006-0).

[10] In the original Russian text, the Pelasgian word '*gure*' is written (in cyrillic letters) as '*гуре*' and its Ukrainian equivalent as '*гора*'. Notice that in Ukrainian the latter is pronounced as '*hora*' though in Russian it would be pronounced '*gora*'.

[11] Formed on the basis of Ukrainian and old Slavic (V. Krasnoholovets).

[12] The term 'Kraventsy' means 'cow-men'. It is mentioned in *The Veles Book* (board 7e) - "And Dazhbo generated us from the cow Zamun, and we were Kraventsy and Skufe" [i.e. 'Cow-men and Bull-ranchers'].

[13] The word for 'glorious' in Russian is 'слав' (slav), and in Ukrainian it is 'слава' (slava).

[14] In ancient Greek literature, Uranus or **Father Sky** was the son and husband of Gaia, Mother Earth. Cronos was his son and Zeus was his grandson.

CHAPTER 9

Fig.84 : **Indo-Aryan names in the Northern Black Sea area** in late-Sarmatian times (according to O. N. Trubachev). 1 – A fragment of a civil oath of Greco-Taurian Chersonese form the 3rd century BCE, which is reminiscent of ΣΑΣΤΗΡΑ[1] (*Saster people*, upper line) – 'the archive of laws' of the Indo-Aryan language; 2a,b.c.d – Tamgi-symbols of Sarmatian rulers of the Greek Bosphorus and the Naples of the Scythians.

THE ORIGIN OF UKRAINE AND RUS

We can now set before us the problem of how to determine the time and circumstances of the origin of Ukraine and Rus. This task has been aided by foregoing consideration of historiographic facts concerning the origin of Slavic ethnoculture in 2300-1700 BCE and its relationship with the Pelasgians [as opposed to the proto- or pre-Slavs, regarded by scientists as fairly advanced, for their time]

Even framing this question concerning the origin may seem unusual, particularly when addressing the relative sequence of the names of those states. The validity of the account given in the *Tale of Bygone Years,* with regard to the name of Ukraine relative to Rus, is not of primary importance to official science, politics and religion, whose disputes tend to cluster around a determination of the date when Kyiv, capital of Rus, first appeared. Meanwhile, *The Veles Book,* amongst other sources, offers several names preceding Kyivan Rus –indicating cities and countries of *Ukruh*, *Ukermark* etc., including references to the mysterious *Ukrians*. They all appeared around the time when Slavs migrated from the Dnipro area of Aratta – the very nucleus of the primary community of Indo-European nations. Apart from Slavs and Pelasgians, even the Hittites and Illyrians came from this same nucleus or its periphery (e.g. the archaeological cultures of Vinca, Gumelniţa and others), although a weak study of the latter and an obscured beginning for the Hittites, precludes the possibility of considering them here. However, concerning the first two, the matter is considerably facilitated by the discoveries of D. A. Chertkov, F. Volanski and E. Klassen.

To this cohort of researchers it is necessary to introduce J. Šavli, P. V. Tulaev and O. N. Trubachev – although, to be clear, they approach the matter from the other side: from the perspective of Aryan-Slavic connections.

1. Leleges – Lida – Ruthenians^.

Fig. 85 : **"Solar barque"** of Sumerian-Egyptian style portrayed at Stone Grave. By B. D. Mykhailov & Yu. Shilov.

In the previous chapter we considered the beginning of the western migration of Slavs whilst among the superior Pelasgians. We shall continue this analysis by first of all examining the relationship between the Pelasgians and the relatively older Leleges. It was probably the latter whom the ancient historians Thucydides and Dionysus of Helicarnassus specifically had in mind when they insisted on the existence of the Pelasgians 17 centuries before the Trojan War (i.e. at the boundary of the 4th – 3rd millennium BCE). If this was so, then **the *Leleges* were forerunners of the Pelasgians and should also be identified with the first seafarers of Oriana**. There are other arguments that also support this reading. According to A. G. Kifishin's commentary on the *Encyclopaedia* of Pauli-Vissova, the ancestor of Lelex was the son of Spartos ('of Stone') and the grandfather of Pelasg. Greco-Roman authors state that the legendary *Leleges* received the name of 'storks' ('lelek', in Ukrainian) owing to the distinctive white sails of their ships as well as their habit of frequently changing their place of residence, (perhaps in accordance with the tradition of Aratta, that of periodically leaving their old settlements and moving into newly built ones.)

According to A. D. Chertkov, the Pelasgians (still known as 'storks', even in another language) were called Leleges by the 'solar' Hellenes, or *Greeks* (i.e. the 'rooks', who are '*graki*'[1] in Ukrainian), just as they were called previously in the language of the Leleges-Pelasgians. This interchange of nicknames could have arisen from the observation that Pelasgians had fair hair (in Ukrainian such hair is called 'rus colour'), but the Greeks had darker hair (closer to black). The implications of this fact should not surprise us in the light of our previous acquaintance with the common origins of the Slavs and Pelasgians, as well as the Ukrainian-Pelasgian dictionary entry of these ethnonyms – it provides another argument in favour of the provenance of Slavs to the demographic and ethnocultural filling of Aratta as the first source of European culture. Furthermore, behind the ethnonyms of the Pelasgians and Greeks, a hint of the legendary struggle between "cranes and pygmies", could be concealed.

The Leleges, who did not initially communicate with the Hellenes, distanced themselves from the ethno-cultural corpus of Riana, instead taking root in the Troad, especially in neighbouring Lydia. The name, Lydia derives from the Slavic word 'lyudy', meaning 'people' – even the Romans were aware of military games [*Ludi Romani*] that went under the literal name of '*Trojan lyudi*' (which were gleaned from the Ruthenian-Etruscans). In addition, the father of legendary Lid was considered to be 'Father'-Atis - a connection which is likely to have originated from the Slavic word 'Otets', meaning 'father'- who was grandson of the patriarch Man-'Muzha'; Slavic 'muzh' means 'husband'. The Vedic prototype for the latter was revealed for the first time in the magical paintings of a Brahmanic tomb dating from mid-3rd mill. BCE in burial No. 3 at High Grave, Starosillia (in the Kherson region). It was possibly Man himself who led the maritime part of the Orianian-Lelegian migration from the lower reaches of the Tiras (Dniester) and Borysthenes (Dnipro), the ancestral homeland of Indo-European people, into Asia Minor. During the course of this migration, other regions of the Northern Black Sea area were seized. Thus, the Roman geographer Ptolemy points to the Tusces (as the Romans called the Etruscans^) near the present city of Piatigorsk^.

As a consequence of earthquakes, droughts, poor harvests in the mid-3rd – 2nd millennium BCE, plus the fore-mentioned circumstances, some of those migrants were compelled, under the leadership of Tyr(s)en (brother of Lid), to trek on further, continuing into Italy, following the Pelasgian-Trojans, Oenotrus and Peucetius. There, under the leadership of Tarhon – whose kin in Troy were still connected with the cult of the 'Conquering Sun', Tarheli (Targelia-Apollo) – the Tyrsenes built 12 cities: Volčini, Kosa, Luka, Vada, Maliuta, Perusia, Artana, *Russela* and others. Their Slavic identity is beyond doubt. The last name, Russela, is connected with the autonym of the Etruscans – *Ruthenians* (whose name, in the same way that Etruscans were associated with the locality of Etruria in Italy, were possibly related to the *Rsa* creek that flowed into Troad). We encounter the city-states of the Voltsi tribe ("volch'i", which means 'wolves', from where we get Volčini, or Volchini), amongst the names in ***Artan,*** which spread away from the city of Potava on the River Medvak, indicating their succession from the Dnipro area of ***Aratta***. One of these migrant tribes, on the southern slopes of the Alps, bearing the name *Tripolyane,* inhabited the valley of Val' *Trimpia*. One may regard the similarity of these names with Kyiv's *Trypillia [Tripolye]* as beyond sheer chance[2]. Spreading away from Trypillia, above the right bank of the Dnipro, were *three* multi-kilometre long "serpent walls", and along both sides (near the villages of Khodosovychi and Trakhtemyriv) lie two old Slavic fortifications, defended by enormous earth banks. Wasn't this very locality the motherland of Tirena and Tarkhon, ancestors of the Ruthenians? Didn't Targitai^ dwell there, the ancestor of the Skolots^, who was related to them? And wasn't the Divych-mountain at Trypillia that same Mount Sian where Tarkh Tarakhovich of Old-Rusian epics lived? [Photo 20].

In the region of Latium, near Rome, there sprang up a considerable number of settlements and villages of the migrants from Lelegi-Pelasgian Troad and Attica: Syt, Medula, Konina, Turana, 'Voly' [which in Ukrainian means 'oxen'], Tri-Kriny(tsi) [which in Ukrainian means 'three-wells'] and Kala(ch)tia. Except for the latter name, the local Latinians (i.e. Romans) adopted much from their more advanced neighbours, even including (kh)lib, which in Ukrainian means 'bread'. The Athenian Pelasgians, since 1570 BCE, had certainly been bringing sacrificial *Pelyanos* for their gods (in Ukrainian 'Palianytsia' is a type of a wheat bread). Whilst the origins of the names of the cities of *Kures* and *Kera* (near the Italic Artan mentioned above), are lost, they are, evidently, related to the meaning of 'Kuren', not so much in the sense of a barrack or hut, but more akin to the concept of the *kureni* (military units, which had separate rooms etc.) of the Ukrainian Zaporizhian-Cossacks. An etymological similarity also existed between *Kera* and the Greek greeting *khaire*. Perhaps there is a more definite convergence here between the Baltic creator-God *Kureias*; the Etruscan priests known as *kuretes,* and the Cossack *kharakternyks^* – keepers of ancestral wisdom and military knowledge.

Fig. 86 : ***Triple* symbolism of earth-walls and hill-forts near Trypillia**, and similar symbols on Ukrainian hand-painted eggs. (*See also Fig. 117).

The Kuretes were considered to have been the founders of the militant dance *Tripudare,* which not only by its name, but also by its performance, resembles the *Tropak* and *Hopak* Cossack dances. Researchers discern a pattern from the military exercises in which the kharakternykes used to achieve incredible concentrations of power and force (no less than in modern "eastern combat sports"). It is already impossible to doubt that the origin of the *Hopak* is cognate with the Aryan *Hopal* (Krishna), which means 'cow protector', whose similarity with the Pelasgian-Greek *Apollo*, Etruscan *Apla*, Venetic *Kupavon* and Slavic *Kupala* were time and again noted by us. It is necessary to seek out the origins of the ancient infantry –the hoplites, in the same ethnocultural environment. The Slavic conjugal customs were also similar to those of the Etruscans, Venedi, Sabians and other descendants of the Leleges. *Marriage* itself was called *faraki* ('брак' meaning 'marriage', 'брать' meaning to 'take') and was connected with the custom of 'abducting Sabian women' (by the Romans; and in Christian Rus Slavs continued to 'abduct maidens' on Kupala night). The Etruscans, just like the Rusy, disapproved of May marriages ("... because you should work!") but welcomed June marriages, timed to coincide with the summer solstice (for the celebration of Ivan Kupala^), a time of maximum natural energy.

Most of the migrants settled in Etruria, from where – as historical tradition would have it – a new ethnonym went with them. But perhaps it was really the other way around? According to the fore-mentioned Greek historian Thucydides: "The Etruscans – these belated Pelasgians, called themselves Ruseny or Raseny [i.e. Ruthenians]". It is simplest of all to derive this from a riparian ethnonym – from the name of local rivers, along whose banks the ancestors of the Ruthenians settled: from the River Rasa (in the Vedas), the Ros' (on the border of Borus'), and the Rsa (near Troy); the prefix *et-* in this case indicates 'belonging to', 'here', 'this is', or even 'from'. Thus, we derive Etruscan to mean 'from the Rus/Ros''. Moreover, Stefanus Byzantinus categorically determined: "The Etruscans – they are Slavic

Fig. 87 : **Grammar of Veneti and Etruscan-Phoenician inscription**, 1st millennium BCE. By M. Bor.

people"; that was also confirmed by F. Volanski and E. Klassen deciphering the Etruscan language during the mid-19th century. It is high time that science researchers accepted this!

Alas - official science, not only in Slavic countries but also elsewhere, persistently maintains that the Etruscans are a nation of unknown origin and relationships, whose writing and language do not yield to decipherment. This is wholly untrue.... it is shameful and inexcusable. Is it possible to believe that given the huge number of inscriptions of Pelasgians and Etruscans, who gave their written language and ethno-cultural origins to the Greeks and Romans, that they did not yield to generations of highly-qualified decipherers from Europe, America and elsewhere? When it was divulged [in 1964] that golden plates had been found in Pyrgi^ which bore duplicate texts in Etruscan and Phoenician languages, the problem could finally be solved ... along with an answer to whether or not that text belonged to "Velianas sloveni" (Velianas sal cluvenias^). This translation, published by Matej Bor (1913-1996) in Vienna, satisfied neither the world, nor our national science. It also ignored the Etruscan-Venedic grammar engraved on another tablet and deciphered by the same researcher – again, it was based on Slavic languages. Academic science is rendered erratic when it is purposefully blocked by politics and religion (which, by lending their most powerful forces to the cause of false doctrines, not only harm all humanity but hides the priority of Slavdom in European and even world culture)...

The migrants from Troad into Etruria called their new motherland *Italy* (from the Slavic 'telenok-*Telets*' [meaning offspring of Taurus]; in Ukrainian, 'telya' means 'calf': thus, *Italy* originated from 'telya' – "The country rich in large horned cattle"... The variety, depth and hard-won blood relationships between the Lelegian-Pelasgian-Etruscan-Venedian peoples with the Slavic world is further revealed by a comparison of words, which extends the fore-mentioned Pelasgian-Ukrainian-Russian dictionary:

Pelasgian	***Ukrainian (& Russian)***	***English***
agn	*yagnia*	lamb
aki	*yak*	as, just as
bageti	*bogaty*	rich
val	*val*	earth wall
vesperina	*vecheria*	diner
zpa	*zpa*	military dance
dukem	*duh*	spirit
elos	*yalynkovy lis* (elovyi les)	spruce forest
zhivas	*zhyvy* (zhivoy)	alive
zar	*zhar*	heat
kaledones	*kolyada, kolyadki*	carol
kondulus	*kaidany* (kandaly)	fetters
korius	*kora*	bark
lar	*lar* (lar')	larder
loena	*l'nyany* (l'nyanoy)	linen
lues	*loy*	boiled fat
mak	*mak*	poppy
mlusna	*mla* (mgla)	mist, darkness
monile	*namysto* (monisto)	necklace
pataks	*ptycya*	bird
peroma	*parom*	ferry
pikun	*pekty* (pech')	to bake, stove
pulu	*pole*	field
r(e)tele	*retel'no* (tshhatel'no)	carefully
ru	*ruka*	arm
runa	*rana*	wound
sekuris	*sokyra* (topor)	axe
skater	*skaterka*	table-cloth
skripium	*skrynya* (sunduk)	trunk
sopil	*sopilka*	pan-pipe

spaka	*sobaka*	dog
spor	*sporuda* (sooruzhenie)	building
sse	*sse (sosat')*	suck
sutina	*sutinky* (sumerki)	twilight
tes	*tes*	boards, planks
una	*yuna* (yunaya)	young woman/girl
cena	*cina*	price
Jenej	*Enej, junej* (Slov., Bulgar.)	Angus [Oeneus/ Aeneus]

2. Eneti – Venedi^.

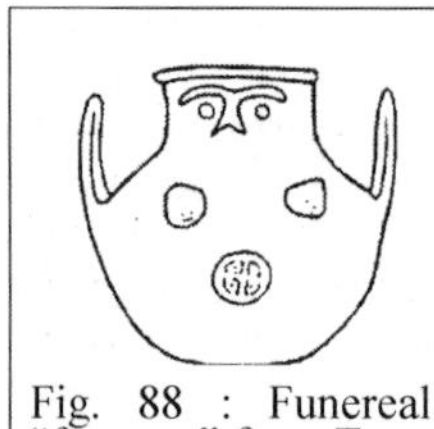

Fig. 88 : Funereal "face urn" from Troy.

The last entry in the list above is a name that is still extant amongst Slavs (i.e. Slovenians and Bulgarians) and is probably cognate with the Sanskrit word *vand* ('to glorify'). In Latin, Oeneus is written as ***Aeneus/Aenei***^, and is pronounced 'Venei'; the Greeks pronounced it (H)Oenei. These connections help to confirm the identity of the (H)Eneti-Veneti-Venedi (as emphasised by Strabo in his *Geography*); the form of ***Aenei*** is similar to Antae [Ants^] and probably goes back to the Aryan Brahmanic name, Vena, and also to the name of the legendary island of Eya (also spelled Aea, Aivan etc., presently the modern Taman peninsula) – a name for which the Aryan sources were proved by O. N. Trubachev. The Aryans and Orianians could also include the Vans whose territory, during the 15th - 8th centuries BCE and later, extended as far as the Transcaucasian Lake Van^ and Lake Sevan, which by that time had formed one of the most vibrant centres of Aryan culture with horses, carts and wonderful metalwork, etc. However, it is possible that these tribes did not arise from Arián or Oriana but from Borusia (the northern part of Aratta in the 3rd millennium BCE). They could have arrived on the north-eastern coasts of the Azov and Black Seas from the Mid-Dnipro area, after going down the valleys of the Donets and the Don. It is necessary to search for archaeological correspondences for the proposed theory in relationships between the northern part of the Late Trypillian culture that led to the Mid-Dnipro, and in the related but later, Fatianov^ culture, which was associated with the Caucasus, namely, the later Balanov variant of this culture.

According to some historians, such as the 12th century Icelandic historian Snorri Sturluson, it is suggested that Europe may have been named after Enaea, perhaps in honour of the people's hero. Nevertheless, there is some agreement with this same northern tradition because a Country of Vans once used to exist in the lower reaches of the River Tanais (the River Don). The Ases waged war against it, led by diys-priests and Odin^ (credited as the "first" creator of writing, by the way!) and their capital was at Asgard. The complexity of these details again brings us closer to the Cimmerian Bosphorus with its island of Eya (Aivan, Oium etc.: see above), and also the cities and localities of Assa, Asandi, Dia and others. In *The Iliad*, Homer mentioned the mysterious Enetia adjoining the cattle breeding Meskhetians (later known as Moskhinikes] of the Caucasus where the Vans, as already mentioned, were also known along with someone called Pilemen who led his people to Paphlagonia in the north of Asia-Minor.

The problem of the (V)enet(d)i was well investigated by the Russian philologist and historian P. V. Tulaev in *The Veneti : Ancestors of Slavs* (Moscow, 2000) in which he supported the research of his Slovenian colleagues – M. Bor and J. Šavli.

According to linguists, the language of the Venedi can be identified as belonging to the earliest form of Slavic language, occupying an intermediary place between ancient Indo-European and the Balto-Slavic languages that were derived from it. The similarity between the Venedi and Etruscan languages can be explained by the common origin of both ethnic groups from the Pelasgian language. These conclusions fit the picture already outlined and will be confirmed by further historical evidence.

The (V-, G-)eneti were descendants or contemporaries of Pilemen who had probably established Pala in Asia Minor and assisted the Trojans during the siege of their city by the Greeks. After the fall of Troy (Ilium) around 1250 BCE, (as currently accepted, although we have justified it already at around 1020) the state of Pala still existed even though a substantial part of the (V)eneti had migrated away from there. Linguists and archaeologists have traced the four directions of that migration.

The first migrants became part of an ethnically different detachment led by Odysseus who returned to their ancestral home of Meotida (the Azov area) where Helon was probably founded.

The second, ethnically very uniform wave of migrants, led by Aeneus, appeared in Italic Etruria. There the (V)eneti became neighbours of the Tir(s)enes and Lides (related to them through the Leleges-Pelasgians) who had migrated from the Troad long before the war and had already settled in the lower reaches of the River Padva, as well as the northern coast of the Adriatic Sea (a name derived from the Slavic word 'Yadrine', i.e. the 'Core', or 'Central' sea for them). Some groups of Pelasgians had also migrated there from Greece.

The third direction of migration was led by Antenor (according to the varying testimonies of ancient authors he had either expelled the Eneti from Troy, or led them away), who turned towards the same coast of the Adriatic Sea where an agreement was reached with the tribe of Aeneus and they went on to found the cities of Aeneus and Potava in the mouth of the River Medvak. Here they were joined by both the Etruscan tribe Evganns, led by Veles, and the Italics, led by Kupavon.

The fourth, most confusing wave of migration reached as far as the Baltic Sea (which was called the Venedian Sea for a long time afterwards) and Scandinavia. This wave could be considered as secondary since it began with the (V)eneti in the northern Adriatic seeking deposits of amber in the Baltic area (the so-called Amber Way) and later, in Cimmerian times, this Way was traversed by the Ases and Vans (Eneti-Veneti) led by Odin. What mitigates against calling this wave secondary are references in Lithuanian legends to Palemon, Julianus, and Ektor – without doubt related to the above-mentioned Pilemen, Odysseus, and Hector. So this wave was not secondary but was entirely brought about by the same Trojan War.

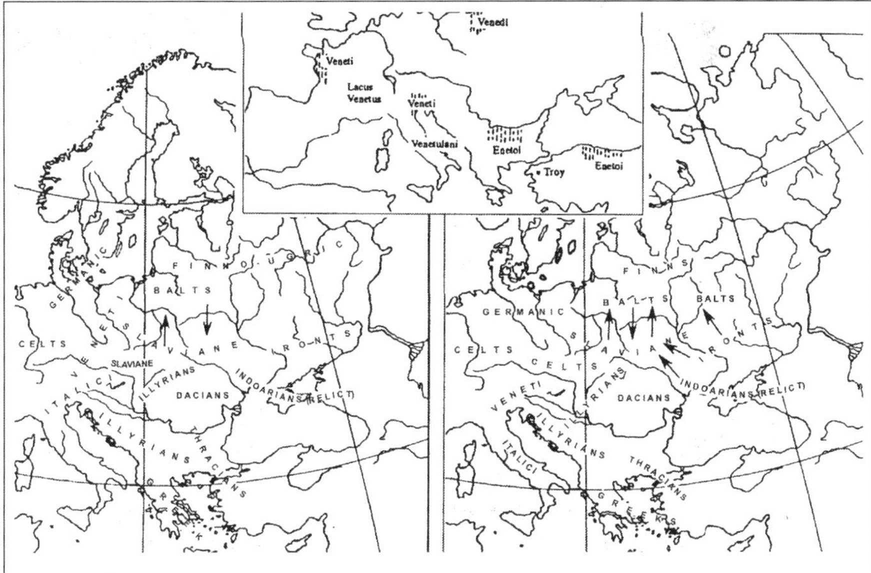

Fig. 89 : **Migration of the Veneti** (above: according to I. Shavli) **and of Slavs** (according to O. N. Trubachev) 3rd–1st millennium BCE.

We shall now look at historical evidence for the migration of the Veneti from Pala and Troy.

The evidence for the first direction of migration is mentioned above; the fourth will be examined in the next chapter but here we will look at the other two.

According to Justinius and Pompeius Trogus^, Antenor banished the Eneti of the northern coast of the Adriatic into Illyria where they occupied the Istrian peninsula opposite the mouth of the Danube as known by the Argonauts (which has now disappeared) where they controlled the start point of the Amber Way to the Baltics. Herodotus (I: 196) knew that the Eneti occupied the beginning of this Way, although Sophocles, despite living during this same 5th century BCE wrote that they reached the coast of the Venedi (Baltic) Sea. Was it just coincidence that made Sophocles call the Eneti the Indus? This could be a feint echo of (S)indica of the Dnipro or Azov area which had been the ancestral home of the Vans-Veneti of the Northern Black Sea. It is entirely possible that during the era of Sophocles they were joined by those who had returned from India (which we will discuss below).

The grave of the Trojan Aeneas was found near the modern Italian city of Crecchio in 1846; there, a stone over the crypt is decorated with an Etruscan inscription which looked quite similar to the 'dashes and cuts' writing-style used by the pre-Christian Rus. F. Volanski, after reading this inscription from Latin and Russian transcripts, then produced his own translations in Russian, Polish, Czech, Illyrian, Wendish, as well as Latin, French and German. The Slavic translations, especially the first, were without doubt closest to the original whilst the west European languages were much further from it. The content of the epitaphs are as follows:

All Heavenly God, higher than Vim and Dim, you are Ezmen' of Rosii,
Take in trusteeship my house and children, best Ezmen'!
Hecate's reign is far; I am going down to the bottom of Earth;
Precisely, really, so it is! As I (am) Aeneus, a ruler by birth!
Sitting with Lado in Eliseus, you draw Leta – and will forget ...
O! dear, remarkable!

In Etruscan this almost sounds like:

All Heavenly God, of high Vim and Dim, Ezmen of Rasiey ...
O! dear, remarkable!

The name Rasiya appears in this inscription along with the names of those gods who would in time become familiar in Rome, including some who were absolutely Slavic. The greatest of the Slavic names is Ezmen – also known as Ovsen, Yasmen, Jason, Iasion etc. We have already discussed the latter form of this name Iasion which originated with the 'Mammoth'-Ishkur of Stone Grave. Ezmen is known to have been the Pelasgian-Etruscan deity of light who conquered the seven dark Kabirs (who evidently embodied the unfavourable months of the half-year, or 'semik'[3] of the Slav calendar). The sources of this mythology have been traced to memorials from the late stage of the Ingul archaeological culture in the Dnipro area at the end of the 18th – 17th centuries BCE where they are linked with the appearance of mythology associated with 'Our God' Dionysus, the son of Diya-Zeus and the brother of Apollo. The ethnohistorical convergence of images of Ezmen and Dionysus is completed by the inclusion of La(t)da, mentioned in the epitaph inscription above; she is the mother of Kupala (and Apollo) and had already merged with the image of her husband Diya-Jupiter as Lado. With regard to Hecate, also recorded in this epitaph, she was the goddess of the netherworld, who, together with the Elysian fields and River Lethe (the river of oblivion), became inherent to the Italian tribes and in time with Rome too (unless they had already been so before the migration of the Trojans lėd by Aeneus and others?).

The ethnonym of the *Eneti-Veneti-Venedi* is not an easy one to understand. Many eminent official scientists (or those who aspire to become such) have speculated on the readings with the aim of separating the genealogy of the Venedi – who were undoubtedly Slavs of the first centuries CE - from the ethnohistorical depth of the first two, the Eneti-Veneti, which nudges us towards a reconsideration of politically established priorities, history and values. Fancy placing Slavs ahead of the Trojans, the Greeks and Romans!? Yu.

V. Pavlenko, for example, in the monograph *Pre-Slavs and Aryans* (Kyiv, 2000) managed to get around this awkward situation by dividing the pre-Veneti into a first group (*Language area* A) "proto-Tocharian and Kelto-Italico-Illyrians" and a second group "Germano-Balto-Slavic" and then completely put to one side the Pelasgians and Etruscans. Evidently someone who knows how to make a career topic scientifically and politically important!...

Despite the plethora of theories and interpretations that have been written about the ethnonym of the *Veneti,* most researchers come down to supporting just two main positions for its meaning: the words 'kin' and 'glory'. Another interesting interpretation, though far less acknowledged, is found in the terms 'dowry', 'sale' and the like. There are rather obvious indicators of just these meanings residing in the suffixes of Slavic names, -*vna*, *-vich* (especially in the latter patronymic), and in the Sanskrit terms of glorification: *vand* and *stavana*. Ptolemy gives the latter name in the *Geography* (III: 5.8) as an ethnonym, placing these people between the northern Sudini-Balts and southern Alans-Iranians. O. N. Trubachev in *Indoarica in the Northern Black Sea coast* (Moscow, 1999) treats this as a reasonable Sanskrit translation [by whom, Ptolemy?] of the autonym of ***Slavs***: "which speaks of a certain degree of contact whilst also acknowledging, in our eyes, a rare example of the unity of folk and scientific etymology".

"The rarest example" is actually what is occurring right now, a time when scientific researchers turn away from national needs in order to serve authority. In the communal state of Aratta, whose traditions persisted into pre-Kyivan Rus, power lay in the hands of 'scientific'-priests who selflessly served the people: they taught them and also continued their own studies. Having constructed the immense system of sanctuary-observatories extending from the Urals even to Britain, for creating their calendars and celebrations of the gods, could the devotees of this system really bypass questions of history, ethnogenesis and, above all, word-formations for international discourse and technologies, etc.? From whom, if not from them, did the 'synthetic language'of Sanskrit originate? In addition to which, by the way, it co-existed with the Prakrit language of the common people... If the esteemed Mr. Trubachev had included these quite well known (but nevertheless, badly investigated) archaeological and ethnographical realities in his searches, his conclusions would be far more specific.

The creation of ethnonyms was the priority of the priests who worked within their figurative-intuitive ideology and therefore perfectly understood the importance of semantics and its necessary 'nodes' which are densely sown in Sanskrit, in the Vedas, and in *The Veles Book.* This must be borne in mind when considering the semantics of the Ruthenians, Etruscans, Rusy and Rus... In completing this consideration of the semantics of the ethnonym of the Veneti, we shall pause to look more closely at the possible significance of the terms 'dowry', 'sales' and 'redemption'. These meanings, if they were actually enveloped within this ethnonym along with the fundamental core meaning of 'glory' (in stark contrast to the analogy with the German 'Sklave' considered as being closer to 'slave') could have been provided by priests for the migrants and people, based on the following considerations. The 'dowry', or *veno* offered to the bride from her parents really did embody the concept of 'glory' for them all. The inhabitants of the motherland offered the migrants who had to leave them (often as a result of of over-population or for other reasons) a *veno* – 'dowry' or 'ransom' – as a compensatory benefit for fleeing their homeland.

In conclusion of this subsection, it is helpful to look more closely at the social order of the Etruscans, the Italic descendants of the Trojans of Asia Minor – descendants of the Venedi of Oriana or Borusia, locations which were, respectively, the coastal or forest-steppe parts of Aratta.

According to A. D. Chertkov's perceptive identification, after the migration of the Eneti and other tribes from the Troad, the Danube-Dnipro Arattan tradition of having city-states (from the 7th – 3rd millennium BCE), was retained after their arrival in Italic Tir(s)enia-Etruria: "By a federal republic, tribes which were too small united amongst themselves (although it seems that all the Etruscans preferred a general council for the consideration of internal relations and disputes). Concerning foreign affairs, each separate city operated independently; it fought, reconciled itself, and concluded agreements independently of other tribes and mutual meetings. For this reason we always see twelve tribes, which were alternately at war with Rome but never together. Hence those devastating consequences for all Etruria when eventually, it transformed into a Roman province."

Substantial changes in the social order and political system of the Pelasgian-Venedi-Slavs, compared to the way they were practised in Aratta and Oriana came about, neither from the Scythians, nor, in anticipated approval by Rurik^ in the second half of the 9th century, as a consequence of having the Varangians in Rus. Instead, the tradition of federal policy can be traced to the subsequent period 'of breaking up the princedoms of Kyivan Rus' (which was not a "breakdown of statehood" *per se* but a return to their multi-millennial Arattan tradition; within just a couple of centuries it was superseded by the totalitarian administration of the first Rurik feudal lords [Rurik Dynasty^]). This brought destruction to Rus at the hands of the Tatar-Mongol hordes (whose totalitarianism at that time turned out to be far more brutal than that of the Varangians). Memories of the same communal tradition lie in the subsequent ordeals suffered even in today's Ukraine; it seems that only imperial-totalitarian Russia succeeded to some degree in ridding itself of the misfortune of such heritage (mutated from the happiness of the truly "Golden Age" of Aratta of the 7th – 3rd millennium BCE).

The Roman historian-geographer Ptolemy mentions some Sevaks[4] in the pre-Danubian province of Noricum^ (they were perhaps derived from Sievy, the brother of Rus and even the son of Bohomyr of *The Veles Book*?). Also worth considering is the statement written by Nestor, the 12th century Kyivan chronicler, that "Slavs are the essence of Narci". Amongst the numerous old names that still survive on the outskirts of modern Venice and Verona there happen to be those such as Slavia and Slavini.[5] The Ants also, since olden times, coexisted with the Venedi and in fact the surname 'Ant' still exists in Verona. Lastly, Ptolemy referred to a tribe called 'Andian' situated to the south of Lake Balaton^. It is entirely probable that these Ants are migrant descendants of the Trojan leader Antenor, who, together with the Eneti led by Aeneus, founded the Italian ***Venedi*** at the end of 13th (or 11th) century BCE.

3. What then is Rus?

Fig. 90 : The symbol of Taurus on an Old-Rusy amulet.

From what has been said already in this chapter it can be safely concluded that the Rusy (Rusychi) and Rus arose in the western migrational movement of the Pelasgians and Slavs who passed through Asia Minor, Troad and Italic Etruria. Whilst it is not known whether the afore-mentioned ethnonyms of *Slavini* and *Ants* existed there at that time, the *Eneti-Veneti,* unquestionably, did.

The dispersal of the latter through the expanses of Europe-Enetia was somewhat less widespread than through Rus. In this case this ethnonym became attached far more frequently to the name of localities and the like, whilst Veneti signified the population. This characteristic of Rus coincides with the observation by O. N. Trubachev that the earliest Rus were mainly the 'Light, western' side. This interpretation approximates the feeling of the historian M. Ilin (*The Banishment of the Varangians*, Paris, 1925) who "understood the name of Rus as shining with moisture, the symbol of life, illuminated by the heavenly light of the Sun..." This is in inherent agreement with the other pre-Indo-European names of Ra-'Sun' and Ras-'River' – and in that same vein the hydronymic name of the River Ros, the ethnicity of Rus, etc.

It is impossible, however, to ignore the conclusions of those linguists who have focused their attention more closely on the ethnic meaning of the term *Rus,* rather than on its territorial meaning. S. I. Nalyvayko takes a somewhat different position from those preceding linguists, suggesting that Rus arises from various names for the 'Bull'. Incidentally all of these attitudes become integrated with Taurus because, since ancient Scythian times at least, it was the astrological symbol identified with the territory of Rus-Ukraine (V. M. Moskovchenko and A. V. Popravko, *The Karma of Ukraine*. Kiev, 1997). This calendar-zodiacal constellation is in any case compatible with an understanding of Rus by all the forementioned researchers including also A. Veltman, according to whom *Rus* inherently meant 'ancient rulers'. Added to this are the semantics of Dazhboh-Taurus, already touched upon earlier, according to which the Rusy (Rusychi) considered themselves to be grandsons of Dazhboh. And yet – isn't that precisely what was said in a recent paragraph about the attendants of the sanctuary-observatories of those times, those involved in the preparation of Sanskrit etc.?

Broadly speaking, have we not solved the problem that was articulated by Bruckner, and before him by Trubachev, i,e: "Whoever correctly interprets the name of Rus, will receive the keys to an explanation of the original history of Rus"? An unambiguous answer was awaited. Well, that unambiguous answer can be now be given as follows: Rus was the successor of Aratta, the first state in the world, where the all-encompassing *figurative-intuitive* world view ruled, consolidated by the shared ideology of its intellectual-rulers, namely the priests. Our modern cut-and-dried, *logical-analytical* science cannot hope to compete with them! Although, if we were to step down from the academic pedestal to at least gather together the disconnected disciplines of science and history, then we might just attempt to contend. What we attempt to do in this book is to stand upon the ancient position, particularly that inherent to the priests, and respectfully consider the poly-semantics (the polysemy of names, which contemporary science aspires to simplify to the point of unambiguity).

First of all let's focus attention on the fact that in comparison to the development of the Veneti – which began like a mosaic, assembled over time perhaps in Italic Venice and also on the south-eastern coast of the Venedian (Baltic) Sea – the statehood of Rus had already matured to the point where it was no longer a *priestly-communal* society any more, especially when compared to Aratta and Oriana which had inspired them both, but had become a *military-totalitarian* system. Despite the opposed developmental polarity of the Veneti and Rus, they were connected by the timeless and stateless concern of the rulers – the elite of people – for their kinfolk. However, the state-system of the Slavs had now turned from the glorification of gods and its people to dominion over those people, and over the gods (though let us recall the religious reforms of Prince Volodymyr [10th century] – a pagan but later a saint). During that profound turn-around in attitudes that played out over the course of some 500 years (compared to Aratta – Arsania which had existed in the same territory for 7 millennia), a radical change of ideologies by society and rulers took place, including amongst the intellectual elite.

There arose, initially, a naturally induced mental shift and in its train came social and other developments[6]. Along with the global process of change, development and the consequent unwinding spiral of the human psyche went a deep alteration in the quality of its world view. Consequently, the contemporary politicians, secret servants, scientists, and artists of the latter centuries are *naturally* not to blame in this matter. Their fault before their peoples, and humanity generally, lies in another plane: in the poor performance of their intent for a *social* elite – to adequately understand the historical process and proactively to choose the best way for society to proceed in its complete natural development. The elite, according to its essence and Arattan past, is the security intelligence service but now, in class societies, it tends towards looting in the wars that it has provoked. Clearly, such lawlessness and its perception (or even awareness) is not part of the mind and conscience of the elite. However, our book is not an accusation nor even a comparison, but a search for a way out from that doomsday promised by the present "world elite". The exit already glimmers before us: in "returning" from the present "winter" to a fresh "springtime" – one that is very similar (however qualitatively new) to that old "springtime" with which civilisation began 8,200 years ago – similar, not because of its forthcoming form and content but because of the quintessence of its content. However, the "world elite" promises mankind not a "doomsday", but only a recovery from the modern "winter" back to a "favourable autumn" and mankind does not understand that this leadership is crazy!

However, let us now return to consider the stages of development of the most ancient Rus. Oriana (Orissa) and Borusia, as already mentioned, together with manifestations in the Trojan-Etruscan world and the names attested by those subjects in *The*

Fig. 91 : Antiquities of Ruthenians (Etruscans).

Veles Book which are set around the time of the 1st millennium BCE and later. These subjects will be considered in the following section. Here we shall call to mind the biblical people or country of *Rosh* in Urartu, where in the 8th century BCE, under the governance of *Rus* I and II, there lived the Vany, Vediny, Albainy, Aces and others. I. Kahanets and his predecessors have assembled numerous manifestations of *Rus* in Asia Minor particularly in the name of Tsur(Sur) – from the name of the Pelasgian-Phoenician city which gave us the name of Suria-Syria. This version deserves further development. Perhaps, from the end of the 5th century BCE the ethnonym of *Rus* began to be concentrated in the main region of the Veneti migration – the Baltic area. Their centre became the island of *Ruyan* or *Ruegen*, where until now about 30 similar names were concentrated: *Rus*, *Rostok* and others. The river *Ros* is referred to as the influx of not only the Dnipro but also of the Neman^, where in the early Middle Ages the gulf of the latter was called the *Rusian* Sea^ and the coast of the gulf was *Rusian* land. South of the Veneti resettlements, in the Smolensk region, such names are far fewer. On the coasts of another *Rusian* (Black) sea – there is a new concentration of names.

So, there seems to have been a degree of over-lapping and competition between the Veneti-"priests" and the Rus-"warriors" on the expanse of the Slavic world of the 1st millennium BCE. Clearly, the Magi and the Princes had to be able to coexist or, at least, adjoin; whilst in some regions they still retained the force of the overlord moving away from communal statehood, in other regions they gained strength in the forthcoming class statehood (with feudal elements of slaveholding); thus the names of these regions, and their ethnonyms were formed accordingly. We will not consider here any smaller caste-ancestral definitions. Take the name *Roxo*lan^, although consonant with *Rusko*lan (the 'Rusian community') and other such in *The Veles Book*, it is nevertheless defined by O. N. Trubachev and his associate-linguists as Persian/Iranian (belonging to the Alans); though by other linguists there is also an interpretation of *Roxolan* as 'Rusian dwellings in the Field i.e. in the Steppes, or "field expanse".

There now follows some well-dated evidence relating to the 2nd century when, according to Saxo Grammaticus in '*Gesta Danorum*' "Hotherus, the son of the Swedish King Hothbrod, fights a battle with Boes/Vali, the son of Princess Rinda of Rus/Ruthenia". According to the epitaph for St. Maximus of Salzburg, Austria, who perished in the year 477, it is written: "Odoacer^, chieftain of the Ruthenians^, raging against the church of God, and blessed Maximus, hiding with 50 followers in his cave, pushed them from the perpendicular cliffs then threw down the [Roman] province of Noricum by fire and sword".

By the year 555 a reference from the Syriac Chronicle^ by Zachariah the Rhetor, mentions *The people of Khros*, and by the year 626 by the Georgian parchment – *The siege and assault of the great and holy city of Constantinople by the Scythians, who in essence are Rusians*. O. N. Trubachev begins an analysis of the notions of 'Rus, Rossia' only from data mentioned in these and following paragraphs, and that is why the conclusion he reaches is less than accurate: "In the first centuries of our era the Northern Black Sea coast was the West for many nomads... The name Rus was, apparently, conceived here, meaning 'White side'. Rus was originally the south-eastern advance post of Slavdom, and this was written in its name".

This understanding of the term 'Rus', as stated above, is merely the start of a comprehension of its complex semantics. During the period when Oriana-Orissa was already dissociated from Aratta, the ethnonym *rus* was principally connected with the Vedic caste of warriors called *raj(an)ia (raya, rassia)*. Although reminiscences of the "white (west) sides" lingered on, the name *Rus*, ever since the establishment of the Venet(d)i in the Baltics after the Trojan War, rapidly began to assume a meaning more akin to social content; in the Caucasus and East this tendency appeared earlier, though it acquired a more self-contained character. Magdeburg law correctly testified the time and situation, when the princes – the leaders of warriors – were separated (by the priest-rulers and the people) from the ordinary Russians, namely the 'subordinates, who were resettled' and formed the 'principal, continuity' [i.e. the native majority].

It was on these foundations that Rus became Kyiv and Novhorod, and in time – an entire state. So ***Rus*** *became, above all, the synonym of a state that was headed not by priests, but by warriors* who then continued as dynasties. Between these two trends an ethnic self-awareness was formed. It began neither from a cardinal point nor a colour, nor from the outlandish name itself because this *Rus* was not identified with a particular environment but was generally rather detached and could by no means become an autonym. Instead, it began from the totemic reflection of the "bull-taur-Taurus" as the ideal warrior, the embodiment of power, alas, rather than of wisdom, as it had been formerly during the times of the reign of priests; the leaders here became the Tauris of Taurida. Hence this ethnonym reached out to its neighbours and began to be synthesised from its tendencies as indicated by O. N. Trubachev, becoming much stronger and more capable because of the spirit of militant authority associated with it, according to A. Veltman. Synthesis occurred in the states of Rus: Carpathian, Surozhian or Black Sea, Venedian or Baltic, Gelonian, and then Kyivan and Novhorodian Rus. Of these, only Kyivan Rus emerged to assume a position (after its baptism and the decline in its composition of Arsania) which enabled it to break up the communal tradition of Aratta and to become a feudal class state. Even after this, the Arattan tradition was still maintained by the people – by peasant communities and Cossack associations – until the abolition of the Sich^, the Cossack Republic, in 1775, and the fall of Russia in 1917; however, its traditions still live on...

It is possible to verify this and draw even deeper conclusions by further consideration of *The Veles Book*.

Suggested reading

1. Chertkov A. D., *Pelasgic-Thracian tribes who colonised Italy,* The Osnova Magazine, Kiev, 1993-1995, No. 24 (2)-No. 28 (6) .
2. Klassen E., *New Materials for the Ancient History of Slavs...* Moscow, 1854; St. Petersburg, 1995.
3. Trubachev O. N., *Indoarica in the Northern Black Sea coast.* Moscow, 1999.
4. Tulaev P. V., *The Veneti: Ancestors of the Slavs*. Moscow, 2000.

---

[1] The Ukrainian word for Greeks is 'Греки' (Greki) , whilst for rooks it is 'граки' (graki).

[2] In Russian, Trypillia is called Tripol'e or Tripolye.

[3] The Slavic word 'semik' is derived from 'sem', or 'sim', which respectively in Russian and Ukrainian means 'seven'.

[4] cf. Kar Sevak^

[5] The modern city of Vinnytsia in Ukraine is similar in pronunciation to Venice. (V. Krasnoholovets).

[6] These are dealt with in the final part of Yuri Shilov's trilogy, the 4th edition of which was published under the title *Sources of Slavic Civilisation*, 2008, Moscow; ISBN: 978-5-98967-006-0. The first part, *Pre-history of Rus,* is presented here, with minor additions, under the title of *Ancient History of Aratta-Ukraine*. Parts II, *The Vedantic Heritage of Ukraine,* & III, *Cosmic Secrets of Kurhans,* are currently only available in Russian.

CHAPTER 10

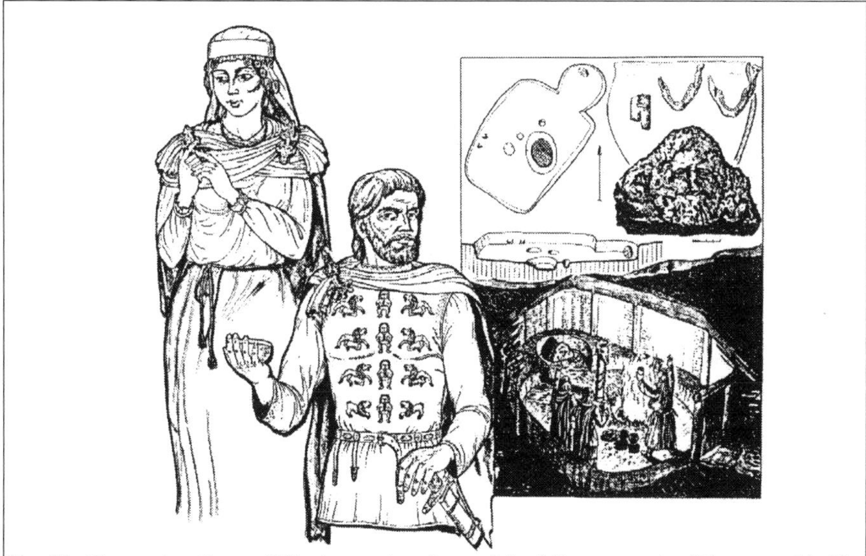

Fig. 92 : **Reconstructions of Slavic sanctuaries and druidic garments** of the second half of first millennium CE by P. L. Kornienko et al.

"THE VELES BOOK" ON THE ORIGINS OF SLAVS AND RUS

With the help of *The Veles Book*, we discovered that Slavs had remembered their ancestral origins as far back as 20 millennia ago and recognised themselves as an ethnic community no later than 2300-1700 years BCE, when they adopted the cult of Svaroh and Dazhboh-Svarozhych – a time when the constellation of Taurus was at the head of the solar zodiac. We will now consider what *The Veles Book* had to say about the origins of the Slavs (or Slovyan, as Ukrainians say) and of Rus; and whether the information of *The Veles Book* confirms or contradicts the above consideration and what new information it injects into the understanding of history.

1. Orissa and Borusia as the general Slo(a)vyan homeland.

In S. I. Nalyvayko's book *Secrets of Sanskrit Revealed* (Kyiv, 2000) – which not only endorses but also expands upon O. N. Trubachev's monograph *Indoarica in Northern Black Sea coast* (Moscow, 1999) – he showed that the territory of future Rus [i.e. modern Ukraine] had an extraordinary saturation of names associated with different breeds of cattle. Although the researcher initially saw Indo-Aryan parallels in this, it is only possible to explain their origin and, most importantly their concentration, by taking into account Aratta and the archaeological cultures making up its antiquities. This is because the most esteemed animal for Aryans and even for modern Ukrainians, was, and still is, the horse rather than the bull; the semantics of the latter prevailed only in Trypillia and some cultures genetically

Fig. 93 :**Model of a sanctuary-observatory from Oriana**. Cultic bowl from a burial at the settlement of Cherkasiv Sad of the Usativ archaeological culture, Trypillia C-I.

connected with it.

Amongst those culturally associated names are Or(d)issa and Borusia. As repeatedly mentioned already, between the 4th – 3rd millennium BCE these names gained a foothold in the two parts of Aratta, i.e. the coastal south and the northern forest-steppe. As a rule, the first of them was called Oriana^ (as in the *Mahabharata* and *The Veles Book*, etc.), and this name reflected the synthesis of its Arattan basis as well as significant Arattan influences on the formation of the first State in the coastal area of modern Odessa and of the Odessa Region. Orissa (as the name appears in Sanskrit, or *Odissa* in Hindi), located on the lower reaches of the Boristhen-Dnipro, was probably an amalgam of names from the Rivers *Tiras^*-Dniester and *Ros*, which are consonant with the name of the Vedic *Rasa,* carrying the meaning of 'lit up' and 'Sunny water'. When discussing the toponym of *Orissa,* S. I. Nalyvayko draws our attention to Indo-Aryan conformity with *Vrish* and *Godesh* – the 'Bull', 'Bull country'. The toponym of Borusia (medieval Beresteyschina) is obviously similar to Borusthen which has been ethno-culturally related, since ancient pre-Slavic times (as well as Indo-European, even then), to the Pelasgian Boristhen and subsequently to the Boristhen of the Greeks. The latter treated this name as the river "from the northern current" but this was derived from "popular etymology" based on consonances; details about the actual sources of the name were mentioned earlier.

As the economic basis of both parts of Aratta consisted of agriculture and cattle breeding, they both tended towards the sea rather than the forests. Indeed the Asia Minor homeland of the proto-Indo-Europeans lay in the hinterland behind the sea from where the patriarchy gained in strength, mainly because of the metals, salt and other products of trade necessary for the economy and rapid enrichment. That is why Orissa in the 3rd millennium BCE appeared to be progressive, an economically and demographically dynamic country predisposed to migrations. Furthermore, it was created as the active destiny of the Aryans – those nomadic steppe inhabitants whose ethnonym underlay the name Oriana and who were the first in the world to tame the horse, invent cavalry, wagons and chariots.

Two clear trends of demographic explosion and migrational movements developed in Orissa-Oriana: westwards, by the sea and eastwards, by the steppe. These took place between the middle of the 3rd – 2nd millennium BCE.

In both cases a more or less distinctive Slavic substrate can be traced because, as we have already discovered, it was identical to the core of the 'Indo-European language community', the ethnocultural basis of Aratta. At the same time, the western migrational movement became the catalyst for the formation of the Pelasgian-Greek ethnic groups, and in the east – the Aryan (Indo-Iranian). Their 'passionary' embryos (the term used by L. N. Gumilev) formed in Orissa-Oriana and then moved – increasing, accumulating like a snowball – in the related environment of the principally Aryan tribes of Asia Minor and the Balkans, as well as in the Eurasian steppe. The specific character of this state is perhaps outlined in one of the bequests of *The Veles Book* (board 17b):

And they should return those steppe horpy [kurhan-barrows]
and to protect, as our fathers and forefathers...
our cities must be encircled, just like our fathers ...

The inter-relationship between Oriana and Borusia, and also the past history of the origin of Rus, are quite clearly outlined in *The Veles Book* at the section which discusses the migration to the Indian 'Pendeb' (Punjab), a prolonged sojourn there, and then a partial return:

31 *Let his name be sanctified – Indra,*
Because that is our god among gods and he knows the Vedas...
Being a child he came from the land of Aryans (the country of Arstia) to the land of In(d)...
And there told the father – at the Veche of Aryans – to his three sons
to divide in three kinds
and go to the noon [south] *and westward suns.*

6a *From Oriy our fathers were with the arrival of Boruses^*
on the Ray-river [Paradise-river], *on the Dnipro and to the Carpathian power.*

5a … *and there they settled down and lived agreeably…*
and the patriarch of the kin was Shchek, who was from Oriana.
7f *And Dazhbo generated us from the cow Zamun,*
and we were Kraventsy and Skufe ['Cow-men and Bull-herdsmen'] –
Ants, Ruses, Borusy and Surozh.
And so began the forefathers of Ruses.
and from Pendeb [Punjab] *we are still going to the sky of blue Svarga* [Svarozh]

As we see, Oriana and Borusia combined to become a union of Aryan tribes which went on campaign to the Indian Punjab, lived there and then came back together. They were accepted on the right bank of the Dnipro by their old hearther-relatives who had not gone on campaign to India; for this hospitality the returners began to praise the glory of Svaroh and Dazhboh (VB: 38a). These gods were already honoured by them before the Indian campaign because the Borusians were said to have been created by Svarozhych-Dazhboh (*The Veles Book*, 7f) and in India *Svarog, chastising the migrants brought a great confusion in the mountains* – i.e., an earthquake (VB: 38a); so that now, returning home did not involve having to adapt to new ways but instead offered an opportunity to reinforce their ancient faith. Hereafter these tribes or their kinfolk who had left the Punjab, were related to the Venet(d)ians, Usians, and also generated the Surozhetsians (and probably the Ants); this union – initially military in character – was called *Rus* (one which was similar, but not the earliest union; see the previous section). All of these details are derived from adjacent texts in *The Veles Book* and can be verified on the basis of the independent sources mentioned earlier. It is necessary to add even more sources to those already examined.

The onset of the migration from coastal Oriana into India in the 18th – 16th centuries BCE is acknowledged by the appearance of the Indo-Aryan Hurrian state of *Mitanni* in northern Mesopotamia. According to Trubachev, the name 'Mitanni' comes from the Indo-Aryan tribe of *Meoto* from the shores of the Meotida (Sea of Azov).

According to Vedic traditions, Indra led the tribes of *Yadu* and *Turvash* into India and we will later be seeing their relationship to the *Yatvyagi* of Lithuania and the *Turovtsy* of Volyn [the Volyn region of modern Ukraine] and indeed to other tribes of those regions. No-one disputes the fact that the indigenous Dravidian population of India (the *Dacu* of the Vedas and *The Veles Book*) was, and remains, dark-skinned and black-haired, whereas Slavs and other peoples of Eastern and Northern Europe are characterised by light eyes, skin and hair. Therefore by indisputable evidence the Aryans migrated to India (but not vice versa, as conjectured by K. Ritter, N. K. Roerich and others), linking the corresponding 'arrival of Indra' and other Vedic gods together with the Aryans. Furthermore, consider the instruction issued by Patanjali in the 2nd century BCE: "For true Brahmans it is necessary to have grey eyes and chestnut hair". Although Krishna is considered to be a native Indian deity (Dravidian) and black, nevertheless his eyes were said to be 'like flax flowers' and such blue eyes are not indigenous to India. Presumably, this God (barely mentioned in the *Rigveda*) came into India with the Aryans. In fact he is described as having 'unnaturally blue skin' and he ritually wore yellow clothes – the opposite of his elder brother Balarama^. On the other hand, the Agathyrsi of the Carpathians and Dniester area were reported by Pliny, Solinus[1] and others, to have dark-blue dyed hair-colour, thickly tattooed faces and were 'greedy with (yellow) gold'. Since then the combination of blue-yellow colours remains characteristic of the Cossacks of Ukraine as it also does for the Nikhang of India (Punjab) who are similar to them, and where such combinations of colour symbolise festivals and happiness. Tridents (trishulas) are especially esteemed there, exactly as in modern Ukraine (and prior to that – in Rus).

What is particularly impressive, besides the natural evidence for the journeys of the Rusy ancestors from Taurida^ as far as India, are the calendar sanctuaries of the Maiden (convincingly shown as embodiments of the God Siva – by Trubachev and Nalyvayko) in the extreme southern, coastal capes of these countries. Also found from those times in India and extending down to its southern borders was the Shaka-Sambat^ (calendar) - is this not similar to verse 38b in *The Veles Book*– the 'Saki (Scythian) feed' calendar? This calendar, together with supporting data, raises some doubt for an absolutely Indian origin for Shiva; this God is

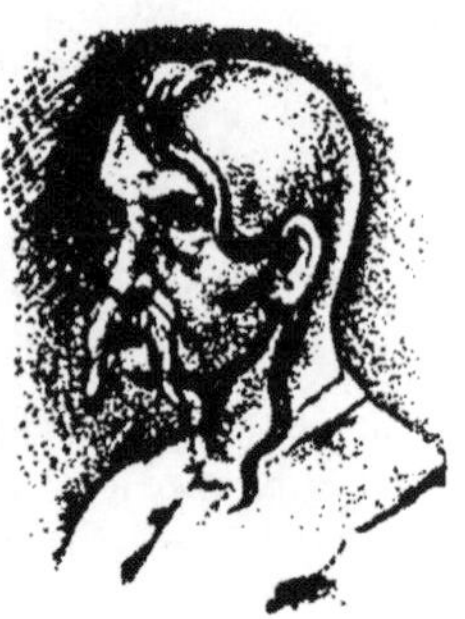

Fig. 94 : Hairstyles of an Indian Brahman and Ukrainian Cossacks.

evidently a synthesis of the local (Dravidian) and alien (Aryan) cultures.

In addition to recording information about the campaign to India, *The Veles Book* also contains much more detail about the stay in India and, especially, details about the return of a certain number of migrants from there to the Dnipro area. This can be supported by archaeological finds of Indian cowrie shells and other such ornaments in Cimmerian graves and subsequently on the Northern Black Sea Coast, together with the presence of specific architectural details. The cult of Siva mentioned in inscriptions in the Odessa Region could have arisen as a synthesis of local cults and the introduction of Orianians from India. Having come back to their homeland with Siva (in Old Scythia or Sindica, territories where manifestations of the cult are concentrated) here the 'slavni-slaviany' [i.e. glorious Slavs^] transformed him into the ancestor of Sieva (VB: 9a), the hero (of the Balga-bull of the Indo-Aryans, Baal-bull of Kinahh of Suria-Syria); and from Savur Grave, is Cossack Mamai – whose primary images are rather similar to those of Siva. The most essential difference between these canons is that the horse is connected with Mamai and the bull with Siva.

The first is connected with the deification of the horse-like Khors – as with the Croatians [the Horvaty, in Russian] – who already had Persian roots (according to Trubachev), and corresponded to Khorev, one of the sons of forefather Oriy^. Some of those who had been forced to move away to India from overcrowded Oriana, or Dandaria (the 'Mace-bearing Aria' of the Aryans) as it began to be referred to then, built for themselves on their return from India a new Sindic and Dandaria (on the Taman peninsula); their centre became Kimoria–Kimmeria (located on each coast of the Kerch strait) with its capital *Surozh^* (modern Sudak). In the authoritative opinions of Nalyvayko and Trubachev, this latter name arose from the Indo-Aryan *Sauvira* and Suria^. Nevertheless it could be said that there was also a connection with the return from Suria (Syria^), which had a district called Khoriv and a city, *Samiria*, the capital of Samaro (<Sumer> Kimoro, which avoided Semitic assimilation and founded Samaria – an area in Palestine). A further migration of Cimmerians from the Northern Black Sea area was directed towards those allies.

It is noted that the old names were not retained but were replaced according to the needs of the moment. "Old Scythia" is obviously pre-Scythian (until the 6th – 7th centuries BCE, when the Scythians, as commonly believed after Herodotus, came to the Northern Black Sea Coast from Asia). It is to "Old *Scythia*" that the 'cast-offs and roamers' from India returned (a name cognate with Persian *Skud,* Greek *Skutkhari,* according to O. N. Trubachev). Then, after the formation of Kimoria by some of these so-called 'Roamers', and after being invaded by other Scythians, the value of the latter ethnonym 'Scythian' was rethought and acquired other meanings. This is a regular occurrence for all nations, countries, and states.

The exodus from the 'country of India' took place during the 9th – 8th centuries BCE (according to the chronology of *The Veles Book* although it would now be more reliable to date it to the boundary of the 1st and 2nd millennium BCE). They travelled along two routes as alternate groups. The section led by Iriy and his sons, went through Persia and

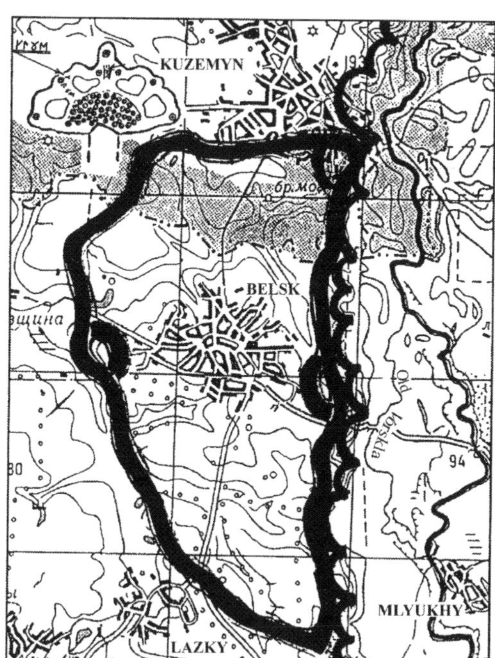

Fig. 95 : **Triple Dnipro-Don of Gelon, follower of Asia Minor's Troy-Illium**. The plan of the ancient city-state (according to *The Veles Book* and Herodotus), conditionally named by archaeologists as Belsk Horodyshche (near the village of Belsk, Poltava region). On the left above – outline of a buckle-fastener with a profane inscription of 6th century CE, using the same script as that used in *The Veles Book*.

Syria, the Caucasus and Kuban and settled on the right bank of the Dnipro together with the local, related population (of Skolots) who permitted Kiy to found or extend the city of Indikyiv (VB: 38a)... The second group led by Oriy and his sons returned by travelling behind the Ray-river [Paradise River] (the Volga) to their Rusy kin, descendants of Bohomyr, where the wandering Orianians and Borusians were also remembered by their compatriots (VB: 4d, 6a, 9b, 10, 36a). They were not welcomed without conflict but they accepted the principals, Shchek and Khoriv[2]; their father Oriy received permission to found the city of Golun (VB: 7c, 35a of *The Veles Book*; Helon, according to Herodotus), which covered an immense area of 44 km², almost equalling the combined area of Carthage, Rome and Babylon. In subsequent legends and editing of *The Veles Book*, these two separate returns from India were merged into one [losing the vital evidence of chronology]. Legends were interpolated about (O)Sedn, a relative of Iriy and Oriy, who was on the Pontic shore of Rosii-city (VB: 33) from where Cimmeria began with Surozh, which subsequently became Surozhian Rus (VB: 4d, 6c, 26).

The arguments for this thesis will be continued later but let us pause here on the ethnonym, Sloviany-Slaviany, which – according to *The Veles Book* – was formed at the time of the Indian migration.

It began from the discord, which preceded the general return from India of some of the Orianians and Borusians:

38a ... a*nd many people spoke :*
"We shall not go to our kin as there is no rest for hearthers,
but we will be better off wandering in woods or mountains".
Thus, by such words relatives were separated (from relatives)...
There were those Slavs (Slavishchi) *in great difficulty,*
unable to live on anything.

And they said to Father-Iriy: "Lead us away [back]"...
And since then the kin of Slavdom (Slaven) *began up to now.*

Thus, **on the boundary of 2nd - 1st millennium BCE, the autonym of *Slovian*, and in a short time *Slavs*, was *attributed to*, and accepted in, India by the union of several kin of Orianians and Borusians separated from other Aryan-immigrants, who returned to the Dnipro and began to glorify Svaroh, Dazhboh and other local gods there**, whilst at the same time not forgetting their former gods. The privilege of creating an ethnonym belonged to the leader-priests, therefore, it is not surprising that its significance was primarily coordinated with a similarly meaningful term for the ethnonym of the Veneti (but without giving the word Slova the same emphasis as *Slavia* [which means glorious]) – which had been conceived in the Northern Black Sea coast, as we already know, even at the beginning of the westward migrations from this place and to the East.

Within the area of nearest distribution and adoption of the ethnonym of passionary *Slavs*, it appeared that the Skoloty and Rusy, etc., were related to them. Borusia was associated with the Rusy, Prusians, Uglichians, Slavs, Slovenes, Serbs, Sorbians and other allies of African Berbers (who were descendants of the Slavic tribe of Vandals). The latter, were apparently mentioned in the Frankish *Song of Roland,* which records events of the 8th century.

2. *The Veles Book* on the Origin of Rus.

Fig. 96 : **Pre-Indian Sanskrit**: Inscription on a vessel of mid-2nd millennium BCE from a kurhan at the city of Artemivsk in the Donets region. According to V. Kulbaka and V. Kachur.

Rus already existed in the Dnipro area when the glorious union of sections of Orianians and Borusians returned there from the Punjab at the beginning of the 1st millennium BCE:

4d *From that darkness issued the wicked tribe of Dasuv* ("The Veles Book" later names them and others as the (Kh)Huni)...
And that old Father-Oriy says:
"Let us go out of this land where the Huni kill our brothers."
10 *After Bohumir*[3] *there was Oriy with his sons.*
And when the Huni began a large war, aiming for the formation of their great land, we went away, there, to Rus.
2a ... *and we were led by father Oriy to the Rusy land, because we had always resided there.*

The founders of Rus derived their lineage from Bohomyr, mentioned earlier, who was more ancient than Oriy and who probably lived on the north coast of the Adriatic Sea. Thus, Rus had existed since Bohomyr, and its long connection with the Dnipro area (VB: 2a, 38a) can be understood through its identification with Orissa (Oriana) and Borusia. There was also an anonymous forefather who came from there, or maybe from the "*mountain of Rusy"* (VB: 17a) in Taurida or the Balkans, who was in due course identified with Kvasur^ or Bohomyr.

16 *In old times there was a knight who was wealthy and valiant,*
and was, they say, [held] *in honour in Rus.*
And he had a wife and two daughters.
22 *And still let it be said about that,*
how Kvasur received from the gods a secret and approved surina [type of drink]...
just like father Blahomir, [Kvasur] *received an exhortation from heaven...*

That because Bohomyr is named tvastyr (creator, the master of divine rank)
and they told him about Slavs...
that Slavs should be such as gods instruct them: behold them.
9a *In ancient times Bohumir lived, a knight of slavy* [= *glory*],
who had three daughters (Dreva, Skreva, Poleva) *and two sons* (Sieve and Rus)...
And here was their mother named Slavuna...
From them three kins have gone, that were Slovian.
From their (daughters) *descended the* [tribes] *of Drevlyan, Krivichi and Polian,*
(from the sons) *descended the tribes of Siverian and Rusy.*

What do we have here? First of all, it is the genealogical legend from the times when patriarchy was taking root although there were still strong traditions of matriarchy, which finally petered out somewhere in the 7th century (when rivalry between Drevlian and Polian tribes had already begun but the latter had still not yet finally secured superiority). It is also evident that Slavs preferred matriarchy and rather dissociated themselves from their Rusy kin who favoured patriarchy. We should take note of the observations of L. I. Akimov concerning a similar collision of allegiances in the Troad and the part played by the Slavs (and, we should add, the Ruthenian-Etruscans)! With this echo from *The Veles Book*, half-forgotten by subsequent authors, we have the name and speciality of the first-ancestor. Bohomyr – Master of the Word, the intermediary between the God Svaroh (and other gods) and the Slavs, who, in a later section on the same board of *The Veles Book*, are still named just as Rusy. In this context, Boh**omyr**'s name may be understood as 'Divine Omir', (i.e. God's story-teller) in the manner of that most famous *Omir* who is now inaccurately called Homer.

The *Kryni* (VB: 30) or the seven 'streams' of *Semyrychia*[4] (VB: 9a, 15a) *where our fathers had cities* (19), is not a feature that necessarily fits geographically in the location of Central Asia. However, that feature of "seven wells" does exist in Crimea, where in the northern part of the peninsula, during Taurian times, there lived the tribes of Satarhi who were related to – 'those who have seven settlements'. A town with a similar name was located near Chersonese [in modern Crimea].

The legendary motherland of Bohomyr is best matched by the area of the Timava River on the northern corner of the Adriatic Sea where there were seven sources and a sacred forest devoted to Diomid ('the God Mid') (Strabo's *Geography*). In the neighbouring region were the Etruscan cities of Slavini, Kyiv, and Perugia, etc., whose rise was enabled in Italic (V)enet(ts)i because of the migration to that region of a tribe with the same name led by Aeneus after the fall of Troy – around the middle of the 13th (or at the end of 11th) century BCE. It is here, near Creccio, that the gravestone of Aeneus, with its reference to Rasii, was found. Is this not a connection with Rus, by the younger son of Bohomyr? This and other cities could be regarded as the second or third wave (after Orissa-Borusia and Ruthenian-Etruria), in Adriatic Rus.

It was apparently from there (VB: 5a, 6e, 9a) that "the great-grandfathers went up to the mountains of Carpathia and settled". In the first instance the Rusy went with the Venedi, but the latter wanted to take their gods away to the Venedian Sea, i.e. the Baltic Sea. Since Oriy's campaign to the Carpathians is indicated to have been 1300 years prior to that of the Gothic ruler Hermanaric^ (VB: 9a) or 1500 years before Kyivan Prince Dir^ (VB: 5a, 6a), these events must have taken place during the 10th – 7th centuries BCE. Two additional Rusy were then founded – the Carpathian Rus and the Baltic Rus, centred on the island of Ruyan^ (now Rugen).

These events took place not later than the 7th century BCE, during the Rusy-Cimmerian occupation in the Middle East, where they became known to the authors of the Persian *Avesta*^. In the '*Geographical Verses*' describing the 16 countries[5] created by Ahura Mazda, there is a reference to *Chakhrem* (the 'Circle', or 'Kolo' in Ukrainian, a concept inherent to S*kolo*tians and the cities of *The Veles Book*, but in particular the city of *Chyhyryn* – according to S. I. Nalyvayko). It belonged to 'True'-Asha (i.e. Aratta in Sanskrit, as befitting the placing of *Chyhyryn*) and was damaged by a ceremony of cremation (which actually existed in Aratta and became evident in the Kyiv region at the end of the Trypillian

Fig. 97 : **Foremother of the Skolots (ancient Slavs)**. The central part of ancient images on a golden diadem from a burial of Scythian archaeological culture at the village of Sakhnivka.

culture). Other countries mentioned in the *Avesta* are also of interest – Hapta-Hindu ('Semyrychia'[6]), Sukhdho [Sogdiana], Badki [Bakhdhim/Bactria] and Rankhi [Rakham/ Ragai]. The last three are located in Central Asia but relate to *The Veles Book*. So, Sugdeya, is connected to the Sogdiana of the Persian-Asian Scythians and to Surozh, the Cimmerian-Slavic city of the Sarmatians. Badki is related with Bolokhov ('Volkhov'[7]) in the combined area of three modern regions of Kyiv, Volyn and Ternopol, and also Wallachia. However, as far as Rankhi is concerned, as a river it can be compared to the Vedic river Rasa: initially by the Dnipro and Ros rivers and in due course, the Volga.

The Carpathian Rusy are apparently first described in *The Veles Book* (board 6a, et al.). However, the history of their origin, which is traced sufficiently clearly above, was later subject to retellings and writings about the sons of Indian Oriy, i.e. Kyi^, Shchek and Khoryv (VB: 4d, 31, 38a). After returning from India they did not want to go along with their father's plans, "after being subdivided on those and others" (VB: 26). Kyi "settled down" near the Dnipro in Indikyiv, which is called Kyiv (VB: 7c, 38a), and he founded the Kyivan dynasty amongst the Rusy sometime during the 9th century BCE (VB: 22, 36a, 7i). Khoryv and Shchek left the area and migrated to the Carpathian mountains where they established other cities (VB: 36b). Subsequently, "Khoryv took his warriors" (VB: 7i) and became the patriarch of a separate tribe (VB: 36a). Whilst Shchek entrenched his people in the Carpathians (VB: 5a), "another part (tribe) of Shchek remained with the Rusy, and formed Ruskolan with them in that area, which was different from the Rus of Kyi" (VB: 7i). When they encountered difficulties with enemies in the Carpathians, they moved to Kyiv-hrad (Kyiv-city) and to Golun and settled there" (VB: 36b).

18a *And we have left the Carpathian mountains for Kyi...*
and sing – because we are Rusy – about those glorious days...
In fact this governor Bobrets that led the Rusy to Golun,
received on his death the rank of Perunian.

19 *Let us also tell the old words of our glory about our sacred Semyrychia,*
where our fathers had cities,
but they returned from that ground, and departed to another land.
And in those times they had power,
and in antiquity had ... the destiny of Rusy named Golun (Kelune)...
and after (expiration) *that land of those days was stolen from us.*
Those stones of Rus'-city call to us.

Some of the events mentioned in these lines occurred centuries after the return of Oriy with his sons from India; we shall examine those events in more detail below.

In *The Veles Book* (board 35a), the establishment of the city of Golun is attributed to Oriy. Maybe, there was such a place – with some Klunia-'Sobranie', as frequently mentioned in the *Book*. However, the city-state of Helon, [Gelon in Ukrainian] described by Herodotus in *The Histories* (IV: 108-109) is the one most likely to be meant since, at that time, it was the greatest fortified settlement in Europe (near the modern village of Bilsk in the region north of Poltava). It arose immediately after the Trojan War and during the period when the name of Troy was replaced by Ilion/Ilium – so, it is quite probable that it was founded by the companions of Odysseus or their descendants. According to O. N. Trubachev, A. I. Asov and others, and partly to S. I. Nalyvayko, Odysseus had sailed along the coast of Odissa-Orissa and ended up in the north-east at the island of Eya (on the Taman peninsula). There, before he founded the city of Helon, (<Ilion/Ilium?) he and his crew were made to suffer: first of al, the crew were turned into pigs by the enchantress Circe and then they were oppressed by local merchants. Later, Helon was built by them on the land of the benevolent Budini in whom it is possible to detect a kindred part of those who returned from India. Their faces corresponded with the Brahmanic ideal: "Light-blue eyes and red hair", according to Herodotus. The ethnonym 'Budini' is cognate with 'Bhuti' – the companions of Siva-Bhutanatha (also a familiar name in Oriana-Orissa) and also with the Irano-Median 'Budiy'. As already stated, there is a relationship between the Indo-Aryan 'Siva', the Slavic 'Sieva' and 'Sevik' of Herodotus' and it is helpful to include (in this ethnological unit of Aryan nations) the Urartian 'Shivani', the Hittite 'Sivam', the Palais 'Tiyat', and so on. The Wolf-like Neuri[8], who found the same Budini rescued from serpents, could also enter the Slavic ethnogenesis.

Thus, we return to the testimony of *The Veles Book* and other written sources describing Rus having arisen from Orissa and Borusia in the chain of events after the Trojan War, in the flow of western migration of Slavic tribes, which somewhere between 2300-1700 BCE started to secede from Oriana-Orissa-Odissa, as the Veneti, and in the process formed the Ruthenians-Etruscans at the beginning of Rus. Its primary composition in the Adriatic, the Carpathians and the Baltic, takes place at some time during the 10th – 7th centuries BCE. At that period there was an adjustment in the relationship between the migrants and their Northern Black Sea ancestral home (Oriana-Borusia), from where a counter impulse came

Fig. 98 : **Odysseus and the Sirens**. An ancient image and sculpture.

from the active migrants who had returned from India, led by Oriy and his sons. S. I. Nalyvayko wrote: "To refuse any discussion on the Indian aspects of *The Veles Book* ... by asserting and alleging that this document is a fake, should be decisively rejected. To describe the history of Slavs, with such knowledge...densely interspersed with specific details (with which researchers still struggle, even now), which reach back into Aryan remoteness - is simply impossible to fake, whatever talent the writers owned". It remains regrettable that the greatest modern Slavist, O. N. Trubachev, doesn't use *The Veles Book* in his researches.

3. Social traditions and faith of pre-Kyivan Rus.

Fig. 99 : **Ceremonial bowl from the kurhan of a Scythian chieftain,** 4th century BCE. (Also Figs. 116, 130).

Those who research the problems concerning the origins of Rus, who do not acknowledge *The Veles Book*, or other "unreliable sources", must remember three simple things that have already been repeatedly touched upon. Let us look at them again:

Firstly, in the mid-20th century, a system of sanctuary-observatories was identified; they were revealed by aerial photography, by mapping and archaeological excavations. The line of these observatories ran from Stonehenge in Britain over to Arkaim in the Trans-Urals. The tradition of constructing such 'Maidans' [sanctuary-observatories] is to this day retained in India, and this exact name is used in Ukraine for these ancient ruins.

Secondly, these constructions were built for specific projects by the people who used them and who communicated with other users, like themselves, across huge expanses of the Indo-European world, by millennia-long adherence to definite, specific calendar-astronomical traditions which are now studied by the academic discipline of archaeo-astronomy.

Thirdly, the attendants of this system were able to follow not only the system of calendars, the economy and selective breeding etc. over many generations but also to record the ethnogenesis of their fellow tribesmen, relatives and neighbours, fixing historical events and from time to time summarising them. Since the priests raised the best strains of cattle breeds and plants, why should they ignore implementing a similar policy for the people?

From these three associated factors grew the Vedas of Indo-European people: the *Veda* of the Slavs, the Rig*Veda* of Indo-Aryans., the A*vesta* of the Persians, and the Icelandic *Edda*. It is evident that *The Veles Book*, in which the *Vedas* are mentioned (VB: 31), has an affinity with these texts. (Could the Veles reference have been to the *Veda Slovena* that was found by S. I. Verkovich around the mid-19th century in the [Bulgarian] Rodope mountains?).

The helplessness of academic science with regard to *The Veles Book* (and the impossibility of it being a fake, which would undoubtedly be acknowledged by all who dared to study it deeply) – is a consequence of traditions started by the ancient 'fathers of history'. Even Herodotus did not understand the context of the pilgrimages of the Hyperboreans to Delos and neither did the Greek Aristeus - even though he was "obsessed by Apollo". Incidentally, Aristeus noted the similarities with places associated with the legendary astronomer-cartographer Atlanta, who continued the same tradition on behalf of Apollo, whose wanderings were even recorded in a poem! It is surprising that these circumstances do not interest science. All the more so since Hecataeus and Diodorus, adherents of Herodotus, left a description of a "spherical Hyperborean temple", where "from the vernal equinox till the rising of the Pleiades" Apollo arrived once every 19 years to specify the calendars, but modern scientists disbelieve these even more vehemently. The specific character of figurative-intuitive thinking and its advantages over logical-analytical thinking was incomprehensible even for the Greeks in their own time so to modern scientists and archaeologists it is completely incomprehensible.

We hope that O. N. Trubachev's decoding of what was meant by "dark places" in the 3rd century BCE oath of the citizens of Chersonese will yield results, as well as the legend of the relics of St. Clement. The Greeks, Tauris and other inhabitants of the famous, ancient Greek city-state swore that they would protect the *Saster* ('Sacred Collection' i.e. the 'Divine book') of their people. Meanwhile the very name of this Book indicates its relationship is not with Hellenic culture but rather with Indo-Aryan, Taurian, or Orianian culture. The divine force of the *Saster* is illustrated by an act of "going from good believers, Digits by name, ... nearer to true Double-knowing". This quote refers to those who trained (and, possibly, ethnically belonged) within the Indo-Aryan tradition of the 'twice-born^ Digits', an expert of the 'Divine book' *Saster*, who belonged to the order of highly educated Taurian or Rusy priests, loyal to Christianity, who helped 9th century St. Cyril [ostensibly 'the creator of Slavic writing'], in Korsun, in searches for the relicts of St. Clement, as well as helping him predict a forthcoming rain-shower... *The Veles Book* complies perfectly with this ethno- and cultural-historical context.

Without repeating the lines from *The Veles Book* already considered, we shall examine new, other illuminating moments in the formation of the State of Rus as the successor to Aratta and Oriana. The reference points for further examination of data will be the names of ancestors and the instructions in ancient testaments.

Deeper than other precepts, reaching far back into Indo-European-Arattan times, is the precept of *Khorig's son from father Khorig, and there is your petitioner before the gods* (VB: 29). He appeals to the ancestors' Mother-S(o)va-Slava and Father Diya, and also to the forefather Oriy – and reminds the people that their traditions "had arrived from the sources of Semiramis"^ (VB: 30). The heavenly god Svarezh was considered to be the husband of the Earth, and the people as their children who honoured this divine pair with sacrifices and at the end of their lives departed to Iriy-Ray (Paradise). Svaroh was the highest God, but a wise man calls on other gods – Vishna^ and Indra – as manifestations [aspects] of Svaroh. And on Indra-Onder too – since there,

exists another Perun
and he lays enemies on their back and so tears off their heads;
and speaks to the sky and throws (them) near the sea and in forests

This is conjuring; the calling down of rains on fellow tribesmen and droughts on strangers. Fortunes were told by casting wooden idols of Indra into a fire and by manipulating the heads of enemies slain in battle; they matched an Indo-Aryan and Taurian tradition of making sacrifices to Deva (Diva, i.e. the Maiden), the female aspect of Siva as the destroyer. By subjugating-killing the bull-like Asura^ ('vital force') named Mahisha ('God of the Earth'), Siva-Mahadevi absorbed this life-giving energy. This ritual has calendric frequency, as symbolised by a necklace of skulls around the neck of the black, terrible goddess. Hence it was the custom of the Tauris (according to Herodotus, IV: 103) to sacrificially kill strangers with a blow to the head from a club-staff and then to exhibit the head on a pole above a chimney – probably, so that it would turn black and rise up to the heaven of the Maiden-Diva (Siva). It is probably specifically associated with the trident which was especially esteemed in Taurida during ancient times, both by the local population and by the Greeks...

To have brought this cult out of India and integrated it [into Slavic culture] could only have been, we repeat, from the Orianians and Borusians whose corresponding migration is described in *The Veles Book*. And from the appearance of the entities described above (each of whom has both female and male aspects) the appearance of the Rusy Mokosh^ could have developed, as conjectured quite justly, by S. I. Nalyvayko, (although as a unisexual goddess she is also represented in two hypostases: with hands pointing downwards (as valleys) and upwards (as mountains), which are directed in prayer either to the heavens or to the earth).

Thus, the first precept under scrutiny here is connected with the western migration of the Rusy (the Trojan-Italics, conventionally speaking), which incorporated some of the lessons learned from the eastern migration. The basic composition of *The precept of the kin of Khorig* concerns the beginning of ancient time and is probably connected with

Taurida. However, the application of the laws/precepts on boards 29-30 of *The Veles Book* is marked, on the first board, from the time of the Kyivan princes, Askold and Ryurik[9] and is connected with the formation of Kyivan Rus.

Here, it is worth deviating momentarily from studying specific precepts to note some of the traditions upheld by the Magi with the help of codified records, one of which was *The Veles Book* (board 16). It would have emerged during the times when legends began about the ancestor Bohomyr; times when the inherent matriarchal position of Aratta had not yet been finally rejected; times when Dazhboh, Veles, Iasus (<Iasion) and magicians on earth were then especially honoured. Veles, as correctly regarded by S. I. Nalyvayko, could have been regarded by the Magi as an aspect-epithet of Siva – as Vrish, the 'Ox, Bull', as 'Sivi, or the Syvi Oxen' of Ukrainians – a transformation of the sacred to the ordinary level of folk culture. The name of Sivash^ could have arisen in this way; a name that features in the surnames of Sivaschenko, Shilo – or, conversely, several sacred names.

A framework for the beginning of written language and also for *The Veles Book*, emerges near Stone Grave, the location of the most ancient annals in the world, dating back to the periods of the (19th) – 12th – 6th – 3rd millennium BCE. The earliest instances of phonetic letters were recently identified there (at the time, these letters were only being found in burials of the Ingul culture, which began in the 2nd millennium BCE and whose carriers were involved in the ethnogenesis of the Pelasgians, Hyksos, Aryans and Slavs); here the alphabet was conceived. In the modern Donetsk region, vessels have been found which were decorated with pre-Sanskrit inscriptions from a time which marked the threshold of the partial migration of the Aryans to India. The implication is that in the course of their

Fig. 100 : Depiction of **Veles** [a Slavic god], a woman and of Lada, on the Zbruch idol of Svitovyd, 9th century.

wanderings in Troad and Etruria, India and Palestine, the heroes of *The Veles Book* could already record events, add to them and periodically summarise them. This assumption is confirmed in two legends. Firstly: the legend recording the arrival of the Argonauts on the isle of Eya (in Colchis – erroneously) in their quest for the fleece-skin that held records. Secondly: the testimony of the Chaldean priest Berossus (perhaps Borusian originally?) in which he drew a considerable amount of information from the ancient books of the Scythians (or rather it would seem, the Rusy?). We should remember the history of the Pelasgian-Trojan-Etruscan books of the Sibyl, which were piously kept in Rome until they were suddenly burned (they were written on oak boards, similar to those of *The Veles Book*) – most fortuitously they were then rediscovered [as copies] in Asia Minor.

G. S. Belyakova (in the magazine *Russian Thought*, Moscow, 1993, No. 3-12), offered a well substantiated hypothesis on the formation of the "alphabet from the Golden fleece", drawn from the symbols of the solar zodiac, multiplied twice. The same formation could well have arisen from Stone Grave and area, whose calendars date back into the Palaeolithic era (according to linguist, A. G. Kifishin). The ascendancy of Aries in the Zodiac began around 1700 BCE, precisely where the cults of Apollo, Zeus, and Dionysus arose, and where myths and writing, etc. were reformed. It is from here that the written language of the Pelasgians – together with the cults of those particular gods – could have reached Troad and Greece (aboard ships, like those depicted in the same Stone Grave) four centuries prior to Deucalion's flood, (according to the *History*, Diodorus V: 57). Could it have been from this specific time that the *Sastri* – the sacred books – started to be amassed, later continuing in Chersonese (see above)? Was it purely accidental that in these territories, on the same Aryan-Rus foundation, as well as on the Zodiac (Orthodox calendar), that the monk Konstantin - who later became St. Cyril, the alleged 'enlightener of illiterate Slavs', reformed the written language yet again? In the year 861, in Korsun (<Chersonese in ancient times), according to *Pannonian Life*, Konstantin found "*The Gospel and Psalter*" written with Rusy letters and met someone who spoke to him, using that priestly language; during their conversation that person showed Konstantin different vowel and consonant letters and offered a prayer to God; Konstantin appreciated what he had been shown and was astonished." Cyril and Methodius therefore only 'processed' a written language which already existed, a very developed written language of the Rusy, which they then fitted into the canon of the Byzantine church.

When Greek-colonisers reached the Northern Black Sea coast during the mid-1st millennium BCE, they were met not by savages but by an ancient people of culture. These people were the root and branch of Pre-Grecian cultures who had, in terms of their understanding, their chronology and to a significant extent, their ethnicity - moved away from the unified Aratto-Orianian past of Slavs, Greeks and other Indo-European people. Rather than the Greeks encountering barbarians they met culture-bearers, keepers of the root of civilisation – whose scion blossomed into the Hellenes – Greeks – Byzantians. The greatness of our Slavic ancestors but also their misfortune when confronted with the slaveholding culture of the Greeks, lay in their inheritance of a pre-class statehood which venerated a spiritual world-view. The whole culture of the primordial civilisation was steeped in a harmonic spiritual consciousness, although it was only sustainable when maintained within a figurative-intuitive perception of the world. In contrast, the Hellenes and their descendants, Greeks and Byzantians, fostered civilisation based on a logical-analytical perception of the world, one which generated and prioritised the form and material manifestations of matter... *The Veles Book* (board 8(3)) very clearly recorded the **tragedy** that arose from the **polar opposition in civilisation between the two types of culture** (the state systems of communal pre-class culture versus class and slave-holding culture):

When our ancestors began to create [the city of] *Surozh,*
Greek merchants came to trade with us, looking for profits,
and, seeking out our ground,
sending us many of their young people
and built houses, and cities for exchange and trade.
However, once they were here (we) saw their warriors with swords.
And soon they put in order our land by their hands
and created other games...

In fact, they have given us their letters [instead of ours],
So (we) had them taken and have lost our memory.
And [our teacher] *who wanted to teach* [our letters]
to our children,
must hide in the houses of those (parents),
only so that, the uneducated (child), *could return to our letters*
and lead in religious rites to our gods...

English	Ukrainian	Greek	Hebrew	Hebrew	Voynich	Etruscan	Phoenician	Pidiysky	Lunas
Английский	Украинский	Греческий	Гибру	Гибру пропись	"Войнич"	Этрусский	Финикийский	Пидийский	Лунас
B	Б	A	ב , כ	ב , כ	Λ	A, A	O	A	O
W	B	E	ו	I	O	Ǝ	⩮	Ψ	⩮
H	Г	Г	ה , ח , ח	ה, ח, ח	⌒	8, 8	Ǝ	1, Ŧ	▷
KH	X	X	ק , ף , ך	ק, ף, ך	8	日	Φ	1, Ŧ	Ч
D	Д	O, Ω	ד , ד	ד , ד	?	O, Φ	日	↿, o	Э
ZH	Ж	I, Ξ	ץ	ץ	⁊	ƚ1	I	Ϯ	H
Z	З	I	ז , ץ	ז, ץ	ᒣ	I	I	I	Щ
K	K	K	ק , ף , ך	ק, ף, ך	8	K	Ƴ	⸸	Ч
L	Л	Λ, Δ	ל	ל	ℓ	⅃	ᒉ, ᒉ	λ	И
M	M	M	מ , ם	N, D	◡	Ш	9, 9	M, M	◪
N	Н,н'нь,нн	N	ן , נ , נ	I, כ, J	ℓ	V	ק	ᒧ	⫪
P	П	Г, П	פ	פ	cz	1	ך, ך, 1	8	1, ך
R	P	P	ר	ר	2	ɑ	9	9	9
S	C, сь	Σ	ס	ס	4	Ƨ, S	w	ʅ	Ш
T	Ть, Т	T	ט , ת	ט , ת	Ⴖ	⸸, ⸸	ƒ	T, Ŧ	T
TS	Ц	ζ	צ	З	⨎	3	Ⴤ	↑	Z, ⱶ
CH	Ч	H	ע	Ɣ	Ɏ	Ͻ,),⟩	Y	ꓘ	ꓘ
SHCH	Щ				⨎	Ѱ	Ƴ, Ѱ	2	
J	Ї;Й	Y	י	י	J, ~	╕	ᒐ, ᒐ	ɿ	L
SH	Ш	Σ	ש	ℓ	9	Ѱ	W	ʅ	Ш
Di	Дї; Дй							ɟ	
	безмолвная		א						

Fig.101 : **The alphabets of various nations** of the last four millennia. [From left to right : English, Ukrainian, Greek, Hebrew, Hebrew hand-written, "Voynich", Etruscan, Phoenician, 'Pidiysky', 'Lunas'].

These 'Rusy letters' were learned and then used by Konstantin (Cyril) for creating Old Slavonic church literature but Christianity, Judaism and other religions, as well as official science "and all cultural mankind (in the manner of Russian researcher Likhachev)", subsequently professed this to be a frank lie, as if the first alphabet for the Rusy had been invented by the holy Christian Cyril who, along with his brother Methodius, introduced it to "the dark Slavs"; and that, supposedly, it was a blessing from the Byzantine church authorities not to be Rus and continue in ignorance. The only grain of truth here is that Byzantium, the direct successor of the powers of Greece and Rome, approved a new type of civilisation-statehood in Europe and the previous one of long standing (existing since the boundary of the 2nd - 3rd century CE, as we now know) ceased to be relevant.

To return to the precepts we started examining earlier, one of the boards of *The Veles Book* (board 38a) begins with the words, "Written by this hand". Here is the second precept under examination, involving an account of the occupation of the "kin of Slavs in the land of In(d)us" and then the return to their kinsmen-hearthers "on the (D)Nieper". Those kin [in the Dnipro area] were living individually as families in dug-outs with fire-hearths and they honoured the cemeteries of ancestors ("each kin had ancestors and pre-ancestors who had died centuries ago"). The 'newcomers' willingly accepted their gods (in fact, they renewed their eternal veneration of Svaroh, whom they had already honoured before their campaign into India; but they had also accepted new gods who appeared during the long Indian campaign), and for this they received residence in the city-state of Kyiv. The precept, dated to the return from India of the carriers of the most ancient ethnonym of Slaviane (Slavdom), reads like this:

For we sing glory to Svaroh and Dazhboh, who exist in the sky very pure,
To Perun and Stryboh who rule by thunder and lightning.
And Stryboh comes to blow winds on earth.
Therefore, Ladoboh that governs lad [harmony] *of the kin and various clemency;*
and Kupalboh who rules by washing and various ablutions;
and Yarboh who governs the spring flowering and mermaids, water-spirits, and forest-dwelling spirits, and house-spirits.
And Svaroh governs them too.

Thus arranged, the returners led by Oriy and his sons settled in so well that in the local "oak forests, forest-dwelling spirits in the branches began to sing lullabies" for them, and calendar matters (economic-ceremonial) came to be connected with the constellation of Dazhboh ("a golden plough on the dark blue wise sky") (VB: 38b). The chronology of boards 38a-b doesn't go beyond the realm of this return of the Slavs from India (between the 2nd – 1st millennium BCE; see above); a settlement was founded of the right bank of the Dnipro and at this location was a fortification of the Chernoles^ culture – (which was, conceivably, at Trypillia or Trakhtemyriv). Although the extent and range of historical memory of boards 38a-b is less than that on boards 29-30 (examined earlier), the time of their creation was nevertheless ancient.

Now let us consider a third precept. On board 25 there is a section which handles the teaching concerning a *penalty*; this section records the actions of the Magi Ukrians, Ukhoriez and his brother Osloven. The translation by B. I. Yatsenko of the "Magi Ukrs[10]" is not accurate, it isn't about the ethnic relationship of the brothers but about their specialisations within the caste of the Magi. Their particular expertise is clearly defined within the names of the "Magusian Ukrians": one is the '(Scribe)-runist (of declarations) who listens and writes' and the other is the 'Herald' (of those declarations) who reads and speaks. If the role of the first – Ukhoriez – was to both write and to speak masterfully, then the second – Osloven – would probably not have been required.

When the Ukri-Magus was teaching a Rusy prince and his soldiers to fight with enemies, he would remind them of the commandments given to Oriy from the creator-God Svaroh, about father-Dazhboh:

And those gods talk to you by present and Oriy's precepts:
"Love green and life-giving light!
Love your friends and be peaceful between kin!"
And after that time (of fore-father Oriy) *there were seventy of our princes ...*
chosen at a Veche [Meeting] *and excommunicated* (from power) *at the Veche too,*
if people (already) did not want them ...
Our memory still holds all that,
since we must glorify them with every funeral feast three-form
and preserve the memory of them in our sons.

In many places *The Veles Book* refers to social order and changes within it. Even with Bohomyr, authority belonged to the priests and then to the priests and Veches [meetings]; with Oriy, authority belonged to the Veches and princes; the usurpation of authority by princes began with the Varangians (when the creation of *The Veles Book* had been completed). The process of replacing the theocratic democracy of Aratta with the feudal statehood of Rus continued, gradually, until after the last Kyi[11] (VB: 37b), and until then the tradition of Aratta (Arta-Arsania in composition) was kept alive, and in many respects remained "primitive-communistic", because:

33 *In that old time fathers gathered many kins.*
And those kins had elders and meetings,
others had princes, whom they selected on the seventh circle from Kolyady till Kolyady.
And any kin was guided by a magician who brought sacrifices.
And each kin had an old magician
who produced gladness to others.

And that the first among them was – Dazhboh, and created by him...
26 *here Father-Oriy told his sons to lead all the kins.*
But they did not want to, being divided on that and others.
So in this way the princes guide their people...
37b *In those times, after Kyi* [Oriy's son], *princes were selected among many fathers,*
and princes very special and different became simple men at the meeting after their reign.
And so the earth blossomed,
and elective princes took care of the people and bread,
gained food and all belongings from their people.
Now we have the opposite: princes take people as property,
and transfer power to their sons –
from father to son and (so) even up to great-grandchild.

Caring about the independence and well-being of the people on the eve of the violent establishment of Varangian authority, the Magi tried to argue with the ideology of the usurper-prince Askold^ who had been baptised by the Byzantine empire. This then brings us to the fourth, the latest precept of *The Veles Book*. In it, the Magi pointed out that the principles of monotheism and spirituality had been inherent to the Slavic-Rusy since time immemorial (see above, 29, etc.), and the claims of Greek-Byzantians concerning this are false (VB: 6f-g, 22, 24b). In confirmation, it must be noted that Oriana and Rus had their own native Saviours with strong Arattan and Aryan fundamentals. There is a discussion about the Arattan's Saviour below. Concerning the second, the Aryan's Saviour, he is repeatedly represented in *The Veles Book* in the form of a horseman: (see: Yu. Shilov, *Gandkharva – the Aryan Saviour*, Moscow, 1997).

8(2) *And we thought about help of Perun.*
And we saw, as in the sky, a messenger galloping on a white horse.
And he raised a sword to heaven
and split the clouds and thunders.
And the living water flows to us, and (yes) we drink that,
Because all from Svaroh is vitality flowing to us.
3a *We prayed to Veles, our father,*
so that he brought about in the sky the cavalry of Surozh [Sun god],
let him come down to hang suris [sun's plenty] *on us, golden circles twirling...*
Let us sing glory to Surozh,
and here the golden cavalry of Surozh cavorts in the skies!
9a *... Slavuna... said to Bohomyr, that... they* (supposedly three) *must*
their daughters (marry) *and grandchildren nurse...*
And he arrived (Bohomyr) at an oak that stood in a field,
and remained at night near his fire.
And saw in the evening three husbands on horses, who approached him...
The three men were the three heralds of morning, midday and evening.
15a *And here, they prayed to Svaroh, the first ancestor:*
For kin – they asked about a source of childbearing women,
and at the oak – they asked the measure of our bread.
Svaroh, who created the world, –
this is the god of light and the god of Prava [heaven], *Yava* [real life] *and Nava* [netherworld/afterlife],
and, indeed, we have them truly.
And this our truth overcomes forces of darkness and leads to blessing.
Like our forefathers, once knowing about it,
brought a white horse to the sacrifice
and went out from the land of Semyrychia...

Did not *Khors* (deity) dedicate such a horse? Were they not there together with the Saviour-Herald on the same horse, the embodiment of *Khros, or Hros* – which was the

Fig.102 : **Solar horse-"skates"** of Rus huts, decorations and embroidery (see Fig. 74), of spinning-wheels.

name for our people recorded by Zacharias Rhetor[12] in the year 555? It is quite obvious, that this image was adapted by the church in due course, though under the name of George Pobedonosets [St. George the Victorious], which serves as a symbol of Rus to the present day.

It is remarkable that before the baptism of Rus, the Magi had started to submit to princely authority – apparently understanding that this was a natural step, a process, (to be understood in terms of periodic mutually-changing priorities between spiritual phenomena and matter, essence and form, the figurative-intuitive and logical-analytical world outlook, bringing changes for themselves and for others). Although there was some resistance – it wasn't so very active. Of course the Magi didn't want to lose the essence of ancestral customs and faith, nor to abandon people of the future to any misfortunes without providing them with a primordial spiritual compass. Alas, the Magi could only operate effectively on their age-old terms, i.e. within figurative-intuitive perceptions of the world; removing the contradiction between life-and-death; operating as a tool to serve the phenomenon of the Saviour with his sacrifices both voluntary, and compulsory. Therefore, when compelled to accept the prevailing authority of those with a logical-analytical attitude, the Magi were forced to renounce their primordial, effective phenomenon of the Saviour, along with its sacrifices and other rituals:

24b *These Rus' gods do not take sacrifices (neither) human, nor animal...*
And these Varangians and Elan give other sacrifices to gods, and terrible human flesh.
And we should not do that, as we – Dazhbo's grandsons,
also should not follow the steps of strangers.

6e *And Greeks wished us to baptise so that we'd forget our gods*
and so we turned (to their faith) *and began to serve them...*
And our fathers made a sacrifice to Dazhboh (by a herb drink – Suritsa),
which was also sanctified in the sky repeatedly.

By *terrible human flesh* is implied, primarily, the crucified Christ – 'the anointed sovereign'. Alas, refusing to worship him, it was necessary to recant the worship of their own Saviour – **Maslenytsia**^ (with the same Aratto-Indo-European basis, as we already know). There was only one eventual outcome from this contradiction – a compromise: acceptance of the authority of the princes with their Christian (slaveholding-feudal) ideology, along with whatever most nourished their native traditions. The Magi, and also the princes, went along with this compromise. As a result, there arose the phenomenon (first promulgated and to a certain extent explained by, B. A. Rybakov) that after the baptism of Rus, in 11th – 12th centuries, there began an unprecedented splash of pagan, pre-Christian culture in which spiritual essence was victorious again – despite the change to 'form' [materiality]. The victory was short-lived however: there came a period of pressure favouring form over essence [spirit]. It was necessary to live through and endure this objectionable period which, according to legends was predicted by the Magi to last for 1000 years following the baptism of Rus in 988.

Suggested reading

1. *The Veles Book.* Translation and comments by Yatsenko B. I. Kyiv, 1995, 2001.
2. Herodotus, *The Histories*, Moscow-Leningrad, 1972.
3. Trubachev O. N., *Indoarica in Northern Black Sea coast*, Moscow, 1999.
4. Nalyvayko S. I., *Secrets of Sanskrit Revealed*, Kyiv, 2000, 2001.
5. Asov A. I., *Slavonic runes and the "Boyan anthem"*, Moscow, 2000.
6. Shilov Yu. A., *The "Veles Book" and the relevance of ancient doctrines*, Kyiv, 2001.

---

[1] Solinus said of the Agathyrsi "that their bodies were painted *colore caerulea*, just as the old Picts were". Tacitus observes of the Arii...."that they had *tincta corpora* i.e. were Picts.

[2] Oriy had three sons: Kyi, Shchek and Khoriv, the latter being the youngest.

[3] Bohomyr is called Bohumir in the *The Veles Book* where it is said he was the father of Slavs and had three daughters and two sons.

[4] The word for Seven in Russian is Семь (Sem)

[5] The main Avestan text of geographical interest is the first chapter of the *Vendidad* which lists the sixteen nations created by Ahura Mazda which were opposed by a corresponding number of counter-creations set up against them by Angra Mainyu. The name of the Chakhrem nation (cf. Persian 'charkh') means wheel or revolving.

[6] The seven Indus Rivers, **Hapta Hindu**, are the Indus (1) and its tributaries the Kabul (2) and Kurram (3) from the west and north, and the Jhelum (4), Chenab (5), Ravi (6) and Sutlej/ Beas (7) from the east and south.

[7] The Cyrillic letter 'B' is pronounced 'V'.

[8] Neuri tribe, according to Herodotus, were driven from their land "one generation before the attack of Darius (512 BC)" by an invasion of serpents. He also reports a Scythian tale that the Neuri changed once a year into wolves, although giving no credence to it. This is perhaps a reference to shamanic practices.

[9] Dir, Askold and Ryurik were Kyivan princes of the beginning of 9th century. (V. Krasnoholovets).

[10] The Ukrs were a priestly caste.

[11] The youngest son of Oriy.

[12] Also known as Zacharias (Bishop) of Mytilene.

CHAPTER 11

Fig.103 : **Cimmerians.** An ancient image.

ANCIENT TIMES

Despite the clear instruction by Nestor the Chronicler that Rus was Great Scythe [Greater Scythia], it was assumed that there was no relationship between them, i.e. no relationship between Rus and Cimmeria (which was, supposedly, not a state!) nor between Rus and Scythia. Furthermore, it was assumed that there would not have been any relations between them and the Bosphorus empire of the Greek-colonists. Officially, they are regarded as completely different ethno-historical formations, who destroyed each other before disappearing almost without trace.

Nevertheless even Herodotus, the promoter of this concept, left us fragments containing considerable details about the agedness and indestructibility of the roots of nations after the end of their rule. He also gives several examples of changes in ethnonyms and names of people. For this reason alone, we should not expect examples of the identity of events and people as recorded by the Greek author of *The Histories* to be necessarily identified with those mentioned by the Rusy compilers of *The Veles Book,* and yet similarities certainly do exist, though they may not be identical.

We will attempt to compare these works so that we can gauge whether or not their details complement each other. In that endeavour we shall turn to the academic text, *Indoarica in Northern Black Sea Coast* by Prof. O. N. Trubachev who, even though he doesn't yet acknowledge *The Veles Book* [as an historical source], was nevertheless one of the first, after perhaps Prof. Dr. B. A. Rybakov, to start dismantling the limitations of the semi-official science just mentioned, enabling him to reveal the real nature of Indo-Aryan-Slavic connections.

1. The Pre-Scythian population of the Northern Black Sea area.

It is generally recognised that the Scythians of the Northern Black Sea area were preceded by the Cimmerians whose roots are discernible in the Sabatynivka archaeological culture from about 1500-1200 BCE and whose most recent memorials date to 800-700 BCE. The archaeology of the Cimmerians is specifically dated to between the 2nd – 1st millennium BCE, though it is not more recent than that of the Scythians of course, who knew only swords of iron, a useful detail which

Fig. 104 : **Legendary objects of the Skolots**, as portrayed by Bulgarians on festive bread.

corresponds with evidence from *The Veles Book* (6c):

From father Oriy until [Prince] *Dir, passed one thousand five hundred years.*
The Persians knew of our copper swords,
because (their) *master told them [how] to make iron ones ...*

This hints at the identification of Slavs with Cimmerians and there is indeed a direct reference to this fact:

6f ... *Kimorias were also* (along with Orianians, Borusians and others) *our fathers ...*

2a *Father Oriy led* [tribes] *to the land of Rus* (from India),
because there they had always remained ...
Ours was a nation, with Kilmerstians as kin,
who appeared from a single root.
Who came later onto Rus territory,
then settled among the Ilmershti.
They are in fact our brothers and similar to us
and in danger they defended us from evil.

6c (Greeks and Scythians) *were yellow,*
And Rusy had fair and were blue-eyed
(just as Herodotus described the Budini).

There is even more concrete evidence to be found in the medieval letters of the Magi of Novhorod Region (according to V. Torop): "We send the words of Perun against a false deed. The Rusy were the Cymru/Kimrams and [where] they lived...the Eternal Borus, stands on their bones "...

Thus, the dual community of Aryans (the 'Indo-Iranians') had continued to exist in the same way since those ancient times when they were called Cimmerians and Scythians. These were the most militarised alliances of tribes (which is why they were so interesting and understandable to the Greek and Roman authors) on whom the life and activities of the ancient colonies of the Northern Black Sea Coast mainly depended. As for being the main ancestors of the Slavs – those keepers of the peaceful traditions of the Arattan farmers – they were already particularly interested in the Latins and Byzantians (ancestors of Romans and Greeks) but only because they had reached a point of militarisation more congruent with the "pre-class period of military democracy" rather than with its communal traditions, but nevertheless... let us try to determine the specific place of Slavs within the community of Cimmerians and Scythians.

First, let's outline the broader background of the Cimmerian ethnogenesis.

As a consequence of the Great Flood which occurred around mid-4th millennium BCE (caused by the Mediterranean Sea breaking through into the Black Sea), parts of Aratta had been flooded and this produced many Sumerian immigrants; the flooding also caused some tribes from the basin of the Azov Sea and the northern shelf of the Black Sea to migrate to the Balkans and to Asia Minor, whilst some of their kinsmen remained in the foothills of Crimea and the Caucasus. We can safely assume that in the first two regions the immigrants were reunited with their relatives who had been living there since the origin of the state of Aratta (7th – 5th millennium BCE), and they formed the Illyrian community along with the relict of the pre-Indo-European tribe (inherent to late Aratta, and its sibling Sumer).

This line of communication was later enhanced by the overland and maritime migrations of the Orianians, Leleges, Pelasgians and Eneti. Migrations like this are specifically reflected in the ancient myth describing the wanderings of Io, daughter of Inachos and sister of Pelasg, who was transformed into a cow by Hera (the same goddess responsible for the wanderings of Hercules). This miserable creature, persecuted by a gad-fly, began to run from the southern coast of the Adriatic Sea, crossed Illyria northwest of the Balkans, crossed the Gemiya ridge, swam across the Bosphorus, appeared in Cimmerian lands, then continued on to Egypt where the Cimmerians had gone in the 7th century BCE... From sources closer to the history of those times comes another example, that of a tribe living on Sikelia^ island in the Adriatic sea whose tribal name – Illyrians – was precisely the same as that in the Io legend and whose land, in the days of Herodotus (VI: 22-24; VII: 153-168), was also crossed by armies of the tyrants of Scyth and Helon, whose destinies were bound up with the city of *Himera* in Sicily.

Is it pure chance to find such a complex of ethnonyms which accord so closely with the countries of the Northern Black Sea area? Obviously, we have built the optimum case for explaining such a complex of coincidences. The names of Mesopotamian *Sumer* and *Cimmeria* found on the coast of the Bosphorus (the Cimmerian strait, which is now the Kerch strait) probably originated in the flooded basin of *Temarunda* (Sea of Azov) – whose name was retained as *Temerossa* until the late Middle Ages and today as Temryuk until being transformed, like the name of Sumer, into the name of the Cimmerian union of tribes led by Ir or Osed(e)n (see above).

The *Cimmerians* were known to the Assyrians under the name of *Gamir*(ra) and the Israelites called them the *Homer*. Perhaps the lineage of Bohomyr should be sought in this direction? The Biblical prophet Ezekiel knew the above-mentioned Kyaxares^ under the name of "*Gog of the Land of Magog, Prince Rosha*". He was the Cimmerian-born king of the Medes and an enemy of the Scythians. *Rosh* is also the name of Urartu ('City-state of Arta'?) near Lake Van where, until the dynasty of Kyaxares-Gog, it was governed by the dynasty of *Rus*. The name *Rus*salem then appeared which means 'Village of the Rusy' (later renamed as Jerusalem), and which twice gained an army of Cimmerians who conquered the thrones near its gate which the biblical Lord had promised (via the prophet Jeremiah) to the "kings of the northern tribes" in exchange for the release of the Israelites from Babylon (V. Torop, *Ancient news of Rus*, Moscow, 1997). We have here quite a range of evidence which tells us more about the relationship of the Cimmerians not only with the Slavs but also with the Rusy.

Strabo subsequently wrote in his *Geography* that the Eneti, who co-existed with the Cappadocians of Asia Minor, were at war there with the Cimmerians and had been driven back to the Adriatic Sea. Herodotus also records the Eneti as being there, though amongst the Illyrians. The relationship between the Slavs and the Celts, through the Skoloty (see below) should be pointed out and *The Veles Book* (28) recorded this:

> *And indeed it is known, as it is told by the forefathers, that the Kielts have helped them.*
> *In fact they* (the forefathers*) went to them and had their help there for a hundred years;*
> *The same is known about the Ilmors, namely Illers; we are relatives.*

Naturally, the Illyrians-Gamirra-Cimmerians established close relations with the Orissians-Ruthenians-Rusy, in effect maintaining and renewing a primordial relationship. Only by looking through the prism of the picture outlined here is there a clearer, more accurate view of the Cimmerian tradition in Europe which had been passed down to the Middle Ages (see below) after centuries of being ignored by the Greeks.

Our outline of the Illyrian-Cimmerian relationship is particularly necessary for understanding their further development. Under the names *Kilmerstians, Ilmenians*, etc., they and other tribal remnants dispersed from the Taman peninsula at the end of antiquity, going into the Balkans, to the Novhorod region and to the Baltic; and as we shall see in due course, we should attribute the *Cimbri* [Cymru] of Western Europe to these same migrations [they became the Welsh]. This is the reason for tributaries in the basin of the River Elbe bearing the names of the Ilm and Ilmenau, and even for the name of the island of Elba itself (Ilva, in Latin), Tuscany, Italy; these names retained their original meaning of '*white*', as it once had been for *Rus*. History has thus come full circle: the Cimmerians were not only related by events but were also close in spirit to the country of Rus, and indeed its most ancient meaning. The priests, who had traced the ethnogenesis as well as the calendars, selective programmes, festivals, creation of words etc. over the course of millennia, evidently still knew their business!

With good reason to trust the logic of those priestly definitions, we shall try to trace the centre of the Cimmerian people, whose settlements were said to be bounded by their 'Cimmerian (earthen) walls' above the banks of the 'Cimmerian Bosphorus', according to Homer, Herodotus, etc., and try to pin down the problem concerning Cimmeria and Rus. Let's think again about the times of Aratta, the time when Sh(S)umer was conceived precisely in this region, in the Temarunda basin of the 'Mother of the Black Sea' (i.e. Meotida, Sea of Azov). Similar names to *Sumer* crop up in the name of Palestinian *Samaria*; in tributaries of the Dnipro and Volga with the same name, and also in *Surashtra^* and *S(a)uvir^* in Indian Aratta (recorded in the *Mahabharata*), names taken from the coast of Sind(h) (i.e., Dnipro) into the Punjab (well known as Pendeb to the authors of *The Veles Book* from the lineage of Oriy). Surashtra means 'Best soldiers', and Suvir, 'Best bulls'; Samara, Sumer and Cimmeria all mean 'the Best ground lit up by the Sun'. But if *Su*mer is more connected with '*Shu*-Nun' ('Hand-Law of The Empress') and '*shu*itsa' (which means left hand/arm), then *shu* is 'the Best Law' or 'the Best (other than left) Hand', and so *-mer* in both cases gravitates to meaning 'the country' [1].

The final form of the ethnonyms and toponyms of Rus was indirectly connected with Surashtra. This relationship was more ethnic than territorial. However, near the modern city of Kremenchuk where the Dnipro rapids begin, there used to be a crossing, together with the most ancient Aryan sanctuaries, burials and a most remarkable settlement with gigantic ramparts and ditches associated with a local legend of Reva the builder. Is it just by chance that the namesake of King Surashtra, founder of this dynasty, was related to Balvir, the elder brother of Krishna, according to the *Mahabharata*? Anyway, all three of these names were inherent to Cossacks of the Kremenchuk area, and still occur amongst Ukrainians. We need to examine here the name of *Surozh*, the capital of the Cimmerians. The name of this city-state is closer to '*Suria-* the Sun', as revered in both Oriana and Rus, as well as Syria and India, but through a connection with the 'warriors' of Kshatriya-Rajania^-rasia-rai, [the latter means 'paradise'], it is inherently derived from the 'Best warriors' of *Sura*shtra.

Indian S(a)uvira was also inhabited by people with the same name of Sind who identified themselves with their well-known namesakes on the Northern Black Sea Coast. In particular, the Sinds of the lower reaches of the Dnipro and Kuban are associated with the times when the river bore its old name of the Sind(hu)-'River'. According to the authors of some ancient texts, e.g. *The Peutinger Table*, living near them in the Caucasus foothills were the Savrika, Savars or Savirs who, according to Ptolemy, lived near the well-known Borusci mentioned in *The Veles Book,* who were direct predecessors of the Sivertsi Slavs. Regarding the latter, the princes of the city of Chernihiv considered their ancestral land to have been Tmutarakan (the Taman peninsula)...

But to return to the Cimmerians. S. I. Nalyvayko researched the Greek pronunciation and spelling of their ethnonym which actually corresponds to the Sanskrit tribal name of *Sauvirs*, even though they came to be known as *Cimmerians*, possibly as a result of an encounter with the pre-Greeks (i.e. through Odysseus and Circe, Helones, and perhaps even the Argonauts, Achilles and Aeneas). Those *Sauvirs*, who were part-Sind, became the *Sivertsi* and therefore had every right to assert their claim that the ***Kimorias were also our fathers*** (*The Veles Book,* 6f). So, yet again, the authors of *The Veles Book* and the Magi of the Novhorod region were correct here, whichever way we view the situation! Let's face it, the authors of *The Veles Book* were much wiser than modern scientists and politicians who long ceased to meet the requirements of that ancient proverb: "Great knowledge does not teach one to be clever, it's the one who knows how to make connections who is clever."

For the most part it is believed that the Scythians, along with their very near contemporaries the Greeks, were migrants into the Northern Black Sea coast and their resettlement, along with other tribes, began around the turn of the 8th – 7th centuries BCE and arose from the territories of Northern Persia and Central Asia, respectively, and from the coastal cities of Ionia and Greece. We have already mentioned that the Hellenic-Greeks arose from Aratta. When it comes to the origin of the Scythians, most researchers rely heavily on the third legend recorded by Herodotus (IV: 11-12), which records the arrival of those peoples in the Dnipro area from beyond the River Araks^, which researchers generally equate with the Volga. In contrast, the outstanding Scythologist B. N. Grakov, considered the Scythians to be a mainly autochthonous nation descended from the Srubna archaeological culture of the Dnipro area in the second half of the 2nd millennium BCE. His reasoning however, was based on the first legend of Herodotus (IV: 5-7):

The first inhabitant of those yet uninhabited countries was a man named Targitai. The parents of Targitai, according to the Scythians, were Zeus and the daughter of the river Borysthen (probably, the serpent-legged goddess – according to IV. 9). *This Targetai had three sons: Lipoksai, Arpoksai and the youngest, Kolaksai. During their reign, gold objects fell [flaming] to the Scythian earth from heaven: a plough, a yoke, an axe and bowl... Seeing that when the third, youngest brother approached the objects, the flame became extinguished, allowing him to carry the gold for himself into the house, the older brothers agreed to give the kingdom to the youngest. So it is said that from Lipoksai, came the Scythian tribe named Auhats; from the middle brother, the tribes of Katiar and Traspi, and from the youngest brother – the chieftain – the tribe of Paralat. All of these tribes were known collectively as the Skoloty, i.e. Royal 'Tsarski'*[2]. *The Hellenes also called them Scythians.*

It is in words such as these that the Scythians talked about the origin of their people, however, they thought that since the times of the first ruler Targitai, only 1000 years had passed up until the time when their lands were invaded by Darius (leader of the Persian army, in 514 or 512 BCE). *The Scythian leaders carefully protected the sacred gold objects mentioned and worshipped them with awe, since they brought rich sacrifices annually. It was the opinion of the Scythians that if anyone at the festival should fall asleep under the open sky with this sacred gold, then they would not live past a year. Therefore, the Scythians would give him only as much land as he could ride on horseback in one day...*

Judging by the nature of this collection of sacred objects, it is obvious that the Skoloty, led by Kolaksai, cannot possibly be considered as nomadic-herdsmen (Herodotus had more to say about the other, "Royal Scythians", in IV: 11-12, 19-20, etc.); those objects typically belonged to a culture of forest-steppe, slash-and-burn husbandry. There were indeed forests along the sea coast at that time – such as Gileya in the lower reaches of the Boristhen (Dnipro). Furthermore, the collection of golden items are still esteemed by Ukrainians at the festival of Rodzdva (or Rizdva, i.e. Ukrainian Christmas - although today the implements are made of iron and other materials instead of gold). Bowls of food stand on the table and a yoke and plough are placed under the table; during the festive supper ("sviata vecheria"^ in Ukrainian), family members must touch these objects with their feet from time to time.

Like the *Cel*ts, the *Skol*oty also absorbed the Vedic word *Kula* into their ethnonym which was also partly familiar to Slavs from the words for knee (*koleno* in Ukrainian), and for clan and village (*selo* in Ukrainian).

In which case, according to S. I. Nalyvayko, S-*kolo*-ty can be assumed as (Co-)*relati*-ves. However, most researchers tend to associate Skoloty and Kolaksai (the Persian *Skolahshaya*) with the Slavic word for 'sun'- *Kolo*^ – from which *Kolyada* derives, celebrated with traditional cottage loaf kalaches^ (Fig.104), and with images of a plough, a yoke and other original objects placed under the table at the festival of Rodzdva of Kolyadi-Dazhboh; (see above). The suffix *-ksai* [ksay] is not foreign to Slavs – it crops up in the Ukrainian surnames *Say, Sayenko, Tsar, Tsarenko*, etc. In the same spirit, it is necessary to interpret Lipo-ksai as meaning 'Fine tsar [king/ruler[3]]'. However, the name is usually explained – though based on Persian rather than Slavic parallels – as meaning "Mountain-king". By the same token, the name of the middle brother would translate as "Deep [interior]-king".

However, it's more likely that Arpoksai originated from Arto-ksai, i.e. the 'Arta-(Sun-like)-king'. The name of Arta is found in the name of the Scythian (or Skoloty?) goddess Artimpasa (Arty in Persian) as well as in the ethnonym of the subsequent Scythian-ploughmen (*aroter*), a name which could be their autonym despite being rather mangled by Greek translation. In any case, Herodotus' delimitation of the Scythians to ploughmen and farmers (not herdsmen?!) is viewed by researchers as being nonsense. But S. I. Nalyvayko came up with a good explanation for this deduction. He noticed that a second name for these Scythians, – *Georgos* – was a poor translation of the Indo-Aryan *Gauvarga*: 'admirers of bulls (and cows)', thereby restoring a proper correspondence between the historical, the ethnological, and the mythological pictures: the farmers coexisted with neighbouring cattlemen whose herds formed the main composition, indicating their Arattan, pre-Aryan roots.

It is appropriate to mention here that the main guardians of the gold of the

Skoloty were the Agathirs, who had a reputation for being 'greedy for gold'. They were of Aryan-Thracian provenance inhabiting Transylvania and Transcarpathia. According to M. S. Bandrivsky (*Faces of Svarog* Lviv, 1992), a treasure horde of gold dating from the 8th – 6th centuries BCE, which was found in 1878 near the village of Mykhalkiv, in the Ternopol Region, had belonged to this tribe. It consisted of well-preserved bowls, jewellery and armour with solar symbolism (swastikas) and, large ornaments of uncertain use divided into three or four-sections; two tiaras crowned with the upright horns of a bull and possibly a ram; brooches in the shapes of deer and wolves; thousands of gold beads; also wrist guards and pommeled daggers... "sacred gold" would later become an obligatory attribute of burials of the Scythian nobility in what is interpreted as a very Skoloty tradition.

Each of the three kings, according to their names, embodied one of the three states of the Sun in the ancient tri-seasonal calendar (present in a legend from *The Veles Book* concerning the three daughters and sons-in-law of forefather Bohomyr). It had to be transformed later into a four-seasonal calendar. In the legend, this was given as the explanation for the origin of four tribes from three kings. The middle king generated two tribes simply because he represented the second season of the most ancient Indo-European calendar which became divided, in due course, into spring and summer. The adoption of the solar "Kolo of Svaroh" [Circle of Svaroh] and its associated zodiacal *calendar*, (derived from the Etruscan calendar name *Kola Dara^*, the *Gift of the Circle*), occurred between 2300-1700 BCE, a time when the Slavs started to see themselves as an ethnic community through the adoption of the cults of Svaroh and Dazhboh (see above). Since the ethnonym of the Slavs only emerged at the turn of the 2nd and 1st millennium BCE , the name *Skoloty* (which originated, according to Herodotus, from mid-2nd millennium BCE) could be the most ancient autonym of the Slavic ethnic group. This assumption is supported by the existence of an intermediate form of the name – *Sklavins^* – which shares just the same meaning of '*glory*' (it is *kleo* in Greek being similar to *kula* and *kolo*). This accords with what has been said already regarding the Veneti.

Their name could be connected to the Slavs through the ethnonym of *Stavany* (according to the evidence of Prof. Trubachev and attested by Ptolemy)... It must not be forgotten that word-formation (in particular, the formation of tribal names) was the sole responsibility and preserve of the highly educated priests, rather like the "primitive intellectuals" of our own time!

Although the genealogical stories of *The Veles Book* (16, 9a) already studied in this chapter had taken place during a later period, they were generally recording the archaic details from matriarchal times as in Herodotus' *The Histories*. The connection between the three riders, the three sons-in-law of Bohomyr, with the three states of the Sun in the first case, is quite obvious, though the significance of the sacrificial horseman described in *The Histories* only becomes clear through studying the [Veles] boards previously mentioned, i.e. 8(2) and 15a.

In order to understand the Aratto-Slavic connection with the Skoloty, we should refer to the Pelasgians, who probably originated in the areas of the *Skol* and *Skolo*poent – which is where the Greek tribes of the Balkan peninsula and Asia Minor were living. The pre-Danube *Celts*, who worshipped the supreme god Dagda and his ancestor Araya; (Dazhboh and Oriy perhaps?), could be an off-shoot of the Skoloty (either through the legendary founding brothers or the historical Agathirs and Alizons). It is acknowledged that the Skolotian god Targitai is more ancient than their gods, based on B. A. Rybakov's well-observed reasoning that Targetai has many parallels in the Indo-European world. Thargeli (Apollo) and similar 'Conquerors (of the Sun)' like him, were known amongst many descendants of Aratta, such as the Etrusco-Roman Tarcheti, the Hitto–Luwian Tarkh-Tarhunt, and Tarkh Tarakhovich who appears in one of the fairy-tales of Old-Rus.

As the legendary ancestor of the Skoloty of the Dnipro area in the 16th century BCE, Targitai can be securely identified with the 18th century BCE relic of a priest from burial No. 13 of kurhan No. 1-II near the village of Kairy^ (on the left banks of the rivers Dnipro and Konka above the town of Kakhovka) who was embodied as Thargeli and lay alongside an embodiment of Zeus (burial No. 11). These burials relate to the Ingul archaeological culture which buried ploughshares in the graves. This agrees very well with

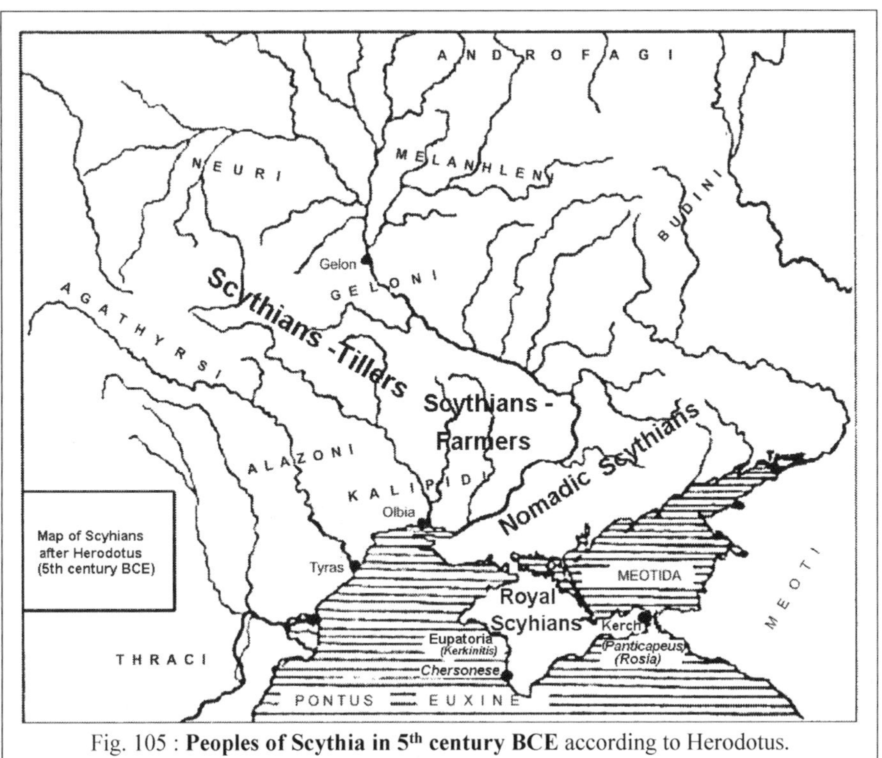

Fig. 105 : **Peoples of Scythia in 5th century BCE** according to Herodotus.

the origin of this culture coming from Oriana and in proximity to the Mid-Dnipro culture originating from the northern part of Aratta, i.e. Borusia... Concerning the relationship between Targitai and Tarkh Tarakhovich we can say this: old-man-***bohatyr***[4] lived on the 'Siyanski[5]' mountain (which means 'radiant/shining', just like the gold of the Skoloty and Scythians). ***Balgatur***, according to O. N. Trubachev, is an Indo-Aryan word which translates as 'radiant hill' (akin to the Zaporozhian *Savur*-grave or Savuryuga containing ***first ancestor Bohatyr***).

Tarkh Tarakhovich fought with an unusual form of Baba-Yaga[6] — she headed the female cavalry who fought with the bull herders. It is probable that they were the 'maternal' Maiotai (i.e., Sarmatians 'subordinate to women'), or the 'man-hating' Amazons, who had already become legendary by the 5th century BCE. Since there are also legends describing the Indian *Traitan* and Persian *Traetaon* who fought the three-headed dragons and who also freed women and bulls, then the appearance of the related *Tarkh Tarakhovich,* an eastern-Slavic fairy-tale, should be attributed to the onset of the resettlement of Aryans from their original Dnipro area homeland and for that date to be no later than the mid 2nd millennium BCE. Herodotus also referred to this when describing the times of Targitai (relevant to the burials near Kairy). However, the presence of agricultural parallels with the Hitto-Luwian thunder-god Tarhu-Tarhunt makes it possible to extend this date back to between the 3rd – 2nd millennium BCE, i.e. prior to the beginning of the belated Arattan (Orianian) migrations and the appearance of Slavdom (2300-1700 years BCE).

Those migrations have already been examined. Herodotus associated *Targitai* with the formation of the Aryan state of Mitanni in the north of Mesopotamia during the 18th – 16th centuries BCE (compare with Meotida[7], the ancient name of the Sea of Azov), since his name corresponds most closely with the Mitannian name of '*Tirgutavia*' and Moeotian '*Tirgitao*' (according to O. N. Trubachev) rather than to the name examined above. This confirms our assumption that Targitai and the Skoloty are associated with the Ingul culture, concentrated along the northern shores of the Azov and Black Seas. It is not ruled out that

Fig. 106 : **Herakles in battle with the Amazons**. Ancient image.

the ethnic identity and matriarchal tradition of these warrioresses named above became transferred into the legendary name of Myrina, the first of the Amazons from the times of Atlantis (according to Diodorus Siculus). Did they battle with Tarkh Tarakhovich? Regarding the Moeotians, their centre lay in Sindic (on the Taman peninsula) for some time and was called Multan (which means 'main place'). Having rejected similar names of this region, O. N. Trubachev proposed a theory that the formation within the Aryans on the eve of their migration into India comprised a triple-composite ethnosystem, as follows: inheritance-'maula', alliance-'mitra', mercenary-'bkhrita' which perhaps could not have been done without including the legend of the three sons of Targitai.

Archaeologists (A. I. Terenozhkin and B. A. Rybakov) are inclined to locate his grandsons – Auhat, Katiar and Traspi, as well as Paralat (descendants of Lipoksai, Arpoksai and Kolaksai) – between the Dniester and Dnipro rivers. This was possibly the area of the tripartite fortification near the settlements of Trypillia, Khodosovychi and Trakhtemyriv – now modern built-up areas but with ancient monuments and names. The account in *The Veles Book*, along with the legend describing the Scythian chieftain Lynceus^ being instructed in agriculture by mythical Triptolemus and Demeter, could have parallels with the story of those who returned from India led by father-Oriy who had to adapt to new skills. According to the legend, this occurred in the lower reaches of the Danube although it was connected, nevertheless, with Trypillia by the system of "Serpent vala [earth walls]", since they were called Valachs, also known as *Trojans*^. In the legend, Lynceus (Linkh) nearly killed his benefactor and the King of the Getae eventually killed one of the winged serpents which pulled the divine chariot. There are analogies here with the Ukrainian legend of the Cossack blacksmiths Kuzma and Demian (names deriving from 'kuznia'-smithy and 'domna'-furnace, who were contemporary with the introduction of iron metallurgy at the turn of the 2nd and 1st millennium BCE). These heroes forced a serpent to pull the plough to build those Walls... all of these legends seem to be recording the reasons which led to the separation of farmers and cattle breeders, the senior and junior ethnic groups.

The second of the legends narrated by Herodotus (IV: 8-10) on the possible origin of Scythians, also portrays them as autochthonous, however they are younger than the Skoloty population and relate to several local nations or tribes:

But the Hellenes that live at the Pontis speak otherwise. Herakles, chasing the bulls of Geryon, now arrived ... in the so-called country of Scythians...

After awakening, Herakles travelled the country in search of the horses (that had escaped from him) *and at last arrived in the land by the name Hilea. There in a cave he found a certain creature of mixed nature – half-maiden, half-serpent... the maiden-serpent said that the horses were with her but she would not return them, unless Herakles would accede to her in love...*

He later passed on to her a bow and a belt (on the end of the belt fastener hung a golden bowl) and after some time he eventually left. When their children grew up, the mother gave them names. One was called Agathyrsus, another Gelonus[8]*, and the youngest was Scythes... Two of the sons – Agathyrsus and Gelonus were not equal to the task* (left by Herakles – to draw his bow and belt the waistband), *and so their mother banished them from the country. However, the youngest son, Scythes, managed to fulfil the task and remained in the country. From this Scythes, the son of Herakles, arose all subsequent Scythian leaders...* (Herodotus 4.9.1, 4.10.1)

Apart from having the familiar motif of three brother-patriarchs, this legend has another connection to the previous mention of Kolaxi (compared to the Kolaksai from the first legend of Herodotus), the ancestor of the Scythians from the maid who was "half human and half serpent-legged". In a legend recorded in the *Argonautica* by Valerius Flaccus (Roman poet in the 1st century A.D.), the father of Kolaxi was Jupiter of the Romans, similar to Zeus of the Greeks. However, there are profound differences: where the ancestor of the first legend is more connected to the Mitanni and the migration to India, the second legend has more connections to Troy-Ilium (in other words the migrations that went eastward and westward, as we have established). When passing Troy with the same bulls mentioned above, Herakles freed from the serpent Laomedon's daughter - sister of Priam who would become king of Troy during the next period of the Trojan War. The prelude for war was initiated by the hero Herakles because Laomedon did not fulfil his promise to give him the [magic] horses in exchange for the safe return of Laomedon's daughter. Evidently, when Herakles later searched for those same horses he arrived at the cave of the serpent-legged goddess Hilea (along the flatlands on the lower reaches of River Dnipro).

It is generally accepted that the Trojan War dates from the middle of the 13th century BCE which correlates with Troy-VI (according to excavations by H. Schliemann). However a more plausible correlation would be with the period of Troy-VII, between 1250-1020 BCE, when Troy had been destroyed twice by enemy invasions – the first of which could have been Herakles (see above). In any event here is a possibility of indirectly dating the second legend of Herodotus, placing it in approximately 13th century BCE. It appears somewhat earlier than the first legend, and also 6-7 centuries before the arrival of the Scythians in Cimmeria (according to the third legend of Herodotus).

The meanings of the names given to the three sons of Herakles, as stated above, are: Agathyrsus – 'Greedy for gold'; Gelonus – 'Solar'; and Scythe – 'Wanderer' (the last named being the one who attained the greatest prize – to own the fatherland, Scythia). It is noticeable that the younger brother falls away from the semantics of the trio, whereas the first two gravitate to the genealogy of the Skoloty or, at least, to the sacred, golden, Old Scythia.

Several interpretations of the name of their father exist. S. I. Nalyvayko insists that the name Her(r)os means 'Crane'; through drawing a connection between this nickname of Herakles with that of Dionysus and Krishna, he connects all of them with the valleys of the Konka and Molochna, and with the local origins of the Indo-European epic. (There are other grounds for this, given above). This approach does not exclude a putative connection between the name of Herakles and the goddess Hera: 'glorified Hero'. The mysterious Pelasgian-Greek Hera is an embodiment of the Indo-European deity, 'Hod', or 'God'[9]. Hera also corresponds to the German word for 'year', i.e. Jahr, but most of all with the Belarusian Yaryla, the female (and, possibly the oldest) hypostasis of the homonymic god of the eastern Slavs. Yaryla was imagined as a white girl on a horse, with a sheaf in one hand and a human head in the other... Thus, the Greek Herakles would be related to the Slavic Yaroslav. They are both connected with the constellation of Taurus (perhaps arising at the same period, during the times of its ascendancy in the zodiac, between 4400-1700 years BCE). In the legend, *Herakles* reached the serpent goddess of the Dnipro area when "he was chasing the bulls of *Geryon*", which had been presented to Herakles by the 'Sun'-Helios, – whereas the usual epithet of Yaroslav was 'Yar-Tur' - 'Sun (of the resurrected, i.e. new year) Taurus'.

In this, as in the previous chapters, the legends of the wanderings of Herakles are put under close scrutiny - both the times when he was alone and also when he was with the Argonauts, covering the same route which was later sailed by Odysseus between Atlantis, Troy-Ilium and Boristhen. The second of them, Troy-Ilium, is connected with the city of the Helonians. It is worth emphasising the circumstances which considerably strengthen the mutual convergence between the legends narrated by Herodotus and those of *The Veles Book*.

First of all, we shall add details about the motives of the legendary three sons, the daughters and the horsemen, as well as the relationship between the names of Trypillia, Troy-Ilium and Helon. We must also take into account the similar tripartite construction of fortresses of both *Helon* and *Ilium* (Troy), as well as noting that Helonians inhabiting the first of these cities, "*spoke partially in Scythian language, and partially in Hellenian*" and had "*sanctuaries of Hellenic gods with statues, altars and wooden temple buildings of Hellenic design*" (Herodotus IV: 108). The "father of history" makes a point of noting such striking similarities between the culture of these barbarians with the Greek culture, by the fact that the "*inhabitants of Helon were anciently Hellenes. After banishment from trade settlements they resettled among the Budinis*" (just like the Neuri) – who also resemble the Hellenes, because "*they celebrate with festivals in honour of Dionysus and go into a bacchanalian frenzy*". As we see, Herodotus' explanation leaves much to be desired with regard to this latter fact and most importantly – it is at odds with the motivation of a Helonian blood relationship with the local Agathyrsi^ and Scythians. Their brotherhood could only have arisen as a result of the age-old relationship between Borusia and Oriana (Orissa), Skoloty-Slavs and Pelasgian-pre-Greeks, which was eventually renewed by the return of the latter (first as companions of Odysseus, then as colonists) after the fall of Troy. The Scythians also returned, at least partly, according to the third and fourth legends.

In the lower reaches of the Dnipro, a legend still exists which is similar to that told by Herodotus concerning Herakles and the serpent-leg goddess, it is connected with the Serpent cave of Perun island. This, allegedly, was the name of the seven-headed serpent, who lived in the cave and there dragged "*beautiful girls, lived with them, and then devoured them. Once it brought the daughter of a ruler and had already begun to jeer over her but God sent there such a hero who killed that fierce serpent, and married the rulers' daughter and from her had three falcon-sons*". Didn't this legend arise here at the very time of the common migration of Slavs and Pelasgians, when there existed on this island, at the beginning of the 2nd millennium BCE, a unique workshop which made the stone "axes of Perun" for the Ingul archaeological culture? These axes were decorated with images of masks, serpents, lightning, ears [cereal], and symbols of female and male sexual union; amongst them I. N. Sharafutdinova perceived the symbols of Zeus and Dionysus (Table XXVIII: 1-2).

There is also a serpent cave on the Dnipro island of Khortytsia. It leads to the river crossing which Konstantinos Porphirogennetos^ knew - as it was known until recently - as Krariyska ('Passage of Aryans') near which was the lowland of Tsokurov Mitus ('cliff base of the Maeotis'?). Both names are Aryan. Archaeologists fairly recently uncovered some sanctuary-observatories dating between the 3rd – 1st millennium BCE, situated on the hills and lowlands of Khortytsia island, which are connected with the main Vedic mythology ritual.

We now turn to the question of discrepancies (or more precisely: mutual additions) recorded by the Scythian authors of *The Veles Book* and the author of *The Histories*. Yes, there are slight differences in their descriptions of the origins of nations but this is understandable given the ethnocultural differences inherent to the books and their objectives. The genealogical legends in both cases bear on the myths of the different nations: in the first case – on the myths of Slavic Oria (Orianians and Borusians) and of Rusy Bohomyr (descended from the same Slavs but from those who passed through Troad and Italy instead of India); in the second case – on the myths of Scythians and Hellenes.

It is perhaps unsurprising that the latter nation composed a legend explaining the origin of those that were foreign to them, such as the Agathirsi, Helonians and Scythians. But why?! Why did they, the Hellenes, purposely name as Scythians those tribes that were actually "called Skoloty" (IV: 6, 8)? It's fairly straightforward to answer this question when we recall those priestly centres located at sanctuary-observatories and the priestly habit of wandering amongst the Hyperboreans etc. Then the ideological, international-political underlying cause of the genealogical legends becomes obvious. Whilst the terminology is clearly modernised that doesn't alter the core significance. Contemporary diplomacy is considerably more primitive than its ancient forms which were based around significant 'nuclei'; a structural form which clearly exceeded current practise. Such legends were meant to eliminate ethnic differences in order to legitimise the validity or desirability of the relationships between various tribes and nationalities.

In the example of *The Veles Book*, which is suffused throughout with communal ideology, pre-class statehood, care for the unity and happiness of their own nation, we find the union of two genealogical legends about the related ethnic groups of Bohomyr and Oriy (with most authors attracted to the latter of the two). In the example found in *The Histories*, it reflects the slaveholding ideology of the foreigner who seeks allies in war. Note that the Scythians organised a repulse to the enemies of the Hellenes (the Persians); the Hellenes had sought alliance with the Scythians since it was necessary for the Hellenes to assert themselves in their colonies and also on the wheat market of the Northern Black Sea area, therefore, the Hellenes were responsible for the legend stating their eternal relationship with the Scythians (through Herakles). They tried to formulate an ideological basis for protecting colonists from being oppressed by aboriginal dwellers, (here, the Helonians became an example for imitation). The second of Herodotus' legends had already come into existence after the Scythian invasion on Cimmeria, and of the Persians on Scythia, who had already assented to the existence of Greek colonies and the Bosphorus empire in its land (or land captured from the Cimmerians). The inclusion of the Agathyrsi in this legend is primarily motivated by their superiority over the Scythians, as they had won against the Persian leader Darius. Agathirs was not the only elder brother of Scythes, his descendants [i.e. the Agathyrsi] (and perhaps descendants of some of the Skoloty) were the only nation which forbade the Scythians to step on their land when they were snooping around (Herodotus IV: 125).

The first of the legends told by Herodotus was considerably less politicised. It allowed for the first returners from India (or their local supporters) who settled in Old Scythia (see below). Their ancestor Targitai could have originated with "*the Maeotae^, who are associated with the tribes of Sindi^, Dandarii, Toretae, Agri, and Arrechi, as well as Tarpetes, Obidiaceni, Sittaceni, Dosci and quite a few others*" (Strabo, *Geography*, XI: 2). Perhaps, the direct recorders of this legend were from this origin and were not very numerous in Scythia; and with the exception of Herodotus, other ancient authors hardly spoke about it; they heard only names and ethnonyms similar to Paralat: Pal, Palak, paly, palei. We shall turn our attention to them shortly.

2. Were the Cimmerians expelled by Scythians?

So, part of the Scythian peoples, this eternal Ukrainian population of the Dnipro area — just as B. N. Grakov hypothesised — were direct descendants of Aratta in its settlements of Borusia and Oriana-Orissa, as well as "Old Scythia" which was formed in the lower reaches of the Dnipro by the first returners from the migration of Aryans into India. Besides the Skoloty (who could subsequently become the Sklavini in the first centuries CE), other nations were named by Herodotus (IV: 17-18): "*Callipedae – the Hellenic Scythians; after them another tribe follows under the name of Alazonians. Together with the Callipedae they conduct a similar way of life with the rest of Scythia, however they also sow grain and eat bread as "Scythian-farmers. The Hellenes ... call them Borysthenites.*" The Scythian-nomads came into that

Fig. 107 : A Persian battling with a Scythian (on the right). Persian image.

part of the Dnipro area which had already been settled by sedentary Scythians and occupied the steppe that was hardly suitable for agriculture. The 'Royal Scythians' described by Herodotus obviously gravitated to the nomadic way of life (IV: 20, 71-72 et al.). Nevertheless Herodotus himself (IV: 6) determined them in this way: the descendants of Targitai.. "*are called Skoloty, i.e. Royal. The Hellenes call them Scythians*".

Such duality/correspondence is not accidental. The contrasts within Old Scythia (which was Sindian), Scythia Minor and ordinary Scythia, bear comparison with the presence of Dandaria, Sindica and Hypanis in the lower reaches of the Dnipro and Kuban. This obvious duality led O. N. Trubachev to a fruitful conjecture to do with certain boundaries of authority between the age-old occupants and the *alien* population that arrived in the Dnipro area in the 7th – 6th centuries BCE. And if all previous researchers had assumed an Irano-Aryan affiliation with the alien [nomadic] Royal Scythians, then Trubachev pulled the emphasis back onto the local Scythian leaders belonging to the Indo-Aryan branch of the Aryan ethnogenesis. This approach, as we already know, allowed us to discover the roots of Slavdom in Scythia, leading us back precisely - through Aratta, Borusia and Oriana - to Indo-Aryan roots (rather than to Irano-Aryan, where the roots of Slavdom were very insignificant – just as the predecessors of Trubachev had deduced, hence reaching the incorrect conclusion for the absence of a Slavic ethnic group in ancient Scythia). The Cimmerians also belonged to the Indo-Aryan ethnogenesis who were allegedly expelled, one and all, by the alien Scythian-Irano-Aryans from their archetypal land.

In order to understand the true relationships between Cimmerians and Scythians, as well as to comprehend the relationships between their leaders and nations, it is necessary to analyse two more legends recorded by Herodotus. We will proceed from the following premises which were partly established earlier in this chapter:

1) The Cimmerians and Scythians are direct descendants of two branches of Aryans ("Indo-Iranians"), whose original homeland was the Steppe of the Dnipro area;

2) It was primarily Scythians who were called 'roamers/wanderers', whose ancestors were drawn into the Aryan migration during the latter part of the 2nd millennium BCE; the Scythian-roamers themselves began to return to the Dnipro area homeland in the first half of the 1st millennium BCE;

3) The first two waves of returners from India, described in *The Veles Book*, are mentioned by Herodotus in his *Histories* and by his ancient followers as "Old Scythians", "Royal Skoloty" etc. and also as "Cimmerians"; the *The Veles Book* links the latter to the Slavs (whose ethnonym was conceived in the second wave of returners from India);

4) The Cimmerians of the ancient authors and the earliest Slavs of *The Veles Book* are two allied unions of tribes who descended directly from Aratta (from Arattan Oriana and Borusia) and were kinfolk of the returners from the two first waves;

5) The Scythians as they are anciently understood (by Herodotus and other Hellenes) were the returners of a third wave emanating not from India, but from Central Asia, more precisely, from Persia. The last two locations can now be considered in more detail.

Thus, according to the **third legend about the origin of Scythians** (IV: 11-12, 1, 3-4; etc) which Herodotus trusted and to which academic science clings, which occurred at the boundary of the 8th-7th centuries CE when the Scythians invaded the land of the Cimmerians in the Northern Black Sea area, these were lands which had belonged to the Cimmerians from ancient times. The Massagetae had dislodged the Scythians from Central Asia forcing the Scythians to cross the Arax River (now known as the River Volga according to the majority of Scythiologists, however we will see that it was actually the Transcaucasian Aras, whose name today is still unchanged from those early times). Prior to the exodus of the Cimmerians from Europe into the Near East, a fratricidal war took place amongst the Cimmerian rulers, some of whom decided to remain in their native land rather than comply with the decision to abandon it to the Scythians. Having buried their heroes on the shores of the Tiras River (modern Dniester), "*the Cimmerians abandoned the land, and Scythians arrived and corralled the uninhabited country*". Having left their women and children along with their slaves, the men set forth after the outcasts into Media (the forerunner of Persia and Iran) and having subdued it, ruled the Middle East for 28 years. Then the Median king, Kiaksar, (having by that time subdued Nabupalassar, ruler of Assyria) poisoned the Scythian leaders at a banquet. After that it became necessary for their army to return to the Northern Black Sea area [after their 28 years absence] and after a struggle with the descendants of their abandoned women and slaves, they were reinstated in depopulated Cimmeria.

Following this, the most acknowledged legend of Herodotus identified Semyrichia [meaning seven-rivers] as the original homeland of Bohomyr of *The Veles Book* with the rivers that flowed into the Central-Asian, Lake Balkhash. Thus, A. I. Asov and B. I. Yatsenko and supporters reached these conclusions about the Scythian affiliation of Slavs. By contrast, we have shown the possibility of it being the other Semyrichia, mentioned in *The Veles Book*, located on the northern shore of the Adriatic Sea. We have also offered a way of combining these two different territories described by the authors of *The Veles Book* with a prospect of aligning them in the legends recording the eastern and western migrations with the ancestors of the Slavs, in which Oriy and Bohomyr participated. This, and similar streamlining of legends by the authors of the *Book,* was prompted by an aspiration to create an ideology of the unity of Slavic tribes, and the unity of Rus. But now let us concentrate our attention on these questions: did the Scythians consider themselves to be Slavs, who had returned from India? Is it possible to co-ordinate the evidence of *The Veles Book* concerning that return with the third legend of Herodotus' *History*? Does it not substitute the Cimmerian

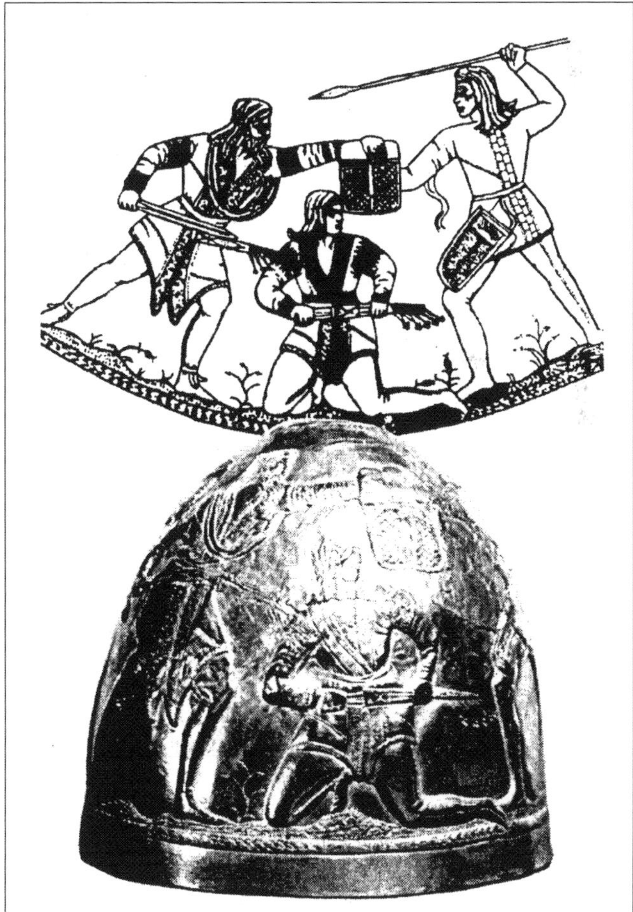

Fig. 108 : **The battle of Pali and Napi – 'senior' and 'junior' people of Scythia.** Image on a royal helmet of the 4th century BCE, found by A. A. Moruzhenko in the kurhan of Perederieva Grave (at the village of Zrubna in the Donetsk region).

history from the "father of history" with the Scythian history (as he had already done with the Scythians' and Skoloty' histories)?

To round-off the second legend recorded by Herodotus we'll look more closely at a legend recorded by Diodorus Siculus, [II: 43], "Scyth[10]*became more famous than his predecessors and called his people by the name Scythian. Amongst the descendants of this leader, two brothers stood out for their virtues; one was called Pal, and second Nap. They subsequently achieved glorious victories and divided the reign between themselves; their people were named after each of the brothers accordingly: one – Pali, the second – Napi.* Pliny (VI: 50) testified to the tragic continuation of this legend: "*at Tanaisa the Napi were destroyed by the Pali*". According to their identification by O. N. Trubachev, the names of these peoples were of Aryan origin, pre-Scythian, and they meant 'ancestors' and 'descendants'.

So, there was war between them in which the first, Pali, conquered the second, Napi. This part entirely corresponds with what Herodotus had said: he thought the Scythians could be considered "senior" only with respect to the "descendants of slaves". With regard to the Cimmerians, they and the others were considered "junior". The distortion of facts in Herodotus occurs where he identifies "Royal Scythians" with the local Skoloty, whereas the alien and allegedly victorious Scythian-nomads are allotted a secondary role. So it was to him, apparently. It is another matter that the local ruling elite would be dissolved over time with the arrival of the military ethnic group of the resettled nomads. Then the military orientation of the new ethnic group prevailed over the priesthood, the keepers of antiquity (Herodotus IV: 67-69). Perhaps, it was precisely these nomads who offered the main repulse to the invasion of Persians led by Darius. Some legends could have arisen favouring this army (from the resettled ethnic group and local priests), in which the places of those considered "junior" and "senior" became exchanged. Herodotus was for this version; it is quite possible that he created it himself.

In any case, the names of Scythian rulers (as Trubachev has shown) were almost exclusively not Irano-Aryan but Indo-Aryan: they were from Old, or Sindic, Scythia also called Dandaria ('the Iron-Wearing Aria'), and before that – Oriana. During difficult times the priests were able to move away to the Taman peninsula, which is why in the ancient world Sindic and Dandarian names also found a more durable position here (as "new" names, unlike their "old" names on the Dnipro). Sometimes these old and new resident custodians of the aboriginal traditions were allied in a united country along the south coasts of the Meotida [Azov Sea], the eastern part of which belonged to Maeotae. Those people lived there even before the Scythians and were living there in the time of the Cimmerians; they remained together with the Cimmerians in Scythia, quite contrary to the ideological narrative offered by the "father of history" (as shown already). *The Veles Book* is much closer to the historical truth as attested by a great number of other sources. We shall now consider them, at the same time verifying the assumptions stated above and if they are confirmed, transferring them to the status of a realistic hypothesis.

Whilst being accepted as relatives on their return from India, the people of Oriy could not live with their old kin for a long time, at least not all of them. They, or at least some of them, returned again from the Dnipro to the Kuban. Probably, as a result of this, two sets of Dandaria and two sets of Sindica and so on, appeared in the lower reaches of those rivers. Here is how *The Veles Book* (26) describes the conflict - compare it to the version presented in *The Histories* which described it as the fratricidal war between Cimmerian leaders caused by those who disagreed with their people concerning the invasion of the Scythians. The latter, according to the *The Veles Book*, had absolutely nothing to do with it:

> *And in those times there was Oseden, a noble warrior fire expert (Ognichanin^), ...*
> *Two* (of his) *sons went to the setting of the sun* [i.e.West]
> *and there they saw a lot of marvellous and lush grass.*
> *And they came to their father and told him, that land was remarkable.*
> *And then many tribes and kins wished to stay on that path and follow Oseden.*
> *And here father-Oreo* [Oriy] *told his sons to lead all the kins.*
> *But they did not want* (to leave the fatherland) *and share with those nor any*

other.
Then the princes (of Oriy and Oseden) *led their people along to the south,*
and Or [Oriy] *took the coastal area ...*
And when they had assembled a large cavalry, they went into the foreign lands.
And warriors there (of local tribes) *stood their ground, forced to fight*
But were defeated (by the people of Oriy).

The fate of the two detachments later resulted differently (6c). It is probable that those who were with Oseden led their *large flock to the setting of the sun – and disappeared there*. However, the people of Oriy *went into the valleys of Nabsursar^, later into Syria and Egypt.* This campaign was traced by chroniclers of *The Veles Book* over several generations.

Contrary to Herodotus, but in accord with the above mentioned section from the *The Veles Book* and other sources, the Cimmerians suffered from regular droughts, as well as strife due to overpopulation and began to migrate to the East (from 783 BCE) long before the appearance of the Scythians in the Northern Black Sea area (considered to be about 700 BCE but in reality, only in 595-594 BCE – see below).

We already know that in ancient times at least three Scythias existed – Old, Minor and plain, most thoroughly described by Herodotus. The first and last of them correspond to the *Pali* and *Napi*, the "old" and "young" descendants of the tribes migrating into India, part of whom returned in three waves over the first half of the 1st millennium BCE. The first two waves, according to *The Veles Book*, were led by Ir and Oriy, their people having come into the Dnipro area through the Caucasus and Volga. The second, as already discussed, turned out to be close to the ancestral homeland where Oriy was associated with the appearance of Cimmeria and his son Khoryv was able to create, or stimulate the

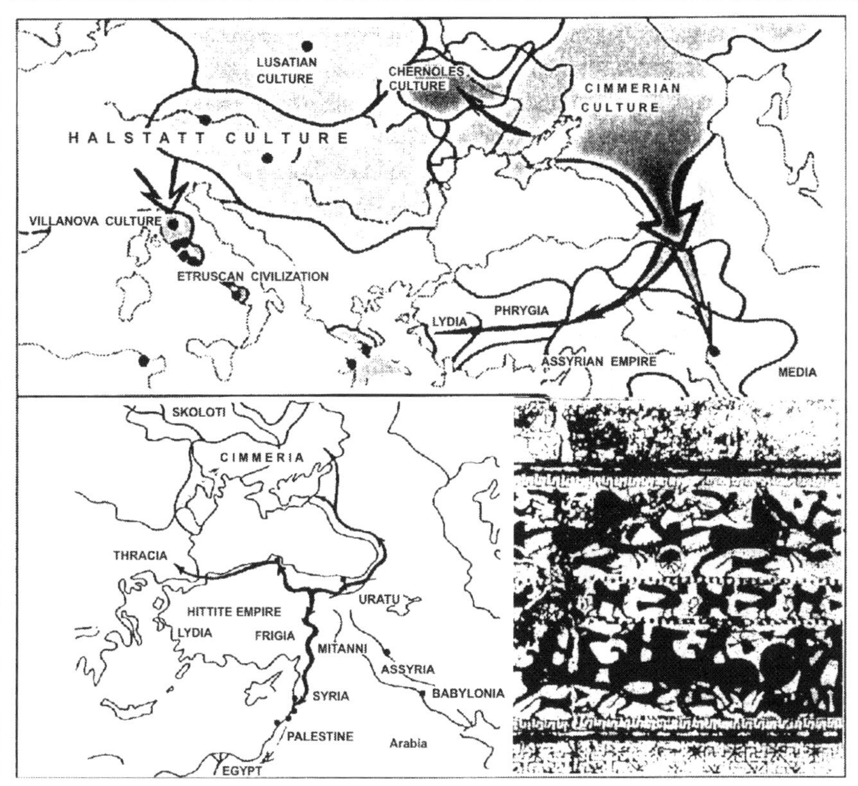

Fig. 109 : **The formation and campaigns of the Cimmerians** in the 12th – 6th centuries BCE. According to A. A. Bilousko et al.

formation of, Scythia Minor in the hinterland of the Danube. The name Khoryv is Persian and the movement of Croats – compatriots of another Khorovatosa – continued from the Caucasus into the Balkans in the 1st millennium CE (according to O. N. Trubachev). It is crucially important here to realise, based on the archaeology, the inter-relationships between the Cimmerians and Illyrians based on linguistic and historical data and from *The Veles Book* – that Kimoria-Surozh, through a chain of tribal bonds along with the kinship of fore-father Oriy along with his sons, joined ranks to create a state in Ruskolan Carpathia. This was the second centre of formation of Rus (after the Adriatic formation). And it alone was the last wave, already an entirely Persian wave of "Minor" Scythian-'wanderers' around the beginning of the 6th century BCE, which was so prejudicially described by Herodotus. More will be said on this later.

We interrupted the sequence and description of events occurring at the boundary of the 9th – 8th centuries BCE, when part of the first two waves of returners from India did not take root in the lands of Scythian Sindica that had been assigned to them, and in their establishment of Cimmeria, were led in two waves by Oriy and Oseden into the sunset [westwards] and sunrise [eastwards]. As noticed by S. I. Nalyvayko, it was probably at this point that we see a correspondence formed between the names of *Yadavi-Satvati-Danavi* of the Indian *Mahabharata* and the *Yatvyagi*[11]*-Sudovity-Dainovi* of the early-Baltic area, whose trail leads out from the Chernihiv region. This became the second homeland (after the Taman Sindica) of the Indo-Aryan-Slavic *Sauvir-Sivertsi* considered earlier and the Cimmerians were derived from the first of them. It is only by taking into account the above mentioned information from *The Veles Book* about the unequivocally explicit convergences between the Arattan ethnonyms etc. – in both cases – to Oriana and Borusia (in the Dnipro area), and to Surashtra and Sauvira (in Punjab), can be revealed, and understood.

It was not the mythical Colchis of the *Argonautica* of Apollonius of Rhodes, but historic Cimmeria that became the first state of Taurida and Ei [Eya Island?] of the Crimea and Taman peninsula, on the boundary of the above-mentioned centuries. However the Cimmerians failed to be consolidated there. The pre-state traditions of Aratta and Oriana as well as the power of the brahmans, were probably too strong for them there; that is why the militant Kshatriya were forced to satisfy their ambitions in a more suitable environment for that – amongst the slaveholding states of the East. In *The Veles Book* this migration of an active part of the population of the Surozh-Kimoria led by the Princes Oriy and Oseden is described thus:

15a ... *they left that land* (Cimmeria) *and went to the Double-river area* (Mesopotamia),
and broke those (enemies) *with the help of their cavalry;*
and went to Syrian land, and stopped there.

6c *How many times they took out swords and came out against enemies*
and cast them away from their lands the fathers of the kin of Or [Oriy], *glorious and strong.*
Those who fought Syria and Egypt.
But in those old times there was no unity among us (Rusy),
and we remained without Veles, as wax...
Therefore the Persians took away the better half of the Rusy and drove them to Nabsur...
And they went, their heads bowed under the enemy whips, –
as strong detachments attacked (us) *from three sides...*
(Others of) *our people went to the valleys of Nabsursar,*
later on to Syria and Egypt.

6d *When they suffered from Babylonian slavery,*
their prince there was Nabsursar,
who ruled them.

Middle-Eastern and Greek sources say that those events happened between 783-595 BCE. In fact, there were two successful Cimmerian campaigns on Egypt (and absolutely none by the Scythians!) – in 663 and 605 BCE, and between them – a palpable

Fig. 110 : **Cimmerians**. Images from the 6th – 5th centuries BCE on a cyst from Klazomen [an ancient Greek city] and "Etruscan" amphora (above).

defeat on the territory of Persia (Iran) from the Assyrian armies led by Ashurbanipal^. The Chronicle for those years lists the names of the Cimmerian leaders: *Kashtarit, Sandakshatra* and *Tugdamma*. In their names, despite severe disfigurement by foreign scribes, one can clearly see they belonged to Indo-Aryan Kshatriyas-'warriors', who perhaps venerated the Celto-Slavic *Dagda*-Dazhboh.

According to the same sources (and comments by V. Torop), during the period 624-585 BCE, the Cimmerian Kiaksar (Cyaxares, in Herodotus) ruled Media and waged war with Assyria. His contemporary and enemy was the Scythian chieftain King Madyes, the son of Protothyes who allegedly (according to Herodotus, I: 103) led the Scythian banishment of the Cimmerians from the Northern Black Sea area in Asia. However Assyrian sources name the Cimmerians as the Umman-Manda, and Madyes (whose name was immortalised in the Biblical place-name, "Land of Magog) was known as the grandson of Esarhaddon^, who had given his daughter to the said Protothyes (Partatua[12]). The wife of Madyes became Zarina, princess of the town of Roxanak, north of Media. A Slavic-Rusy connection between the latter two names is quite possible; especially since the Irano-Arabic tradition from that time considered Slavs to be the descendants of Madyes (according to Al-Masudi: "*The Slavs are the essence of Madyes*"). This does not mean that these events relate only to the Slavs but their presence in the ethnic and cultural diversity of the Cimmerian-Scythian-Saki world certainly has Indo-Aryan (rather than Irano-Aryan) roots and is entirely consistent with the corresponding data from *The Veles Book* (rather than with *The Histories* by Herodotus).

During the time of Kiaksar/Cyaxares, circa 595 BCE, part of the suffering Cimmerian tribe from Babylon erupted into Asia Minor and passed out through the Balkans into Europe. Behind them were the Scythians, though before leaving, their insolent leaders had been killed at a banquet by the people of Kiaksar (Herodotus I: 106). Nothing is known about the death of Madyes but his wife Zarina, as reported in Assyrian archives, arranged a defence against Kiaksar, repelled his onslaught, made peace with Media then returned to the city of Roxanak. The location of this mysterious city is "*indicated in the country of Sako-Amirgi, in the mountains*". According to Diodorus, Roxanak was next to Parthia; Nicolas of Damascus also pointed to north of the Caucasus. In any event, this group of Slavs or their kinsmen can be understood in terms of the migration between the Punjab and Dnipro area (or vice versa): either they hadn't reached as far as India or they didn't return from there to Rus.

The Veles Book highlights some aspects of the return of the Cimmerians to the Northern Black Sea area (VB: 6d et al.), as well as recording a version of the **fourth, most plausible legend** which also appears in *The Histories* (IV: 13) but was barely considered by Herodotus, nor by his followers. Here is that legend:

"*However, Aristeas, the son of Canstrobia, a man of Proconnesa, reports in his epic poem how he came to the land of the Issedones, obsessed by Pheobus. According to his prose,... the Arimaspi drove the Issedones out of their country, then the Issendones banished the Scythians, and so the Cimmerians, who dwelt on the Southern Sea, being pressed by the Scythians, left their land. Thus the story of Aristeas does not agree with the Scythians legends about these countries*".

Aristeas, who is already known to us as the servant of Apollo, belonged to the clan of "wandering Hyperboreans" who travelled along the line of Maidan sanctuary-observatories. From this evidence, some compilers of *The Veles Book* could well have belonged to the same clans, Aratto-Indo-European in their origin. We already know that the activities and very existence of this clan were virtually unknown to the ancient Greek "father of history" which is why neither Herodotus (nor almost all his contemporaries) was able to understand them, so we cannot trust their information about this clan. This is reinforced by the last sentence of Herodotus' fourth legend that is consistent with the position of both *The Veles Book* and the Middle Eastern chronicles of the 8th – 6th centuries BCE.

After living for 200 years in Asia Minor, the coast of the Southern Sea (as the Greeks called the Red Sea) became home to the Cimmerian migrants. Not all descendants of Oriy had left Surozhian Rus (i.e., Cimmeria) but only one Cimmerian tribe of Treres[13], left for foreign lands and then returned to their abandoned native land (where amongst others tribes named by Strabo in his *Geography* were the *Toretae* and *Tarpetes* – perhaps relatives of the returned Treres?). Behind them went the nomadic Scythians, dislodged by the Issedones (one of the tribes of Saki, related to Massagetae, Sarmatians and Scythians) from the southeastern area of the Caspian Sea, with their advance guard making their way through unfamiliar lands trying to catch up. After passing through Asia Minor, crossing the Bosphorus and Danube, they arrived at the Dniester. Here the Cimmerians tried to hold off the Scythian-Napi (the 'young outcast-wanderers') who had followed the Cimmerians on to the territory of their original homeland and whilst this is described by Herodotus (IV: 11) in legend III, it is in terms of a dramatic discord amongst the Cimmerians themselves.

One of the possible prototypes for a similar discord was described in *The Veles Book* (26) earlier on. In that scenario, the disagreement between the kings and the people concerning the threat of invasion by the Scythians can now be better understood: the Cimmerian-returners were keen to please their local relatives by meting out a strong rebuff to the Scythians who had arrived immediately after them. However, their relatives didn't

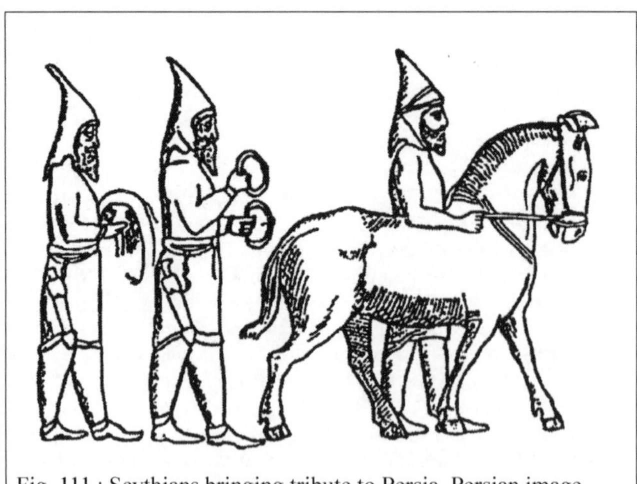

Fig. 111 : Scythians bringing tribute to Persia. Persian image.

hang around and moved far away from that dangerous place (rather as the Scythians themselves hadn't waited around when the Persian armies of Darius invaded their land). Then the returners formed an alliance with their former enemies and with their combined forces they themselves recaptured the Royal Scythians and nomadic tribes, as described by Herodotus (IV: 19-20). The first of them could have been formed, primarily, from the descendants of the Cimmerian-Treres who had returned from Asia. Genetically they were close to the aboriginal Skoloty and, as we have suggested, their inter-relationships with the related local population is linked with the legend described by Valerius Flaccus: Arpoksai (from the first legend by Herodotus, the leader of Traspi and Katiar) apparently killed his brother Kolaks (Kolaxsai) in a battle... However, whether that was the case or not, O. N. Trubachev convincingly showed an Indo-Aryan affiliation in the names of the Scythian rulers mentioned in *The Histories* of Herodotus (rather than Irano-Aryan, as they should have been in the case of the migrant Scythian-nomads, the Napi).

As so often happens with heroes, their actions and personalities fall outside the limits of canons; people even create new canons to accommodate them, which are not always appropriate and timely. This is how it happened with the Cimmerians and with the Kimoria they created. They were burned out at the crossroads of epochs and statehoods – communal and slaveholding societies. That is how Cimmeria is presented in *The Histories* of the foreign wanderer Herodotus, the great son of slaveholding Hellas.

However, it is not the ashes but the radiance that is the real legacy left by Kimoria, recorded on the best pages of the holy book of Slavs, *The Veles Book*. To this day it blazes the same call: do not tread on the unsteady pathway of untruths; venerate God's peace and respect human life; do not be pulled behind the corruptible but save immortal souls; follow the precepts of the winged Mother-Glory of our ancestors!

The light was never once extinguished but revived again and again – by *The Veles Book* and *Tale of the Campaign of Ihor Svyatoslavlich*, by Cossacks and kobzari^, by Taras Shevchenko^ and Batko [i.e. Father] Makhno^... Even now – it will never fade! For the tablets of Stone Grave, the cities of Aratta and kurhans of Oriana have become the foundation of this beacon ... an unconquerable foundation!

Behold, before us is our land and that is why we defend it, just like our fathers. And let us marry the Sky and the Earth, and let us celebrate their wedding, — for we are their children.

3. Rus and Bosphorus.

So, Scythian-Persians came into the Northern Black Sea area after the Slavs who had returned from India, and after the partial return of the Cimmerians from the Middle East. The attitude of the local population to these Scythian-nomads and Cimmerian-Treres was initially unfriendly (6c). Nevertheless, following a short-lived conflict at the start of the 6th century BCE between the Cimmerians and Scythians, according to *The Veles Book*, they were no longer considered to be enemies. The partial identification of the Rusy with the Scythians in *The Veles Book* came later — and although it speaks of the brothers Slaven and Scyth (as recorded in the lost Yakimov's chronicle, according to V. N. Tatishchev) as sworn brothers, in fact they also, separately, had a subordinate Celtic ally in "*Bastar*[14], *their son*" who was ethnically foreign to them, (17a). And the evidence in "*bedekhshemo kraventse a skufe antíve rusy borusen' a surenzhetsy Tako sme stakhom ded' rusove*"[15] (7e) can be understood as: "*we were Korovychi and Skotychi* [children of Zamun and Dazhboh, i.e. cow-like Earth and bovine/Taurean Heaven]: *Ants, Rusy, Boruses and Surozhtsi – in this way were formed the Rusy grandfathers*".

Fig. 112 : **Scythian King Ateas**. A coin of the 4th century BCE.

In 549 BCE, power in Media passed to another of its ethnic groups – to the Persians. They gravitated not to the Indian, but to the Persian offshoot of Aryans; correspondingly the politics changed too. In 522 BCE power in Persia came to Darius I who accepted Zoroastrianism, a belief system inherent to the Persians – which, although it had grown from the Aratto-Aryan Vedas, now stood in opposition to them. After being affirmed in the Middle East, King Darius moved without delay into Scythia – in 514, (or 512) BCE – allegedly aiming to punish it (according to Herodotus IV: 1) "*for their invasion of Media and for the fact that the Scythians, after conquering the Median adversaries, were first to violate the peace*". Admirers of the "father of history" swallowed this frivolous reasoning about the Scythians being the motive for this immense and rather risky campaign – but it is an

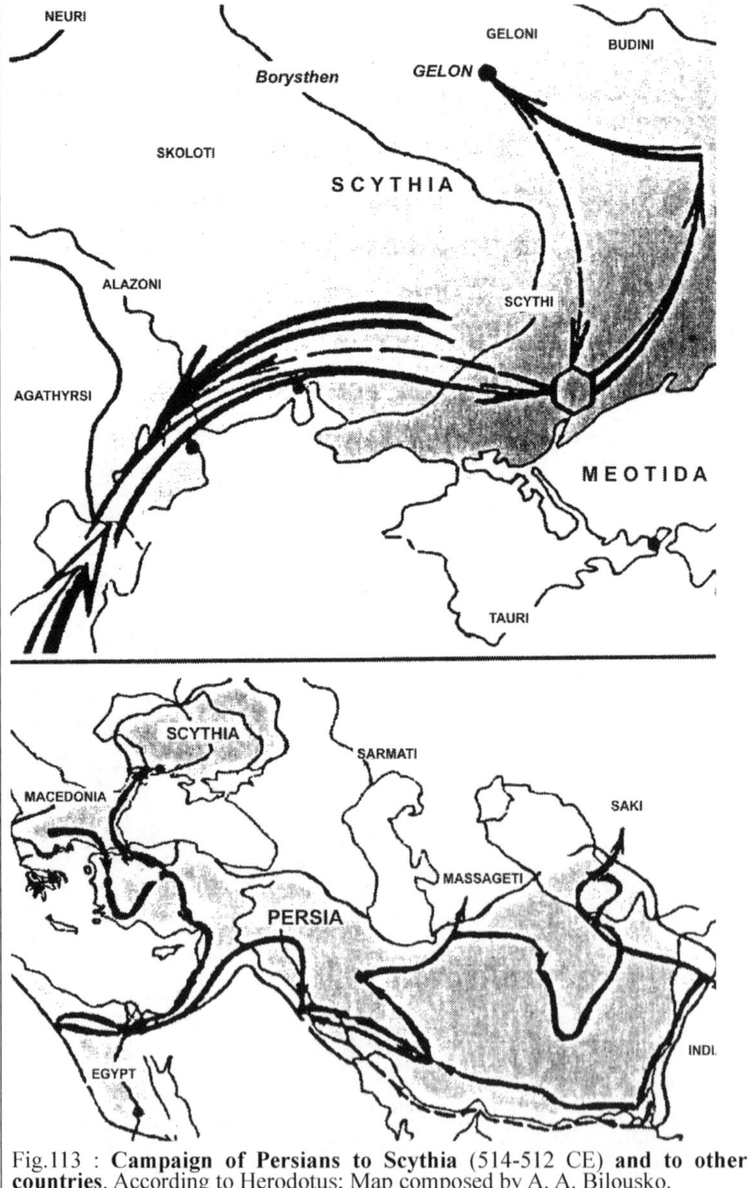

Fig.113 : **Campaign of Persians to Scythia** (514-512 CE) **and to other countries**. According to Herodotus; Map composed by A. A. Bilousko.

unacceptable motive as we have seen. We shall aim to show that the root cause of this lamentable gamble (really?!) by Darius I was far from foolish.

We will proceed from the well-known theory which postulates that diplomacy in those times was securely based on religious principles and therefore this should be regarded as the root cause for the Persian campaign on Scythia and thus, the real reason was to be sought in religious reforms carried out by Darius in Persia on the eve of the campaign. *The Veles Book* (6d) hints rather transparently at this primary reason and motive:

> *And came the day, when the Rusy went from Nabsursar.*
> *The Persians did not chase after them, but came into our lands*
> *and there they heard our songs to Intra and claimed,*
> *that if they would begin* (for first time) *to believe, then they would be with our gods,*
> *and to their gods they would not force us* (among themselves in the East).

There may be an imputation here that it was not the Persians *per se*, but those Scythians related with them, who came into the Northern Black Sea area from the Middle East on the trail of the Cimmerians; indeed further on in the book it is said: "let us recall Darius of Persia who came to us and beat us through our disunity and civil wars" (8). However this does not change the main point. It is clear that Darius – even despite the fact that he united the Persians – sought to destroy **in Scythia** the cradle of pre-Zoroastrian Indo-

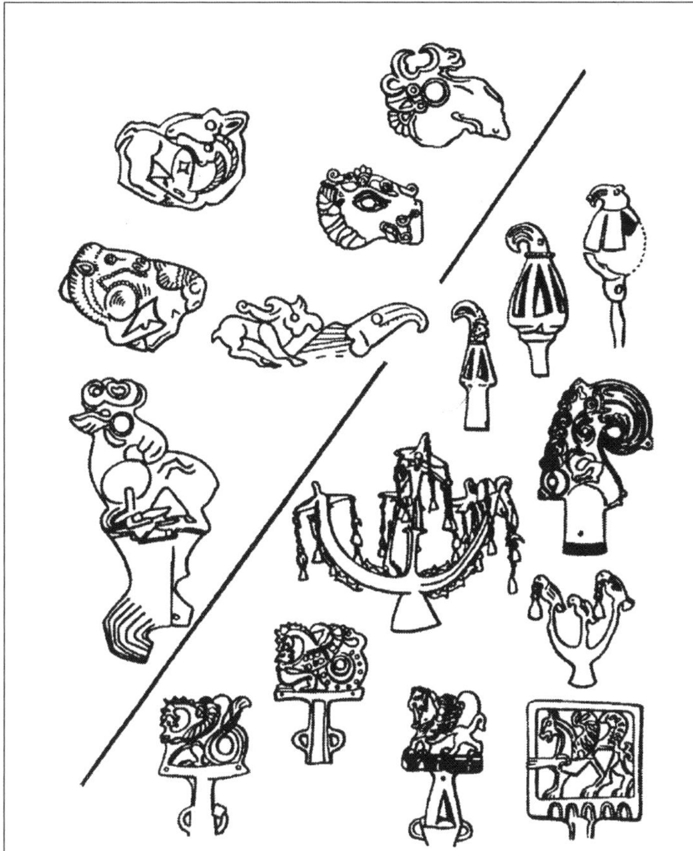

Fig.114 : **Venerations of eagles and deer, etc. Totems of Pre-Slavs and Scythians** in the 6th – 4th centuries BCE (according to B. A. Rybakov, *Paganism of Ancient Slavs*, Nauka, Kyiv, 1987; pp. 554-555).

Aryan faith; to annihilate it in the name of the same association and to initiate a faith founded not on the basis of an archetypal-community but on a qualitatively new (slaveholding) basis.

It is clear that the authors of *The Veles Book* by no means shared the militancy of the Royal Scythians (who were already acquainted with slaveholding in the East) and sought a peace agreement with the Persians. However, a military resistance was organised by the Scythian kings who bore *Indo*-Aryan names rather than *Irano*-Aryan names. Chief amongst them, Idanthirs, was only part Aryan, judging by his name. This was 'Thirsty *Thirs*', whose ethnicity was sought by O. N. Trubachev in the chronicled names of *Toursi* and *Tivertsi* (namely, amongst the *Tauri, Rusy and* Slavs). Although it is noticeable that the name *Idanthirs* was close to that of *Agathirs* (Aryans with a Dacian admixture or vice versa), his actions contradict that association. After all, if the Royal and other Scythians together with the Holuns[16], Budini and Sarmatians actively opposed the Persian invasion, then at the forefront of those who did not wish to defend Scythia, according to Herodotus (IV: 119), were the Agathirsi (together with the Neuri, Androphagi^, Melanhlens and Tauros^). The un-mentioned Rusy or Cimmerians could be part of a tribal alliance.

For example it is known from *The Veles Book* that the Holuns (Gelons) were occupying the land of the Budini that had been burned by the Persians (IV. 123). Incidentally, the first of the ethnonyms mentioned earlier have not yet been fixed (still identified more particularly with the militarised tribes of the Skoloty-Slavs), and the second had already fallen into disuse having lost (along with the breakup of the Surozh Cimmerians) their original essence after being absorbed into the new, up-to-date regime of the Scythian 'Wanderers'[17] becoming established again on their original ancestral homeland. The position of the Agathirsi in this war consisted of an observance of armed neutrality (IV: 119, 125): "*To us it seems, that the Persians came not against us, but against their offenders* (who had returned from Media)... *After that Agathirs came forward with armies to the borders, in order to resist the attack*" (of both the Scythians and Persians, if they encroached on their territory).

The authors of *The Veles Book* regarded the Greeks and Romans as the foremost enemies of ancient times. Antagonism with the Greeks even went back to the time of the fall of Troy and was maintained until at least the baptism of Rus in Byzantine times. As we already know, there was a clash here between two very distinct types of civilisation – communal and slaveholding.

Although sources of information from the times of Homeric Troy are not very detailed, they are sufficiently and usefully revealing. The earliest reference to the fact that *the Greeks attacked Rus* (perhaps at Troy), is framed within the myth describing the creation of the world by Dazhboh (VB: 1) – more specifically, the detail indicating the approximate time of of the svarga-zodiac[18] which spans the period 4400-1700 BCE during the supremacy of the constellation of Taurus (which has been repeatedly discussed above). These were the times when ancestors *elected princes from among the eldest kin, ... and did not consult the Greeks about their preference*, they were related to Bohomyr (VB: 10) who lived shortly after the Trojan War, approximately 13th or 11th century BCE. Perhaps there has been a mistaken interpretation of the source [VB: 2a) about it referring to reasons for the resettlement led by father Oriy "[when our ancestors] *went from the southern borders to take the lands for us and for our children. And the Greeks attacked us there, because we were settled on their land. And there was great carnage for many months*". Because this is most likely to have been a reference to the Cimmerian return from the shores of [what the Greeks called] the Red Sea through Asia Minor, where many Ionian Greeks were living at that time.

There were also mentions of quarrels and of trade concomitant with the spread of the ancient city-colonies in the Northern Black Sea area, which were partially merged, during the 5th century BCE, into the Bosphorus kingdom (Gretskolun of *The Veles Book*, 19). This helped the colonists repel the Athenian fleet led by Pericles in 437 BCE, "*the barbarians showed the strength, courage and daring of Athenians, by sailing anywhere and subjugating the entire Pontis to themselves*" for the sake of supplying stony Greece with the high-quality and cheap bread of Scythia. There is evidence for the capture of the city of Surozh^ by Athenians and its later reconstruction as Greek Athenion.

This kind of force is non-human, as it is black,
and this serpent - those enemies come from the south, namely Bosphorus.
Whipped and discarded by the armies of our grandfathers,
the Greeks want to surround our land.

Some of the city-colonies – Khorusun (Chersonese) and Surozh (Athenion, later renamed as Sudak) – could precede Slavic settlements in the composition of Kimoria and Surozhian Rus (VB: 6c, 8(3), 19). Just like the city-state of Holun (the Gelon of Herodotus]), they were also surrounded by ditches and earth wall ramparts, which the Greeks said were Cimmerian, and the remnants of which are still evident on the Kerch and Taman peninsulas. And although the expulsion of the Greeks is said to have been from there (VB: 23), in reality (and then only partially) this was during later antiquity and during the Middle Ages. However, in ancient Scythian times the interests of commerce predominated (VB: 7b):

The Greeks wanted to subdue us near Khorusun,
but we struggled against our slavery.
And that struggle and great battle lasted for thirty years;
and they left us alone.
And then the Greeks went to our trading...
Here we trade so till this time,
though even after (that war) *the Greeks sought in us a weakness,*
seeking for opportunities to take us into captivity.

One of those opportunities became *The Histories* written by Herodotus. We have seen that the historical acts and the very name of the Cimmerians were stolen at that time in order to favour the Greek-colonists and "the youngest of the Scythians" who by the end of the 5th century BCE became the mainstay of the colonialists in their commercial and political affairs. It was no accident that Herodotus had undertaken a mission to their city (as reconnaissance?) and to Scythia just a few years prior to the military expedition of Pericles; for these outstanding figures of their state were personally acquainted and supported each other's activities.

Apart from the Scythian wars of 339-331 BCE with the troops of Philip II and his son Alexander of Macedonia, which took place with variable success on the right bank of the Danube and Dnipro (and the final defeat of commander Zopirio under the walls of Greek Olvia and the neighbouring "trading place of the Scythian-Borysthenians"), there were no other serious clashes with the Greeks up until the 2nd century BCE. However, in Thrace

Fig. 115 : **Origin legend of the Scythians**. A ceremonial bowl (see. Fig. 100 and 130) from a royal kurhan of the 4th century BCE (Haimanova Grave at the village of Balka in the Zaporizhia region, excavated by V. I. Bidzylia).

(where the 90 year-old Scythian King Ateas perished in battle with the Macedonians), except for Scythia Minor^, there was still the kingdom of Odrs-Odris in the coastal valley of the River Hebrus (Evros, or Maritsa). It existed from the 5th century BCE to the 1st century CE, although the nation itself was ancient (and represented, possibly, a conservative group from Oriana-Orissa. Moreover there is a correspondence with the *Mahabharata* in the form of "Odrs of Orissa who aided the Pandavas").

In the mid-3rd century BCE, Scythia sharply reduced its holdings, leaving the noble cemetery of their kings at Guerra and their capital(?) city of Metropolis near the Dnipro rapids. Their primary reasons for doing so, above all, were climatic-environmental-demographic reasons as well as drought, migration and so on. However another influencing factor was intensified activity from the Sarmatian tribes which must have stimulated that reduction; those tribes were considered to be descendants of the Amazons and Scythians (Herodotus IV: 110-117), probably from the 'maternal' Meotians of eastern Meotida. According to the testimony of Diodorus Siculus (II: 43) and previous authors of the 2nd - 1st centuries BCE, the extinction of the Greater Scythians of the Sarmatian period was devastating, "*and, one and all exterminated the vanquished, turning most of the country into a desert.*" The remaining Scythians formed a new capital, Naples, in Taurida/Tauris, near present-day Simferopol – later called 'Novhorod' by the Rusy (who had either seized it or it had already emerged from one of the tribes of Tauro-Rusy or Tauro-Scythians).

The next Scythian kings were Skilur and his son Palak^ ('Palka-Kyi', meaning 'stick, staff or club' in English, who were perhaps from the same dynasty as Kyis of *The Veles Book* etc.). Palak, supported by the Roxolani (a Sarmatian or Ruskolan tribe), started a war with the Greco-Taurean Chersonese. Afterwards, its inhabitants appealed to Bosphorus and Pontis – Greek states on the opposite shore of the Black Sea – for aid. The king of Pontis, Mithridates Eupator^, sent an army led by general Diophantes, during which period, 110-107 BCE, the Bosphorean king took power over the Pontis kingdom. There is evidence that Mithridates, as ruler of the Bosphorus, used the Rusy to wage wars, first against local Greeks (19), and then in 89-63 BCE against the advance of the Romans (32):

> *And Mithridates said to the Rusy that they could settle nearby.*
> *But when they agreed, those Greeks called them (the Rusy) into a battle, then called a second time and* (so on) *without end...*
> *The Rusy went away from the Greeks and set themselves down on the Don and Donets, later going up to the Dnipro and Danube, and there lived peacefully...*
> *And we intermarried with those Mithridians.*

It is appropriate to emphasise here the relative differences between the Slavic, Greek and Roman cultures. We have already looked at their eternal similarity, namely, their common origins from Aratta – the core of the "linguistic community of Indo-European nations". In the Northern Black Sea area, up until the end of antiquity, the tribes who existed there retained their ethnogenetic connections, i.e. the Borysthenes, Scythian-Hellenes, Gelons/Holuns, Callipedae, Vans and a certain measure of Venedi. In Holun, ancient Dionysus was esteemed; Chersonese was under the guardian Deva with roots in Pelasgian Artemis and Aryan Devi. It was perhaps the cult of Devi that was linked to the 'divine books' of Sastri and their 'twice born' keepers. In addition, the Greek-colonists vaguely remembered the origin of Achilles, Odysseus and others from these places... All of which explains the relative tolerance of the Slavic Volhvs [i.e. Magi] and their people towards the Greeks, as well as the subsequent baptism of Prince Vladimir in Korsune (Khorsun, or Chersonese).

For *"Thousands of years we fought against the Romans and Goths"* (VB: 7c), and during their feuding with the Romans, the Rusy reached as far as the Etruscan remoteness of Adriatic Semyrychia. Clashes in the Northern Black Sea area started from 74 BCE, when Rus supported Mithridates VI Eupator in his third war with Rome. The latter victory was helped by a terrible earthquake in 63 BCE, which happened just "*at that moment, when Mithridates celebrated the holiday of Ceres in Bosphorus*" (Paul Orosius, 5th century). This terrible catastrophe that destroyed cities and caused hydrosulphuric eruptions of the Black Sea, was remembered for centuries; a description of it was introduced in the apocalyptic *Revelation of Theologian Johannes*. We agree with A. I. Asov that this was the precise catastrophe referred to as the "Bosphorus serpent" on Board 19 of *The Veles Book* as cited here (and maybe other sources where a similar catastrophe is described in the Punjab). Most frightful was that Ceres (Demeter), to whom the tyrant Mithridates brought sacrifice, was considered to be the mother-in-law of Aides/Hades whom the Pelasgians and Greeks traditionally placed at the Cimmerian Bosphorus (known today as the Kerch strait) in Meotida [the Azov Sea]. One can imagine the inevitable conclusion of the Bosphoran people: "Aides of the underworld rejected Mithridates' sacrifice!" Against the enemy of Rome [i.e. Mithridates] even his army and son rebelled – and Mithridates killed himself.

In 62-61 BCE, the year following his suicide, the Roman army was defeated in Macedonia by a coalition of Greeks, Getae, Bastarnians and Rusy. From that time a fairly prolonged period of peace began, which is recalled in the fore-mentioned portion from *The Veles Book* 7b. However, the peace was violated by Pharmakes, the treacherous son of Mithridates VI Eupator. He destroyed the temple of the Scythians-Meskhetians^, in which, according to legends, the Golden Fleece was stored along with holy manuscripts. For this, Pharmakes was apparently deposed and killed by his lieutenant-general Asandr (probably a Sarmatian or Slav). He ruled in the years 47-17 BCE, followed by his wife Dinamia who reigned until 7 CE. These were relatively happy years despite the construction of the Perekop earthen wall against incursions on Taurida and only minor wars east of the Bosphorus realm. Their son, Aspurg, ruled until 38 CE – he placated the inhabitants of Taurida, and afterwards the Bosphorus was ruled by members of the Aspurg dynasty until 335 CE. At the end of their rule the Rusy returned and rebuilt their original Surozh as recorded in *The Veles Book*.

The Sarmatian state of King Pharzoi and his son Irismey existed in the northwestern Black Sea area for twenty years at the end of the 1st century CE. At that time even Rome paid tribute to the Roxolani, because along with the Bastarnians and Dacians, they had conquered the Romans in Moesia^ and the Carpathians in 86-87 CE. "*And* (then) *Rus, conquered by Greeks and Romans, went to the sea shores as far as Surozh and there they created Surozh; on the side that was sunny and was subject to Kyiv*" (6f). Here we are put in mind, perhaps, of the victories of the Romans over the Dacians in 101-106 CE, and then in 193 CE – the victory of the Bosphorus troops over the Tauro-Scythians who were supported by Rome". Slavic tribes could have been amongst them. The reference to Kyiv does not mean the Kyiv which began to rise in the 5th century on the site of the present capital of Ukraine. It is possible that here (as in some other cases), these quotations do not relate to the events that were intended by the authors of *The Veles Book*.

When it became untenable to continue maintaining the Bosphorus kingdom, Chersonese and other city-states of the Northern Black Sea area, around the middle of 3rd century, the Roman troops left this region. Over the following century the Bosphorus kingdom ceased to exist. From that time the Slavs could believe that their fathers *"had shaken the Romans and swept away the Greeks, like frightened piglets*" (VB: 6e). It was only commercial trade interests that restrained the victors from inflicting the final crushing defeat on the remnants of the Ancient Greek colonies.

Clearly, the historian cannot rely wholly on the evidence of *The Veles Book* and other sources; more than once we have mentioned the need to recheck them. We shall reiterate that again here when considering references to the victory of Dulebs^ and Rusy over the legions of the Roman emperor Trajan^ "*for three hundred years before our time or for five hundred years before the Goths*" (29), i.e. from the 3rd century BCE to the 6th century CE. This date range cannot be accepted, particularly because Trajan actually waged a victorious war with the Dacians (ancestors of Romanians and Moldavians) in 101-106 CE, and the victories of the Slavs and their allies relate to the years 86-87 CE, as already mentioned. In any case, it was not as respected enemies of that emperor but by him for his own honour that the 'Trojan centuries', 'Trojan lands' etc. were glorified. The origins and semantics of these concepts deserve special attention but before we begin to consider the problem, we shall round off the outline of the relationship between the Slavs and the Bosphorus kingdom.

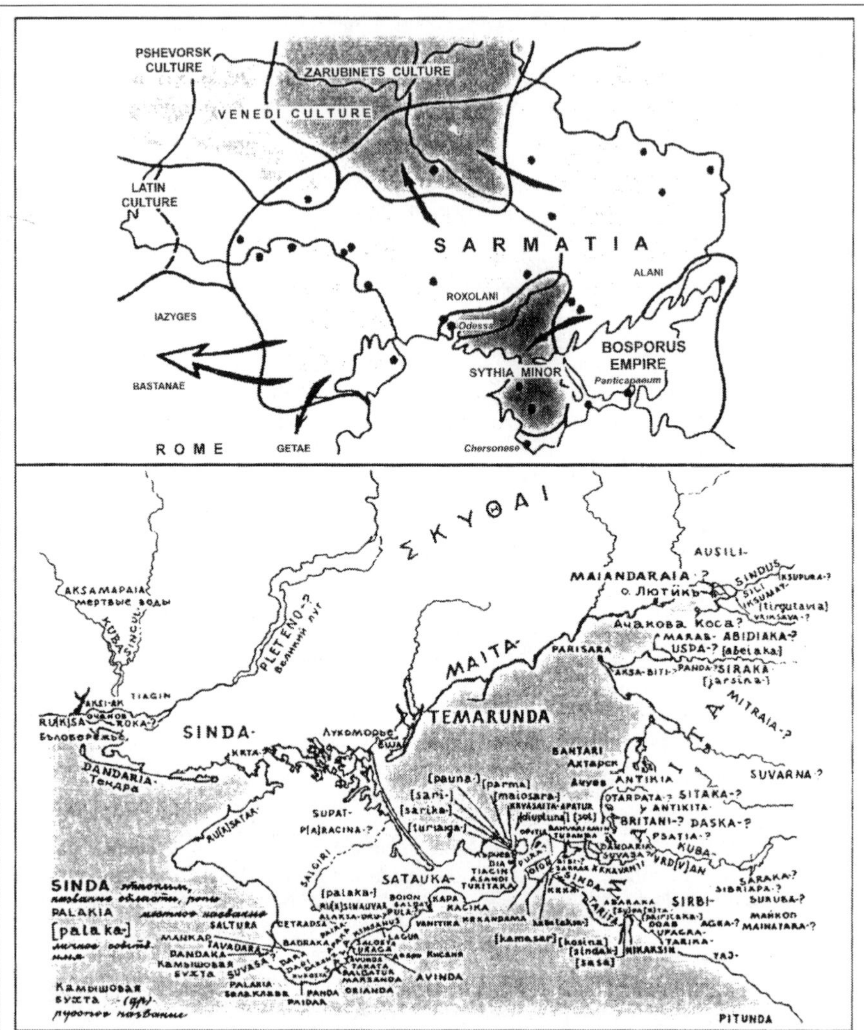

Fig. 116 : **The ethnoculturnal environment** of Indo-Aryan toponymy of the **Northern Black Sea area at the end of ancient time** (according to O. N. Trubachev).

In 395 CE the Eastern part of the Roman empire, settled principally by Greeks, became separated and later became the Byzantine empire. Having a fleet, it established commercial and political relations with the remnants of the Bosphorus kingdom and the city-states on the opposite side of the Black Sea. In 410 CE Rome was taken over by barbarians, but the empire struggled on until 476 CE. In the preceding year Odoacer had become emperor – he was a mercenary who had previously been a Prince of the Rugi (according to Jordanes; but according to other authors – the Roxolani, Ruthenians[19], Rusy; perhaps related to each other). Having become heir to the Roman empire, Byzantium established power in 518 CE over part of the territory of former Bosphorus and continued its policies of pressure, fraud and commerce with Rus which was seen as the continuation of Scythia. According to the 11th century Radziwill^ chronicle: "*And Dulebs lived along the* [River] *Buh, and the Uluchi-Tivertsi were sitting on the Buh and the Dnipro towards the sea. Their cities stand to this day and they are called by Greeks, Great Scythia.*"

Concerning the relationship of Cimmerians with Slavs as remembered in the

Middle Ages (VB: 6f), the ethnoculture of the Cimmerians was probably inherited by immigrants into the Baltics and Novhorod region (VB: 8, 15a), as well as Western Europe – including the Cimbri [Cymru/Britons] of Britain, though [incorrectly] attributed as Celts or Germans by researchers. According to Plutarch (46-130 CE), "*When rumours reached Rome about the Cimbri and Teutons... most believed that they belonged to German tribes... some argued that the land of the Celts was so large and so spacious that it extended from the Exterior* (Baltic/Outer) *Sea to the most northern areas of the settled world extending east as far as Meotida and the borders of Pontic Scythia. Here the Celts and Scythians were mixed... still others said that the Cimmerians, familiar to the Ancient Greeks, constituted only a small part of the tribe, ... with the greatest and most militant part of the Cimmerians living near the Exterior Sea ...*".

Fig. 117 : The surroundings of the village of Trypillia in the Dnipro area. An aerial photo from the early 1940s (above).
*2008 satellite image below (courtesy of Google Earth). In both images, northwest is uppermost. (See also Fig 86).

On the other hand, it is not accidental that there was a tendency to extend the history of Rus, identifying them with Tauro-Scythians and Tauros (Leo Diaconus[20] and Ioann Tsets, of the 10th and 12th centuries, respectively). According to this tradition – the supported part of the Cimbri probably migrated to Britain and were adopted there in the 5th century with their Rusy prince **Yar-tur** (from the tribe of Uliches?^), collaborating with the friendly local druid-priest Merlin on the formation of the British state and entering history as the glorious king **Arthur**.

We won't argue with B. A. Rybakov and other authoritative researchers on matters pertaining to the approval of their concept about Trojan lands (!?) during the times of Emperor Trajan. Instead, let us broaden the origin of this concept back to the time of the Skoloto-Cimmerians, and if possible to more ancient times, when construction really did began of the 'Trojan earthen walls'– as these structures were called in former Walachia (Romania, Moldova and Bessarabia). The name of Veles and the Volhvs [Magi], who "*prayed to Trihlav^, adult and young, and this Trihlav of ours gathers us*" (VB: 25), could be derived from those earthen walls[21]. A Trojan earth wall is also mentioned near the Danube (VB: 7g). And let us not forget that from Trypillia in the Dnipro area, the 'Serpent earth walls' are dispersed precisely like a Trident – in the direction of the Danube. They were probably built during the times of Aratta, Oriana and Troy – even up to the time of Emperor Trajan and beyond (VB: 29):

And let us recall how the Trojan was broken by our grandfathers,
and the legions of captives [Romans] *were taken on our fields,*
and so (the captives) *worked ten hard years for us and were released by us.*
But (now) *these Romans say that we are thieves.*

But weren't the Trojan earth walls supposed to have taken ten years to build under the supervision of the victors, those liars?

At the very heart of all these sacred site concepts, the main mytho-ritual of the Indo-Aryan Vedas is to be found: in this ritual, the hero Indra frees the new year 'shell' of Vala from the serpent Vritra. *The Veles Book* repeatedly makes reference to these characters: the first of them through Vparuni (the Vedic Varuna) who was transformed into Perun and "*Parun gave all the weapons*" (VB: 31, 6d); and the second, (possibly, through "*Intra and Vola*", which means an 'ox': (VB: 6d)), turned on the name of Veles, who not only taught the ancestors "*to call to* (to plough) *the land and sow grain*" (4b) but also became "*our father*" (VB: 3a) after "*grandfathers*" Svaroh and Dazhboh (VB: 36b).

After his victory over the serpent, Indra is blessed by 'All-encompassing' Vishnu, another Vedic character of *The Veles Book* (VB: 11a, 15b, 31). Associated with him is Sheshi, the truly Vala-like world serpent. When Aryan kurhans from the mid 2nd millennium BCE were excavated by archaeologists in the Bilozirka valley of Zaporizhia region and the Chongar^ peninsula of Sivash, they actually contained the self-same symbols of Sheshi. Research shows that these constructions were not only appointed places for burial and calendar practises but also centres of the mytho-rituals of 'Rajasuia' ('rada sviata', the 'Holy Council' of Ukrainians) which were visited in the annual tour around the lands of his nation by the ruler-priest, namely the *Brahman* (in Ukrainian *Rahman*). Perhaps the Serpent and the Trojan earth walls of Rus, besides being defensive, had the same purpose. They were a type of memorial in honour of the triune God Trihlav (i.e. Svaroh-Perun-Svitovyd, Khors-Veles-Stryboh, Vishen-Lial-Litych and others: *The Veles Book*, 11), a sign of holiness and ownership of Rus on their own "Trojan land" that began to unite (by the efforts of the authors of *The Veles Book* and similar public figures) in Oriana, Borusia and Ruskolan.

In concluding this essay about the Slavs, and their earliest origin as members of the indigenous parts of the Cimmerian and Scythian tribes, we emphasise the key facts of the eternal right of Slavs to the lands of the Dnipro-Danube region, now mostly owned by Ukraine. In *The Veles Book* and the *Tale of the Campaign of Ihor Svyatoslavlich*, this right is referred to as the '*earth of Troyanna*' and embodied in the original memorials, namely, the Trojan earth-walls situated near the village of Trypillia (south of Kyiv) bearing the form of a trident. **This is one of the few examples in the world that certified the rights of the people – by reason of their multi-millennia old sanctuaries – to their archetypal land**

and to their historical identity.

Suggested reading

1. *The Veles Book*. Translation and comments by B. Yatsenko, Kyiv, 1995, 2001.
2. Herodotus, *The Histories*, Moscow – Leningrad, 1972.
3. O. N. Trubachev, *Indoarica in the Northern Black Sea area*, Moscow, 1999.
4. V. Torop, *Earliest News of Rus*, Moscow, 1997.
5. B. A. Rybakov, *Paganism of Ancient Rus*, Moscow, 1987; *Scythia by Herodotus*, Moscow, 1979.
6. A. A. Terenozhkin, *Cimmerians*, Kyiv, 1976.
7. B. N. Grakov, *Scythians*, Moscow, 1971.
8. R. F. Smirnov, *Sauromatians*, Moscow, 1964.
9. V. F. Gaidukevich, *Bosphorus Empire*, Moscow-Leningrad, 1949.
10. *Archive of the earliest written information on the Slavs*, Compilers L. A. Gindin, S. A. Ivans, Volumes 1-2, Moscow, 1994-1995.

---

[1] In Russian the word 'мире' (mir) means 'world'.

[2] Concordant with *Sakai*. Ancient Greek and Roman scholars believed all Sakai were Scythians, but not all Scythians were *Sakai* (B. N. Mukerjee, Political History of Ancient India, 1996, p 690-91).The Persians called all Scythians by the name *Sakas* (Herodotus Book VII, 64).

[3] The title of 'Tsar' originated as a medieval Bulgarian title, derived from the Latin 'Caesar' to designate the supreme ruler or monarch. It is therefore inaccurate and inappropriate to refer to the Scythian/Skoloty rulers as 'tsars'.

[4] ***Bohatyr*** means 'hero'.

[5] In modern Ukrainian this is 'siayuchiy', meaning 'radiant' in English.

[6] The old-woman Yaga is a fairytale character.

[7] Maiotis in Greek, or Moeotis in Latin.

[8] Transliterated as Helonus (in Ukrainian).

[9] The Slavic word 'Год' (transliterated as 'god') means 'year' in English.

[10] This is the same person that Herodotus called Scythes. According to Herodotus Scythes was the son of Herakles and the serpent-legged goddess, whereas Diodorus wrote that Scyth was the son of Zeus and the serpent-legged goddess.

[11] Jatvingorum, or Jetvorum gens in Lithuanian. (V.Krasnoholovets).

[12] In 673 Esarhaddon slew the Scythian king who was replaced by Bartatua. Bartatua became the Scythian ruler and entered into alliance with the Assyrians, which entailed marrying Esarhaddon's daughter.

[13] Cimmerian Treres - a people repeatedly mentioned by Strabo, generally as a tribe of, or at least. as closely connected with, the Cimmerii, but in a few passages as Thracians. They are not named by Homer or Herodotus. Strabo was evidently undecided whether to regard them as a distinct race, or as identical with the Cimmerii, in whose company they several times made destructive inroads into Asia Minor. "The Cimmerii, whom they name Treres also, or some tribe of them, often overran the southern shores of the Euxine and the adjoining countries, sometimes throwing themselves upon the Paphlagonians, at other times upon the Phrygians, at the time when they say Midas died from drinking bull's blood. And Lygdamis led his army as far as Lydia and Ionia, and took Sardes, but perished in Cilicia. And the Cimmerii and Treres often made such expeditions. But they say that the Treres and Cobus [their leader] were at last driven out [of Asia] by Madys, the king of the Scythians." [1] (*Strab. i. p.61*). "Callisthenes states [p. 2.1226]that Sardes was taken several times; first by the Cimmerians; then by the Treres and Lycians, as Callinus also shows; lastly in the time of Cyrus and Croesus." (Id. xiii. p. 627). "In olden times, it befell the Magnetes [the people of Magnesia on the Maeander] to be utterly destroyed by the Treres, a Cimmerian tribe."

[14] An alliance against Rome in 62-61 BCE of the Greeks, Getae, Bastarnians and Rusy is mentioned below.

[15] This italicised text is a transliteration from the old Rusy text : *бедехшемо кравенце а скуфе антіве русы борусень а суренжецы Тако сме стахом дедь русове.*

[16] Herodotus called them Gelons.

[17] The word "Scythia" may be derived from the word 'Skytaltsia' which in Old Slavonic language meant 'wanderer'. (V. Krasnoholovets).

[18] Svarga means swastika, which is treated as a protective talisman. (V. Krasnoholovets).

[19] The Ruthenians (or Ruthenes) were the ancient Rusy people who migrated to Italy and were known under that name.

[20] A Byzantine historian.

[21] These are called 'Vala' in Ukrainian and Russian.

CHAPTER 12

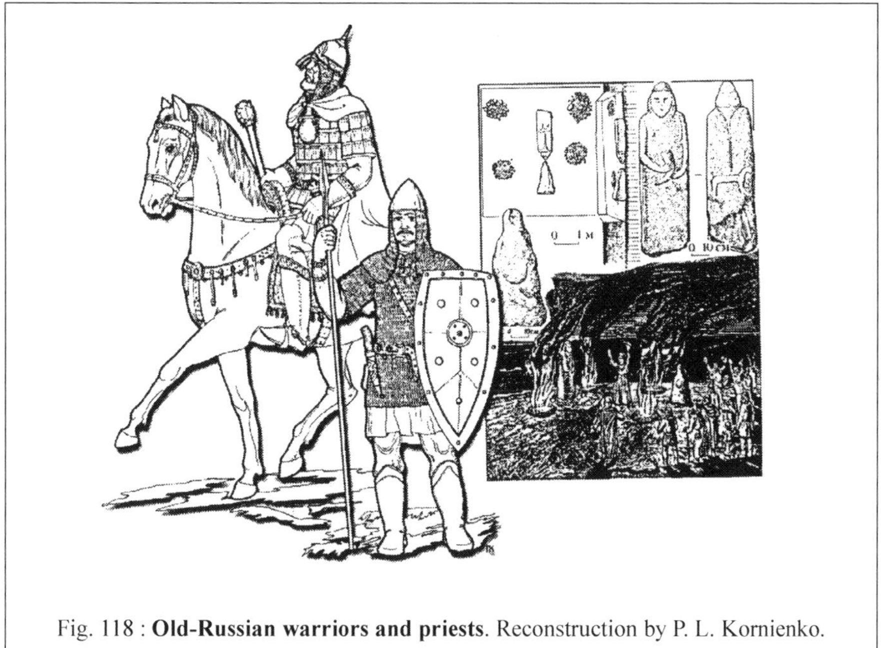

Fig. 118 : **Old-Russian warriors and priests**. Reconstruction by P. L. Kornienko.

THE EMERGENCE OF KYIVAN RUS

We have already examined the earliest, most complex. principal historic periods of the Indo-European world. At its nucleus were the Slavs, the direct descendants of Aratta, confirming the 21,000-year-old heritage of their Proto-Pre-Slavic ethnogenesis as recorded in sources such as *The Veles Book*, the myths of the Kyiv Region, the annals of Stone Grave, in folklore and traditional symbolism. Their evidence pointed to the existence of subsequent links between their ethnogenesis and history ever since the time of the mammoths, proceeding along the time chain to the "Age of Trojans". In order to understand the issue of the formation of Kyivan Rus (in the 9th century) however, we must go back to the (G)Eneti-Veneti-Venedi of the Baltic area, mentioned earlier, who arrived there from Borusia or Oriana through Troad and Etruria. For reasons unknown, some authors considered them to be amongst the earliest Slavs. Why? What was happening at the northern borders of the Slavic world from where, in due course, the Varangians and the family of Ruriks came, and where Kyivan Rus began?

1. The Venedi, Ants and Sklavins.

Fig.119 : Old-Russian symbol of the annual cycle.

The problem of finding a start for the ethnogenesis of the Slavs is probably best summarised by looking at the most recent approaches to it in academic science - such as an article by B. A. Rybakov called *Ancient Slavs and the Ancient World* (Vseslavianskii Sobor, Moscow, 1998), in the booklet by A. N. Lebedev *The Formation of the Slavic World* (Kyiv, 1997) and the monograph of Yu. V. Pavlenko *Pre-Slavs and Aryans* (Kyiv, 2000). The principal disadvantage of their approach has already been presented:

each of them severs the root back to the Trypillian culture (through the Mid-Dnipro archaeological culture) from the Tshinets culture of the 15th – 12th centuries BCE, and also separate this same root (through the Usativ culture of the later Trypillian culture) from its branches which extended into the Pelasgian-Etruscan world. Consequently, this artificially demarcated the Vans of the Northern Black Sea area, Asia Minor's (G)Eneti of Paphlagonia, Troad and the North Adriatic, and the Veneti-Venedi of the Baltic area; only later were these considered to be Slavs. Moreover, the Slavs weren't even considered to have started in the 5th century BCE when they established themselves along with the Pomor archaeological culture but only from the 2nd century BCE, when that culture overgrew into the Pshevorsk culture.

We have referred to the Aryan Brahman Vena as the possible founder of the Veneti and also referred to an unconventionally written monograph by P. V. Tulaev, *Veneti: Ancestors of Slavs* (Moscow, 2000) which acknowledged to a considerable degree, the suggestion of Johann Christoph Jordan (18th century author of *De Originibus Slavicis*) that the Venedi were the ancestors, then contemporaries, of the Ants and Slavs. This assertion is correct about those historic depths where the events of the Trojan War were revealed and where the ethnogenesis of the pre-Venedi Slavs was traced back even further, even though they did not then call themselves Slavs but came to recognise their ethnic singularity, no later than 2300-1700 BCE. At this moment it will be helpful to remember Pilemen who led the (g)Eneti into Paphlagonia to the north of Asia Minor; let us also recollect the migration of the Eneti after the fall of Troy..... In a legend from the *Chronicle of the Great Prince of Lithuania and Zhjamajtija*[1], the Roman Prince Palemon is mentioned, a relative of Caesar Nero who, along with Rus Ulianus and Ro(u)gom Hector, led the search for new lands for their kinsmen. These nomads selected for themselves the lower reaches of the River Neman where they founded cities. We have already noted that improbable similarity between the names Pilemon and Palemon, which at first sight could be explained by the presence of the neighbouring Trojans, Odysseus and Hector. The Romans, who absorbed the culture of the Rusy-Etruscans [i.e. the Ruthenians] knew the Greek hero Odysseus by the alternative name of Ulysses; Nero was a relative of Julius Caesar^, therefore also a descendant of Aeneas who led the partial migration of the Eneti from Asia Minor's Troad to Etruria. At this juncture we won't dwell over-long on the conclusion reached by E. Klassen: "The Trojan Oeneus was not only Slav but also specifically Rus!"; and that from the legendary Palemon could have arisen not only the Lithuanians but also their relatives the Prussians^.

Thus the Balto-Slavic language community, which had allegedly already separated from the Indo-European and divided into two others, could instead have arisen the other way round: i.e. from uniting with the migrant Veneti-Slavs in the local Baltic area. In any case, as has already been pointed out, the authoritative linguist O. N. Trubachev found no grounds for placing some intermediary link between the "Indo-Europeans" and the genesis of Slavs. We have gone even further: we discovered that Slavdom (the direct descendant of the Arattans) actually constitutes the original nucleus of the "Indo-European language".

In the meantime Scandinavian historiography, represented by the Icelandic *Edda* compiled by Snorri Sturluson (1179-1241 CE), recorded sagas describing the migration of Ases and Van tribes during Cimmerian-Scythian times, from their original Northern Black Sea homeland. This occurred, perhaps, after the other legendary events mentioned above. Nevertheless, the Vans-Eneti step forward here as self-sufficient, indigenous masters of their fatherland, rather than as descendants of hypothetical "Balto-Slavs":

A country in Asia east of Tanakvislya [the River Tanais, or Don] *is called the country of the Ases, or home of the Ases, and the capital city of that land was called Asgard. There was a ruler there, who was called Odin, and a large altar was there. According to ancient custom it had twelve supreme priests. They were obliged to create sacrifices and to judge people. They were called Diyas, or rulers... Odin went to war against the Vans, but they were not captured immediately and they defended their country, and victory was first in favour of the Ases and then for the Vans. They devastated the lands of each other and when all this tired them, they called a meeting for reconciliation... They narrated as truth, that when Odin and his Diyas came into the North Lands, they began to teach the local people those arts which the people still possess from that time... He and his priests are called masters of songs because this skill in the North Lands came from them. Odin could do likewise, such that in battle his enemies became blind or deaf and they were filled with horror, and their weapons wounded no more than sticks and his warriors dashed into battle without armour; they fought, as furious mad dogs or wolves, bit shields and were strong, like bears or bulls. They slew men and neither fire nor iron had effect upon them. Such warriors were called Berserks.*

It should be noted that patriarch Odin (probably an ancestor of the Udins, relatives of the Vans), was also called Votan/Wotan or 'Vedun' i.e. a knowledgeable person. He was also called Bor, whilst amongst the Ases we have Khemir. These names are consonant with the Borusians and Cimmerians (Borysthenes, Gamirs and so on). Some researchers consider the Divine Ases to be an offshoot of the Agathyrsi who were related to the Geloni and Scythians. Since the 6th century BCE that offshoot was known as Aorses in the western Pre-Caspian region. Some historians see in them the forerunners of the Roxolani who can often be identified as the Ruskolans of *The Veles Book* where Bohomyr and Kvasura (VB: 22) correspond to Mimir and Kvasir of Snorri's *Edda* who were descendants or heirs of Odin. Since Odin was considered to be the inventor of runic writing but came into northern Europe from the territory of the truly earliest writing, we may assume that Odin and his priests were familiar with the beginning of *The Veles Book*. The upper date for the start of *The Veles Book* does not fall outside the limits of antiquity and the Pshevorsk archaeological culture: according to A. I. Asov there are metal figurines from the Slavic temple of Retra^ pertaining to that time bearing the inscriptions: *holy Kvasura, Bohumir, Siva*. Thus, we have another line of evidence affirming the reliability of this outstanding historical source that is still ignored by official science.

In the migrations described earlier, apart from the Slavic centres that have already been mentioned, two others formed, they were in the Alps and the Mid-Danube area. Despite academic proscription, which considered their formation to have taken place during the Great migration of nations in the 4th – 6th centuries, Slovenian researchers and P. V. Tulaev point out that the foundations of these centres, which existed on the "Amber Way"^ that ran from the Adriatic to the Baltic, were actually formed during ancient Veneti times. A particularly high level of development was reached at Noricum, the first state formation on the territory of modern Slovenia. Its ethno-historical root is traced back into Asia Minor to the time when the Vans-Eneti arrived there from the Azov area. In the Hittite Kingdom at that time a cultic centre called Nerik existed which was connected in some respects with the Pelasgian-Greek God Nereus and the Etruscan Goddess Nortia. The capital of Noricum was named in honour of the goddess, Noreia. Its highest mountain honoured the pagan temple of Trihlav although they also honoured the Mistress of the mountain, its Golden-Horned goat and an old linden-tree [lime] that was the embodiment of the Tree of Life. The Veneti population of Noricum was very advanced in agriculture and husbandry, especially in horse breeding; even in pre-Roman Europe they were the most skilled iron blacksmiths. When Rome annexed Noricum to its empire, it was obliged to recognise a particular "Slavic right", which not only placed the local population on a par with Roman citizens but also had to acknowledge their local customs, nevertheless, this did not save the Romans from an insurrection headed by Odoacer, the chief of the Scirii^. In 476 he not only freed the fatherland but also became emperor of Rome... It is now clear that when Nestor the Chronicler stated that "the Narci are in essence Slovenian", he was not mistaken in recording the ancient times of Slavic history (especially his indication of their origin from Japhet's tribe, hinting at Asia, though not Asia Minor). In *The Tale of Bygone Years,* the chronicler also mentions that "in old times the Slovenians set along the Danube", and he considered this to have been a re-settlement of Slavic tribes from Noricum, rather than a migration of tribes from the Dnipro-Danube interfluve that was the result of all the migrations from the 4th – 6th centuries, mentioned previously.

A combination of the legendary events described above and the transformation of the Pomor culture into the Pshevorsk culture, led to the creation of unions between Slavs (not only of Veneti) with Bastarnians and other local tribes of Celts, Teutons, Balts and Finns. Then an opposite migration of the Veneti and miscellaneous unions of tribes began to the south, "*to our lands, to the old steppes, in order to look at their hearths, as in the days of the exodus from Piatyrichia* (meaning 'five-rivers', i.e. of Punjab) *and Semyrychia* (meaning 'seven-rivers', i.e. the Timava River), *when at the sunrise* [i.e. East] *they moved from us* (i.e. Rusy, descendants of Bohomyr)" (*The Veles Book*, 36a). The name of the wife of ancestor Bohomyr was Slavunia. Perhaps her name was inherited by the prince whose kin "*came to the Ilm River and settled down with the Goths and were there for 1000 years*" (*The Veles Book,* 8) until the first centuries CE. That migration formed two Sverenze[2] (Northern groups) in the Baltics: "*One Venedian, and the second Gothic*" (*The Veles Book,* 8(27)). At the same time there was also movement from the south to the north. In fact a legend is recorded in the *Mazurinsky Chronicle,* describing a campaign of Slaven and Rusy Princes from the Euxine Pontis (Black Sea) to Lake Ilmer, so-named in honour of their sister. The Serbs and Kostoboks from near the River Tanais (the modern River Don), well known to Pliny in the 1st century, turned up in Dacia a hundred years later. It seems the 'passionate' ardor of the Kostoboks finished there; according to *The Veles Book*, they began to die out owing to laziness and were absorbed by the Illyrians until those in turn were absorbed by Slavs.

O. N. Trubachev translates the ethnonym 'Bastarnians' from the Indo-Aryan language as the 'offspring of slaves', which goes along nicely with the mythology mentioned below from *The Veles Book* about Bastarn being a (subordinate) son of Slaven and Skiv(f)a (VB: 17a). Clearly such a name for a "son" had been given to someone by "parents". If those were Scythians, then the name originated from the "old" Indo-Aryans, namely, the Skoloty or Cimmerians. However, in Ukrainian-Slavic the word 'baistriuk' carries the same significance [meaning bastard]. In any case we can see the continuity of the traditions of Pali

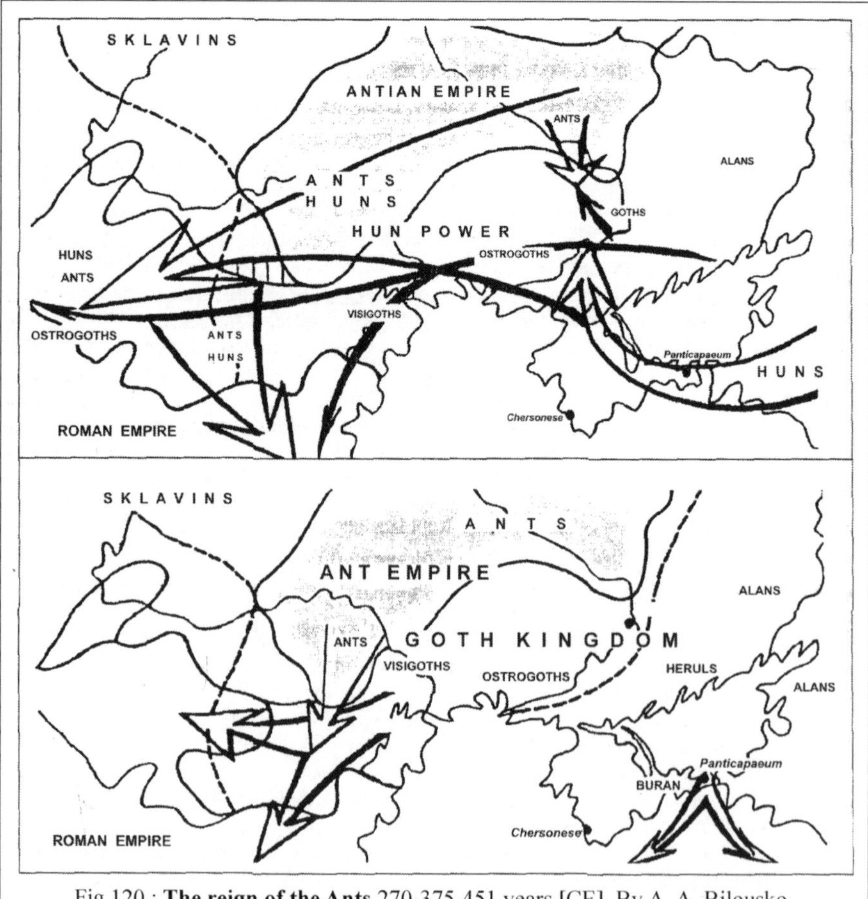

Fig.120 : **The reign of the Ants** 270-375-451 years [CE]. By A. A. Bilousko.

and Napi, which started in the Northern Black Sea area during Cimmerian times. The veneration of this tradition in the Baltic area could have been sponsored by the priests of Retra, the temple city in the lower reaches of the Elbe, perhaps akin to Roden at the mouth of the Ros River in the Dnipro area. Retra's central temple in particular incorporated about a hundred metal figurines inscribed with the runic names of Veles and Perun, as well as names of the pre-ancestors, Bohomyr, Siva and Kvasura, as mentioned already.

The Pshevorsk culture spread from the upper rivers of the Oder and Wisla to the Volyn region and then along the River Pripyat to the Dnipro where it was transformed into the Zarubinets^ culture at the boundary of the 1st millennium. "This is saying that Volyn came first, that beat the enemies, since [Volyn land] is brave. And that Volyn was the first kin, being their (the Ants) beginning" (*The Veles Book,* 24b). The ethnogenesis of Slavs intensified just as it did with the Germanic tribes (Goths and others) both nations flocked into the steppes of the Black Sea area where they must have fraternised and fought amongst themselves, as well as with the local Sarmatians, successors of the Scythians. At that time the ancient hierarchy of the 'senior' Pali and 'junior' Napi was consumed by the idea of slavery. This all happened under the strong pressure of slaveholding Rome with its mighty troops and corresponding ideology.

When the Germanic people are mentioned as going opposite the Baltic Slavs, followed by the Black Sea and Mediterranean Slavs, we should not forget that at that time there was no clear distinction between those ethnic cultures. Even now, it is only maps which separate them and give them distinct borders. For example, the ancient Vandals are considered as tribes of Germans even though in the 11th century, the German Adam^ of Bremen clearly recorded: "Slavia is a very extensive area of Germany populated by Vinules who in the past were called Vandals" (according to the name of the river along which this tribe was living initially). "Vandals and Slavs were the same people" as indicated in the beginning of the 17th century by Mavro Orbin based on the *History of Vandals* by Albert Kranz. The Vandals became famous not only for their campaigns (led by Radegasius and then by Gunderic and Genseric), which ended with the downfall of Carthage (in 447) and of Rome (in 455), or by their capture in the Mediterranean Sea of Sicily, Corsica and Sardinia, but also for their establishment of a state in "African Rome". When this state was annihilated in the 6th century by the Byzantians, the Vandals were converted into Berbers ('barbarians', mixed with the conquerors and local population) who then successfully fought with Spain, Italy and France, thereby maintaining their union with Slavic tribes. Part of those Sakaliba-Berbers remained in Europe, having taken precedence over the Moors of Al-Mansur^. Some aspects of those events were reflected in the *Song of Roland,* mentioned earlier.

Around the 2nd century BCE the 500-year history of Carpathian Ruskolan came to an end. "And then they moved to the sunrise [i.e. east] and came to the Dnipro... and the fathers named it Nepre Prepente [Dnipro Prypiat, i.e. crowded Dnipro]" (VB: 5a); "One part went to the city of Holun and remained there and the other part remained near the city of Kyiv; and the first part is Ruskolan, and the second belongs to [Prince] Kyi, which honours Suren [the south]" (VB: 22). Similarly, archaeologists divide the Zarubinets culture into Volyn and Kyiv groups, and the "Thracian gold state" in the Carpathians was changed first of all by the alien carriers of the Pshevorsk culture (Venedi, as we already know), and then in the 1st century by the Lypytska culture that also embraced Sarmatian and Thracian kin.

In *The Veles Book* the ethnogenesis of Slavs, that is, the Baltic Veneti and north-Carpathian Rusy outlined above, is described as follows (VB: 17a):

And those were Prince Slaven with brother Skiv.
And they led large wars in the east.
And they said: "Let us go to the Ilmer land on the Danube
and look for Bastar, our son
who was left there (by us) *to stay as a guard".*
And Ilmerians went north and there founded the town of Slaven.
And brother Scyth was near the sea and brought his son Bastar.
And after them there was grandson Kisek^ who was the ruler of the south steppe and many [cows, or relatives].
And there was a great war there for the crops along both shores of the Danube to

the Rus mountain and slopes of the Carpathian mountains.
And there they got settled, made a kolo [circle of earth walls] *and were inside the circle...*
and there, the Earth [Trojan wall] *stood five hundreds years.*
Once again strife appeared there among the Rusy and they began to quarrel,
and having altercation and disorder the power was lost.
So enemies came to our fathers in the south,
and the fathers lost the Scyth land on the sea coast and in the steppe,
and they moved on north, and faced the Fretse [Friagi or Thracians]
who gave aid (to our fathers) *to* [their] *enemies.*
And those Scyth-fathers returned and gave battle against the enemy power and crushed it.

The story proceeds to give details of somebody named Kyi (neither the original, nor the chronicler) and of the Dnipro where he founded a city and fought with the tribes of Oszesche and Onezva (*The Veles Book,* 33, et al.); maybe they were a Celtic or German tribe of Esths related to the Ostrogoths who participated in the formation of the previously mentioned Kyivan group of the Zarubinets culture and subsequent Kyivan archaeological culture.

In both the southern steppes and the forest-steppe of the Dnipro area "Kishek was great and wise" (*The Veles Book,* 25). He acted together with Oriy, although (like the Kyi just mentioned) not with the famous ancestor but with the next representative of his dynasty: "now and again he is born among us" (*The Veles Book,* 4d). So, there was a clan of keepers of ancient traditions. "And that Kiska was glorious, and the people of father Oriy were glorious because their glory had grown" (*The Veles Book,* 35a). At first the allies fought successfully with their enemies, but since Kiska (Kishek) did not wish to join them, his "people were killed by the swords of those Yazyches and Yases" (*The Veles Book,* 35b), i.e. later Sarmatian tribes of the 2nd – 4th centuries from the Caucasus foothills.

Since those times, when Tamarkha (Tmutarakan principality, now the modern Taman peninsula) was Aryan (S)Indic and Orianian Cimmeria, there one of the major centres of Rus began to emerge. By the end of the ancient times this centre was replaced by Borusia (Borysthenians) in the lower reaches of the Dnipro. Before Kiska, "seventy of our princes, such as Mezislav, Boruslav, Komonebranych and Horyslav" were there (*The Veles Book,* 25). Perhaps the name 'Kiska-Kishek' (of *The Veles Book*) arises from the name of the Kiseisky mountains which were indicated by the Roman geographer Pliny to be where the modern city of Pyatigorsk is now located. It is quite possible that the Ukry Volhvs (Magus-priests) visited those places, perhaps reviving the authority of primogenitor Oriy when compiling what was to become *The Veles Book*? Possibly they retained the words of dying Kiska for the next generations (VB: 17c):

Where our blood is poured, our land exists...,
Be it, as in the old times of our fathers...
You will be sons of your gods –
and their force will be with you to the end.

According to A. A. Asov, it is possible that the statue of a 4th century warrior from a kurhan above the River Etoko, bearing letters similar to those found in *The Veles Book,* belongs to Kiska rather than to the subsequent Bus Beloyar^ (*The Veles Book,* 8-9). It was moved from Pyatigorsk to Moscow in 1849 where it now resides in a storeroom at the State Historic Museum.

According to the understanding of Tacitus, Jordanes and other Roman-Byzantian historians (who continue to dominate modern understanding), the 'earliest' Slavs of the first half of the 1st millennium BCE were subdivided into three branches: Venedi, Ants and Sklavins. Jordanes considered the first as the earliest, noting in his *Getica*: "Sklavins and Ants alike were previously called the Veneti". Perhaps the author was guided by ancient written sources and data on the Veneti of the Adriatic, Noricum and the Baltics. Jordanes' opinion aligns with the ethnogenesis of the Slavs considered earlier, where the ethnonym

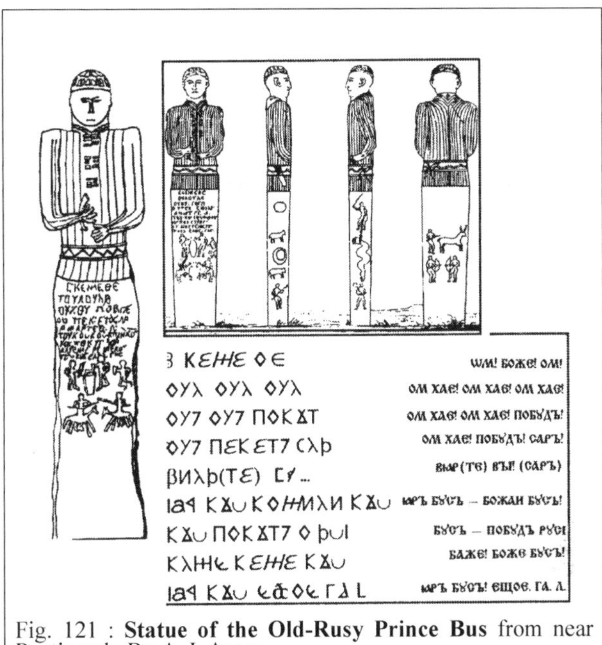

Fig. 121 : **Statue of the Old-Rusy Prince Bus** from near Pyatigorsk. By A. I. Asov.

(G)Eneti-(V)Eneti-Venedi is the most ancient of those known, only competing in this respect with the Orianians, Borusians (Borysthenians), and Skoloty.

The first reference to the Ants in *The Veles Book* (board 4d) is connected with the return of Oriy's people from India. Indeed, the Ants-'krayane' could also have been there (according to O. N. Trubachev). Their manifestation in the Dnipro area may be associated with the Scythian ruler *Arianta*s who ordered a monument to be set up at Exampaios (between the Dnipro and Buh): a huge cauldron was filled with molten bronze arrow-heads which had been brought by all the Scythians, one arrow-head from each Scythian warrior (Herodotus IV: 81). In Julius Caesar's *Memories of the Gallic Wars,* written in mid-1st century BCE, he recalled the Baltic *Ands* together with the Veneti, Ruthenians and Nevri/Neuri (called Neuri by Herodotus?). They possibly had a relationship with the Vandals during their campaign to Gibraltar in the 5th century in the territory of future Spain, since the city of Antiya emerged there and probably, the province of *Anda*lusia too. Roman authors in the first centuries of the new era point to a separate tribe of Ants in the Northern Azov area. Nevertheless the formation of the Ant Union of Eastern-Slavic tribes dates back to times of the Gothic invasion.

The Goths appeared in the lower reaches of Danube at the end of the 2nd century; it is possible those Visigoths were led by Konorih (*The Veles Book,* 27). An invasion was arranged by the Ostrogoths who (according to *Getica* by Jordanes, mid-6th century) invaded the Black Sea steppes through the swamps of "Oium land", a land known to Odin and the people from Ei (the Taman peninsula). The Ostrogoths came to the sea about 230 CE; *The Veles Book* (board 27) names their chieftains to have been Aldoric to whom they gave tribute, Gotoric who was the grandfather of the best known Gothic chief and Hermanaric (Germanarik, Ermanarich, or Iermonreha). In 237 the Goths destroyed the city of Tanais at the mouth of the Don and then captured Scythian Novhorod and other cities of Semihradia in Taurida. The local population intensified. In 262 the Scythian chieftains Respa, Veduk and Tarvar (which seem to be Slavic names, though mis-spelled by Roman authors) led their warriors into Asia Minor. Within a year, a marine detachment of other "Scythians" captured Athens and Corinth, having freed the Roman slaves. In 267 the Roman fleet defeated about 500 "Scythian" ships and in the following year they gathered thousands of ships and landed in Greece with up to 300,000 warriors.

Historical testimonies concerning an invasion of Goths revitalising the local population in the Northern Black Sea area agree quite well with archaeological data. In the 3rd century, the Velbar culture, which spread into the Volyn and Kyiv areas displacing the Kyivan culture of Slavs and their allies, is considered to have been completely Gothic. The mixed Cherniakhov^ archaeological culture formed later; specialists were able to differentiate pure Slavic, Gothic and Thracian settlements, however traces of campaigns, particularly maritime, are very difficult to reveal by archaeological means and methods.

Poorly defined borders, which were even in a state of flux during the times of slaveholding states of Greece, Bosphorus, Rome and Byzantium, were a fact and should be borne in mind. For example, the 4th century Gothic "empire of Hermanaric" was represented by migrants temporarily occupying the lands of local tribes over a series of regions before leaving them as part of the process of Gothic movement. They moved further along the south-eastern coast of the Baltic, then through the Novhorod and Volga area into the Caspian region and from there to the Caucasus and Danube. A second part of the "empire" turned out to be rather more stable, settling for a while along the Northern Black Sea area between the Taman [peninsula] and the Carpathians (B. A. Rybakov, *Paganism in Ancient Rus*, Moscow, 1987).

Around the middle of the 4th century when the ephemeral "empire of Hermanaric" was developed, Rus began to arise not from the Kyiv region (since the capital as such did not yet exist), but from coastal Surozh, the nucleus of the future Tmutarakan principality;

> *So Rus was cut off from the sunset of the sun* [west]
> *and some went to Sur, to midday* [south]
> *and found Surozh-hrad* [Surozh-city] *near the sea that belonged to Greeks.*
> *There Beloyar fortified Surozh.*
> *In that time Kryvoroh was the prince of Rus...*
> *And they, Greeks, were on Holun* [Herodotus' Gelon].
> *Kryvoroh reached an agreement that Rusy would be opened there.*
> *And then Greeks sent warriors in iron to them and killed them...*
> *Ilirmoshche* (Ilmery-Novohorodians or Illyrians, relations of the offspring of Cimmerians) *said that we are foolish, and would come to help us...*(*The Veles Book*, 4c)

In rising up, Rus had first of all to overcome its main infirmity, i.e. internal discord. *The Veles Book* refers to this time and again (VB: 36a):

> *It was foretold since olden times*
> *that we have to create a uniform country in an alliance with others,*
> *we have to revive our Rusken with Holun* [the capital] *and three hundred cities and villages.*

The authors of the sacred book, being concerned about this implementation, had a high expectation of the return of their kinsmen, namely, the Baltic Veneti, to the Northern Black Sea area. By that time the Veneti were certainly strong enough, having two glorious cultic centres, one in the Baltic island of Ruyan (Rugen, [Ruegen is the modern German island]) and the other in the city of Retra in the mouth of the Laby (Elba). In 57 BCE their fleet clashed with the navy of the belligerent Roman commander Julius Caesar who wrote of anticipating the next victory in his notices. However, Gaius Suetonius Tranquillius in his book *The Lives of the Twelve Caesars,* reported instead the loss of the whole Roman fleet, allegedly through a storm. Actually, what is known for certain is that the battering-rams of Roman ships were unable to penetrate the Venedian ships.

From the year 230 onwards, Rus groaned for 120 years under the invasion of Goths and then for 50 years suffered the Greeks of the Bosphorus kingdom and the Romans of the Danube area (*The Veles Book*, 6b, 34):

> *And there we began to battle with the Goths,*
> *and the force of people drove them away...*
> *And we went to Holun and to the Surents-land* [Surozh], *to the sea of Dulebs.*

And on the left there were Goths and right onto the south there were Elans (Hellenes, Greek-Byzantians)...
And we stayed against them, by the front
and committed a great fighting.
And the Greek state asked about a peace;
and we ended our war.

Having reached peace with the Greeks, Surozhian Rus began a campaign against the "empire of Hermanaric": "There was a great battle, the Goths were marginalised and pushed back as far as the Donets and Don. And Hermanaric drank wine (in oath) that he would be a brother (and) our outside governor". But when a new enemy then came from behind the River Ray (the Volga) in 375, then :

Hermanaric agreed to a union with the Huni tribes and supported them.
That is why we have two enemies at the two ends of our land.
But that Bolorev... defeated the Huns^ and then turned onto the Goths.
Over there he defeated the son of Hermanaric and killed him. (VB: 9b, 8)

This particular feat was elsewhere ascribed to boyar Segen (*The Veles Book,* 6e). Maybe he himself fatally wounded Hermanaric also, although that act was ascribed to Rosomon (i.e. to Rusy people in general) in Jordanes *Getica*. There are other minor discrepancies between these books.

According to Jordanes, Vinitar was the successor of Hermanaric and he revenged the Ants, having captured and crucified their leaders: Bozh^ and 70 elders. According to *The Veles Book* (board 32), those were Ruskolans:

and Hermanaric defeated them,
and killed the Rusy Bozh-Bus and crucified another seventy.
And at that time a great unrest was among the Rusy.
And there arose young Vendeslav and he gathered all the Rusy, and led them (onto the executioners of Bozh).
And completely defeated the Goths...
As also the Gothic land became Rusy and (this) *will be forever.*

A monument to Bozh and his elders was recently established near the foot of the Bozh Mountain on the River Ros at the village of Syniava in the Kyiv region. Its inscription states: "To the people of the Ants – primogenitors of Ukrainians. From the inhabitants of the

Fig. 122 : Modern **memorial to Bozh, the chieftain of the Ants,** and his elders **at the foot of God's Mountain** (at the village of Syniava in the Kyiv region) in the surroundings of Slavic neopaganism "Triitsi" of E. I. Dobzhansky (seated third on the right).

Rokytnte area. 1993". Somebody has hacked at the figure of Bozh with a chisel. It is unlikely to have been someone German... so alas, the struggle continues.

During the punishment over Bozh-Bus the Ants were located somewhere in the lower reaches of the Dnipro – where the Baltic Veneti continued to move between the interfluve of the Vistula and Oder. The Penkov archaeological culture, which some researchers consider to have been the earliest Ant culture, came from south of the River Ros; "For behold, we Ants were Ruskolan, but previously we were Rusy and left them" (*The Veles Book,* 24b). The victory over the Goths can be traced back to the creation of the union of Antian tribes by the Veneti (by Segen and Vendeslav); following that, from the end of the 4th century to the beginning of the 7th century, this union played a significant role in the formation of Kyivan Rus.

After the victories over the Goths and Huns by the Union (the Prague archaeological culture was a synthesis of the Penkov culture and some of the later groups of Pshevorska, Lypytska and Cherniakhov cultures), "Kyiska Rus was created. And since then the Goths were afraid and went away to Sverenze" – i,e, to the north, to the Baltic area (*The Veles Book,* 8(27)). Nevertheless, the Ants did not found Kyivan Rus, they supported Surozhian Rus (*The Veles Book,* 7c). The tradition of Surozhian Rus was preserved for a long time in Kerch-Taman (i.e. the Tmutarakan principality), right up to the end of Kyivan Rus.

2. The establishment of Kyiv, capital of Rus.

Fig.123 : Old-Rusy idol.

There are many places in Europe which bear the name 'Kyiv' and its variants, O. N. Trubachev counted more than 60, this is attributable to many towns being walled with 'kyis' (staves made from trees), or having rulers who carried the *kyi*-staff (from which ancestral Kyi of *The Veles Book* also took his homonym perhaps,: *The Veles Book,* 22, et al.), or they had carriers called 'kitovans' (still called by this name in remote Ukrainian villages). Similarly, as we have learned, there was not just one Rus in existence in the Slavic world; not just the Rus allegedly founded by Kyi, later headed by the Rurik family...We will now consider the origins of that particular Rus, as well as its capital. *The Veles Book* records the life of a later prince Kyi (i.e. one subsequent to the primogenitor) who lived sometime during 2nd century BCE, a period which also coincides with the time when the unified centre of Rus was transferred from the Carpathians to the Dnipro (*The Veles Book,* 17a-18a). However, the most recent of those princes named Kyi mentioned by Nestor and other chronicler,s is said to have ruled in the 5th century :

After the Gothic war and all was destroyed, [we] *left Ruskolan,*
we moved to Kyi and settled down on that land...
And this was in a thousand and three hundred years after father Kyi,
three hundred years after residing in the Carpathians. (*The Veles Book,* 22)

The history of the city, let alone its history as the capital, must have begun with some urban settlements (since there was already evidence for settlements standing on the territory of Kyiv at the time of the mammoths!), as would be expected for any location suitable for habitation. *The Veles Book* hints at the establishment of Kyiv in the Dnipro area by the son of primogenitor Oriy (*The Veles Book,* 7i); this hint is traced in the final compilation (about 879 CE) of this book (*The Veles Book,* 15).

The origin of the city began during the times of Aratta from the seven settlements located at the place which would become the future Kyiv. In ancient times, fourteen local Slavic hamlets (of the Zarubinets archaeological culture) could have combined to become a city or could at least have had a trade centre or market in common; there is evidence for this in one of the most massive coin hordes found in the north, consisting of Roman coins dating between 2nd century BCE to the 4th century CE. It may be conjectured that the foundation of

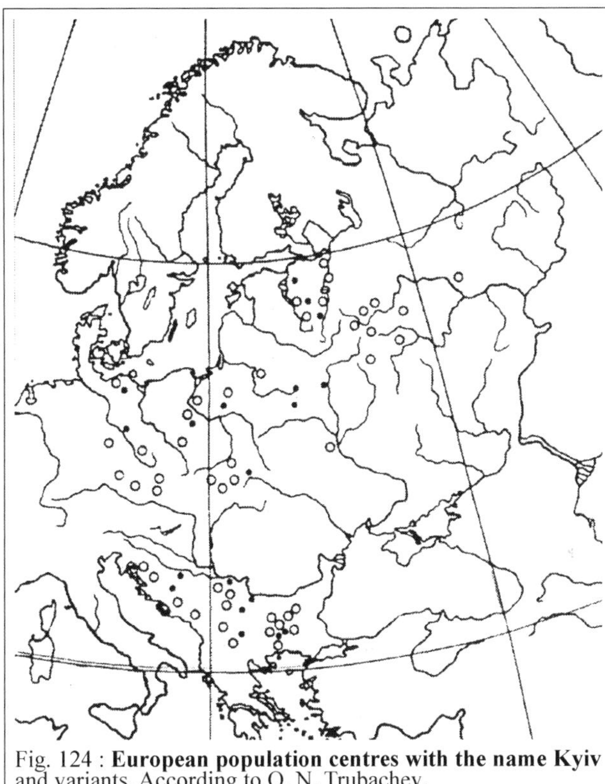

Fig. 124 : **European population centres with the name Kyiv** and variants. According to O. N. Trubachev.

the monetary system of Kyivan Rus was laid just here (along the Roman rather than Byzantine model). Initially the city may have been called Amadoka, probably owing to this name being associated with the location ever since the times of Aratta ('amadoka' in Greek can be understood as a *log deck or passage*). The ancient geographer Ptolemy placed the city of Amadoka in the area of future Kyiv, in proximity with the cities of Sar, Azagari and Serim. In about 370 CE a tragedy was played out in these locations; its participants were the Gothic chief Hermanaric, the local princess Lebed (Sunilda, or Svanhild, i.e. 'the swan maiden' of Germano-Scandinavian legends) and her brothers known in Slavic tradition as Kyi, Shchek and Khoryv.

The Kyiv Chronicle [Rusian Primary Chronicle^] was established in 430 according to the testimonies of annals no longer extant but from which excerpts were published in the 18th – 19th centuries. The birth of Kyivan Rus should begin from this date. It seems that even then it spread its ownership over two banks of the River Ray, i.e. the Volga (*The Veles Book,* 6b, 34), maintaining the tradition established in the time of father-Oriy, when he returned from India (*The Veles Book,* 10).

The impetus for the appearance of Kyivan Rus, which started in Carpathian Ruskolan, did not come directly from the shores of the Baltic Sea but from the Black Sea, following the Rusy victory over the Greeks, Romans, Goths and Huns (*The Veles Book,* 33):

And this is our funeral for Seden, our father
who was on the Pont shore in Rosia-city.
And, indeed, Rusy went from Bila Vezha and Rosia to the Dnipro land.
And over there Kyi founded the city of Kyiv.
And the tribes of Polian, Derevlian, Kryvychi, Liakhov [settled down] *on the bush of Rus.* [See Fig. 128]
And everybody became Rusychi.

At the same time as Kyi founded Kyiv in 430, someone called Maukhu, living in the Black Sea area of Rus, "gathered Slavs to one bush and he brought all the lands into unity" (*The Veles Book*, fragments). It seems that there were two centres in existence in the 5th century, when "Rus gathered its forces and defeated the Huns, having created the Land of the Ants and the Kyivan Skuf [Scyths]" (*The Veles Book*, 7c). Thus Kyiv was initially subject to the residue of the longstanding Scythian state and its old-order, whose founder Skuf [Scyth] was a sworn brother of Slaven (*The Veles Book*, 17a). It is possible that the latter was the son or successor of founder-Kyi and either went by the name Lebeden (*The Veles Book*, 36b) or else he was a brother of the latter. Prince Kyi drove the Bulgarians to the north and "up to Voronents (for which the Rusy had previously fought with the Goths, then later, with the Varangians). There he united with the Polians^ and took back the Rusy city of Holun. Lebeden, though seated in the city of Kyiv, could not rule for he was struck by mental illness and impoverished. Owing to his rank, he still managed the Greek and Arab markets (*The Veles Book*, 34). It is likely that before his illness (possibly from a battle wound?) Lebeden founded the land of Lebedia, which Constantine Porphyrogennetos, in his essay, placed near Khazaria which was populated by Turks. However, O. N. Trubachev noted that those were the Tourtsy, or Turovtsy, founders of the city of Turov.

In 451 - 452 Attila, leader of the Huns, successfully acted against the Franks and Romans; it seems that Kyi was his ally for aiding the Slavs and this is noted in *The Veles Book*: "And in this moment Attila supported us and we conquered our enemies". If the testimony describing Kyi's victory over the Goths from Taurida is true (the ten-year war is mentioned on wooden plaque 37a) and the temporary extending of his possessions "beyond the Volga and to Surents land, to the sea of Duleb", then this evidence can be compared with that recorded in *Getica* by Jordanes with regard to the breakdown of the Hun empire after the death of its founder in 453. After that, Jordanes makes no mention of the Black Sea Ostrogoths. If Kyiv, the "Rusy mother of cities", was indeed founded by Kyi, who ruled for 30 years (*The Veles Book*, 36b) in the area of the much more ancient Holun (which is now the village of Belsk in the Poltava region) in 430, then the year 453 can be considered as the date for the appearance of Kyivan Rus (which actually never had this name; this epithet was created by modern historians). Its border even spread, temporarily, behind Moravia since the Czechs began to migrate there and from that place Prince Veren was invited to rule in Kyiv - and all of this was considered to constitute a unified Rus.

However, the later dates are more probable because of the tradition of Oriana-Orissa-Borusia which, in the lower reaches of Dnipro and the adjacent Black Sea area, had remained unchanged since at least 2300 BCE and furthermore had not been extinguished. The above-mentioned cities of Bila Vezha and Rosia were probably located in the places of the former Greek colonies of Tyra (the modern city of Bilhorod-Dniestrovsk) and Panticapaeum (Kerch). One of these two cities was the capital of the Land of Ants, a tribe which retained very old traditions. According to O. N. Trubachev (*Indoarica in Northern Black Sea Area*, Moscow, 1999) 'anta' means 'land', but only in the Aryan language; perhaps the local *Dand*arians, 'Mace-bearing Aryans' (according to S. I. Nalyvayko), were semantically related to the above mentioned Kyivs, Kyis, Pali and Polians...

Irano-Arabic travellers of the 9th – 11th centuries witnessed the conservation of the tripartite division of Rus (Ruskolan-Borusia, in agreement with the first codifications of *The Veles Book*); they wrote that Rus was composed of Kuyaba, Slavia and Arsania with the capital Arta. Contrary to the credible treatment of these areas as the Kyiv region, Chernihiv region and Cherkasy region, some commentators (V. Torop, *Earliest News About Rus*, Moscow, 1997) insist on the Caucasus foothills, placing Arta-Arsania in the lower reaches of the Kuban – in Tmutarakan. It is possible that these names, as an imitation of the territorial division of Rus, came from the Dnipro area according to an ancient tradition which we have considered in connection with Dandaria and Sindica. Whatever the case, Arta-Arsania was the successor of Aratta, whose centre was located in the modern Cherkasy region... The fact is that the class society of Kyivan Rus could not have begun from the establishment of its future capital [Kyiv]; it first of all had to have overcome the multi-millennial tradition of the other pre-class type of statehood. The same problem that had faced former Cimmeria and Scythia couldn't be resolved, however, Kyivan Rus did resolve it.

By means of a gradual saturation with the traditions of class statehood, Rus managed to overcome the traditions of the former communal statehood of Aratta-Oriana-Arsania. This did not come entirely from its inner structure but rather leaked from the dying slaveholding states (of Sumer, Babylon, Assyria, Persia, Greece, Bosphorus and Rome) and from feudal Byzantium arising from them.

At the end of the 5th century the Goths tried to return from the Baltic to the Black Sea area where their small principality remained in the mountains of Taurida. However after a ten-year war they were finally expelled from Rus if not by Kyi, then by the Ants led by Mezenmyr (*The Veles Book*, 24b).When the Goths went to the north, where they disappeared, they were led by Deteric (known as Theodoric^) (*The Veles Book*, 8). In a short time he went against the Romans and during negotiations in 492 he slew their emperor Odoacer, already familiar to us (mentioned as leader of the Rusy on the tombstone of St. Maxim who was slain in 477). It is possible that Odoacer was a secret protégé of the Ukrs-Volhvs (Magus-priests) who took vengeance for his death upon the leader of the Goths (*The Veles Book*, 28):

And we went on the Romans and struggled there with legions,
and were taking big tribute from them.
And we invaded their land.
And, indeed, Deterik was killed by Ukrs.
And, indeed, those Goths were nasty to gods and the latter weeded them out.

Another similar protégé of the Volhvs (Magus-priests) could have been Khalabuti (*The Veles Book*, 33 fragments); Procopius of Caesarea called him Khilbudi, Prince of the Ants. He allegedly served the Byzantine empire in 533-546, unsuccessfully defending it against Slavs at the Danube border; traces of Khilbudi's detachment were lost in Constantinople. It is notable that linguist-Indianologist S. I. Nalyvayko sees the Persian version of Khilbudi's name - 'Leader of the tribe'- as reminiscent of the ruler Kolaksai of the Paralat-Skoloty. A connection between Khilbudi and the chronicler Kyi, a view defended by B. A. Rybakov, is too doubtful as by that time Kyi had been long dead.

At the beginning of the 6th century the Byzantine historian Procopius of Caesarea wrote that the provinces bordering the empire were annually filled with Huns, Sklavins and Ants; during every invasion more than 200,000 people of the empire perished or became prisoners. Emperor Justinian believed the Ants also belonged to the empire and entrusted them to protect the borders (though not without paying a bountiful payment and cherishing a secret intention of splitting them from the Sklavins). The Ants regularly gained a salary, namely tribute, but they did not serve diligently. In the middle of 6th century the Slavs

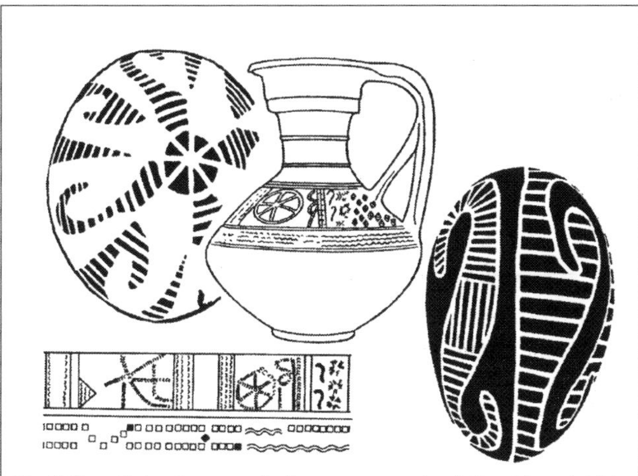

Fig.125 : **Calendar symbols** on a vessel of the Cherniakhiv archaeological culture of the 3rd – 5th centuries and decorating modern Ukrainian hand-painted eggs.

successfully negotiated amongst themselves and fought against Byzantium, sometimes approaching its capital on the shore of Thracian Bosphorus, Asia Minor.

On the other side, the Byzantians incited the Goths of Taurida and Tamarkha in their rear, at the same time turning them towards adopting Christianity. It is from there that Christianity moved to Rus in 547 from the episcopal department that had been approved by Justinian for the Goths (the Bosphorus bishopric had existed since the 4th century). God's word was maintained by fire and sword, as it had been already when used by the same emperor in 550 against tribes in the Caucasus foothills who were disturbed by forcible Christianisation (and where Prince Kisko had acted previously and perished). From that time, acting in revenge, the tribes of that region began to raid the Byzantine provinces situated behind the Danube, each time passing through the land of Rus. The Avars, referred to as 'the terrible Obry' in Rusy chronicles and *The Veles Book*, stretching beyond the Volga, also started to follow those tribes. In this way the migration to the Balkans began, which is known as a part of 'the great migration of nations'. In *The Veles Book,* (board 32) the beginning of that migration is described as follows:

After the Huns found themselves in great trouble, the Obry came to us,
Like the sand of the sea.
And they took in captivity the entire (coastal) *Rus and left it for the Obry.*
Though we fought, but there was no order among the Rusy.

History records that in 560 the Ant's Prince Mezenmyr tried to reach an agreement with the Obry (Avars), but they "went to the prince and killed him. And behold the Blue Sea moved away from Rus" (*The Veles Book,* 24a,b). Only Tamarkha (later the Tmutarakan principality) remained with Surozhian Rus to the end of the 12th century. It should be said that after the final breakdown of the Ants union of tribes between the 6th – 7th centuries some remnants of the Slavs of the Black Sea area were able to found the Duleb union, but it crumpled after 670, when Khazaria gained in strength.

I. Nalyvayko detected the very earliest testimonies for the Dulebs in the *Mahabharata* and *Iliad* (namely, the Vidarbha kingdom and the tribe of Dolopians on the island of Skyros). They travelled northwards from the sea into the forests and from that time they were called the Drevlians (from 'derevo', which means tree). It may be that their ancestors "had originally turned to Borus" (*The Veles Book,* 7g), and that Kyiv had unified with Ruskolan and become related to the Polians. – but hostility was inflamed between the Polians and the Drevlians which ended in tragedy during the time of the reign of Ihor and Olga. The root of this antagonism could have been even deeper if the ethnonym of the 'Dulebs' had arisen from the Indo-Aryan *dulospor* – 'children of slaves' (according to Trubachev), namely the descendants of the Napi who were obliged to obey the Pali-(Polian)-princes of Kyiv.

3. "Great land of ours..."

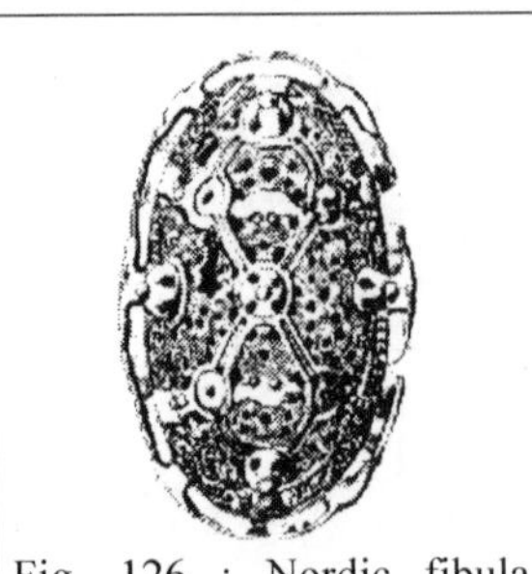
Fig. 126 : Nordic fibula from Shestovytsi's kurhans of the Kyiv Region.

Somewhere toward the end of the 7th century following the division of Slavs into new tribes – Drevlians, Krivichi, Polians, Siverians etc. – the next codification of *The Veles Book* commenced. Beginning with references to Bohomyr and Slavunia (and their daughters Dreva, Skreva and Poleva, and their sons Sieva and Rus), it was edited by the Volhvs (Magi) in a form consistent with the prevalent Kyivan Rus in the Slavic world. This codification is especially notable for its inversion of the titles of tribes: Polians, Krivichi and Drevlians (*The Veles Book,* 33) with respect to the names of the three daughters (VB: 9a, see above) and also in ascribing heroic deeds to the founder of Kyiv from the former Rus and those which he could have carried out in the 5th century (*The Veles Book,* 34).

At the end of the 6th century Rus not only separated the Obry (Avars) from the coastal steppe but also the Bulgarians and Khazars who passed after them from the Volga to the Danube. The Khazars defeated the Duleb union (*The Veles Book,* 3b) and in 670 pursued Asparuh^ – the last Bulgarian khan of the Volga region who then founded the Danubian Bulgaria that included (as the major part) seven Slavic tribes.

Regarding the Rusy (*The Veles Book,* 4b), from the time of the Trojan War somewhere in the 13th century BCE, they :

came under partition during the second millennium, and remained all alone,
and began to work for others in captivity...
– for Khazars, when those appeared with the kagan [chief]...
And he was our friend and initially (his Khazars) *were merchants in Rus.*
At first they were equivocal, but later became angry
and began to oppress the Rusy.

What took place half a millennia ago in the relationships between Slavs and the Greek-colonists is worth repeating again: the Slavs, adhering to the age-old traditions of social order, fell into difficulties when faced with the treachery of their foreign guests who already espoused the laws of the next, slaveholding formation. In such cases the victories achieved by the Slavs were not only due to the concentration of their own forces but also to learning at least some features of their adversaries. The poison of class statehood came to take superiority over Aratta's heritage… The situation just described corresponds to that in the second half of the 8th century when the Khazarian chief Bulan^ (Sabriel in Hebraic) laid the foundation of a Jewish state which included those expelled from Persia in 529 for insurrection against the government. Since that time they had lived in the Caucasus near Derbent^, gradually laying their hands on the rulers of neighbouring Khazaria and hence, capturing control over this important area of trade and migration routes. Whatever the basis of Judaism, by that time the Jews were much more successful than the Rusy in mastering the specifics of slavery and for the first time in several centuries they were openly able to realise their secret art [slaveholding] worldwide. On the one hand, Khazaria, and on the other hand, Rus (no longer community based but not yet class based either), became test areas for the implementation of the 'secret art'.

The indigenous people of Khazaria belonged to the later Sarmatians and other Aryan tribes. The state initially rose with great difficulties after the rule of the Turkish Khaganate and the following Bulgarian domination. Gradually, Khazaria became the Khaganate itself and repelled attacks by Byzantium, and halted an invasion of Arabs, who had crossed the Caucasus in 737, before they reached the 'Slavic river' (the Don). When forming their own statehood, the Khazar Khagan (leader) and his court had a choice of religions at hand; in that situation the most financially favourable for them, because it was thickly mired in money from usury, mercantile trade and related connections, was Judaism.

In agreement with *The Veles Book* (board 4a), in 787-788, after the Rus had been oppressed by the enslavement policy of Judaic Khazaria, assistance came from Ironts-Ossetians^, distant relatives of the Khazars who still maintained communal traditions:

And boyar Skoten was here in the steppes,
who did not surrender to the Khozars.
Being an Ironets himself, he asked help from Iron,
and they sent cavalry
and the Khozars were driven off.
Other boyars remained under the Khozars,
who reached the city of Kyiv and settled there.
Those Rusy who did not want to be under the Khozars,
went to Skoten; Rusy camped there near (his army),

And some people became Cossacks on the steppes, the same as free Khazars independent of the Khagan-Jew.

This became one of the notable milestones in the formation of Cossacks at the southern boundaries of Rus, which remained in the legends of the future Zaporozhian

Cossacks. An interesting detail from the episode described above is that Skoten, who belonged to the other ethnic group, served Rus and achieved a high rank during his service. (His name 'Skoten' is the reinterpreted translation of 'Skuf'<'Scyth', which had been obsolete until that time). We can see that Khazaria was not the only state absorbing strangers who were needed for building the state – there was a natural formation process underway of people from tribes and nationalities from which real nations emerged, – nevertheless, the choices of Rus were for the time being fundamentally different.

At the same time that Rus first clashed with Khazaria, there was an attack from the remaining Goths which was stopped by the Ironts and Rusy led by Skotich and Sviatoyar (*The Veles Book,* 4b). They were the Goths of Taurida, who since 815 had been under the principality of Byzantium. The Rusy prayed for help to "our Dazhboh and Perun-zlatousa" [Perun with a golden moustache] whom father Oriy had borrowed from the Persian pantheon (which featured Perun, a relative of the Indian Varuna – Vparuni of *The Veles Book,* 31, 20 fragments).

Over time the "Khozars took people to work for them and created the great evil [of slavery] for children and wives" (*The Veles Book,* 4a), and then in the early 9th century the "Varangians came and took the land away from the Khozars for their own hands" (*The Veles Book,* 2a). The Khazar khagan of that time appealed to Skoten for help, but Skoten replied "Help yourselves", refusing to defend the city of Voronzhents against the Varangians (*The Veles Book,* 4c).

The invasion of Varangians preceded the migration of the descendants of the Veneti and others Slavs from the banks of the River Laba in 800-809. Perhaps they were called up by Kyiv's prince Boreven (Bravelen; Bravlin, according to *The Life of Stephen Surozhsky*) who had previously united the cities of Rus and defeated the Elans (Byzantians and descendants of Greek colonists) on the coast (*The Veles Book,* 28, 18b). It should be emphasised (according to O. N. Trubachev) that the compilation of the *Life of Stephen Surozhsky,* used a legend which testified to "a great Rusy army of Novhorod" (whilst in another list: "warriors *from* Rusy Novhorod"), which perhaps implies, the former Scythian 'Naples'... In the time of Bravlin, they probably wished to return to Khorsun and Amastrida (*The Veles Book,* 8(3)), a port city near Constantinople, which at the beginning of 840s was twice attacked by Rusy from the sea. These campaigns were inspired by the example of Foma Slavianin. Having led a corps of the Imperial army (basically formed of Slavs), Foma in 820 raised an insurrection in the capital of Byzantium under the slogan: "Those who do not work – so shall they not eat!"... As we have seen, the Slavs not only absorbed the influences of class statehood but also infused them with their original communal statehood of the Arattan type. Despite being untimely and contrary to the general course of history at that time, such attempts, nevertheless, built bridges from the pre-class past to a classless future of human civilisation.

The intended return of Rus to the coast was terminated by the intervention of the Varangians. They appeared under the previously mentioned boyar Skoten, paving the way 'from Varangians to Greeks' and he helped the Greeks not only to become firmly established again on the northern shores of the Black and Azov Seas but also for Diros of Elan to become the prince in Kyiv; he was later slain by one of three Askolds who were Varangian (*The Veles Book,* 18b, 29).

The Varangians were not really an ethnic group but rather naval warriors (maritime and riverine), who accompanied the merchant caravans (*The Veles Book,* 29):

> *And this Askold is an armed Varangian, in order to guard Elan merchants,*
> *who went along the river Dnipro...*
> *And those Varangians brought sacrifices,*
> *and* (they) *are not ours, but not strangers to the princes, as they do not* [have] *princes at all,*
> *but are simple warriors who seized power by force.*

An important testimony in *The Veles Book* states: "The Varangians went to Kyiv with merchants and killed the Khazars" (*The Veles Book,* 4b). Thus, Kyiv was a commercial city, at the crossroads of 'the route from the Varangians to the Greeks' which is why it attracted merchants and warriors of diverse ethnicity who fought for their positions in this important centre. Those foundations had been laid in Aratto-Aryan times, since the times of enigmatic Sambatos on the borders of Kyiv, mentioned by Constantine Porphyrogenitus and then known as Subotka [a settlement], which arose from the Sanskrit name su-nam – meaning 'good way'. Since the superior local population had remained Slavic since the time when the city was founded, that name could have been left there by local attendants of the maidans (sanctuary-observatories), one of which was excavated near the village of Kozarovichi by the archaeologist V. A. Kruts.

Armed squads were hired by merchants or communities for protection against incursions, on land and water, and similar armed detachments often of differing ethnicity were composed of mercenary warriors whose actions (crime and expulsion, etc.) disturbed community relationships; such people were without either 'kin or tribe'. In the south of the Baltics the predominant detachments were Veneti-Slavic, while in the north they were Scandinavian-German, together with Celts, Balts and others. The armed detachments of the south and north, which were principally marine, were called Varangians and Vikings respectively. The first of them appeared earlier according to Julius Caesar, (in the mid-1st century BCE): "the tribe of Veneti has the most influence along the whole maritime coast, since the Veneti has the greatest number of ships in which they go to Britain, and they also exceed the other Gauls in their knowledge and experience of maritime affairs. They made all the tributaries floating in this sea." Amongst the Veneti, the best sailors were the Varias (Variny, Vahry). The Danish/German author Helmond, in his 12th century *Chronicle of the Slavs*, put the Veneti "ahead of all Slavic nations" and he called their lands "the marine area of Slavs". The Varangian name probably originated from those 'Varias', their ethnonym retaining memories of the Aryans. On the other hand, in the north of Rus the word 'variazhyt' meant 'to travel along the sea, to navigate'.

An account of the Vikings and Varangians is well illustrated in the testimony of *The Tale of Bygone Years*: "and they went across the sea to the Varangians, to Rus. And the name of those Varangians was Rus. Others [of the Vikings-'Variags'] have the name Svei [Swedes]; others are Urmany, Angliane, and others are Goths". Caring for booty and income

Fig. 127 : **Images and swords of Norse and Rusy.**

above all else, (i.e. caring about the traditions of their community), the Varangians were able to locate and defend their gains. Thus, in 839 the embassy at the court of the Byzantine emperor, Theophilos, consisted principally of Swedes (who therefore supported the Vikings), but they introduced themselves as belonging to Rus headed by the khagan. We can see here an arbitrary mixture of three ethnic cultures with an emphasis not so much on the native but on what was deemed prestigious at that time. A well-known narrative involving the Slovenes of Ladoga and Novhorod calling upon Rurik, the Rusy Varangian, in 862-864 to rule in their lands, was intended to protect them from other, less ethnically indigenous groups, which a few years earlier had imposed an excessive tribute on the Slovenes. Rurik and his two brothers may have originated from Raroh, the capital of coastal Pomerania. When in 867-870 this "relative let himself go", Novhorod's people drove him away. However, Rurik was not accepted [as a prince] by Kyiv's townsfolk (*The Veles Book,* 14) and later, when he came to his senses he ruled in Novhorod for five more years, until his death in 879.

As we can see, the Varangians were Slavs, and not Normans (Scandinavians and Germans). ***The root of the tragedy of Rus' association with the Variagian reign was not ethnic but social: having replacing the power of the priests*** (the Volhvs, Ukrs, Rahmans and so on). ***The time of the power of warriors had come*** (Rusy, Rarohes, Varangians and others). ***The traditional communal statehood of Aratta-Arsania*** (i.e. social, hierarchical, "primitive communism") ***became changed to the class statehood of Rus*** (feudal, with elements of slaveholding)**.** ***The catalyst for this transformation came from the caste of warriors*** (Rajania^–Rusy), ***and the decisive factor was the Varangian-Rus of the 9th century***.

When the citizens of Kyiv "drove Rurik away from our land, and sent him back whence he came" (*The Veles Book,* 14), he was not alone but accompanied by Askold, the third (representative of the kin?). This one was far luckier and far more treacherous than his partner: "He did not hesitate to rob the merchants who trusted him" (*The Veles Book,* 8(27)).

At first, Askold did not stay in Kyiv but sailed to Constantinople where it seems he was baptised by Patriarch Photios. The latter entrusted him with the task concerning the mission of Cyril and Methodius (from the end of 860), and he sent him to the Slavs and Khazars to draw them into Christianity. The prince of Kyiv was Borevlan, great-grandson of the above mentioned Boreven (*The Veles Book,* 18b). He also began to call for a campaign against the Byzantians. However, it seems Askold then returned and "Askold by force smashed our prince and pounded him" (*The Veles Book,* 6f). That violence occurred in 862 according to testimonies from *The Tale of Bygone Years*. Settling down in Kyiv, Askold tolerated the Byzantine emissary Diros, giving him shelter. This patronage was probably payment from the usurper-'prince' for his own baptism, which he had accepted when maintaining support for the side of Byzantium.

Two years later Byzantium occupied Bulgaria and, taking advantage of a drought and famine (saying those misfortunes were sent down on the people by biblical God for Bulgarian paganism), baptised the Bulgarian people. At that time Surozh land was also taken from Rus and baptised. Then in *The District Message* for 866 Patriarch Photios boasted that he had baptised not only Bulgarians, but "also the nation that often is mentioned and glorified by many others, that excels all other nations by its bloodiness, I speak about the Rusy... Now they have changed their wicked pagan superstition to the clean and pure Christian faith"... Well, not so much by choice it would seem: Byzantium acted in Surozh land just as it had in Bulgaria, spreading the pure message with the aid of soldiers, sermons, hunger and promises. So, the faith implanted by Byzantium was not so pure but in fact rather bloodthirsty. The misanthropy and chauvinism of the clergymen, who were later canonised as attendants of biblical God, is entirely evident…{Although centuries have passed, in this same luscious, Northern Black Sea area, the ethnic descendants of the creators of biblical God still use just the same methods – soldiers, sermons, famine and promises – to introduce a "clear and chaste" doctrine offering a "bright future for all humanity", bloodthirstily eradicating in this case both pagan and Christian "profane prejudices". {Against Judaism there will be no persecution. O sacrificial, infinitely good Rus!.. did you ever abandon Aratta's traditions or will you recover yourself and revive the traditions for the benefit of all mankind? Recover, mother! Retain the spirit of Brahmanic Aratta, become stronger by living the precepts of its Bharata. Do not allow any suicidal "end of the world" or sizzling "bright future" schemes which would accord with Jewish scenarios, for they have already brought a manner of stasis to civilisation on Earth}.

But to pick up again... Having now become securely entrenched by the aid of Christian Byzantium, Askold killed its emissary, the Elanian Diros, who had become unnecessary to him, superfluous to his requirements. Then, in 882 Askold was killed by Oleh^, the successor of Novhorod's Rurik... So, Rus "for the first time gained statehood" and "entered the bosom of civilised European nations". On that stood the ideologies of the church, state (tsarist, communist-commissars, democratic) and the forthcoming world government. {Recover, mother!..}

The Veles Book ascribed the formation of Kyivan Rus to the 850s because its authors (up until 879 when the book ended) knew of the last dates and events mentioned above. However, a specific record that can be ascribed to 864-866 in *The District Message* of Patriarch Photios (VB: 38b, fragment) notes "and Rus was baptised of that day". There is also information which records the baptism of part of Kyiv by Askold in 867. Perhaps, it was precisely this which triggered desperate calls to the Rusy to change their mind, as expounded

Fig. 128 : **Kyivan Rus and neighbours**. Map by M. M. Ievlevym.

by the Volhvs in the final lines of the great book, *The Veles Book* – Holy Testament of outgoing Ruskolan.

As a consequence of social disruption by Varangian-warriors and being enmeshed by the biblical ideology of the "slaves of the Lord" during 9th – 10th centuries, Rus (having now become Kyivan), lost its Arattan tradition of eternal statehood (primal for all humanity) which had been exemplified by its hierarchical, communal or "primitive communism" quality, although remnants of it were later preserved in peasant communities and Cossack siches (Cossack republics). The official statehood became class-based, feudal and totalitarian and in this form it entered an established regime (initiated by Sumer, Babylon, Greece, Rome etc.) which was well-suited for that era of polarisation, for "decompression/expansion" of the pulsating heart of history [i.e. stressing the heart intolerably].

{From the standpoint of such a regime, many of the convulsions of subsequent stages of Rusy history are at best represented in acts of anachronistic barbarism or hopeful dreams. In reality (or, in the worst case, due to its repressed spirit), such convulsions which happen in other countries are a stark testament – represented by those worst instances, those bad moments – to past and future "compressions". "Expansion", which is characteristic of modern Europe and other continents, should not be over-eulogised because ultimately it will be accompanied by a 'heart attack' for terrestrial civilisation, infected, moreover, by biblical suicide. Life is a harmonic co-existence of nations and the cultures created by them, a rhythm of priorities! Here, the deadly Bible could be generally helpful, if it was proportional for the time and place.}

Starting with the usurpation of power in Rus by the Varangians, subsequent princes and rulers, along with the Byzantine type of statehood, were wholly foreign to the nation. That is why, since those times, the people who cherished the tradition of communal collegiality going back to 6,200 BCE (if not to 19,121 BCE) were cursed for 1000 years as predicted by the Volhvs (counting from the baptism of Rus in 988) up to the present day: they were on their own, and initially foreign to the people in authority with a 1013-year history (in the opinion of a representative of that power, the Muscovite (Moscowian) academic Likhachev, and others like him).

{Do not accuse the author of these lines of inciting discord. The author is an historian who generalises the well known, though constantly distorted, facts. However, one must be true and seek out the facts, looking at the outcomes of deadly conflicts, which the author is doing according to his own understanding of civic duty and God. Is this understanding criminal or is it beneficial?.. Should professional historians, like physicians, tell people the truth, the only truth and nothing but the truth? Or should they continue to prescribe bed rest for the regime, right up to last rites on the death bed? What is more useful for the people and authorities – an explicit understanding, adrenaline in the blood, or blood in the ditches?}

Neither the Cossacks in general, nor their genius Bohdan Khmelnytsky, nor imperial Russia, nor the present independent Ukraine were able to overcome this discord between the people and government. As it was, so it remains: the power, either consecrated or formally opposing the Bible, parasitised and parasitises the eternal-communal culture of people. And neither the Russian Prince Kropotkin^, nor the Ukrainian peasant was able to remove this contradiction, not to mention the Marxist-Leninist communists of, for example, Zionist orientation, proclaiming their course on "world revolution, which should burn down the Slavic nations" (i.e. burn down the root of human civilisation enshrined by Slavdom, whose Slavic lands cherished Aratta).

The millennia-long period of abhorrence predicted by the Volhvs (Magus-priests) has now elapsed and the despair of those rulers of Aratta-Oriana-Borusia-Rus presented in *The Veles Book* comes through to us right now not as a call, but a plea:

6f *Askold and Dir settled down on our lands...*
But (Ohneboh, i.e. 'fire god') *turned his face away from them,*
Because they were baptised Greeks.
Askold was a dark warrior, but now educated as Greek
was not Rusy at all, but carried the essence of thieves...

6g *And Greeks wish to baptise us so that we forget our gods*
and are converted, and will come to serve them.
Beware of that, as do shepherds who guard their flock
and do not allow wolves to prey on lambs
who are, after all, also children of the Sun...

Let us come back to the Sun – Svaroh of our pre-ancestors!

Suggested reading

1. B. A. Yatsenko, *The Veles Book.* Translation and Comments: Kyiv, 1995, 2001.
2. Nestor, *The Tale of Bygone Years.* Complete collection of Rusy annals. Moscow, 1962-1965.
3. *Tale of the Campaign of Ihor Svyatoslavlich.* Kyiv, 1985, and others.
4. B. A. Rybakov, *Paganism of Ancient Rus.* Moscow, 1987.
5. P. V. Tulaev, *Veneti: Primogenitors of Slavs.* Moscow, 2000.
6. A. A. Asov, *Atlanteans, Arias, Slaviane (Slavdom): History and Faith.* Moscow, 2000.
7. N. A. Lebedev, *Formation of Slavic world.* Kyiv, 1997.

---

[1] Traditionally Lithuania is divided into four ethnographic regions: Aukštaitija, Zhjamajtija, Suvalkija, Dzūkija. Each region is distinguished by its own dialect, customs, national costume and architecture. (http://www.smalvos.ru/EN/Index.html).

[2] Severenze, (in Russian ' Сверензе' resembles the Russian word 'Севера', meaning 'northern').

EPILOGUE

Fig. 129 : **Scythian Patriarchs**. Fragment from an image on a ceremonial bowl from the royal kurhan of Haimanova Grave (see Figs. 100, 116).

THE KYANI – INDO-EUROPEAN DYNASTY

The ancient sages were not only wise in thought and word but also used their wisdom to actively guide people, shouldering the gravest of tasks during times of difficulty.

Mezhybor arrived. And Mezhybor said: "The arm is lightning. The foot is thunder. The hand is a sword, the foot, a hammer. Death to untruth for truth!" And Mezhybor struck the Pecheneh^ Prince in the face with his foot – he cried out terribly, calling upon the prince of darkness for help. And he punched the Pecheneh with his fist under the heart and the prince fell dead. "This is not for a battle, but for a clean way, in accord with the way of truth", said Mezhybor. And he hit an oak with his fist. And the oak shook and dropped foliage with acorns. And Div [Slavic god] *cried out from the forest, and a Bull ran out of the forest, falling down at Mezhybor's legs. And with great horror the Pechenehs ran away, astonished by the power of Mezhybor.*

This account is similar to the tale of "*Volkhovnik*", the same Magian who foretold the death, "by his horse", of the rather conceited Prince Oleh [Oleh had the horse killed and whilst gloating that he had outlived the threat, was struck dead by a snake amongst the bones] ; M. F. Slaboshpytsky also cites the case of the ancient Magian Dobrohast (from *Klio's Voice, Klio*, Kyiv, 2000). When Prince Ihor offended the old man, shortly before he was killed by Drevlians, Dobrohast called out his thirty armed combatants to do battle and – unarmed – conquered all of them.

Following the baptism of the state of Kyivan Rus, the Magi retired into the forests. From time to time, through effective insurrections, they were able to keep alive their body of knowledge which they passed on to the Cossacks and thence on to [modern] researchers. Their last actions were observed during the years of the Civil War [1918-1920] (V. N. Demin. *Secrets of the Russian people. The search for the beginnings of Rus*, Moscow,

1997); perhaps the remarkable enthusiasm of Father Makhno^ was inspired by their example?

It is said that the Magi cursed the baptism of Rus in 988 for a thousand years. Now, it is said, a revival has begun ... but what has been revived? What is relevant in terms of the ancient precepts?

1. Kyani, the Indo-European dynasty of Oriana-Dandaria.

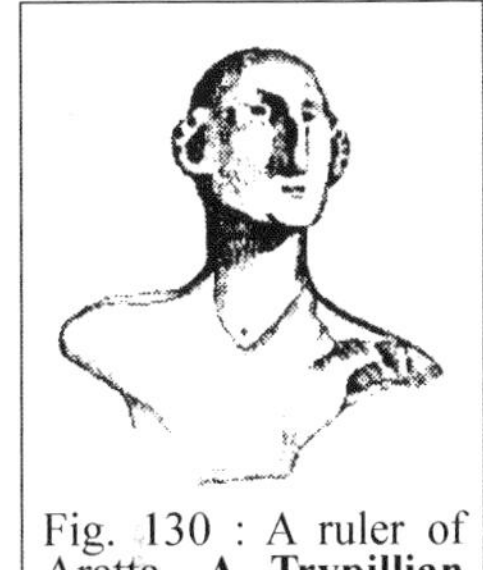

Fig. 130 : A ruler of Aratta. **A Trypillian figurine** between the 4th – 3rd mill. BCE.

Contrary to the prevailing opinion that prior to its conversion to Christianity, Slavdom offered nothing to world culture, we would like to mention the discovery made by the linguists N. Ya. Marr, O. N. Trubachev and S. I. Nalyvayko, and put in order by the historian Yu. Shilov. This discovery is only one of many examples of the genuine place of Slavic culture within the general human civilisation of the Earth.

From the 6th century BCE to the 2nd century CE there were references to the country of Dandarica^ by Greek and Roman geographers. Although the extent of its territory changed along with prevailing ethno-political conflicts, in general it extended between the lower reaches of the Southern Buh and the Kuban. At the time these rivers were each named alike as Hipanis, meaning 'Horse (?) Water'. There were also two Sindic rivers, the "Old one" along the common estuary of the Buh and Dnipro, and the "New one" at the mouth of the Kuban. Dandaka, located between these rivers as recorded in the 4th century, lay on the south-western coast of Taurida. Furthermore, ancient authors wrote about a King Dandaria as the leader of the homonymous tribe.

O. N. Trubachev, and later S. I. Nalyvayko, drew attention to the Indo-Aryan correspondences within the famous epic poems of the *Ramayana* and *Mahabharata*, noting that these sources had not been focused upon for such correspondences hitherto.

Arica clearly signified the 'Country of Aryans'. *Danda*, however, did not simply mean 'cane', 'root', 'stick', 'oar' or other variations of 'rod', 'mace', and 'support'. Danda was symbolic of power over the world and humanity, thus, Dandaria, meaning 'mace-bearing Aryans', can be treated as Dand(dh)aria – the 'mace-bearers'; the essence of this meaning does not change.

There is a similar relationship between the Ukrainian words ***kyi***, ***Kyi***, ***Kyiv*** – where the last two names are connected with the beginnings of Rus. As explained in 1773 by the Petersburg writer V. K. Trediakovskii in *Three discourses concerning the three principal antiquities of Rossians*, "In Slavic language, Kyi is a baton [sceptre or mace] and this word was hitherto in usage amongst Little Rossians [i.e. Ukraine-Rus] as a portent", Since then, the time when academic science could well have understood the Slavic contribution to the foundations of world culture, had passed.. We shall try to go back to unravel it right now.

The symbolism of the ***kyi*** [the sceptre/staff] has a long history in Rus, reaching back at least to the time of Aryan burial kurhans, stelae and amulets, etc. The sceptre-staff is present in these kurhans as a symbol of cosmogonic myths involving the Almighty-Serpent Sheshi and the Creator-God Vishnu. This tradition was transferred to the batons [maces] of the Slavic gods Radhost^, Veles and others, as well as rusalska^ (Fig.131). Traditional Ukrainian pysanky [hand-painted eggs] portray many variations on the shape of the sceptre.

Ancient inscriptions indicate that the Dandaria (mace-bearing Aryans) were associated with the Sindi, Torety, Psesy, Tanaity, and Meoty tribes whose ethnonyms accord with the names of local features e.g. creeks. Similar tribal names are found in the *Mahabharata*, where the Sinds, Suviry, Kauravas, and Magadshi coexisted with Dandaria. This leads us to agree with S. I. Nalyvayko's observation that the Dandaria belonged to the "military camp which included the Sindo-Meoty tribes with whom they shared the same status, just like the so-called 'Royal' Scythians and Rusy chroniclers". As we know already, the ancestors of the Rusy were related to Aratta (Indo-Europeans) and to Oriana (Indo-

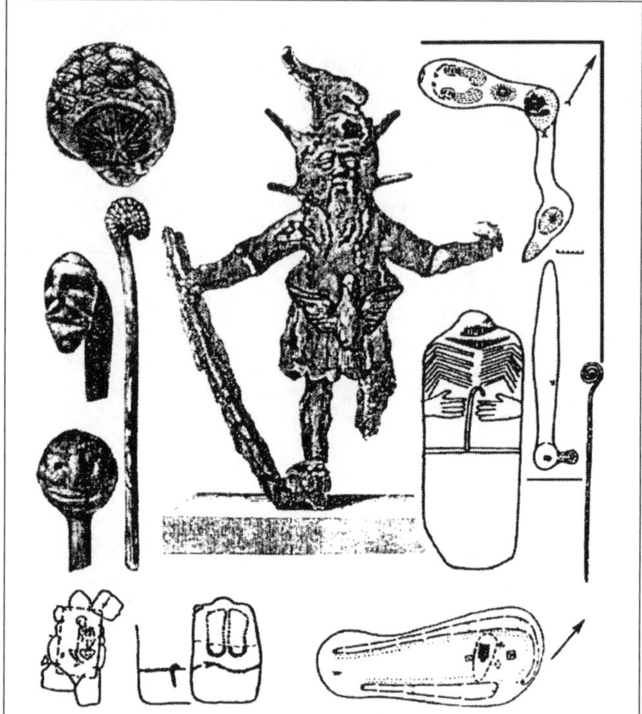

Fig. 131 : **The sacred staff** [sceptres] (Slavic Kyi, Aryan Danda) in archaeological finds from the mid-3rd millennium BCE to the end of the 1st millennium CE.

Aryans) and therefore, after borrowing the term "mace-bearing" from their more militant neighbours, they translated it into their native language as "kiyanstvo", with intermediate forms in between. Compare this with the ethno-historical sequence of Paralat, Pali and Polian. *Danda, cane* and ***sceptre*** also correspond to a series, which has just been discussed.. We have drawn attention to the relationship between their earliest ancestor, Targitai, and the Celtic Dagda and also Slavic Dazhboh. Dynda as a surname exists amongst Ukrainians and a lanky person is styled "dylda". In the Lama vocabulary [Tibetan Buddhism]; **kiya** is a synonym for the club or vajra, the weapon of Vedic Indra and other gods.

The term *kyi* is not found later than the term Danda(ria). With regard to the latter term, S. I. Nalyvayko is reminded of the Vedic concept of Sky-Earth unity in the compound name Diava (from Dyaus-Prithivi; Dyaus the Sky Father, Prithivi the Earth Mother). Since the Kyivans, just like the Dandarians, arose from the region of Stone Grave, site of the world's earliest chronicle, it is possible that the appearance of the sacred Kyia(na) is derived from the Pre-Indo-European sacred concept of ***Ki-Anu*** – the sacred 'Earth-Sky' bond which was forcibly separated in the course of time by Enlil. When considering the memory of this mythology which was enshrined in the Slavic Red Hill celebration, we referred to its Pre-Slavic antiquity, a time steeped in matriarchy. In the Red Hill celebration, the axis of the universe is represented by a "burned stump", [symbolising Father Sky] on which sits Le(ya)la [symbolising Mother Earth], decorated with flowers. She is considered to be the daughter of Lada (Lata etc. of Pelasgians and Greeks); her father was *Kol* (the Titan ***Koios/ Koeus/Coeus***), the Pole Star. The mythology of this family was connected, as we already know, with the initial developments of the Arattan system of sanctuary-observatories (maidans), between the 5th – 4th millennium BCE. This is the origin of the ***Kyan*** dynasty who were probably the builders and keepers of the system. Our assumption is confirmed by the presence of a city called *Kyan* in Sumer and also by the Sumerian poem "The City – The bond between Earth and Sky [Dur.an.ki]", where *youthful Enlil lives – young man of the town.*

In previous chapters there was convincing evidence that the Slavic ethnic group (which superseded the Pre-Slavic) formed between 2300-1700 BCE when there was a change in the canon of the celestial calendar (from lunar to solar). Clearly, the importance of Polaris [the Pole Star] as ***Koya-Kola*** of the universe remained unchanged. At the same time, and together with the migrations of the Slavs and Pelasgians of Aratta (Borusia and Oriana), as well as their neighbouring Aryans, an expansion of the system of maidans began along with the spread of their attendants, who, one way or another, belonged to the ***Kyan*** dynasty. Its earliest manifestation is found in the *Ramayana* as the ***Keka*** tribe, from which came ***Kaikeya***i who was the third and junior wife of the father [King Dasaratha] of the main hero [Bharata]. This correspondence to the citizens of the Black Sea area is all the more probable since the main actions of the poem occur in Dandaka, the similarly-named location in the forementioned locality in Crimea, where we have indicated other specific correspondences in the *Ramayana.*

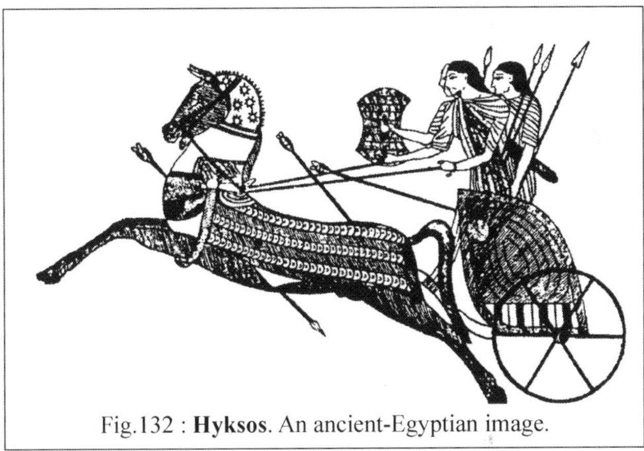

Fig.132 : **Hyksos**. An ancient-Egyptian image.

The path from the Northern Black Sea area through Palestine into Egypt is traced to the 19th – 18th centuries BCE. The route of this path is referenced in the myth of the wandering. unfortunate Io, the sister of Pelasg, as well as in the histories of the Hyksos. It is not certain whether the beginning of their migration from the "northern land Ta-Ru" was from Dandaria, on the shores of the Hypanis where that ethnic group of 'equestrians' emerged (related to Indo-European 'equestrians' of Pre-Palestine – the Canaanites or Kinakhs), or whether it was from Taurida. The assumption makes it all the more possible that amongst the Hyksos tribes – besides the Pelasgians-Peleset-Pelishtim-Philistines etc. – were the *Tursha* and *Danuna*. Possibly they were related to the Vedic tribes of *Turvash*[1] and *Danava* or Anu; or even the ancestors of the Tanaity and *Toreti* of ancient Sindica (Taman peninsula), as well as of the *Turovtsy* of Rus? The fact that these riders and horsemen also invented phonetic letters brings them together with the carriers of the Ingul archaeological culture whose borders, in the 20th – 17th centuries BCE, largely coincided with the original homeland of the Aryans. The first manifestations of phonetic letters are found in several Ingul burials in the area of Stone Grave where similar inscriptions are also known and even images of a "solar barque" inherent to Egypt are found there as well as an amulet in the form of a scarab beetle.

After settling in Palestine and perhaps having founded the Aryan-Hurrian state of Mitanni (from Meots of Meotida, the Sea of Azov) in the north of Mesopotamia, the Hyksos captured Egypt at the end of the 18th century BCE and built there a new capital, Avaris, (whose name, coincidentally, is possibly consonant with that of the eminent Hyperborean sage, Abaris, a learned colleague of Pythagoras). They founded a new, 15th dynasty of kings, the first of whom was ***Kh(K)yan***. According to O. N. Trubachev, a city with a similar name to our ***Kyiv*** also existed in Egypt in ancient times.

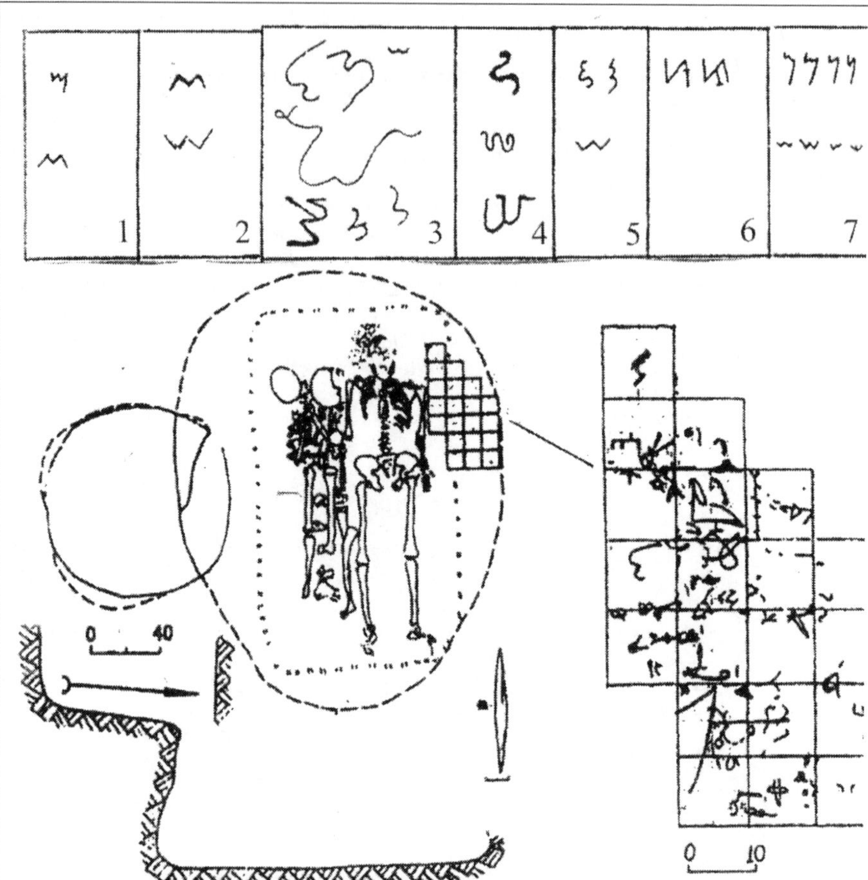

Fig. 133 : **The inverse image of the Golden Fleece** in burial 2 of kurhan 13 at the village of Vinohrad, Tokmak District, Zaporizhia Region. One of the signs of the scrolls and its analogues in other monuments, 6th–2nd millennium BCE Trypillian (7), Catacomb (2) culture, as well as letters of Stone Grave (6), Crete (5), Phoenicians (4) and the northern Semites (3). (S. J. Pustovalov. *Social structure of catacomb society of the Northern Black Sea*. - Kyiv: "Path", 2005. -p. 162-163).

It is not known whether Kyi arrived in India from Oriana along with his father Oriy, brothers Shchek and Khoryv or whether he was born there and had grown up in India (amongst the above mentioned Keka tribe, for example); *The Veles Book* focuses attention on their return to the Dnipro from Punjab. Here it is necessary to focus on the canonicities [i.e. accepted history] of this family: the ancestor Oriy and three of his sons correspond to legends of the Skoloty, Scythians, Hellenes and Ukrainians from the Dnipro area. If Oriy, figuratively speaking, provides an indication on the ancestral home of the majority of migrants, and Kyi reflects the canon of its sanctuary-observatories, then who were Shchek and Khoryv? On board 4d [of *The Veles Book*] the names Pashchek and Horovato, appear thus revealing the primary form of the two names, Shchek and Khoryv. The first name can be considered synonymous with the ancient meaning of Shchek as 'Serpent'; the second as 'Mountain'[2]. So, we return again to the characteristics of the Red Hill celebration, supposedly started in association with these two brothers of Carpathian Rus (VB: 7a). As stated earlier, the 'grief-grief mound', and particularly Vratar of this Slavic celebration, is identified by researchers with the serpent Vritra in the main mythology of the Indo-European *Rigveda*. Indeed the canon of the this family in India was also connected with the foundation of the Aryan and

Indo-European culture and thus of all human culture. According to F. B. J. Kuiper and other researchers of archetypes and prenatal memory, the "serpent-warrior memories" recreate conception, development of the embryo, and birth, etc. It is appropriate here to recall the serpent-warrior Indra – highly revered in *The Veles Book* by experts of the Vedas as the forerunner of Perun [the Slavic thunder god], to whom Indra handed *all his weapons in order that Perun use them to defeat the serpent* (VB: 6d). The ***kyi*** corresponds most closely to the magical club-vajra of the hero Indra, as confirmed by the name ***kiya*** used for the staff of the Tibetan Lama. According to *The Veles Book* Indra gave his weapons to Perun, then indeed in the same way we see the sceptre (and its variants) amongst the attributes of Perun on figurines from the city of Retra, on stelas from Zbruch^ and Danube River areas, and on one of the reliefs of the Demetrius Cathedral in Vladimir [modern Russia] etc. All of these are staffs or clubs.

It may have been during the precise time when the Slavs (Orianians and Borusians) settled in the Punjab that the name of the territory became called Aratta[3] (according to the *Mahabharata*) in homage to their homeland. Their sorcerer-priests were called ***kavi*** or ***kei,*** which means 'word-composer' or 'poet'. The ruler Ushanas was the son of the ruler Kavi who was the son of Brahman Bhrigu, the latter being one of compilers of the *Rigveda*. Their descendants are considered to be the patriarchs of the tribes of Yadu and Turvash who were allegedly led into India by Indra. The Yadu tribe was also referred to by the names Satvati and Danava. According to S. I. Nalyvayko, they correspond to the Yotvingian tribe recorded in the Baltic states (who were also called Sudovity and Dainovi), and to the Turovtsy tribe of Volyn. On its neighbouring expanses there also dwelt the Drehovychi (Drehva), Ants and Polians. Their names correspond to three (of the five) other Aryan tribes which according to Vedic tradition, came into India from the north-east: the

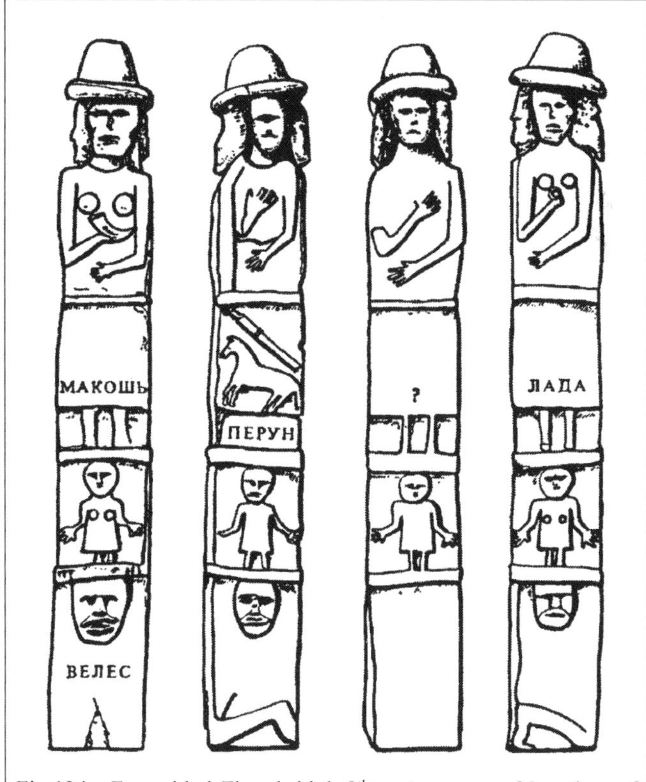

Fig.134 : Four-sided Zbruch idol, 9th century, **eve of baptism of Rus**. By B. A. Rybakov.

Druhyu, Anu and Puru... So, we have enough evidence for establishing the offshoots of the dynasty of ***Kyan*** not only in Egypt but now also in India.

The Indian and Ukrainian linguists, S. K. Chatterji and S. I. Nalyvayko respectively, believe that after a period in India, part of the Aryan tribe of Bhrigu (see above) appeared in Asia Minor, where they gave rise to the nation of Brigs or Phrygians. In *The Veles Book*, (board 26 and others) this is perhaps described as the march of father Oriy from Punjab into the Dnipro area, from where he (or Oseden), having left his sons behind, then led the people "as far as the edge of the sea". Since Strabo writes that the Phrygians arrived in Asia Minor from Thracia prior to the Trojan War (1030-1020 BCE?) that migration of the Bhrigu tribe can also be compared to the Sigynnes of Herodotus and also the earlier (e)Hun tribes of *The Veles Book* (board 4d and others), who supposedly displaced the Slavs from India... With these two related migrations, we may coordinate the beginnings of at least two other dynasties of ***Kyan***.

According to the testimonies of *The Veles Book*, on the way from India to the Dnipro area, somewhere near the sea and large mountains:

4d *Kyi who was the founder of Kyiv settled down.*
Over there was the throne of Rus.
31 *There they lived in the winter and by Spring went again to the South...*
Our land stretched from sun till sun of Svarozh.
And indeed great meadows of Khors...

It would seem that the similarity between and the Indian ***Kavi*** Ushanas^ and the Persian ***Kei*** Usan^, representative of the ***Keyanids*** of Khwarezm, emerged from ***Kyiv*** of the Caspian Sea area. Kei Usan, just like Rustam, was considered to be the father of Siyavush, semantically identical to the Ukrainian 'Chornovil' [meaning 'black ox', hence the further semantic link with Sivash^ in Crimea with the bull/Taurida], which has counterparts in India. Another counterpart of the Indian ***Kavi-kei*** appears in the Persian *Avesta*, although he was not a 'poet', but a 'warrior'. The latter, just like the Keyanids, were opponents of Zoroaster, whose holy book, the *Avesta*, was composed by Zarathustra later than the composition of the *Rigveda*, at the beginning of the 1st millennium BCE. By these means (perhaps arising from the acquaintance of the orthodox chroniclers with the holy books of the heathens/pagans^) the echo of these events was incorporated into *The Tale of Bygone Years* by Nestor in the 12th century. He spoke positively about the Bactrians (Iuktrians), considering them not as Khwarezmians, but rather as Indian Brahmans: *The law in Iuktrian, the same as that called Vrahmans and Ostrovits, was taken from the great-grandfathers for their example and piety, under great fear not to eat meat, drink wine, fornicate and not to create malice*.

It is entirely probable that the above-named ***Kyi***, Hora and *Khoryv*[4], as well as the name of Khors that appears in the "meadows *of Khors*", refer to *Key Khorses*, the son of Siyavush, and also refer to to the establishment of Khwarezm. Having founded the dynasty, the Orianians and Borusians continued their way from India to the Dnipro area ancestral homeland. This is reflected in Khwarezmian legends (possibly not the ancestors of Sigynnes-Huns, as mentioned above?) as the banishment of some of his people by king *Keyani* to somewhere in the fishing margin, where they were called Mitany or Miuyten. S. I. Nalyvayko correctly correlates these ethnonyms (according to O. N. Trubachev) with the related Mitanni kingdom and Meotida that we mentioned earlier in connection with the past history of the Egyptian ***Kyan***.

The question was raised in the Chapter 11 concerning the underlying root causes of the Persian campaign, led by Darius, into Scythia. There we paused on the ideological contradictions within the Vedic doctrine primarily inherent to the Aryans and to the Zoroastrian off-shoot of Persian Aryans. Having adopted Zoroastrianism as the religion of Persia – within the Achemaenid dynasty, one of the founders of which was Darius himself – he became an enemy not only of the Vedic doctrine but also of the former Keyanid dynasty which was based on that doctrine. Since the shared cradle-land of the Vedas and Kyan lay in the Northern Black Sea area, Darius, being an ardent champion for the superiority of the new dynasty and faith, could not disregard that cradle-land. We now know the underlying reason for that seemingly senseless campaign of the Persians against the Scythians. The campaign was similar to the military march of Cyrus, predecessor of Darius, into the Trans-Caspian steppe-lands of the Massagetae and Saki to attain the hand of the widowed princess Tamiris; perhaps to resolve the same problem of dynastic priorities.

We will now consider another dynasty of ***Kyan***, formed on foreign land by the returners from India – although perhaps not those who went with progenitor Oriy and his sons.

According to *The Histories* by Herodotus, the Phrygians, together with the Armenians, went from the Balkans [into Asia (VII: 73)]. The Armenians were probably the same as the Mitany-Miuyten of the Khwarezmian legends. At that time, or later, there was a different legend, this version was introduced into scientific circulation for the first time by N. I. Marr (*Book legends about the foundation of Kyiv in Rus and Kuar in Armenia*, Moscow, 1924). It had been recorded in the 8th century *History of Taron* by Zenon Amartol[5] and described the Indian princes Demetri and Gisane who escaped from one of the rulers of India and found asylum with the king of Armenia. He allotted them the land of Taron (in Asia Minor), where they built the city Vishapu. Subsequently Demetri and Gisane fell out of favour and were executed by their benefactor and the king of Armenia transferred their possessions to the sons of the executed princes – Kuar, Meltey (who was also a 'Serpent', just like Shchek) and Khorean. Each of them built himself a city bearing his name. *The Histories* also mentions a region called Palun, in which the third brother settled. Then they all ascended Mount Kerkey, where they established a settlement and placed idols to their parents to serve a cult to which they later dedicated themselves.

When the rehabilitation N. I. Marr's^ scientific legacy began, B. A. Rybakov tried to explain the amazing coincidences of this legend with that recorded by Nestor in *The Tale of Bygone Years* of the 12th century. According to Rybakov, Nestor's narrative claims that captive Slavs were relocated to the Caucasus by Arabs in the 8th century. Closer to the truth (and perhaps entirely correct) is the hypothesis substantiated by S. I. Nalyvayko. It is known that in the 1st century many Indians migrated into Armenian Taron. In the 3rd century, when Christianity began to take root in Armenia and the oppression of pagans began, some of the Indians migrated into the still 'un-Christianised' region of the Roman empire. The above-mentioned legend may have formed under those conditions. In any event, it is older than the narrative recorded by chronicler Nestor and it originates from the Indian tradition, which was founded there by the Aryan migrants from the Northern Black Sea area. Therefore the legend from Taron should be considered as a reflection, if not a retelling (complemented by subsequent details) of the ancient canon of the ***Kyan*** dynasty.

Let us consider the version of S. I. Nalyvayko (*Secrets of Sanskrit Revealed*, Kyiv, 2000):

The parents, especially the idols of Demetri and Gisane on Mount Kerkey (the ancient Druidic centre near the Kerch strait), are already familiar to us from the wanderings of Odysseus, also, according to the Ukrs of *The Veles Book* (board 25), they are the embodiment of Mitra and Shiva who are represented in monuments in the Northern Black Sea area. The epithet of the second prince (Gisane) was Keshava^, 'He, who bears a kosa' (meaning a "tress" in Slavic languages). The attributes of Shiva – besides the kosa (a particular type of the "oseledets" of the Zaporozhian Cossacks) include the trishula-trident and his seated position, etc., bringing together his iconography with the canonical images of the Ukrainian Cossack Mamai^. Such an approximation of detail could have originated only from the Indian campaign of Slavs, described in *The Veles Book* and considered above.

The region of *Palun* that is mentioned in the legend, is associated with ancient Rus, as well as with Taurida where, between the 3rd – 2nd century BCE, the fortresses of Pali and Napi were built, according to the Scythian legend of the forefather's sons, Pali and Napi. Khorean, according to Khwarezmian and Rusy traditions, was one of the ***Kyan**-captains*. Perhaps it was this specific Khoryv who began to build Khorsun (Chersonese), at the beginning of the 1st millennium BCE when the Orianians and Borusians returned from India through Khwarezm Zamore (*The Veles Book*, 6a).

In the general context of the legend, *Kuar* is comparable to ***Kyi*** of *The Veles Book* and *The Tale of Bygone Years*. At the same time, Kuar is cognate with Kuru, the ruler of *the* Kauravas of the *Mahabharata*. Remember that the Kauravas have been compared to the

Toreti of Taurida and Sindica, which in turn exposes the Pelasgian-Etruscan liaisons with this tribe, then it is pertinent to recall the ancient tribe of *Koretians* and Trojan *Kuritian*-priests, who were the forerunners of the *kharakternyks* of the Zaporozhian Cossacks[6]…

The name of legendary Visapur[7] [in India] can be translated as 'high, elevated city'; going deeper into Aryan languages leads us back to a meaning closer to 'generative city'; 'city of the nation'; 'capital'. All of these meanings can be attributed to Vyshhorod ['horod' meaning 'city'], the historic centre of Kyiv.

Before we examine *The Veles Book* further, beginning from the earliest Kyi, and the fate of this dynasty in their native land, let us pause to consider the Germanic-Gothic offshoot of the dynasty which can be considered as Slavic-Venedian because it belonged to the union of Vandals and Veneti in the 3rd century. The common ancestor of this union was considered to be Arias, whose son was ***Kyi***, and whose grandson was Ostrogoth, and whose great-grandson was ***Cniva***. The indicated union of Vandals and Veneti grew up at the time of Cniva who defeated the troops, in 251-283 CE, of Sauromates IV, a Roman lieutenant general and ruler of the Bosphorus, then captured Semihradia and thereby established the Gothic principality of Taurida, whose borders at times reached the Carpathians and the Caucasus. In the course of time this dynasty became more and more Teutonised, and increasingly antagonistic to the Slavs. The treacherous affairs of Hermanaric, grandson of *Cniva*, and his infamous death in 375 CE, have already been examined.

It is impossible to give up entirely the version of history which records that the capital of Kyivan Rus had originated from the legendary founder ***Kuar*** from Armenian-Indian Taron, especially because a relationship did exist between them through **Kisek** (*The Veles Book*: 17c, 19, 25, 35a), who operated in the North Caucasus along with Or, the heir of the homonymic patriarch of the dynasty. However in any event, *The Veles Book* and other sources point to the existence amongst the Slavs of their own dynasty of ***Kyan***, as the main dynasty in the Indo-European world. It formed, as was shown, long before the migration into India and the partial return to their homeland. After returning to the Dnipro area, the son of legendary Oriy allegedly did not build ***Kyiv*** but received the town as his ancestral right:

Fig. 135 : Bohdan Khmelnytsky [Hetman of the Zaporozhian Cossacks] with the Hetman's indian club.

38a *And* [they] *placed the first altar of the kin of Slavs in the city Indikyiv, named: Kyiv.*
And they began to settle in it.
7i *Kyi settled down at Kyiv, and they obeyed,*
and together with him until this time we are building Rus

– that is, they continued to adhere to the dynasty of **Kyan** (for almost two millennia, until Askold and the kin of Rurik came to Kyiv). Not one, but many members of this dynasty knew *The Veles Book* (board 22 et al.). The knowledge of *The Tale of Bygone Years* is much impoverished in comparison. The status of Kyi and Kyiv was built upon a tradition of riverine transportation (Ukrainian '*kytovane*') [across the Dnipro River] and shipbuilding in the area of the suburban fortress Sambatos (in Greek, *collection of canoes*) and the Busov (in Slavic, *Ladeine*) field [of the Rooks].

Over time the traditions of the ***Kyan*** dynasty were passed on, perhaps, to the Cossacks – and were sustained by them until the liquidation of the Zaporozhian Sich [the old Republic of Cossacks by the Muscovite (Moscowian) Empress at the end of the 18th century]. People still preserve the memory of the Zaporozhian Sich^ to this day. One of the legends of the Ukrainian Dnipro area (*Savur-graves*, Kyiv, 1990) derives the Cossacks from ***Kyiv*** (***kyїiv***) who "went into campaigns with ***kyikamy*** [sceptres/maces]" and began to rally together in the forests near ***Kyiv***.

Kyans were known, as we have seen, by many other countries of the Indo-European world. Mankind is obliged to acknowledge the essential contribution of this dynasty – generated by the ancestors of Slavs of the land of Ukraine – in the development of both the Indo-European and worldwide civilisation.

2. The precepts of the Volhvs [Magus-priests]

The social traditions and beliefs of the times prior to the creation of Kyivan Rus have been investigated in terms of the testimonies in *The Veles Book* – namely the eternal, pre-class Aratta type of statehood, protected by generations of priests and their subordinate warriors (the Kyan, as we have just explained). We shall try to improve this review by posing the following questions: What was deemed most valuable in those precepts of the "primeval elite"? Are they relevant for our time? Are the precepts of the ancestors suitable for building the future?

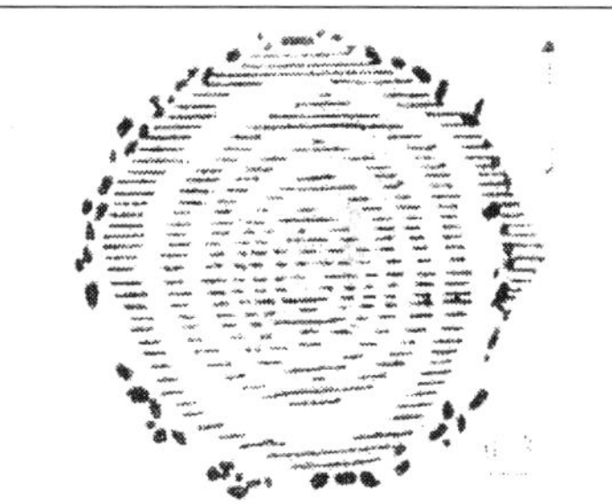

Fig. 136 : **Rollright Stones** (U.K.), at the centre of the circle, the Earth's magnetic field is weakened i.e. the average intensity of the magnetic field of each of the seven turns of the spiral is significantly lower than that occurring outside the stones.

To answer these questions, it is necessary to know what to look out for. If we rely upon the methodology of historical materialism (in which until recently, historians placed their academic skills), then once again – like Marx, Lenin and their apologists – we will be restricted to the secondary and incidental issues of economics, social attitudes, and the formation of class struggles etc. The most important issues for most human beings – the meaning of life and death, their spiritual culture and prospects – would still stay unresolved, just like the many manifestations of so-called material culture that are inaccessible to the methodology of istmat [historical materialism]. Such important issues, which are practically uninvestigated by academic science, include: the pre-Grecian written language of Stone Grave and across the entire Eurasian steppes; the system of maidans (sanctuary-observatories) of Aratta; the very fact of the existence of this earliest-in-the-world type of pre-class state; its wooden cities and villages, which were periodically completely burned by the population; the pre-Christian Saviour, on which the traditions of Aratta and of Arián were based; the origins of the Vedic culture of the latter that are reflected in the kurhans of the Dnipro steppe area and elsewhere; the foundations of the teachings of immortality and the reincarnation of souls, imprinted in the Aratto-Aryan culture; the ethnogenesis of Slavs, their direct heirs… the list goes on...and on. Just like a list of facts, separately well known and even researched by the official science paradigm of historical materialism – but ultimately irreconcilable within that system (because of the danger of self-destruction of the paradigm itself, due to this system being unable to accommodate such information).

We examined the situation outlined here in the Introduction. We will now build on the methodology presented there of Tri-Gnosis and focus our attention on the spiritual culture of all nations and times: on the removal of the antagonism between existence and non-existence, of life and death[8].

In considering the social traditions and beliefs of pre-Kyivan Rus, we touched upon their principal paradigm of Tri-Gnosis to successfully resolve this superhuman challenge [i.e. the removal of the antagonism between existence and non-existence]. The name of that paradigm is **SAVIOUR**. We will now consider how it operated – cementing the structure of pre-class states and communities without exploitation, slavery, militancy and other such lovely Marxist-Leninist realities of the subsequent class states (to say nothing even about Judaism, etc.).

The Saviour, in the form of a rider, a concept inherent to the Aryan culture (Yu. Shilov, *Gandkharva – the Aryan Saviour*, Moscow, 1997), is repeatedly described in *The Veles Book* (board 8(2) and elsewhere) and in various expressions. The Saviour appears to ancestor Bohomyr in the form of husbands for his three daughters – the ancestresses of the Slavic tribes (truly saved from inexistence by such a marriage!). He takes the form of *three husbands on horses, the heralds of morning, noon and evening* (*The Veles Book,* 9a) at the single Kolo [circle] of Svaroh, symbolised here by a campfire near a lone oak. Here, Boh*omyr* expressed the precepts of the Saviour in the following terms (*The Veles Book,* 22): to begin the kin and to take care of its continuation and regulation, to be an omyr[9]-'narrator' and to convey to the Slavs a sermon from heaven: *they have to be as the gods ordered them: this is theirs; and Svaroh – he is Father* (to them), *but others* (the people themselves, the Slavs) *– are the sons* (of Father-God)". The ancestor Bohomyr was also obliged to support the Saviour by the drinking of a beverage Kvasura[10] that he had created, for those deemed worthy, calling on them with these words: "*to the gods, rejoice and dance, and create glory to the gods by singing songs and by* [drinking] *suryna,*" which is a solar (intoxicating) beverage. In doing so it was emphasised that the intoxicating drink must be consumed by people with intellect, under the control of priests and gods who attend to the poles [axes] of the universe (*The Veles Book,* 22):

> *This we must have for all the days after, as the harvest-work shall be carried out, and rejoice to that.*
> *These things cannot be at another time, when one person was unable to hold back from speaking unreasonably about Chornoboh* [Black God],
> *and another, also joyfully about Beloboh* [White God].

Having thus taken care of the everyday welfare of the paradigm of the Saviour, the authors of *The Veles Book* began to delve deeper into His appointed business for the two brothers Kyi and Shchek -'serpent'. It was barely noticeable that Shchek belonged to the caste of warriors whereas it was evident that he belonged to the caste priests, especially the highest caste:

5a ... *great-grandfathers went to the Carpathian mountain*
and settled down there and lived well.
Because those kins were ruled by fathers-relatives,
and the elder of the kin was Shchek, he was from the Orians.
Parkun favoured us, and owing to him lived in peace.
7d *Except for Svaroh we have nothing, only death.*
But that is not frightful, when we are encouraged by speeches of Shchek.
Behold the Sky calls on us, and we go to it.
We go, as Matyr-Sva (our Foremother) *sings* (to us) *a military song...*

So, in removing the fear of death from the Rusy, Shchek relied on the cult of our-Mother-Owl-Glory[11] as this goddess was named even during the times of Aratta, and as she was sometimes named in parts of *The Veles Book*, as well as relying on the cult of Perun. We shall attempt to unravel the truth of this and to clarify the truths concerning Bohomyr and Kvasura. Also, how did Shchek and his followers operate, and what did they introduce into the development of the paradigm of the Saviour?

Let us begin with the fact that they regulated and arranged their craftsmanship in Carpathian Rus. Temples and trade places were constructed which co-existed without friction. Merchant-guests, who moved into Ruskolan from different countries of the world, received *welcoming honour and honorary shirts, as gods honour them and as they commanded us* (*The Veles Book,* 14). It was there, allegedly, that began the celebration of *Red Hill and also the field sacrifice [ritual] with millet, milk, and fat* (*The Veles Book,* 7a). The doctrine of the followers of Shchek was not meditative nor detached from general human life. There was no shadow of redemption from "original sin" and the procuring of daily bread, nor abasement of dissidents and foreigners, – quite the contrary!

In moving from Punjab [back to the Dnipro] the Slavic-Rusy carried with them their pre-Indian veneration of Indra, Dazhboh and Svaroh, *to whose sky we are still going.* Subsequently, they knew that aspects of the creator Svaroh (the annual Solar zodiac) existed in his many manifestations such as the god of light, as well as Prava, Yava and Nava (*The Veles Book,* 15a) i.e. as heaven, earth and the netherworld. Perhaps at the same time, the synthesis of the cults of Matyr-Slava [Mother-Glory] and of Perun emerged in Slavic culture. *The Veles Book* (board 7g) calls this synthesised deity Perunytsia; she is even closer to the Vedic Matarisvan^ (the 'Swelling/Pregnant Mother(-earth)' precursor of the Greek Creator God, Prometheus) whom S. I. Nalyvayko considers as corresponding to Matyr-Slava. Here we have a link to Hindu penetration of the secret of immortality of the soul, and its reincarnation (*The Veles Book*, 26):

And so let us each accept our fate, and live.
And I say that, my son,
that time is not abolished but is always there before us.
But there (after death) *we shall see our ancestors and mothers will*
who order the sky and their flocks graze (there)...
There are neither Huns nor Elans, and Prava reigns over them.
And that Prava is true, as Nava is downcast or given to Yava,
and abides for eternal centuries beside Svitovyd.
And there Zareboh goes along that land and says to our ancestors,
how we should live on earth, and how we suffer, and how much is evil.
And there there is no evil, and green grass will meet them...
And [we must also] *look to the paradisical steppes in the blue sky,*
and that blue comes from god Svaroh...
And so proclaim Glory to the gods, who are our fathers, and we are their sons,
and must be in bodily purity, just like our souls,
that never die and do not die in the moment of the death of our bodies.
And to whoever has perished on the battlefield, Perunytsia gives living water,
and, after drinking it, (they) go to the sky on a white horse [like the Saviour]...
And [after] *remaining there for some time* [the deceased] *receive a new body* [for the next earthly life] ...

The existence of the netherworld and its relationship with burial ceremonies is now better known, based on research material from Aryan kurhans of the Dnipro area; this research traced the ceremony as it was performed by Brahmans for over two thousand years – from the emergence of the Aryans until their partial migration to India from their original homeland (Yu. Shilov, *Ancestral Homeland of Aryans*, Kyiv, 1995; *Gandkharva – Aryan Saviour*, Moscow, 1997). How is this finding recorded in *The Veles Book*?[12]

First of all, let us focus attention on the fact that Matyr-Sova-Slava [Mother-Owl-Glory] embraced the concept of the Indo-European Earthly-Foremother, the spouse of Dyaus-'Sky', the next embodiment of whom became Svaroh (*The Veles Book,* 30) – the Solar zodiac with corresponding celestial-calendar knowledge, festivals etc. His constellations were imagined as immortal ancestors... Matyr-Slava [Mother-Glory] is more ancient and ingrained than Matarisvan who was born to Prithivi-'Earth', and she is associated with the image of the resurrected dead ascending from fire to the netherworld in the sky where the gods give them mortality again. And here is Mother-Glory, Goddess of the Slavs, who personally brought them fire! More specific and socially determined manifestations of this myth were transformed into the home fire-places and funeral pyres of communal people, the fire-keepers (*The Veles Book,* 36a and others). Those sparks, and the radiance of the fire-places and bonfires, transferred the bodies and souls of the ancestors to heaven... There was a third, *really divine,* hypostasis of Matyr, but we shall talk about her at the end.

The formation of Perun's image came about in a similar way. The adaptation of this deity as an instrument **of Saviourhood, namely for the removal of the contradiction between life and inexistence**, arose from cattle-raising Indra, *our god amongst gods (who) knows the Vedas* (*The Veles Book,* 31) although in the Vedas there is a *different Perunets*. In the second hypostasis Indra was not only the god of war but also of human sacrifices, connected with rains and drought and through those atmospheric phenomena with 'Father'-Pitar Dyaus, fire, Svaroh and the light of Iri-'Ray (celestial)' (*The Veles Book,* 30). It was not Matyr but Indra who had the bird Magura. She was heiress of the Vedic Maruts [goddesses] – the spiralling flocks of warlike 'Corpses' whose father (Rudra – meaning 'Growling' but also 'Rod', meaning 'Kin') stole the phallus-shaped vajri-club^ for Indra. When the descendants of Oriy returned to their native Black Sea area from fighting in the Middle East, *Intra gave Parun every weapon, so that he would use it to bring a heavy rain onto the meadows* (*The Veles Book,* 6d). Thus the importance of having power over the rains increased and human sacrifices mutually merged with the killing of enemies on the battlefield to the extent that the authors of *The Veles Book* could subsequently candidly say (*The Veles Book,* 7a):

> *We have true faith that does not require human sacrifice.*
> *But that which operates with the Varangians, who always brought it,*
> *naming Perun* as *Parkun* – as he was called in the past by relatives of Shchek (*The Veles Book,* 5a).

Aside from the series of transitions described above from living-mortal to eternal-immortal through linked mytho-ritual actions with blood-suritsa-water and fire-light-stars, – the priests composed other links: for example, with body-meat-earth (*The Veles Book,* 23):

> *They lived in such a way on that land...*
> *And there was a great massacre there.*
> *And crows cawed above the food of men,*
> *that were cast on the field, and drank their eyes...*
> *But that land will be ours, since we shed blood for it.*

Fig.137 : The coins of Kyivan princes of Varangians.

The mortally wounded had to press earth into their wounds to ensure that the netherworldly Mar-Moria could not then separate a Rusy warrior from the earth and accuse him, together with the land, of any sins (*The Veles Book,* 37b). From the dust of this Earth, *from ashes, thrown to heaven, the celestial warriors rise up and they flow on our enemies and entomb them; ashes that were able to exorcise wizards, who created great miracles* (*The Veles Book,* 14). These miracles also had a divine basis.

It is apparent from these examples that the qualitative cultural hallmark that distinguished the ancient wise men from those who came later (i.e. from the time of chronicler Nestor down to modern scholars, cherished in polarised-totalitarian societies) was the ability to remove that polarity, the deadly polarisation of reality. Furthermore, that polarisation of attitude and perception of the world, social structure and natural economy, etc., became so deadly that in fact everything flipped head over heels! This can be illustrated by the change of symbols:

Tri-Gnosis in the Aryan Vedas was not really emphasised: there was no need for that in the circumstances of prevailing harmony. Veneration of Trihlav [three-headed] and the trinomial division of the different manifestations of a complex God (*The Veles Book,* 11, 30) had hardly been expressed for the first time in *The Veles Book*. The next step was made by the wise men in later Vedic literature and Hinduism where the complex Trimurthy [three-headed] consisted of Brahma (the creator of existence), Vishnu (the protector of beings) and Shiva (the destroyer-and-rejuvenator mediator between them). This is similar to the overlap of Mother-Glory between fire and water, and others considered above, but that was already accented as ***dualism***. From its infinite manifestations we shall point out only one, specifically, the androgynous Mahadeva-and-Mahadevi: the Great 'God-Goddess'. The embryo of the Trinity, as well as this duality in the Vedas, was already most essentially expressed in the image of Mitra-Varuna. This particular fraternal pair of 'Peace-War' and others, were sons of the real Foremother, 'Everlasting' Aditi – they became the basis for the polarised, militarised, class ideology of Kyivan Rus. It was not entirely by chance that it affirmed and baptised Prince Volodymyr as 'Varuna-Mitra', "War-Peace", – whose name would become the favourite for Rurik's warrior-Varangians. Since then, and up to the present time, it has been traditional in Ukrainian land that the national flag consists of two dominating colours (blue water and heavenly yellow sunshine) that are reversed (with the solar yellow below), without the obligatory crimson band (symbol of blossoming Earth), and including the tripartite peace trident symbolic of destruction-renovation. According to *The Veles Book* (board 29):

> *Let go our word about truth, and in this way we will receive truth.*
> *And this is said from old sayings that come from our fathers, who indeed were strong.*
> *And hence we have to return into their furrows and thus able to get to it.*

3. The divine essence of *The Veles Book*.

What can we learn from these precepts if we cannot take advantage of the ancient methods of removing the contradiction between living-and-inexistence? While it is still possible to accept the underlying philosophy, it is difficult these days for us to identify blood with rain and the body with earth... The world has changed.

Fig. 138 : A **Sirin Bird** on a female decoration from the times of Kyivan Rus.

The point in all this is that the identification must take place at the sub-conscious and even genetic level – only then can it operate. We must not judge the figurative-intuitive or "mythological" ideology of our ancestors by the modern standards of our logical-analytical, i.e. "scientific" reasoning! The priest-rulers of Aratta (and later) guided people along that "furrow" but today the understanding of charms now requires enormous effort: algebra doesn't equate to music!

Yes, the harmonic and totalitarian ***forms*** of civilisations ("pre-class and class") have changed immensely and the ***content*** has also considerably changed. But the ***essence*** itself remains almost unchanged; they successfully removed that contradiction but now that it is removed, there is no culture without it. A different matter is how much is best, what sacrifices are needed from humanity, bringing more suffering or happiness… One could say that the quality of modern culture does away with the primitive one but as yet how can we evaluate the civil and world wars, the ecological catastrophes and famines of the last centuries? And can it be said that such sacred texts as the archives of Shu-Nun and Sumer, the *Rigveda* and *Avesta*, the *Edda* and Vedas, were given to people as a compass to guide them to that essence for thousands of years; perhaps the same could be said of *The Veles Book*?

'Essence' is attracted to the primary field principle of the material world, rather like a compass needle points to the North Pole. But 'form' is material and pulls in the opposite direction. Modern civilisation, whose origins we have considered inseparable from those of ancient Rus, still took a long time, in general, to complete mastering the real world (i.e. "material" world, as it seemed to be to the founders of "historical materialism", although in reality the basis of the material world is the field, namely "idealism" or "divinity").

Facts for the existence of field-based civilisations were amassed in science long ago. Only recently in the homeland of the former "triumph of Leninism" has a new discipline within natural sciences been acknowledged – Ufology, 'The Science of unidentified flying objects' (V. G. Azhazha, Fundamentals of Ufology. Instructional material, Institute of Government Administration, Moscow, 1995). Its historical section surveys mysterious archaeological objects, ancient fables and texts, where contacts are described with "incomers from the sky". It is possible to say with complete confidence that every holy book contains such evidence for the appearances of gods. Let us suppose that these were bearers of minds similar to ours. Although their civilisations are qualitatively different from ours we cannot regard them as gods; perhaps we could include in this concept a particular meaning corresponding to our modern time and suggest another term, one that is more scientific (see above).

So, to make *The Veles Book* absolutely sacred it should include testimonies about ufological objects that indicate the direction of further development of the Slavs. So does it? Indeed it does! For amongst the numerous descriptions of the Saviour-rider, Perun and Mother-Glory there are several which approximate ufological manifestations encountered by witnesses in our own time. Although these [ancient] manifestations of non-human civilisations prefer to masquerade as rainbows and other earthly phenomena, nevertheless they exhibit their mind and flying capabilities, etc. (see underlined below):

7h *And Mother-Owl-Glory beats her wings*
and tells the descendants of those
who yielded to neither Greeks, nor Varangians...
As soon as dawn poured onto the steppes,
Mother calls us, so that we make haste.

7g *Mother-owl beats her wings and sings a song to battle*
And that bird is not the dawn sun,
but that she (dawn) *came from it.*

7i *We have our strength in the steppes which was built by Mother – our Sun*
(Her) *wings are mutually spread and the body is in the middle,*
and the head of a hawk – on her shoulders.

7f *And Mother-Owl beats her wings about her sides;*
from both her sides fire shines light to us.
And each feather is different, fine – dark red, blue, light blue, yellow and silver, golden and white.
And she shines, as the streaming sun, and the circle is the sun.
That (Mother-Owl) *gleamed by seven beauties,*
as bequeathed from our gods.
And Perun, looking at her, thunders in the clear sky.

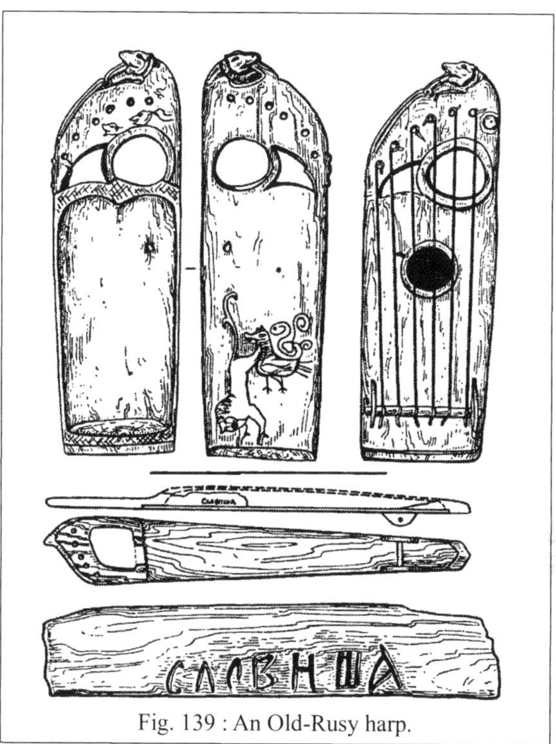

Fig. 139 : An Old-Rusy harp.

24c *Mother-Glory chose us to sing of victory over our enemies, and we believe in it, for it is the word of the Supreme Bird, which flew from us to the celestial verdure...*
Since our fathers saw Oriy walking to the clouds, after he was abducted.
And abducted by force to Perun's blacksmiths;
There Oriy saw how Perun forges swords to enemies.
Forging (Perun) *declares* (to Oriy):
"*These are the arrows and swords against those warriors* (enemy)
and do not dare to fear them (...)".
And Oriy told that to our fathers.
And such was our struggle for life and victory many centuries ago, –
and now we believe in that, that it was so.

Beside Oriy and Bohomyr, the agents of God's will could be Ukhorenz, Osloven, Seden and others mentioned in the texts of the Magi and princes. It is possible that it was specifically from them that the tradition of the prophecy of the new era came, which would begin, it is said, on the shores of Borysthenes-Dnipro with the fall of Marxism ("Law of Mor"). This is according to quatrain XCV: III of Nostradamus:

The law of Mor will gradually fade away.
Later another, considerably more enticing,
of Borysthen first will come to establish
Attractive law – (by its) *talents and language.*

We hope that by this, our book, we contribute to the creation of this Law.

The sacred *Veles Book* reflected the pre-history of Rus in the best way, having achieved its 20-millennial span. It appeared in the circumstances of an extraordinary ethnocultural impulse, which noted the Rusy-Slavs between the fall of Troy and the formation of the Scythians; it accompanied the creation of the Rusy state between Aratta and

Orissa, Arsania and Rus; it reappeared from inexistence in the 20th century of our modern era, at the cusp of epochs.

We have to raise and carry this banner! In the glory of Rus, to the pride of Slavs, for the strengthening of Indo-European peoples, for the sake of all mankind.

Suggested reading

1. B. I. Yatsenko, *The Veles Book. Translation and comments*, Kyiv, 1995, 2001.
2. S. I. Nalyvayko, *Secrets of Sanskrit Revealed*, Kyiv, 2000.
3. M. F. Slaboshpytsky, *From the voice of our Klio*. – Kyiv, 2000.
4. A. I. Asov, Atlant*eans, Arias, Slaviane: History and Belief*, Moscow, 2000.
5. Yu. Shilov, *The Veles Book and the actuality of ancient doctrines*, Kyiv, 2001.

---

[1] Vedic ancestor.

[2] The Ukrainian word for 'mountain' is 'гора' (pronounced 'hora').

[3] Aratta was the origin for Bharata, the early name for India, as recorded in the great historical book of the nation, *The Mahabharata* - which means Great Bharata/Aratta.

[4] In the original Russian edition, the author wrote '***Кий*** и Гора да *Хорив*' which translates as 'Kyi and Hora and *Khoryv*' (V. Krasnoholovets). However, the word 'Гора' (when not a name) also means 'mountain', and *Хорив* transliterates as Horeb. Note that in the Biblical Exodus Mount Horeb is referred to as "the mountain of God" (Exodus 3).

[5] cf. *History of Taron* by Zenon Glack, V-VI centuries? (V. Krasnoholovets).

[6] The Zaporozhian Cossacks were elite fighters; they were spiritual people with strong psychic powers. (V. Krasnoholovets).

[7] Visapur [Maharashtra, India] has a water well which local legend says was built by the Pandavas who fought the Kaurava tribe in the great battles described in *The Mahabharata.*

[8] The distinction between existence and non-existence is not quite the same as that between life and death since where there is a soul that transcends death, there can be no meaning to non-existence.

[9] Compare 'omyr' with the homonymic Ancient Greek narrator Homer (Ὅμηρος, Hómēros). Thus, Boh*omyr* literally means 'narrator of God'.

[10] Kvasura. In most countries east of the Carpathians, Kvass has been the number one thirst-quenching drink for more than 1000 years. Its malty-fruity flavour makes Kvass a unique refreshment experience. It is all natural and according to Slavic folklore, Kvass can cure most known ailments. The Kvas-wagons are still a ubiquitous feature of most street-corners across Ukraine and Russia.

[11] In the original Russian text the author writes "Матери-нашей-С(о)вы-Славы", transliterated as "Materi-nashyei-S(o)vy-Slavy" - thus equating our-Matyr-Sva with our-Mother-Owl. ('Slavy' means Glorious, not to be confused with 'Славистик' ('Slavistik') meaning Slavonic/Slavic).

[12] The author explores the "scientific insight into that superhuman reality" in the third part of his trilogy of which the present volume is Part I only. Part II, *The Vedantic Heritage of Ukraine*, and Part III, *Cosmic Secrets of Kurhans* are presently only available in the original Russian edition, under the title *Origins of Slavic Civilisation,* 2008, Moscow. ISBN: 978-5-98967-006-0.

CONCLUSION AND OUTLOOKS

To the Reader:

This book belongs to the genre of conceptual science since its format is based on a course of lectures that may be termed popular-science. However, in order to affirm its scientific status, the conclusion is now presented in the spirit of a monograph rather than as a popularised account of the book. Here, we proceed systematically along the chronology of facts – dealing not only those that are well known but also those that are rarely drawn upon. We also include facts that have been completely covered-up by the 'official science' that is directed more towards compliance with State orders than towards seeking the Truth - facts that have been restricted whether they are Biblical, historical-materialistic, democratic or of any other doctrine. That doctrinaire approach, unlike (true) Science, does not support those concepts where *descriptive* and analytical genres dominate, and its supremacy has already become a habit in the treatment and evaluation of factual information. We now have to take account of this and that is why I have summarised this book in a "strictly scientific" form, giving references [in square brackets] to all the research that is cited at the end of the chapter.

So, let us proceed...

THE ORIGINS, STATUS AND FUTURE OF SLAVIC STUDIES

In the historiography of this theme, two directions were taken which, although partly complimentary, are generally opposed. The self-educated historian, Yu. P. Mirolyubov, formulated this dualism as follows: "It is necessary to listen to the opinion of the people, rather than to the fabrications of scientists" [30, p. 49]. In academic science, this duality is most clearly indicated in the following monograph, *Paganism of the Ancient Slavs* by the outstanding archaeologist, historian and ethnologist, B. A. Rybakov [45]. In that work, he shows the priority of the ***historical memory of the people*** preserved in their lifestyle, customs, language, folklore, ornamentation, characters and monuments over the *official writings* which have been dominated by and subjected to, ideological changes. The essence of their opposition amounts to the fact that *the first is rooted in the* communal society of aboriginal times whereas the *second does not go beyond the realm of the* totalitarian formations of the last five millennia.

Contrary to prevailing opinion, that the formation of the Slavic ethnoculture began from the middle of the 2nd millennium BCE with the Tshinets archaeological culture and the Skoloty [47] or from the 1st millennium CE [18; 54, p. 117-119], Rybakov reasoned that, "relicts discovered in the ethnographic material were associated with the belief systems of the hunters of the Palaeolithic (...), of the Mesolithic (...), of the first farmers of the Eneolithic, and of many of those who followed closer to our time. The depth of popular memory turned out to be very significant"; relict memories of mammoths that had become extinct in Europe about 12 millennia ago had been preserved by Slavs [45, p. 754 et al.]. *The Veles Book,* which was completed about 879 CE, dates the historical memory of Slavs from the glacial periods of 20,000 years ago, indicating myths of the Kyiv Region from 198 centuries ago [14, p. 13-14]. However, neither Professor Rybakov nor any other reputable scholars writing at the end of the 20th century chose to bring such specific popular historiography to their research since it had been stigmatised by totalitarian officialdom as being "fake", too far removed from the doctrine of "historical materialism" and from "the servants of the Lord".

Subsequently however, by developing their own methods, the archaeologists-ethnologists V. A. Safronov and N. A. Nikolaeva [40] came to the conclusion that the historical memory of the Slavs extended back to the Palaeolithic era. They expanded the origins of Slavic folklore out to the Black Sea area of Asia Minor, with this being the original homeland of the Pre-Indo-Europeans. In addition, the Sumerologist-linguist A. G. Kifishin [22] pointed out that both a mnemonical and a graphical method had been used to preserve the image of the Mammoth-Ishkur (Yashcher, according to Rybakov, or Iasi[1], according to Safronov and Nikolaeva). The method involved a subdivision of the established calendars and translation of the recently discovered proto-writing that began, if not together with, the pictorial art of *Homo sapiens sapiens* around 20 millennia ago. At that time, the extent of maximum glaciation in Europe drove people to follow and record the long-term changes: thus, chronicle writing originated to fix events, participants, places and dates [22, p. 534-550; 59, p. 335-357] (see Table XIII: 10-19). The reality of this is verified by the scholarly discipline of archaeo-astronomy which reveals the "domestic calendars" of ancient fables and myths and helps to compare folklore with images and other artefacts of the past [59; 64 et al.]. The world's earliest archive of Stone Grave in the Azov area, which has been scientifically recorded and dated to [active periods] 19th –12th – 3rd millennium BCE, is partially synchronous with [written] characters from Trypillia and concurrent with the archaeological cultures of Europe and Asia [22, p. 23-57; 35, p. 98-109; 50, p. 71-72], including inscriptions derived from the Catacomb and Srubna cultures [26, p. 49-52; 42, p. 94-99], and with the extension of traditional calendar-dedicative inscriptions from Troy up to the zenith of Kyivan Rus [22, p. 39-48; 72, p. 19-25]. Accordingly, the above named scientists, and even [the esteemed archaeologist] V. M. Danylenko [16], established a sound basis for researching the prehistory of Slavs and indeed the entire community of Indo-European people – a common root shared by the "civilised Hellenes" and their "barbarian environment".

The written language of Stone Grave, Trypillia and Vinca has already been acknowledged, with various reservations, by many researchers of this subject [16, 17, 22, 33, 35, 36, 42, 50, 68]. Over the last decade, discoveries at Stone Grave have shown that Indo-Aryan Sanskrit arose in the Northern Azov region [26, p. 49-52; 42, p. 94-99] in the mid-2nd millennium BCE. Its local context is close to the pre-ecclesiastical Glagolitic^ alphabet and *The Supoi Legend* of the keepers of Ukrainian Cossack customs [5; 75, p. 9-10; 77, p. 39-40]. However, the Sanskrit characters discovered in *The Veles Book* are closer to Runic characters [3]. This script is a 'Revelation' (even in the event of it having been significantly processed by Yu. P. Mirolyubov) and just like *The Veda Slovena*, the Indo-Aryan *Vedas*, the Irano-Aryan *Avesta* and the Icelandic *Edda* it was probably written down for the first time in the 1st millennium BCE. In this case, records hitherto considered (such as the oracles of India and Tibet), become secondary sources: the truly sacred texts were not written, but memorised. To these, in addition to those mentioned above, belong the Ukrainian *Tales of Zakharikha* [31] and Rusy heroic poems as well as a vast amount of folklore. Alongside them exist the multitude of synoptic records from Stone Grave and Troy, the sanctuaries and cemeteries of the Ruthenians, Rusy, Celts and others. That is why it is not surprising that the Byzantine-Bulgarian monk Constantine (afterwards Saint Cyril) indicated in *Panonnian Life* the existence of "Rusy-characters" which were so well developed that they were used for translations of Christian books even before "the creation of a script by Cyril and Methodius for backward Slavs".

In summarising all the above facts, it is necessary to acknowledge the accuracy of the ancient historians – Babylonian Berossus, Roman Pompeius Trogus and Byzantine Stephanus. They consistently regarded the books of Scythia as being the earliest in the world, that the Skoloty were the first civilised nation and that the Etruscans were Slavic people. Historians of the 15th – 19th centuries, i.e. the Italian M. Orbini, French P-C. Levesque and the Russians V. M. Tatishchev, M. V. Lomonosov, A. D. Chertkov et al, worked in a collaborative direction that was also supported by the autocrats Catherine II and Alexander II [3, p. 322; 52, p. 679-692]. In the wake of the assassination of the Russian Tsar Alexander II in 1881 there was a dramatic increase in the number of politicians and scientists who ignored the above-cited facts, deliberately severing the root of Slavic history and ethnoculture. It seems that Alexander II's patronage and identification with the Petersburg publication of *The Veda Slovena* was one of the significant reasons for his assassination. Only in the second half of the 20th century was this devastating process discontinued with the indicated publications of Yu. P. Mirolyubov, B. A. Rybakov and others. The officially recognised work of Professor Rybakov then opened the way for the innovative monographs of V. M. Danylenko [15-16], O. N. Trubachev [56-57], E. K. Chernysh [29], Yu. Shilov [61-66], M. Chmykhov [59] and others.

With the collapse of the USSR, the opposition, which had been evident 90 years before, intensified again. An example of this can be shown by the trouble caused over the discussion of Shilov's monograph, *Ancestral Homeland of the Aryans* [66; 76, p. 116-127]. A few days after its publication by the 'House of Scientists' publishing agency (Kyiv: SINTO, 1995), the author, Shilov, was falsely accused of unpaid debts, arrested, office property was seized and removed from the printing house, including part of a print run of "fascist composition" (these words are quoted from the judicial trial). That political persecution was supported by Shilov's colleagues from the Institute of Archaeology at the National Academy of Sciences of Ukraine. Leading scientists of the Institute of Archaeology headed by the Director of the Institute, Professor P. P. Tolochko, Vice President of N.A.S.U., presented their own version of the problem [of the ancestral homeland] in a collective monograph entitled *The Ethnic History of Ancient Ukraine* [54]. Despite Tolochko's co-authors and supporters quiet conclusions (made in the past by Rybakov, Danylenko and others) concerning the relationship of the Trypillian culture to Indo-European peoples and the ethnogenesis of Aryans and Slavs [15, p. 149-151; 16, p. 99-100], the opposition attempted to "pass off" the Trypillian culture as being Pre-Semitic [18, p. 84-91 > 54, p. 26 > 17, I, p. 526], ignoring the enormous quantity of factual ethnological data [17, I, p. 528 et al.] [74, p. 55-92] (see Tables XXIII-XXXVII). This was done not only by manipulating the sources and historiography, but also by making incorrect statements. Thus, from the singular evidence of thousands of anthropomorphous figurines (of Trypillia A-C, 4800-3000 BCE) that had heads of tortoises and birds [16, p. 44, 99-100], L. L. Zaliznyak and V. V. Otroshchenko concluded from "the large hooked noses of the Trypillians that they were distant pre-Semitic missionaries from the Middle East" [18, p. 85-86; 54, p. 26]. Reconstructions of the faces of Trypillian people were deliberately made, in the time of M. M. Gerasimov[2] [29, p. 222-223, Table III], so that their faces had a Semitic appearance and these were placed by N. B. Burdo and M. Yu. Videyko in the *Encyclopaedia of Trypillian Civilisation* [17, t. I, p. 474-475] which declared that "Aratta has nothing to do with our land" and that "Yu. Shilov is sculpting Aratta from the position of an ethnic Russian-internationalist" [54, p. 23].

At the same time, historical science of post-Soviet Russia introduced the other side of the same coin - that "the Black Sea area is the ancestral homeland of Semites and that the ancestral homeland of Slavs is in the Arctic". Responding to this, N. R. Guseva published an article *On the Fanciful and Real Aryans* (in the magazine *Heritage of Ancestors*, Ruspechat Ltd., Moscow, 1997, No. 4, 33) where she linked "Aratta – Trypillia (...) with the flowering of Ukrainian national-chauvinism", the leader of which, in this [particular] subject, is the "Ukrainian archaeologist Yu. Shilov". That article was published soon after the Minister of Education for Russia tried to exclude the teaching of history. When the "active intervention of a number of scientists helped to end this sabotage", Guseva, a doctor of historical sciences, together with her political adherents, started to seek a "new cradle-land for Russia other than Kyiv" in the tundra [25, p. 9-10]. However, Shilov's monograph *Ancestral Homeland of Aryans* (which pointed to the Ukrainian Dnipro area) became the banner of historical truth not only in domestic [i.e. Ukrainian] science but also in Russian science [25, p. 83, 368; 55; 56, p. 301 et al.]. B. A. Rybakov, Professor at the Russian Academy of Sciences, appealed to Ukrainian scientists with a call to anchor the discovery of the formation of the Indo-Aryan *Rigveda* to the banks of the Dnipro, saying "this will restore the connection between times", quoted by N. A. Kikeshev (from the introduction to Rybakov's book) in *Appeal to the Slavs*, Vseslavianskii Sobor, Moscow, 1998, p. 3.

The awareness of the truly significant position of modern Slavs in the history of mankind now becomes even the more urgent – not just for the repulsion of enemies but also for the fulfilment of their destiny by GOD (where 'god' from Slavic < Vedic BHAGA means '**happy fate**'). An examination of this mission is the objective of the concluding remarks of this book.

It is now necessary to emphasise some particular features of the methodology that I developed instead of using the obsolete methodology of 'historical materialism'. The weakest and most fatally-erroneous area of 'ist-mat' [i.e. Historical Materialism] is the identification of matter with its *material manifestations,* and the rejection of "idealism and religious relicts" (since their *field basis* had not yet been discovered by the physicists of Marxist-Leninist times). However, since the basis of culture is figurative-intuitive ("*mythological*") rather than logical-analytical ("*scientific*"), the 'ist-mat' approach disconnects researchers, and people in general, from the mode of '*auto-pilot*' [a cognitive state in which one acts without self-awareness] within the energy-information field of the Universe (i.e. science ≈ religion and Almighty-Omniscient GOD) [44; 77, p. 19-31]. That disconnecting approach separates the individual from an essence-based understanding of the fundamentals of culture, effectively locking historians and others (e.g. archaeologists, politicians and society) into a formal-material mode of consciousness, akin to 'steering on *manual pilot*'. We can understand therefore why the *Revelations* of sacred literature are closer to life-giving Truth than the scientific *monographs* which rationally attempt to dissect and thereby reduce it. Hence a change of approach to scientific sources is relevant and I propose a formula, represented below [77, p. 26-27] that I developed in the process of extending my researches into the field essence of the Universe and the removal of the contradictions of existence-nonexistence (including universal, natural, ethnic, social, educational factors and cultural elements in general):

	F	*F* –	[the material world]
	+ **Z** –		[reality]
+*E*	E		[the field essence]

[EXISTENCE ⟷ NON-EXISTENCE]

As represented here, the 'F' term tends towards the real manifestations of the material world and the 'E' term tends towards its field essence, "+" being the connection of reality with existence and "–" with the trend to non-existence. The '**Z**' term represents the content of Reality (from Ukrainian '**zmist'**, meaning '*content*'), which is created by the interaction of four designated forces of which +*E* to *F*– are the main trends for all phenomena. Their oppositions exist objectively and necessarily and the interaction of their polarities generates the space-time energy-information [field] of the Universe (see above for the convergence of Vedic and modern understanding of BHAGA-GOD as 'happy fate' [76, p. 276-281; 77, p. 19-31]). Consistent with the law of growth of asymmetries, the poles are unequal: thus existence (+) predominates over inexistence (–), i.e. the field essence (E) predominates over material form (F), and the regime +*E* predominates over *F*–. That is why the Worldwide system outlined by the formula is constantly dynamic: the strategic prevalence of +*E* coexists with periodic strengthening of the trend towards *F*–, i.e. to the "doomsday" state. The whole system pulsates and revolves with the resultant motions representing a conical spiral of existence and development... So, when the +*E* regime dominates unconditionally (which corresponds to the communal self-governing formations of history) "the heart of history" is compressed [i.e. strengthened] and "stands on its own two feet", and people live in resilient harmony; but in the *F*– regime (which corresponds to totalitarian formations) everything is contrary and the periods of world wars in the cause of finance and over farming, etc., can be considered as the greatest example of "humanity standing on its head with a decompressed [or weak] heart".

The formula represents a methodological framework for the objective analysis of any phenomena and processes.

Its subsystems +*E* and *F*– include both collaborative directions of historiography, outlined at the start of this chapter. We now move to its main part, presented in divisions that correlate with links in the historic memory of Slavs (from the unknown pre-ancestors of the upper Palaeolithic period to the well known tribes of the Middle Ages).

1. Upper Palaeolithic (…19th – 10th millennium BCE.)

With regard to the above mentioned 21,000 year remoteness of the historical memory of Slavs, it is now necessary to include additional data (see Table I). It is no accident that this date coincides with the maximum glacial advance as far as the mid-Dnipro Rapids, 20,000-17,000 years ago. Clearly, this specific circumstance became the primary reason for people to regularly monitor and record the flow of events and it marked the beginning of the druidic collection of written chronicles and fables [68, p. 145-148]. The proto-Sumerian archives of the 19th – 12th – 3rd millennium BCE at Stone Grave [22; 34] may be studied in the light of the Ukrainian fairy-tale *Hero Dymko and his brother-in-law Andrushka* [58] and also, perhaps, the less reliable *Tales of Zakharikha* [31, p.17]. In addition, there are memories of times hunting the Mammoth (Sura Lamie) in songs of *The Veda Slovena* [52, p. 218-357], which links its earliest mythology of Kalitsa-statehood with the main Vedic mythology of the Aryans:

God strikes Suria Lame,
who closed the gates (to the source)...
Snehynia angered God
as he asked the servant of Lightning
to fill the fields with snow...
The king sacrificed
a black bird to the Fire God,
so that it would bring bright fire from heaven,
let bright fire burn Suri Lame...

The Upper Palaeolithic was marked by the emergence of Paganism (meaning Communal Belief System in ancient-Rusian), in which the rudiments of future "world religions" were already evident. The ideogram of the earliest Creator-GOD – 'Ruler-of-Wind' Enlil (Slavic 'Lel', Hurrian 'Lelvan', Indo-Aryan 'Lilith' < Sumerian En.Lil; An 'Sky' > Biblical 'ELOHIM) – grew out of the sanctuaries of the Mammoth hunters of the 14th – 12th millenia BCE reaching from Mizyn and Stone Grave (Ukraine) as far as Las Monedas, Spain [22, p. 545, 826-827 et al.]. The Syllabarium of Stone Grave, makes it possible to embark upon the recovery of a **Pre-Slavic** vocabulary (see Tables XIII-XIV) during the period under discussion here, 12th – 7th millennium BCE [22, p. 658-659 et al.] Aside from *Lel*, this heritage is evident in the closeness of the words which designate 'man' (*pa-*) and 'woman' (*ma-*), and for 'smoke' (Rus. *dyma*) and 'house' (Rus. *doma*) although there is a slight difference in the last term between the notions of 'abode' and 'family'[3] [57 , I, p. 247-252].

2. **Mesolithic** (9th – 7th millennium BCE.)

The mammoths died out at the beginning of the Mesolithic epoch when elks then became the beasts of economy. Such light-footed prey led to the invention of the bow and to the breeding of dogs. The domestication of small animals also began. Together with the ancient lunar calendar there now emerged a zodiacal calendar with the central constellation in the form of a gigantic Deer (Greek ελαφος 'elafos' < Pre-Slavic ols > elk); however, the celestial picture is complicated by the addition of fawns (Ukr. 'olenyatko'), hunters, dogs, and the Milky Way, etc. [68, p. 149]. The "Palaeolithic Venus", the keeper of kin, was transformed into the hunter Divanna (Slavic < pre-Indo-European Div-Anu 'Celestial-Sky' in its male and female hypostasis; Inanna 'Mistress of Heaven', 'Venus' > Diana of the Etruscans and Rome) [9, p. 149-151; 13, p. 37] (see Table I:7). "In the depths of the hunting economy, perhaps as early as the Palaeolithic or Mesolithic era, the cult of vampires and Berehynia[4] appeared" – with whom the periodisation of pre-Christian Slavic beliefs began - as recorded in *Account of Pagan Idolatry* (12th century) [45, p. 24]. The earliest male gods of *The Veda Slovena* [52, p. 8-195, 360-369] are Kolyada, Yognitsa, and Vishna. Besides these images from folklore we also have a significant number of ornamental and more realistic images on hand-painted eggs, embroideries etc. (see Tables XV, XXIV-XXV). Numerous horned animals and dogs were featured in the ornamentation and form of figurines or on housewares of the Trypillian archaeological culture which served as an intermediate stage between Eurasian and Slavic details.

The most progressive culture in the Mesolithic epoch (with its achievements outlined above) was established by tribes of the Upper-Carpathian-Baltic region which archaeologists relate to the Svidertian culture and which linguists consider to be the carriers of the boreal or Eurasian language community [40, p. 238-306]. As a result of the population explosion and subsequent migration of "Svidertian-Eurasians" and their Mesolithic relatives who were settled in Europe, they reached as far as Altai and Sinai. This accounts for the similarity of names between the *Kets* of the Trans-Urals (who generally inhabited the valleys of the rivers *Khatanga, Kotui* and *Keta* of the modern Krasnoyarsk territory) and the *Khattians* of Asia Minor who survived, along with their descendants, as carriers of Sino-Caucasian and Indo-European language communities until the beginning of the New Era [21, p. 43-59; 40, p. 238-250 et al.].

So, one group of carriers of the Svidertian culture or its kin travelled along the northern coast of the Black Sea whilst another group travelled along the southern coast. The rulers of the former were concentrated in the Northern Azov area, having reunited with the custodians of the sanctuaries in the caves, grottoes and shelters of Stone Grave (the mound near the village of Mirny, Melitopol District, Zaporizhia Region). The second group, the Takhuny archaeological culture, became centred on a settlement near the village of Çatal Höyük (in Anatolia, Asia Minor). The next demographic explosion, brought about by the new economic achievements and an ecological catastrophe, forced the "Takhuny-Proto-Indo-Europeans" to seek land for resettlement with their already rather remote kinsmen of the Northern Black Sea area. After the corresponding contact between the priests of Stone Grave and Çatal Höyük in 7000-6200 BCE [16, p. 102-103; 22, p. 448-524] there stood, on the one hand, the tribes of the archetypal hunter gatherers and on the other, the earliest farmers and cattle breeders whose economic complexity was generated by the beginning of the Great Neolithic Revolution that was marked by the transition from an appropriating [hunter-gatherer] economy to a reproductive [agricultural] economy.

It was in these circumstances that the domestication of large animals began on the rich pastureland of the Dnipro area. The Palaeo-zoologist O. P. Zhuravlev [17, I, p. 152-168] discovered evidence of the initial domestication of the horse around 7650-7450 BCE in a Mesolithic settlement at Vyazivok (in the Poltava Region, on a promontory above the inflow of the Sliporod into the Sula River). Evidence of the earliest large cattle and domesticated animals, around 6600 BCE, was discovered in the settlement at Stone Grave [15, p. 125-131; 17, I, p. 510]. Linguist O. N. Trubachev rightly supposes that the domestication of cattle occurred at a stage of **Proto-Slavic** existence, prior to the appearance of the words *ox* and *cow* – when they were called 'alinia' (in the Russian dialect), which is similar to 'olenykha' ['female deer' in Russian-Ukrainian], and 'bull' (in Hattian) [57, I, p. 254, 272]. *The Veda Slovena* mentions the appearance of the pre-ancestor Ima (Hattian > Sumer, Ya.ama from the Transcaucasian outpost of Aratta [43, p. 211-219] > Yama in the Indo-Aryan *Rigveda*, which is reminiscent of Imu in the Slavic *Veles Book*) where he is described as a herdsman specifically cultivating large cattle [52, p. 361-365]. From here the GOD Vlas then commanded them. Later on he also became Volokh, Veles, Asura-Varuna and others [10, I, p. 209-213] but here he is Vlas < Ox-Ace [Rus./Ukr. Вол–*АС*/Віл-*АС* (transliterated as Vol-*AS*/Vil-*AS*)] < goat ('bocc' [voss] in Armenian, 'bus' [vus] in Tajikian > Greek βους, Latin. 'bos') – ag > až > as (which is the Indo-European root of words for the designation of small livestock [15, p.115-116, 125-126]; see the previous reference to the zodiacal Deer and alinia-cow).

In this case the Vedic Adžah of the Indo-Aryans supported the World Tree, and the Sumerian Abzu embodied the Celestial Stream, better known by the Greeks and other Indo-European nations as the Milky Way (Млечный Путь), which apparently owes its origin to the goat Amalthea (Амалфее), the nurse of Zeus. In this context Ima-'Gemini' (see the following reference to Berehynia) should also be understood as the constellation which headed the zodiac in 6680 BCE, subsequently transferring to Taurus in 4400 BCE. [59, p. 232 et al.]. In a Proto-Sumerian inscription of the 7th millennium BCE from the "Grotto of the Bull" (9/7) at Stone Grave, the following identities operated together [22, p. 657]: the legendary Mammoth (AM.SI^{5}), the 'Sky' Anu (AN), the "Goat and fate of Defeated Taurus", and the GOD Urash (URAŠ) who was the forerunner of Uranus (> Slavic Uray > Yuri [9, p. 550-553]) and grandfather of Zeus. Myths involving Oceanus and Pontus – as father and son of Uranus in the earliest Greek ideas about the Black Sea – should be compared with geological data from the postglacial basins (see Table I): the primary basin then having been divided into 3-4 inland seas (Lake Balkhash, the Aral, Caspian and Black Seas without the Azov).

Ima's instruction in agriculture will be considered later: *The Veda Slovena* presents the beginning of this agricultural sector as already being quite well developed. Findings show the precursors of barley and wheat existed in Asia Minor and its associated lands of the south-eastern "fertile crescent". In the Northern Azov area the earliest traces of cultivated cereals are dated between 6800-6300 BCE [17, I, p. 510]. Nevertheless the Slavic ethnoculture – together with the entire proto-, and maybe pre-Indo-European community – participated in this beginning which correlated with the above-mentioned origin and movements of the "Takhuny-Svidertians" or "Eurasian-Proto-Indo-Europeans". Names of the life-supporting <u>rye</u> [Ukrainian 'zhyta'] (Slavic 'zhyto' ← Greek ςιτος [sitos]← Prusian 'geits' ← Hattian 'kait', i.e. grain) and <u>barley</u> [Ukrainian 'zachmenya'] (Tadzhic 'džan' → Nepal 'diuvo' → Slavic 'zhito' < Sanskrit yávah, i.e. life) retain the echo of gathering and harvesting. This is consistent with the sanctity of a particular sheaf – the 'Baba' or, more often, the 'Didukh'^ (the Ukrainian 'Spirit' of the grandfathers) – the earliest examples of which were found by archaeologists in the Jericho-B primary Takhuny culture of the 8th millennium BCE. These didukhs represented a backbone made of "bunches of reeds or straw" (which later became symbols of Inanna[6]), which were coated with red clay and leaned against walls in the form of two symbolic 'family' groups, "each of which consisted of miniature figures of men, women and children" [40, p. 166-167]. The word <u>wheat</u> [Ukrainian *пшениця* 'pshenytsya'] is indicative of its selection from wild cereals (Tadzhic gandunam 'bluegrass' [пырей 'pyrey'] > gandum 'wheat' [пшеница 'pshenitsa'] > Indo-European 'gad-',and Ukrainian wheatgrass or couchgrass [пирій 'piríy'] → Lithuanian pūrai 'пшеница' [pshenitsa, i.e. wheat]) [15, p. 121-122]. The earliest images and dedications known in Europe concerning this subject are familiar to us in the "Grotto of the Bull" at Stone Grave. This composition comprises the bull-Taurus set against a background of calendar ploughing and field irrigation (see Table XXX: 15). Here, in the opinion of the Sumerologist-linguist A. G. Kifishin [22, p. 340-409 et al.], are the Proto-Sumerian phrases PA (meaning 'bough', 'baton' and 'elder'), PI ('mind'), še ('grain'), and Nin-a-zu ('Princess-seed-learn'; ziz 'wheat'). Thus the selective cultivation of wheat from the bluegrass is shown by *p*(-a,-i) *še ni*(na)*zu*, which means: "*the grain created by the mind of sages with the help of the Goddess of conception*". It is unlikely that formation of the name of this cereal had been based on 'pounded (porridge oats)' [Ukrainian 'kashi'] [57, I, p.258] or on 'food' [Ukrainian yizhi] [15, p. 122].

The antiquity of Proto-Indo-European culture is also revealed in the vocabulary associated with collecting, processing and consumption of cereals. The earliest words for the use of cereals in German, Etruscan and Chinese languages (not for the grain-growers and gatherers of pre-Indo-European times) mean "baked", 'oblational gift' (cleva) and 'rice grains' (gliep). The first two, later relative to the third, correlate with the Early Greek κλιβανος [kilvanos'][7] – "clay vessel to bake bread [Ukrainian 'khliba'" (> Slavic 'kolobok', a small round loaf) [36, p. 63-64; 57, I, p. 718 et al.]. The third meaning (which the first farmers of the Chinese Yangshao culture could have learned from the Arattan culture of Trypillia (see Table XLII: 10-22) tends towards the Slavic 'obilye', i.e. 'threshed (grain)' [Ukrainian 'obmolochennoe (zerno)'] > 'cereals, bread' [Ukrainian 'zlaky, khlib'] and 'well-being'. Since "pounding by a hand flail, known as the earliest method of threshing, was then partly displaced by the use of domestic cattle for threshing by means of trampling the sheaves" [57, I, p. 600], the idea of an "abundance of <u>threshed grain</u>-bread" could only have formed at the beginning of the reproductive economy in early Aratta (i.e. the Keresh, Boyan and Buh-Dniester archaeological cultures (see Tables II-III)). Here, and somewhat later (Cucuteni, Trypillia A), the vocabulary relates to the simplest processing and consumption of bread, prior to baking, viz.: "1. Breaking and grinding grains between stones – Slavic 'boršno': Ukrainian 'boroshno', i.e. 'bread-stuffs'; 2. Pounded in a mortar – Slavic 'ršeno', Rusian-Ukrainian psheno, Slavic 'tolkno'[38], i.e. millet; 3. Chaffing and crushing by manual grindstones (and other) mills – Slavic 'moka', Rusian-Ukrainian 'muka', i.e. flour;

(…) in general the Slavic 'kaša' (kasha) belongs here and means porridge in the most original sense of the word [pounded]" [57, I, p. 718-720 etc.]…

So, somewhere between 7000-6200 BCE, contact was made between the priests of Çatal Höyük and Stone Grave from, respectively, the southern and northern coasts of the Black Sea. The Great Neolithic Revolution with its profound change of economic management and division of labour in production and management, led to an unprecedented population explosion and immense overgrowth of settlements (> "proto-cities" of 3 to 14 hectares) before the prospect of *cities* (Slavic 'horod/hrad') became the primary manifestation of '*civilisation*' (Latin). This contact legitimised the advancement of the earliest farmers and cattle breeders of Asia Minor onto the fertile lands of the related hunter-gatherers of the Danube-Dnipro region. A reverse motion is traced, particularly in the spread of horse-breeding into Asia Minor from the Dnipro area (see above) from the inflows of the Rivers Konka[8], Kobilyachka and the like. Hence it is possible to derive an etymological line of the Slavic 'Kobyla'^ > Thracian 'Kabula' > Phrygian 'Kubela' and the Foremother 'Κυβέλη' [Cybele], or 'Mountain' who in ancient Crete was called "Lady of Horses" [36, p. 29-31; 57, II, p. 348-353].

The burial grounds of Zaporizhia show evidence of a tense co-existence between the carriers of the two cultures and two anthropological types: the local Palaeo-European and the alien East-Mediterranean. Thus there appeared a transformation from the proto- to pre-Indo-European community, in which the germination of the **Pre-Slavic** ethnoculture is traced [40, p. 220 et al.]. The key indicator of the beginning of not only this civilisation, but also of civilisation *per se*, common to all mankind, is the canonical image of Berehynia (giving birth to Gemini which headed the zodiac in 6680-4400 BCE), as depicted on Ukrainian decorated eggs. She herself is connected with a figure from temple 23/VII at **Çatal Höyük**, whose walls are covered with a duplicated copy of the first part of the original Chronicle text recorded at **Stone Grave** [22, p. 660-665] and also with subsequent Arattan ("Trypillian") images of ancient Scythian cultures [73, p. 120-121] (see Table XXIV). This copy is unique, being the earliest written agreement in the world between two nations (i.e. those descendants of the "Svidertian-Eurasians" of the northern-Carpathian region who had diverged in the Mesolithic epoch along the **northern** and **southern** coasts of the Black Sea), and it holds evidence for the germination of the **Indo-European** community arising from an original nucleus, which appeared in Aratta, the earliest world state. Its territory, according to A. G. Kifishin [22, p. 68-70], was based on the ceremonial 'Quadrangle' of Palaeolithic origin (the Aryan forerunner of the Vary and Scythians), whose socio-economic aspects become meaningful within its natural environment. The corners of this territory were located near the modern Ukrainian villages of Polunochne (Lviv Region), Poludenne (Cherkasy Region), Polutory (Ternopil Region) and Polumyate (Luhansk Region).

Apparently Berehynia became the protector of Aratta to whom reference has already been made. (Her name derives from the Slavic word 'berech′' meaning 'save', or from 'bereh' meaning 'protect' < Indo-European 'bhergh', i.e. storehouse, cache; > Sanskrit 'bharana', i.e. conserve. Slavs have retained up to the present day the memory of this symbol as a representation of the beginning of earthly civilisation. Ever since that time there has been the annual custom (in Ukraine) to commemorate the renewal of Velykden [Great Day] with hand-coloured eggs. The celebration of Velykden (at first, probably, Babski[9]) is similar to the Great Day of Sumer which also had the custom of exchanging painted eggs. Unfortunately, finds such as eggs, especially ancient ones, do not survive in the soil, although similar painted "churinga"^-stones are known to archaeologists. Ethnographers also know of "karukovani hand-painted eggs" – which typologically (and probably, also historically) preceded the painted eggs, including those in the style of Berehynia and in the earliest (Buh-Dniester, pre-Trypillian) ceramics [73, II-III, p. 25-26]. It is significant, that the author of the ecclesiastical *Account of Pagan Idolatry* (12th century), considered the first deities of the Slavs to be "vampires and Berehynias" [46, p. 755-756].

Evidence of the official 'civilised' appearance of Velykden [Great Day] with its hand-decorated eggs [pysanky^) and painted eggs [krashanky^] is found in the Testament of Rahman (< Vedic 'praying' Brahman) of Ukrainian legends) [74, p. 32-33]. Departing from the Blue Sea (Azov), the best of those pre-ancestors left a legacy to annually decorate eggs and throw their shells into the river at the end of Velykden, in order for them to sail across the sea to Rahman; "*Old people say: as people cease to write on eggs and "warm Grandfather", then the end of the world will come. Whilst eggs are written, while carollers stroll, then Rusy Faith will be in the world*".

3. Neolithic.

(Dating of the 'New Stone Age' differs across Slavic regions, varying between the 7th – 4th millennium BCE.)

At the end of approximately three million years of the "Stone Age" the Great Neolithic Revolution led not only to a change in the appropriating economy (hunting and gathering) and the reproductive economy (stock raising and agriculture) but also to other profound changes occurring in the communal culture of the tribes. The pioneers of the Great Neolithic Revolution in Eastern Europe became the carriers of the Buh-Dniester culture and from them, in 6400-5300 BCE, derived the Sursk-Dnipro archaeological culture [17, II, p. 72-73]. The ornamentation of their earliest ceramic housewares still persists on some Ukrainian decorated eggs [68, p. 49, 53]. Ceramic, a hard-burned clay material with various additives, became the first artificially-created material and the most massive expressive source for archaeological and ethnological research. Weaving also appeared at this time together with nets and canoes (see Table XXIX). The New Year [Springtime] 'Great Day' became 'Navski' ([derived from 'nava', i.e. the past] which means 'boat-vessel' and 'departed' in the languages of Slavs and other Indo-European nations. It originated specifically from the funeral rites of the carriers of the Dnipro-Donets culture of 5850 BCE – 4th millennium BCE). Characteristic images of catfish-like vishaps[10] and fish are interwoven with folklore motifs. (The "Black stone" of Khortytsia island has the features of a carp – the antediluvian primary living creature 'Sukhur' of Stone Grave and Sumerian mythology [22, p. 823 et al.; 34, p. 103-105]). The Kyiv legend of Lake Ovrut (a queen in a canoe and a golden reed that grew from the body of a drowned boy) corresponds to a legend in the Indo-Aryan Vedas and is reliably dated to the 5th millennium BCE. [14, p. 7-24].

The end of the Stone Age is commensurate with the time of an immense deluge in Europe (see Table I) where, as a consequence of the formation of the Bosphorus Strait, the level of the previously disconnected Pontis (Black Sea) rapidly rose by 160m and the northern coasts shifted by as much as 400km, forming the Maiotis (Sea of Azov). American geologists date this event to 5550 ± 20 BCE, but there are grounds for extending that date back to 6700 BCE [17, I, p. 510]. In the archive of Stone Grave, inscriptions from the 7th – 4th millennium BCE mention the "Sea" and "Marine Abyss" [and other more obscure details] [22, p. 671, 817]: "*For the court of water Dumuzi designated 40 asses (and) 40 of the best chariots. The best chariots were destined to carry the dead // to knowledge of [taken into] the Marine Abyss. Chariot-birds (were even mentioned in the Epic of) Gilgamesh (and) Abukuna – the ruler, having the Tree of the Bull*". Global science associates this Deluge with the floods described in the Sumerian 'Epic of Gilgamesh' and in the Bible. Hypotheses have also been expressed with regard to the sinking of Atlantis by a deluge in the basin that formed the Meotida [Sea of Azov] [3, p. 411; 78, r. 91-154]. This is where the Greeks placed mythical Hades – the 'impenetrable' kingdom of our pre-ancestors. Hence, it seems, the Hyperborean 'beyond-the-North' Zeus arose here as well as his consorts Metida [Metis] and Hera (cf. the River Herros-Molochna in the Azov area, above which stands Stone Grave). They were the daughters of Oceanus and Cronos, (respectively) the latter being the father of Zeus. From the limits of Hades (on the island of Eya at the entrance to the Cimmerian Bosphorus, i.e the Kerch strait) steered the greatest heroes of Hellas, i.e. the crew of the "Argo" (who even saw the kingdom of Atlantis) and the crew of the Odyssey [33]. Historic Greek legends placed Atlantis on the shore of Lake Triton, which was converted, as a consequence of the Deluge, into the Marmara Sea^. This accords with Russian (Muscovite) fairy-tales describing the Altyn-kingdom beyond the Blue Sea, giving grounds for a comparison between Atlant and Sviatohor [3, p. 208-212, 411].

Since Aratta was the core of the Indo-European community from its proto-stage, it offers a common origin for the mythological and chronicled similarities between Slavic and Greek histories (see Tables XIII-XIV, XXIV-XXVII). Today, the earliest historian in the world can be considered to have been Kaskisim (the 'Itinerant Ant') from Stone Grave (Location 25[11]) who in 6003 BCE founded a dynasty of rulers who were appropriate for editing his stone tablets several times and continued them into 4231-3452 BCE. Achilles, the Argonaut and hero of the Trojan War, was possibly a descendant of that dynasty [22, p. 252-257], from the kin of the Mirmex-'*Ants*', whose names are attached to locations at the entrance to the Meotida (Sea of Azov) en route to Stone Grave. According to L. I. Akimova, it was the priests of this sanctuary [1, p. 9, 22-23; 2, p. 270] who laid foundations for the mythologies of "Sumer, Egypt, Greece, Italy (...) Taurida, Colchis, the Caucasus and Hyperborean countries"; here "Slavs had their ancestral home on that *northern* territory, which then became the centre for the future 'history of Troy' ".

In the Neolithic epoch the zodiacal calendar began to assume its modern appearance (see Table XV) with the Deer and Gemini finally giving way to Taurus in 4400-1700 BCE [59, p. 232]. This change is reflected, in particular, in the numerous designs of ecclesiastical table linen (Orthodox, viz. Pravoslavny^, but not Christian) in the Arkhangel Province of Russia, which was settled by southern fugitives from the invading Mongol Horde in the 13th century. Following the summer solstice and religious Petrovka^ festivals they sacrificed bulls for general feasting, as narrated in the legend: "Earlier there came to our church two deer and it was said one should be taken for slaughter and the second was to be released, at liberty". On one of the table-linen designs was embroidered a calendar featuring the Goddess Oranta^ surrounded by two fawns, and beneath them is shown a pair of deer around an altar with a bull [45; 68, p. 143, 155-156]. The image for Gemini accords with the brother-and-sister first-ancestors; these motifs are united in the Ukrainian fairy-tale of *Princess Olenka and her brother Ivan*, which contains a complex of correspondences with the Indo-Aryan *Ramayana* [60, p. 30-32]. We find an even clearer complex in Crimea, where they are found together with the deification of *deer* in the Ramos tribe, in the locality of Dandaka; the pair are shown on the stela of an archer-GOD (Siva?) from Verkhniorichia along with a couple (Rama and Sita?) and struggling heroes (Rama and Ravan?) (see Table XXI: 6). In addition, in the *Ramayana* there is a description of the wedding custom of Svayamvara [an Indian folktale] (> Ukrainian svayba [a Ukrainian folktale] and Russian svad'ba [wedding]), concerning the match-making of a girl and boy, which goes back to the matriarchy of Aratta. It is similarly reflected in the Ukrainian song *Oh iziydy misiats...* [Oh, the Moon comes up...], in which the mother of the bride offers the rejected bridegroom a "black horse" rather than a garbuz (i.e. pumpkin) [68, 304-305]. This custom lived on beyond the time of the Amazons and still existed in Ukraine in the 18th century[12].

Aratta had taken root, though its name (Arita) in the *Veda Slovena* was now replaced by the naming of the state as Kalitsa (> Kolo 'Sun' and 'Circle', where both meanings indicate the importance of the relationship between the concentrically-circular layout of the city-states of Trypillia (see Tables XVI-XVIII), the characteristics of its calendaric ornamentation, and the periodic incineration and construction of its villages). The term is connected with the success of the Great Neolithic Revolution and can be derived from an analysis of the changes in systems of kinship of that period. According to studies by the linguist O. N. Trubachev [57, I, p. 249 et al.], from the times of the appropriating economy and the ancestral times of Indo-Europeans, the "overwhelming mass of names for parts of the body were formed from *gend*, from which the ancient *gends*, i.e. 'kin'", is formed. The subsequent transformation to a reproductive economy and the formation of the Indo-European community led to a change of terminology: "Kuel- which at this ancient stage behaves like another, technical term, meaning 'to spin', cf. the archaic kolo / koles- (Pre-Slavic basis in consonance) and the Lithuanian kaklas (kal-kl-as), i.e. 'neck'". The Sumerologist A. G. Kifishin [21, p. 66-67] came to the conclusion that since then the names of the Ukrainian cities Kalnev and Kolomyia preserve the significance of the '(sacred) bull' in the (proto) Hattian 'kal': (< *Kal-lam-ASU*, i.e. Bull-flame-God, meaning "Country under the guardianship of Taurus", etc.).

At Stone Grave there is the term *Kalam=un* meaning 'Country(Sumer)= people' [22, p. 61, 667, 822] from which can be derived such names as Kalitsa and Kaile-grad of *The Veda Slovena* [52, p. 370 et al.], Kolunekh, or Keloune of *The Veles Book* [8, boards 4-c, 19, 37-a] as well as its Hol(o)une (> the Greek city of Gelon mentioned by Herodotus, the "father of history" [12, IV, 108]). These notions are mutually interchangeable [8, board 17b]:

> *Our Kolune we left to enemies.*
> *And that Holune, being a circle, with great difficulties became the property of enemies.*
> *So we must place cities as a circle, just like our fathers...*

These concepts are unified by the semantics associated with the Ukrainian 'kolo': the 'sun', 'circle', 'congregations', and 'communities'. Also connected with these ideas of the circle is the most frequently mentioned GOD of *The Veda Slovena* [52, p. 8-195], Kolyada (< Kola Diy, i.e. 'GOD Kola', the calendar^-zodiacal 'Circle' > Kolody). But *The Veles Book* harks back to the onset of statehood 10,000 years ago, when "*we settled our cities by cup, fire playing around*" [8, board 2-b], which accords with the custom of the Trypillian culture to lay out cities in concentric cities and periodically renew them by burning the old ones [17, I, p. 316-320, 419]. Perhaps in this connection the prayer of the settler "fire-people" was composed for the Indo-European "*Patar Dyeus* so that he would extinguish the fire which Matyr-Sva-Slava (i.e. mother-owl-glory) brought on wings to our forefathers" [8, board 19]. The origins of this mythology are described in *The Veda Slovena* [52, p. 368-371]: it involved a fire sacrifice to Surya Agni^ which was employed on the field of "Kalitsa White-town"; the GOD Yognitsa, who "burns fire on that field"; the divine "mothers and girls" of the matriarchal state, and the first man Ima.

It is relevant to mention here the linguistic correspondences between Slavic-Ukrainian terminology for construction and destruction [22, p. 681-696; 36, p. 31-33, 62-63]: the realities of Trypillia and Kalitsa are reflected in the following Aratto-Sumerian terms:

ki meaning 'land, place, city' (> kèš 'city K(i)esh' > Cossack *kosh,* 'camp');
kisal-bar meaning 'outside yard' (> *kosh zala y dvir,* 'camp and courtyard');
bàd meaning 'strengthening' (> *budynok,* 'house, building');
dù, dím meaning 'to build, to plant' (> *dim*, 'home, house');
éš-hal meaning 'sanctuary of sacraments'(> *tse zala,* 'this hall');
uru meaning 'city' (> *uryte* 'dug in') meaning 'city' (< basis of Ur);
LAM-KUR (-ru) meaning 'Aratta';
lam-ma (-ta) meaning 'from Aratta (- fire)'(> *lamaty*, to destroy by incineration);
kára meaning 'to burn' (> *kara,* 'punishment') ;
gibil meaning 'fiery, new; to renew by fire'(> *(za)hybel,* 'death') .

The tradition of periodic incineration-reconstruction associated with Trypillian settlements is traced in temples of Sumer and Troy I-III and with the Slavs – in the self-immolation of old believers, ancient things and festive effigies. The arrangement of houses and villages doomed to destruction are mentioned in *Poem of the Sea* by O. Dovzhenko, *Farewell to Matera* by V. Rasputin, and *Overturned Soil* by M. Sholokhova.

Based on A. G. Kifishin's research of Ukrainian place names, it can be stated that the "Proto-Sumerians first lived on the Volyn-Podolian and Pre-Dnipro hills from where they were dislodged by proto-Hattians into the Black Sea steppe, after which the Trypillian culture began to develop". Those names, just like the preceding Buh-Dniester local cultures of Proto-Sumerian provenance, "gained a Proto-Slavic 'interpretation' in the 3rd – 2nd millennium BCE" [21, p. 66-70] (see Table II-IX). Along with translations of hitherto existing settlements bearing Proto-Sumerian names, several were transformed under Slavic influence: Urych, Urozh, etc., and "in Transcarpathia, Lahash[13], Ur and Uruk stand aligned and come forward in ritual bond, just as they did later in Sumer" [21, p. 88]. Much the same can be said with regard to many elements of ceremonies, ornamentation and everyday life of Carpathian Ukrainians (see Tables XVII, XXXVII). The considerable *Trypillian Dictionary of Ukrainian Language* was compiled from pre-Indo-European, Hattian and Sumerian roots by Yu. L. Mosenkis [36]; this vocabulary [see also 15 and 50] and the dictionary of Stone Grave [22, p. 681-696] can be related to the language of Aratta and the neighbouring tribes of that time [66, p. 614-622; 73, p. 27-34] (see Table XIII).

4. Eneolithic^, or Copper-Stone Age.

(5400-2200 BCE, according to the latest dating of Trypillia.)

According to B. A. Rybakov's interpretation of the manuscript *Account of Pagan Idolatry* [45, p. 11-30; 46, p. 755-756], after the time of the previously mentioned Berehynia, and together with the advent of agriculture, "Slavs began to offer food to [the god] Rod and to birth-mothers". These were features of the archaeological cultures of the Trypillian circle. Ipatiev's continuation[14] from *The Tale of Bygone Years* (1114 CE) draws on traditional knowledge of the Rusychi [i.e. Rusy] that "they fought with clubs and stones" until "in the time of his reign [i.e. god Svaroh], tongs fell from heaven and the forging of weapons began" [45, p. 9-10; 59, p. 181-183].

In Eastern Europe, researchers connect the Trypillian culture with the beginning of the epoch of copper and other metals [17, I, p. 220-260]. This culture which appeared in 7000-6200 BCE represents the apotheosis of the most ancient State of Aratta [17, II-supplement, p. 45-47; 74 et al.] (see Tables III-V). In this case "with Trypillia in the east and Tordas in the west, these plough-based agrarian farming cultures were, indisputably, the nucleus of the Indo-European area which completely dominated ethno-historical development in Europe for no less than five centuries" [15, p. 130-131]. Here for the first time, there is a connection between plough-based agriculture which boosted the production of ploughshares (see Table XXX), i.e. "plough – *cuprum* < *curpum*, etc.", and metallurgy (Sumerian 'urudu', Latin 'raudus' meaning 'ore, lump of copper' > 'aeris' meaning 'metal, copper, [bronze]', Slavic mědь < Hattian-Hittite 'miti' – 'red' > Greek 'μεταλλεα' [metallea] 'mine') [15, p. 109; 36, p. 44]. This historically preceded the Slavic *sapa* and *sokha* (< soh-) [hoe, sap] which originate from *suk* [bough] and *sokhaty* [elk], whose antlers are found as farm implements in Trypillia [17, I, p. 136-138]. At that time horns were identified with the sacred sag-'head' of Taurus (both for the Proto-Sumerians at Stone Grave and for the Trypillians with their "horned thrones"). The Ukrainian New Year ceremony of "seed sowing", accompanied by the chorus of "be sown and thrive, rye, wheat and every grain", preserves the tradition of Aratta-"Trypillia" being central for the emergence of wheat, arable implements, and ploughed land. Only then, and only from Aratta of the Danube-Dnipro area, could the similarity between the agricultural terminology of Ukraine, Sumer and India have emerged, including such words as: (Sumerian) abba [father], nana [ancestral mother], bara[15] [royal prince or king], hari, dim [create]; (Sanskrit) bap [father], amba [mother of all], vira[16] [hero], ariya [devoted], dhama [Lord's abode]; (Ukrainian) bat'ko [father], nenya [mother], vira [faith], harny [nice, beautiful], dim [home]; (Russian) papa [father], mama [mother], vera [faith], krasivy [beautiful], dom [house], – and many others [68, p. 162-163].

Later, under the influence of Aratta's missionary-priests (carriers of the Lower-Mykhaylivka, Usativ, and Kemi Oba archaeological cultures), the formation of Aryan culture developed from the Sursk-Dnipro, Dnipro-Donets, and Seredny Stoh cultures that were already established in 5850-5300 BCE (see Tables II-III, V). Due to the interactions of both the early Seredny Stoh and the developed Dnipro-Donets cultures with the Lower-Mykhaylivka or even Trypillian cultures, the onset of this process in the first half of the 5th millennium BCE is found in the appearance of ceremonial kurhans e.g. Tsehelnia, Stovbuvata Grave, and Kormylytsia near the upper reaches of the Dnipro rapids (see Table XXXVIII), in the Kobilyachka valley (where the appearance of horse-riders has already been mentioned). The basic mythology of the *Rigveda* had already appeared there in the pre-kurhan sanctuaries, i.e. the creation myth of the New Year embryo universe, Vala, protected by the serpent Vritra and freed by the hero Indra and the creator-GOD Vishnu [27; 51, p. 81-82, 112-115; 66, p. 691-694 et al.]. This theme was probably introduced from the ceremonies and rituals of Aratta-"Trypillia" (see Table XXXVIII-XL). *The Veda Slovena* reveals the text source [52, p. 62-87 et al.] for the mythology, transformed by the authors of the *Rigveda*. In the beginning GOD-Vishnu reigned, protecting the birth of God-Koleda on the *Kharapska zeme* ('kurhanian land'). The birth of Koliada^ is described thus:

On the face of the clear sun,
In the year of the Star book (…)
The Clear book[17] *is gold-plated,*

Koleda we are Defne,
Defne, Previta,
Previta, Arita,

Faf[18] *book is a clear song:*
We are near Kola, near Koleda,
Arita, Denita,
Denita, Apita".

The difficulties of Koliada's birth are stressed in another song, brought on by the outrage of *arny* and *afitsi* (boys and girls) who, not having been brought up in the tradition of Kola-Arita, decided to bathe in the holy Danube spring (i.e. in the Danube at the holiday of Idra). (Here, *arii*-parii and *afitsi* became the modern terms *parni, parubky* and *devitsy, divchata* [in Ukraine and Russia respectively] for young men and maidens, derived from Aratta). Wrathful Vishnu appealed to Siva (> Shiva > Sieva, the son of forefather Bohomyr from *The Veles Book*) requesting a thunder stone, which GOD [Vishnu] intended to hurl at the field near the unrighteous – so that the ground would open up and the withering snake *Sura Lamie* would crawl out of the crack. However, the still unborn Koliada persuades GOD Vishnu not to punish unreasonably but to permit himself the possibility of teaching them. He does this, after being born. However, Vishnu vents his wrath on the "Kharapska beauty, Queen Kharapine" who decided "to cut off the golden head" of Koliada… and there are other such scenes. The noted opposition between the Arattans and Aryans relates to the way they are represented in the *Mahabharata* but as that was created by principally Aryan authors it therefore presents Aratta in an unfavourable light [38, p. 42-57]. In *The Veda Slovena*, as we see, it is the other way round. However, it should be noted that the heroic pair, Indra and GOD Vishnu, who are characters of the Aryan *Rigveda* are also known in *The Veles Book* [board 6e]:

And now bright son Intra lives in darkness
and also we have our assistant Vishnu,
and in the old time there was our blessing.

A universal formula was given earlier in which the dominance of $+E$ for the communal civilisation of Aratta (see Tables IV-V, XVIII, XLII :11-22) corresponds to the "golden age" in the fables of the Indo-European people. In its culture a figurative-intuitive perception of the world prevailed which strongly connected people and society with the ("divine") foundation field of the Universe through the subconscious mind (see Tables XL-XLII). This regime of $+E$ is represented in the ornamentation of Trypillian ceramics. On almost all the dishes and on many of the figurines there are representations of the human archetypes of conception, embryo and birth. Amongst these archetypal symbols (i.e. of *nature*), the "yin-yang", "trident", and "Mother-Earth" are each more-or-less obviously associated with the calendars – lunar, zodiacal and solar, and their combinations [59, p. 346-347 et al.]. Hence, these are the reasons for the main Vedic mythology already outlined [27]. The combination of archetypes and calendars was most expressive in the compositions of "Mother-Earth and Father-Sky". The first corresponds to matriarchal Aratta (see Tables XXIV-XXV). The second is embodied in the thrones, named by archaeologists as the "*small horned armchair*". The "horns" of the earliest armchairs (up to 4400 BCE) were formed by the figurines of Gemini, and subsequently, by the actual horns of Taurus. Hence (from the 'arc' of the horns of the celestial luminaries and from "horned hearth stands" with similar symbols) the name, Taurus, of that time can apparently be traced to 'beautiful' Dug and Hurrian Dagi > Aryan Daksha [meaning] 'hot, southern, energetic, giving' and to Slavic Dazh(d)Boh, (i.e. from the Indo-European dah meaning 'burn' > Sumerian dug). [Here, it is necessary to know that the word for 'arc' in Ukrainian and Russian is 'дуга' ('duha/duga'].

The Veles Book and *The Supoi Legend* of Ukrainian Cossacks, written in the traditions of Arattan-Aryan Sanskrit and the Glagolitics of Orianian origin, indicate the involvement of (Pre-) Slavs from the very beginning of the circumscribed process of the deification of the bull-Taurus in Aratta [26, p. 49-52; 42, c. 326-339; 68, p. 20, 119-137, 211, 298]. In the first text, Dazhboh[19]-Taurus impregnates the cow-Earth [8; board 7f], and the second begins thus [75, p. 9]: "Once, in ancient times, Father Kolo and thunderstorm Mother Dazh-Earth gave birth during the night to vkrainski [Ukrainian] people. (…)". Here, in the names of Father and Mother, the earliest terms for the designation of civilisation and the place of Taurus are reversed, wherein "Mother Dazh-earth" preserved the matriarchal priority of "Foremother on the Throne". The antiquity of this tradition is confirmed by its domination of the lunar calendar and the 8-division zodiac that was later superseded by the 12-division solar zodiac around 2400 BCE [11, p. 207-208; 64, p. 285-288] (see Table XV). From that moment, the opportunity presented itself to represent Dazhboh (Svarozhych) as the look-alike-son of Svaroh [Slavic sky god] (< Vedic Suvar Agni, which means 'Golden Fire' of the solar zodiac), the supreme GOD of Slavic people [8, board 25]:

Thus our SVAROH said to Or:
"*Like my creations I created you from my fingers* (…)
Be like my children, and Dazhbo will be your Father (…)".

The origins of GOD Svaroh in Trypillia are marked by the proliferation of swastika-svarha[20] symbols, (see Tables XXXV-XXXVI), which are illustrative of Indo-European people. This Slavic god (< Persian baga- < Indo-Aryan bhágah: 'Lord, bearer of blessings', 'fate, happiness, wealth') is connected, as noted above, with the bull-Taurus. However its immediate origin is from the Indo-Aryan Bhága: 'Endower, Distributor' of blessings. Bhaga was one of the 6 (>12) main sons[21] of Foremother Aditi ('Eternal never-ending' cycle of years). In this sense, GOD [Svaroh] (boh ← boh-atъ, sъ-bož-ьje, according to Trubachev) primarily meant the zodiacal calendar of Taurus of the autumn equinox (when that constellation began to descend from its night zenith and became the Sumerian 'bukun', i.e. 'Prostrated Taurus') completing the favourable half-year with its harvest, etc. Aditi and her closest offspring in the Indo-Aryan *Rigveda* (derived from 'ryech vyedaty[22]' meaning 'knowledge of anthems') arose from the netherworldly "life forces" of Asur (see earlier reference to Vlas > Veles). However, they relate more to the 'radiant' celestial maidens (< Indo-European 'Sky-Father' Dyaus-Pitar, – Pytare Diaie of *The Veles Book* > Dii > Divas > Did [which means *grandfather* to Slavs], and Greek Dii > Dzeus > Ζεύς and others). Thus the contradiction of the night-and-day sky is resolved. Remember, the boundary period when the classes of Gods shifted from the lunar to solar calendar, which occurred around 2400 BCE, reinforced Svaroh as the Solar zodiac. This was apparently in accord with a change of the principal viziers at Stonehenge, High Grave and other Arattan sanctuary observatories (the kurhan-like maidans of Ukraine and India, and aidans of Persia) and of other Indo-European countries [11; 64] (see Tables XV-XIX).

In earlier times, Trypillia was the source of Asura-Varuna [45, p. 205-206] (< Arattan-Sumerian Urash [sky god], Pelasgian-Greek Uran > Slavic Urai > Jura and Varuna > Paruna > Perun [8, Boards 20, 31, 6-d, 4 et al.]) who, known as 'The Grumbler' and similar names, Lord of the night sky and netherworld, was the most formidable of all the sons of Foremother Aditi. In the Aryan kurhan of High Grave (at the village of Starosillia in the Velyko-Olexandrivsk district of the Kherson region [66, p. 695-696]) the family of Aditi was manifested through the calendars and images of Soma-'Moon' in mytho-ritual burials Nos. 3 & 4 of the Kemi Oba culture (who were brahmans of Arattan origin) in the first half of the 3rd millennium BCE. Perhaps the earliest solar zodiac is shown by the image of the Hurrian-Aryan-Slavic 'Sun'-Surya found in Starosillia's burial No. 8, dated between 2240-2230 BCE, (see Table XV: 9,15).

It can be established that the primarily Arattan names of the supreme POWER of the Universe, En > An > As ('Overlord' > 'Sky' > 'Taurus'), of the 7th – 4th millennium BCE, were eased out between 4400-2400 BCE by the terms Dii and Boh^, etc. It was towards the end of the first of these periods, in the environment of the earliest Aryans between the 6th – 5th millennium BCE, that kurhans appeared (< kurhals of *The Veles Book*; also called khorpi/horpy[23] etc. in *The Veda Slovena*). Their name originates from the epithet of Enlil – *Kur-Gal*[24] 'Great Mountain' – which is already familiar to us (i.e. from Stone Grave [кам'яна Могила, Kamyana Mohyla], which could be regarded as the prototype kurhan, and also the Ukrainian 'mohyl' [grave] < Proto-Sumerian Me-gal[25] 'Great Mission/predestination' > Albanian magulle, Romanian and Ukrainian magura > Greek μεγάρα(-ον), i.e. 'cave' or 'temple'). The appearance of the earliest kurhans of the state of Arián, not without the influence of missionaries from Aratta (see Tables XVI-XX, XXXVIII), can be traced to the formerly convenient crossings in the headstream Rapids of the Dnipro (i.e. near the modern cities of Kremenchuk, Komsomolsk and Svitlovodsk), on the boundary between the steppe and the forest-steppe. This is between the mouths of the Rivers Psel and Vorskla in the lower reaches of the River Kobilyachka (see the previous section on the Mesolithic). The names of these three rivers could have arisen in that time, revealing their pre-Indo-European roots and their Sumerian analogues [36, p. 14, 24-31, 50], akin with sources of Slavic ethnoculture, in the same way that the Red Hill Spring festival of *Lel* (< of *En-lil*; see above) usually takes place over a *kurhan* (< Kur-Gal) [8, board 7-a, 37-a; 10, vol. II: pp. 21-47]… Incidentally, it is specifically from the research of the earliest mounds at Komsomolsk [66, p. 623-625; 76, p. 261-281] that we have succeeded in understanding the astro-geo-biophysical field basis of the Vedas, GOD, and Immortality.

Having considered the bases of economy and faith of the period that interests us here, we shall continue with a consideration of Ima^ from *The Veda Slovena* [52, p. 364-391] (see Table XLI: 5).

In order to instruct Ima about agriculture (see Table XXXVIII: 13-15), GOD designated nine "malka momi [i.e. good-looking mothers] and girls" of whom the eldest was Iuda Samovila. This keeper of the Veda is directly comparable with the prophetess Sibyl (daughter of Zeus) of the Greeks and Romans who regarded her as the creator of nine sacred books [33, vol. II, p. 430-431]. She is comparable to Iuda ('yudol', 'dolia' [which in Ukrainian means 'fate'] < Tibetan 'yi-dam', meaning 'welcome GOD'; Yiuda < Slavic 'obo-jǫdu' 'oboyudno, (meaning mutually embrace)' <-jętьnъ 'yat, (obni)-mat', (to embrace)). She is also comparable to *Ida* (=Ila Indo-Aryan 'Íḷā' < Slavic 'idol'[26]), the Vedic Foremother of mankind, who arose from sacrificial food brought by Forefather Manu^ after the Deluge. Ida of the Pelasgians and Greeks (see Tables XXIV: 14, XXVI: 6, 11, 13) was the goddess of sacrifices, and the mountains named after her on Crete, and near Troy, were considered to be the birth-places and residences of Zeus as a child. His wife Metide [Metis] and the Meotida Sea have already been mentioned in connection with the Deluge. The name of his daughter Artemis (> Slavic Artemitii) can be understood as Ar(at)ti-m(at)-Ida. The earliest reliable image of "pre-Artemis" [16, p. 33, 99] is to be found on a stela from the Orianian (Arattan-Aryan) kurhan I-3 at the village of Usativ (in the Odessa region) (see Tables XXIV: 12, XXI: 16).

Ima was taught by the subordinate Iuda Samovila not only "to plough, sow seed, and reap white wheat", but also to knead dough and bake "pure bread as an offering to God". An early Trypillian sanctuary for baking ceremonial bread is being investigated by archaeologists in a settlement near the village of Sabatynivka (in the River Buh area); it corresponds to the Ukrainian custom of making bridal karavai [a special festive bread] [35, p. 143-147]. The horned throne was appointed, perhaps, for the karavai-making matchmaker, from whom the young pair "fenced by the Moon and tied by the dawn", inherit the Vedic (Aratto-Aryan) expression "svadkha!" which means "bless!" and was accompanied by a fire sacrifice to the celestial Gods. Several models of temples corresponding to Sumerian "birthing huts" and "houses of the Great GODDESS Ninhursag, Mother of all children" are also known, [17, I, p. 380-384; 33, II, p. 222] (see Table XVII). They contained grain shredders and dishes for washing and baking bread and there was also an oven and cross-shaped ('krestovidnyy') altar (the pair creating a "lexical family" based on kresaty in Slavic languages with the words 'vykresat' meaning 'to strike fire', 'tvorit' krasu' meaning 'to create beauty', 'voskresat' meaning 'to resurrect or resuscitate' [i.e. rise up], and 'krest'yane' meaning 'peasants' [57, I, p. 136-138]). This complex can be compared with a bakery and also with the popular custom of accepting delivery of newborn babies. After washing the babies, a Baba-[old woman]-midwife, (in essence, the village Foremother), immediately baptised[27] them ("so that those not already given to God would not die unbaptised"), coordinating their name with the parents and with the calendar. When a baby had grown a little, the priest in church simply asserted the previously held ceremony. The Arattan-"Trypillian" antiquity of this custom (see Tables XXV: 1-7; XXXIV) is indicated by the fable of the Cossack kin of Skulski (from the city of Mykolaiv) concerning the origins of the pre-Christian 'Spas' [i.e. Saviour], which agrees with the fore-mentioned datings and theories concerning the "malka momi" [good-looking mothers] and Dazhboh, as well as chakras and the others aspects of yoga: "(…) *The Science of the Great Spas is lost, only small Spasas remain: witchcraft, sorcery, incantations, and small "miracles" (...) That was related by your grandfather and my father, when on the steppe kurhan he "bound" me to the Sun (...)*

That was so that Malka could well cover Dazh, Radiance and body; a child has to be baptised, then it will be difficult for any creature to seize it to gnaw (…)" [77, p. 41].

After bringing sacrifice to the God Yognitsa, [according to the fable], Ima then went with the "mothers and girls" to Bel-hrad [White City] of holy Kalitsa. Here they celebrated the summer Masina Asunitsa, with every mother holding the Clear Book [28] in her hands. (In addition to the archive of Stone Grave, rather expressive inscriptions of that time are also known to science from the Danube-Dnipro Trypillians [35, p. 98-109] and related cultures of Central Europe [50, p. 71-72]: see Table XIII). The pre-ancestor Ima then climbed the Holy Mountain again, where "he appeased GOD-Vishnu", for which GOD gave him the "Clear Book" (which is also known to Persians and probably corresponds to the the Indo-Aryan *Yajur-Veda*^ – 'Knowledge of Sacrifices). Having promised Vishnu "to sing the Clear song", Ima returned in the Spring to the City and to his Goddesses with his precious gift. It is possible that the following Ukrainian carol appeared at that time:

From the visni[29]
God Vishni was born.
He descended to the ground,
He called us from the world.

The most widespread symbol of Vishnu in India to this day is the image of feet, and it was the same in other Indo-European countries, beginning from the Eneolithic period. In one location at Stone Grave[30] [Grotto 34a] V. N. Danylenko and others defined a feature called "Footprints on stone" as mapping the cult of Vishnu, while others make assumptions about his connection with agriculture [34, p. 108-109]. Along with images on stelae etc. in Aryan kurhans [66, p. 709-710, 723 et al.], the "foot of Vishnu" also exists amongst monuments of Aratta (see Tables XVIII: 1; XXI; XXXIX: 6,11). Particularly impressive is the foot-shaped layout of the largest city of the "Trypillian culture" situated between the modern villages of Talianky and *Vishnopol* in the Cherkasy region (Vedic 'protected by Vishnu' > Ukrainian 'Vishnu pole [field]') [17, II, p. 510-512; 66, p. 676]. Hence, through Arattan-Aryan-Ukrainian-Indian connections, there is a similarity between the Sanskrit *viš(s)i-grama* and the Ukrainian *vsieyu hromadoyu*[31], which means 'whole community', and also with the old-Rusian '*Vesi* i hrady' [which means *villages* and cities]. But *vishnu* [which means 'cherry' in Russian and Ukrainian] is possibly the "public tree of Vishnu", which would have been just as abundant in the gardens of Aratta as in villages of the Northern Black Sea area today.

The *Veda Slovena* also records details about a Spring festival at Kaile-grad – one of the cities related with 'Mace-bearing' Kyiv [37, p. 222-236]. Resettling from Aratta and its related surroundings, the Indo-European tribes in Europe (including the earliest Slavs) created about 60 settlements with similar names; also known are cities called Kyan in Sumer and Kyiv in Egypt. Even the ruling dynasties of Kyan and Keyanid existed between the mid 2nd – 1st millennium BCE in Khwarezm and Persia, and in Rus such a dynasty of Indo-European rulers existed until 862 CE [73, p. 111-115]).

By the law of Kalitsa, GOD established the Clear book. Iuda-Zhiva Samovila was taught that God came down from heaven to Earth, in order that she in turn, would teach the book to "*our good-looking ruler Ima (...), he is singing, he is writing*". And then our forefather went "to our villages and our koshes [settlements]" to teach …

... little children
to sing to the Clear book,
Clear book and Military,
Military and Stellar,
and Stellar and Earthly,
also Iuda,
let little children learn,
let them write the Golden Canon.

Upon that, they grew up to help ruler-Ima; from those children grew young voivodes^ – "the first reskitsa", 'the first Rus'. This term arose from the Vedic rajania or rasia (< Indo-European Tau(u)rus 'bull') – and it means to command a 'warrior-host'. In general the state of Aratta was led by Brahman-priests (> Ukrainian Rahmans). Their caste-'colour' was an aide to the *Kshatriya*-warriors, *Vaishia*-communal people and Sudra-rogues (i.e. those not accepted for any reason into the three main castes). From those times, there are a multitude of Arattan-Aryan surnames in the register lists of Ukrainian Cossacks of the 17th century: Rohmanenko, Koshovy, Vashchuk, Shudrenko, and also Krishnenko, Putrenko, Ranjida, Rudrimenko, Shekera, Reva, Balavir, Shamshur, Panikar, and others [23; 38, p. 185-310]. We also note here the appearance of complex features of the Cossacks that began to emerge since time immemorial, of the use of ochre in funeral rites, of horse-riders and of Indian clubs [maces] (see Tables XXIII, XXVIII; XXXIII). Particularly indicative are the "Zaporozhian oseledets [forelock]", of which the earliest manifestations are found on late-Trypillian figurines and skulls from burial grounds in the Odessa region [19; 73, p. 232]. It is here, in Oriana (see below), "based on the Greek system and concept of beauty, that the image of combed, orderly hair is reconstructed – κόσμος [kosmos] < Indo-European *kes-/kos-*» [57, I, p. 140] – from which the term '*kosak*' > '*Cossack*' was derived. The name 'Gosak' is known in inscriptions from 220-225 CE of ancient (S)Indica (subsequently the Tmutarakan principality of Rus and presently the modern Taman peninsula) [38, p. 83-89]. One of the covenants of the Cossacks states [5]: "Cut hair, retain a forelock to conform to the Parental Covenant: These are Kolo's solar brother-rays brought to the edge". We already know about the characteristic Kalitsa-Kola [culture] from *The Veda Slovena* where we find that male braids are mentioned [52, p. 120, 126, 338]:

A small child left the competition standing,
His braid plaited with gold.

There are few finds of human remains from the era of early Aratta-"Trypillia"; only some tens of skulls originate from kurhans and burial grounds of those times. Evidently, the majority of the dead were burned, floated away over water and scattered by the wind (as formerly practised in Bharata-India). Ceremonial cremation appeared in the burial grounds of the forest-steppe zone of Late Trypillia, which by then had become characteristic for the Indo-European peoples of pre-Christian Eurasia. Anthropological studies by S. P. Segeda et al. led to the following conclusions [17, I, p. 474-477] (see Table III): Men, principally of the "western variant of the ancient-Mediterranean type" of Çatal Höyük and the like, migrated from Asia Minor to their distant kinsmen in the Danube-Dnipro region. Similar migrations of men, thereafter militarised, are "well known in other early Indo-European societies" [20, p. 223]. The female part of the Indo-European population of the state of Aratta was principally of the local "proto-European" type, and remained a characteristic of the Seredny Stoh and subsequent archaeological cultures of neighbouring Arián. "Tribes, whose number at the zenith of the Cucuteni-Trypillia epoch could attain hundreds of thousands, played an important role in forming the gene pool of ancestors of the Ukrainian people – the autochthonous ethnic group of South Eastern Europe – whose physical features began to be formed long before the appearance of Slavdom in the historical arena" [17, I, p. 477].

Besides anthropological data, comparisons have accumulated instances of Arattan, Ukrainian and Romanian-Moldavian dwellings [17, t. I, p. 320-340], clothing and hairstyles [6, p. 50-93]. In addition, even "numerous ethnographic parallels to Trypillian ceremonial dances", songs [29, p. 250; 60, p. 121-252], and language have been investigated [36; 73, p. 68-71]. Thus, the previously mentioned [9, p. 149-151; 13, p. 37] Slavic Divanna (> Diva, Dana, Hanna Panna, Zhyva and Iva > I(Iu)van) is of Pre-Slavic origin, derived from the Arattan-Sumerian Goddess-*nenia*[32] Inanna (Ukrainian 'matusia', Russian 'nyanya'), as well as the Rusy-Etruscan Diana[33] with her companion Verbius [the woodland god]. Even to this day, branches of Russian/Ukrainian 'iva/verby' [willow] – the earliest of "world trees" or "Tree of Life" of the Indo-European peoples – decorate the skirts of Bulgarian women performing the Spring ceremonial dance of "Dodol". B. A. Rybakov [45, p. 187-209] noted the correspondence of this dance and its fineries to images on some Trypillian housewares (see Table XXV), and M. I. Chumarna and V. F. Mytsik [60; 35] considered the "Curve dance" and "Round dance" from the position of this culture with their ceremonial songs. The fragments that are presented here from The *Veda Slovena* also offer evidence about the relationship of Slavdom to Aratta and reflect its apotheosis with Trypillia (and to the cultures of Arita and Kalitsa).

In addition to the terms Kolomyia-Kalitsa-Kolun-Kolo (see Table XVIII,6), the Slavs also used three other terms to designate the world's most ancient pre-slaveholding civilisation . Closely related with the first, the second term [Tauro-] spread into the Ternopol, Kyiv and Cherkasy Regions, consistent with the mythologies of 'Bull-city' Tauropolisa of proto-Hattian origin [21, p. 67-68] (> Tauropolia festival of Artemis), and then to the ascendancy of Taurus in the calendars of 4400-1700 BCE [59, p. 232]. In these circumstances, the notion of the **state** could have emerged (< Indo-European guōu > Sumerian 'gud' [bull. ox. cattle]; Sanskrit 'gō' [bull/cow] > ancient-Rusy 'govyado' [beef]; Latin 'bos' [ox]): hence go(vyad) [beef] (Volu-A)SU meaning bestowing community, [or in modern parlance] "the community bring large horned cattle for sacrifice to the GOD-Taurus"**.** It was earlier, rather than later, that these two terms arose [i.e. Kolo- and Tauro-], from which *The Skupa legend* of the Ukrainian Cossacks emerged [77, p. 40]: "Our country was named Skupa Krayu [Land of Assembly/Gathering], as related by the word Slovo [which means Word i.e. a congress/a parliament/a place of speaking]; it arose about 5,190 years ago. It was populated by Chornukhi Derevlyani (Burned/blackened trees), a swarm of Cossack families – Kimy, Anty, Roxy (…) and with them – the Vkraintsi, because we lived in the land of their ancestors, amongst the graves of Saints. Skupa Vkrainska existed for thousands of years (…)". The words I have highlighted fit the realities of Aratta-"Trypillia", while the date mentioned indicates 3226 BCE (i.e. 5190-1964, since it was in 1964 that Cossack Chorny passed on the text to his grandson Bezkluby). We will shortly provide several more recent dates, indicating the time when Slavs became distinct from the Indo-European community of nations.

The [third] term, 'skupa' (< Ukrainian 'kupa' meaning 'group'), still exists in the Balkans where the Serbian term 'skupina' means 'group', 'skupa' means 'assembly' and 'Skupshtina' means 'Parliament'. In addition to these associations with 'Skupa Krayu' [see above], the Serbs called their country "Kraina"[34]. The above legend may have formed in the Cossack settlement of Berladi (up to the 12th century) in the lower reaches of the Danube [39]. 'Skupa' may also be derived from the Hittite 'Kurara(s)' < Hattian '*Kamamas*' > Hurrian 'Kuba(ba)' > Phrygian '*Kybele*' [36, p. 30-31, 34-36]. The Slavic '*Kupava*'-'Kupala' also belongs to these bisexual deities, gravitating to Gemini and the Foremother. The antiquity of their local roots in the Poltava region was indicated in connection with the onset of the domestication and veneration of horses (see Tables V:2; XXI: 3,6,11,16; XXXIII). "In Slavic, 'kobyla' [female horse] means transmission of fertility and vitality (notice that even the gender of this Slavic word is feminine), and the rudiments of this ritual practice can still be felt" [36, p. 31]. 'Kobyla' is associated with the Slavic *kob* meaning 'talisman, fortune, chance, augury and witchcraft' [57, I, p. 704-706], which is consistent with the concept underlying female and other Aratta-"Trypillia ceremonial figurines found with holes at the shoulders, as though meant to be suspended, like a charm or amulet. These figurines were manufactured in enormous quantities judging by the number found[35]" [17, II, p. 229-233 et al.].

A fourth linguistic term for the designation of 'urban' or 'civilisation' (a word which is etymologically Latin) arose later in the community of Aratta – this was derzhava (< Sanskrit 'dairghya-va', which means 'possess by an extended loan') [23, p. 147]. Here the beginning of a Sumerian type of totalitarianism is perceived, as well as the influence from the Aryan vicinity of Oriana (the Usativ version of later the Trypillia culture) [37, p. 142-152; 38, p. 42-57; 74, p. 37-48] which was the coastal part of Aratta in 3200-2650-2200 BCE. Apparently, at the same time, its northern pre-Dnipro part gained the name Borusia (> Greek Borysthenes [12, IV: 18, 53 et al.]). *The Veles Book* refers to both parts [8, boards 29, 31 et al.].

Oriana links together the beginnings of the ancient histories of Slavs and Greeks and their general ancient origin through Troy of Asia Minor (so named because of its *three* founding-tribes and its *tri*angular walls, etc.). According to A. G. Kifishin [22, p. 48], the culture of Troy II-IV "was differentiated from the Pre-Slavic culture from which it had grown and shared common roots (as indicated by their use of the same ceremonial calendar), but they evidently still used the Pre-Slavic form of ancient Proto-Sumerian letters". Researchers have found that the hill of Hissarlik had the remains of ten sequential hill forts of Troy and others [1-2]; those contemporary with late Aratta and early Oriana are as follows: 0 – a settlement of 3700-3400 BCE; I (2920-2450 BCE), II (2600-2450 BCE), and III (2390-2220 BCE). Settlements I-II were neighbours, whose differences are particularly noticeable in the adobe buildings of Troy-I and the wooden buildings of Troy-II; at the same time they were thoroughly burned – perhaps in accordance with the Arattan-"Trypillian" custom of deliberate incineration and reconstruction of villages. Troy-III was a poor recreation of the previous ones.

The Cossack legends [48] of Savur-grave^ or Savuryuga (Ukrainian < Sanskrit *suvar-yuga*), appeared no later than 3102 BCE (which according to Vedic tradition marked the end of the 'Golden Age'). The image of a buried rider – the Heroic first-ancestor conquering the intrigues of his own sister and her beloved serpent – indicates the boundary between matriarchy and patriarchy that is most characteristic of Oriana. The Ukrainian hero Bohatyr (< Indo-Aryan Balga-tur 'Radiant mountain' [56, p. 230-231]) coincides with the mythical heroes Sviatohor and "Tarkh Tarakhovich on Mount Siyansky[36]" mentioned in a Russian bylina [heroic poem] [46, p. 45 et al.]. The latter, who co-existed with the Amazons and, perhaps, with Queen Targitao of Meotidian ancient times, was the successor of Targitai, the first-ancestor of the Skoloty, as well as Apollo-Thargeli (see below). Both of the named ethnic groups are related to the Scythian-Aroteres ('Oratanians'), direct successors of Aratta, and through Arián, the rider from Savuryuga was the successor of the Saviour Gandkharva (> Greek Centaur > Slavic Kitovras) – a mythology which emerged with the spread of the earliest horsemen [15, p. 87-106; 65; [68, p. 323-334, 569-573]. Gandkhava was the forerunner of *Cossack Mamai, the righteous soul* (but without the cross), who was a "popular icon" of pre-Christian origin [39; 73] (see Table XXXIII).

Pointing to the year 3099 of the Christian-Byzantine chronology (i.e. 2591 BCE), *Chronicler Mazurinsky* described this legend [3, p. 43]: "The Slovenes and the Rusy went with their kin from the Pontis Euxine (Black Sea) away from their clan and their brothers and wandered in various countries, like winding eagles". It is unlikely chance that this date just happens to coincide with the demise of Oriana (around 2650-2200 BCE) and the beginning of Troy-II (2600 B.C), and with the names of the patriarchs, spouses and younger son of forefather Bohomyr from *The Veles Book,* who are also connected with the end of the Trojan War [8, boards 9a, 10; 72, p. 82-84]. Similar writings and calendar were preserved by the Celts, relatives of the Skoloty-Slavs, and the authors of *The Veles Book* were aware of this [8, board 28 et al.]. The years 2910-2951 of the "unknown chronology" of Celtic Dan (five centuries before the Byzantine chronology) correspond to the time of Troy-II, i.e. not to some strange Slav name of a hero but to the Danai-Greeks of the subsequent Trojan War. The chronicled words to which I have drawn attention can be understood as the final dissociation of the Slavic ethnoculture from the mother community of Aryan peoples. This is indicated by the belief in the tandem supreme deities of the Slavic world, Svaroh and Dazhboh-Svarozhych, with [their] obvious Indo-European basis. As established above, their roots grew in Aratta and are traced from the beginning of the Trypillian archaeological culture (5400-4600 BCE). However, reflecting on the solar zodiac (rooted about 2400 BCE) and the superiority of its constellation of Taurus (4400-1700 BCE), such a belief could only have taken root around 2400-1700 BCE (see Tables XV, XXXI).

Summing up all the above mentioned dates and arguments, we come to the following conclusion: **the beginning of Slavic ethnoculture from the ethnogenetic chain of their early pre-proto-ancestors goes back to 2600-2400 BCE.** This coincided with the end of the Trypillian archaeological culture and other cultures which derived from it, viz. Usativ, Lukashivka and Sofiivka (see Tables IV:VI), and their transformation into the Mid-Dnipro, Ingul, Multi-roller Ware/Corded Ware^ and Tshinets cultures – the latter culture is acknowledged by most archaeologists as Pre-Slavic. The above-mentioned period expresses the national character of Oriana, Borusia and also, evidently, the (G)Eneti (who are identified as migrants from the north-eastern Azov area into Lydia in Asia Minor, from the 18th century BCE). In the opinion of B. A. Rybakov and others concerning the transition from the Pre-Slavic to the Slavic stage of ethnogenesis, the true onset of Slavdom occurred in the environment of the Tshinets culture and later Skoloty culture during "the times of the Greek argonauts and classical Hellas" [47, p. 10], i.e. in the 8th – 5th centuries BCE (see Tables VII-IX). However, in contrast, but consistent with *The Skupa Legend* and the traditions of Savur-grave, the threshold of this origin goes back to the beginning of Trypillia C-II and Sumer, to approximately 3300 BCE.

5. Bronze Age.

(2,200-1,020 BCE, between the end of the wars of the "peoples of the North" with Sumer-Akkad, and Dorians with Achaeans of Troy.)

Pre-Indo-European Sumer originated as a result of the Deluge (either in 5550 or 3300 BCE), spread its influence to Egypt [34, p. 38; 43; 74; 78, r. 112-114], and "Trypillian" Aratta faded away along with the seizure of Sumer by the semitic dynasty of Akkad. At the end of 2400 BCE this event extended as far as the right bank of the Dnipro, as reflected in kurhans at the village of Starosillia with the appearance of the Hurrian culture (a Starosillian type Alazan-Bedensk culture) amongst the circle of Arattan-Aryan archaeological cultures [50, p. 205-217; 66, p. 616, 681-685, 695-696 et al.] (see Table XV: 9-15). The formation of the Aryan-Hurrian union, carriers of the Yamna and Starosillia cultures, can be traced in the lower reaches of the Dnipro and by their migrational movements into Northern Mesopotamia and back (see Tables V-VI). The completion of this campaign around 2200 BCE is marked, on the one hand, by the assertion and codification of *The Epic of Gilgamesh* in the Sumerian-Akkadian or early Babylonian empire, and on the other hand, by its manifestation in the burial implements of the Catacomb culture near Stone Grave [66, p. 713] (see Table XXXII: 6). It is also indicated by the joint construction of a fortress above the Dnipro crossing (at the village of Mykhaylivka in the Novo-Vorontsovky district of the Kherson region [42, p. 42-43]). Thereby, the foundation of the future state of Mitanni was laid, which then moved into the area of Mesopotamia taken over by the migrants [56, p. 253-254; 68, p. 92-95]. Around 1700 BCE there was a new campaign by the Hyksos ('horse-men' from the shores of Hypanis of future Scythia?, cf. Greek Ἰξῖων [Ixion^], father of centaurs) who took over Egypt, bringing their horses and chariots (see Table VI) and their alphabet (which first appeared in the Steppe of the Dnipro area between the 3rd – 2nd millennium BCE), together with Khyan^, founder of the 15th dynasty of pharaohs [see: 42, p. 59-61, 79-86, 94-99 et al.].

The events as presented exemplify the appearance in ancient legends of Scythian invasions along the Tanais (River Don), and of Skolopit (father of the Skoloty) going into Egypt during the times of the 12th Dynasty (2000-1785 BCE) until the birth of Tezeya (13th century BCE), – whereas two subsequent, well known Cimmerian invasions (Scythian, according to Herodotus) only took place in the 7th century BCE [20, p. 208-244]. As we see, from Pompeius Trogus, Diodorus Siculus and other authors of voluminous compositions on worldwide history, there were grounds for maintaining the dispute concerning the victory of the Skoloty (> Sklavs > Slavs-Oratas < Aroteres < Arattans) over the Egyptians and over which nation founded the earliest civilisation.

The remark made above about the alphabet requires a detailed explanation (see Tables XII-XIV). Having deciphered the well-known earliest chronicle of Stone Grave, 19th – 12th – 3rd millennium BCE, at the town of Melitopol (which contains, in particular, the mythology of the Trojan circle [34, p. 131-137; 67 et al.]), Kifishin came to the conclusion that until 2600-2000 BCE Troy continued to use Proto-Sumerian letters, as did its Pre-Slavic relations [22, p. 48]. Furthermore, a tentative dotted line is traced from the earliest chronicler known to science, Kas-Kisim (the 'Itinerant Ant'), from Stone Grave in 6003 BCE up to, in subsequent years, the Trojan-Argonaut Achilles from the kin of the Myrmidons^-'Ants' [22, p. 252-257] whose names were used to designate districts at the entrance to the Meotida (the Sea of Azov, beyond which stands Stone Grave). This hypothesis can be supported by interpreting the sequence of a multitude of additional facts. Thus, according to Palaephatus, the value of the Golden Fleece lay in the fact that it was "a book written on skins" [4, p. 109-110]. In the 2nd millennium BCE this fleece was the objective of the wandering crew of the "Argo" on the island of Eya (before the Meotida; the Caucasian Colchis was included in a later legend). Apparently, the guardian of this book – regarded as the earliest Holy Scripture in the world (which the Babylonian historian Berossus also believed was located in Scythia) – was considered by the Greeks, and after them the Romans, to be the Trojan priestess Sibyl [33, II, p. 430-431], an undoubted believer of Samovila of *The Veda Slovena* [52, p. 388, 670-671 et al.]. Moreover the most sacred shrine of the Greek-migrants of Chersonese was the originally local ΣΑΣΤΗΡΑ [SASTIRA] – 'Divine Book' in translation from Sanskrit [56, p. 103-105, 271-272] (see Table XI: 1). Its earliest, pre-Indian inscriptions were recently found in the Azov area [26, p. 49-52]. Furthermore, the matter of the common origin of the Sumerian, Indo-Aryan, and Greek epic is set forth in the river valleys of the Molochna and Konka between Stone Grave and the Dnipro island of Khortytsia [1, p. 9; 22, p. 558-562 and others; 37; 56, p. 207-212; 61-65; 68, p. 119-133, 529-536] (see Tables XXV-XXVII). The presence of local Vedic literature is consistent with the similarity between Slavs and Aryans, as indicated by *The Veles Book* and the *Boyan Anthem* [8, 31; 3, p. 23, 26], and also confirmed by the 12th century Trojan lines of the *Tale of the Campaign of Ihor Svyatoslavlich* – particularly the legend describing the ruins of Homeric Troy "in Kyivan land" that existed until the 16th century [25, p. 398].

Contrary to A. G. Kifishin, B. D. Mykhailov supposes [34, p. 121-122] that the archive of Stone Grave is not confined to Proto-Sumerian characters but comprises "numerous ideograms, pictographic symbols and written letters, distinctly related to the period of the appearance of syllabic and alphabetic letters resembling characters from Sumer, Crete and Phoenicia dated from the beginning of the 3rd – 1st millennium BCE". In the same district, upstream of the River Molochna, six examples of Catacomb graves have been found, dated to the boundary between the 3rd – 2nd millennium BCE, in which rugs etc., covered with signs which "confusingly hide a specific content", were found arranged in a location between the deceased and the entrance. Having alluded to the previous memorial and its researcher, and also having mentioned symbols of Trypillia and the Middle East, S. J. Pustovalov [42, p. 94-99] (see Table XIV: 8-9) came to the conclusion, with regard to their similarity, that they were factual "proto-alphabetical and early-alphabetical, consonant systems". All of the above are also applicable to the Aryans of the Azov area, the Yamna and Catacomb archaeological cultures, the Pre-Grecian Pelasgians and, probably, to the Hyksos of the Ingul cultures, together with their descendants of the local Srubna culture of the mid 2nd millennium BCE. This poses a question concerning the appearance of the earliest Sanskrit in the latter [26, p. 49-52] (see Table XIV: 4-5); from the Azov area of Ukraine "this system of writing, as well as proper mythological texts, was carried into India and Asia, its foundation having already been made in the Yamna-Catacomb period from the late 3rd to early 2nd millennium BCE". At the same time, the tradition of calendar-dedicatory inscriptions on amulets placed in Oriana and Troy-I about 2500 BCE [22, p. 39-48], survived up to the zenith of Rus (10th – 12th centuries) [25, p. 199-203, 398; 72, p. 19-25] (see Tables XIII: 2-3; XIV: 3). The name of the Trojan-Rusy-Etruscan writing, "Chitala" [which means "to read'], that was preserved by Spartans, also indicates its relationship to Slavic culture. As we truly see, "Slavs had letters long before the birth of Christ" (as declared by Catherine the Great) [3, p. 322].

The ancient Greek-born Myrmidon-'Ants' mentioned above were related to the Telchines^-'worms' who were related to the Kabiri^. The latter two were considered to be excellent metallurgists and escorts of the goddess Rhea – the mother of Hades, Hera, and Zeus. They all gravitated, beginning from the Myrmidons, to Hyperborea 'Beyond-the-north', beyond the Meotida-Azov (as I have repeatedly indicated). Here are found, in Ingul burials Nos. 11 and 13 of kurhan 1-II at the village of Kairy (in the Hornostaivka district of the Kherson region), druidic embodiments of Zeus Taleisky and Apollo-Thargeli of 2000-1800 BCE, reflected in the remains of men bearing the tools and items of a metallurgist and archer [62; 66, p. 715-716 et al.]. Since this is the earliest pre-Cretan complex of the Divine father-and-son, [33, I, p. 92-96, 463-466] we can consider that their early images and ancestors remained upon the ancestral homeland, in the Ukrainian ethnoculture. These include [73, p. 45-49, 179-183]:

Dii or Divas (< Indo-European Dyaus 'Sky' > Greek Dii, Dzeus > Zeus);
Kupala (< Hittite Kurara > Etruscan Kupavon, Aplu > pre-Hittite Apollonius > Greek Apollo, originally connected with Taurus);

Lad(a) (Slavic 'Order', 'Wife' < Indo-European Rato, Vedic Rita, 'Kolovorot', Zodiac, Zakon [Law] > Lat(on)a, lover of Zeus and mother of Apollo);
Kol (Ukrainian 'Core' of Universe, Pole Star > Greek Koios, the Titanic father of Lata);
Ha(i)ster (Ukrainian 'Star, Venus' > Greek 'Asteria' [star], sister of Lata-Leta 'Night');
Obida (the sea maiden from the *Tale of the Campaign of Ihor Svyatoslavlich* < Hyperborean Opis 'Berehynia' and Arga escorting the children of Lata to the island of Delos > "Argo", the vessel of the greatest heroes of Greece, who sailed to Meotida for the Golden Fleece with the sacred text).

The relationship between Slavic and Greek mythologies is traditionally considered to rest upon the maidans – the sanctuary observatories for calendric and other purposes that are embodied in Arattan pre-Indo-European times (see Tables XV-XVI, XXVI-XXVII). They existed in the kapishche [pagan temples] of Rus before the assertion of Christianity. However, their meaning began to be lost even in classical Greece since, as Herodotus, "the father of history", recorded in *Pilgrimages of the Hyperboreans* the role of the [maid]servants of the indicated [maidan] sanctuaries [64]) was no longer understood [12, IV, 13-15. 32-36].

The etymology of the Slavic ethnonyms < Sklavin < Skoloty > Celts whom we mentioned above are also related to Ancient Greece since all these named nations, and many others, resemble and derive from the Indo-European language community (see Tables III-IV). Herodotus [12, IV, 5-7] incorrectly likened the Scythian cattle breeders and their tribesmen to the farming Skolotians (Σκολότοι [Skolotoi], meaning 'glorious[37] kinsmen' [i.e. Slavs] ≈ Greek κλεο [kleo] meaning 'glory, kin' ≈ Slavic 'kin' clan [Ukr. kolino] > Slavic 'okolotok' [meaning 'district'], sun-blessed from the times of Arattan city building [17, I, p. 341 et al.]). However, the [Greek] epithet of "Scythians" – ἀροτηρες, i.e. 'aroteres' [ploughmen] can only be applied to the Arattans [12, IV, 18-19]. The suggestions of the "father of history" attribute the appearance of the Skolotians to the 16th century BCE – but such a date has evidently been underestimated.

As already noted, the similarity between Targitai, the mythical father of Kolaksai, progenitor of Skolotians, with the more ancient hero Apollo Thargeli from Savur-grave, makes it possible to date the first of them to the 4th millennium BCE. Targitai and Kolaksai are then comparable with the father-and-son Sun-king from *The Veda Slovena* [52, p. 197-359] – whose struggle against the serpentine Sura Lamie living in the White Danube is not only considered to be the source of the main mythology of the Aryan *Rigveda* [66, p. 615, 683-685 et al.], but even memories of mammoth hunting (see above). Arpoksai, the second of the three sons of Targitai, could be the descendant of the late rulers of Aratta (see Ima above) and the ancestor of Aroteres. A more probable connection to Arpoksai is with the Orianian g(kh)orb(p)-kurhans[38] (mentioned in *The Veles Book*), as well as with the "ruler of Kharap land" mentioned in *The Veda Slovena* [52, p. 36-39 et al.]. On the other hand, the myth narrated by Herodotus about golden objects that fell from heaven – a plough, yoke, axe, and bowl, which the youngest brother Kolaksai carried into his own house – is the basis for the celebration of Christmas by Ukrainian peasantry. It is pointed out that the birth-renewal of the Sun (i.e. at the solstice) embodied Kolyada[39] in the winter position of the annual course of Dazhboh (Taurus) – who is related (through Targitai) to the Celtic D(T)agda [9, p. 124-15; 33, I, p. 633-637]. Even now, on Holy-Night [in Ukraine], one is supposed to lay 12 platters on the table (representing the number of the months of the year), put an axe and ploughshare from a plough beneath the table, and place a yoke and horse-collar in the Red corner beside a Didukh-sheaf (< Indo-European Dyaus [sky] > Celtic Dis [god]). On introducing a Didukh into the home, the head of the family declares his "gold", and the children must touch the items placed under the table with their bare feet [10, I, p. 65-66].

If we are now speaking of the 16th century BCE as approximately the beginning of the next stage in the ethnogenesis of the Slavs, then it is not necessary to start from the Skoloty, but from the above mentioned (g)Eneti (> Veneti-Slavs of the Baltics) [3; 21; 53] from Asia Minor. Memories were preserved in Roman historiography about their similarity with the Rusy of Troy, about the calendar [Kolyada's gift] of the Ra(u)senov-Etruscans, and of their commemoration of Kolyada in 1570 BCE, when according to ancient custom, they threw bread-*Pelyanos* (> Ukrainian Palianytsia[40]) into the Labu (presently the Italian river

Tiber). The temples of the Ruthenians were arranged in oak-wood groves (Ukrainian dibrova) which are sometimes called Dodon. All this is close to the Celtic druid-priests (who are also known in *The Veda Slovena*), and (in connection with "Trypillian"-Aratta) to the above mentioned Dodol Bulgarians, as well as to Dodole who was the spouse of the god Perun. A. D. Chertkov points out in his book *Concerning the language of Pelasgians populating Italy, and comparison of them with ancient Slavs* (Moscow, 1855) that many of the names of Gods and cities, and so on, are cognate with, even identical to, Slavic names. Concerning the problem of the Indo-European relationship between Slavs and Greeks, it is constantly necessary to reiterate the fact that the specific source of this relationship was Pelasgian pre-Slavic Oriana as well as pre-Greek Pelasgia. Herodotus noted the similar ethnos of each of the latter pair and modern researchers have not raised objections to this but the fact is that an understanding of the Pelasgians and other Peoples of the Sea (see Table VII), where "everything was clearly preserved most precisely in Slavic languages", needs further research [25, p. 95-103]. Indeed, kindred inter-relationships between Oriana and Troy in the 3rd millennium BCE can be extended to Pelasgian-Ukrainian correspondences: Haimon-Haiman, Halia-Halia, Himalia-Hamaliya, Hrai-Hrai [play], Hraikos-Hrak [rook], Gurton-Hurt [band], Danaos-Danya, Kutos-Kutok [corner], Lebedos-Lebid, Lelex-Leleka [stork], Pelasgia-Palazhka [a Slavic goddess], Pero-Pero, Sullis-Sulima and others. The overall Arattan-"Indo-European" basis of the Pelasgian-Eneti-Slavs is also inherent in Asia Minor's Lidy-Liudy [people] with their ancestor Atis-Otets [father]; the term "Trojanski liudy" [Trojan people] is a Roman transcription of a Rutheno-Etruscan phrase. Within this series one can also include the 'Storytellers'- the Omirs, one of whom became the forefather of Bohomyr of *The Veles Book*, and another – Homer, author of the *Illiad* and *Odyssey*.

Legends describing the advent of the 'man-hating' Amazons are an echo of the struggle between the ancient matriarchal and patriarchal traditions that were already inherent in Oriana (c. 3200 BCE). According to Pompeius Trogus, they were the widows of soldiers led by Skolopit somewhere in the mid-2nd millennium BCE. The legendary 'Father of the Skoloty', their mythical patriarch Kolaksai [20, p. 223], the youngest son of Targitai [12, IV, 5], is comparable with the epic of Tarkh Tarakhovich, who similarly fought with the Amazons [46, p. 45 et al.]. The second of the mentioned dates and related characters, just like the Argonaut Herakles, a victor over the Amazons, constitutes the threshold of the ideology and events of the Trojan War. They now connect, for the most part, with the ruins of Troy-VI (1700-1250 BCE) and the city that perished in an earthquake [1, p. 23], therefore it is more expedient to connect the legendary war with Troy-VIIa-b (1250-1020), which was twice destroyed by invaders. The Ruins "A" correspond to the legendary capture of the city by Herakles travelling with the Argonauts as far as the island of Eya in the Cimmerian Bosphorus whereas Ruins "B" correspond to the Trojan War (1030-1020 BCE). The conclusion is all the more admissible because in command of the "Argo" was Laertes, father of Odysseus – hero of the war that would change the course of Greek, European and worldwide civilisation.

The Eneti of Asia Minor's Paphlagonia, who came to the aid of besieged Troy, merged after its fall into the ethnogenesis of European Slavs as the Venedi [25, p. 89-95; 53, p. 39-40]. "Those two 'glories', 'father glory' and 'mother glory', for the sake of which Zeus settled the greatest war, have a particular, ritual-heroic meaning. They pertain to the glory of the dead in the cause of the living. Glory of this kind is extremely ingrained in the ethno-psychology of Slavs whose very name is possibly connected with this concept[41]. It is evident that the Slavs had their ancestral home on that northern territory, which became the centre of development for the future 'history of Troy'". As already mentioned, L. A. Akimova theorised that Stone Grave, the place where this history was germinated [2, p. 270], abounds with specific correspondences to the mythological rituals of Troad [34, p. 131-137; 67 et al.] (see Table XXVI: 12).

Thus, due to the many reasons that have been indicated (see particularly, below, details of board 26 of *The Veles Book*), the Trojan centuries etc. turned out to be in Rus, "at the centre of a princely genealogy similar to that in the *Tale of the Campaign of Ihor Svyatoslavlich* in 1185 CE. This tradition only faded away with the fall of the princely-ruling dynasty of Ruriks [25, p. 201-203].

6. Ancient times

A portion of the *The Skupa legend* given above, preserved by the keepers of Cossack traditions, listed the ethnonyms of the pre-ancestors: "*Chornukhi Derevlyani (burned trees), Kimy* [Cimmerians], *Antes, Roxy* [Roxolani], *Berends, Tatrans, Olbers, Topchaky, Revuhs, Shelbyrs* – a host of Cossack families, including the Vkraintsi, who lived in the 'krai' [i.e. land] of ancestors (...)". {Not everything here will be appreciated by a patriot, and it is possible to doubt the authenticity of the list, as well as the legends. If that is so, let the specialists work further; my objective is to put in order that which is well known, little known and practically unknown, and to present an updated concept of history for people to assess it from the perspective of *+E* (the science of *F-* having been already manifest since the times of "the father of history"). In meeting this challenge, I too, of course, have not overlooked criticisms of sources, the assessment of their authenticity and so on; for me, the supreme criterion of truth is the congruence, complementary relationship (i.e. internal coherence) and verification of facts across the whole system under consideration, and its viability. Hence my assessment of the list presented above is that it specifically reflects the Indo-European and even the Eurasian basis of Slavdom from the position of the archetypal-Cossack. It is wholly and essentially different (*+E* reflecting communal) from our usual military doctrines (*F-* reflecting totalitarian formations). It is impossible to expect to read in the statutes of totalitarian formations such concepts as: "Do not completely finish off the enemy; while the enemy exists – there will be our strength; they have power until we defend ourselves, but we are respected" [5; 77, p. 39-42 etc.]} There are echoes here of the reality of "Trypillian" Aratta, and confirmation of *The Veles Book* (which mentions "Kimoria – our fathers"), where ethnonyms of Gothic and Pecheneh roots exist. They resonate with Zaporozhian legends detailing the origin of Cossacks [48] and are also the source of the latest discoveries of the Aryan origins of Cossacks flourishing in the world of Pechenehs-Polovtsy^ [23; 37; 56; 70-75], extending up to the time of the demise of Kyivan Rus, in accordance with the traditional complementary co-existence of Aratta-and-Arián [38; 69 et al.] (see Tables V-XI, XXI-XXII).

Orthodox science inclines to the strong (blemished[42]) attitude that *Slavs* (*Cossacks*, and others) just appeared on the world stage when their competing neighbours began to write about them *under these names.* However, such an approach vitally misses, no less than it favours, the politics complicit in the Biblical ideology of alien subordination, the common sense of everyday experience. For example, we can look at the self-evident truth that as people, families and nations pass through different stages of development, there are changes in both their names and their status. For instance, some Pelasgians became Greeks, who at the dawn of antiquity were initially named Hellenes, but then in the early Middle Ages they were called Byzantians... not forgetting the many tribes, allies and other ethnonyms that have already been mentioned. The same happened to the Slavs who also had blood-related ancestors whose descendants have settled around the world (see Tables IV, IX).

According to *The Veles Book* [8, boards 9a, 38a] the ethnonym **Sla(o)viany** had two sources (and the point where the ethnonym divided/changed [compared to the Arattan root] became coastal Oriana of Arattan-Aryan roots) but there is a noticeable desire amongst authors to bring them together again. In general, it seems to me that *The Veles Book* is a collection of processed texts, composed by priests of particular specialisations. Such "'Magi-koshchunnyky', were story-tellers of 'koshchun'^-myths, the keepers of ancient myths and epic legends" but who in fact, (according to B. A. Rybakov [46, p. 770-771]) tracked the destiny of tribes and nations; evidently their places of work and relationships were the maidans [11; 59; 64 et al.] see Tables XII-XVI).

The first line of historiography of *The Veles Book* is mythologised (see Tables VII; IX; XIV: 1) but the beginning of the related *Tale of Bygone Years* by Chronicler Nestor agrees with the above mentioned "Chronicler Mazurinsky". It begins from the post-Trojan time of the 10th – 7th centuries BCE – when the Eneti of Troy, defeated by the Dorians, resettled in Europe, led by Aeneus and Antenor. *The Veles Book* [boards 5a, 6a, 9a] describes the family of forefather Bohomyr as the primary source of the Rusy and the Veneti, who settled across territory extending from the Adriatic to the Carpathians and into the Baltic

States; the names of the Drevlians, Kryvychis and Polians [see Fig. 128] were derived from the names of his daughters, and were also generalised by an ethnonym [derived from their mother], '*from the consort of God's narrator*':

And their mother was Slavunia (…)
And that is why three kins generated by her were slavny [glorious].

Chronicler Nestor, however, begins the history of Slavs no later than the 5th century BCE when the Venedian city-state of Noricum emerged in the Danube area [53, p. 40-53], where they were usually called (g)Eneti > Venedi, thus providing a second name of ancient Europe – Enetia. (Hitherto they were the numerically predominant ethnic group of the carriers of European culture). According to Strabo's *Geography* (64 BCE – 20 CE), the power of the Enedi extended between the shores of the Adriatic and the Danube. Their capital, Potava (cognate with the name of modern Ukrainian city Poltava), located above the coastal River Medvak, was the "best and the most populous city of Northern Italy which was so rich that it could arm and advance an army of up to a hundred and twenty thousand people". Numerous other cities also had Slavic names, e.g. Hrad, Hradisha, and Turios. Rusy-Etruscan cities also should be included here as they settled close to one another (according to Titus Livius) "from the shores of the Tiber to the Alps and from sea to sea". Their cities were Artana, Oriana, Porusia, Rusalia, Halychi, Cordon, Kosa, Kuma, Kuren, Luka, Maliuta, Spina [which are all Ukrainian names].

The second line [of historiography] in *The Veles Book* is more comparable to legends I, III and IV in the *The Histories* of Herodotus [IV, 5-7, 11-13] (see Tables VI; VIII-XI). A short account there outlining the ancestral veneration of Indra, who came to them as a child "to the land of Arstia, to the Insk land", should be attributed to the partial migration of Aryans into India during the mid- 2nd millennium BCE, from their original homeland of the Lower Dnipro and more easterly areas [37-38; 55-56; 66]. At that time, on the Chongar peninsula of the Azov, the Aryans completed the Garman^ kurhan (a Ukrainian 'Tok'[43] and Indo-Aryan changar: hardan, khirman, etc.). It embodied the mytho-ritual boundary of the "Day and Night of Brahma" that involved the Almighty-Serpent Shesha^ and the life-giving staff (Ukrainian *kyi*; see below) of the Creator-GOD Vishnu [63; 66, p. 688, 724 et al.] (see Tables XXXIX: 11; XL: 16). The monument directly shows the beginnings of eastern-Slavic legends concerning the origins of their Serpent Walls (which were called '*Trojans*' in Moldavia "… fallen Romans left when the Danaos crossed the Trojan Wall" [*The Veles Book*, board 7h]). The settlements and camps of Arattans, Aryans, Cimmerians and the like continued to exist uninterrupted on the Chongar peninsula. Thousands of years after the completion of Garman a number of Scythian kurhans appeared there and 12-15 centuries later the Pechenehs (Patzinaks, Kanhary) and the Polovtsy – followers of Aryans – justly constructed a burial ground there, above those mounds [38, p. 57-71]. Old-Rusian items (and relics?) in that burial ground indicate that contacts existed between these corresponding populations. We should also mention here Ukrainian legends about the ancestral Rahmans (< Arattan-Aryan Brahman-priests) who were the best of people who "went from Ukraine beyond the Blue Sea" (Azov or Aral Sea) [probably via the Chongar peninsula], [73, p. 124-128].

The migrants residing in India (not only at the indicated time but also from the time of Punjabian Aratta), established there the Indo-European dynasty of Kyians. Linked with that dynasty are Kavi and Kei – 'poets' and sorcerers who subsequently became 'warriors' [37-38]. Amongst the earliest of them was Brahman Bhrigu who was one of the compilers of the *Rigveda* and whose son, Ushanas, became a ruler of Kavia. From them came the tribe of Turvash [a Vedic ancestor] (> Slavic Turovtsy?) who considered themselves to have come to Bharata-India under the patronage of Indra, whose magical vajra-club is called 'keya' (< Ukrainian '*kyi*') by Tibetan Lamas... The authors [8, Boards 5-a, 6-a, 31, 38-a] then outline a picture of the return from Indian Pendeb-Punjab to the homeland of their tribesmen fire-hearthers, as far as the Nepre-Dnipro. Not everyone from Oriana and Borusia had left with that section of the Aryans in that campaign to India, and likewise not everyone came back. Those kinfolk who had not become accustomed to that foreign land and decided to return, united under the name of Slo(a)vyane, and having sought permission from the Aryan

Veche (i.e Assembly Chamber), father Oriy and his three sons (Kyi, Shchek and Khoryv) were elected as leaders and the tribes then moved back, where the tribesmen of the Dnipro area accepted them.

And since that beginning till now, the kin of Slaven began (...)
On that Nepre [Dnipro] *the kin of Slavs sat.*
And those fire-people [settlers], *each of them had an earth hole* [hearth] *for a fire.*
We glorified Svaroh and Dazhboh who were involved in their development (...)

The time of this return was reflected in the Chornolis^ archaeological culture of the Skolots on the forest-steppe on the [Dnipro] right bank, whose tribes were allegedly "subjected to attack from Cimmerians inhabiting the steppe. They repelled their onslaught and built a number of powerful fortifications on the southern border. They even turned on the offensive in the 8th century BCE and began to colonise the Vorskla river valley on the steppe on the left bank of the Dnipro" [45, p. 224]. Expressive artefacts were found in this region by the expedition of A. B. Suprunenko [51, p. 47-139; et al.] at the extensive necropolis of Stovbuvata^ Grave (see above). The co-existence of both flexed and extended body positions of the deceased set out in these burials indicate that the carriers of the Chornolis and, probably, the post-Ingul archaeological cultures had been assimilated into the Scythian environment of the 6th – 3rd centuries BCE. The ceremonial aspect of mound 12/III is particularly indicative. This grave, of a priestess with amulets of Median origin [the fore-runner of Persia] (see Table VIII: 1), was encompassed by the arc of a serpentine ditch (reflecting the mythologies of Vala and Vritra that are already familiar to us). Close to her head was buried the flexed body of a maidservant. Similar facts can be connected with the narrative by Herodotus which describes the co-existence in these places of the Budini and Geloni (in the modern Poltava region)... *The Veles Book* [board 38a] describes the tension associated with the ethnogenetic process in the forest-steppe of the Dnipro area between the 9th – 8th centuries BCE which was otherwise without onslaughts and repulsions.

The returners from India to the right bank of the Dnipro were given the opportunity by their local relatives to settle "in the city of Indi-Kyiv, which is called Kyiv". Prince Kyi remained there with his people whilst his brothers Shchek and Khoryv "went to the Carpathian Mountains and began to create cities there" [board 36-b]. It was Oriy, the father of all three, who settled on the left bank next to local Oseden [board 26], having founded there the city of Holun [board 35-a]. The patriarchs then moved to the south and "Oriy led his people to the coastal area" where he possibly established Surozh [board 4-d, 6-c] on the Cimmerian shore of the Bosphorus (Kerch strait). The connection between the Surozh-Cimmerian-(S)Indics with the Skoloty is indicated by their names [in common] of their pre-ancestor Targitai – and also queen Targitao who was the empress of the Meots [Maiotai in Greek or Maeotae in Latin] and of the (S)inds. In addition, the Scythian chieftain Skopasiy ruled on the shores of Meotida [Azov Sea]. In that area, since ancient times, was the island of Eya (also known as Aenei, Aivan) where the Eneti that are already familiar to us had formerly lived, close to the Vans of Transcaucasian Aratta and Urartu [43, p. 60-251]. Opposite the island, on both shores of the strait, were situated <u>Keka</u> and <u>Kasika</u>, and beyond (S)Indica were the <u>Kiseisky</u> mountain range (near the modern city of Pyatigorsk). Kiska (Kishek), an associated descendant of father-Oriy, was the ruler there [25, 35a]. Here we should remember the Urartian dynasty of Rus, which ruled the lands on the shores of the Transcaucasian Lakes <u>Van</u> and Se<u>van</u>.

The name of Gelon mentioned by Herodotus [12, IV, 10, 108 et al.] is derived from the homonymous son of Herakles. The Gelon described by Herodotus (< [the city of] Holun in *The Veles Book* > Ilium in *The Iliad*) emerged at the beginning of the 8th century BCE and is identified by most researchers with "Belske horodyshche" Belsk hill-fort, (which is located on the border of the Poltava, Kharkiv and Sumy regions). Not by chance, this date coincides with the return of Slavs from the Punjab campaign and with the foundation of Ilium on the ruins of Homeric Troy [1, p. 22-23]. The named city-states of both Asia Minor and the Dnipro-Don interfluve also coincide, with regard to their solar names and tripartite defensive walls and also specific legends about the itinerant Argonaut <u>Herakles</u>. His name and his 12 <u>heroic</u> feats are associated with the goddess <u>Hera</u>-'Hod' [=year], and the source of each of them originated from the Azov vicinity of the river Gerros/Herros in the locality of Stone Grave which holds the world's most ancient archive and is the origin of the Indo-European epic [2; 12; 67; 68, p. 118, 228-229] (see Tables XII-XIII). Travelling with the Argonauts, Herakles rescued the sister of Priam, future king of doomed Troy, from the serpent and for this he received a pair of horses. Later, Herakles was evidently searching for these [lost] horses when he arrived at the abode of the serpent-legged maiden of the Borysthenes-Dnipro who later bore to him Agathirs, Gelon and Scythes.

It is necessary to draw attention to the account by Herodotus [IV, 102, 108-109, 120, 136] of the close ties between the tribes of Geloni and the Budini (see Table IX: 7), who shared their fatherland with the migrants and who lived alongside them in Gelon. The facts connecting them with the Budini of Media in the 1st millennium BCE (in addition to the aforesaid finds in kurhan12/III at Stovbuvata Grave) are given below. Researchers keep accentuating the connection of the Geloni with forest lands, thereby excluding them from the numerous agricultural-stock-raising ancestors of the Slavs. The fact that the "Budini celebrate festivals in honour of Dionysus" is evidence that they, at least, were farmers who had adapted to the new living conditions. However, their "light-blue eyes and red hair" which were different from the Geloni are entirely comparable with the Slavs. Moreover, *The Veles Book* considers the city of Holun (i.e. Gelon by Herodotus) as a construction of the Budini – in the area of which, in the modern Poltava region, we find an agglomeration of names such as Buda, Budno, Budina, Budaky, etc. In this way, ancient tribes with Indo-European roots (e.g. Tirites and Alazonians, like the Geloni) could be merged into the ethnogenesis of the Slavic community as the Turovtsy, Halychans, and Ulychis. However, "the Callipidae, Hellenic Scythians" reveal a relationship with the Indian Goddess Kali, the hypostatic wife of Shiva – the veneration of whom is found in ancient inscriptions of the same Dnipro-Dniester region [56, p. 114-115, 205]. Once more, this confirms the veracity of information in *The Veles Book* describing the Slavic-Aryan migrations. An equally ponderable confirmation is found in an Indian-Armenian legend of the 1st – 8th centuries recording the names Kuar, Meltei and Khorean [37, p. 222-236].

So, having lived in India and then partially returned again, the migrants left their legacy in a trace of the Kyans dynasty of Indo-European origin. Reference has already been made to Keya(k)h and Ushanas Kavi. The Indian ruler was related to Kei Usan, the founder of the Khwarezmian dynasty of the Keyanids. Whether or not Usan belonged to the 'warrior'-Rus (like his fellow tribesman Rustam), it was clearly not coincidental that when his grandson Kay Khusra returned, he travelled so closely through those lands of his brother-Slavs, Kyi and Khoryv. In addition there is the opinion that Khwarezm^ is the 'Land of Khwars'. Its connection with the Slavic ancestral homeland is supported by a Khwarezmian legend recording the expulsion by King Keyani of part of his subjects somewhere in the fishing region, where they received the ethnonym Mitany or Miuyten (see above reference to Kasika, etc., near the Meotida). This confirms the hypothesis of O. N. Trubachev, that there is a relationship between the names of the Meotida and Mitanni; on the other hand, it offers a possible explanation for the appearance of Slavic parallels in post-Mitanni Media.

We mentioned this state in connection with the theory which examines the similarity between the Budini and Budiev [12, I, 101, p. 557]. The latter, just like other Indo-European tribes, migrated (in the second half of the 9th century BCE) into Media [the forerunner of Persia and Iran] from the territories of Bactria and Sogdiana, which were adjacent to, and related to, Khwarezm. Greek sources link the emergence on the historic arena of Media with its deliverance from Assyria, which was led by King Deioces^ (727-675 BCE). In 625-584 BCE the State was led by Kiaksar (Uvakshatra in Persian) who was a great-grandchild of Fraort and the son of his namesake. These names can be interpreted as a slightly garbled Slavic Pre-(father) Or(iy), 'God's eye' and 'Kiyok-tsar'. All the more so because they turn out to be allies of the Cimmerians who *The Veles Book* [boards 2a, 6] names as consanguineous[44] relatives and even that their fathers "*in essence they are our brothers and they are similar to us*". Meanwhile, there are more Slavic correspondences (other than Median) in the names of three Cimmerian leaders in the Middle East – greatly misspelled incidentally - by Assyrian scribes: Kashtarit, Sandakshatra (< Indo-Aryan *Kshatriya* 'warrior, warlord' > Slavic '*Koshevy*' (of Aryans and Sinds), and Tugdamm (<

'*Dazhd* blessed'?).

As shown with regard to the earlier Aryans (Indo-Iranians), the authors of *The Veles Book* connect the movement of Slavs in the Middle East with their Indian branch – the Cimmerians of 783-595 BCE. That was the beginning of the Iron Age [8, board 6c]:

Hitherto the Persians knew our copper swords.
So the Creator told Ima to make iron ones
and to take horse-riders, passed to us from God.

Here are the kin of Oriy and his dynasty "who beat Syria and Egypt, and Assyria. (…) Our people went into the valleys of Ashurbanipal". The chronicles of this Assyrian ruler called the Cimmerians *Umman-Manda* (a name influenced by the Persian Medes who were captured by the Scythian chieftain Madyes); later, the Arabs considered the Slavs to be descendants of the Cimmerians: Al-Masudi recorded that "Slavs are the essence of Madya". It is also possible to identify several traces of the presence of ancient Slavs in the texts of Urartu and Palestine… The migratory branch of the Slavs returned to the Northern Black Sea area, with the Cimmerians and, after them, the hostile Scythians, in the years following the defeat of the Babylonian leader Nebuchadnezzar II (604-562 BCE). One of the routes taken by the returning migrants went through the Caucasus; a second went through Asia Minor, where Slavs came face to face with the Greeks for the second time (after the Trojan War). The authors of *The Veles Book* [board 2a] describes this return in the following way:

We went as far as southern parts, just to take land for us and our children.
And there Greeks attacked us, as we sat on their [land].
And there was a great battle for many months… (…)
So, our fore-fathers led the cattle,
and father Oriy led us to the Rusy land.
Because we were always there. (…)
As [our] *people are relatives with the Kilmerians,*
From the same root our kin are growing.
Who came later to the Rusy land,
Settled among Ilmerians. (…)
And an evil clan came to us, and attacked us (Scythian or Persian?).
And so we were forced to spring back into the forest (where Budini appeared).

The Chornolis archaeological culture, with a complex of Skoloto-Cimmero-Scythian features, existed in the forest-steppe of the Dnipro area up until Hellenic times and in the 3rd – 2nd centuries BCE, having experienced a Celtic influence, developed into the Zarubinets^ culture of Slavs of late antiquity [45, p. 220-229] (see Table XI). Regarding their relationships with Scythians (see Tables IX-XI), the tension was aggravated by the alliance of the latter with the Greeks – based not only on their victories over the Persians but also on trade. Stimulated by trade, which had become the main cultural conductor of slaveholding Greece, Scythia reached the same point of destruction as the local, traditionally communal civilisation of Aratta>Arta>Arsania [68, p. 231-250]. The controversy focused on Taurida, the Bosphorus (Kerch) coast, which has traditionally been called Surozhia and Cimmeria [8, board 6-c]:

… two branches were named, Great and Small Borusia,
Surenzhe were called Surenzhka Rus.
And Boruses carried out a war (…)
That is why Boruses could not stand against the attack of Greeks and Scythians.
Those were yellow [haired], but Rusy had brown hair and blue eyes.
A strong restless war was going on uninterrupted…

The greatest war in Scythia, according to the opinions of the ancient Greek "father of history" Herodotus and his followers, was the conflict in 514-512 BCE between the alliance of local nations with the Persian army led by King Darius. The official version stated the reason for the invasion stemmed from the anxiety to punish the Scythians for their invasion into Media [the forerunner of Persia and Iran], from which Persia then grew [12, IV,

1]. However, a comparison between this campaign and the very reckless previous campaign [12, I, 204-214] directed by Cyrus, founder of Persia, against the Massagetae, who were Scythian allies, unveils the true cause of the war. In the world of the Persian branch of Aryan nationalities (known as 'Indo-Iranian Aryans') there was a power struggle for precedence and accordingly, the named rulers, in asserting [preference for] the young dynasty of *Achaemenid* over *Keyanid* (see above), as well as preferring the superiority of the *Avestan* over *Vedic* ideology, could not ignore the Northern Black Sea area. For it was here, in Aratta that civilisation had originated together with the earliest dynastic rulers of 'rod-bearing'-Kyans (see above), who were similar to the Arián Dandines (in Indo-Aryan languages) and to the Palak (in Irano-Aryan languages) [37, p. 18-27]. Their sacred centre of Dandaria (Δανδάριοι, [Dandarioi] < ancient-Greek 'Δανδάκη' [Dandaki], ancient-Indus 'Dandaka' > Turkish 'Tentere' and modern 'Tendra' [island]), gravitating to the traditions of Aratta-Oriana, was transferred – through Tauridian Dandaka (see earlier for origins of the Indo-Aryan *Ramayana*) – to the region between the lower reaches of the Old and New (S)Indic (i.e. the Dnipro and Kuban rivers) [56, p. 40-41, 233-234]. Ancient authors mentioned Dandaka-Dandaria between the 6th century BCE to the 4th century CE (see Table X-XI). A guerrilla raid by the Scythians kept at bay the Persians from 'Iron-wearing Aria', and whose victory outlived [the times of] Cimmerians, Scythians, Sarmatians and even during the same times of Hellas, Bosphorus and Rome. It laid the foundations of military art for the subsequent Tauris and Rusy, Roxolani and Pechenehs, Rusy and Polovtsy, and the Tatars and Cossacks. Some Cossack origin legends [48] recall the times when, "they went into battle with 'kyikamy'" (i.e clubs) and had been born in the environment of Kyiv,

We have already mentioned the ancient Covenants of the Cossacks of Ukraine, however, it is appropriate here to give a description of the ceremony of sworn brothers – reflecting more deeply their antiquity relative to the Scythians than that mentioned by Herodotus [12, IV, 70] (see Table X: 1). "Mazepstvo: one by one, one hand on the sabre, the other hand on the belt, they incise and mix a smear [of blood]; at dawn near the Holy Tomb of the mother or parent they turn to the eight sides and keep saying: "God, our father and the grove steppe are witnesses" ('Rodzhypittya chas' [which in translation means 'the time of birth-life-drinking']). After that they sprinkle [the smear of blood] in a goblet with wine and drink it one at a time. When one is a simple brother, he drinks it himself in camaraderie" [5]. There is another variant [77, p. 41]: "At the Holy Tomb, near the mother or parent, as Father Kolo Yaryla [the sun] rises, one by one, each puts their hand on the sabre, the second on the belt, cuts near the bones of the fist and mixes the smear [of blood] – turning to the eight sides and keeps saying: 'we protect the Homeland Custom, each other by folklore; God, our Father and the grove steppe are our witnesses'. After that they sprinkle [the smear] in a goblet with wine and drink it one at a time." This is the Principal Cossack testament [5, 77, pp. 41]: "Do not strike each other. As long as youths will drink with mother's milk, reject supremacy over themselves and in themselves, and in the family, then the Swarm of families of the Ukrainian Skupa [assembly] will be able to protect their lands as blood brothers for their own benefit... in dying I bequeath [this]: keep forever the custom of the smear and you will dominate with strength forever."

I bring this section to a conclusion with the final lines of *The Boyan Anthem*. A. I. Asov connects its origin with the victory of the Rusy over the Goths in 368 (375) CE [3]:

Slavs, you did not reduce glory.
The sword of Boyan is truthful in battle,
Recognise the memory of Magian- Zlatohor!
Memory of Aria, and give loud exclamation to Scyth,
We pour gold from bowls at the funeral feast!

7. Early Middle Ages

The names Artaplot and Orativ (cf. Etruscan Artana and Greek Ortopolis) and also Tendra (< Ancient Dandaria), persisted in Ukraine to this day even though those communal civilisations of Indo-European derivation ceased in the second half of the 1st millennium BCE with the rise of totalitarian-feudal Rus [old Kyivan Rus]. There is evidence that subsequent manifestations of Aratta lay in the region of the greatest collection of its cities, i.e. in the Cherkasy region, although in texts of Arab travellers it is more obvious in the Taman peninsula (< Ancient-Rusy Tmutarakan). This affected the tradition of duplication of the historic phenomena in these two territories, i.e. in the lower reaches of the Dnipro and Kuban rivers. Al-Istarhi (in the 10th century) wrote about three groups of Rusy who were centred on the cities Kuiaba (Kyiv), Slaviya (in the Volyn region?) and Art(s)a, the capital of Art(s)ania. It is not accidental that the latter names are confirmed by the Arabic names of *Rashtri* [Rus], which considered only two 'Lands' – Bharati-India and Artania-Rus [38, p. 42-57]. "Concerning Arta, it is unknown whether any travellers reached it because there they kill any foreigner coming into their land. They themselves only sail along the river and trade (...)". It is also known that the Rusy were sometimes called Art(s)ami by Arabs. And no matter how dubious their information, it is still possible to reconstruct an ethno-cultural chain for such a genesis (viz. Indo-European Arattans > ancient-Grecian Aroteres > Persian-Arabian Art(s)es > ancient-Rusy Oratai > Ukrainian Orachi), which emanates from the beginning of terrestrial civilisation and still lives on in the same Northern Black Sea region right up to modern times (see Tables IV-XL).

The characteristics of the earliest Indo-European co-existence between settled Aratta and nomadic Arián were sustained through subsequent millennia, surviving until mid-1st millennium CE, paired together as Arta-Arsania and Dandaria-Dandaka, which stimulated the later co-existence of Borusia and Oriana, Skolotia and Cimmeria, Bosphorus and Scythia, Rus and nomads [38; 56], thus revealing the Arattan basis of the peasantry [45] and the Aryan basis of the Cossacks [23; 38]. They both kept alive the 9 millennia-long tradition of communal civilisation up until the end of the 18th century [28; 39] and at the beginning of the 20th century, constituted an effective opposition to the totalitarian civilisations of slaveholding, feudal, capitalist formations of the last 5 - 2.5 millennia.

The process of calculating the above tradition of *+E*, and its prevailing coexistence with the *F-* tradition, led to a reconsideration of that version of history which had, from ancient times, formed in favour of the latter [i.e. the *F-* tradition associated with military totalitarianism]. According to that picture (which was summarised but somewhat corrected by "historical materialism"), the primitive communal structure of Slavs was protracted until the beginning of the new era [CE], when there was a 'period of military democracy' and their appearance on the historical arena was then established by virtue of the chroniclers of neighbouring civilised nations; the Slavs only being organised for safeguarding their civilisation-statehood (relative to the bloody chaos of the military democracy period) in the 7th - 9th centuries, i.e. later than almost all other peoples of Europe. But no, that is far from right! **Pre-Slavic Civilisation arose, as shown above, along with their origin, within the environment of Indo-European peoples but that *primary, communal civilisation* *was not known to historical materialism*** (see Tables IV, XIII-XL). With regard to the second, i.e. class-based civilisation – yes, the Slavs were somewhat delayed in that, possibly even to their own detriment but very much for the benefit of all humanity.

The transition in the traditionally Slavic Dnipro area was effected through the arrival of foreign princes of Baltic origin rather than having been resolved locally. The process of transition from communal to totalitarian civilisation (see Tables IV-XI) was objective (because the 'see-saw', dynamic nature of history was subject – just like all things – to the laws of interaction between *+E* and *F-*). Society became increasingly militarised as the control of it passed from the priests to the warriors. In the Slavic world the term 'Rusy' began to apply not only to the warriors of the prince and the tribes he controlled but also to united tribes and their lands. *The Veles Book* [board 7g] ranks the tribes of that time in the following way:

And Dazhbo gave birth to us through the cow Zamun,
And we were Kraventse and Skife, – Ants, Rusy, Boruses and Surozhets, –
And thus began the grandfathers of Rusy.

All the descendant tribes of Taurus-Dazhboh and Cow-Earth were already Rusy (< Indo-European Taurus, i.e. 'bull'), bearing both matriarchal and patriarchal traditions of the 'Korovychi' and 'Skotychi' of Aratta and Arián (see above for the "two glories" of Troad [2, p. 270]). Their original "period of sacred democracy" however, now became "militant".

Turning now to an examination of the gathering of the Rusy into Surozhian Rus (Black Sea), Venedian (Baltic) and Kyivan Rus, we must begin with the appearance of the capital city of the Kyivan Rus – which was different from the above-mentioned Indikyiv of Skolotian-Cimmerian times.

People have taken a fancy to living in comfortable places since ancient times. In Cyril Street of Kyiv[45], archaeologists identified the remains of a camp of mammoth hunters whose dates coincide with a myth, from the Kyivan Region, which dates the origin of the world to 198 centuries ago [14, p.13-14]. Much later than that, at the time of Aratta between the 6th – 5th millennium BCE, a unique sanctuary was found which marked the beginning of the Kyiv Pechersk Caves as well as 7 settlements of the Trypillian archaeological culture. Perhaps the name of the area as Subotka (< Sanskrit 'Su-path', i.e. 'good path' > Byzantian 'Sambatos') could have arisen at that time and been called 'Amadoka' (Greek 'log-deck' [or 'plank-bridge'] crossing) during the ancient Scythian epoch. Furthermore, 14 settlements of the Zarubinets culture formed here; this was also the location of the most northerly accumulation of Roman coins ever found which spanned a period of five centuries, dating from the 2nd century BCE. It was during that time that the military-trade route began "from the Varyags^ to the Greeks" (i.e. from the Slavic south-eastern Baltic into maritime Byzantium on the Black Sea) along which flourished passage and trade centred on the site of the future capital (i.e. Kyiv). The "Zarubinets"-Slavs (see Table XI) made contact with the related Celts (through the former Skoloty) and began to form a path, in the 3rd century, that connected with the Slavic-German alliance of the Veneti, Vandals and Goths. Those alliances were held together and sustained by virtue of their generic genealogical legends. The subject of one was ancestor Ariy (see above: *The Boyan Anthem* < Oriy of *The Veles Book* > Fraort, the founder of Media) and his son Kyi (also in *The Veles Book*) whose descendant allegedly became Hermanaric. It is probable that, at this time, though not earlier than the foundation of Cimmerians, there was a partial migration consisting of Aces/Ases and Vans headed by the later deified Odin – from the Kuban-Don region into Scandinavia [21, p. 46-50]. Its Lesser Sweold (> Sweden) arose from Greater Sweold – Scythia, and Rus in Europe was treated as its successor up to the late Middle Ages.

Kyiv is first mentioned in the chronicles of the city in the year 334 CE. *Kyi* of that time (prior even to the rulers of the dynasty of that name) could be a carrier at the Dnipro crossing. The carrier was a very valuable person at such an important passage, (which Ukrainians even now in some places call 'Kytovan', referring to his 'kyi', i.e. staff). In any case, there may have been such a title, which had been unknown to Chronicler Nestor in the 11th – 12th centuries. The origins of the title 'Kyi-kytovan' go back to Rus of the Chermne Sea ("Black Sea" or "Red Sea[46]" < Tauridan Surozh Rus) and to the preceding Cimmerians who were located on both shores of the Bosphorus (Kerch) Strait. *The Veles Book* [8, board 33] describes this succession of generations as follows:

Here is our funeral feast about Seden, our father,
Who was at the Pontian coast in the city of Rosia.
And those are Rusy who went from Bila Vezha [white tower] *and from Rosia to the lands of the Dnipro area.*
And there, Kyi created the city of Kyiv.
And there, Poliany, Drevliany, Kryvychi and Liakhove settled on the Rusy bush.
And all became Rusychi [Rusy].

Subsequent events, leading up to the Christendom of Rus, are sufficiently well understood. Nevertheless, it is still necessary to outline them here.

The wickedness of Hermanaric, chieftain of the Goths, resulted in the dissolution of the indicated alliance in 368 CE. The battles that occurred between the Rusy and the Goths from the Kyiv Region to as far as the Kiseisky mountains (to the modern city of Pyatigorsk) were reflected in *The Veles Book* [boards 17, 19, 22, 35], *The Older Edda*, and in the Circassian, Adygei version of the *Narts saga* [3, p. 94-119] (see Table XXII: 8). In 375 CE a new adversary appeared, the Huns but by about 450 CE the Kyiv prince became an ally of

Attila, the chieftain of the Huns, who started a successful war against the Franks and Romans. After the death of Attila in 453 CE Kyivan Rus inherited part of his conquests. It stretched across the Volga and Danube, to where the (G)enety > Venedi had migrated (see above), and it was from there that Verena was invited into Kyiv to rule.

At the beginning of the 4th century the Rugi appeared at Noricum in the Danube area. This is the name of a community which provided warriors from amongst ancient Slavs < the 'ragabs' of Aratta) [43, p. 144]) to serve as mercenary legionaries in the Roman Empire. In 476 their chieftain Odoacer (according to Jordanes) led the capture of Rome, where he became emperor. (According to other authors Odoacer was King of the Geruls [Heruli or Sciri], and Prince of the Rusy). At this time the Goths decided to come back from the Baltic region into the Black Sea area where their small principality remained in the mountains of Taurida; however, after a ten-year war, the Goths were banished by the Slavs who were led by Antes. On their departure, the Goths met the Romans and at the moment of negotiations they disloyally killed Odoacer (from whom the Ukrainian Hetman, Bohdan Khmelnytsky^, derived his genealogy 11 centuries later) : see Table XXVIII: 6.

In 518, having become the successor of the declining Rome, the Byzantine empire established authority over the Greek-migrants of the former Bosphorus empire of the Northern Black Sea and it continued its policy of dishonest trading with Rus, as well as increasing its ideological, political and military enforcement. Christianity increasingly became the leading Byzantine influence on Rus, which was already flush with migrants from Palestine in the first centuries CE. The Bosphorus and Scythian dioceses arose between the 3rd – 4th centuries [24, p. 41-46]. In 547, Emperor Justinian had already affirmed the pontifical department for Taurida, and three years later the Byzantians began the forcible baptism of tribes in the northern foothills of the Caucasus. In revenge, those tribes began to annually attack and plunder the Byzantine provinces behind the Danube, time after time breaking through the coastal lands of Rus. They especially rampaged the Avars and Obry who are known from *The Veles Book* [board 32] and subsequent chronicles.

In 560, the Antian prince Mezenmyr tried to agree a treaty with the nomads but he was killed. The Avars' yoke was thrown off by the Slovenes of Carantania, the successors of Noricum. Here in 623-658 Governor Samo united four Slavic nations with a strong communal basis and established their power which stretched as far as the Vistula and the Adriatic [53, p. 54]. At the turn of the 6th – 7th centuries, after the break-up of the 'lands of the Ants' (i.e. the Ant alliance of tribes), the Slavs of the Black Sea area were combined into the Duleb alliance – but this also broke down after 670, when the Khazar Khaganate arose. Bulgaria of the Volga region also suffered from the Khaganate. The Bulgarian khan Asparuh went with a small party beyond the Danube where he united seven Slavic tribes and by 681 he had created the state of Bulgaria. However, Turkish Khazaria took Taurida away from Byzantium with whom it concluded an alliance. The Khazarian direction against Rus was strengthened under the influence of Hebrew outcasts from Persia, who took control of the Eastern European section of trade routes between the East and West. The ruling elite of the Khaganate embraced Judaism around the end of the 8th century and that became the instrument of Jewish management of Khazar finance and politics. Thus, the interests of the Khazar Khaganate and Byzantine empire were interwoven as two Biblical religions. Since trading with people brought the greatest profit in those centuries, the collaborative efforts of this Biblical pairing somehow fuelled wars of conquest, the main object of which became Rus. In 787-788, within a significant part of Rus, "fighting was continued by the Khazars, who scaled the city of Kyiv and sat there" (*The Veles Book* [board 4a]).

In the conflict with the Khazars the first aid to reach eastern Slavs was rendered by the Ossetians (also known as Ironts) who were descendants of the Scythian-Sarmatian branch of the Aryan community. The union of their cavalry with the Rusy army initiated the formation of the steppe Cossacks and, apparently, it was due to those Cossacks that Prince Bravlin took Tauridian Surozh from the Khazars and Byzantians in 787. A second aid then came to Kyivan Rus from the Varangians of Venedi (Baltic) Rus. For several centuries their armed detachments had already been using the military-trade routes to Greece (see above), either accompanying or plundering the caravans of merchants; in their campaigns this army had long ago looked towards rich and convenient Kyiv.

Somehow, according to *The Veles Book* [board 4c], the "Varangians going to Kyiv together with guests [merchants] had killed Khazars". Then, or later, Kyiv was engaged by the Varangian governor Askold. At the same time, in Ladoga and Novhorod Rus, another Varangian – Rurik, son of Gotleib, prince of the Baltic Slavs-Obodrites^ – tried to usurp power. In 867 the Novhorodians banished this impostor, Rurik, but after three years they accepted him back again to defend their city-state from similar mercenaries and other enemies; Rurik remained in this ruling position until his death in 879.

In addition to the aforesaid common origins of the Venedi-Gothic alliance of Slavs and Germans of the Baltic States (moving away from their Indo-European, Arattan-Aryan past, i.e. Varangians < *Varias*) – it is appropriate here to emphasise that the Varangian-Slavs of the South-East Baltics were quite different from the Viking-Germans of the North-Western Baltics and were somewhat closer to the Slavs from the Dnipro and Black Sea area. However at that time all of them were already identified as Rus, since they were drawn into the "period of 'military' democracy". That is why the author [Nestor] of *The Tale of Bygone Years*, completed in 1113, did not emphasise the ethnic differences within that army: "Rusy, being those named Varangian Rus, included Svie, and the allies Upmane, Angliane, and Gete [Goths?]". Consequently, **the reign of the Varangians in Rus was shaped more by events than by race** (as it seemed to [Russian] patriots, from M. V. Lomonosov up to B. A. Rybakov), **and not even by society. The crux of the problem amounted to the shift in power and the civilisations associated with them: the *priests*** (i.e. the [B]Rahmans, Volhvs[Magi], Ukrs and others) **and the *communal traditions* of Aratta which they preserved were replaced by *warriors*** (the Rugi, Rarogi-Ruriks, Rusy and others) **thereby imposing a *ring of totalitarianism* upon the growing, explosive contradictions of Arsania** and other components of Great Rus.

The impostor, Prince Askold, having initially not been accepted by the Kyivans, departed with his armed detachments to Constantinople which was probably not only the place of his baptism but also where he pledged to set Dir of Byzantium on the Kyivan throne. In 862 Askold killed the legal prince Borevlen (*The Veles Book* [board 6f]) – the **latter being from the aboriginal dynasty of Kyans – and he once again captured Kyiv. That point, *marked the end of communal* Rus and *the start of feudal* Rus**. In line with these events, at the end of 860, Patriarch Photius^ blessed the Bulgarian monks Cyril and Methodius with the task of bringing Christianity to the Rusy and Khazars. When they arrived in Taurida, Cyril saw the "Gospel and Psalter, written in Rusy characters" – "from there they composed books in the Rusy tongue" [3, p. 322-330]... Indeed, long before the Christian era and actually up until Volodymyr "the Slavs and the Slavic-Rusy had letters, and many ancient writers offer evidence for this" (V. N. Tatishchev) (see Tables XII-XIV). Modern supporters of the fallacy that "Slavic written language was initially created by Cyril and Methodius on the basis of ecclesiastical-Byzantine letters" do not want to reckon with this fact and are freely or unwittingly promoting totalitarianism.

Operating by the cross and the sword, as well as making strategic use of drought and famine, Byzantium, – "God's help against the pagans" – occupied Bulgaria and baptised the whole nation. At the same time, with the help of the government of Kyiv [where Dir reigned] the Byzantians captured and baptised the long-suffering Surozh. In *The Epistle* of 866, Patriarch Photius of Constantinople was praised for allegedly having subdued the Christian church[47], not only of the Bulgarians "but also the people who are frequently remembered and glorified by many as those whose bloodthirstiness surpassed that of all other nations – I speak of the Rusy (...). Now they themselves reverted from profane superstitions to the pure and virginal Christian faith". Well, not entirely - all of the hierarchy since, according to moral-ethical evaluations, was sinfully corrupt... moreover the proteges of Byzantium had not even been able to baptise Kyiv – let alone the whole of Rus.

Having strengthened his own power, the Varangian Askold decided to do away with Byzantine Dir. Then in 882 Askold was murdered by the Novhorod governor Oleh, who brought to the Kyivans the infant son of the late Rurik – the successor of the "legitimate prince". From that time Rurik's dynasty started in Rus. The latter of these events, however, remained unknown to the authors of *The Veles Book* which was evidently completed in 879.

It goes without saying that the *totalitarian-biblical* ideology worked deeply and extensively in order to denigrate and exterminate the traditions of the preceding, *communal-Vedic* civilisation. This was natural: the transition gravitated towards the 'autumnal withering' associated with feudalism that was far removed from, and hostile to, the flowering associated with the previous 'springtime'. Now, however, the present intellectual elite has to think hard about the new 'springtime' of popular *self-government* and cease to serve the outgoing *totalitarianism* of rulers – let the capitalists bustle about over grubby deathbed policies: these are their earnings and hence their cross to bear.

Alas! Even though the Academy of Sciences [of Ukraine] has until now supervised the celebration of Slavic writing, they still study the eradication of paganism by Prince Volodymyr. Disregarding the chronicle, "Volodymyr lived by ancestral principles" even after the baptism of Rus which, in the honest opinion of Professor B. A. Rybakov [46, p. 763-782], considering the controversy with Christianity in the 9th – 12th centuries, generated the "revival of paganism". The basis of this phenomenon is outlined by the authoritative researcher A. G. Kuzmin [25, p. 345-353].

All the facts of this matter, systematically organised by the above mentioned two scientists, are based upon an understanding of several axioms: Firstly, Paganism (whether 'populist or 'nationalist', accursed by churchmen and biblical politicians for "antigentile-internationalist" ferment) represents a cultural quality of communal origin, embracing the indivisible unity of elements of science, arts and religions, etc. Secondly, Pagan harmonic unity is incompatible with the religion of totalitarian formations which are isolated from culture and which are inflated by serving state politics, both domestic and foreign. Thirdly, the censure of populism and peasantry. (The Ukrainian word for 'paganism' is 'поганство' (poganstvo) < Latin 'poganus', meaning the [archetypal] 'peasant' of catholic ministration). The pursuit of their annihilation, by church and policy, cannot be deemed righteous in any circumstances whatever (and although 'Photiuses' or 'Lenins' may believe that such annihilation is righteous, this thought will not succeed since the number of "elitist"-intellectuals and other associates is vast). Fourthly, the natural calendaric-economic everyday basis of Paganism is ineradicable; the typical citizen of even such a super-industrial and ultra-religious country as the USA remains a cowboy at heart. Therefore, Prince Volodymyr was neither desirous of, nor able to, "shake the un-shakeable" (Veda). Having vainly attempted in 980 to strengthen the young feudal state by communal "pagan"-Pravoslavny^ (< to praise 'Prava'-Heaven: (The Veles Book [board 1])), Volodymyr adopted another decision in 988 – in accord with the dictates and circumstances of the era, and very different from his previous attempt to mate 'spring' with 'autumn'. By adopting the ideology and religion of Byzantium, Volodymyr the Baptist showed brilliant wisdom as both a ruler and a politician for it was not the Byzantine Christianity of that time which he adopted but the original form into which Byzantium was baptised in 330, and that, fulfilling the decision of the Synod of 381, was proclaimed "Aryan heresy".

Was the hierarchy of the empire displeased by the actions of its enlightened Aryan First-Baptist, who by that time had died? He had remained loyal to the principle of the ancient civilisation with its religious ideology: that a citizen should be obliged to venerate the state GOD first but after that may esteem any Gods, that was his own private affair. In Rus, this principle of dual-faith and dual-power (the archaic communal and contemporary totalitarian principle that had been preserved by the people and by rulers) became known as 'Pravoslavny Khrystyianstvo', i.e. Orthodox Christianity. Byzantium was forced to at least acknowledge its favouring of Rus, especially since Byzantium itself also did not cross over. However, for a long time conventional churchmen considered Prince Volodymyr to have been an Aryan-heretic just like, coincidentally, Cyril and Methodius, who were only canonised by the Orthodox Church many centuries after their deaths.

8. Conclusions and outlooks

It seems that this ***symbiosis*** [of christianity and paganism] facilitated not just ***the priests*** but also the ***Magi*** – the higher rank, who were inseparable from the art of clairvoyance and other properties of priests immersed in the Energy-Information FIELD (this scientific notion corresponds to the religious 'Almighty, All-knowing GOD'). These sacred ministers apparently laid the ***foundation of the Pravoslavny-Church elders*** and Black Monasticism. They worked hard to link the past 'spring' with the forthcoming 'spring' and to strengthen this connection during the adverse conditions of the intermediate 'season' of totalitarian formations... For the post-baptismal history of Rus and Slavdom, this fact is the principal secret of what followed – the "secret of the Rusy soul". {The West European (*F*-) type capitalist civilisation that opposed our Slavic (+*E*) communist civilisation (neither of which were in naturally pure forms), embodied this secret in Freemasonry; its source in the traditions of Paganism was retained underground by those fleeing from the church-state orthodoxy (i.e. by the artisan-townsfolk, strained by the subsequent opposition of the nobility but also driven by the financially persecuted Jewry)}.

The primary carrier of the energy-information field of the Universe is *gravity*, then light (and *water*) – such is the framework that links the *field* basis of the Universe with its tangible, material manifestations, i.e. its *essence*-and-form. The Magi, at the level of wisdom for their time (i.e. intuition, magnified by knowledge), had to seek that connection through water and, especially, through light. And they did precisely that! In analysing the renewal of Paganism (because of its controversy with Christianity), Professor Rybakov drew particular attention to the "abyss of celestial water" and to the fact that "for Rusy people in the 12th century, the daily illumination of the world was attributed not only to the Sun but also to a special, indescribable non-material light which, apparently, in later times was called 'white light' " [46, p. 763-764]. It is a pity that he did not dare to acknowledge the authenticity of *The Veles Book* (see Table XIV: 1) and draw on its immense information, which I do draw upon, since I do acknowledge its authenticity. Even if someone eventually happens to prove that the author of *The Veles Book* is Yu. P. Mirolyubov or someone else – nevertheless this Book exists by GOD-GIVEN Revelation from a number of Holy writings. This work is still overlooked by the Academies of Science, the consortia of authors and even by geniuses.

So, let us turn to those verses of *The Veles Book* which, in starting to update Orthodoxy, lay the foundation for a future understanding of GOD (i.e. more scientific than religious) as 'happy Fate', akin to the "Information Field" or +*E* [44; 77, p. 19-31].

Greeks honour neither gods nor people.
They make stone images in the likeness of men.
But our gods ***express*** *essence...*

[*The Veles Book*, board 22]

Contrary to popular opinion with regard to the polytheism of Paganism, it should be recognised that within the communal-state **Pravoslavny** [Orthodoxy], and at least from the time of the accession of Svaroh (the Solar zodiac being the **embodiment of the annual-calendar cycle** from 2400 BCE onwards), **Paganism naturally tended towards Monotheism**. Only one god represented the Year, consequently, it was not possible to squeeze two or more [primary] gods into one Year. However a year includes the set of seasons, months and days, and the various works and phenomena of nature – and all these are manifestations of GOD or equate with relatively independent Gods with different functions and names (see Table XV):

If anyone mischievously distinguishes those gods,
as separate in Svarzi ('Heaven')
– he will be thrown from his kin.
Because we don't have different gods: (and) Vyshen, and Svaroh,
and others are multiple, –
since GOD is one-and-many.
And nobody divides that multitude,
and does not say that we have many gods.
For behold the light of Ira(ya) goes before us and let us be worthy of that.
[board 30]

The line that I have highlighted may be treated as an illustration of Professor Rybakov's above mentioned conclusion. However, it may also be interpreted as the call of the priests to adequately perceive the Truth (i.e. the Information FIELD). *The Veles Book* [board 1, and others] provides evidence of this interpretation, and specifically defines the perception of Truth:

For behold Da(zh)bo(h) created us an egg,
which shines for us like the real dawn-light. (…)
So behold the essence of the souls of ancestors,
Those that shine the dawns on us from Iru... (…)
By praying to gods, we clean our souls and bodies,
and yes, we have life from our ancestors – the gods merged into one.
The Truth is this: behold, here are Dazhboh's grandsons
(behold: Rusy to the Mind).
As God's Great Mind is united with us –
(and) therefore we create and talk with gods put together...

We can see how this instruction would satisfactorily connect to the Information FIELD (i.e. to DazhBOH, [boh = god]): the Living being purified with the radiance of the ancestors (from the burning dawn of DazhBOH) and together with them, merge with the Gods; thus uniting their minds with the mind of GOD and becoming suitable (by their words and actions) for HIS Godly-manifestations.

The above passage holds the extremely important description of the removal of the contradiction between life-and-death – by means of light and mind-information (see Table XV: 5,9,15). The authors of *The Veles Book* [board 26 and others] repeatedly immersed themselves in the problem of "the glory of the dead in the name of the living", so characteristic of the "ethno-psychology of Slavs, whose name is possibly connected with this concept[48]" [2, p. 270; see above about the Trojan War].

I tell you my son, that time is indestructible and eternally before us.
And there (in Prava, i.e. the Sky) *we see our ancestors and mothers,*
who talk to Svarha [Svarozh] (as constellations) *and there his cattle graze,*
and they bind their sheaves, and have lives similar to ours. (…)
And so we praise the glory of the gods,
who are our fathers and we are their sons.
And deserving of purity in body and soul
that never dies and does not disappear at the hour of our bodily death.
And Perun gives living water to drink to the fallen on the battlefield,
and, after drinking it, [the warrior] *goes to Svarha on a white horse.*
There Perun meets him and leads him to blessing in his halls,
and there he will stay a certain time and will get a new body.
And so life becomes a joy for ever into the eternity of ages,
creating a prayer about us.

The resurrection of warrior-heroes agrees with the image of the Divine Rider (< Aryan Saviour *Gandkharva* > Ukrainian "folk icon" Cossack Mamai [65; 73]), who we suppose to be the basis of the *Cossack Saviour* [*The Veles Book*, board 8(2)] (see Tables XXI: 3,6,11,16; XXII:8; XXXIII; XL: 10,6):

And then seen, galloping in Svarzi a herald on a white horse.
And he raised his sword to heaven
to rend the clouds and thunder.
And living water flows to us, and we drink that –
because anything from Svaroh flows to us with life.
And we drink that as the outflow of the life of GOD on Earth.
That – since the Earth-cow comes to the blue fields
and starts to eat grass and to give milk,
and that milk flows right down to the abyss
and shines at night by the stars above us.

The last lines may serve to illustrate both the conclusion reached by Rybakov about the *abyss*, or 'troughs' (the openings in the vault of heaven, above which extend the "supply of rainwater" - in this case in the stream of the Milky Way) as well as to my own conclusions about the distribution of energies within the Universe (equated with the power of God in the galloping rider) through the means of gravity, light and water.

Having dealt with the updated understanding of GOD from the pagan authors of Christian times – i.e. with that update extending a bridge between ancient philosophy, with its figurative-intuitive worldview, and the logical-analytical worldview of modern physics – we shall go on to consider (in addition to *The Vedas*, *The Veles Book* etc.) those tangible accomplishments which amount to the supports of the bridge.

Contrary to the historical-materialist understanding of the "driving force of history" as a class struggle in totalitarian formations, we have to focus attention on the six-century cycle of Renaissance-Reformation-Enlightenment-Neo Orthodoxy [or rather the true Neo ***Pravoslavny***]. This chain of overall cultural transformation changed the links between the emergence of capitalist-linked (*F-*) and communist (*+E*) formations, but the main point is that it completed the first round of human civilisation with the characteristic mastery of the ***material*** manifestations of the physical world and began the second with the onset of gaining mastery over its ***field*** basis. Note also that the links in this chain were successively formed by Italians (in the 14th – 15th centuries), by Germans, French and British (in the Scientific-Industrial Revolution) and from the activities of Helena Blavatsky and the Roerichs in the 19th – 20th centuries.

Referring to the fact that the [anonymous] author of *Tale of the Campaign of Ihor Svyatoslavlich*, anticipating the poets of the Italian Renaissance, "made extensive use of images of ancient Paganism, revitalising the native Pagan romance for his readers" [46, p. 775], we must not forget other immense works of this circle: the inexhaustible ornamentation and folklore of *The Veda Slovena*, *The Veles Book* and *The Boyan Anthem*, or the 'bylinas' [heroic poems] and 'dumas' [ballads]. As we see, the discussion should focus not so much on revival but on continuity. From the ruins of the Aryan, Cimmerian, Scythian and Slavic fortresses of the island of Khortytsia arose the Zaporozhian Sich of the medieval Cossacks [42, p. 44-47]. Here, in 1710, from the environment of those 'custodians' of communal statehood-civilisation, appeared (in both Latin and Russian-Ukrainian languages) the forthcoming Charter: *Pacta et Constitutiones lecum libertatumque Exercitus Zaporoviensis,* "Agreement and Regulation between Hetman P. Orlyk and the Zaporozhian Army" [41, p. 10-111], – the Constitution which, after half a century and more, became the model for the republican legislations of USA, France and other nations. Figuratively speaking, the seeds from the last communality (of Rus), preserved in the hothouse of Slavic-Ukrainian ethnoculture [when the state was ruled by all the people], were sown into the **upcoming communism** [when the state had to be self-managed by the people].

We will not emphasise here the troubles of the transitional period, from the 'February thaws' to the 'March frosts' – they are inevitable. However, the heritage of the 'springtime' concept was not interrupted and in order to adequately understand what happened, it is necessary to compare the legislative-ideological foundations of the totalitarian and communal civilisations, i.e. the foundation of the first one, which had prevailed in Europe since the time of Hellas and Rome (see Tables VII-XI), and the foundation of the second one, which was preserved, though modernised, by Zaporizhia since the times of Aratta-Arta-Arsania (see Tables IV-V, XIII-XXXIII).

So, Europe in the 18th century was dominated by the following schematic model: at the top – the anthropomorphic Lord of Biblical-type, a slave-holder, who made people his slaves "according to his image and likeness"; below the Lord – the priesthood headed by the Pope, "the vicar of God on Earth"; below them – the "pastors, servants of the Lord" affirmed by the priesthood nobility headed by the king etc.; at the bottom – the subservient people, over whom reigned the supreme Lord, blessed by the vicars and pastors. And here is what was *introduced by the Cossacks*, the guardians of the Slavic, European, Indo-European, and the entire human basis of civilisation: at the top – GOD, 'happy FATE' (i.e. the Information FIELD, as we now know); below GOD – "God's children", i.e. the people; then at the bottom – "servants of the people", i.e. the foremen and officers led by the Hetman and so on. The Power-Management of society is subdivided accordingly into three inter-connected parts: the Legislature, held by the assembly-council of "God's children" (since "the voice of the people is the voice of God"), the Executive, in the hands (of course!) of the "people's servants", and the Judiciary, the most influential members of the community and who are subject only to GOD and the traditions of Customary Law. This is the ideal of democracy… which attracts (!) Slavs (!!) to the "civilised West" (!!!).

{Yes, we have scattered! – you were behind us (from the beginning of the 18th century), and now we are behind you (from the middle of the 20th century). Oh! – the beacon of light exhibited by our Cossacks is by no means extinguished, its light is for all and for many millennia to come. Moreover this light includes all spectra, not only the sciences, religion and politics but also, indeed, art and culture as a whole. Here Jung humanised Freud, renewing (by means of "Neo-Paganism"!) the subconscious basis of modern culture; but Freud indeed, through Dostoevsky, "came out of Gogol's *The Overcoat*, and Gogol came out of the Zaporozhian-Cossacks (see Tables XXIII: 2-5; XXXIII: 7), from the archetypes of Ukrainian hand-painted eggs, etc. And if Slavs, as well as all humanity, would know and understand history, they will indeed learn the lessons… Alas!

Alas-Alas, the problem is basically insoluble. The stumbling-block here is not human stupidity or laziness – no, the situation is much more serious. It rests against the context of human existence in general (that is one more, crucial spectrum). And the meaning is very simple: the natural necessity for the development of anthropological types. This is like the problem about an egg: should it be kept as it is, or should we allow the chick to destroy it from within? Homo sapiens (Neanderthal) reigned at the apex of the hierarchy of the animal world, indeed became its 'fate'-god. Then, Homo sapiens sapiens (we ourselves, Cro-Magnon) mastered the material manifestations of the entire physical world, mastered the expanse of the planet and of time, past and present. In the future, in cosmic space[49], the field basis of the material world will begin to develop the already conceived *Homo noeticus* (the typological-anthropological forerunner of 'aliens' who are barely known to science).

Our present position is that of the hatching chick piercing its egg shell in its nest during the seasonal change of early-March [i.e. at the cusp of a new springtime for civilisation]. So, here we are – needing a change of anthropology that has been the root cause of revolutions, wars, and catastrophes, but… who is right: the keepers of the egg [who want to conserve it] or the parents of the chick [who want it to develop]? The answer lies only with GOD; for people, and even 'aliens', the answer is beyond their capabilities. Thus although we are improving, experiencing troubles as they arrive, the effectiveness of the teachings (including this book too), alas, is not high. However, we have already found the key for the successful universal settlement of all the problems of the foreseeable future. The key is this: it is $+E$ (in the system of the entire aforesaid formula), the reality of the Almighty & Omniscient GOD being the Energy-Information FIELD (see Table XLI) and, hence, the credibility of "the netherworld". Biofield-souls, cultivated by our bodies, periodically move away to the "netherworld" [i.e. to the network of the energy-information field] and return again, and again; these "transmigrations" ensure the conception of new bodies… }

Finally, let us consider a lesson from the same *Cossack Testaments*, concerning the "servants of the people" (who were capable of substantially favouring or playing dirty tricks on *people*, as the experience of democratisation has convinced us since the times of the Zaporozhian Sich centred on Khortytsia. (The Vedic word 'khardis' (хардис) means 'protection', from which evolved *Khortytsia* (Хортица), Charter (хартия 'khartiya'), the Khurites, Khairo! [*Greek*, i.e. be glad!], Khi!-ura!, 'glory!' and so forth).

Thus, *the leader and other chieftains were elected for a year according to the ancient tradition of the Saviour* [*Spas*]. If he endured, he would be held in respect and enjoy privileges to the end of his days; if he did not endure, the Gromada (< Vedic 'community') would slay him, i.e. bring him to sacrifice ("devour" him or bring him down, as it is now expressed in "civilised society"). The Otaman/Ataman, i.e. chieftain, was the best (Rahman (*Rusy*), or Brahman (*Vedic*) 'worshipper') of the best, who amongst the Cossacks were the *Kharakternyks* – the priest-custodians of military art. A Cossack had no right to renounce such chieftainship – the penalty for refusal was death. He was obliged to serve society. The *essence (+E) of public service* was not simply to make the right decisions (that is only the Z component ['zmist' in *Ukrainian* means 'content', see p. 343] which the kharakternyk possessed faultlessly); instead, the essence of public service was to *ensure its success* (in other words: "the people's servant" formed an in-depth, adequate connection to the GOD-'FATE', i.e. to the Energy-Information FIELD). This is yet another aspect of the Slavic beacon of democracy for humanity – it may seem rather remote but there is a very real prospect of it gaining the desired result.

Glory to Slavs! Glory to the Heroes!

References cited in the Conclusion.
(Unless otherwise stated, these works are in Russian).

1. L. I. Akimova, *Troy and Schliemann*, GMII, Moscow & Leonardo Arte, Milan, 1996; 24 pages.
2. L. I. Akimova, 'The Dardan World in Ancient Mythological Ritual Tradition' in *Treasures of Troy*, GMII, Moscow and Publishing "Leonardo Arta," Milan, 1996; pp. 241-280.
3. A. I. Asov, *Slavonic Runes and the Boyan Anthem*, Veche, Moscow, 2000; 416 pages.
4. G. S. Belyakova, 'Sources of the pre-writing system of Slavic letters', in *Russkaya mysl*, Obshchestvennaya Polza, Moscow, Nos. 3-12, pp. 109-114, 1993.
5. L. Bezkluby, 'From ancient customs', in *Spas. Ukrainian custom*, Zaporizhzhia, 2000; p. 8 [in Ukrainian].
6. Z. Vasina, *The Ukrainian annals of attire*, Mystetstvo, Kyiv, Vol. 1, 2003; 446 pages [in Ukrainian].
7. Yu. I. Venelin, *Ancient and present Slovene in their political, national, historic and religious attitude to Russians*, D-r France Preshern, Moscow, 2004; 384 pages.
8. *The Veles Book*. Ukrainian translation and comments by B. Yatsenko, Indoeurope, Kyiv, 1995; 316 pages; Russian translation by V. Yatsenko, Veles, Kyiv, 2001, 256 pages
9. V. M. Voitovych, *Ukrainian mythology*, Lybid, Kyiv, 2002; 664 pages [in Ukrainian].
10. O. Voropai, *The customs of our people. Ethnographical essay*, two volumes, Munich, 1958, 1966; Oberih, Kyiv, 1991; 456 pages & 448 pages [in Ukrainian].
11. J. Wood, *Sun, Moon and ancient stones*, Mir, Moscow, 1981; 269 pages. [in Russian, but first published [in English] as *Sun, Moon and Standing Stones*. Oxford University Press, 1978, ISBN 0-19-211443-3].
12. Herodotus, *The Histories*, Translation to Russian and comments by G. A. Stratanovskii, Nauka, Leningrad, 1972; 600 pages.
13. Ya. F. Holovatsky, *Exposition of old Slavic legends, or mythology*, Dovira, Kyiv, 1991; 94 pages [in Ukrainian].
14. V. M. Huzy, *A golden cane*, Ukr. idea, Brovary, 1997; 400 pages [in Ukrainian].
15. V. Danylenko, *Eneolithic Ukraine*, Scientific thought, Kyiv, 1974; 176 pages.
16. V. Danylenko, 'The cosmogony of barbaric society', in V. Danylenko and Yu. Shilov, *Beginning of Civilisation*, - Ekaterinburg: "Business Book", Moscow: "Rarity", 1999, pp. 3-216.
17. *Encyclopaedia of Trypillian Civilisation*, two volumes, Ed. M. Yu. Videyko, TOV Ukrpoligrafmedia, Kyiv, 2004; 704 pages [in Ukrainian].
18. L. L. Zaliznyak, *Essays on the Ancient History of Ukraine*, Abris, Kyiv, 1994; 248 pages [in Ukrainian].
19. K. V. Zinkovsky and V. H. Petrenko, 'Burials with ochre in Usativ burial grounds', in *Soviet Archaeology*, No. 4. pp. 24-39, Nauka, Moscow, 1987.
20. I. A. Ivanchyk, *On the eve of Colonisation*, Palaeographer, Moscow-Berlin, 2005; 312 pages.

21. N. I. Kikeshev, *Original Homeland and Ancestors*, Belye alvy, Moscow, 2003; 400 pages.
22. A. G. Kifishin, *Ancient Sanctuary of Stone Grave. The experience of the decipherment of the Proto-Sumerian archive of XII-III millennia BCE*, Aratta, Kyiv, 2001; 846 pages.
23. V. O. Kobyliukh, *Ukrainian Cossack names in Sanskrit*, IPShI Nauka I osvita, Lviv-Kyiv-Donetsk, 2003; 244 pages [in Ukrainian].
24. I. V. Kahanets, *Aryan Standard*, A.S.Kyiv, Kyiv, 2004; 336 pages [in Ukrainian].
25. A. G. Kuzmin, *The Beginning of Rus*, Veche, Moscow, 2003; 380 pages.
26. V. Kulbaka and V. Kachur, *The Systemic Cults of the Bronze Age of south-eastern Europe*, PGTU, Mariupol, 1998; 60 pages [in Ukrainian].
27. F. B. J. Kuiper, *Transactions on Vedic Mythology*, Nauka, Moscow, 1986; 196 pages (Russian translation).
28. N. I. Makhno, *Recollections*, three books; Paris, 1926, 1936; Scorpion, Kharkiv, 1998; 213, 163, 184 pages.
29. V. M. Masson and E. K. Chernysh, 'The Eneolithic Right bank of Ukraine and Moldavia', in *Eneolithic USSR*, Nauka, Moscow, 1982; p. 165-320.
30. Yu. P. Mirolyubov, 'Prehistory of Slavic-Rus', in *Collected works*, Vol. 14, KLIEMO-Euren, Aachen, 1988; 188 pages.
31. Yu. P. Mirolyubov, 'Tales of Zakharikhi', *Collected works*, Vol. 16, KLIEMO-Euren, Aachen, 1990; 224 pages.
32. Yu. P. Mirolyubov, 'Gogol and revolution', in *Collected works*, Vol. 18, KLIEMO-Euren, Aachen, 1992; 86 pages.
33. *Myths of the World Nations*, two volumes, Ed. S. A. Tokarev, Soviet Encyclopedia, Moscow, 1991, 1992; 672 pages, 720 pages.
34. B. D. Mykhailov, *The Petroglyphs of Stone Grave*, Dikoe Pole, Zaporizhia & Institut obshchegumanitarnykh issledovanii, 1999; 238 pages [in Ukrainian].
35. V. F. Mitsyk, *Sacred Country of the Grain growers*, Taki spravy, Kyiv, 2006; 264 pages [in Ukrainian].
36. Yu. L. Mosenkis, *Trypillian pre-dictionary of Ukrainian Language*, NDITIAM, Kyiv, 2001; 80 pages [in Ukrainian].
37. S. I. Nalyvayko, *Secrets of Sanskrit Revealed*, Prosvita, Kyiv, 2000; 288 pages [in Ukrainian].
38. S. I. Nalyvayko, *IndoAryan Secrets of Ukraine*, Prosvita, Kyiv, 2004; 448 pages [in Ukrainian].
39. V. Nedyak, Ukraine – 'A Cossack Country', EMMA, Kyiv, 2004; 1216 pages (in Ukrainian).
40. N. A. Nikolaeva and V. A. Safronov, *Sources of Slavic and Eurasian Mythology*, Belyi volk, KRAFT, GUP "Oblizdat", Moscow, 1999; 312 pages.
41. P. Orlyk, *Constitution, Manifests and the Literary Heritage*, MAUP, Kyiv, 2006; 736 pages [in Ukrainian].
42. S. Zh. Pustovalov, *The Social Order of the Catacomb society of Northern Black Sea area*, Shliakh, Kyiv, 2005; 412 pages [in Ukrainian].
43. D. Rol, *Genesis of Civilisation*, Eksmo, Moscow, 2002; 478 pages.
44. M. D. Rudenko, *Gnosis and the Present Time (Architecture of Universe)*, Jura, Ternopol, 2001; 248 pages [in Ukrainian].
45. B. A. Rybakov, *Paganism of Ancient Slavs*, Nauka, Moscow, 1981; 606 pages.
46. B. A. Rybakov, *Paganism of Ancient Rus*, Nauka, 1987; 784 pages.
47. B. A. Rybakov, 'Ancient Slavdom and the Ancient World', in *All-Slavic Council*, Vseslavianskii Sobor, Moscow, 1998; pp. 7-13.
48. *Savur-Grave. Legends and Remittances of Lower part of the Dnipro River region*, Compiler: V. Chabanenko, Dnipro, Kyiv, 1990; 262 pages [in Ukrainian].
49. L. P. Sannikova, *The Holy Language of the Creator in Customs of People: Eniological phenomenology of old-Ukrainian culture*, Aratta, Kyiv, 2005; 776 pages [in Ukrainian].
50. V. A. Safronov, *The Indo-European Original Homeland.* – Gorky: Volgo-Vyatskoe

knizhnoe izdatelstvo, Gorkii, 1989; 402 pages.
51. A. B. Suprunenko, I. M. Kulatova, K. M. Myronenko, A. V. Artem'ev and S. V. Maevska, *Ancient Residences of Outskirts of Komsomolsk*, Part I, ASMI, Kyiv-Poltava, 2005; 140 pages [in Ukrainian].
52. A. I. Asov, *The Veda Slovena*, Translation and comments, FAIR-PRESS, Moscow, 2003; 704 pages.
53. P. V. Tulaev, *The Veneti: Ancestors of the Slavs*, Belye alvy, Moscow, 2000; 192 pages.
54. P. P. Tolochko V. V. Otroshchenko, et al., *The Ethnic History of Ancient Ukraine*, Institute of Archeology, Nat. Acad. Sci., Kyiv, 2000; 280 pages [in Ukrainian].
55. O. N. Trubachev, 'On the Ancestral Homeland of the Aryans' (Concerning the output of the book: Yu. Shilov, *Ancestral homeland of the Aryans: History, Ceremonies and Myths*, Kyiv, 1995), in *Questions of Linguistics*, No. 3, pp. 3-12, Nauka, Moscow, 1996.
56. O. N. Trubachev, *Indoarica in the Northern Black Sea area*, Nauka, Moscow, 1999; 320 pages.
57. O. N. Trubachev, *Transactions on Etymology: Word. History. Culture*, two volumes, Yazyki Slavianskoi Kultury, Moscow, 2004, 2005; 800 pages, 664 pages.
58. *Ukrainian national tales*, Perun, Kyiv-Irpin, 1996; 680 pages [in Ukrainian].
59. M. Chmykhov, *Sources of the Paganism of Rus*, Lybid, Kyiv, 1990; 384 pages.
60. M. I. Chumarna, *From the Beginning of the World. Ukraine in Symbols*, – Privatna avtorska shkola M. Chumarnoi, Lviv, 1996. – 256 pages [in Ukrainian].
61. Yu. Shilov, 'Earliest Mounds and Myth-Creation', in *Macedonian folklore*. XX, br. 39-40, p. 45-61, Institut za folklor "Marko Cepenkov", Skopje, 1987.
62. Yu. Shilov, 'Embodiment of Apollo in Late-Catacomb Burial in the Lower Dnipro', in *Ancient Black Sea area*", Odesky Derzhavny Univeritet, Odesa, 1991, pp. 110-112.
63. Yu. Shilov, 'On the name of the Chongar peninsula', in *Problems of the History of Crimea*, issue II, pp. 14-15, Simpheropol Derzhavny Univeritet, Simferopol, 1991.
64. Yu. Shilov, *Myths about "Space Nomads" and the Employment of the Calendar in Europe, VI millennia BCE*, Moscow, 1992; 32 pages; also in *On the Frontiers of Knowledge of the Universe. Historical-astronomical research*, XXIII, Nauka, Moscow, 1992; p. 272-303.
65. Yu. Shilov, Gandkharva – 'Aryan Saviour', in *Ancient Black Sea area*, Odesky Derzhavny Univeritet, Odesa, 1993; pp. 22-25.
66. Yu. Shilov, *Ancestral Homeland of the Aryans: History, ceremonies and myths'*, "SINTO", Kyiv, 1995; 744 pages.
67. Yu. Shilov, Trypillia, Troy, Illium and Helon, in *The Third International Philosophical Symposium "Dialogue of Civilisations: East is West*, Publishing house of Russia. The University of Friendship of Peoples, Moscow, 1997; pp. 44-46.
68. Yu. Shilov, *Sources of Slavic Civilisation*, MAUP, Kyiv, 2004; 704 pages [in Russian].
69. Yu. Shilov, Aratta and Ariana. 'Pre-roots of Rus', in *Theses of All-Ukrainian Scientific Conference "Pereyaslav land and its place in the development of the Ukrainian nation, statehood and culture"*, MPP "Booklet", Pereyaslav-Khmelnytsky, 1992; pp. 46-47 [in Ukrainian].
70. Yu. Shilov, 'On the Cosmogonical Origins of Fancies of Zaporizhia Cossacks', in *Ukrainian Cossacks: Origins, Evolution, and Heritage*, issue II, ANU, Kyiv II, 1993; pp. 147-153 (n Ukrainian).
71. Yu. Shilov, 'The Population of Ukrainian Lands during the Indo-European Community: pre-roots of Ukrainian folk-ceremonial culture', in *Materials for Ukrainian Ethnology*, Vol. 1(4), UFETS IMFE of Nat. Acad. Sci. of Ukraine, Kyiv, 1995; pp. 145-155 [in Ukrainian].

[1] A Polish god.

[2] Gerasimov (1907-1970) developed the technique of forensic sculpture and meticulously reconstructed the faces of more than 200 people, including Yaroslav the Wise and Ivan the Terrible.

[3] In Russian, the word for 'man' is *muzhchina* and 'woman' is *zhenshchina*; 'abode' is *zhilishche* and 'home' is *sem'ya.*

[4] 'Beregynia' in Russian.

[5] AM.SI and other capitalised words in this section are Proto-Sumerian (Ref. Kifishin, A. G., *Ancient Sanctuary of Stone Grave. The experience of the decipherment of the Proto-Sumerian archive of XII-III millennia BCE*, Aratta, Kyiv, 2001, pp. 681-686, ProtoSumerian-Russian dictionary.

[6] In astrology, Virgo is depicted holding a sheaf of grain.

[7] The Greek word 'klivanos' means 'oven'.

[8] The Russian-Ukrainian word 'koni' means 'horses'.

[9] In Ukraine there are several different forms of Velykden (Great Day). Babski is one of these but there is also a Rahmanski Velykden. This is not as widespread as the conventional Velykden but both involve baking cakes and decorating eggs "which are consecrated in the church (though not without complaints of some priests about paganism)". The essential difference from the conventional Velykden is the specific imitation of the allied Red Hill celebration. (Ref. Shilov, *Origins of Slavic Civilisation*, Part II: *The Vedantic Heritage of Ukraine*. 2008. Moscow. ISBN 978-98967-006-0).

[10] Vishaps are a form of dragon which, in Armenian mythology, are associated with water.

[11] Within Stone Grave, there have been investigated 63 caves, grottoes and rock slabs with images and symbols dated from 12,000 BCE to 1000 CE.

[12] The groom would visit the bride's parent's house and offer a ransom to get his bride. Initially the offer would usually be money or jewellery for the bride, whereupon the bride's parents would bring out a woman or man dressed as the bride and covered with a veil. When the groom realized that it is not his bride, and asked for his true love, and the family would demand a bigger ransom for the bride. However, if the bridegroom was met at the door with a pumpkin, it meant that his offer of marriage was not accepted and the pumpkin was something for him to carry away so that he wouldn't leave empty-handed.

[13] Note that the cyrillic letter 'Г' ('G' in Russian but 'H' in Ukrainian) transliterates the Ukrainian name 'Лагаш' as Lahash but in Russian as the more familiar Lagash of Sumer.

[14] The Hypatian Codex (also known as the Ipatiev Chronicle) is a 15th century compilation of several much older documents from the Ipatiev Monastery in Russia.

[15] L.A. Waddell noted that the Indian name for the Bharat royal line is derived from this Sumerian word - 'Bara'. (Ref. Catherine Obianuju Acholonu *Eden in Sumer on the Niger : Archaeological, Linguistic and Genetic Evidence of 450,000 years of Atlantis, Eden and Sumer in West Africa*, 2013, Wuse, Abuja, Nigeria. ISBN: 978-978-910-259-4.)

[16] Notice that cyrillic letter 'B' is pronounced as 'V', hence the derivation here of 'vira' from 'bara'.

[17] Translated from the old Slavic 'Ясна Книга' as 'Clear Book' (V.Krasnoholovets) the term transliterates as 'Yasna Book'. (In the Avesta the principal litergical text is called the Yasna Book and the entire book is recited in the *Yasna* ceremony, which takes about two hours).

[18] Faf (Фафъ) is not a recognised word; maybe this is a name; Faf has the pronunciation [FΛF] (V. Krasnoholovets).

[19] The Slavic sun god.

[20] 'Swastika' is a synonym of 'svarha', which originated from Svaroh. (V. Krasnoholovets).

[21] In the Vedas, Aditi is the mother of 12 Adityas whose names include Vivasvan, Aryama, Pusa, Tyasta, Savita, Bhaga, Dhata, Vidhata, Varuna, Mitra, Sakra, and Urukrama. (Vishnu was born as Urukrama, the son of Nabhi and Meru. Ref. *Srimad Bhagavatam* Canto 6, Chapter 6, Verses 38-39).

[22] Transliteration of the Russian 'Речь ведать' meaning 'to know or be in charge of speech'.

[23] In Slavic languages 'horby' means 'humps', (V. Krasnoholovets).

[24] Note that Kur-Gal, written in Cyrillic as 'Кур-Гал', is pronounced Kur-Hal in Ukraine.

[25] As above, Me-gal (pronounced as Me-hal) is the probable root of Mohyl (могыл).

[26] 'Idol' is translated, and equally transliterated, from the Russian 'идол' and the Ukrainian 'ідол'.

[27] The Russian word for baptised is 'крестила' (krestila), i.e. 'christened'.

[28] In Russian, 'Clear Book' is written as 'Ясна-книга', which transliterates as 'Yasna' Book.

[29] From Ukrainian, this means 'cherry tree'. (V. Krasnoholovets).

[30] Compositions of petroglyphs have been described from 65 separate locations inside the caves and grottoes within the hill of Stone Grave. (Mykhailov, B. D., 1999, 'The petroglyphs of Stone Grave', Zaporizhia, Moscow).

[31] Ukrainian 'hromadoyu' is pronounced as 'gromadoyu' in Russian, hence the similarity to the previously mentioned Sanskrit 'grama'.

[32] In the original Russian edition of this book the 'Goddess-*nenia*' is written as 'Богиня-*нэня*' which transliterates respectively in Russian and Ukrainian as 'Boginya-*nenya*' and 'Bohinia-*nenia*', from whom the Slavic goddess Berehynia is perhaps derived?

[33] There is a sanctuary to Diana on the northern shore of Lake Nemi, 25 miles southeast of Rome.

[34] The Republic of Serbian Krajina (1991-95) was a self-proclaimed Serbian state within the Republic of Croatia. The name 'Krajina' (meaning 'frontier') was adopted from the historical borderland of the Austro-Hungarian Empire.

[35] Female figurines often have small holes through the shoulders, presumably for thread from which they could be hung.

[36] The name 'Siyansky' (transliterated from the Russian 'Сиянской' has the same etymology as 'Сияющая' - which means 'radiant' or 'shining').

[37] Remember, the Ukrainian word for 'glory' is 'слава' ('slava').

[38] In Slavic languages 'horby' means 'humps', (V. Krasnoholovets).

[39] A male god in the *Veda Slovena*.

[40] In Ukraine, 'Palianytsia' is a type of a wheat bread.

[41] 'Slava' means glory; Slavs are people who glorify the glorious, i.e. praise the gods. (V. Krasnoholovets).

[42] The author is using word-play here, having specifically written п(о)рочной (p(o)rochnoy: in Russian 'прочный' (prochnoy) means strong, but 'порочный' (porochnoy) means blemish. (V. Krasnoholovets).

[43] 'Tok', in this context, means a 'threshing floor'.

[44] 'Of the same blood', i.e. descended from the same ancestor.

[45] The name of Cyril Street (which leads to the Cyril Monastery) dates back to 1869, before which it was simply called 'Flat'. In 1935 it was renamed Frunze Street in honour of a Soviet military commander although there have been recent moves (2012) to restore the name of Cyril Street.

[46] The origin of the name of the Chermne Sea is derived from the Ukrainian words 'chervony, chermleny' which mean 'red'. However, 'cherne' means black; so this reveals the name of the Black Sea. However, the term "Chervona Rus", as a synonym, initially corresponded to Tauridian Rus, or Surozhian Rus. (V. Krasnoholovets).

[47] The sudden promotion of Photios as Patriarch of Constantinople had caused an ecclesiastical division with Pope Nicholas and the western bishops, and in 863 the Pope deposed Photios. Four years later, Photios responded by calling a Council and excommunicating the Pope on grounds of heresy over the question of the double procession of the Holy Spirit. (Fortescue, A. (2001). *The Orthodox Eastern Church.* pp.147–148. Piscataway, New Jersey: Gorgias Press LLC. ISBN 0-9715986-1-4). The situation was additionally complicated by the question of papal authority over the entire Church and by disputed jurisdiction over newly-converted Bulgaria.(Chadwick, Henry (2003). *East and West: The Making of a Rift in the Church: From Apostolic Times until the Council of Florence*. p.146. Oxford, United Kingdom: Oxford University Press. ISBN 978-0-19-926457-5).

[48] In both Ukrainian and Russian the word 'славити' ('slavyty') means 'to glorify' or 'praise'.

[49] In common parlance, the term 'cosmos' is generally equated with 'outer space' but, in reality, it more accurately means an 'orderly universe' or 'orderly harmonious system'. The latter is more appropriate in the context of this passage since it encompasses "the field basis of the material world". Thus, the author is referring to future human development not necessarily in the physical 'outer' cosmos but in the more abstract 'inner' cosmic space.

REFERENCES

(in Russian, unless stated otherwise)

CITATIONS

Bhagavad-Gita. – Kyiv, 2000.
Chabanenko, V., Compiler: *Savur-Tomb. Legends and Remittances of Lower part of the Dnipro river region*, Dnipro, Kyiv, 1990; 262 pages (in Ukrainian).
Diyakonov, I. M. 'Epic of Gilgamesh'. – Translation and commentary. – Moscow, 1961.
Elizarenkovoi, T. Ya. 'Rigveda'. Translation and commentary – Moscow, 1989, 1999. – 3 vols..
Gindin, L. A., Ivanov, S. A. Compilers. 'Archive of earliest written information about Slavs'. – Moscow, 1994-1995. – 2 vols.
Golovatskii, I. F. Compiler. 'Descriptions of Ancient-Slav legends or mythology'. – Kyiv, 1991.
Herodotus, *The Histories*, Translation to Russian and comments by G. A. Stratanovskii, Nauka, Leningrad, 1972; 600 pages. ..
Homer. 'Iliad'. 'Odyssey'. – Moscow, 1967.
Jordan. 'On the origin and deeds of Goths'. – Moscow, 1960.
Moskalenko, M., 'Golden words. Poetic space of Old Rus'. – Compiled legends, comments. – Kyiv, 1988.
Nestor. 'Tale of Bygone years' / Complete works. Rus. Annals. – Moscow, 1962-1965. – 15 vols.
Rajish, B. Sh., 'Diamond Sutra'. Commentary – Kyiv, 1993.
Tokarev, S. A., Principal Editor. 'Myths of the peoples of the world'. – Moscow, 1991-1992. – 2 vols.
Tokarev, S. A., Ed., *Myths of the World Nations*, two volumes, Soviet Encyclopedia, Moscow, 1991, 1992; 2 vols: 672 & 720 pages.
Yatsenko, B., *The Veles Book*. Ukrainian translation and comments. Indoeurope, Kyiv, 1995; 316 pages; Russian translation by V. Yatsenko, Veles, Kyiv, 2001, 256 pages.
'Tale of the Campaign of Ihor'. – Kyiv, 1985.
'Tibetan Book of the Dead'. – Moscow, 1999.
'Ukrainian folk fairy-tales'. – Kyiv-Irpin, 1996.

HISTORIOGRAPHY

Asov, A. I., *Slavonic Runes and the Boyan Anthem*, Veche, Moscow, 2000; 416 pages.
Bandrovskii, M. S. 'Svarozhie faces'. – Lviv, 1992.
Bibikov, S. M. Principal Editor.'Archaeology of Ukrainian SSR'. – Kyiv, 1972-1974. – 3 vols.
Chertkov, A. D. 'Pelasgian-Thracian tribes which colonised Italy' / Osnova (Journal). – Kyiv, 1993-1995, No. 24-28.
Chumarna, M. I., *From the Beginning of the World. Ukraine in Symbols*, – Privatna avtorska shkola M. Chumarnoi, Lviv, 1996. – 256 pages (in Ukrainian).
Danylenko, V. N. 'Neolithic Ukraine'. – Kyiv, 1969.
Danylenko, V., *Eneolithic Ukraine*, Naukova dumka, Kyiv, 1974; 176 pages.
Danylenko, V., 'The cosmogony of barbaric society', in V. Danylenko and Yu. Shilov, *Beginning of Civilisation*, Business book, Ekaterinburg and Raritet, Moscow, 1999; pp. 3-216.
Dobzhansky, E. I. 'Rodzdva'. – Kyiv, 2000.
Dobzhansky, E. I. 'Velykden [Great Day]. Pysanky [decorated eggs]'. – Kyiv, 2001.
Fraser, J. 'Golden branch'. – Moscow, 1983.
Gamkrelidze, T. V., Ivanov, V. V. 'Indo-European language and Indo-Europeans'. – Tbilisi, 1984. – 2 vols.
Huzy, V. M., *A golden cane*, Ukrainska idea, Brovary, 1997; 400 pages (in Ukrainian).
Keuper, F. B. Ya. 'Proceedings of Vedic mythology'. – Moscow, 1986.
Kifishin, A. G. 'Geno-structure of Pre-Grecian and Ancient Greek myth/image in the context of ancient culture'. – Moscow, 1990.

Kifishin, A. G. 'Palaeolithic Proto-writing. The earliest inscriptions of Stone Grave and their West European analogues / Features of the development of the upper Palaeolithic of East Europe'. – St. Petersburg, 1999.

Kifishin, A. G. '"The frightful wrath" of gods and the "Exodus of people". On the reconstruction of one cultic anthem / Sacrifice'. – Moscow, 2000.

Kifishin, A. G., *Ancient Sanctuary of Stone Grave. The experience of the decipherment of the Proto-Sumerian archive of XII-III millennia BCE*, Aratta, Kyiv, 2001; 846 pages.

Klassen, E. 'New materials for the ancient history of Slavs' – Moscow, 1854; St. Petersburg, 1995.

Kovaleva, I. F. 'The social and spiritual culture of the tribes of the Bronze Age'. – Dnipropetrovsk, 1989.

Kulbaka, V., Selezeny, V. 'Somatic cults of the Bronze Age of South-East Europe'. – Mariupol, 1998.

Kyzlasov, L. R. 'Ancient Kakasia'. – Moscow, 1986.

Lebedev, A. N. 'Formation of the Slavic world'. – Kyiv, 1997.

Losev, A F. 'Ancient mythology in its historical development'. – Moscow, 1957.

Masson, V. M. and Merpert, N. Ya. 'Eneolithic USSR'. – edited correspondence – Moscow, 1982.

Mellaart, J. 'Earliest civilisation in the Middle East'. – Moscow, 1982.

Mirolyubov, YU. P. 'Collected works'. – Cologne, 1981, 1987, 1989. – Vol. 4: 'Rigveda and Paganism'; Vol. 13: 'Formation of Kyivan Rus and its statehood'; Vol. 14: 'Prehistory of Slaviane-Rus'.

Mykhailov, B. D. 'The petroglyphs of Stone Grave'. – Zaporizhia - Moscow, 1999.

Nalyvayko, S. I., *Secrets of Sanskrit Revealed*, Prosvita, Kyiv, 2000; 288 pages (in Ukrainian).

Nikolaeva, N. A. and Safronov, V. A., *Sources of Slavic and Eurasian Mythology*, "White wolf", KRAFT, GUP "Oblizdat", Moscow, 1999; 312 pages.

Popova, T. B. 'Borodino treasure'. – Moscow, 1985.

Pritula, A. L. 'Ukrainian martial art of the "Saviour"'. – Zaporizhia, 2001.

Profet, E. K. 'Lost years of Jesus'. – Moscow, 1999.

Rybakov, B. A., *Paganism of Ancient Slavs*, Nauka, Moscow, 1981; 606 pages.

Rybakov, B. A., *Paganism of Ancient Rus*, Nauka, 1987; 784 pages.

Safronov, V. A., *The Indo-European Original Homeland.* – Gorky: Volgo-Vyatskoe knizhnoe izdatelstvo, Gorkii, 1989; 402 pages.

Sementsov, V. S. 'The problems of interpretation of Brahmanical prose'. – Moscow, 1981.

Sharafutdinova, I. N. 'Steppe of the Dnipro area in the late Bronze Age'. – Kyiv, 1982.

Shilov, Yu., *Ancestral Homeland of the Aryans: History, ceremonies and myths'*, "SINTO", Kyiv, 1995; 744 pages.

Shovkun, V. 'Mysterious Kalka'. – Zaporizhia, 2000.

Stingl, M. 'Worshipped stars'. – Moscow, 1983.

Torop, V. 'Earliest proceedings about Rus'. – Moscow, 1997.

Trubachev, O. N., 'On the Ancestral Homeland of the Aryans' (Concerning the output of the book: Yu. Shilov, *Ancestral homeland of the Aryans: History, Ceremonies and Myths*, Kyiv, 1995), in *Questions of Linguistics*, No. 3, pp. 3-12, Nauka, Moscow, 1996.

Trubachev, O. N., *Indoarica in the Northern Black Sea area*, Nauka, Moscow, 1999; 320 pages.

Veletskoi, N. N. 'Profane symbols of Slavic archaic rites'. – Moscow, 1978.

Voropay, O. 'Customs of our people'. – Munich, 1958, 1966; Kyiv, 1991. – 2 vols.

Wood, J., *Sun, Moon and ancient stones*, Mir, Moscow, 1981; 269 pages.

Zdanovich, G. B. Principal Editor. 'Arkaim. Researches. Findings. Revelations'. – Chelyabinsk, 1995.

METHODS AND METHODOLOGY

Adamenko, N. P. 'Tripleness of the Absolute. Tripleness of souls' / Reports of the International Chertkov, A. D. 'Essay on the ancient history of Proto-Slavs'. – Moscow, 1851.

Azhazha, V. G. 'Fundamentals of ufology'. – Moscow, 1995.
Bolotov, B. V. 'Immortality – this is real'. – St. Petersburg, 1994.
Chmykhov, N. A., Shilov, Yu. A., Kornienko, P. L. 'Archaeological investigations of kurhans'. – Kyiv, 1989.
Convention of Trinitarian knowledge. – Kyiv, 1997-1998, No. 1.
Freidenberg, L. M. 'Myth and literature of antiquity'. – Moscow, 1978.
Furduy, R. S., Shvaidak, Yu. M. 'Intriguing Mysteries'. – Kyiv, 1992.
Grof, S., Moudi, R. et al. 'Life after death'. – Moscow, 1991.
Gumilev, L. N. 'Ancient Rus and the Great Steppe'. – Moscow, 1992.
Kharchenko, P. A. 'Tri-Gnosis'. – Kyiv, 1998.
Krushinskii, V. Yu., Levenets, Yu. A. 'The History of Ukraine'. – Kyiv, 1993.
Lazarev, S. N. 'Karma diagnostics'. – St. Petersburg, 1993.
Martynov, A. 'Confessional path'. – Moscow, 1989.
Safronov, V. A. 'Problems of the Aryan original homeland'. – Ordzhonikidze (city), 1983.
Shilov, Yu., *Myths about "Space Nomads" and the Employment of the Calendar in Europe, VI millennia BCE*, Moscow, 1992; 32 pages; also in *On the Frontiers of Knowledge of the Universe. Historical-astronomical research*, XXIII, Nauka, Moscow, 1992; p. 272-303.
Shilov, Yu. A. '*The Veles Book* and the relevance of ancient doctrines'. – Kyiv, 2001.
Shiure, E. 'Dedicated to the Great. – Kaluga', 1914; Moscow, 1990.

OTHER LITERATURE

Akimova. L. I., *Troy and Schliemann*, GMII, Moscow & Leonardo Arte, Milan, 1996; 24 pages.
Akimova, L. I., 'The Dardan World in Ancient Mythological Ritual Tradition' in *Treasures of Troy*, GMII, Moscow and Publishing "Leonardo Arta," Milan, 1996; pp. 241-280.
Asov, A. I. 'Atlanteans, Aryans, Slaviane (Slavdom): History and Faith'. – Moscow, 2000.
Childe, G. 'Ancient East in the light of new excavations'. – Moscow, 1956.
Chmykhov, M., *Sources of the Paganism of Rus*, Lybid, Kyiv, 1990; 384 pages.
Gusev, N. R. 'Hinduism. Aryans. Slaviane (Slavdom)'. – Moscow, 1995.
David-Nil, A. 'Mystics and Magicians of Tibet'. – Rostov-on-Don, 1991.
Kahanets, I. 'Aryan standard. Ukrainian concept of the epoch of the Great Transition / Transition-IV'. – Kyiv, 2000, No. 2.
Kalinovskii, P. 'Transformation. The last sickness, death and aftermath'. – Moscow, 1991.
Kikeshev, N. I. 'Appeal to the Slavs'. – Moscow, 1998.
Kikeshev, N. I. Principal Editor. 'All-Slavic Church'. Almanac of the international union of social associations. – Moscow, 1998Lozko, G. 'Ukrainian Paganism'. – Kyiv, 1994.
Mavrodin, V. V. 'Origin of Russian people'. – Leningrad, 1978.
Mozolevskii, B. N. 'The Scythian steppe'. – Kyiv, 1983.
Moskovchenko V. M., Popravko ,A. V. 'Karma of Ukraine'. – Kyiv, 1997.
Pavlenko, Yu.V. 'Past history of old Rus in a world context'. – Kyiv, 1994.
Pavlenko, Yu. V. 'Pre-Slavs and Aryans'. – Kyiv, 2000.
Pervukhin, V. YA. 'Slaviane (Slavdom)'. – Moscow, 1997.
Poleshchuk, V. V., Shepa, V. V. 'Historic biogeography of the Danube'. – Kyiv, 1998.
Sedov, V. V. 'Slaviane (Slavdom) in antiquity'. – Moscow, 1994.
Silenko Lev. 'MAHA FAITH'. – New York and others, 1979.
Slaboshpytsky, M. F. 'From the voice of our Klio'. – Kyiv, 2000.
Smirnov, K. F., Kuzmina, E. E. 'Origin of Indo-Aryans in the light of latest archaeological discoveries'. – Moscow, 1977.
Trubachev, O. N. 'Ethnogenesis and earliest culture of Slavs'. – Moscow., 1991.
Tulaev, P. V., *The Veneti: Ancestors of the Slavs*, Belye alvy, Moscow, 2000; 192 pages.
Shayan, V. 'Faith of our ancestors'. – Hamilton, 1987.
Shilov, Yu., Gandkharva – 'Aryan Saviour', in *Ancient Black Sea area*, Odesky Derzhavny Univeritet, Odesa, 1993; pp. 22-25.
Shilov, Yu. A. 'Sacred objects'. – Kyiv, 2001.
Zablotska, Yu. 'The history of the Middle East in antiquity'. – Moscow, 1989.

References

Zaliznyak, L. L., *Essays on the Ancient History of Ukraine*, Abris, Kyiv, 1994; 248 pages (in Ukrainian).

Zaliznyak, L. L. 'Prehistory of Ukraine 10,000 – 5,000 BCE'. – Kyiv, 1998.

Znoyko, A. P. 'Myths of Kyiv land and ancient events'. – Kyiv, 1989.

TABLES

APPEARANCE and FORMATION OF SLAVS

Tables I - XI
Maps and archaeological findings.

Tables XII - XIV
Appearance of writing.

Tables XV - XVI
Calendars and Sanctuary-observatories.

Tables XVII - XIX
Abodes, settlements and kurhans.

Tables XX - XXIII
Anthropomorphous kurhans, idols, figurines and masks.

Tables XXIV - XXVII
Image of the Foremother. Origin of the Epos.

Tables XXVIII - XXXI
Weapons, means of transport and ploughs.

Tables XXXII - XXXIII
Human sacrifices. The image of the Saviour-Rider.

Tables XXXIV - XXXVII
Symbols.

Tables XXXVIII - XL
Serpentine archetypes of conception and revival.

Tables XLI - XLII
Geocosmic connections of the biofield.

Table I

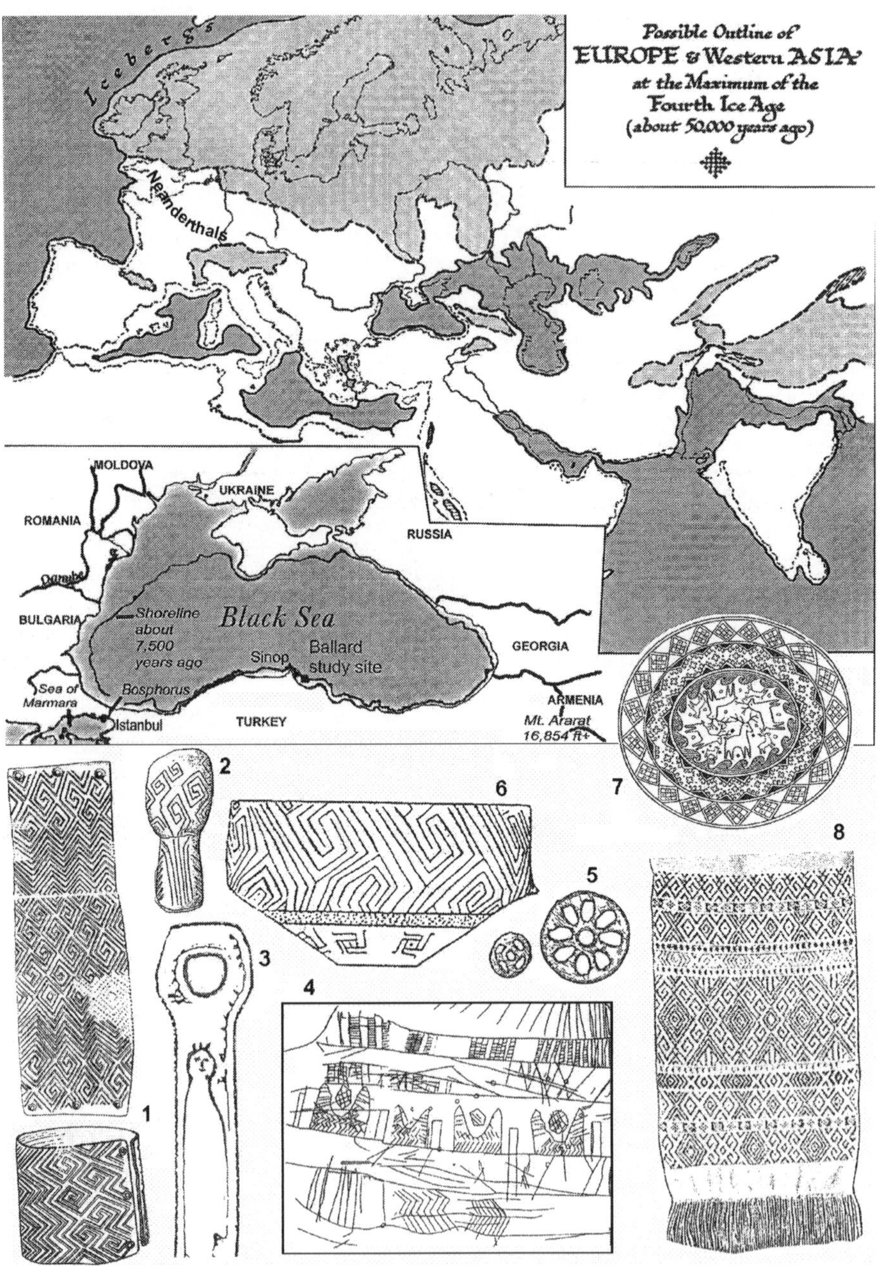

Possible Outline of
EUROPE & Western ASIA
at the Maximum of the
Fourth Ice Age
(about 50,000 years ago)
Icebergs
Neanderthals
MOLDOVA
UKRAINE
ROMANIA
RUSSIA
Danube
BULGARIA
Shoreline
about
7,500
years ago
Black Sea
Sinop
Ballard
study site
GEORGIA
Sea of
Marmara
Bosphorus
ARMENIA
Istanbul
TURKEY
Mt. Ararat
16,854 ft+
1
2
3
4
5
6
7
8

Table I

***The Floods of the 50th – 8th millennium BCE** (above) **and 6700-5550-3300 BCE** (below).*

The Basin formed in the 8th millennium BCE after the melting of the glaciers, decomposed then to Lake Balkhash and the Aral, Caspian and Black Seas. The latter, unlike other isolated basins, remained as such until 6700-5550 (possibly even 3300) BCE, – and then, due to the formation of the Bosphorus Strait, rapidly broadened by the inflow of waters from the Mediterranean Sea and Atlantic (according to R. Ballard et al.). The advance of up to 400 km of water on the northern coasts of the Black Sea and formation of the Azov Sea has left the biblical legend about the "worldwide flood" – sources, which are tracked in the references to the *Sea Abyss, the Court of Water* and such like in Stone Grave (A. G. Kifishin, *Ancient sanctuary of Stone Grave. The experience of the decipherment of Proto-Sumerian archive XII-III millennia BCE*, Aratta, Kyiv, 2001; p. 817, 822 et al.).

The onset of the historic memory of Slavs, according to archaeological data and ethnography (as far back as 21-12 millennia ago, according to *The Veles Book* and B. A. Rybakov's *Paganism of ancient Slavs*):
Ornamentation of bangles and figurines from Upper-Palaeolithic sites near Myzino village in the Korop district of the Chernihiv region formed by emphasising a natural pattern in cuts [sliding fractures] on the tusks of mammoths (1, 2). Later this pattern was preserved in Slavic traditional hand-coloured eggs and embroideries (7, 8) and passed through the emergence of the Aryan community in the Circum-Pontic zone, 'Around the Black Sea' (6: Gian-khasan, Anatolia, 6th millennium BCE).
Palaeolithic origins of the trident and crown indicated on a deer-antler javelin-thrower from a site near the village of Molodovo in the Kelments district in the Chernvitsi region (3), a fragment of an image on a mammoth tusk from the site near Mezhyrich village in the Kaniv district of the Cherkasy region (4), and a simple cross, and paired cross or "Cossack" 8-radial star in bony amulets from Palaeolithic burials near Sunhir village in the Voronezh region (5).

Table II

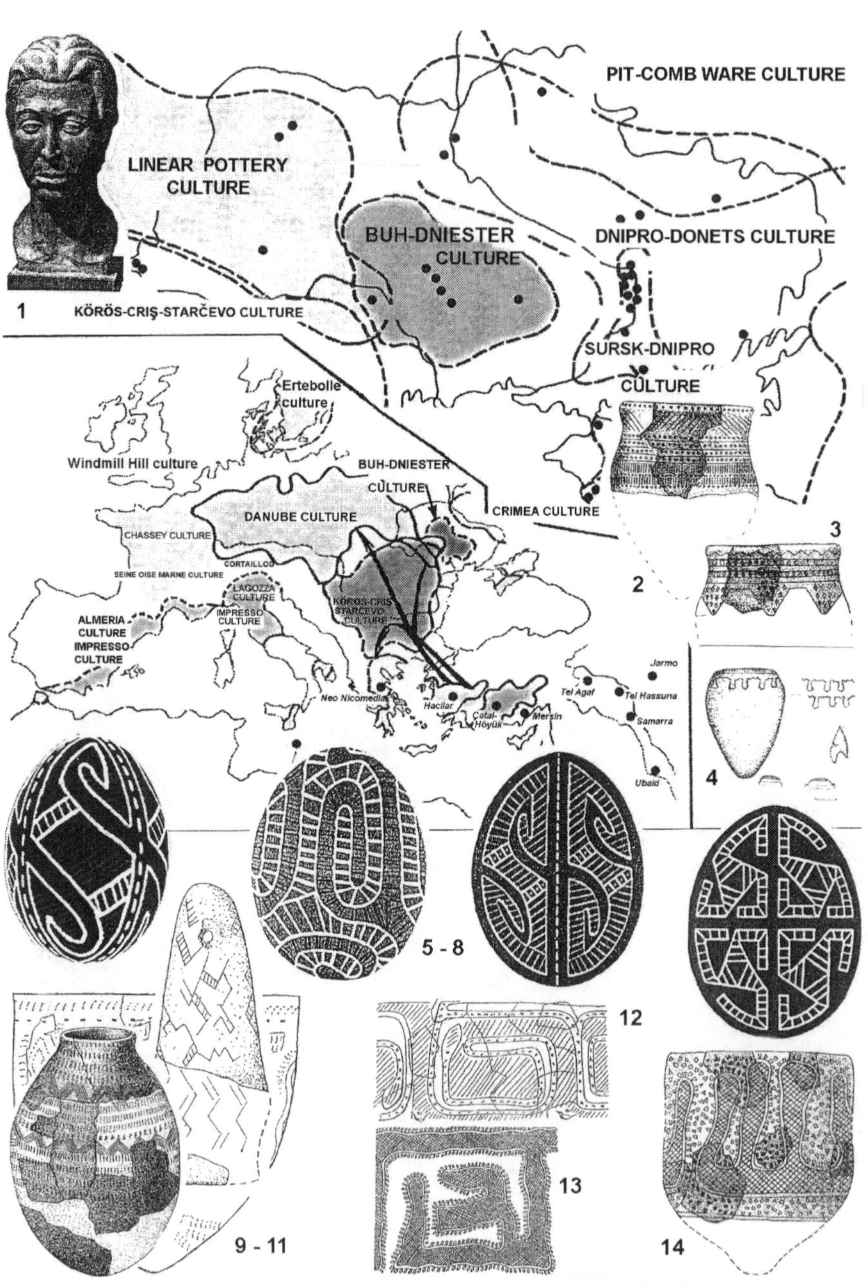

PIT-COMB WARE CULTURE
LINEAR POTTERY CULTURE
BUH-DNIESTER CULTURE
DNIPRO-DONETS CULTURE
KÖRÖS-CRIŞ-STARČEVO CULTURE
SURSK-DNIPRO CULTURE
Ertebolle culture
Windmill Hill culture
BUH-DNIESTER CULTURE
DANUBE CULTURE
CRIMEA CULTURE
CHASSEY CULTURE
CORTAILLOD
SEINE OISE MARNE CULTURE
LAGOZZA CULTURE
IMPRESSO CULTURE
KÖRÖS-CRIŞ STARČEVO CULTURE
ALMERIA CULTURE
IMPRESSO CULTURE
Jarmo
Tel Agaf
Tel Hassuna
Samarra
Neo Nicomedia
Hacilar
Çatal-Höyük
Mersin
Ubaid
1
2
3
4
5 - 8
9 - 11
12
13
14

Table II

The Great Neolithic Revolution reflected in the archaeological cultures of Europe and the Middle East.
Ukrainian hand-painted eggs^ (5-8) **displaying specific ornamentation** of Sursk-Dnipro (2-4) and Buh-Dniester (9-14) cultures, **of the earliest agricultural-stock-raising cultures of eastern Europe** (according to the monograph *The Neolithic Ukraine* by V. Danylenko).

1. A woman of that time, possibly from the same Mediterranean region, form a burial on Sursky Island located on the Samara River (Reconstruction by L. T. Yablonsky).

4. A specific type of stone vessel, 7th – 6th millennium BCE from the settlement at Stone Grave that has analogies at Çatal Höyük in Asia Minor.

Table III

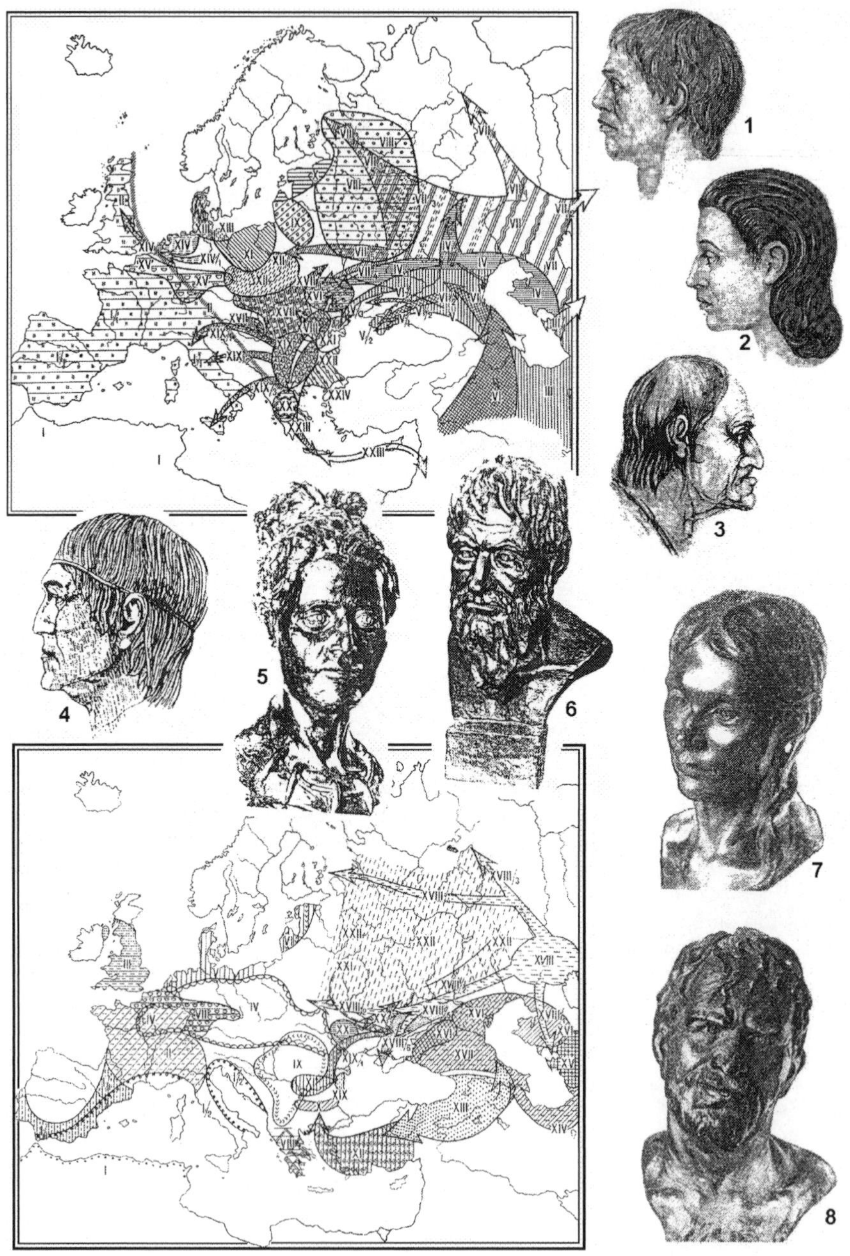

Table III

Indo-European resettlements of the 7th – 3rd millennium BCE and iconic reconstructions by M. M. Gerasimov (1-4, 7-8), S. A. Horbenko (5), T. S. Surnina (6) and V. Danylenko (maps).

1, 2 – From burials 19 and 35 (Trypillia SII) of the burial ground at the village of Vykhvatynts in the Rybnitsy district of Moldova.

3 – Burial (VII) at the settlement of Nezvisko in the Horodenka district of the Ivano-Frankivsk region.

4 – Burial beneath a kurhan of the Yamna culture from Novo-Fylypivka in the Melitopol district of Zaporizhia region.

5, 6 – From Seredny Stoh burial ground at the town of Alexandria.

7, 8 – From graves of the Sursk-Dnipro culture on Sursky Island (in the river of Samara).

The Neolithic and Eneolithic epochs of Dniester-Dnipro region are both characterised by the coexistence of the ancient local populations of the proto-European type (4-8) with the alien south-European Caucasians (i.e western branch of the ancient Mediterranean type). The first was distinctive of Aryan cattle breeding steppe inhabitants who constructed kurhans, and the second of Arattans who founded the agricultural forest-steppe culture of Trypillia. However, it is evident that "among Trypillian tribes and their neighbouring cattle breeders there existed not only economic links but also conjugal, i.e. there were ethnic contacts" (S. P. Segeda, *The anthropological composition of the ancient population of Ukraine: ethnogenetic aspects*, in *The ethnic history of ancient Ukraine. – Collective monographs*, Institute of Archaeology Nat. Acad. Sci. Ukraine, Kyiv, 2000; p. 254 et al. [in Ukrainian]). Generally, these **dual-compound** contacts should be understood as the formation of the **Indo-European community**, whose language can also "be considered as the result of hybridisation of two basically different types" (see below).

The lower map (V. Danylenko, *Eneolithic Ukraine*, Naukova Dumka, Kyiv, 1974; p. 148) reflects the transformation of archaeological cultures from the Neolithic to the Eneolithic. V. Danylenko linked the start of the formation of the Indo-European community with the hybridisation of "local and alien Mesolithic cultures from the East", the latter of which "genetically preceded the Kukrek culture". The continuation of the process [shown on the lower map] is connected, in particular, with the linear-banded ceramics culture (IV) and the Buh-Dniester culture (XX). Later on "the process of Indo-Europeanisation of part of south-eastern Europe, touched upon by the expansion of Dnipro-Donets tribes (XXI, northern Palaeo-Europeans, according to Yu. Shilov), was slowed down, though it continued to grow in the steppe behind the Don and in the Northern Caspian region – being, in essence, the process of the ethnic consolidation of eastern Indo-European" (i.e. Aryan type. – Yu. Shilov). "Indo-Europeans in the earliest stages of their history were initially cattle breeders who later on became nomadic herdsmen" (ibid. – pp. 149, 157).

The upper map (ibid. – p. 150) shows the appearance of Trypillia (XVI) at the location of the Buh-Dniester culture and its genetic relationships with the cultures of the Balkans and Asia Minor's Anatolia. "There is no doubt that in all the above-mentioned cultures we are dealing with Indo-Europeans" (ibid. – pp. 149-151). To the "Indo-Iranian, that is Proto-Aryan, group of tribes" the researcher attributes the Suyarhin culture of the Caspian region, in the same group (directly connected with the "Azov-Black Sea line of development of the steppe Eneolithic" between Trypillia and the civilisations of Mesopotamia) with which he also enlists the Maikop, Kemi Oba, Lower-Mykhaylivka, Usativ "and probably others" (ibid. – p. 153 et al.)

Table IV

V
VI
III
IV
I
II
1
2
GERMANIC
CELTIC
BALTO - SLAVIC
ITALIC
VENETIAN
ILLYRIAN
MOESIA - DACIA
INDO-IRANIAN
GREEK
PELASGIANS
THRACIANS
HITTITE
-LUWIAN
ETEO-CRETE

Table IV

The stages of development of the Cucuteni-Trypillia culture, 6th – 3rd millennium BCE (according to E. K. Chernysh) and **<u>the spread of Indo-European languages</u>** by 3500-2500 BCE (according to V. Georgiev).

<u>Maps</u>:

I – 1-3 steps of the development of the territorial groups of Cucuteni-Trypillia culture (states of Aratta) of Stage A.

II – A (4-6).

III – BI (1-4).

IV – BII (5-7).

V – CI (1-6).

VI – CII (7-11).

<u>Figures</u>:

1 – Early image of an Aryan (military captive), from the tomb of the Egyptian ruler Horemheb 1314 BCE.

2 – Male figurine from the Trypillian (CI) settlement Krutukha-Zholob (according to G. M. Buzyan).

Table V

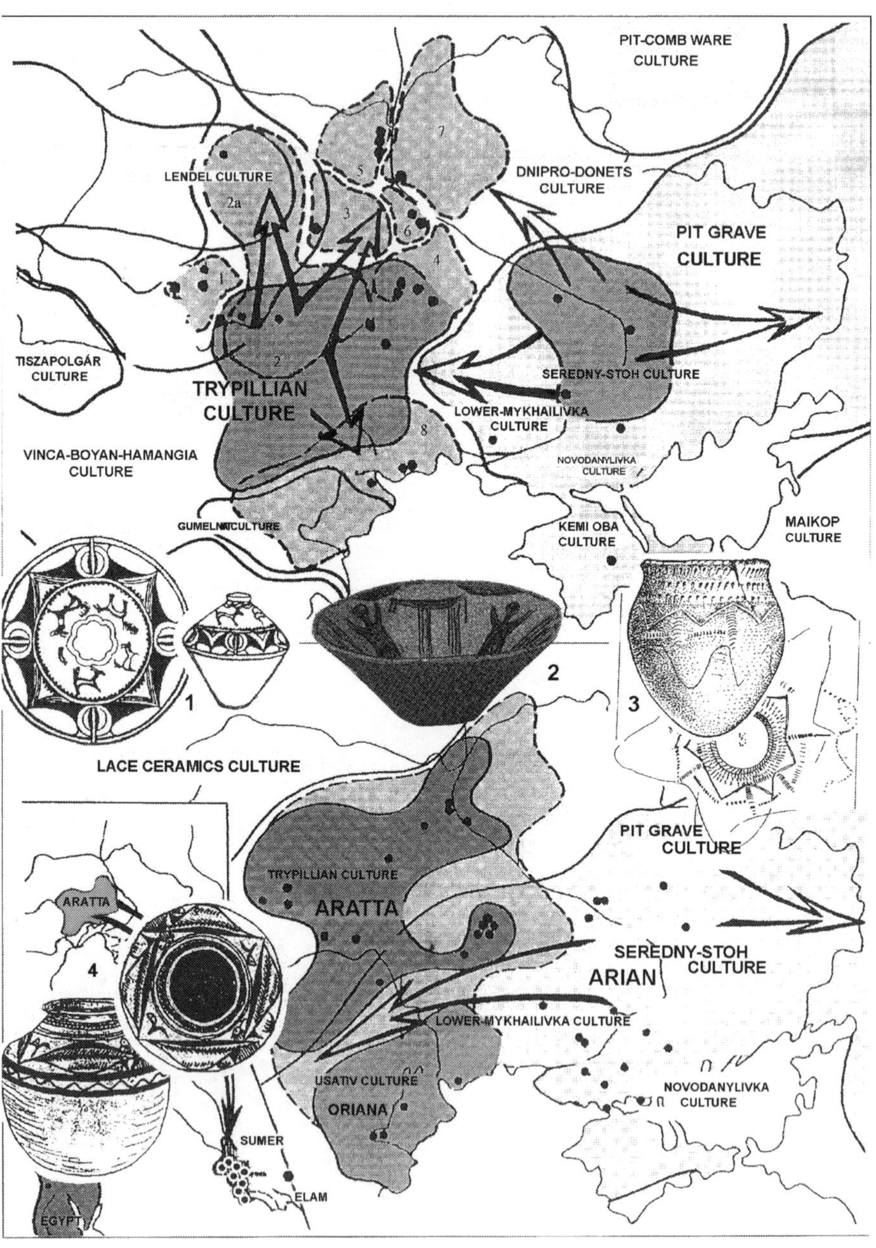
PIT-COMB WARE CULTURE
LENDEL CULTURE
DNIPRO-DONETS CULTURE
PIT GRAVE CULTURE
TISZAPOLGÁR CULTURE
TRYPILLIAN CULTURE
SEREDNY-STOH CULTURE
LOWER-MYKHAILIVKA CULTURE
VINCA-BOYAN-HAMANGIA CULTURE
NOVODANYLIVKA CULTURE
KEMI OBA CULTURE
MAIKOP CULTURE
1
2
3
LACE CERAMICS CULTURE
PIT GRAVE CULTURE
TRYPILLIAN CULTURE
ARATTA
ARATTA
4
SEREDNY-STOH CULTURE
ARIAN
LOWER-MYKHAILIVKA CULTURE
USATIV CULTURE
ORIANA
NOVODANYLIVKA CULTURE
SUMER
ELAM
EGYPT

Table V

Aratta and Arián; The appearance of Sumer between the 4th – 3rd millennium BCE (according to Yu. A. Shilov; Maps composed by A. A. Belous'ko et al.).

Calendar-Zodiacal ornamentation of Trypillian vessels CI-CII. (1, 2), **Early-Yamna** (3), and **Samarra** (4) **cultures**:

1 – Settlement I at the village of Krutoborodyntsi in the Letychiv district of the Khmelnytsky region.
2 – From the collection of A. S. Polishchuk.
3 – Burial 13 of kurhan 9 from Sofiivka in the Kakhovka district in the Kherson region.
4 – According to V. Danylenko (*Cosmogony of primitive society*, Beginning of Civilisation, Moscow-Ekaterinburg: Rarity, Delovaja book, 1999; p. 154, tabl. XIX: 2].

Table VI

GREECE
HITTITE KINGDOM
EGYPT
GREECE
HITTITE KINGDOM
AEGEAN CIVILIZATION
MITANNI KINGDOM
IRAN
EGYPT
1
2
3
4
5
7
8
6
9
10
CHINA
LACE CERAMICS CULTURE
PIT GRAVE CULTURE
Ari ans
TIBET
Harappa
Mohenjo Daro
HITITTE CIVILIZATION
MITANNI
IRAN
HARAPPAN CIVILIZATION
INDIA
AEGEAN CIVILIZATION

Table VI

Campaigns of the Hyksos (2) **and Aryans** 1700-1400 BCE.
The invention of carts in Danube-Dnipro Aratta (10) **of and composite wheels and chariots in Arián, in the Lower-Dnipro ancestral home.**

1 – Starosillia-Yamna burial 8 of kurhan 1 from Zarichne (2110 BCE, by C14 dating).
2 – Ancient Egyptian image of the Hyksos.
3 – Reconstruction (by V. F. Gening et al.) of a chariot of 1700-1600 BCE from the burial ground of Sintashta (Arkaim valley, South Trans-Urals).
4-6 – Images from Caves 27 and 37 of Stone Grave.
7 – Reconstruction (by L. A. Chernykh) of carts from Yamna burial 9 of kurhan 11 at the town of Kamianka-Dniprovska, regional centre of the Zaporizhia region.
8 – Reconstruction (by N. N. Cherednychenko and S. Zh. Pustovalov) of a chariot from Catacomb burial 27 of kurhan 11 at the village of Mar'ivka of Zaporizhia region.
9 – Starosillia burial 8 of kurhan 1 at the village of Starosillia.
10 – Reconstruction (by S. A. Gusev) of a toy cart from a Trypillian settlement (VII, 4100-3800 BCE) at the village of Voroshylovka in the Tyvrovsk district of the Vinnytsia region.

Table VII

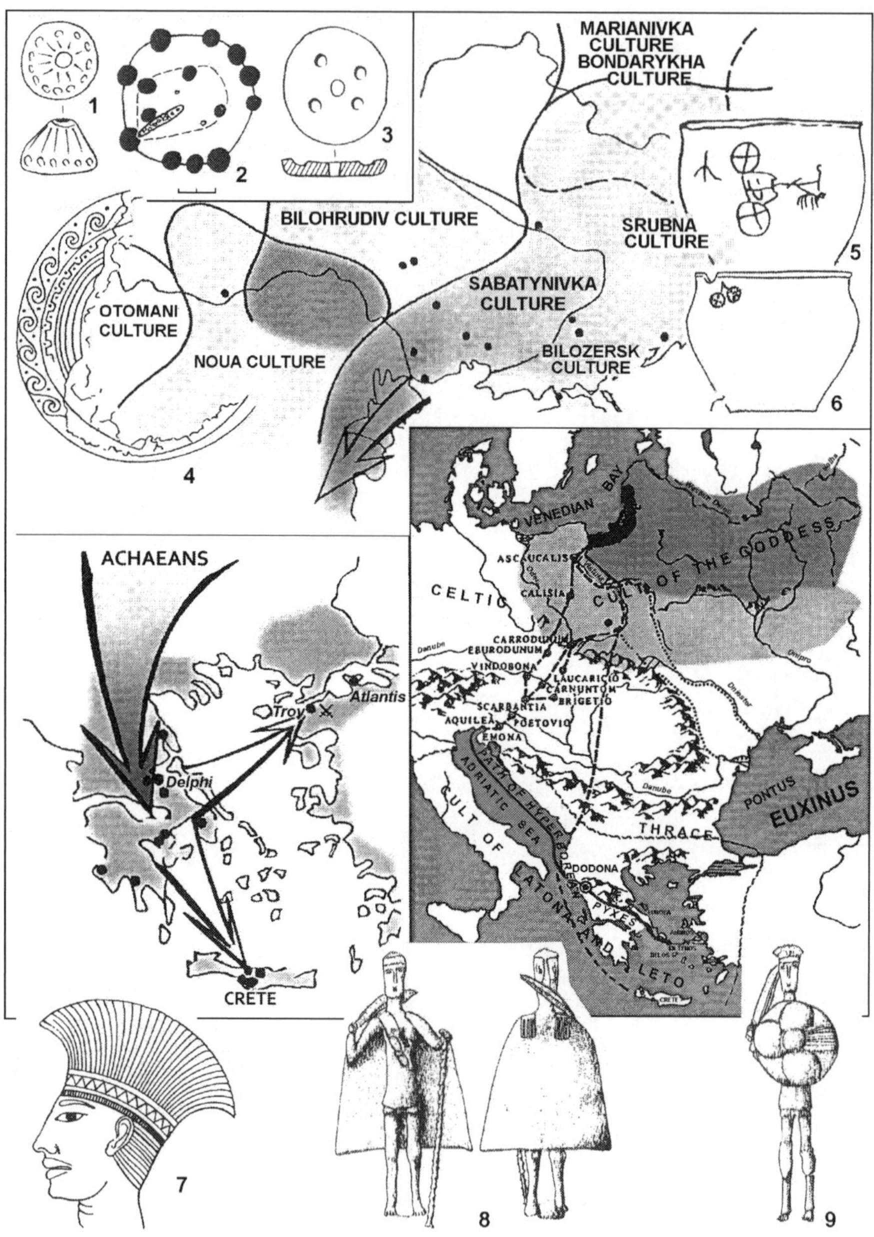

1
2
3
MARIANIVKA CULTURE
BONDARYKHA CULTURE
BILOHRUDIV CULTURE
SRUBNA CULTURE
5
SABATYNIVKA CULTURE
OTOMANI CULTURE
NOUA CULTURE
BILOZERSK CULTURE
6
4
VENEDIAN BAY
CULT OF THE GODDESS
CELTICA
ASCAUCALIS
CALISIA
CARRODUNUM
EBURODUNUM
VINDOBONA
LAUCARICIO
CARNUNTOM
BRIGETIO
SCARBANTIA
AQUILEA
POETOVIO
EMONA
PATH OF HYPERBOREA
ADRIATIC SEA
CULT OF LATONA AND LETO
Danube
Dnipro
Dniester
PONTUS
EUXINUS
THRACE
DODONA
PYXES
CRETE
ACHAEANS
Atlantis
Troy
Delphi
CRETE
7
8
9

Table VII

Campaigns of the "sea people" 1400-1100 BCE **and "Hyperboreans"** (bottom right) of subsequent centuries, according to Herodotus and B. A. Rybakov.

Calendar ornamentation of a distaff (1), luminaire (3) and sanctuary-observatory settlement (2) of Pustynka of the Chernihiv region of the Tshinets archaeological culture of the Mid-Dnipro area 1500-1200 BCE.

4 – Altar at the settlement of Zhabotyn; images of chariots on vessels of the Srubna culture of the lower reaches of the Volga and Dnipro.

5 – Burial 2 of kurhan 2 at the river of Sukha Saratovka, Trans-Volga region.

6 – Burial 5 of kurhan 1 from Lvovo-Beryslav district of the Kherson region.

7 – Egyptian image of 1192 BCE of a *Pulasaty* (Philistine/Pelasgi) man from the island of Crete.

8, 9 – Bronze figurines from the island of Sardinia; the sword and shield are similar to those found in the Sabatynivka kurhan near the village of Borysivka in the Odessa region.

Table VIII

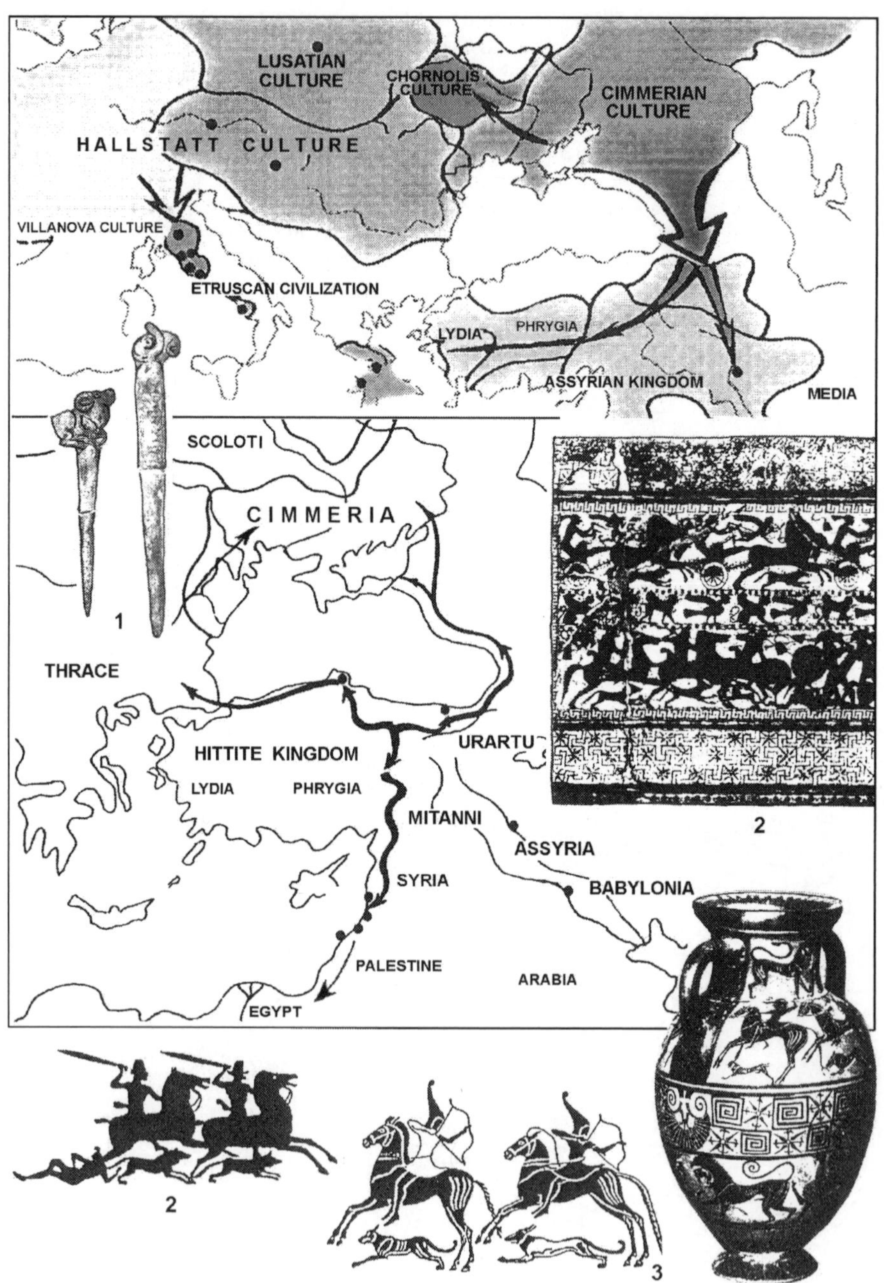
LUSATIAN CULTURE
CHORNOLIS CULTURE
CIMMERIAN CULTURE
HALLSTATT CULTURE
VILLANOVA CULTURE
ETRUSCAN CIVILIZATION
LYDIA
PHRYGIA
ASSYRIAN KINGDOM
MEDIA
SCOLOTI
CIMMERIA
1
THRACE
HITTITE KINGDOM
LYDIA
PHRYGIA
URARTU
MITANNI
ASSYRIA
SYRIA
BABYLONIA
PALESTINE
ARABIA
EGYPT
2
2
3

Table VIII

Campaigns of the Cimmerian, "Indian" branch of the late Aryan ("Indo-Iranian") community 783-595 BCE.

1 – Persian based "Scythian style animal" from an 8th century BCE Skoloty-Cimmerian kurhan at Stovbuvata Grave, near the town of Komsomolsk in the Kremenchuk district of the Poltava region. (Excavation by A. B. Suprunenko, I. N. Kulatova and S. A. Skory)

2, 3 – Images of Cimmerian cavalry on a sarcophagus from Klazomenai [ancient Greek city on the coast of Iona] and on "Etruscan" amphora, 6th – 5th centuries BCE.

Table IX

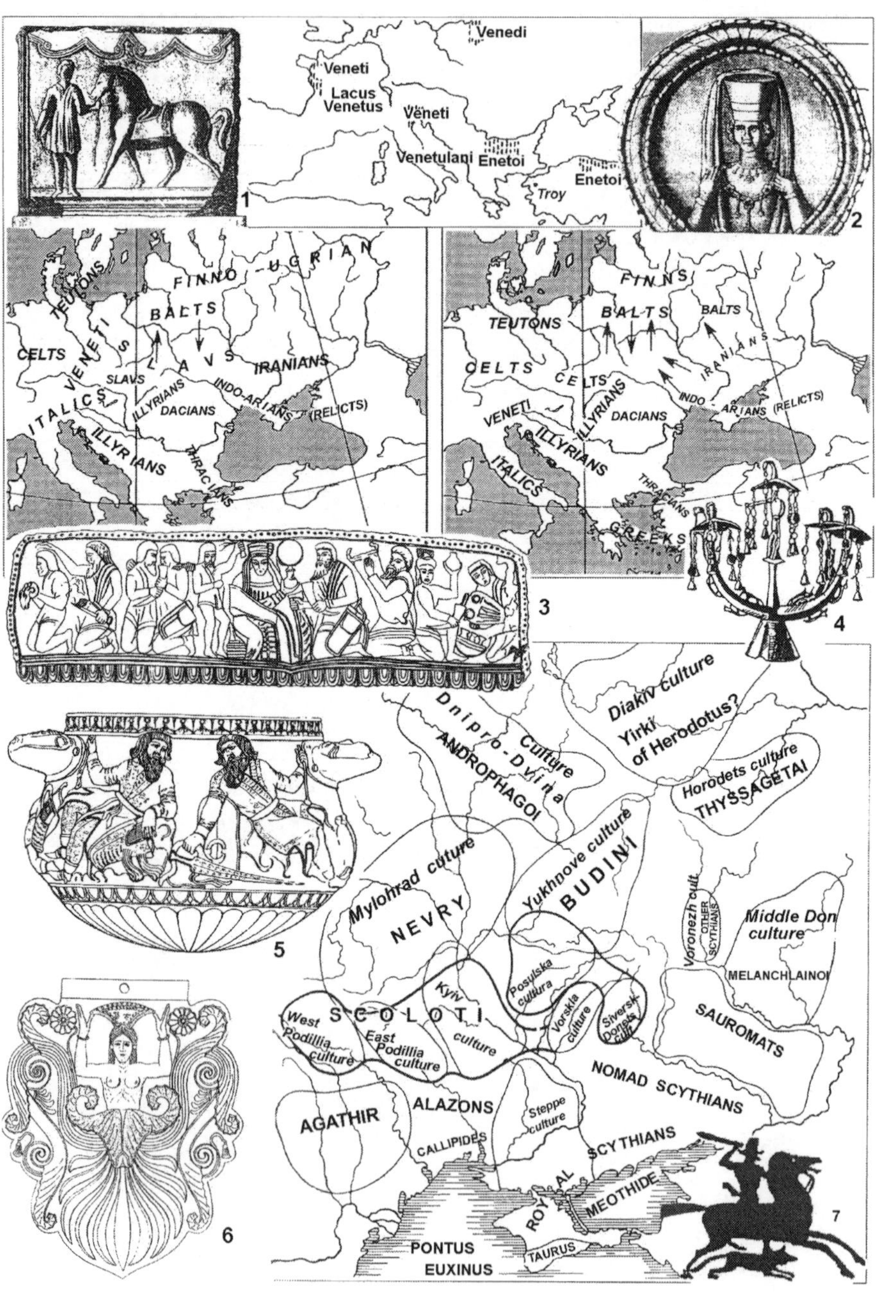

1
Venedi
Veneti
Lacus Venetus
Veneti
Venetulani
Enetoi
Enetoi
Troy
2
TEUTONS
FINNO-UGRIAN
BALTS
VENETI
SLAVS
CELTS
ITALICS
SLAVS
ILLYRIANS
DACIANS
IRANIANS
INDO-ARIANS
(RELICTS)
ILLYRIANS
THRACIANS
FINNS
BALTS
BALTS
TEUTONS
CELTS
CELTS
ILLYRIANS
IRANIANS
INDO-ARIANS (RELICTS)
DACIANS
VENETI
ILLYRIANS
ITALICS
THRACIANS
GREEKS
3
4
5
6
7
Dnipro-Dvina Culture
ANDROPHAGOI
Diakiv culture
Yirki of Herodotus?
Horodets culture
THYSSAGETAI
Mylohrad culture
NEVRY
Yukhnove culture
BUDINI
Voronezh cult.
OTHER SCYTHIANS
Middle Don culture
MELANCHLAINOI
SCOLOTI
West Podillia culture
East Podillia culture
Kyiv culture
Posulska cultura
Vorskla culture
Siversk-Donets cult.
SAUROMATS
NOMAD SCYTHIANS
AGATHIR
ALAZONS
CALLIPIDES
Steppe culture
ROYAL SCYTHIANS
MEOTHIDE
PONTUS EUXINUS
TAURUS

Table IX

"Scythia of Herodotus" (according to B. A. Rybakov and V. I. Petruk, *Great Scythia – About Ukraine*, Spalakh, Kyiv, 2001; p. 145 et al.) **and Venedi-Slavdom**, 1st millennium BCE (I. Shavli, *The Veneti: Our old ancestors*, Zerkalo, Moscow, 2003; p. 48 and et al.; O. N. Trubachev, *Ethnogenesis and culture of the early Slavs. Linguistic research*, Science, Moscow, 2003; pp. 29-30 et al.).

1 – Ancient image of a rider from (V)eneti's Noricum.

2 – 2nd century Noricum woman (from a gravestone from the church of St. Jakob, above Celovec, Klagenfurt).

3 – Scene of Skolotian festivals (according to B. A. Rybakov: A ruler knelt down before a GODDESS) on a golden plate from the village of Sakhnivka on the River Ros.

4 – Scythian bronze top-piece, 4th century BCE (from the bald mountain sanctuary at the city of Dnipropetrovsk) having the aspect of two crossed bows, crowned by figurines of Goitosir or Papai (answering to Apollo and Zeus, according to Herodotus), eagles and wolves.

5 – Reflection of the second legend by Herodotus (according to D. S. Raevskii) about the origin of the Scythians on a 4th century BCE chalice from Haimanova Grave in the Zaporizhia region. (Excavation by V. I. Bidzylia).

6 – Image of the "serpent-legged Goddess" of Herodotus on a bronze bowl of a Scythian chieftain from Chertomlyk kurhan, 340-320 BCE.

7 – Cimmerian rider on a sarcophagus from Klazomen 6th century BCE.

Table X

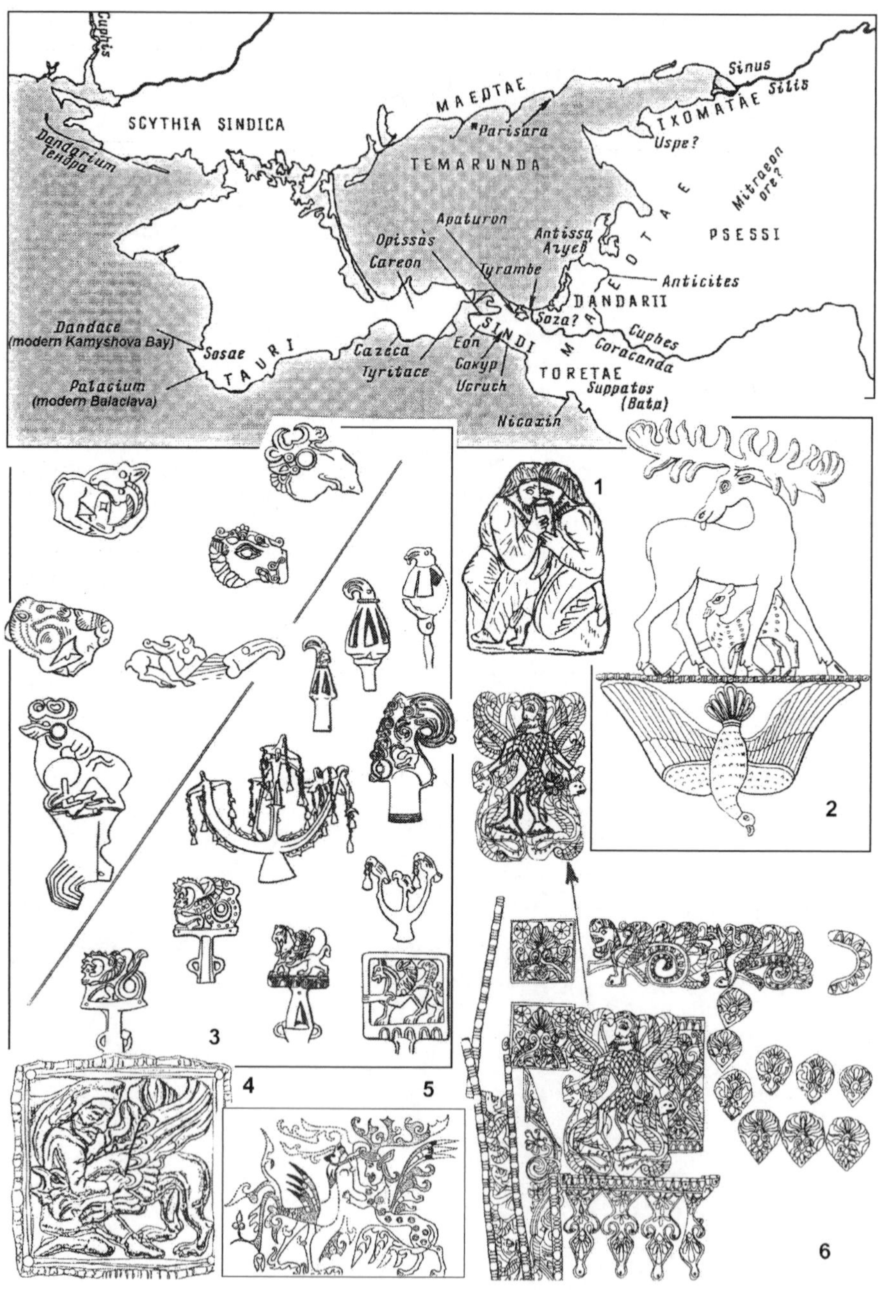
Cuphis
SCYTHIA SINDICA
Dandarium
Тендра
MAEDTAE
*Parisara
TEMARUNDA
Sinus
IXOMATAE Silis
Uspe?
Mitraeon ore?
MAEOTAE
PSESSI
Apaturon
Opissàs
Careon
Antissa
Azyeß
Tyrambe
Anticites
DANDARII
Dandace
(modern Kamyshova Bay)
Sosae
TAURI
Cazeca
Tyritace
Eon
Сакур
Ucruch
SINDI
Soza?
Cuphes
Coracanda
TORETAE
Suppatos
(Bata)
Palacium
(modern Balaclava)
Nicaxin
1
2
3
4
5
6

Table X

Major Indo-Aryan names of the Northern Black Sea area (O. N. Trubachev, *Indoarica in the Northern Black Sea area*, Science, Moscow, 1999; p. 6 et al.) and Scythian (Irano-Aryan) cultic accessories reflecting the Indo-Iranian duality of the Aryan community.

1	–	Image of the Scythian ceremony of sworn brothers on a golden pendant from a Kul-Oba^ royal kurhan, 4th century BCE.
2-6	–	Mythologised contra-representations of a predatory bird and peaceful forest creatures, which stand, in particular for "symbolic imagination of the first Scythian raids on the frontier of Pre-Slavic lands". (B. A. Rybakov, *Paganism of ancient Slavs*, Science, Moscow, 1987; pp. 554-555),
2	–	Kuban.
3	–	Forest-steppe subjects with elks (on the left) and grass-steppe gryphons, and others, (on the right).
4, 5	–	Image of fighting with gryphons from kurhans of Scythia and Altai (Pazyryk).
6	–	Sheath from the burial of a noble Scythian, 4th century BCE (burial 2 of Soboleva Grave at the city of Ordzhonikidze of the Nikopo district in the Dnipropetrovsk region) portraying "two pacing wyverns [winged dragons]", and below them – a priest "in the ritual costume of a rooster" conquering a similar pair, and below – 4+1 "platelets with anthropomorphous projections" (B. N. Mozolevsky, S. V. Polin, *Kurhans of IV century BCE Scythian Gerros*, Stilos, Kyiv, 2005; pp. 168-181). The main person embodies (according to Yu. Shilov) Sraosha – the Avestan receiver of Vedic Mitra, the guide of the souls of the dead. Echoing with the Indo-European-Greek Geronomachia (war of pygmies with cranes), the origin of the image of Sraosha is traced from Aratta and Sumer (see Table XVI).

Table XI

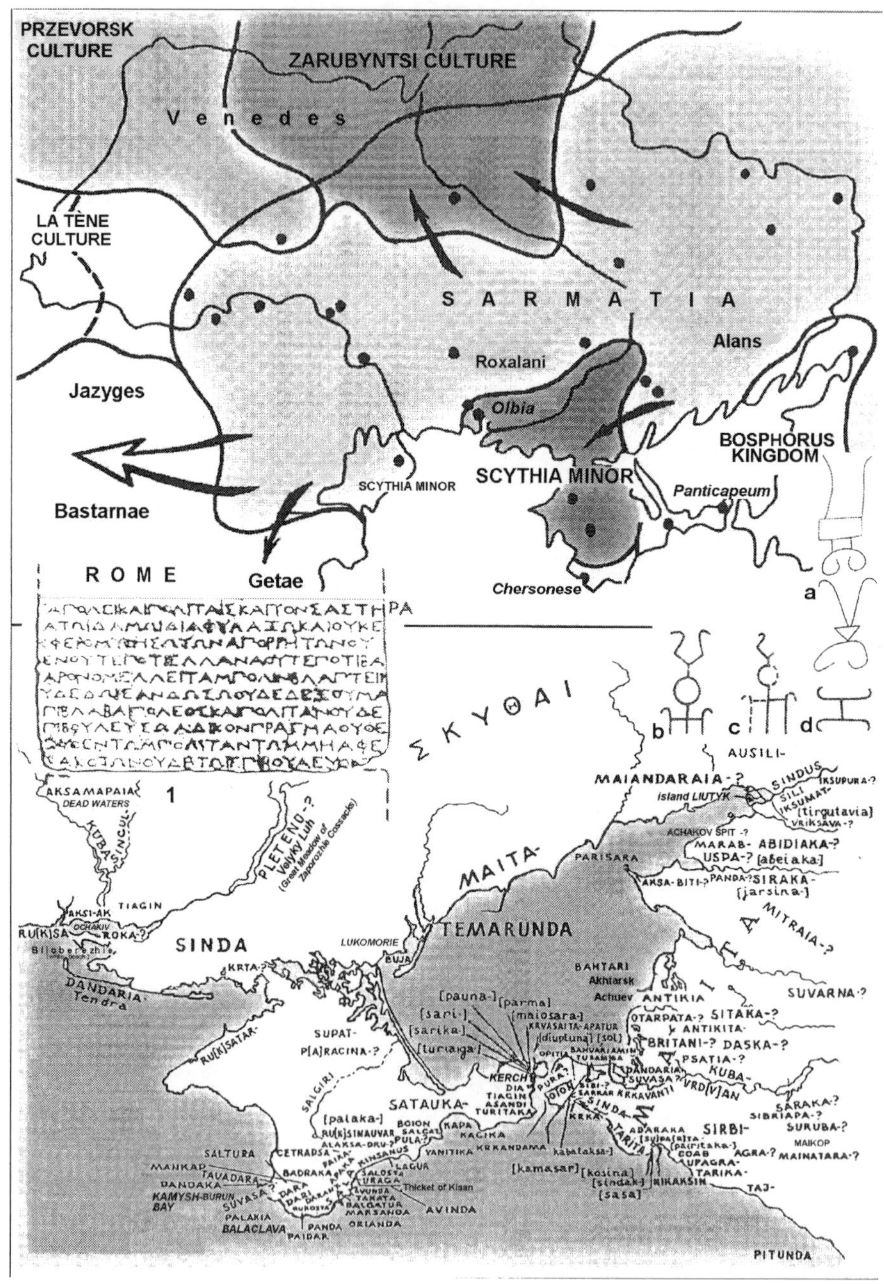
PRZEVORSK CULTURE
ZARUBYNTSI CULTURE
V e n e d e s
LA TÈNE CULTURE
S A R M A T I A
Roxalani
Alans
Jazyges
Olbia
BOSPHORUS KINGDOM
SCYTHIA MINOR
SCYTHIA MINOR
Panticapeum
Bastarnae
R O M E
Getae
Chersonese
a
b
c
d
1
ΣΚΥΘΑΙ
AUSILI-
MAIANDARAIA-?
SINDUS
island LIUTYK
ACHAKOV SPIT -?
MARAB- ABIDIAKA-?
USPA-?
PARISARA
MAITA-
AKSA-BITI-?
SIRAKA-
MITRAIA-?
AKSAMAPAIA
DEAD WATERS
TIAGIN
SINDA
LUKOMORIE
TEMARUNDA
BAHTARI
Akhtarsk
Achuev
ANTIKIA
SUVARNA-?
SITAKA-?
ANTIKITA-
BRITANI-?
DASKA-?
PSATIA-?
KUBA-
KERCH
SATAUKA-
SIRBI-
SURUBA-?
MAIKOP
SALTURA
CETRADSA
AVINDA
Thicket of Kisan
BALACLAVA
PAIDAR
KAMYSH-BURUN BAY
PITUNDA
TAJ-

Table XI

Indo-Aryan names of the Northern Black Sea area, in later ancient-Sarmatian time (O. N. Trubachev, *Indoarica in the Northern Black Sea area*, Science, Moscow, 1999; pp. 7, 271-272 et al.).

1 – Fragment of a civil oath of Greek-Taurian Chersonese, 3rd century BCE, in which ΣΑΣΤΗΡΑ (Sastera people) are mentioned – 'the archive of laws', in the language of Indo-Aryans;

2 – Tamgi-symbols of Sarmatian rulers (b – Sauromates II; c – Rhescuporis III; d – Ininthimeus) of "barbarian"-Greek Bosphorus, and (a) placed on a wall in Scythian Naples.

Table XII

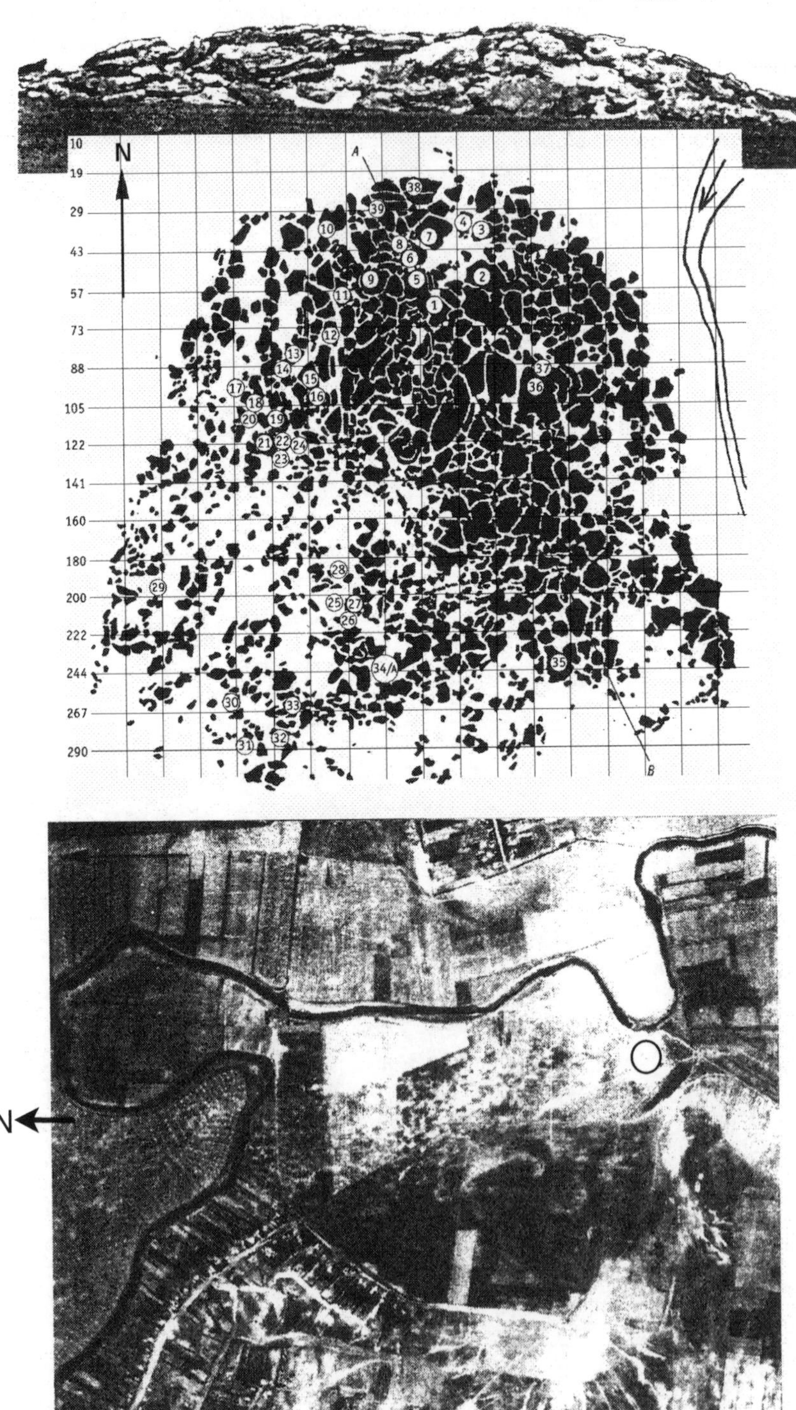
N
A
B
10
19
29
43
57
73
88
105
122
141
160
180
200
222
244
267
290
1
2
3
4
5
6
7
8
9
10
11
12
13
14
15
16
17
18
19
20
21
22
23
24
25
26
27
28
29
30
31
32
33
34/A
35
36
37
38
39
N

Table XII

Stone Grave at the settlement of Myrny in the Melitopol district of the Zaporizhia region. Aerial photo and layout plan showing some of the numbered grotto locations. The position of Stone Grave is shown on the aerial photo beside the River Molochna, indicated by a circle. It was formed from the crater of a type of "mud volcano" geyser, which ceased activity about 5 million years ago. In ancient times the river meandered more to the west, enclosing the sandstone hill on a riverine promontory (See also Fig. 29, p.59).

Table XIII

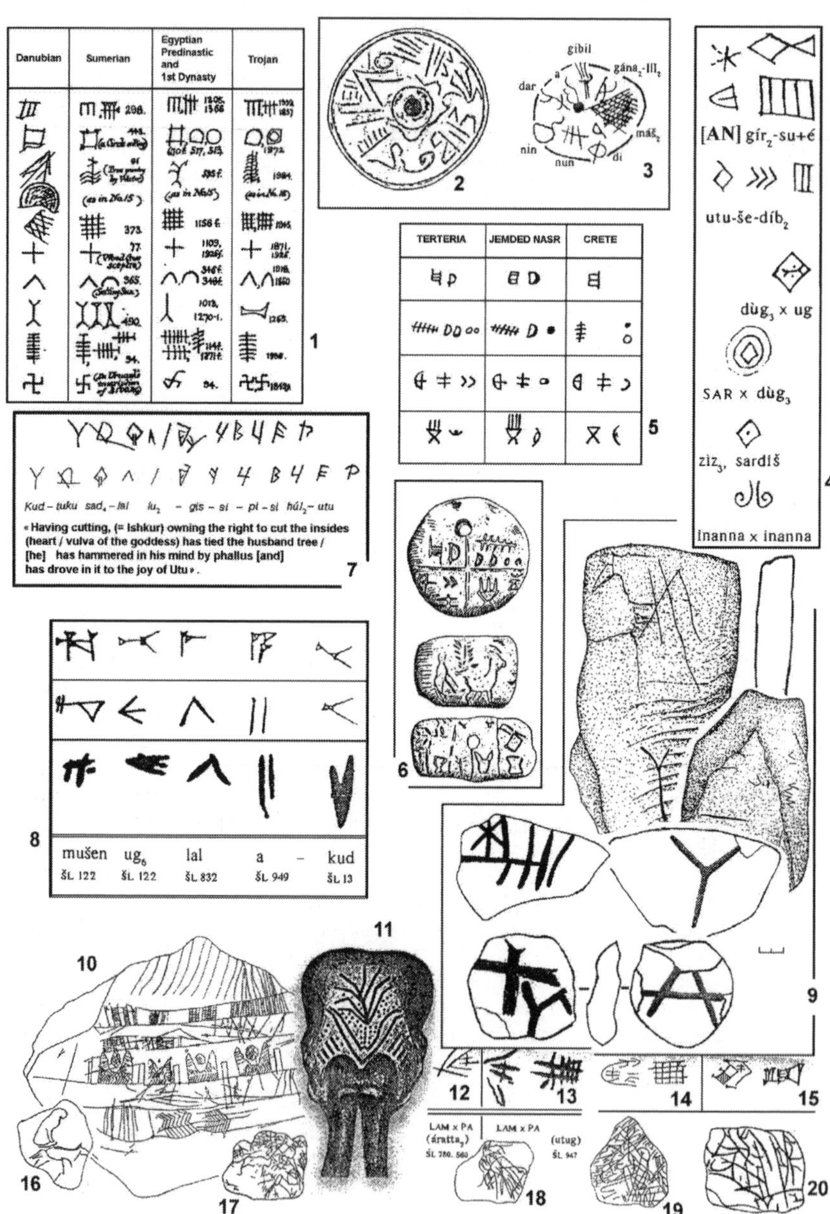

Danubian
Sumerian
Egyptian Predinastic and 1st Dynasty
Trojan
1
2
gibil
gána₂-III₂
dar
máš₂
nin
nun
di
3
[AN] gír₂-su+é
utu-še-díb₂
dùg₃ × ug
SAR × dùg₃
zìz₃, sardìš
inanna × inanna
4
TERTERIA
JEMDED NASR
CRETE
5
6
Kud – tuku sad₄ – lal iu₂ – gis – si – pi – si húl₂ – utu
« Having cutting, (= Ishkur) owning the right to cut the insides (heart / vulva of the goddess) has tied the husband tree / [he] has hammered in his mind by phallus [and] has drove in it to the joy of Utu ».
7
mušen ug₆ lal a – kud
ŠL 122 ŠL 122 ŠL 832 ŠL 949 ŠL 13
8
9
10
11
12
13
14
15
16
17
LAM x PA (áratta₂) ŠL 780, 560
LAM x PA
(utug) ŠL 947
18
19
20

Table XIII

The earliest written language in the world at Stone Grave (7-9, 12-13, 16-19), **its Palaeolithic origins and spread into Aryan and other cultures** of the 7th – 2nd millennium BCE according to L. A. Waddell (1), N. Vlassa and A. Falkenstein (6), A. G. Kifishin (2-5, 7-8, 10-19), B. D. Mykhailov (9).

1 – Relationship of Proto-Sumerian writing of the Danube area (Aratta-I, according to Yu. A. Shilov) with Sumer, Egypt, and Troy.

2-3 – Clay amulet with dedicatory inscriptions from Troy-II 2600-2450 BCE ('Nindara on a fiery field (of spirits) (for) Queen (of hell) (creates) the court of Goatling' (A. G. Kifishin, *Ancient sanctuary of Stone Grave*, Aratta, Kyiv, 2001; pp. 39-40)).

4 – Writing on figurines, etc., from the Dniester area settlement at Luka-Vrublevetscka (archaeological culture of Trypillia A, reflecting the onset of the apotheosis of the state of Aratta-I; according to A. G. Kifishin: III, the later Eneolithic group of Balkan-Danube script, inscriptions which reads (from top to bottom): *The temple of GOD Girsu; Utu seized grain; blessing of the slain* (or the priests of funeral ritual)*; reaches blessing of all; soul?* or *multitude, 3600; Inanna x Inanna* (V. F. Mitsyk, *Sacred Country of grain growers*, pub. These Affairs, Kyiv, 2006; pp. 104-107)).

5 – Similar writing of Tartaria (at the end of the 6th millennium BCE), Sumer (between the 4th – 3rd millennia BCE) and Crete (beginning of the 2nd millennium BCE).

6 – Proto-Sumerian tablets from the sanctuary of Telya of Tartaria, Romania (5300-5050 BCE: M. Merlini, G. Lazarovici, *Settling the circumstances of discovery, dating and utilisation of the Tartaria tablets*, Acta Terrae Septemcastrensis, VII, p. 156, 2008).

7 – Location 63 at Stone Grave: "Early Sumerian symbols" (B. D. Mykhailov, *Petroglyphs of Stone Grave*, Dyke Pole, Zaporizhia & Institute of Humanities Research, Moscow, 1999; p. 138), identification and translation by A. G. Kifishin.

8 – The method of decoding by A. G. Kifishin of Proto-Sumerian the writing at Stone Grave (bottom) compared with the most ancient [viz. Stone Grave] and successive characters of Sumer 4th – 3rd millennia BCE [top] and Balkan letters, 6th millenniumBCE [centre].

9 – 65/KM: Stelas and "tile-discs with 'writing'" that "have an outward similarity with symbols from Mesopotamia (Sumer)" and are "early-Neolithic written symbols which are dated 6th – 5th millennia BCE" (B. D. Mykhailov, *Petroglyphs of Stone Grave*, MAUP, Kyiv, 2004; pp. 155, 259-266).

10-11 – Proto-writing, 18th millennium BCE, on the bones of mammoths from the Palaeolithic settlement from Mezhyrich of the Kaniv district in the Cherkasy region, which indicate 'Aratta' (11) and others (A. G. Kifishin, *Ancient sanctuary of Stone Grave*..., pp. 536-538); 'Aratta' amongst other Proto-Sumerian inscriptions at Stone Grave (12-13) and in archives of Sumer (14-15).

16-19 – Stone tile-tablets with figures (according to V. Danylenko and B. D. Mykhailov) and characters (according to A. G. Kifishin) from the special depositories of Stone Grave, 20th – 12th – 3rd millennium BCE.

Table XIV

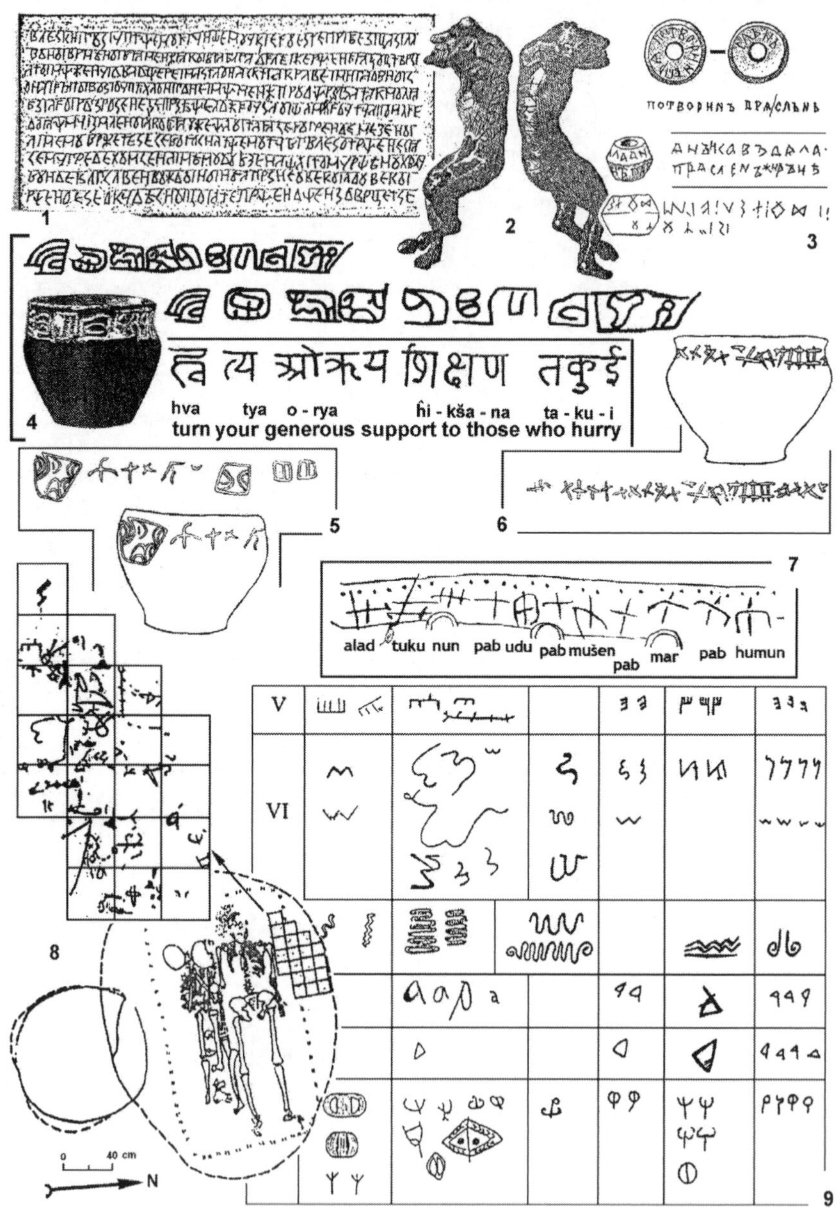
1
2
ПОТВОРННЪ ПРАСЛЬНЬ
3
4
त्व त्य ओ्रत्य शिक्षण तकुई
hva tya o - rya ĥi - kša - na ta - ku - i
turn your generous support to those who hurry
5
6
7
alad tuku nun pab udu pab mušen pab mar pab humun
V
VI
8
0 40 cm
N
9

Table XIV

Formation of Slavonic writing (1-3) – **examples of Trojan** ("Gothic": 1-3 , 6-9; according to A. G. Kifishin) **and Sanskrit** which was a 'synthetic'language: 1, 4-5, 8-9; according to V. Kulbaka and V. Kachur) seen in monuments of Ingul (8-9, according to S. Zh. Pustovalov) and Srubna (5-6, according to A. A. Formozov, V. V. Otroshchenko et al.) archaeological cultures.

1 – One of the boards of *The Veles Book,* 2nd millennium BCE – 879 CE.

2 – One of the metal figurines with an inscription from the 10th – 12th century heathen temple of the city of Retra, of the Ratar tribe (Veneti-Slavs of the Baltic area).

3 – Clay and stone spindles with inscriptions (see Table XIII: 2-3) 1st millennium BCE – 1st millennium CE.

4 – Burial 1 of kurhan 1 at the city of Artemivsk in the Donetsk region, mid 2nd millennium BCE (V. Kulbaka and V. Kachur, *The somatic cults of the Bronze Age of south-eastern Europe*, PGTU, Mariupol, 1998; pp. 49-50).

5 – Burial 1 of kurhan 1 at the village of Pereizdne in the Artemivsk district of the Donetsk region.

6 – Burial 1 of kurhan 1 on a Golden Spit at the city of Tahanrog [northeast Azov] in the Rostov Region, Russia.

7 – Inscription on a ceramic vessel from Troy-II, 2600-2450 BCE: 'Bulls – this (for) Queen (dead), (as well as) the ancestor of sheep, the ancestor of birds, the ancestor of insects, ancestor Khumum(-Saru)' (A. G. Kifishin, *Ancient sanctuary of Stone Grave…*, p. 40).

8 – Writing on a rolled mat (like the Golden Fleece of the Argonauts? – Yu. Shilov) from burial 2 of kurhan 13 at the village of Vynohradne of the Tokmak district in the Zaporizhia region.

9 – Comparative table of written signs, from left to right, of Trypillian, Ingul and Catacomb archaeological cultures of Aratta, Oriana and Arián, as well as Babylonia, Crete, Phoenicia, Stone Grave and Trypillia (among the signs of the last two countries). From the monograph by S. Zh. Pustovalov, *The social world of the Catacomb society of the Northern Black Sea area*, The Path, Kyiv, 2005; pp. 94-99, 338-339.

Table XV

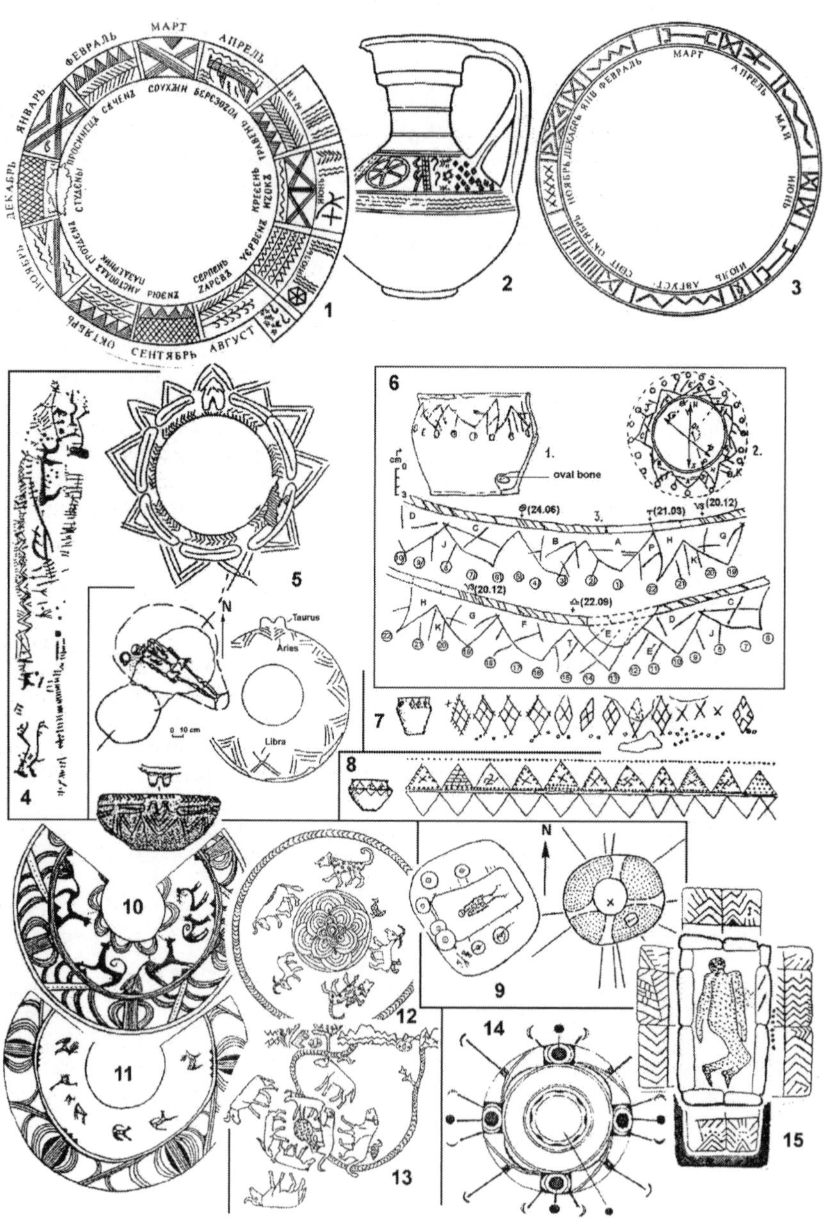
МАРТ
АПРЕЛЬ
ФЕВРАЛЬ
ЯНВАРЬ
ДЕКАБРЬ
НОЯБРЬ
ОКТЯБРЬ
СЕНТЯБРЬ
АВГУСТ
1
2
МАРТ
АПРЕЛЬ
МАЙ
ИЮНЬ
ИЮЛЬ
АВГУСТ
СЕНТ
ОКТЯБРЬ
НОЯБРЬ
ДЕКАБРЬ
ЯНВ
ФЕВРАЛЬ
3
6
oval bone
(24.06)
(21.03)
(20.12)
(22.09)
4
5
N
Taurus
Aries
Libra
0 10 cm
7
8
10
11
12
N
9
13
14
15

Table XV

Calendars of Slavs (1-2), **Pelasgians** (3, 5), **Aryans** (6-8, 15), **Hurrians** (9, 12-13), **Aratta** (10-11, 14), **and Proto-Sumer** (4).

1-3 – Annual and seasonal calendars on ceramic vessels of the Cherniakhov archaeological culture, 4th century BCE, from the villages of Lepesivka in the Volyn region and Romashky in the Kyiv region, and a Bell-Beaker culture pitcher, 18th century BCE, from the Hungarian village of Almásfüzitőről (B. A. Rybakov, *Paganism of ancient Slavs*, Science, Moscow, 1981; pp. 320-326).

4 – Calendar from the "Grotto of the Bull" at Stone Grave, the Spring equinox is preceded by a pair of horses (corresponding to Aryan Ashvin twins) opposing the ploughing bull [Taurus] (similar to Parjanya in the *Rigveda*).

5 – Sextant-cup, 1720 BCE, of the Ingul culture from burial 16 of kurhan 3-IV in the city of Makiivka in the Donetsk region (N. A. Chmykhov, *The sources of Paganism of Rus*, Lybid, Kyiv, 1990; pp. 22, 232 et al.).

6 – Vessel of the Srubna culture, mid 2nd millennium BCE, from burial 6 of kurhan 1 from Novo-Vasylivka in the Krasnoarmiysk district in the Donetsk region. According to the opinion of Yu. V. Kudlay (Bronze Age stellar pictogram from the Donbass region, in *Our heaven*, Republican Planetarium, Kyiv, vol. 2/2, pp. 24-27, 1999 (III-IV quarters)), it is taken here, as the basis of Calendar ornaments XIII-XIV, [showing] the zodiac headed by the Pleiades in the constellation of Taurus, and also the phases of the Moon and eclipse of the Sun. The sunrise on the day of the winter solstice (GKH Calendar) "is the Novo-Vasylivka analogue to the main Indo-Aryan myth – the duel of the thunder-god Indra with the Heavenly Dragon Vritra".

7 – A discovery at the village of Luzanovka, Middle Volga area.

8 – Calendar ornamentation on a vessel of Srubna culture from burial 2 of kurhan 1-I from Pereshchepyno, Ukraine.

9 – Solar-zodiacal calendar and astral observatory of the 23rd century BCE from a Starosillia culture burial, (burial No.8 of kurhan 1 from Starosillia in the Velyko-Olexandrivsk district in the Kherson region), showing wheels that designated the 7 months of the favourable half-year, that point at constellations by sightline-roads diverging from the kurhan.

10, 11 – Lunar-zodiacal calendars on ceramic vessels from Trypillian (C-I, 3700-3200 BCE) settlements of Varvarivka-VIII (according to V. I. Markevych).

12, 13 – Solar-zodiacal calendars on silver vessels of a major burial of a priest-ruler from the Maikop mound, 24th – 23rd century BCE (according to V. A. Safronov and N. A. Nikolaeva).

14 – Lunar calendars (by T. M. Tkachuk and Ya. G. Melnyk (*The symbol system of the Trypillian-Cucuteni cultural-historic community* (*painted dishes*), Nova Knyha, Vinnytsia, 2005; Ch. II, pp. 111-112) before "waxing and waning of the Moon was associated with the increase and decrease of the contents within housewares") shown on Trypillian C-I vessels of the Tomaszów district.

15 – Lunar calendar of the Kemi Oba culture of grave No. 4 of kurhan 1 from the village of Starosillia (see 9).

Table XVI

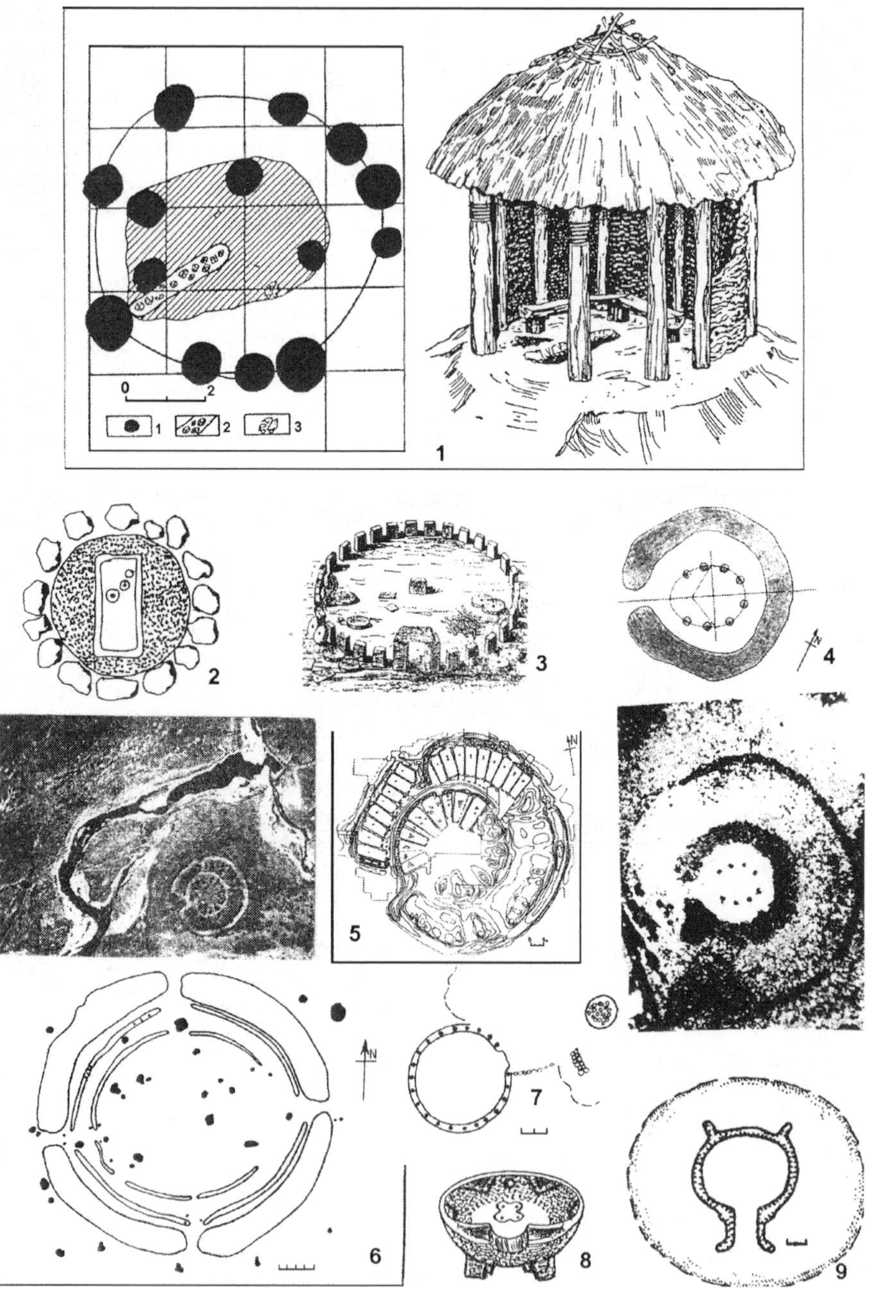

Table XVI

Maidans (sanctuary-observatories) **of Aryan nations**, 5th – 2nd millennium BCE.

1 – Sanctuary-observatory ("'temple'-rotunda" connected with the annual "idea of cyclic renovation" (B. A. Rybakov, *Paganism of ancient Slavs*..., pp. 259-260 et al.)). From a settlement of the Tshinets archaeological culture of the second half of the 2nd millennium BCE, at Pustynka near Chernihiv (reconstruction by S. S. Berezanska); the ditch, orientated along a sightline to the sunrise of the summer solstice, was rammed down with fragments of charred grain-chaff and bones, etc.

2 – Stone circle with the burial of cremated remains, India.

3 – Stone circle with altars, Palestine (according to A. Olesnitskii).

4 – Majestic 'calendric-temple' of Arminghall Henge^, Norfolk, England (aerial photo and plan, according to P. Lancaster-Brown).

5 – Aryan settlement, mid 2nd millennium BCE, in the valley of Arkaim, Southern Urals.

6 – Lendel 'rotunda' of Kijovic, Slovakia.

7 – North Caucasian culture, Pyatigorsk plateau.

8 – Model of a sanctuary-observatory from Trypillian (C-I) settlements Cherkasiv Sad II (at the village of Kyrylivka in the Kodym district of the Odessa region), the legs and shape of which are associated with the "udder of the Heavenly Cow-Kormylytsia" (Vasha of the *Rigveda*), and the cross-like altar opposite the entrance and small window-viewfinder guarded by two bull's horns (possibly, two calendric half-yearly incarnations of Parjani-Taurus, husband of Vasha).

9 – A ditch of zoo-anthropomorphic outline under the earth-fill of kurhan-sanctuary 14 at the village of Zhovty Yar in the Tatarbunar district of the Odessa region; V. G. Petrenko compared the symbolism of this construction with "early-Artemis", as depicted on a stela from kurhan 3-I at Usativ to according to V. Danylenko, (see table XXI: 16).

Table XVII

Table XVII

Ritual constructions of Aryan peoples, from the 7th millennium BCE.

1 – Bridal chest of between the 19th – 20th centuries from the Ukrainian Carpathians (collection of A. S. Polishchuk) retaining (according to Yu. Shilov) the traditional association with Aratta-Sumerian "birth temples" (M. Yu. Videyko, *Trypillian Civilisation*, Akademperiodyka, Kyiv, 2003; pp. 90-92).

2 – Mykolaivska church, 1470 CE, Transcarpathia.

3 – Temple mudhif [reed house] of the "Moorish Arabs" of southern Iraq [formerly Mesopotamia].

4 – Ancient-Egyptian sanctuary Heb-sed [courtyard], Saqqara.

5 – Reconstruction of dwellings; 2-4 settlements at village of Kosenivka (Pereyaslav district in the Kyiv region) of the Trypillian C-II archaeological culture. (by G. N. Buzyan and A. A. Yakubenko).

6 – Image of a foreign tree which "resembles a palm and has prototypes in the iconographic tradition of the Ancient East" (according to M. Yu. Videyko), on a granary-vessel from the "PLATAR" collection.

7 – Model of a Volodymyr type of temple (Trypillia B-II) from the "PLATAR" collection.

8 – Images of similar temples on seals of Sumer (according to D. Rohl et al.).

9 – Interior of temple VII/31 at Çatal Höyük (according to J. Mellaart).

10 – Clay altar from the settlement of Trusesti-I (Cucuteni-Trypillia C-I).

11 – Clay model of a dwelling [seen from above] (from the "PLATAR" collection); the Ψ-like symbol before the entrance, small round window and cross-like altar between them could be used as sight-line for astronomical-calendar observations.

Table XVIII

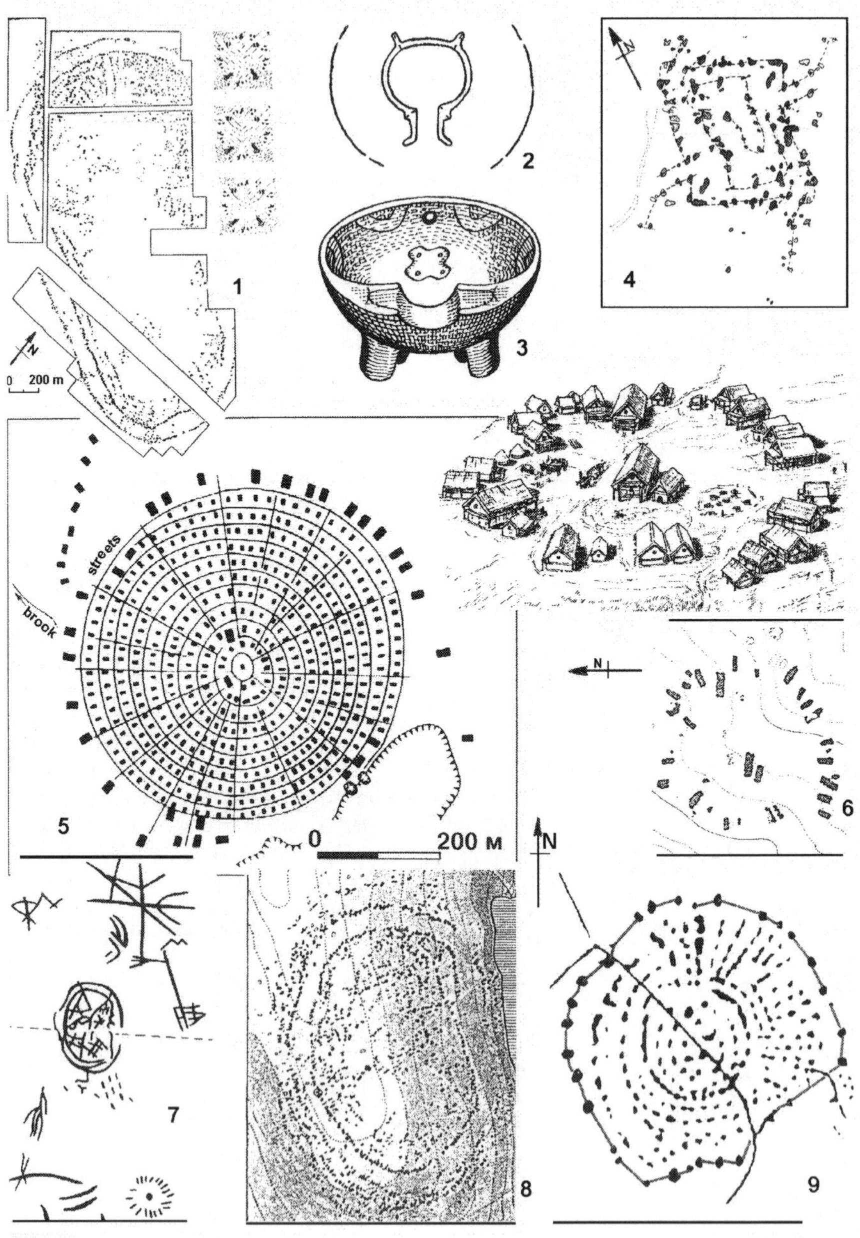

Table XVIII

Embryonic development of the main mythology of the Aryan-Bharatan *Rigveda* reflected in the layout of cities and sanctuaries (2, 3, 7) **in Buh-Dnipro Aratta,** 7th – 3rd millennium BCE. The Vala-'Receptacle' of the embryonic New Year/Universe (represented as forms of the sun (3, 5, 9), swastika (4) and egg (7, 8), is protected by the serpent (3-6, 9) of Almighty 'Rustling'-Shesha or the demon Vritra-'Vrata'*. Images are also portrayed of the Hero serpent-warrior, Indra-and-'Egg' (2) and his protector, the 'all-embracing' Creator-GOD-Vishnu, (1) [shown by the outline of the foot of Vishnu].

1 & 8 – Plans of the largest cities of Aratta and accompanying villages the first of them (the "capital and three small hamlets" of Trypillia C-I with areas of 450 and 2-4 hectares, according to M. Yu. Videyko), located between the villages of Talianky, Vishnopol and Maydanets in the Talne district of the Cherkasy region.

2, 3 – Maidan (sanctuary-observatory) in the form of a zoo-anthropomorphic ditch near the Trypillian (C-II) kurhan 14 at the village Zhovty Yar in the Odessa region and a ceramic model (C-I) found on the nearby settlement of Cherkasiv Sad II.

4 – Settlement (Trypillia A) near the village of Mohylna in the Haivoronsky district of the Kirovohrad region.

5 & 9 – Plans of the settlement of "Petreni" (C-I; near the village of Sofia in the Drokiev district of Moldova) according to aerial photo by K. V. Shishkin [9] and attempted reconstruction by V. A. Markevych (5).

6 – Plan and reconstruction of the village of "Kolomyishchina-I" (C-I; according to E. Yu. Krychevsky and T. S. Passek) at village of Khalepie in the Obukhiv district of the Kyiv region.

7 – Petroglyphs in the "Grotto of the dogs" (sites 15-16) at Stone Grave, 6th – 4th millennium BCE. The central image reveals the symbolism of the 'Pre-egg' and resembles typical outline plans of settlements of Aratta; Proto-Sumerian text, made inside this symbol and adjacent to it, reads: "*Ishkur* (Thunder-GOD), *whose ancestor Namtar* (GOD of Fate) – *Lyra, Plough, Great Dragon* (constellations from the Milky Way), and *Ashnan* (Goddess of grain) – *who like Utu* (Sun GOD), *sails souls of strangers after the Court of Water; Who put the soul inside, – poured out the seed (for rebirth) of people 60+19*" (A. G. Kifishin, *Ancient sanctuary of Stone Grave*, Aratta, Kyiv, 2001; pp. 410-425). It speaks, perhaps, of the time and conditions (after the Flood, as the result of resettlement: see Table I) of the foundation of the city under the protection of the Gods with their corresponding name, IM+TIR (= Ishkur + Ashnan) traced inside the Pre-egg.

* 'Vrata' can be translated as 'gate'.

Table XIX

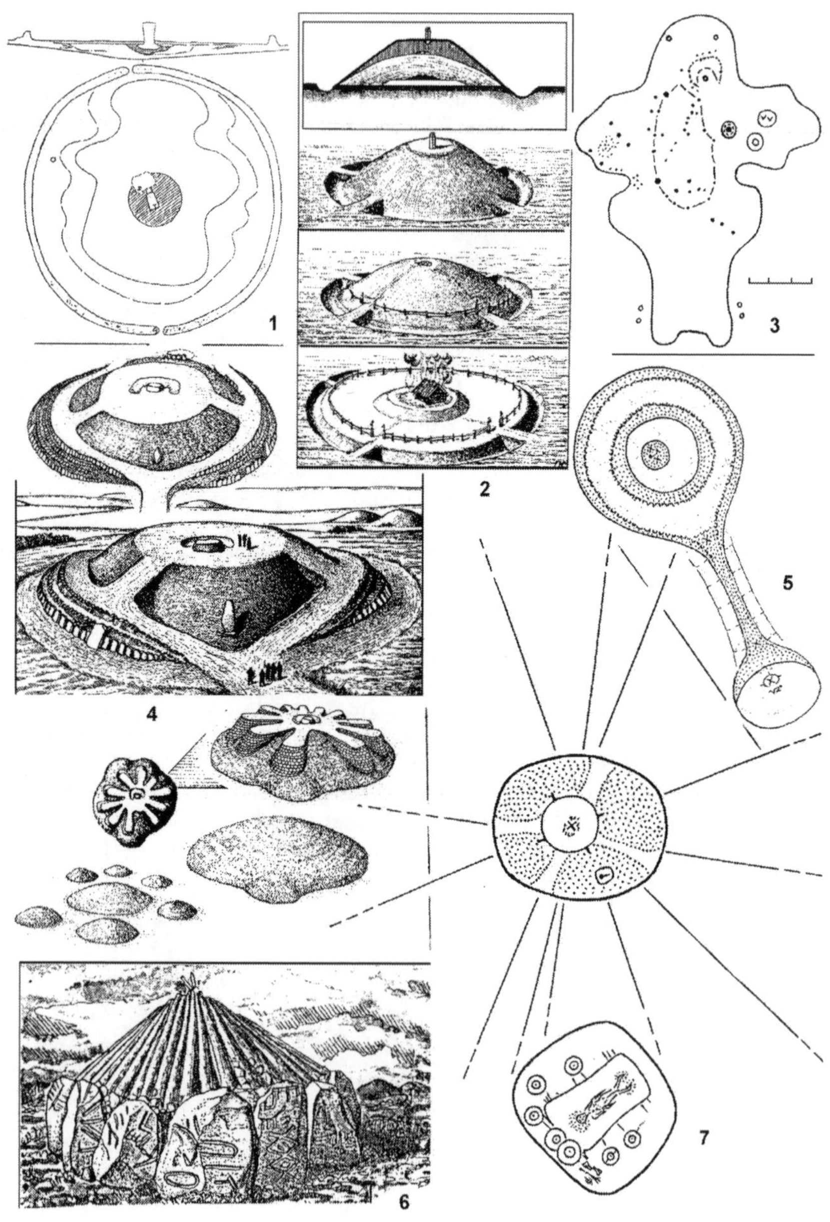

Table XIX

Anthropomorphous and astral constructions of Hurrians (7), **Aryans** (4, 5), **Scythians** (1) **and Rusy** (2, 3), 24th century BCE – 9th century CE.

1 – Base of kurhan 1 from Vodoslavka in the Novo-Troitsk district of the Kherson region, (excavated by V. V. Dorofeeva); the excavated area up to the nearest forest, is coated by silt and lined with grass; above the excavated grave at this site, the layering over it was arranged as a "pregnant womb", split by a thrust iron axe with a gryphon on the axe head (see an analogue in Table XXVIII: 3).

2 – Stages of construction of Chorna Grave (near the city of Chernihiv) above the cremation of a family of an Old-Rusy prince.

3 – Ceremonial half-dugout Slavic sanctuary, 9th – 10th century, in the form of a "Giantess" (according to I. P. Rusanova and B. A. Rybakov), at the settlement of Shumsk near the city of Zhytomyr.

4 – Stages of construction of the kurhan-sanctuary of Yamna-Catacomb period at the settlement at Molochansk in the Tokmak district of Zaporizhia region (reconstruction by S. Zh. Pustovalov, P. L. Kornienko et al.): a group of 1 + 6 small kurhans overlaid by an overall earth-fill, on the summit of which they built an altar at the centre of an 11(?)-radial star (cf. 7).

5 – The upper layering of High Grave (kurhan 1) at the village Starosillia, which connected it with mound 4, forming the symbol of Universe – with symbols of the Sun, Moon and Divine (Milky) Way, – also corresponding to the complex of Shruta altars, from which the *Vedas* are proclaimed to this day in India.

6 – The primary mound of the kurhan at the village of Verbivka^ in the Chyhyryn district of Cherkasy region (excavated by A. A. Bobrinsky, reconstruction by A. S. Trofimova); Proto-Sumerian inscriptions on the plates refer to the First Creator-Ruler *Sukhur-alal*, Goddess-Foremother *Gatumdug* and *Inanna*, *Country of Good*, *sanctuaries*, *court of law*, and *murder* (A. G. Kifishin, *Ancient sanctuary of Stone Grave*…, pp. 525-528).

7 – Starosillia type entombment 8 of kurhan 1 at the village of Starosillia in the Velyko-Olexandrivsk district of the Kherson region; the grave is crowned by a [7-wheeled] cart, which symbolised (see Table XV: 9) the constellation of Parjani-'Taurus', and filling over it with ray-like highways symbolising Surya-'Sun'.

Table XX

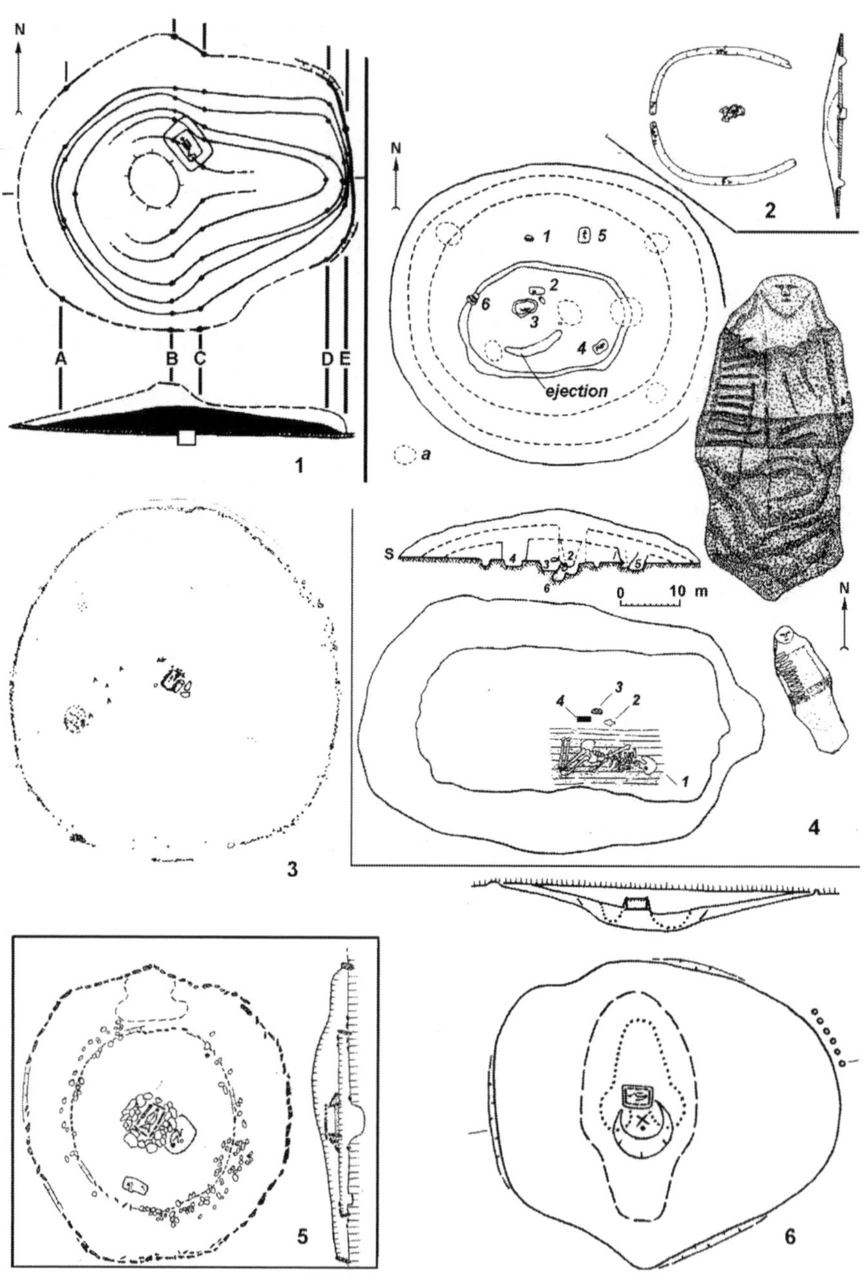

Table XX

Anthropomorphous constructions of Aryans – carriers of the Kemi Oba (3, 5, 6) and Yamna archaeological cultures, 3rd millennium BCE.

1 – Reconstruction of the layering over Yamna archaeological culture burial 25 of kurhan 3 near the village of Starosillia.

2 – Ditch around Yamna burial 6 of kurhan 23 from Sofiivka in the Kakhovka district of the Kherson region.

3 – Grave of Kemi Oba culture, burial 10 at kurhan 41 at Sofiivka; grave situated in womb of the figure oriented with the head facing south, with an altar near the heart and with a human sacrifice under the left shoulder.

4 – Stela, grave and ditch of Yamna burial 3 at kurhan 1 from Konstantynivka in the Melitopol district of Zaporizhia region (excavation by B. D. Mykhailov); the deceased was placed in the area of the heart of an anthropomorphous pit.

5 – Plan of the Velyko-Olexandrivsk kurhan; dolmen-I over a Kura-Araxes (Sumerian) burial 24 and Trypillian (Arattan) burial 23 is endowed with celestial-zodiacal symbols, and dolmen-II over Kemi Oba burial 7 is similar anthropomorphous stela with the grave outlined by a head and "pregnant" belly.

6 – Layering over Kemi Oba burial 3 at kurhan 1 at Starosillia composed of two anthropomorphous figures with (external) features of female and male sex; the filled-"chaos" funnel in their overall womb consists of the main elements of "cosmic"-world order: burned straw mixed with fat and fragments of a human skull deposited in a fire, filled with silt (thus representing plants, animals, people; fire, water, and earth).

Table XXI

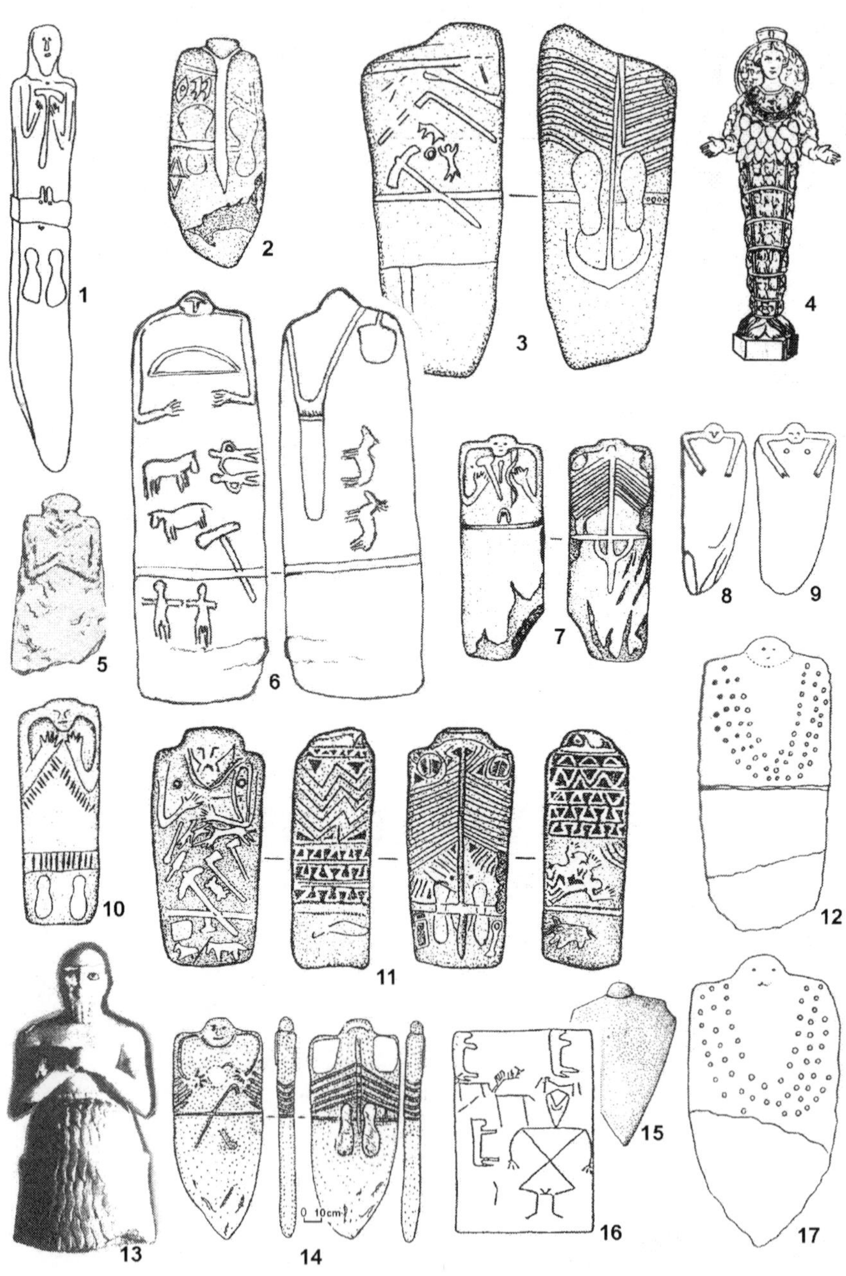

Table XXI

Aratto-Sumerian roots (15-16, 13) **and ancient traditions** (4) **of Aryan stelas,** 3rd – 2nd millennium BCE.

1	–	Chobruch (Moldova).
2	–	Svatovo.
3	–	Fedorivka^ village in the Karlivka district of the Poltava region.
4	–	Statue of Artemis of Ephesus.
5	–	Pervomaivka village.
6	–	Verkhniorichia (Crimea); a bisexual couple at the bottom, pairs of wrestlers and deer above, and the Divine archer reveal a complex of convergences with characters of the Indo-Aryan epic *Ramayana* (Rama and Sita, Rama and Ravan, Solar Deer and the GOD Siva).
7	–	Natalivka village.
8, 9	–	Tiritaka village.
10	–	Belohrudivka.
11	–	Kernosivka^ village; the Creator-GOD Vishnu-Prajapati, or Tvashtar.
12	–	Burial 1 at kurhan 6 at the village of Utkonosivka in the Odessa region.
13	–	Figurine of a Sumerian official, 2500-2315 BCE, from the temple of GODDESS Ishtar in Mari.
14	–	Novoselivka.
15,16	–	Kurhans 11-I and 3-I (see Table XVI: 9 and XVIII: 2) in the village of Usativ, presently in line with the city of Odessa.
17	–	Burial 3 at kurhan 13 from Shevchenkovo in the Odessa region.

Table XXII

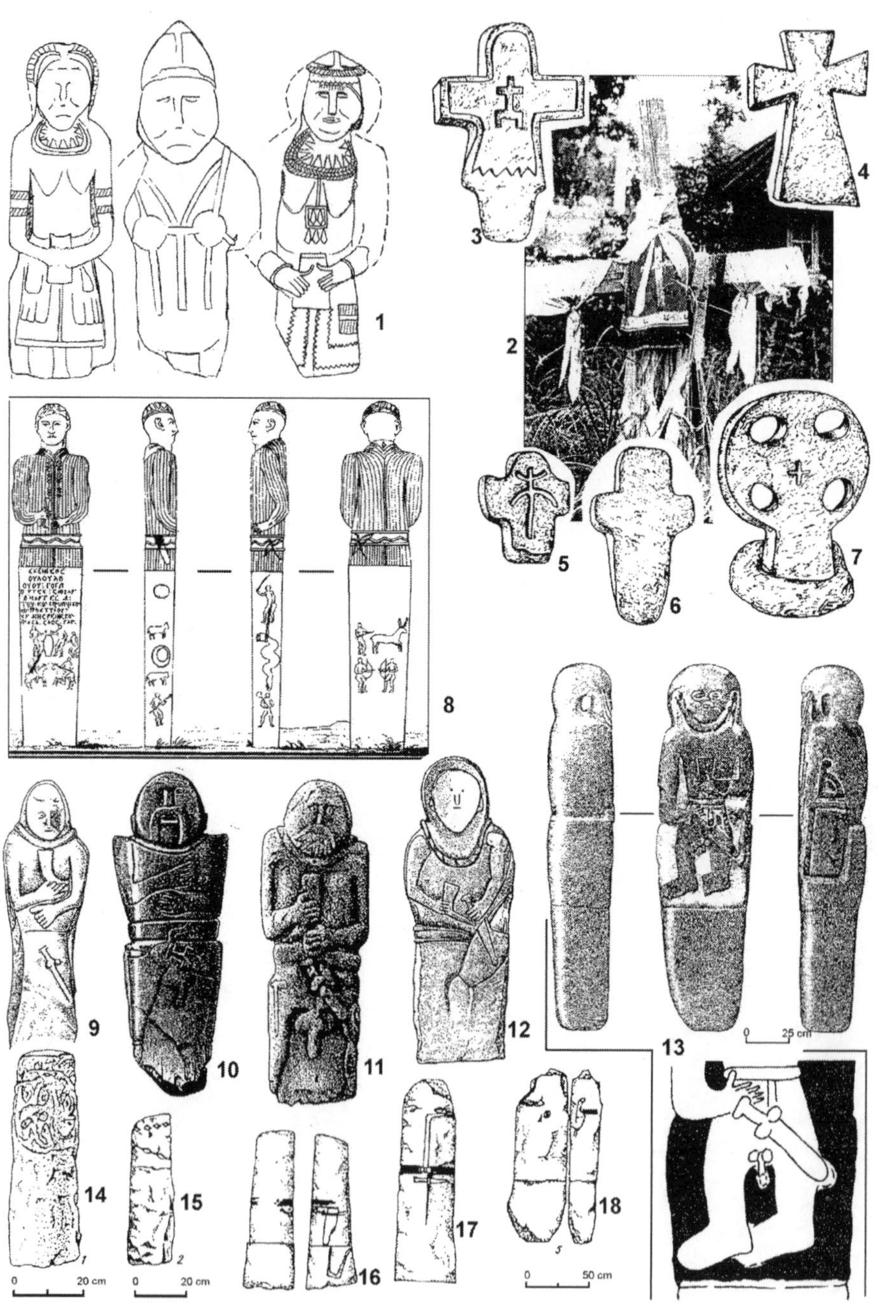

Table XXII

The tradition of Aryan stelas in the cults of the steppe cattle breeders, early 1st millennium BCE to 2nd millennium CE.

1	–	Idols of a Polovets' sanctuary, 1223 CE, on the apex of Aryan kurhan 3 from Nove in the Akymiv district of the Zaporizhia region.
2	–	Grave cross near the village of Vezhytsia in the Rivne region.
3-7	–	Ukrainian grave crosses from the 18th – 20th centuries.
8	–	Old-Rusy statue, 368 CE, which stood on the kurhan over the Antian Prince Bus Beloyar (A. I. Asov, *Slavonic runes and the "Boyan Anthem*", Veche, Moscow, 2000; pp. 80-87 et al.), by the river Etoko at the city of Pyatigorsk in the Northern Caucasus.
9-13	–	Scythian statues (13: from sanctuaries of the 5th – 4th century BCE placed into an Aryan kurhan [perhaps Chaush^ or Tsyhancha?^] above Novoselska^ ferry across the Lower Danube, at the village of Plavni in the Reni district of Odessa region).
14-18	–	Cimmerian anthropomorphous stelas.

Table XXIII

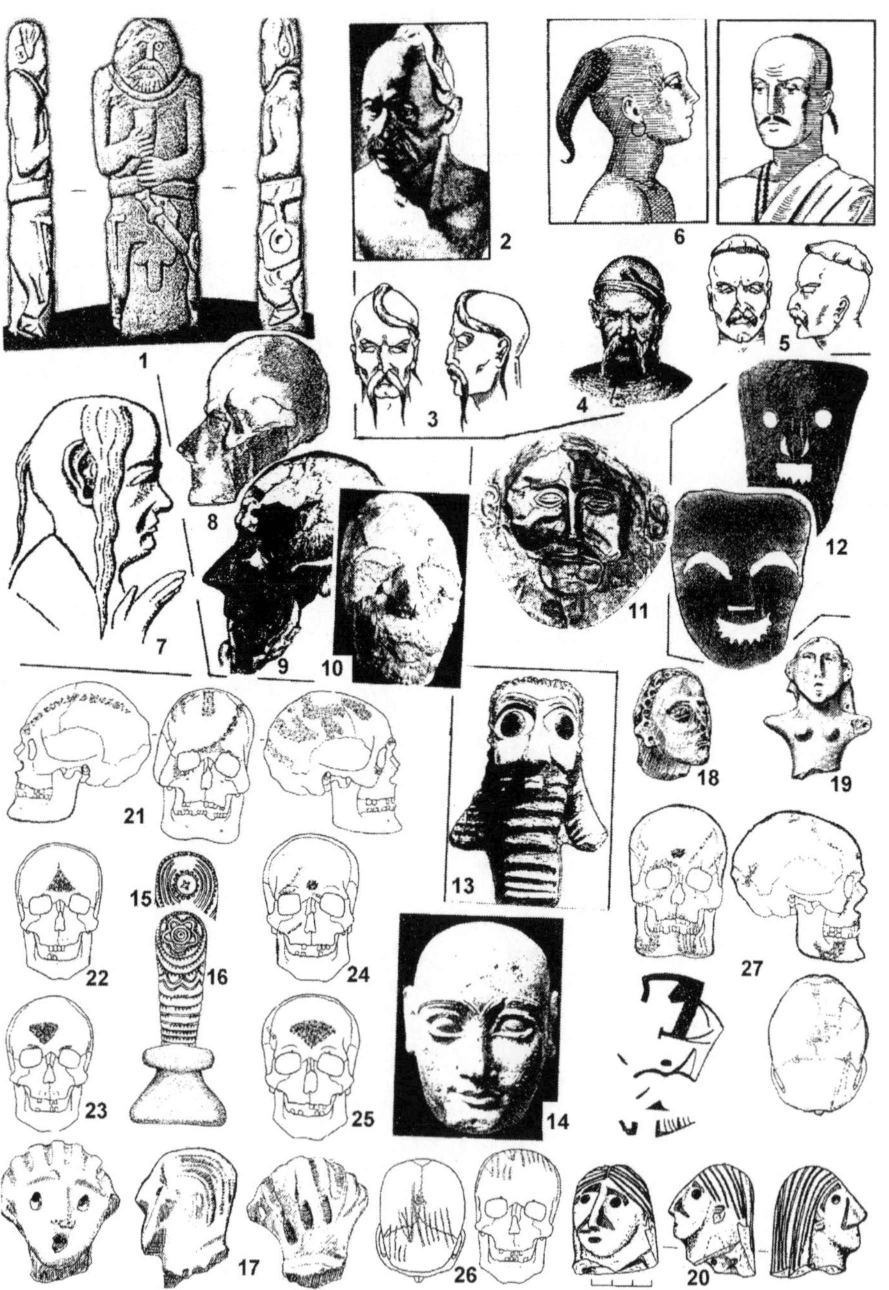

Table XXIII

Hairstyles, characteristic of people and masks, from Aratto-Aryan to Cossack times.

1	–	GOD-Forefather (Papai?) with several "Zaporozhian Cossack's oseledets^" (see 2-5, 6, 7, 21) from Scythian kurhan 9 from Vasylivka in the Snihyrivsky district of the Mykolaiv region (discovery and illustration by V. P. Haychųk).
2	–	Iconic reconstruction (by G. V. Lebedynska) of a Cossack-Zaporozhian who died in 1651 CE near Berestechko.
3-5	–	Hairstyles of Ukrainian Cossacks.
6	–	Indian Brahmans.
7	–	Image of a captive warrior (see Table IV: 1) from an Egyptian tomb, 1314 BCE.
8-10	–	Model (in clay with ochre, etc.) of a skull from an Ingul burial in Zaporizhia region, early 2nd millennium BCE (according to V. V. Otroshchenko et al.).
11	–	The golden "mask of Agamemnon" from a pit tomb of Ancient Greek Mycenae, about 1600 BCE.
12	–	Leather masks of an Old-Rusy scomorokh (i.e. medieval harlequin), 13th century.
13-14	–	Two anthropological types of Sumerians (according to D. Rohl).
15-16	–	Ornamented caps of anthropomorphous figurines (of the Usativ culture circle of Trypillia S-II) from burial 15 at kurhan 6 at Novo-Oleksiivka in the Skadovsk district of Kherson region.
17-20	–	Fragments of figurines from [Trypillian] B-I – C-II settlements: village of Ozarintsy in the Mohyliv-Podolian district of the Vinnytsia region, village of Maydanets (19), village of Krynychky and others.
21-27	–	Male and female (22-26) skulls from Trypillia C-II burials near the villages of Usativ and Mayaky, Odessa region (according to K. V. Zinkovsky and V. P. Petrenko).

Table XXIV

Table XXIV

The Aryan tradition of Foremother veneration.

The Goddess portrayed in sacred images of modern *Slavs* (1-4), *Bharata-Indians* (7-10); ancient *Tauris, Greeks and Scythians* (5, 6, 14); *Arattans* (11, 17-21) and *Aryans* (12, 13); *Hattians* of Asia Minor (15-16), and *Babylonians* of Mesopotamia (22):

1, 2, 4 – Embroidery of eastern Slavs.

3 – Ukrainian painted egg [pysanka] with Berehynia (Oranta*-woman giving birth to Gemini – who headed the zodiac in 6680-4400 BCE (N. A. Chmykhov, *Sources of Rus Paganism*, Lybid, Kyiv, 1990; p. 232).

5, 6 – "Serpent-legged virgin" (according to Herodotus) from Chersonese and the golden front strap of a horse from a 4th century BCE grave of a chieftain in the kurhan at Velyka Tsymbalka in the Zaporizhia region.

7-10 – Figures on a ceremonial vessels. (N. R. Gusev, *Slavs and Aryans. The Way of the Gods and Words*. – FAIR-PRESS, Moscow, 2002; p. 126 et al.).

11 – Bone platelet, late 4th millennium BCE from the Verteba Cave at the village of Bilche-Zloto in the Borshchiv district of the Ternopol region.

12 – Foundation [outline] of kurhan 3 (Yamna culture, end of the 3rd millennium BCE) at the village of Atmanai in the Akimov district of the Zaporizhia region.

13 – Stone figurine between the 3rd – 2nd millennia BCE from Yamna burial 2 in kurhan 17 at the village of Zlatopol in the Zaporizhia region.

14 – Paintings on a Greek vessel from the beginning of the 1st BCE.

15,16 – Relief images of an Oranta[1]-woman in childbirth (comp. 3) from temples VII/23 and VI/A.8 of Anatolian Çatal Höyük, (6200 ± 97 BCE, according to J. Mellaart) upper walls decorated with a copy of the beginning of the Chronicle at Stone Grave (A. G. Kifishin, *Ancient sanctuary of Stone Grave*, Kyiv, Aratta, 2001; p. 441-487).

17 – Ceramic figurine from the settlement at the village of Cucuteni-Cetecuia (synchronous with Trypillia B).

18 – Hamangia culture, settlement at Cernavoda (Romania).

19 – Burial ground at the village of Vykhvatynts above the River Dniester.

20,21 – [Ceramics] from the settlements at Trusesti-I and Birlesti (Cucuteni-Trypillia B).

22 – Sumerian-Babylonian Lilith (?), beginning of the 2nd millennium BCE.

***Oranta** - The Praying Virgin of Eastern Orthodoxy.

Table XXV

Table XXV

Combined images of Woman, Tree of Life, birds and such like in mythological rituals of Aratta (19-24), Mesopotamia (12-18), Egypt (8-11), Ukraine (2-5), Rus (1, 7) and Indian-Bharata (6).

1, 6	–	Clay toys.
2	–	Festival biscuit.
3, 4	–	"Nodular dolls" formed on a *phallic base* (O. Naiden, *National Dolls of Middle Upper-Dnipro region*, Svaroh magazine No. 13-14, pp. 36-38 (2003)) (see Table XXIII: 15-16).
5	–	Ukrainian decorated egg.
7	–	Curtain with embroidered images of various birds and Orant^-women giving birth, (B. A. Rybakov, *Paganism in ancient Slavs*, Science, Moscow, 1981; p. 489).
8, 9, 11	–	Egypt, Naiad II period (influenced by Mesopotamian Ubaid, Uruk, Jemdet-Nasr periods, 6th – 4th millennia BCE): Funerary figurine and vessels with images of ships, birds, women (D. Rohl, *Genesis of Civilisation*, Eskimo, Moscow, 2002; pp. 341-343).
10	–	Winged Goddess from the Egyptian *Book of the Dead*, chapter CLXIV.
12	–	Figurine, Ubaid culture, Mesopotamia, 5th millennium BCE.
13,16-18	–	Ceramics from Suziana and Samarra^, 6th – 5th millennia BCE (V. N. Danylenko, *The Cosmogony of Primitive Society*, in *Beginnings of Civilisation*, Akademproekt, Ekaterinburg-Moscow, 1999; p. 154, tabl. XIX: 3, 5-7).
14	–	Images on a temple seal from Babylonian Nippur 1311-1286 BCE (Mesopotamian *Paradise-griffins* and their GODDESS or GOD, before whom kneels God Ea/Enki) (D. Rol, p. 445).
15	–	Reed temple, Sumerian pre-cuneiform letters.
19	–	Vase from the settlement of Concesti (Moldova; today in Romania), draped by plants and figures performing the "dodol" rain dance (B. A. Rybakov, pp. 187-209).
20	–	Two-headed bird-canoe, settlement at Nemyriv.
21	–	Figurine of approximately Trypillia Stage C-II from a settlement at the village of Koshylivtsi-Oboz in the Zalischyky district of the Ternopol region.
22,23	–	Figures on ceramic [fragments] from the settlement of Costesti-IV [Moldova].
24	–	Characteristic fragment of a vessel from the Brynzen-III settlement of the Edinets district of Moldova (according to V. I. Markevych).

Table XXVI

Table XXVI

Images of women in the mythology of Aryan peoples.

1 – Etruscan-Roman Diana and Dioscuri^.

2 – Rusy embroidery: Mokosh^ and equestrian women with ploughs greet Springtime (according to B. A. Rybakov).

3 – Image on a Greek vessel: Herakles fighting the Amazons of Asia Minor.

4 – Silver gilt rhyton^ honouring 'our God' Dionysus, 4th century BCE, from the Northern Black Sea area.

5 – Image on a Greek vessel of Odysseus listening to the woeful songs of the deadly sirens.

6 – Seal from Ancient Greek Mycenae.

7 – Picture on ancient vase of the Serpent Python pursuing the Hyperborean Lata with the young twins Artemis and Apollo.

8 – Apollo and Artemis shoot the children of Princess Niobe for disrespect to Lata.

9 – Painting of the sacrifice of a bull at a Cretan palace.

10 – Golden plaque from the 4th century kurhan at Kul-Oba showing the Scythian Goddess Api, the "serpent-legged virgin" progenitress of the Scyth, Gelon and Agathirs (according to Herodotus).

11,13 – Similar images of women with serpents from Cretan Knossos 2200-1600-1450 BCE (compare also with other more ancient images in Table XX: 20-24).

12 – Image in the "Grotto of the Bison" of Stone Grave (according to B. D. Mykhailov): Artemis – in accordance with a rare myth from Troad – fights with Orion for (the constellation) of the Golden Hound, which embodies the soul of Zeus, the "father of gods". (Yu. A. Shilov, *Slavic Sources of Civilisation*, MAUP, Kyiv, 2004; pp. 111-112)

Table XXVII

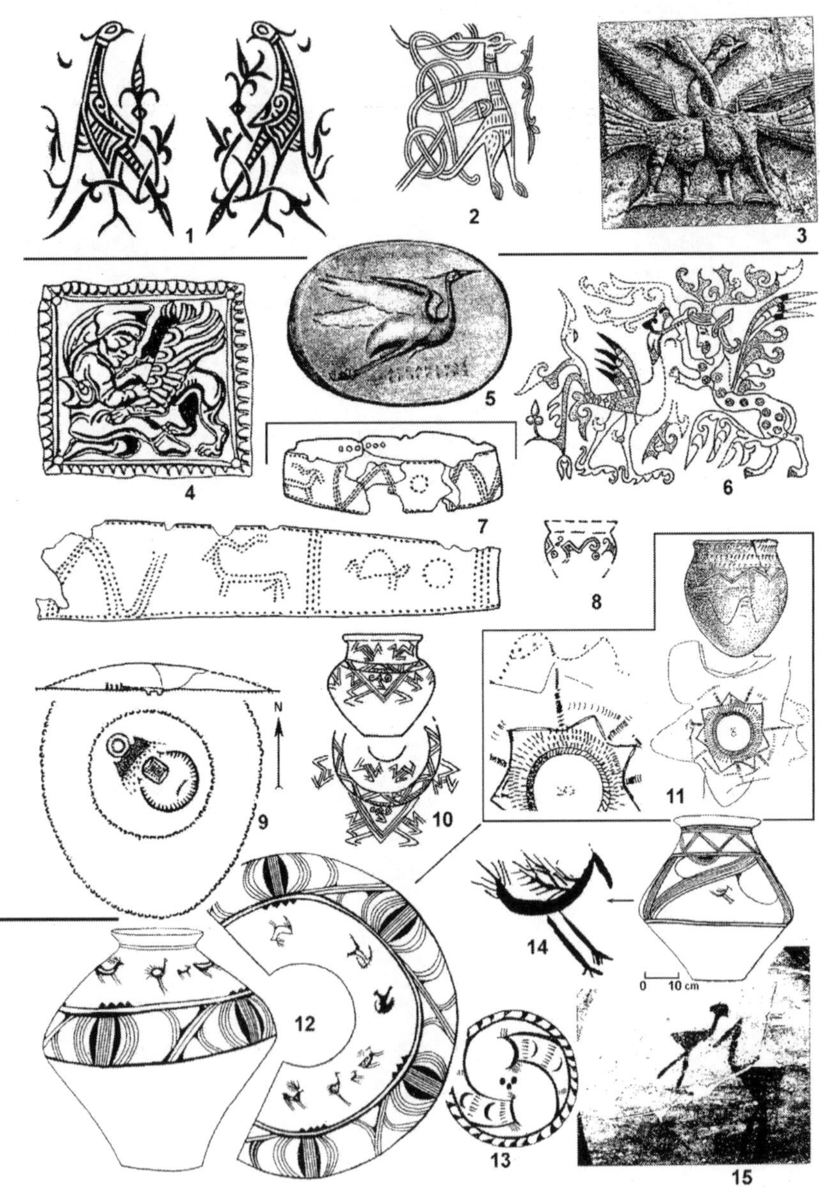

Table XXVII

Mythologies of Geronomachia ("Battle of the Cranes and Pygmies", see also Table XXV: 7, 10, 11, 13, 14, 16, 19, 20) in the Aryan tradition of the middle of the 4th millennium BCE to the beginning of the 2nd millennium CE.

1-4	–	Spring and similar dances of cranes (***zharav-birds****) in Rusy art of the 12th – 13th centuries (B. A. Rybakov, *Paganism of ancient Slavs…*, pp. 709-713).
5, 6	–	Cranes and gryphons in early art of Scythia, Bosphorus, and Altai.
7	–	Copper diadem from a burial ground of the Kura-Araxes archaeological culture at the village of Kvatskhelebi, Georgia.
8, 10	–	Vessels of the Kura-Araxes archaeological culture with images of cranes laying eggs and dancing.
9	–	Symbols of the Primary Egg and Bird placed in an Alazan-Bedensk kurhan at the village of Tsnori^ (excavated by Sh. Sh. Dedabrishvili).
11	–	Image of a crane (above, left) and Taurus (in centre) on a Calendar-Zodiacal ornamented vessel from burial 13 in kurhan 9 (Early-Yamna culture) at the village of Sofiivka in the Kakhovka district of the Kherson region.
12	–	Dogs, deer and a crane (compare with 6) in a Calendar-Zodiacal ornamented seed storage vessel from a Trypillian-VIII settlement at the village of Varvarivka (in Moldova, between the Rivers Prut and Dniester).
13	–	From the settlement at the village of Tomashivsk in the Uman district of the Cherkasy region, Trypillia C-I.
14	–	Figure of a crane from Brynzen-IV settlement.
15	–	Crane birds on a vessel from a Trypillian settlement at the village of Zhvanets in the Kamianets-Podilsky district of the Khmelnytsky region.

* The name is derived from the Slavic term 'zhar' which means heat. [The Ukrainian word for cranes is журавлей (zhuravlei)].

Table XXVIII

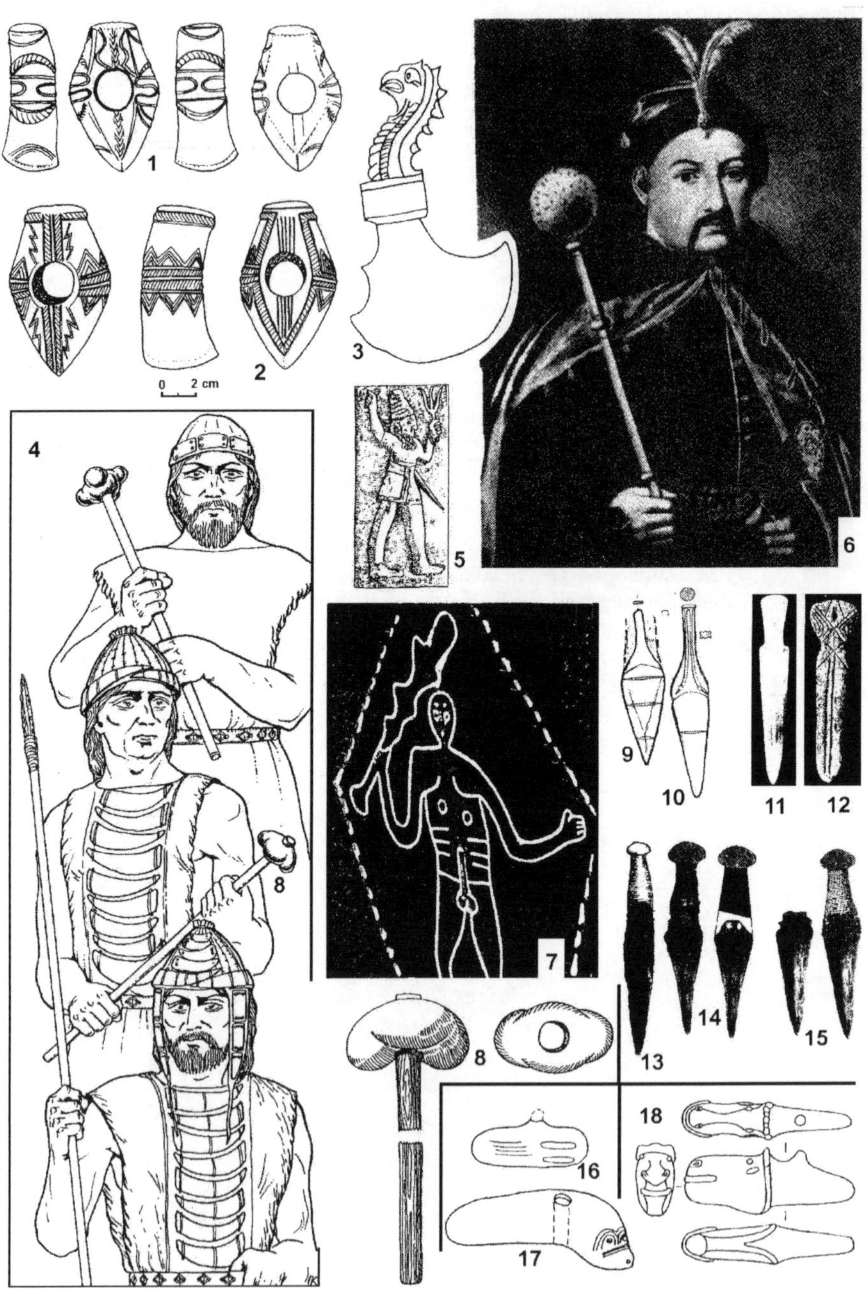

Table XXVIII

Weapons as power symbols in Indo-European traditions from the middle of the 5th millennium BCE to the 17th century CE.

1, 2	–	Burials from kurhans of the Ingul archaeological culture at the village of Barativka in the Novobuh district and the village of Horozhyno in the Bashtan district of the Mykolaiv region.
3	–	Bronze axe from the embankment of a Scythian kurhan, 4th century BCE, at the village of Lvovo in the Berislav district in the Kherson region.
4, 8	–	Indian club from burial 24 of the Mariupol burial ground that also had a spear, defence breast-plates and belts with wild-boar teeth. (Excavation by N. I. Makarenko and reconstruction by P. L. Kornienko).
5	–	Hurrian Thunder-GOD Teshub with a sword and trident.
6	–	Portrait of Hetman Bohdan (1648-1657 CE) of Khmelnytsky with a mace, the symbol of authority amongst the Cossacks of Ukraine.
7	–	The 55m phallic image of the "naked giant of Cerne Abbas" on a hillside meadow in the county of Dorset (England), armed with a club.
9,10	–	Bronze daggers of the Yamna culture (from the kurhan at the village of Vinohrad in the Kherson region) and of a Starosillia type culture (from burial 17 in kurhan 1 at the village of Starohorozheno in the Bashtan district of the Mykolaiv region).
11,12	–	Bone daggers (Trypillia C-II) from Verteba Cave at the village of Bilche-Zlote in the Borshchiv district of the Ternopil region.
13-15	–	Reconstruction of daggers (Trypillia C-II) with flint and bronze sword-blades, from Sofiivka type burials and central burials in kurhan I-3 in the village of Usativ.
16-18	–	"Horse-head sceptres" (according to V. Danylenko and others) found near the Berezovska Hydroelectric Station, Casimca (Romania), in burial 1 in kurhan 1-II at the village of Suvorovo (Lower Danube).

Table XXIX

Table XXIX

Images and symbols of boats beginning from the 7th millennium BCE.

1 – Images (from left to right, according to D. Rohl) of warrior Enkidu, chieftain of Gilgamesh, who survived the Flood of Utnapishtim, and of Gilgamesh and the ferryman, Urshanabi, on a seal from Fara (Sumerian Shuruppak, II Early-dynastic period), 2615-2500 BCE.

2 – Ancient Greek image on a vessel, 850-800 BCE, from the necropolis of Eleusia.

3 – Ukrainian Cossack coat of arms of 1776 CE.

4 – Magical boat over Yamna burial 8 in kurhan 8 at the village of Semenivka in the Odessa region.

5 – Embroidered "barque-horses" (according to B. A. Rybakov).

6 – Magical raft on the bottom of Yamna burial 6 in kurhan 1 at the village of Bychok, Moldova.

7 – Image on a vessel of the Kura-Araxes culture.

8 – Yamna burial 14 in kurhan 3 above the River Konka at the village of Hrihorivka in the Zaporizhia area; the burial of a child in a "wooden log" (according to G. N. Toshchevu and G. I. Shakhrov) has been reinterpreted as a "log canoe" (G. I. Shapovalov, *Boats of faith. Navigation in the spiritual life of ancient Ukraine*, Dyke Pole, Zaporizhia, 1997; pp. 30-31).

9 – "Image of a canoe with several 'arrows' on an anthropomorphous stela from a demolished kurhan of the Yamna period near Stone Grave" 4250-2200 BCE (B. D. Mykhailov, *Petroglyphs of Stone Grave*, MAUP, Kyiv, 2004; pp. 150, 280). It is more appropriate to consider the 'arrows' as symbolic of people and oars (according G. I. Shapovalov, p. 37), although they could be linked with the 7 favourable months of the half-year. (N. A. Chmykhov, *The sources of Paganism of Rus*, Lybid, Kyiv, 1990; p. 232 et al.).

10 – Sumerian seal, mid 3rd millennium BCE.

11,12 – Petroglyphs of boats of Sumerian style (D. Rohl, *The Genesis of Civilisation*. EKSMO, Moscow, 2002; pp. 304-319 et al.) from Kanais [opposite the town of Edfu] and the Egyptian Eastern Desert.

13 – Images of waves and the Sun between canoes on the elevation of a clay model of an Arattan temple (Trypillia B-II) from the PLATAR collection.

14,15 – Images of a "solar barque" on vessels from settlements (Trypillia B-I to C-I) at the city of Nemyriv in the Vinnytsia region and from Blyshchanka in the Zalischyky district of the Ternopol region.

16 – A model of a canoe of the same period and culture from the settlement of Horodnytsa-Horodyshche in the Horodenka district of the Ivano-Frankivsk region.

17 – Images of canoes, arks and ships from Stone Grave (according to B. D. Mykhailov at grotto locations 1 (a), 13 (b), 51 (c), 46 (d), 33 (e), 7 (f), 56 (g), 60 (h), 51-b (i).

Table XXX

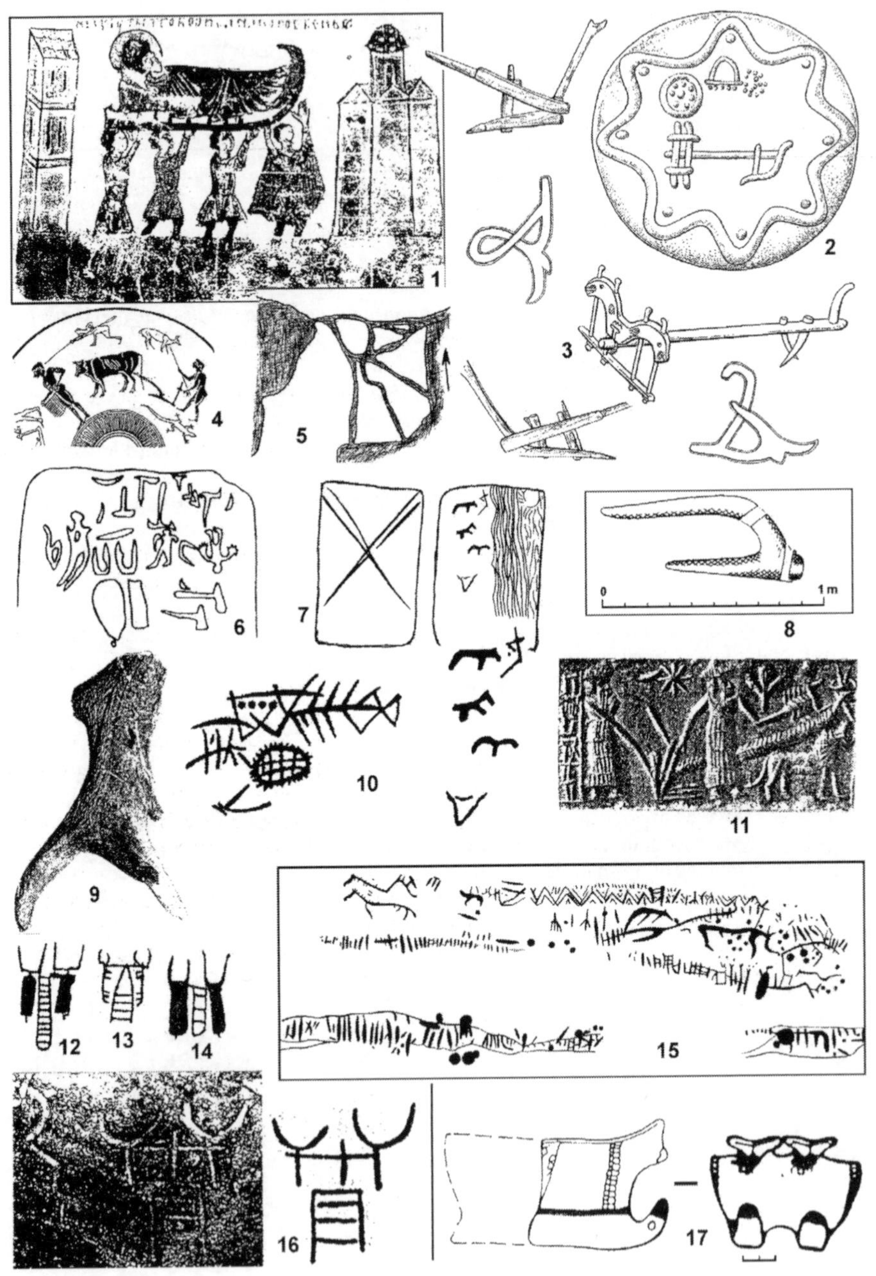

Table XXX

Ancient drag harrows (12-14, 16), **ploughs** (6-11, 15) **and sledge** (17), 7th – 3rd millennia BCE, and their subsequent tradition.

1 – The funeral sledge of Prince Boris (1015 CE), from a 14th century miniature painting.

2, 3 – A celebratory rich-loaf (Bulgarian) with an image of a Slavic wooden plough from the 2nd millennium BCE.

4 – Ancient Greek image, 5th century BCE, of ploughing and sowing.

5 – Ancient drainage system on the bank of the crossing of the Lower Danube at the village of Novosillia in the Reni district of the Odessa region; The location is called Kartal (< Indo-Aryan word 'kṛta' means 'canal' (O. N. Trubachev, *Indoarica in Northern Black Sea coast*, Science, Moscow, 1999; p. 250)).

6 – The ritual fertilising of a plough by a priest (on the left) and others (according to B. A. Shramko) on a stela of the Kemi Oba archaeological culture, Bakhchi-Eli in the city of Simferopol.

7 – Images on plates in Kemi Oba burial 8 of kurhan 1 at the village of Barativka in the Mykolaiv region, showing a plough (above), animals and bull's head (Taurus), as well as the symbol 'X' representing the netherworldly Sun (Savitar-'life-creator').

8 – Bronze Age wooden plough from the village of Tokari in Chernihiv region (according to B. A. Shramko).

9 – Plough made from an elk horn, from the early Trypillian settlement of Hrebeniukov Yar at the village of Maydanets in the Talne district of the Cherkasy region.

10 – Image of a plough on a sacrificial altar with people and calendar [marks], from Location 1 at Stone Grave.

11 – Print of a Sumerian temple seal with an image of a plough.

12-14 – Images of drag harrows from Fontanalba (Spain) and Syunik (Armenia: 13).

15 – Calendar frieze (according to Yu. Shilov), mid 3rd millennium BCE, from the "Grotto of the Bull" of Stone Grave (see Table XV: 15), in which a pair of Aryan New Year Ashvin-'horses'- [cf. Aryan Ashvins twin concept] couple with scenes of ploughing (showing a plough drawn by the bull-Taurus from whose mouth a stream is flowing), characteristic of Aratta-'Trypillia'.

16 – Image of a drag harrow from Stone Grave (Location 37).

17 – Clay model of a sledge from the largest settlement of Aratta (stage Trypillia C-I) at the village of Talianky in the Talne district of the Cherkasy region.

Table XXXI

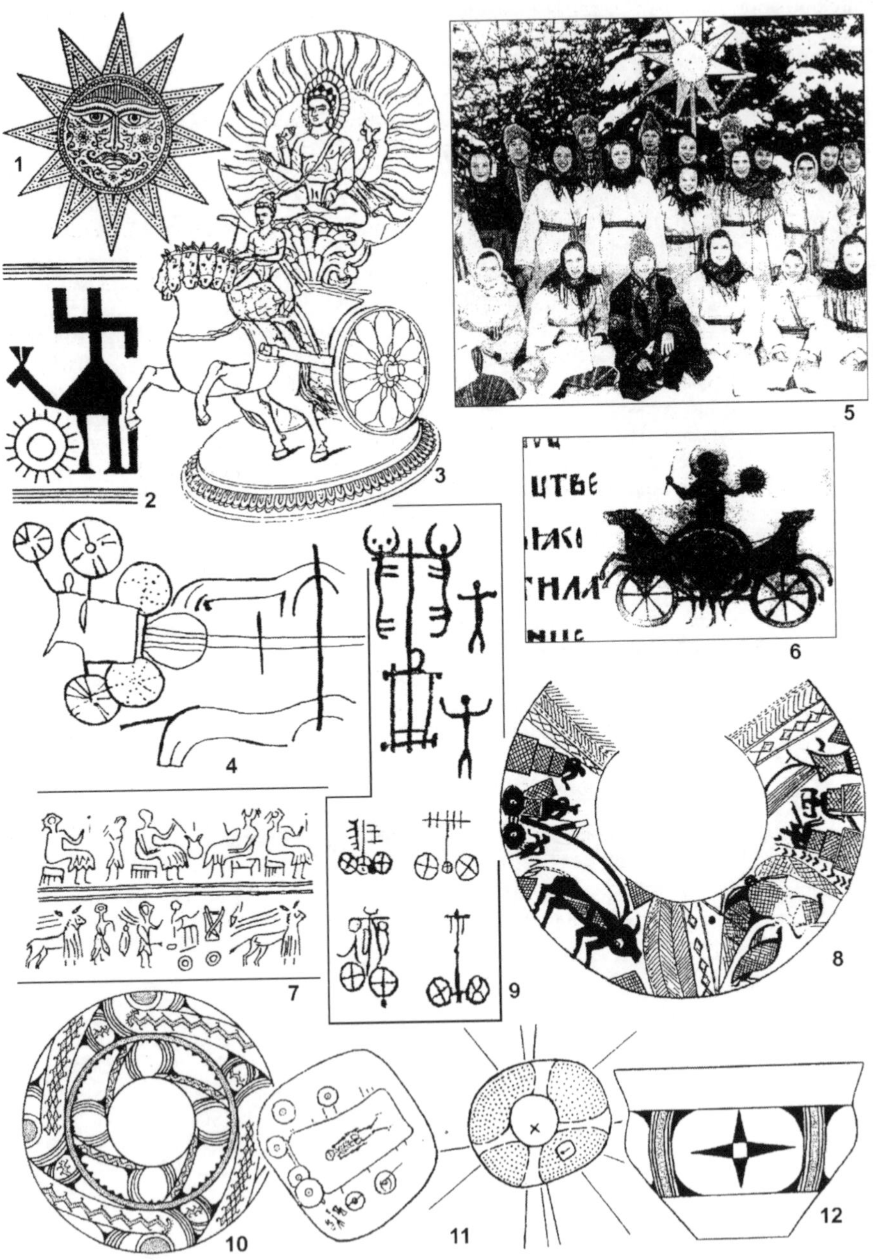

Table XXXI

Symbolism of the God Surya-'Sun' in memorials of Arattans (10, 12), Aryans and Hurrians (9, 11), Indo-Aryans (4), Bharata-Indians (1-3), and Slavs (5, 6).

1-3	–	Traditional images of the Sun (1, 3 – 'Surya') in Bharata-India (according to N. R. Guseva).
4	–	Petroglyph of a cart with 4+1 wheels (compare with image 11 where there are 7 wheels), North India.
5	–	Ukrainian carol singers in the Rivne region (celebrating the Christmas New Year of the Solar God Koliada) with a "star".
6	–	Old-Rusian deity of the Sun; a miniature from the *Kyiv Psalter*, 1397 CE;
7, 8	–	Images of carts on a Sumerian seal and vessel, 3rd millennium BCE.
9	–	Petroglyph of a cart and chariots (including a "chariot of three-wheels" of Aryan twin Ashvins), from Syunik (Caucasus).
10,12	–	View of the upper parts of vessel and basin of Trypillian C-I period from settlements at the village of Konivka in the Kelments district and the village of Shypintsy in the Kitsman district of the Chernivtsi region (according to T. M. Tkachuk).
11	–	Starosillia burial 8 in kurhan 1 at the village Starosillia in the Kherson region, covered by a cart with 2+ (2+1)+2 wheels and [the kurhan] layering with symbols of Surya-'Sun'.

Table XXXII

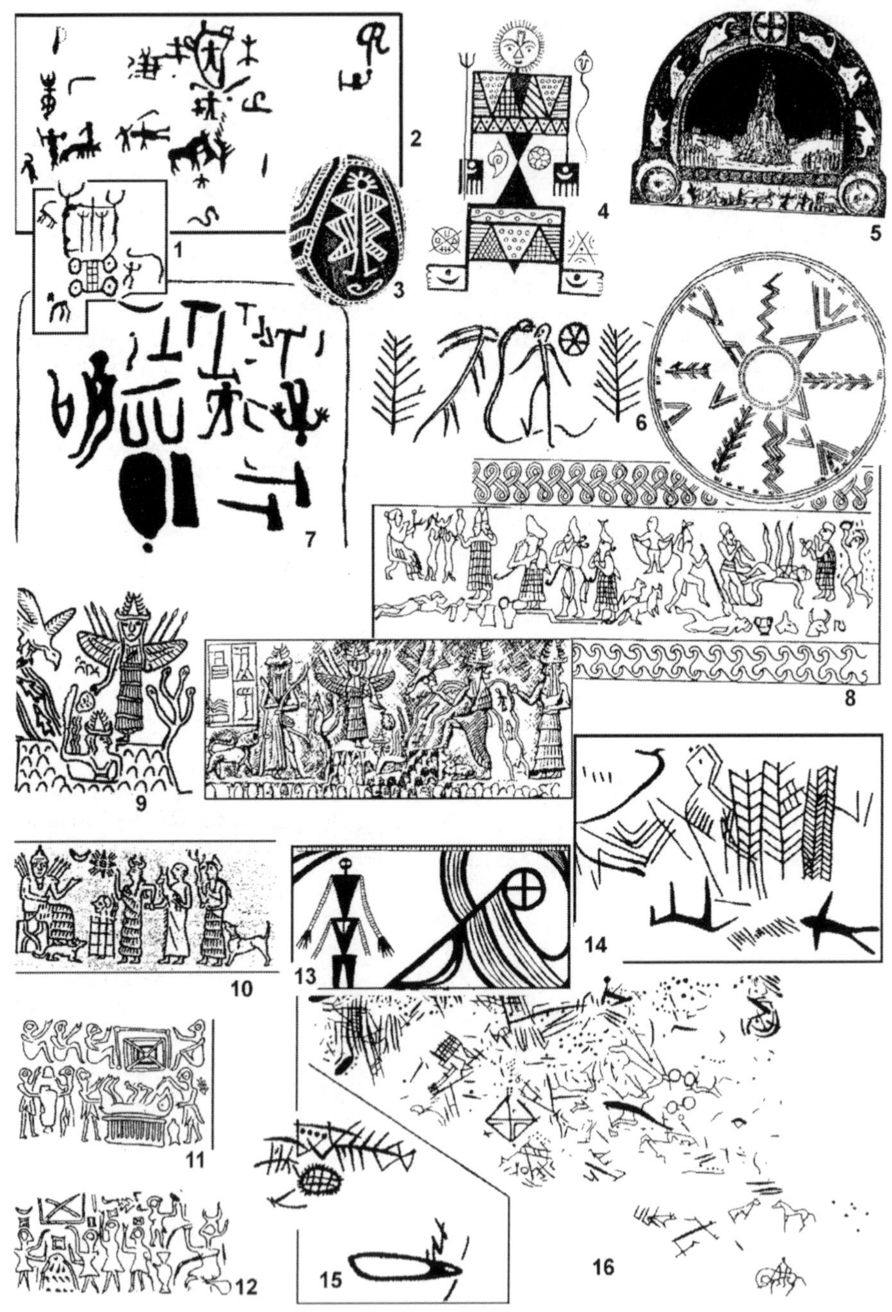

Table XXXII

Images of human and other sacrifices (see also Table XXXIII: 5, 8, 13) from the 7th – 4th millennium BCE.

1 – Image of a ritual cart from Syunik, Caucasus (V. A. Novozhenov, *Petroglyphs of carts from Middle and Central Asia* (*relating to the problem of the migration of the population of steppe Eurasia in period of the Eneolithic and Bronze Age*), Arguments and Facts, Almaty, 1994; p. 65 et al.).

2 – Image from the canopy of Tash-Air Cave in Crimea, Kemi Oba archaeological culture, (copied by A. A. Shchepinsky, interpretation by Yu. A. Shilov): military executions and sacrifices of people and horses at sacrificial pillars called Ashvatthi^ ('horse tree') with subsequent rebirth (in the centre above).

3 – Cosmic serpent-warrior on a Ukrainian painted egg.

4 – Indian folk image of the sacrificial Cosmic [first man] Purusha^.

5 – Skoloto-Slavonic altar of Kola-Diya (Masliana^), 6th – 5th century BCE, at the village of Pozharna Balka^ in the Poltava district (according to I. I. Lyapushkin, B. A. Rybakov, and N. N. Veletskoi; artistic reconstruction by G. Yu. Tymoshenko).

6 – Culmination of the Sumerian *Epic of Gilgamesh* on a temple seal and 12th century BCE vessel (see below) from Catacomb burial 11 in kurhan 2 in the village of Voznesenka near Stone Grave; with the help of Utu [the Sun] the ruler-priest Gilgamesh, and his bull-like companion Enkidu, conquer the serpent-like Humbaba (who was one of the forerunners of Slavonic Kupala), the custodian of the Sacred Grove upon Mount of the Immortals.

7 – Kemi Oba stele from Bakhchi-Eli (city of Simferopol) with scenes of human sacrifice involving agricultural rites and instruments [see also Table XXX, 6].

8 – Temple seal from the beginning of the 2nd millennium BCE from the Aryan-Hurrian kingdom of Mitanni showing 2-3 types of human and other sacrifices to Gods.

9-12 – Sumerian-Babylonian seals from the 3rd millennium BCE with scenes of the sacrifice of people (9, 10), animals, bread and drinks (12).

13 – Image of Purusha, or Purusha-Mithra (related to deities of Persian territory, 5th – 4th millennia BCE, the 4-armed hypostasis of Greek Apollo) on a vessel from the Trypillian (C-I: 3700-3200 BCE) settlement of Petreni, where a painting "with two deities and two suns is valuable because it allows us to date the beginnings of the Vedic myths to a much earlier time than primarily fixed in Indian mythology" at 1200-600 BCE (B. A. Rybakov, *Paganism of ancient Slavs*, Science, Moscow, 1981; pp. 204-205).

14 – Sacrificial rider (Gandkharva) seen at the pedestal of God (Prajapati, the 'Father of creatures') in the surroundings of a Calendar (before the Deity), of 'swastikas' ([representing?] 'Shining'-Viraj*) and others from the "Grotto of the Bull" at Stone Grave. [See also Table XXXIII, 13].

15 – Image of a plough on a sacrificial altar with people and calendar [marks], from Location 1 at Stone Grave.

16 – Scenes of sacrifices and others on the location called "Wall with horses" at Stone Grave.

* In the *Rigveda* (X 90, 5) Viraj was born from Purusha and Purusha from Viraj.

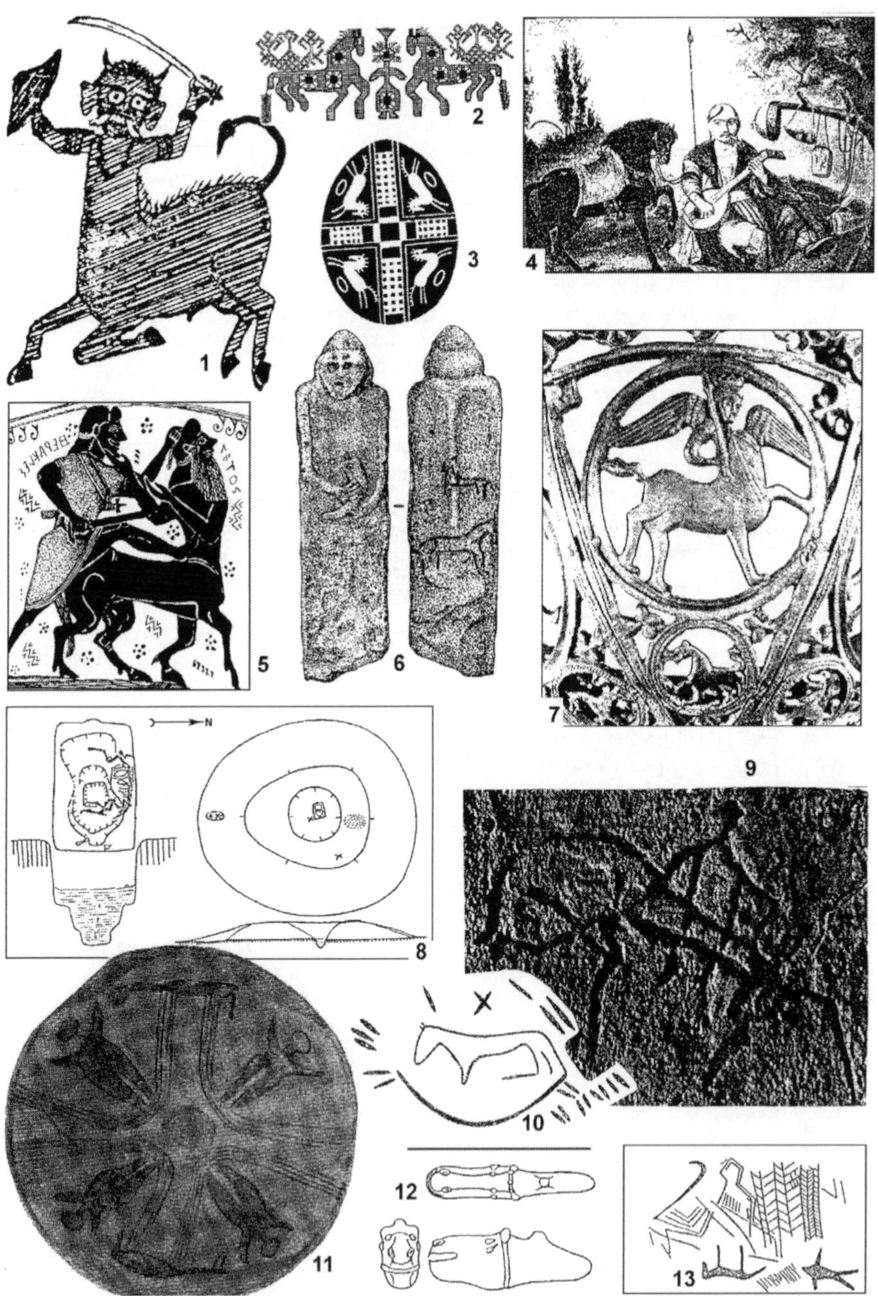

1
2
3
4
5
6
7
8
9
10
11
12
13

Table XXXIII

Images of the horse and rider beginning from the 5th millennium BCE.

1 – Folk image from India (according to N. R. Guseva).

2, 3 – Russian embroidery and Ukrainian painted eggs.

4 – Cossack Mamai, the saintly soul: a "Popular Ukrainian icon".

5 – Hero Herakles and the centaur Nessus: detail of a painted amphora, 675-600 BCE, from the Dipylon necropolis in Athens.

6 – Old-Rusy idol with two horses (cf. the twin concept of "Aryan Ashvins" or "Dioscuri") from sanctuaries of the "solar" Cherniakhov culture, 3rd – 4th century, (according to I. S. Vinokur (I. I. Zaets, *Sources of Spiritual Culture of Ukrainian people*, Aratta, Kyiv, 2006; pp. 203-204)), from the village of Stavchany in the Khmelnytsky region.

7 – Traditional image of Old-Rusy ***Kitovras*** on an ecclesiastical horse-chandelier (< Greek 'krug' [=circle]', Indo-European > hunting dog-hound and Khors^, the horse-like solar Deity of Slavs and other Aryan nations (V. M. Voitovych, *Ukrainian mythology*, Lybid, Kyiv, 2002; pp. 564-565)), Kyiv, 3rd century. (This image is more like the Aryan winged **Gandkharva** than the Greek **Centaurus**; see also ancient images of Cimmerian riders with dogs: Table VIII).

8 – Aryan sanctuary between the 4th – 3rd millennia BCE with the remains of a sacrificial rider and cow-"prayer offering", from the base of the Chaush kurhan just above the Novoselska ferry across the Lower Danube.

9,10 – Images of a rider and netherworldly Sun-Savitar from Locations 25 and 51 at Stone Grave.

11 – Seasonal-calendar image of the Foremother Cybele (horses and creatures) on a bowl of Trypillia C, from the collection of A. S. Polishchuk. (O. N. Trubachev, *Transactions on Etymology*, Languages of Slavonic culture, Moscow, 2005; Vol. 2, pp. 348-353).

12 – "Horse-like sceptre" from Novo-Danylivka burial 1 of kurhan 1-II at the village of Suvorovo in the Odessa region.

13 – Image of the sacrifice of a rider from the "Grotto of the Bull" at Stone Grave. [See also Table XXXII, 14].

Table XXXIV

Table XXXIV

Crosses **in the culture of Aryan peoples** (6th – 4th millennia BCE).

1 – Solar deity (Surya with 'Horses' [cf. the twin concept of Aryan-Ashvins]), from modern India.

2 – Solar horse (Khors as a "horse" on a facade and roof) and Calendar-solar ornamental symbols on a the home in northern Russia.

3 – Dazhboh^ in 19th century Slavic embroidery (according to V. A. Gorodtsov and B. A. Rybakov).

4-7 – Ukrainian hand-painted eggs [pysanky].

8 – Painted fragment from Kemi Oba culture burial 9 in kurhan 4 at the village of Rakhmanivka in the Kryvyi Rih district of the Dnipropetrovsk region; the X-like symbol here means union of Sky-Earth, and crosses are linked with the sacrifice of man (see Table XXXII: 10).

9 – Bone decoration of a horse harness from Cimmerian burials in the kurhan at the village of Zolne near the city of Simferopol.

10,11 – Pre-Christian symbols of crosses of Kyivan Rus (according to B. A. Rybakov).

12 – Solar horse (see 1-3) from Location 51 of Stone Grave (see also Table XXXIII: 13).

13,14 – Pre-Christian Ruseno-Etruscan-Roman Diana (< Arattan Divana > Dana Slavic [cf. Celtic god Dan]) with a star, cross, and crescent (13) – and the Christian Virgin Mary (14) with the same symbols.

15 – Yamna burial 9 in kurhan 36 at the village of Otradne in the Mykolaiv region.

16 – Plan of the upper layers of kurhan 2 at the village of Velyka Bilozirka; early period of Srubna culture.

17 – Sextant-bowl of between the 18th – 17th centuries BCE from Ingul burial 7 in kurhan 10 at the village of Bahachivka in Crimea.

18-20 – Bowls of the Northern-Mesopotamian culture of Samarra; it is notable that the oblique cross is connected with the turtle-Earth (19), and straight cross (18) with the Sky-eagle.

21-24 – Bowls of Trypillia B-II to C-I: Konivka-Putsyta, Bernashivka-III, Brynzen-III, Varvarivka-XV.

25 – Seal from a Sumerian temple, 3rd millennium BCE.

Table XXXV

1
2
3
4
5
6
7
8
9
10
11
а б в г
д є ж з
і к л м н
о п р с т
у ф х
ц ч
ш щ е
12
13
14
15
16
17
18
19

Table XXXV

***Swastikas* in the cultures of Aryan peoples.**

1 – Ukrainian basin from the end of 19th century from the town of Obukhoiv in the Kyiv region.

2-4,5-7 – Ukrainian hand-painted eggs and embroidery (19th century, Eastern Podillia).

8 – 'Protection'-charms "for happiness" used by Indian women to decorate walls and thresholds of dwellings (according to N. R. Guseva).

9,10 – Embroidery from India and Tajikistan.

11 – Swastika motifs in folk art of Eurasia (according to S. V. Zharnikova (N. R. Gusev, *Slavdom and Aryans. The path of gods and words*. FAIR-PRESS, Moscow, 2002; p. 45, fig. 7)): н-о – Eneolithic Trypillia; The Bronze Age of Northern Caucasus (х-ц), Western Caspian Area (ч), Andronov culture of Kazakhstan and Southern Siberia (у-ф); п-т – Scythian-Sarmatian culture; а-м – Rus and Russia 12th – 20th centuries; э – Tajikistan; ш-щ – India.

12 – Burial 6 in kurhan 1 at the village of Mala Bilozirka in the Vasylivka district of the Zaporizhia region, Srubna archaeologic culture, mid 2nd millennium BCE.

13 – Vessel of the Andronov culture.

14 – Vessel from the Baltic region, Scythian times, (according to B. A. Rybakov).

15,16 – Bowls of the Samarra culture, northern Mesopotamia, 6th – 5th millennia BCE.

17,18 – Bowls of Trypillian (C) culture from the villages of Petreni (Moldova) and Usativ (Odessa region).

19 – Fragment of a seal from the Aryan-Hurrian state of Mitanni, 2nd millennium BCE, (see Table XXXII: 8).

Table XXXVI

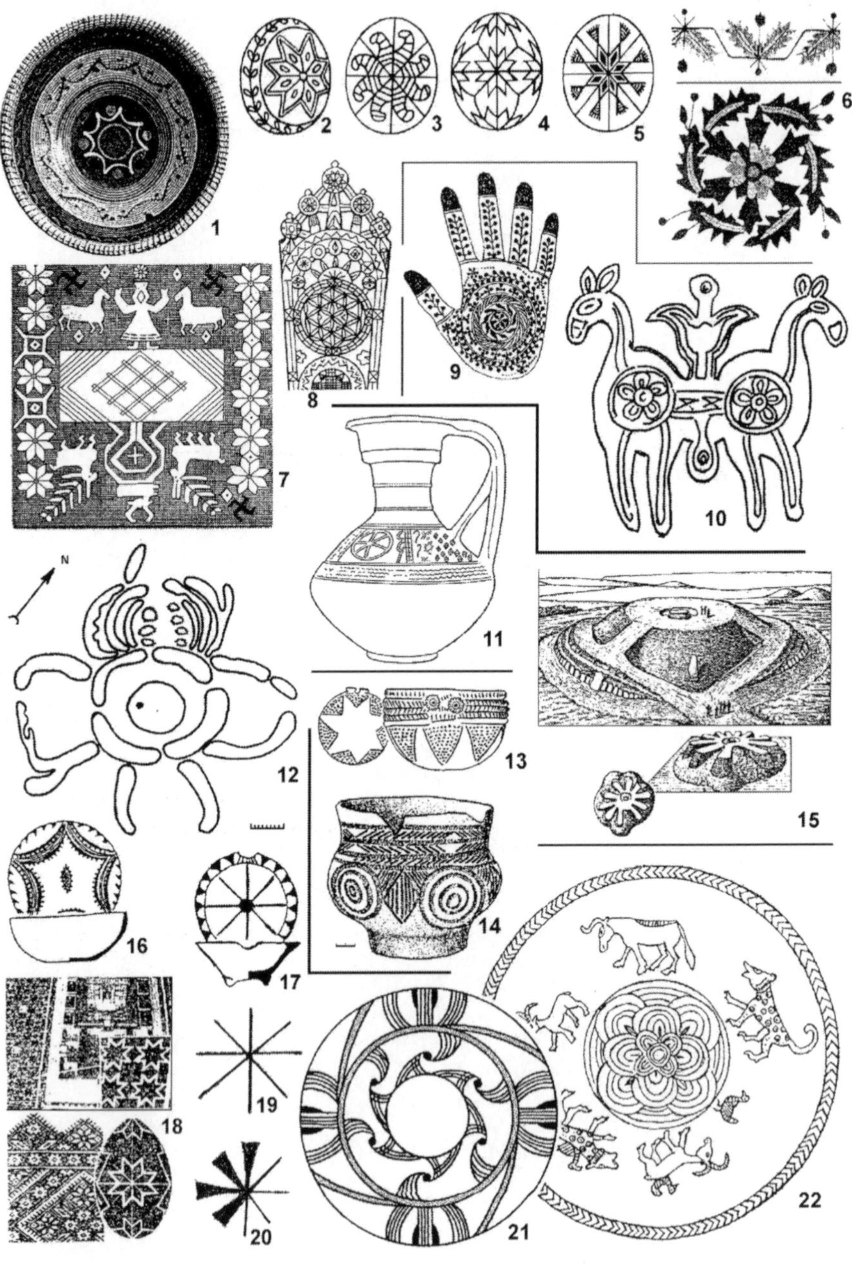

Table XXXVI

***Stars* in the culture of Aryan peoples.**

1 – Ukrainian bowl, from the beginning of the 20th century, from Minkovtsy in the Khmelnytsky region.

2-5 – Ukrainian pysanky, hand-painted [Easter] celebratory eggs.

6,8,9 – Solar brace in ritual ornamentation in Ukrainian embroidery (of a curtain), a Russian carving (of a spinning-wheel), and Indian painting (left female hand).

7 – Ritual table cloth (Arkhangel province, Russia); scene with deer and the sacrifice of a bull on which, the 1+5+6 stars signify the springtime new year and the division of annual cycle into the blessed and unfavourable half-years.

10 – Folk illustration, India [cf. Table XXVI: 1-2; XXXIV: 1-3].

11 – 4th century "ceremonial calendric-vessel for summer rain prayers" with the Slavic thunder sign acquainted with Perun (B. A. Rybakov, *Paganism in ancient Rus*, Science, Moscow, 1987; pp. 177-191; [see Table XV: 2]) which corresponds to the Roman *wheel of Jupiter*, as well as to the Indo-Aryan *wheel of Brahma*.

12 – Maidan Burty^ at the village of Tsvitne near the town of Chyhyryn: a sanctuary-observatory until Scythian times (according to A. A. Bobrinsky), that was supplemented by military strengthening in the 17th century (according to D. I. Yavornytsky). [See Table XVI]

13 – 17th century BCE sextant-bowl of the Ingul culture from burial 9 in kurhan 2 [see also Table XV: 5] at the regional centre of Snihyrivka of the Mykolaiv region; the central part of the ornament resembles the bearded mask of Dionysus.

14 – Vessel of the Donets version of the Catacomb culture, influenced by the Ingul culture.

15 – Kurhan sanctuary of between the 3rd – 2nd millennia BCE, of the settlement at Molochansk in the Zaporizhia region [see Table XIX, 4].

16,17 – Bowls of Trypillian C-I culture from the largest cities of Aratta (between the villages of Talianky and Maydanets in the Talne district of the Cherkasy region: Table XVIII: 1.8) , cf. 19-20.

18 – "Aryan designs from the temple of Jerusalem" (above) compared with Ukrainian embroidery and decorated eggs (I. V. Kaganets, *Aryan standard: The Ukrainian idea of the epoch of great transformation*, A.S.K., Kyiv, 2004; p. 264 et al.).

19,20 – Sumerian-Babylonian symbol of GOD, cf. 16-17.

21 – Sun with 6x2 rays-months in the centre of an image of a solar-lunar-zodiacal calendar on a vessel from the settlement at Varvarivka-XV, Trypillian archaeologic culture C-I.

22 – Sun with 4x3 rays-months in the centre of an image of a solar-zodiacal calendar on a silver vessel from the main grave of the Maikop kurhan, 24th – 23rd centuries BCE (see Table XV).

Table XXXVII

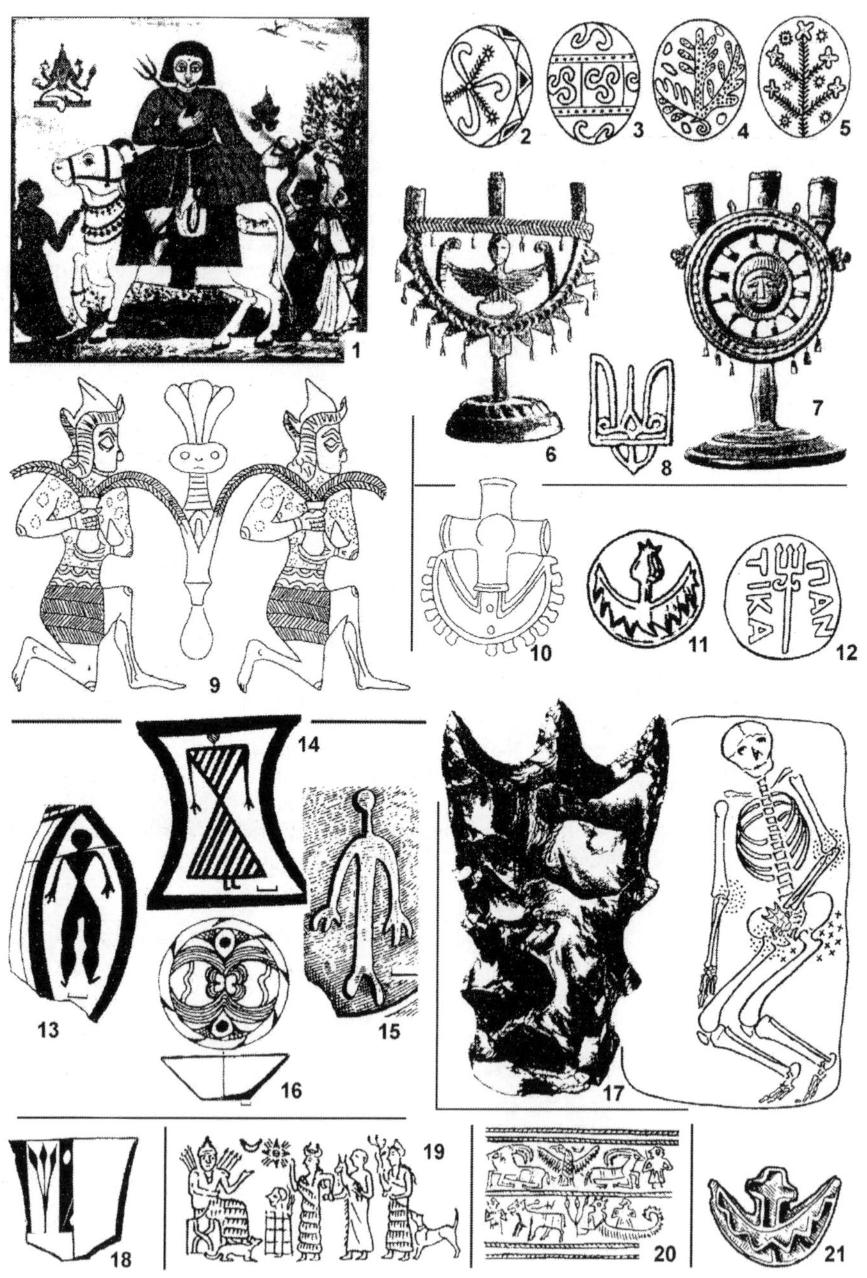

Table XXXVII

***Tridents* in the culture of Aryan peoples.**

1 – Indian image of GOD Shiva (according to N. R. Guseva).

2-5 – Ukrainian hand-painted eggs.

6,7 – Hutsul (Carpathian Ukrainians) 19th century candlesticks with noticeable reminiscences of the "thrice born" Agni-'Fire' and Savitar-'Life-giver', netherworldly Sun.

8 – Symbol of the Rurik Princes of the times of Kyivan Rus.

9 – Image on a golden vessel from Gilan (Northern Iran), mid 2nd millennium BCE; the trident (which Ukrainians also call trisuttya meaning 'Triple entity') is linked here with opening the subconscious mind, with the help of the hypnotic poppy plant (seen in the centre), which provided the juice for the holy drink of 'soma' in vessels held by priests (V. Kulbaka and V. Kachur, *The Somatic cults of the Bronze Age of South-Eastern Europe*, PGTU, Mariupol, 1998; p. 21 et al.). The head of the poppy-plant forms the centre of *trisuttya* on the stamp from burial 10 in the settlement of Toholok-I (Bactria), 13th century BCE.

10,12 – Cimmerian plaque (from Kosovo, Yugoslavia) and an ancient coin (from Panticapaeum, capital of the Bosphorus realm in Taurus-Crimea).

11 – Seal from Altyn-Tepe, between the 3rd – 2nd millennia BCE

13-15 – Tridactyl deities on Cucuteni-Trypillian ceramics (from the settlements of Rzhyshchiv and Zhukavets [Kyiv region] and Traian 'Hill Fantanilor' [Neamt County, Romania]).

16 – Trypillian C-II bowl from a burial ground at the village of Mayaky in the Odessa region.

17 – Burial 5 of kurhan 1 (Yamna archaeological culture, late 3rd millennium BCE) at the village of Vasylivka in the Novo-Troitsk district of the Kherson region; a flint trident embodied the "triple-headed Agni", and the deceased is a revival 'swelling in Mother (Earth)' Matarisvan carrying this 'Fire' from the netherworld.

18 – Vessel from Tel-Abada, Iraq, (Ubaid-II, archaeologic culture, 5th millennium BCE).

19, 20 – Sumerian temple seals, 3rd millennium BCE with images of triple-stemmed plants in the hands of netherworldly entities.

21 – Seal from Altyn-Tepe, between the 3rd – 2nd millennia BCE, where the centre is represented by a cross.

Table XXXVIII

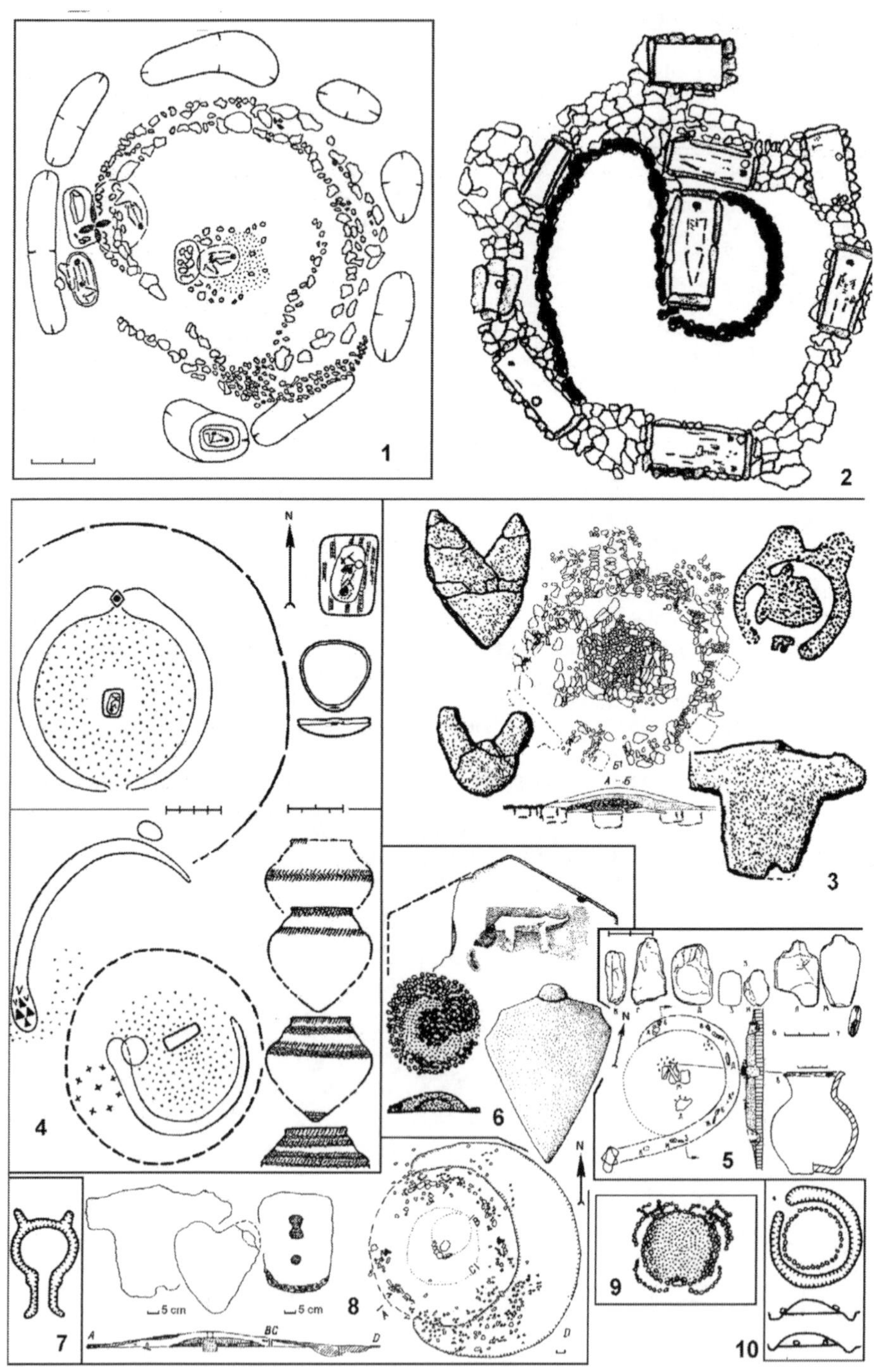

Table XXXVIII

The appearance of the main (serpent-slaying) mythology of the *Rigveda* in the construction of kurhans of Oriana (3, 6-10) in the areas of the Dnipro and Buh (1, 4, 5), and Caucasian foothills of Arián (2), 5th – 2nd millennia BCE. The embryo new year universe of Vala (2, 3, 7 and the central parts 1, 4, 6, 8-10), guarded by the serpent Vritra (1, 2, 4-6, 10) who was conquered by the Hero-serpent-slaying Indra and Creator-GOD Vishnu (stelas in 5 and 6, as well as the "+" symbol of the vajry-club in construction 1).

1 – Kurhan 2 at the village of Kremenchuk* in the Mykolaiv region (excavation by Yu. S. Grebennikov), at the boundary of the Yamna and Catacomb cultures at the end of the 3rd millennium BCE.

2 – Kurhan of North Caucasian culture, beginning at 2nd millennium BCE, (according to V. I. Markovin) on a plateau at the city of Pyatigorsk.

3 – Plan and scheme of kurhan 12-I at the village of Usativ (Odessa region); excavations by E. F. Patokova, interpretation by V. G. Petrenko: stelas and stone constructions in the form of the heads of bulls, cows and a calf (representing Aryan Dyaus, Prithivi, and Parjani – according to Yu. A. Shilov).

4 – Central foundation of a pre-kurhan sanctuary of Seredny Stoh culture, from the beginning of the 5th millennium BCE, the primary mound and its initial layering forming the Tsehelnia kurhan at the village of Podluzhie in the Kremenchuk district of the Poltava region. The layering (above) reflects the transformation from previous solitary serpentine ditches into their paired form; in general, all 1+1+2 ditches reflect reincarnation (according to F. B. J. Kuiper of the mythical Vritra into yogic Kundalini, which metamorphosed into Pingala and Ida.

5 – Foundation of the kurhan at Kormylytsia near the adjacent village of Erystivka. The serpentine ditch encircles an altar with a pair of fallen anthropomorphous stelas, previously dug into the ditch "head down". The presence of phallic and foot-shaped stelas are signs of Indra and Vishnu who, it turns out, after their transient new year victory "devour" the serpent Vritra (the sacrificial victim, sending it into the netherworld).

6 – Kurhan 11-I in the village of Usativ; arrow-shaped stelas embody the dog Sarama^ (with corresponding image) and Indra armed with a vajra, i.e. mace-bearing Indra.

7 – Sanctuary of Usativ kurhan 14 at the village of Zhovty Yar.

8 – Kurhan 9-I at Usativ.

9,10 – Kurhan Usativ-I with characteristic toads and serpents (according to V. G. Petrenko).

* The village of Kremenchuk was situated in the Voznesensk district of the Mykolaiv region; This is now a flooded area in the zone of the South-Ukrainian Atomic Power Plant. [V. Krasnoholovets] Thus, Kremenchuk village is not to be confused with the city of Kremenchuk in the Poltava region.

Table XXXIX

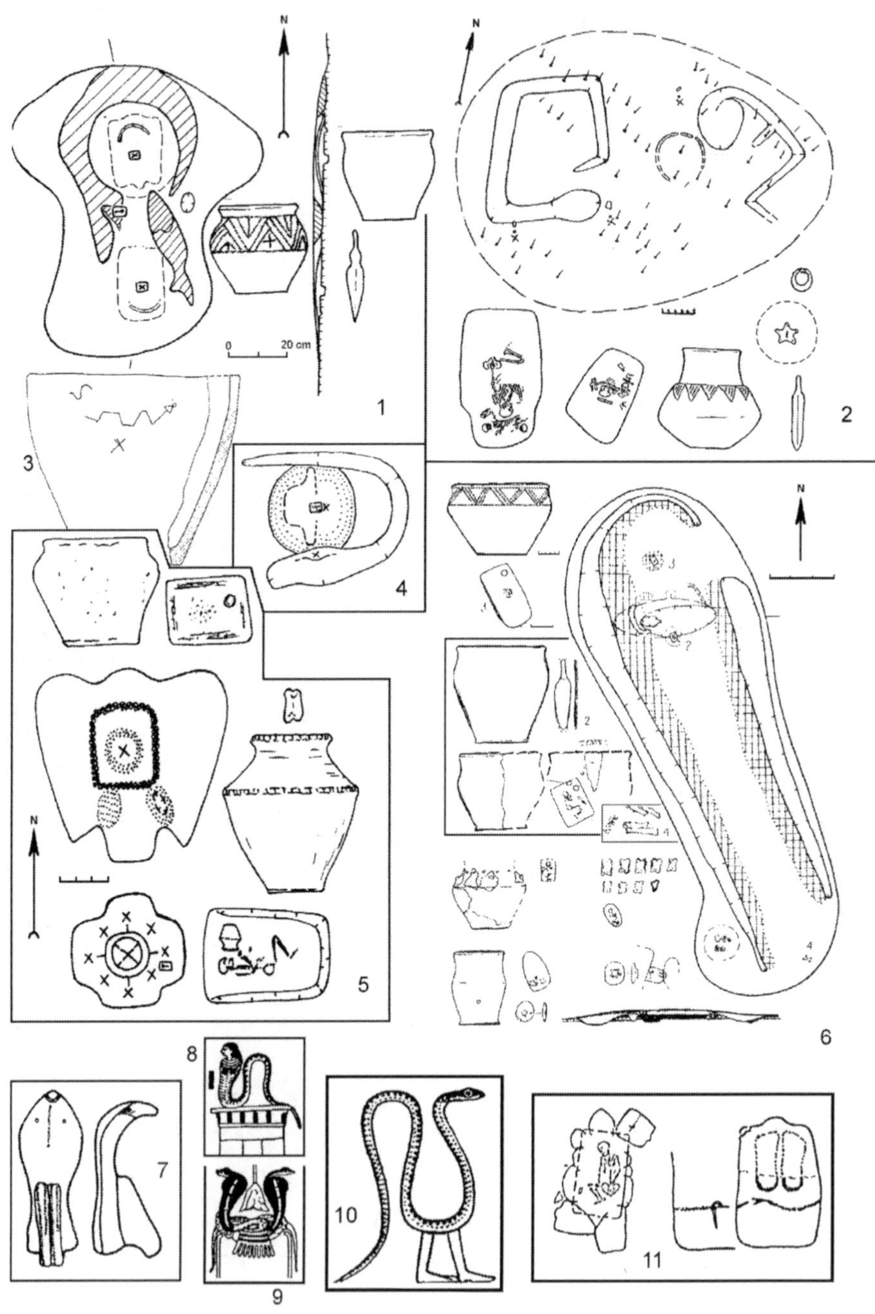

Table XXXIX

The existence of main mythology of the *Rigveda* in the construction of kurhans and burial grounds in the Dnipro area of Arián, in the 17th – 12th centuries BCE, as well as its previous corresponding manifestations in the cultures of Aratta-I, Arián and Egypt (7, 11, 8-10).

1	–	Smolovska^ Grave, mid 2nd millennium BCE, at the village of Novo-Mykolaivka. A Srubna culture grave showing the serpent-warrior Indra between two mounds and the figures of a Vishap-fish (the symbol of spring dampness) and Sheshna, the serpent of droughts (i.e. summer heat) which had to be defeated to resurrect the hero.
2	–	Burial grounds of 12-I Bilozersk culture at the village of Kairy in the Hornostaivka district of the Kherson region; anthropomorphous grave of burial 25 containing the skeletons of a man and dogs. A late 2nd millennium BCE Cimmerian cemetery, its burials characterise the battle of Indra with serpent Vritra for Vala (the embryo of the annual cycle of the Universe), in which the dog Sarama helps the hero.
3	–	A related scene of the main mythology of the *Rigveda,* from burial 11 in kurhan 3 at the village of Mykhaylivka, portrayed on an Aryan (Srubna culture) vessel, mid 2nd millennium BCE.
4	–	The base of the kurhan of the Srubna archaeological culture at the regional centre of Chaplynsk of the Kherson region showing the Vritra-Ditch and Vala-earthfill with a cup-like area (representing the container for the "living water" soma).
5	–	The upper filling of kurhan 2 at the village of Velyka Bilozirka in the Velyko Bilozirka district of the Zaporizhia region showing symbols of *Vala-Agni* [fire] and *Vala-Suparna* [bird] as an eagle with the symbol of the sun-circle over the earth-square.
6	–	Kurhan of the Multi-cordoned* Ware and Srubna cultures, 17th – 15th centuries BCE, at the village of Skvortsovka in the Kakhovka district of the Kherson region, symbolising the 'three steps of Vishnu' by three burials and ditches representing the staff of Vishnu and club of Indra).
7	–	Figurine of the cobra-Goddess from Usativ culture burials of Trypillia C-II at the village of Krasnohorka in the Odessa region.
8,9	–	Images of cobras in the Egyptian *Book of the Dead*, chapter CLXVIII verse IV and chapter XXXVII.
10	–	"Transformation into the serpent Sata" by the deceased: "I lie down in death, and I am born again; I become new, I renew my youth every day" (Chapter LXXXVII of the Egyptian *Book of the Dead*).
11	–	Burial 1 of kurhan 3 at the village of Starohorozheno in the Bashtan district of the Mykolaiv region, Yamna archaeological culture. The image of feet and staff on the stela corresponds to the image of the Aratto-Aryan GOD-nomad Vishnu, and his serpentine belt – the Almighty-Serpent Shesha.

* **Multi-cordoned Ware culture** (Russian: Культура многоваликовой керамики; also known as **Mnogovalikovaya**, **Multiple-Relief-band Ware culture**, and **Babyno culture**) is an archaeological culture of the Middle Bronze Age (22nd – 18th centuries BCE). Tribes of this culture inhabited an area stretching from the Don to Moldavia, including the Right-bank Dnipro, and part of the modern Ternopil region, and was bordered by the Volga to the east.The culture succeeded the western Catacomb culture. (Ref. Kohl, P.L., 2007, *The Making of Bronze Age Eurasia.* Cambridge University Press. p.146. ISBN 9781139461993). Cordons are ridges around the shoulder of the pot (2 or 3) below the rim.

Table XL

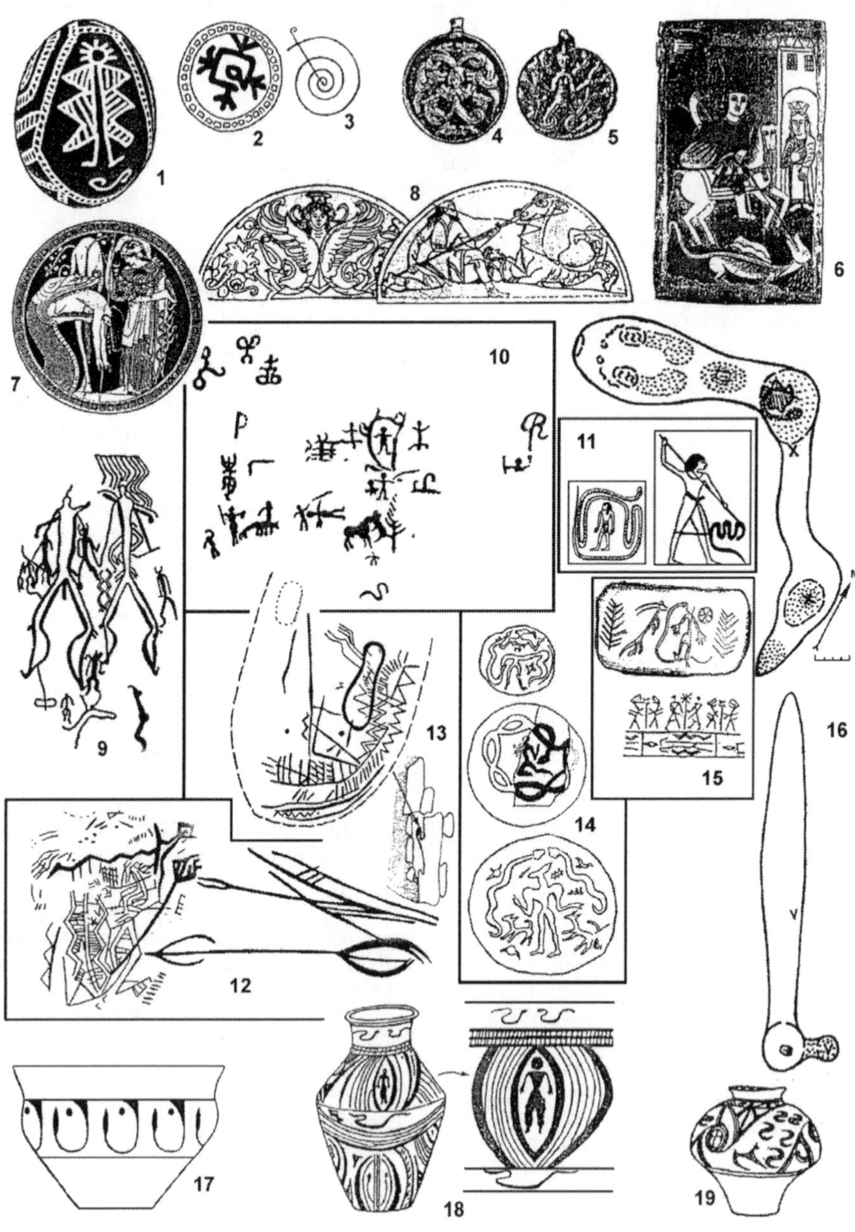

Table XL

The tradition of the main mythology of the *Rigveda* in archaeological finds of Aratta (17-19), Stone Grave (12-13), Arián (16), Taurida (10) and Caucasus (9), Mesopotamia (14-15), Egypt (11), Hellas (7), Scythia (8), Rus (2, 4-5), and Ukraine (1, 3, 6):

Cosmic-serpent warriors:

1 – Ukrainian painted egg (see also Tables XXXII: 1.6; XXXIII: 1.5; XXXIX 1.2).

5 – Old-Rusy "serpent"-medallion, 12th – 13th centuries.

8 – Greek casket from the 4th century BCE from the Scythian kurhan of Haimanova Grave in the Zaporizhia region.

11,14,15 – Depictions from monuments of the Ancient East;

"Serpent-legged" and interrelated serpent Goddesses:

4 – Old-Rusy medallion in the image of St. George the Victorious (< Yuri* dragon-fighter (cf. 8) < Aryan serpent-god Indra and his Arattan forerunners).

6 – Icon from the village of Havrylchichi in Polissia [NW Ukraine], 17th – 18th centuries.

7 – Ancient Greek "kylix by Duris[‡]", 490 BCE, where Athena is portrayed helping Jason to conquer the Dragon who guarded the Golden Fleece.

Others

2 – Medieval decoration (from the Poltava region): a cruciform arrangement that corresponds to an image of Vala and the guardian-serpent Vritra, slain by Indra's vajra (which could be seen as a club, Indian mace, spear, arrow or other symbolically phallic implements: Sanskrit vájra < vája which means 'seed').

3 – Scheme of the "curve dance" (from the Transcarpathian village of Berehiv) resembling a serpent slain by a spear (cf. 6, 8, 11).

9 – Petroglyph from Gobustan (Caucasus), connecting mythological scenes of Location 19-b of Stone Grave (12) with scenes on Sumerian temple seals (15; see Table XXXII: 6).

10 – Kemi Oba image from the canopy of Tash-Air Cave in Crimea (see Table XXXII: 2): a serpent is portrayed at the base of the central composition of the sacrifice-and-rebirth of a rider.

11 – Headpieces from chapters LCXVIII and VII of the Egyptian *Book of the Dead*, which describe the netherworldly journeys and deeds of the dead.

12 – see 9.

13 – Image in the "Grotto of the Dragon" of Stone Grave (location shown on the plan of the grotto) showing the head of the serpent Vritra, defeated by the foot of Vishnu (upper image) and by the arrow-vajra of Indra (lower image) – the first two of which B. D. Mykhailov (*Petroglyphs of Stone Grave*, MAUP, Kyiv, 2004; pp. 126-129) connects more with the fishlike Vishap of the Caucasus region and Middle East, as well as with Cosmic Purusha of Vedic Aryans;

14 – Origins of the main myth of the *Rigveda* on the seals of the Middle East from Tepe Giyan and Tel Asmar, 6th millennium BCE

15 – Sumerian seal with the central scene of the epic of Gilgamesh: the hero and his bull-like companion Enkidu with the help of Sun-Utu conquer the serpent-like Humbaba (one of the forerunners of the Slavic Kupala), guardian of the sacred grove on the "Mount of the Immortals".

16 – Kurhan Garman (on the Chongar peninsula of the Azov Sea; Srubna archaeological culture, mid 2nd millennium BCE) symbolising the Almighty Serpent Shesha who with the help of the staff of the Creator-GOD Vishnu (see Table XXI: 11.14 and XXXIX: 6.11) vivifies the embryo of the New Year/ Universe of Vala (at the tail) and Hiraniagarbha^ (behind the head).

17 – Vessel of Trypillia B-II archaeological culture (from settlement III at the village of Nezvisko in the Horodenka district of the Ivano-Frankivsk region) with a repetitive design corresponding to the serpent Vritra guarding the

embryonic New Year/Universe of Vala (according to the Indo-Aryan *Rigveda*).

18 – Trypillian (C-I) vessel from the settlement of "Rzhyshchiv" at the village of Balyko-Shchuchinka in the Kaharlyk district of the Kyiv region; B. A. Rybakov associates to portrayal of the tridactyl male figure with the image of the "god of elemental water, similar to Varuna (Urana)", (*Paganism of Ancient Slavs*, Science, Moscow, 1981; pp. 205-206).

19 – Trypillian (C-II) vessel from the settlement at the village of Stari Badrazhy of the Edinets district in Moldova, portraying a serpent, a cross in a circle and a dog, etc. They are comparable with the Vedic subject of the dog Sarama who found the "living and dead water" (soma and amrita) for serpent-warrior Indra on the eve of battle with Vritra for Vala.

* The name Yuri (Yuriy, or Jurij) is the Russian/Ukrainian variant of George.

‡ A kylix is a type of drinking cup with a broad, relatively shallow body raised on a stem from a foot, usually with two horizontal handles. Many have mythological scenes painted on them by Duris, some of whose best examples are in the collection of the Pushkin Museum, Moscow.

Turn over

Table XLI

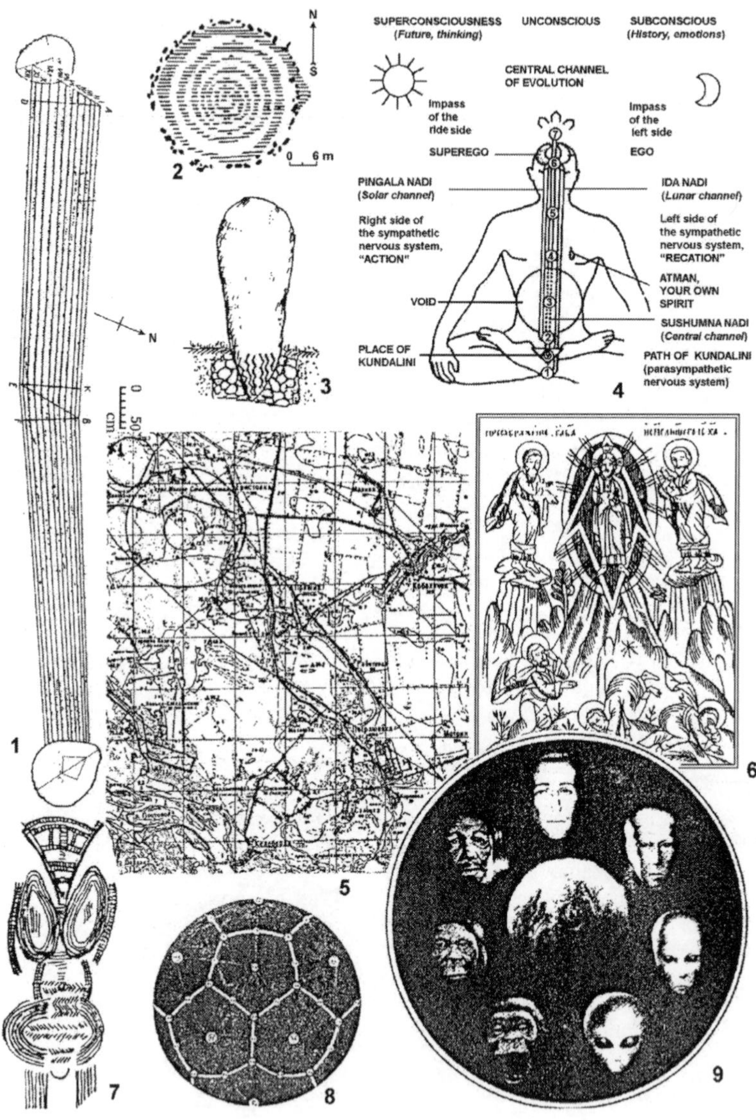

1 2 3 4 5 6 7 8 9

Table XLI

Interactions of planetary fields and man.

1 – Stone rows at Ménec near the town of Carnac (French Brittany) reflecting the "tunnel of immortality of R. Moudi" (see also Table XIX: 5; XXXIX: 6; XL: 16).

2 – Rollright Stones (England), which "before sunrise (...) radiate impulses of ultrasound that fade shortly after sunrise" (R. S. Furduy, '*Intriguing Mysteries - 2*, Lybid, Kyiv, 2001; pp. 167-169).
[See Fig. 136. At the centre of the circle, the Earth's magnetic field is weakened i.e. the average intensity of the magnetic field of each of the seven turns of the spiral is significantly lower than that occurring outside the stones. Ref. C. Brooker, *Magnetism and the Standing Stones,* New Scientist, 97, p.105 (1983)].

3 – "Energetic" ornamentation on the base of a quartzite menhir from Ménec. Geophysicists and geologists (R. S. Furduy, [above] p. 166) note the fact that quartz "has the property to generate an electric current under the action of mechanical deformations" (e.g. by dropping a heavy quartzite menhir down on the pointed end), and that owing to the generated current the "crystals of quartz emit ultrasound" and radio waves. This supports the evidence for the ancient priests being sensitive to the field basis of the material world. (See Table XLII, and, for further reading, the documentary novel about the archaeological research at the Aryan kurhan Stovbuvata Grave: Yu. Shilov, *What GOD has given*, Aratta, Kyiv, 2005)).

4 – Bioenergetic chakra-nodes of man (according to the Indo-Aryan doctrine of Yoga; see 7).

5 – Fault lines and mantle channels in the Earth's crust, which generate "subtle energy" physical fields. Between the 6th – 5th millennia BCE Aratto-Aryan priests built the hitherto earliest renowned kurhans of Tsehelnia, Kormylytsia and Stovbuvata Grave at those locations (near the mouth of the river Psel, at the headstream of the Dnipro rapids).

6 – Iconography of the 'superpower' biofield of Christ the Saviour. (Icon: "The Transfiguration of the Lord", Kyiv, CE 1619).

7 – Palaeolithic image of the energetic nodes of man (from Predmost, Moravia).

8 – Geophysics of the Earth as a 12-facet crystal. The nodes linking its edges are "energetically, particularly strong. This leads to the remarkably peculiar phenomena in nature of stimulating the creative potential in man" (T. M. Fadeeva, *The Crimea in the sacred space*, Business-Inform, Simferopol, 2002; pp. 83-84 et al.). In Europe, two of these powerful interconnected nodes are located in the British Isles (with Stonehenge, etc.) and in the Ukrainian Black Sea area (with Dnipro rapids, and shrines of Aratta and Arián).

9 – "Evolution or Involution?" (V. G. Azhazha, *Under the "cap" of Another Mind*, RIPOL CLASSIC, Moscow, 2002; p. 338 et al.).

Table XLII

Table XLII

Comparison of ceramics of Danube-Dnipro Aratta with those of other cultures, viz. ceramics of Arattan from the 6th – 3rd millennia BCE (11-22), the Chinese Yangshao archaeological culture from the 5th – 3rd millennia BCE (10) and Indian cultures of Central America from the 2nd millennium CE (1-9).

The dubious hypothesis about a genetic relationship to account for the similarity of the first two cultures cannot be applied to the third culture which was isolated from them in time, space and ethnicity. However, the topographical-climatic conditions, economy and stage of historical evolution for all three ethnocultures are similar (i.e. they are primary civilisations of the communal type). Such correspondence evidently led to other similarities, e.g. revitalisation of the unconscious mind, connection to the Energy-information FIELD (i.e. the "Almighty-All-knowing GOD") and expressions of universal human archetypes.

1-2, 4-9	–	New Mexico, USA: 9th century (7-8) and 11th – 12th centuries (4, 6, 9); CE 1890 (2) and 1920 (1, 5).
3	–	Yalisko, Mexico: 10th – 11th centuries (I. Poshyvailo, *Phenomenology of pottery: Semeiotic-ethnological aspects*, Ukrainske Narodoznavstvo, Opishne, 2000).
10	–	Yangshao culture and similar Eneolithic cultures of various areas of China, 5th–3rd millennia BCE.
11	–	Petreni, Trypillia C-I.
12	–	Konivka, Trypillia B-II.
13,14	–	Bernashivka, Trypillia C-I.
15	–	Volodymyrivka, Trypillia B-II.
16, 22	–	Collection of A. S. Polishchuk, C.
17	–	Cucuteni-Cetecuia IV.
18	–	Trusesti I.
19	–	Klyshchev.
20	–	Shypintsy B, Trypillia C-I.
21	–	Nemyriv, V-II. (T. Tkachuk, *The sign systems of Trypillia-Cucuteni cultural-historical union* (*painted dishes*), Nova Knyga, Vinnytsia, 2005).

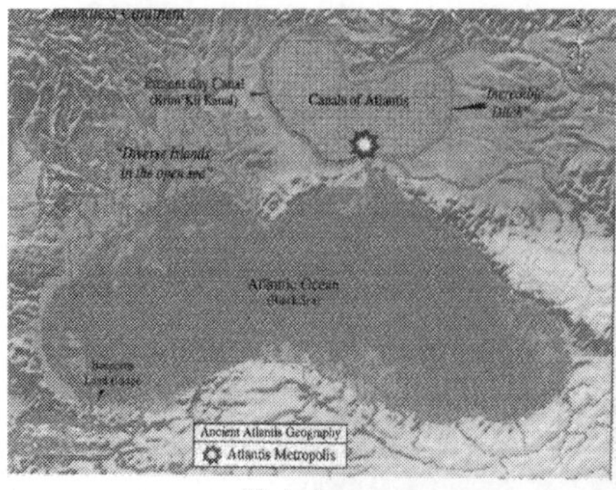

Photo 1

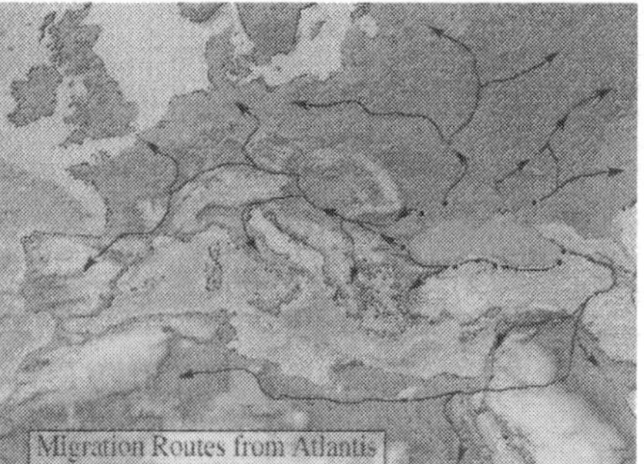

Photo 2

Photo 3

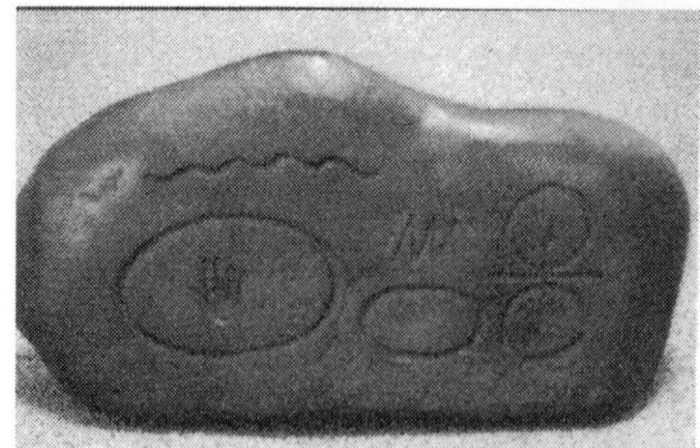

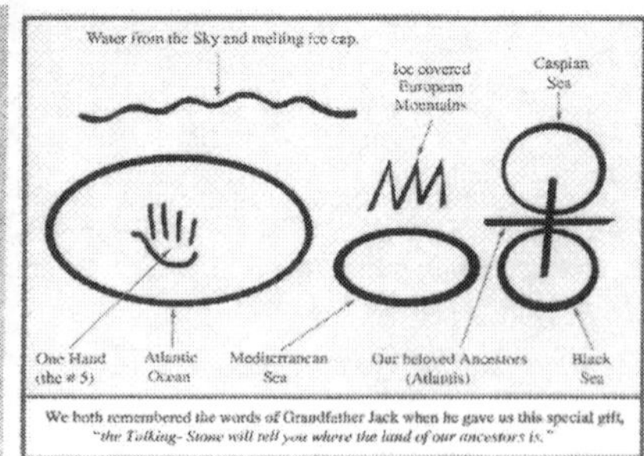

Photos 4-5

EXAMPLE FROM FOREIGN REPRESENTATIVES

THE ORIGINS OF EARTH'S CIVILISATION.
(from the book "ATLANTIS MOTHERLAND" by Flying Eagle & Whispering Wind; **Pukalani, Maui: COSMIC VORTEX; Tetra XII inc.; T. A.** Ernist Nelson; 2003. – 168p.)
(see also Table 1 and Fig. 20)

Photo 1.
Atlantis, the primary civilisation prior to the Flood of 5600 BCE (p. 95). The capital city of legendary Atlantis is shown at the site of what later became Kerch (p. 104), where Professor O. N. Trubachev (*Indoarica in the Northern Black Sea coast*, Science, Moscow, 1999, pp. 7, 235-236) locates the Aryan-Taurian city (?) Δῖα ('God's', though the meaning is "closer to the Slavic 'děva' [which means] 'Maid'"). According to the authors, prior to the flood, the marshy lowlands of the Rivers Don and Kuban (the future Azov basin) were domesticated by the Atlanteans through a network of canals. Is it by chance or another coincidence that "an ancient network of canals is known in the Kuban area (p. 250). As a further "coincidence" an Ancient-Greek tribe of Atlanteans is actually known (A. G. Kifishin, *Genostructure of Ancient-Greek and Greek myth*, GMII, Moscow, 1990, pp. 10-11, 28, 48), amongst whose ancestors were Boristhenes and Achilles, who gravitated to the lower reaches of the Dnipro (including Tendra).

Photo 2.
Resettlement of the carriers of the Atlantean civilisation (p. 112) from the coasts of the Meotida and Pontis (Sea of Azov and Black Sea).

Photo 3.
Book Cover of ATLANTIS MOTHERLAND by *Flying Eagle & Whispering Wind*, Pukalani, Maui: COSMIC VORTEX: Tetra XII inc.; T. A. Ernist Nelson, 2003. The form of the Atlantean 'spacecraft' exactly coincides with the emblem of Ukraine. This fantasy does not contradict UFO records: "extraterrestrial" sightings are fairly firmly associated with the Azov.

Photos 4-5.
Sacred 'Talking-Stone' of North American Indians, and interpretation of its images by Flying Eagle – the principal author of the book *Atlantis Motherland*. The cross between the Black and Caspian Seas indicates the location of Atlantis.

Photo 6

Photo 7

Photo 8

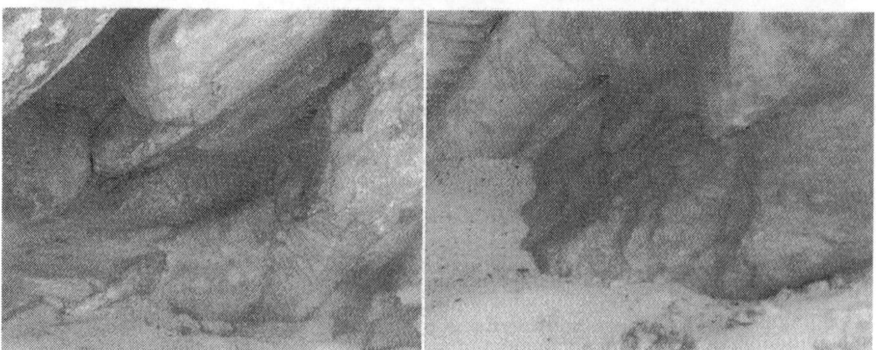

Photo 9

Photo 10

SOURCE OF HUMAN CIVILISATION, DISCOVERIES BY SCIENTISTS OF UKRAINE AND RUSSIA

in 1992-2002.

Photo 6.
On the right bank of the ancient bed of the River Molochna, north-west hollow of Stone Grave, was a settlement of its priests, 19th – 12th – 3rd millennium BCE.
(Photos 6 - 10 by A. P. Samodrina).

Photo 7.
View of Stone Grave (near the village of Mirny in the Melitopol district of the Zaporizhia region) showing the right bank of the modern River Molochna.

Photo 8.
View of the opposite, west side.

Photos 9-10.
Natural projections at Stone Grave, serpentine patterns which were emphasised with ochre, where archaeologist V. N. Danylenko (in his 1986 monograph [*Kamyana Mohyla]*) identified the signs of "footprints of wanderer-God Vishnu" etc; Yu. A. Shilov - "Enlil wandering in the netherworld" (1989-1990). According to our colleague B. D. Mykhailov (*Petroglyphs of Stone Grave*. Zaporizhia.

Photo 11

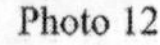

Photo 12

Photo 13

Photo 14

Photo 15

"HAVING VISITED 25 COUNTRIES, I FINALLY SAW THE HOME OF THE ANCIENT ARYANS" IN 1992-2002.

(Statement of Dr. Alok Arvinla at a press conference on 12.05.2000, on his return from a trip to the upper reaches of the Dnipro Threshold)

Photo 11.
The tomb of Stovbuvata Grave, mid 3rd millennium BCE (at the village of Voloshyne in the Kremenchuk district of the Poltava region).

Photo 12.
Completion of excavations at Stovbuvata Grave. (2004 expedition, site leader A. B. Suprunenko)

Photo 13.
Researchers Yu. O. Shilov (right) and Dr. A. Alok (left), Director of the Institute of National Monuments of India, at Stovbuvata Grave. Early May 2000.
(Photo by N. Stakhiv).

Photo 14.
Ore mining quarry (Komsomolsk, in Kremenchuk district) **in the anomalous zone at the beginning of the Dnipro threshold, which stimulated the emergence of the Aratta-Aryan *Rigveda*.**

Photo 15.
A. B. Suprunenko, head of the excavation of Stovbuvata Grave. August 2004.
(Photo N. Radchenko).

Photo 16

Photo 17

Photo 18

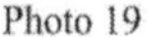

Photo 19

Photo 20

"ARATTA - UKRAINE" MUSEUM

in the village of Trypillia, Kyiv region.

Photo 16.
West pediment of the exhibition rooms of the Museum. In the background is a reconstructed Arattan home (Trypillian archaeological culture, 5400-2200 BCE).

Photo 17.
East pediment of the Museum.

Photo 18.
Entrance to the Museum and the reconstructed Arattan home (left). (Photos 16-18 by I. Blinovoy).

Photo 19.
View of Trypillia and the Dnipro from the heights of the right bank. (Photos, here and below (except where noted), by B. Kolosyuk).

Photo 20.
Divych-Mountain - 'Mountain of God', one of many in the lands of Indo-European people. View from the museum.

Photo 21 Photo 22

Photo 23

Photo 24 Photo 25

Photo 21.
The facade of a typical small family home of Aratta, from the 5th millennium BCE to the beginning of the 3rd millennium BCE. Reconstruction (by builder V. M. Lazorenko) carried out in the summer of 2004 under the direction of Dr. M. Yu. Videyko, fellow of the Institute of Archaeology at the National Academy of Sciences of Ukraine.

Photo 22, 24, 25.
Arattan houses in various stages of reconstruction (unfinished in the photo).

Photo 23.
Rural cottage of a Ukrainian family in 19th century. State Historical-Cultural Museum-Reserve of the town Pereyaslav-Khmelnitsky.

Photo 26

Photo 27

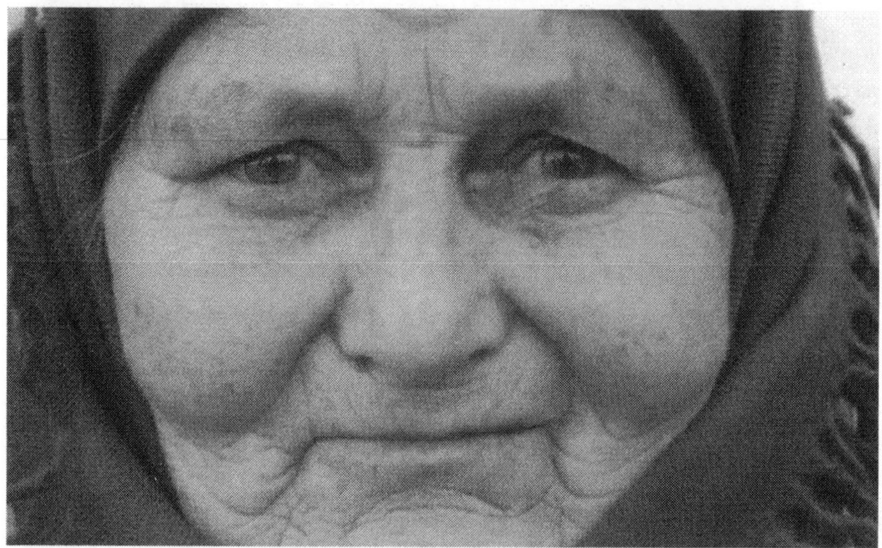

Photo 28

Photo 29

Photo 30

Photo 26.
Enlarged composition (also Photos 27, 30) of the "**Foremother on a throne in the form of the head of Taurus'**" at the early-Trypillian settlement of Luke Vrublevetskaya. Note the serpent's head and X-like mark on the stomach of the Goddess.

Photo 27.
Outside the entrance to the Museum (circle of life-sized, throned Foremothers).

Photo 28.
Portrait of a Slavic peasant. Pereyaslav district of Kyiv region.

Photo 29.
Foremother figurine. Trypillian archaeological culture.
(Here and below, all the museum exhibits were collected by A. S. Polishchuk).

Photo 30.
Note the **turtle with owlish head, serpentine ornamentation and X-like mark on the abdomen of the Goddess.** (See captions of Photos 26-27).
Allusions that the noses on the heads of these Trypillian archaeological culture figurines supposedly "reflect people's faces of the East (Orient) (...) certainly with large hooked noses" (Ref. V. V. Otroshchenko, P. P. Tolochko et al. Ethnic history of ancient Ukraine. – Kyiv: Institute of Archaeology, National Academy of Sciences of Ukraine, 2000. – p. 26) has been the main argument in an attempt by members of the Institute of Archaeology of the National Academy of Sciences of Ukraine to attribute this culture to being "pre-Semitic" (L. Zaliznyak. Sketches of ancient history of Ukraine. – Kyiv: Abrys, 1994, pp. 84-101). This is despite the fact that research on most of these and other heads were published in the 1950s (see: V. N. Danylenko: *The Cosmogony of Primitive Society*, in *Beginnings of Civilisation*, Akademproekt, Ekaterinburg-Moscow, 1999).

Photo 31

Photo 32

Photo 33

Photo 34

Photo 35

Photo 31.
Reconstruction of a stove of an Aratta-"Trypillian home.
Notice the Foremother-and-Daughter figurines (bottom sides), also the cross-shaped altar and the vessel - **evidence of pre-Christian ritual baptism of infants,** also known in the ethnography of the Slavs and covenants of the Cossack Saviour.

Photo 32.
Folk kobzarist V. Nechepa.

Photo 33.
Kobzarist V. Nechepa and the founders of the People's Museum "Aratta-Ukraine": A. Polishchuk, V. Lazorenko & Yu Shilov (right to left).

Photos 34-35.
Tools of the oldest state in the world Aratta, ('civilisation' from 7000-6200 BCE), the apotheosis of which is reflected in the **Trypillian archaeological culture** of 5400-2200 BCE. Products made of flint and basalt.

Photo 36

Photo 37

Photo 38

Photo 39

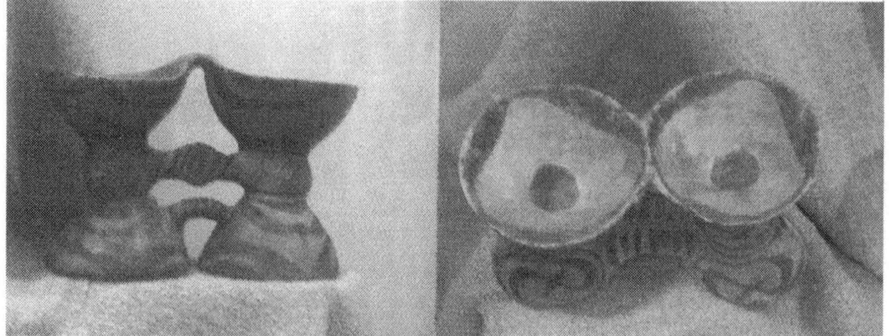

Photo 40

Photo 41

Photo 36.
Yoke of a bullock cart. From Ukraine, 19th – early 20th century.

Photo 37.
Didukh ("Spirit of Father-ancestor", "God's spirit') or Paradise Tree, from the time of Arattan corn-sheaves decorating peasant shrines. The earliest prototypes are found in Proto-Indo-European Çatal Höyük, 7th millennium BCE (H. Nikolaeva, V. A. Safronov. *Sources of Slavic and Eurasian mythology*. Moscow: "White Wolf", KRAFT, GUP "Oblizdat". 1999. – p. 196 et al).

Photo 38.
Ceremonial model (clay mixed with flour and grain) of Arattan bread and Slavic *korovai*^ with symbols of the solar calendar of Svarga. **A Trypillian salt cellar in between resembles *Cow*-udders and Tree of Life** (cf. Didukh).

Photo 39.
Sacrificial vessel for Fire-and-Water.

Photos 40-41.
"Trypillian binocular vessels" (an unofficial archaeological term) **for magically enhancing the unity of Earth-and-Heaven**, saturation of the first moisture, heat and light.

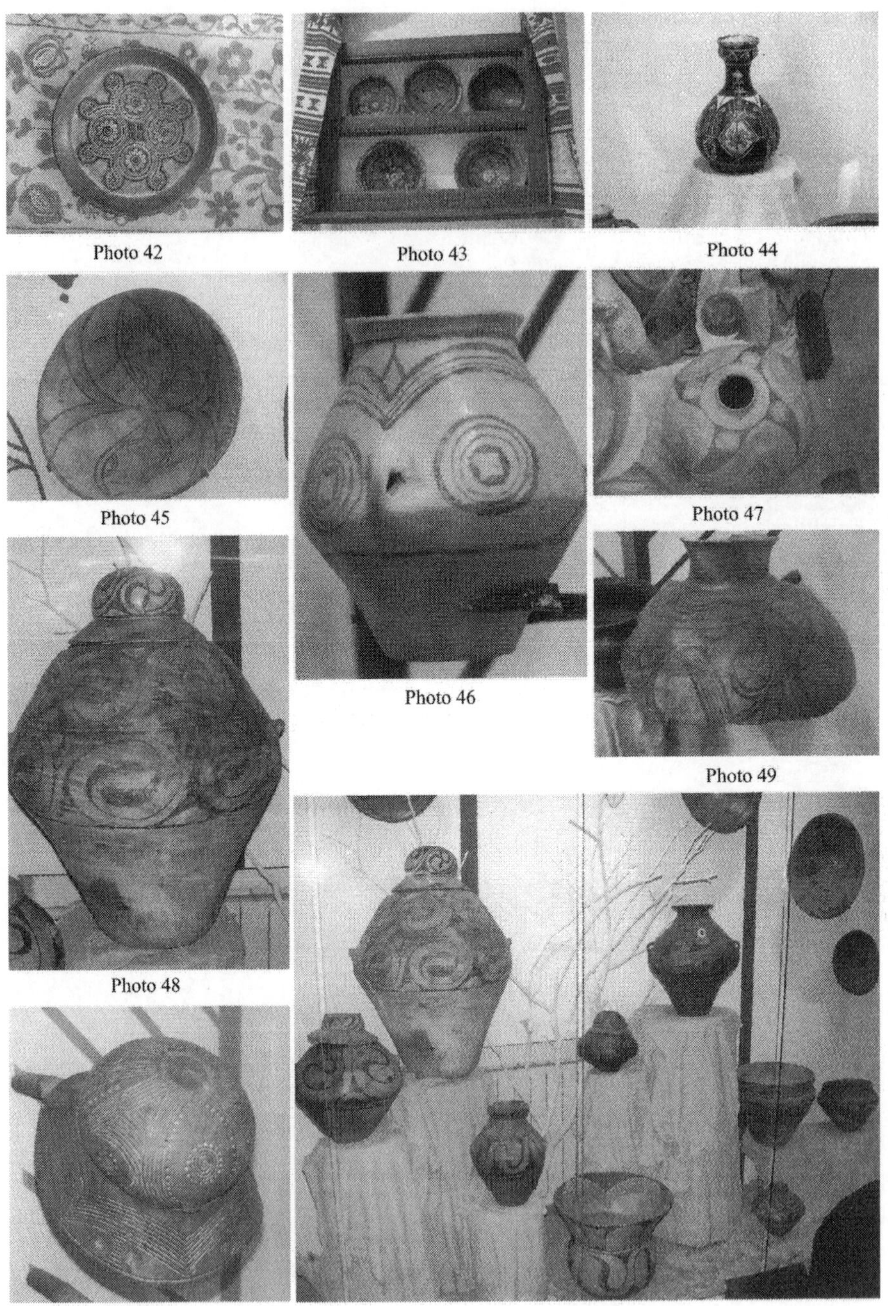
Photo 42
Photo 43
Photo 44
Photo 45
Photo 46
Photo 47
Photo 48
Photo 49
Photo 50
Photo 51

Photo 42.
Ukrainian wooden bowl carved with traditional designs.

Photo 43.
Ukrainian misnik [cupboard] **with bowls**. Notice the swastika-like and other traditional designs.

Photo 44.
Modern pitcher (foreign 19th – 20th century) with swastikas, fertility **rhombuses**, stylised tree of life and Berehynia.

Photo 45.
Trypillian bowl with ornamentation that reflects the archetypal embryo (transformation of the Yogic Kundalini serpent into the veins of Pingala and Ida).

Photo 46.
Trypillian vase displaying the archetype of birth in the form and ornamentation of a "owl-face vessel" (unofficial archaeological term; the "face" eyes mimic the breasts of a wet nurse).

Photo 47.
Swastikas are extremely widespread and diverse in Trypillian culture – clear evidence of its Indo-European affiliation (see the caption to Photo. 30).

Photo 48.
Characteristic complex of anthropomorphic Trypillian ceramics: a pair of vessels, the lower (main) one opening to a covering-cup. This pair is decorated with the yin-yang symbol reflecting the archetype of conception.

Photo 49.
A cross - direct or oblique, usually inscribed in a circle or a square (the four-parts of which open and create a *swastika*) is very characteristic of the Aratta-"Trypillian" culture. **While the circle means the Sun and Sky, the square means the Land and the Earth, and their combination corresponds to Aratta as the 'Land under the Sun', "Country of grain farmers". A cross in a confined space means stability in the open – the dynamics of the annual-calendar cycles, of eternal life.**

Photo 50.
Bowl-lid of an early-Trypillian vessel with calendar designs (cf. Photo 49).

Photo 51.
Museum showcase with Trypillian ceramics.

Photo 52

Photo 53

Photo 54

Photo 55

Photo 56

Photo 57

Photo 52.
A vessel with the calendar symbolism, combining their earth-celestial hypostasis and netherworldly realms.

Photo 53.
Vessel with a *moulded ornament*, head of the bull Taurus.

Photo 54.
An early Trypillian bowl-dish, whose shape and pattern express the mytho-ritual of the "embryonic Gracious Universe, protected by the Almighty-Serpent" (the Milky Way).
Archaeologically, and also in the texts of the "Veda Slovena", the way the missionary-priests of Aratta-"Trypillian" implemented this mytho-ritual (and hence the idea of cultural superiority and sacred authority of Aratta) on the emerging Aryan surroundings, can be traced in their collection of sacred hymns of the Rigveda (see photos 11 - 15, and 45 - 49).
In this manner the elements of Indo-European kinship was streamlined and controlled, but the borderland of settled agricultural Aratta lay between the pastoral-nomadic steppe and the forest-steppe. It avoided the "period of military democracy" (of the later, secondary, slave-holding civilisations of Sumer, etc.) by preserving the sanctity of "sacred democracy" organised the primary, communal civilisation of the Brahmin-rulers of Aratta.

Photo 55.
Ukrainian bowls with traditional carvings (see photo 49). (Photo by V. Makovsky).

Photo 56.
Vessel with symbols of *yin and yang* (see Photo 48).

Photo 57.
Calendar-cosmological ornamentation with symbolism of the Moon, Sun and others.

Photo 58

Photo 59

Photo 60

Photo 61

Photo 62

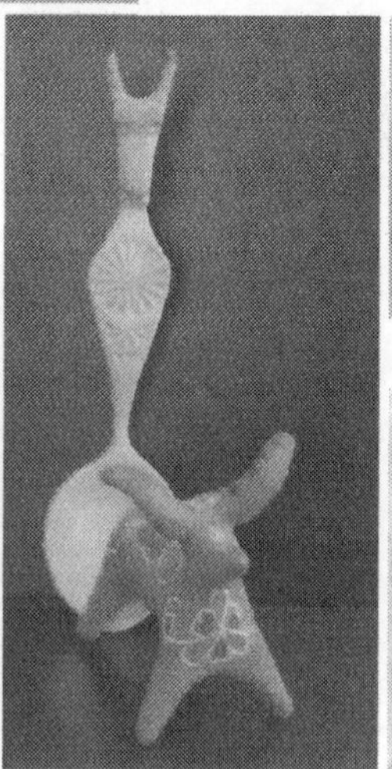

Photo 63

Photo 64

Photo 58.

Ukrainian pysanky eggs with the most developed symbolism of *archetypical* depths in the world, which can be understood only in the light of the powerful heritage of Aratta (see photos 44-49, and the Cossack Covenants (Yu. A. Shilov. *What we deserve* - Kyiv: Aratta, 2006. - p. 128-134, etc.) and the *Veda Slovena* preserved by Bulgarian Pomaks, (A. I. Asov. *Slavic Veda*. Moscow: Fair-Press, 2003. – 714p)). (Photos 58-64, 71, 73, 90-92 made by V. Makovsky).

Photo 59.

Traditional Ukrainian candlestick-trisuttya^. Shown with three colour candles which traditionally (as also in India) correspond with the netherworldly water of Nava (blue), the blossoming earth of Yava (magenta) and sunlit heaven of Prava (yellow), see *The Veles Book* (board 1, etc.).

Photo 60, 62.

Bilateral Pysanky, the Tree of Life protected by pairs of birds and rams. The 6 berries on top of the 1st tree and its guardians correlate with the favourable months of both spring and summer seasons, and with the "mystery-hymns" of the *Rigveda*. The 7 (+ 2?) branches of the 2nd tree and its guardians, and Svarga-swastikas, correlate with the months of the unfavourable half-year and the lunar calendar (with its "devil's dozen" [i.e. 13] months). Transformation of the traditional deer > goats into sheep indicates the time when Aries reigned in the zodiac (from about 1700 BCE). The pysanky illustrate the covenant of Ukrainian *Rahman* (<Vedic *Brahman*) "written-pysanky", annually updating them for the spring Velykden (Great Day).

Photo 61. **Popular toys with Vedic symbols** (Arattan-Indo-Aryan *Rigveda*, etc.) **of Pushan and Adzhashvy** (from the vicinity of modern Uman in the Cherkasy region, former centre of Aratta-"Trypillian" cities). The first represented himself as 'Prosperous, Ample' (with zodiacal signs representing the Deer and Taurus) protector of wealth, etc., (see below). The second is a 'Goat-horse'.

Photo 63.

The image of Pushan^ in a traditional toy and spoon from the Uman area.

The second toy figure embodies the idea of ampleness and prosperity, and corresponds to particular characteristics of Vedic Deities. According to the *Rigveda*, "The gods have given Pushan to Surya" to '*Sunny*' Slavs, Aryans and Indians; Pushan's image (as a goat's head) and self-sacrifice (the cross under the Sun) are represented on the spoon, perhaps sacrificially broken in reference to Pushan and Rudra* (> Rod‡, who particularly patronised Pushan).

Photo 64.

The 'Goat-horse' is not accidental, and the form of its rider (in the style of the head, arms and torso) **specifically corresponds to late-Trypillian figurines of the Orianian-"Usativ" culture**.

* Rudra (or Shiva) had kicked Pushan and knocked out his teeth as Pushan was eating an oblation at a sacrifice that he (Rudra/Shiva) had not been invited to. (Ref. Dowson, J. (1888). *A Classical Dictionary of Hindu Mythology and Religion, Geography, History and Literature* (2nd ed.). London: Trübner & Co. pp. 249–50. ISBN 978-0-7661-7589-1

‡ According to B. A. Rybakov's interpretation of the manuscript *Account of Pagan Idolatry* [45, p. 11-30; 46, p. 755-756], after the time of the previously mentioned Berehynia, and together with the advent of agriculture, "Slavs began to offer food to [the god] Rod and to birthmothers". These were features of the archaeological cultures of the Trypillian circle. (See p. 258)

Photo 65

Photo 66

Photo 67

Photo 68

Photo 69

Photo 70

Photos 65-70.

Chests from the Carpathian region of Ukraine with the traditional form and ornamentation of specific temples of Aratta and Sumer. Besides the rather obvious solar-calendar symbols and fortuitous number 9 (see below), notice the symbols of *Berehynia* and *Gemini* on the ends, and the "horned" cover of the left chest (symbolic of Taurus and the Moon).

Trypillian clay models of temples, that are reminiscent of the same specific temples of Sumer, are interpreted by archaeologists to represent the "birth house" custom of the Iraqi "Marsh Arabs" (which is consistent with the wedding and dowry chests of brides, and 9-personal symbolic ornaments), dedicated to the Birth Goddess Nintur-Ninhursag (M. Yu. Videyko. *Trypillian Civilisation.* Kyiv: Akademperiodika, 2003, -S. 90-91).

'Sumerian traditions' have also been preserved in Ukrainian Carpathian place names, etc. For example "proto-Sumerian names like Orov appear in the south-western part of the Ivano-Frankivsk region beyond the Magura Mountains", and "Lagash, Ur and Uruk stand adjacent to each other in Transcarpathia, performing a ritual group, as later in Sumer" (H. I. Hikeshev. *Ancestral home of the ancestors.* M. White Alva, 2003, pp. 87-88, etc., referring to an unpublished study by A. G. Kifishin. See also the captions to photos 1-13).

Photo 71

Photo 72

Photo 73

Photo 74

Photo 75

Photo 76

Photos 71, 73.

Traditional embroidered rushniki [towels] from the Uman region (<Arattan-Sumerian Uma?) with a rare image of "mares" and other beings as 'Mountains' who represent the Foremother Κυβέλη [Cybele] (< Slavic kobyla [a female horse in Czech and Slovak languages] > Kupala [the Slavic form of Pelasgian-Greek Apollo] (see: O. N. Trubachev. *Proceedings on etymology*. Moscow: Slavic Languages of the department, 2005, Volume 2, p. 348-353)).
The oldest (7650-7450 BCE.) traces of the domestication of horses were identified by Palaeo-zoologist O. P. Zhuravlev in the Poltava region, at Stovbuvata Grave (see photos 11-15) and the river valleys of the Kobyliachka, Vorskla and Psel etc., in whose names are detected the "Sumerian or even pre-Sumerian substrate called the *Abzu / Apsu,* 'the fresh water abyss'" (Yu. L. Mosenkis. *Trypillian pre-Slavic Ukrainian language*. Kyiv: NDITIAM, 2001, p.14, 26-36, 50, with references to publications of O. N. Trubachev. See also photo 2).

Photo 72.

Fragment of a *rushnik* [embroidered towel] **with a dual-headed image of *Berehynia* (an allusion to Gemini?) beneath the roots of the *Tree of Life.*** Notice the birdlike [representation of] Berehynia (see photo 94). This is probably *Mother-sva-Glory* of *The Veles Book* because the red colour of the owl ("phoenix") specifically corresponds to her fiery image - which goes back to the Arattan tradition of Trypillians periodically burning and rebuilding their wooden towns and villages.

Photo 74

Ukrainian wedding chest showing the traditional Aryan kibitka^ [a covered vehicle]. The chest is traditionally marked with functionally redundant wheels as well as the "national icon of *Kozak Mamai, the righteous soul*" who is shown without a neck cross, as also shown on hundreds of other [chests]! (see photos 75-76). Researchers might compare his iconography with Buddhist tanks^ and the canon of Shiva.

Photos 75-76 (see above).

Photo 77 Photo 78

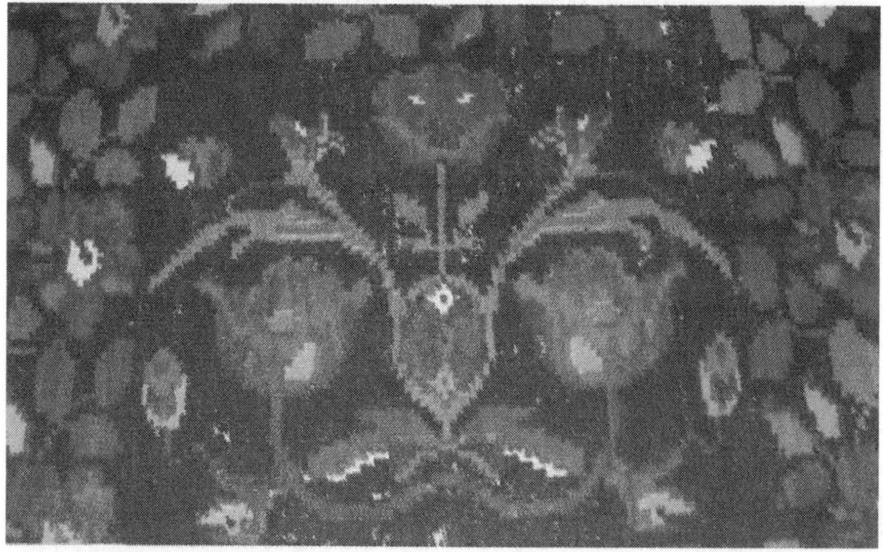

Photo 79

Photo 80

Photo 81

Photos 77-80.

Ukrainian kilimi (carpets, tapestries) **as family talismans, which are pre-Christian Orthodox canons** (see photo 59) **to Berehynia (>Virgin-Protection*) and Yuri (<young Orianian-ploughman [i.e. citizen of Oriana] > George).**

The rugs come from Carpathian Pokuttya.

Blooming *Berehynia* in the compound form of a *trisuttya and pregnant woman* is seen in the upper centre of the more antique carpet (second half of the 19th century) [Photos 79 & 80]. On both sides she is guarded by two *Rahmans* horses (*Brahmans*, see photos 60, 62, 71 and 73), embodying Yava^ trampling Nava^ as the serpent. Prava^ (see above) is represented as a composition of 5+4 characters (see photos 65-70) over the 1st and 2nd horses. The composition consists of *Berehynia*, a square-like sign of the *fertility of Yava-Earth*, a birdlike *trisuttya*, and a *swastika > happiness* (and *blessing* of the cross). In both cases, a pair of celestial bird-"tridents" blow *Berehynia* to Earth, corresponding to the representation of the spring and summer incarnation of 'Mother harvest' Ma-koshi (according to B. A. Rybakov).

For some reason the weavers of the lower carpet talisman transformed the above outlined matriarchal tradition of Aratta to the correspondingly patriarchal tradition of Oriana or Arián. There is the distinct sign of *Berehynia* present here but and in the centre is placed the cosmological *Rahman Horse* (and hidden behind *Yuri*, possibly *Kozak Mamai*) protected by his bird and the sign of a cuckoo. Symbolic trident-falcons provide a framing, supporting role.

(Photos 77-79, 81 by I. Blinova).

*In the original Russian, "Virgin-Protection" is written as "Богородицы-Покровы". Significantly, "**Покрова**" is a big holiday, the Festival of Protection (on 14 October by the modern calendar), celebrating the Goddess having descended and covered people with a veil against the Saracens. (V. Krasnoholovets).

The Pokrova holiday was also regarded as the turning point between autumn and winter, when faithful Ukrainians celebrated in churches to the Holy Mother of God, the Virgin Mary. Before Christianity, the pagans celebrated the same day with a traditional cult of remembering memorising their ancestors, praying for the souls of the dead, the happiness of their families, and for their harvest. The Mother of God, who was also called Pokrova, was also an idol for Zaporozhian Cossacks.

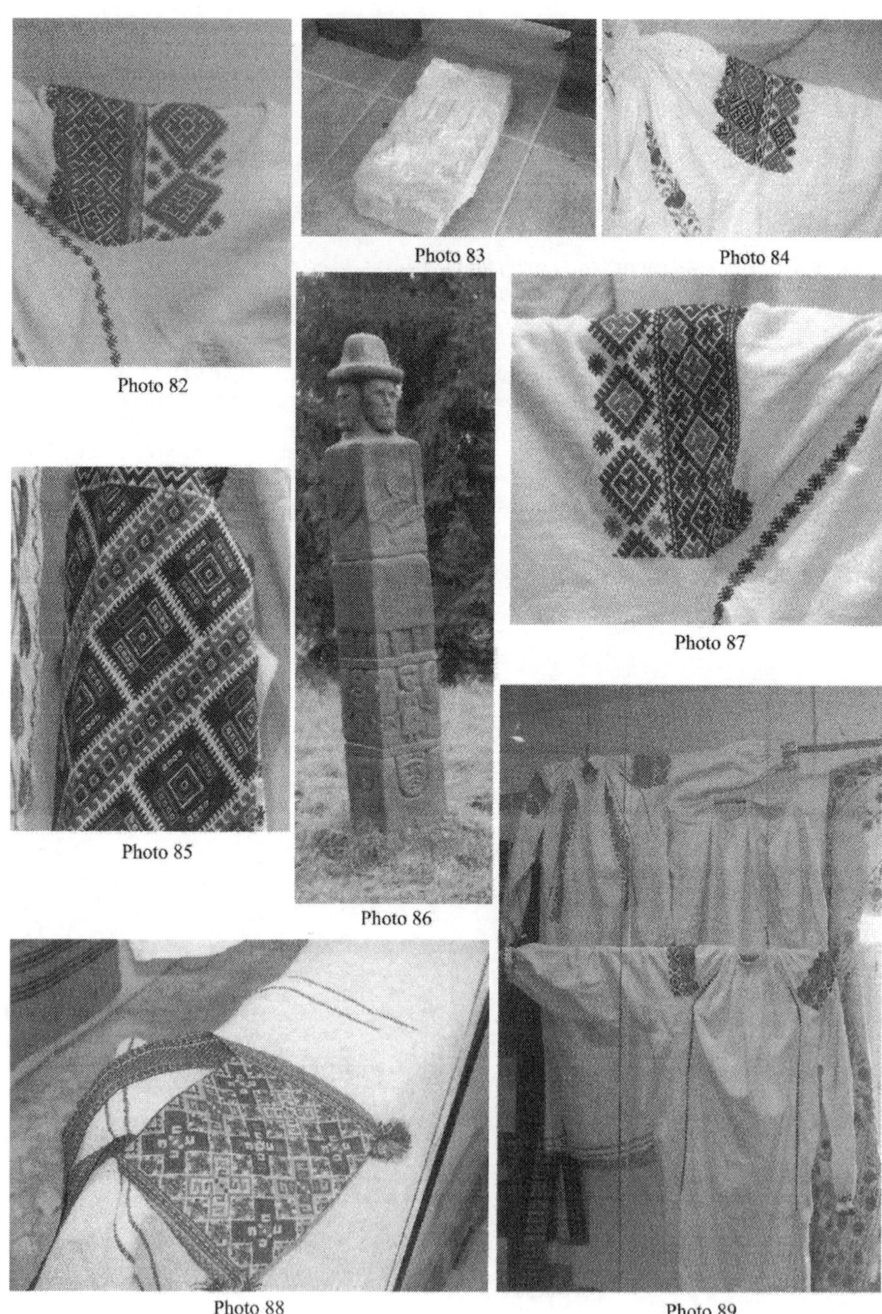

Photo 82

Photo 83

Photo 84

Photo 85

Photo 86

Photo 87

Photo 88

Photo 89

Photos 82, 84, 85, 87-89.
Swastika, trident, crosses, diamonds, Berehynia and other symbols in Ukrainian traditional embroideries. It follows to pay tribute to the Pravoslavny^-'pagan'-beliefs and courage of the Ukrainian peasants for preserving precious rarities in the communist "eradication of fascist ideology" (see photos 77-80), and to collector A. Polishchuk for his dedication to collecting these and other rarities. These and other "ornamental compositions" presented here are also amenable to being read with the above tapestry (photos 77-81).

Photo 83.
Sign of a trisuttya-"trident" on a medieval brick from Kyiv.

Photo 86.
A copy of the **Zbruch^ idol** standing in the Pereyaslav-Khmelnytsky State Historical and Cultural Museum.

Photo 91

Photo 90

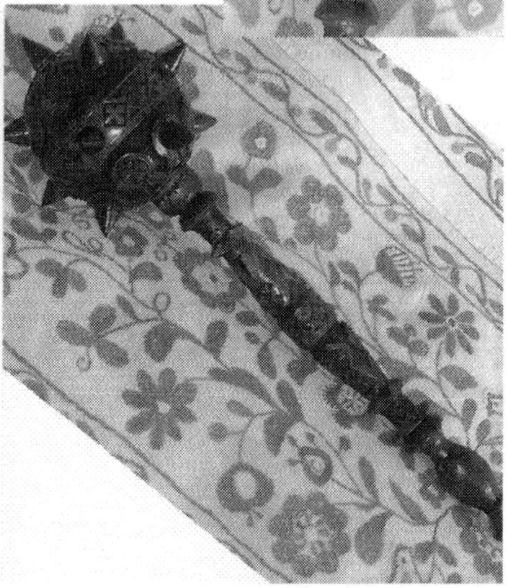

Photo 92

Photo 93

Photo 94

Photo 90.
Towel with the Tree of Life **and pairs of guardian birds at its roots and apex**.

Photo 91-92.
Traditional rod-mace with calendar symbols and signs of Aryan *vajra*, diagonally splting the embryonic New Year UNIVERSAL *Vala.*

Photo 93.
Weaving loom surrounded by the finished product.

Photo 94.
Towel with the Tree of Life and *Berehynia* surrounded by roosters at its roots (see photo 72).

GLOSSARY

* Additional terms and definitions added by the translators.

Achaeans* – one of the ancient Greek people, identified by Homer, along with the Danaoi and the Argeioi, as the Greeks who besieged Troy. Their area as described by Homer – the mainland and western isles of Greece, Crete, Rhodes, and adjacent isles, except the Cyclades – is precisely that covered by the activities of the Mycenaeans in the 14th – 13th century BCE, as revealed by archaeology. From this and other evidence, some authorities have identified the Achaeans with the Mycenaeans. Other evidence suggests that the Achaeans did not enter Greece until the so-called Dorian invasions of the 12th century BCE. (Encyclopaedia Britannica).

Achelous* – in Greek mythology he was the patron deity of the "silver-swirling" River Achelous, which is the largest river of Greece, and thus the chief of all river deities, every river having its own river spirit. (Hesiod, *Theogony* 337f).

Adam of Bremen* – 11th century German historian whose work on the archbishops of Hamburg-Bremen provides valuable information on German politics under the Salian emperors and is also one of the great books of medieval geography. Of Franconian origin, he was probably educated at the cathedral school in Bamberg but was introduced in 1066 or 1067 into the cathedral chapter at Bremen by Archbishop Adalbert. In 1069 Adam was head of the Bremen cathedral school. Adam began his *Gesta Hammaburgensis ecclesiae pontificum - History of the Archbishops of Hamburg-Bremen*), comprising four books, after Adalbert's death (1072). (Encyclopaedia Britannica).

Aditi – the 'Infinite' Foremother of reality, daughter of Aryan Prithivi and progenitor of Aryan deities of the *Rigveda*.

Adriatic Sea – a 'Sound', the sea at the centre of the Slavic western migration during late 3rd millennium to the 1st millennium BCE.

Aeneus – The leader of the Slavic-Rusen tribe of the (V)Eneti who brought them out from Troy, destroyed by the Greeks in the 13th or 11th century BCE, to [their] relatives (Rusen-Etruscans) in Italia. It is there, near the town of Crecchio, that the tomb of Aeneas was found in 1846.

Afanasievo* – or Afanasevo culture, 3500–2500 BC, an archaeological culture of the late copper and early Bronze Age. It became known from excavations in the Minusinsk area of the Krasnoyarsk Krai, southern Siberia, but the culture was also widespread in western Mongolia, northern Xinjiang, and eastern and central Kazakhstan, with connections or extensions in Tajikistan and the Aral area. The culture is mainly known from its inhumations, with the deceased buried in conic or rectangular enclosures, often in a supine position, bearing a remarkable resemblance to those much further west in the Yamna culture, the Seredny Stoh culture, the Catacomb culture and the Poltavka culture, all of which are believed to be Indo-European in nature, particularly within the context of the Kurgan hypothesis as put forward by Marija Gimbutas and her followers. (Mallory, J. P. (1997), "Afanasevo Culture", *Encyclopedia of Indo-European Culture*, Fitzroy Dearborn.)

Agathyrsi* — a people of Scythian, Thracian, or mixed Thraco-Scythic origin, who in the time of Herodotus occupied the plain of the Maris (Mures), in the mountainous part of ancient Dacia now known as Transylvania, Romania. According to most authorities, the Agathyrsi were of Thracian stock, although their ruling class seems to have been of Scythian origin (William Bayne Fisher, Ilya Gershevitch, Ehsan Yar Shater (1993) *The Median and Achaemenian Periods, The Cambridge History of Iran*, Volume 2, ISBN 978-0-521-20091-2). Herodotus also reported that Greeks viewed the Agathyrsi, Gelons, and Scythians as brothers. He described their habits as luxurious, wearing many gold ornaments (the district is still auriferous) and having many wives. The description of the pomp and splendour of the Agathyrsi of Transylvania is most strikingly confirmed by the discoveries made at Tufalau (Romania) – though this pomp is itself really pre-Scythian (Bronze Age local nobility) in character. (Parvan Vasile (1928) *Dacia*, Cambridge University Press). Herodotus recorded the Pontic Greek myth that the Agathyrsi were named after a legendary ancestor Agathyrsus.

Agni – Vedic 'Fire' in various manifestations.

Aides – 'Impenetrable' netherworld, the afterlife realm of Pelasgians and Greeks. According to their viewpoints, Aides lay beyond the islands of Lefkada and Eya (perhaps created by flooding of the lowland mud volcanoes in the Taman peninsula during the "World Flood, which created the Sea of Azov").

Akkad* – (Sumerian: *Agade)* the central city of the Akkadian Empire and its surrounding region in Mesopotamia. (Mish, Frederick C., Editor in Chief. "Akkad" *Webster's Ninth New Collegiate Dictionary*. ninth ed. Springfield, MA: Merriam-Webster 1985. ISBN 0-87779-508-8). It reached the height of its power between the 24th and 22nd centuries BCE, following the conquests of King Sargon of Akkad (2334-2279 BCE), often referred to as Sargon the Great. Under Sargon and his successors, Akkadian language was briefly imposed on neighbouring conquered states such as Elam. Akkad is sometimes regarded as the first empire in history. (Liverani, Mario, *Akkad: The First World Empire* (1993)).

Al-Mansur* – the second Abbasid Caliph (754-775 CE). He is generally regarded as the real founder of the Abbāsid caliphate. He established the capital city at Baghdad (762–763). (Encyclopaedia Britannica).

Amazons* – a nation of all-female warriors in Classical and Greek mythology. Herodotus placed them in a region bordering Scythia in Sarmatia (the territory of modern Ukraine).

Amber Way – in ancient times this stretched from the northern coast of the Adriatic Sea to the amber rich south-eastern coast of the Venedi Sea (also called Rusian; presently the Baltic Sea). At the same and former times amber was gathered in the lower reaches of the Dnipro.

Androphagi* – (meaning "man-eaters") an ancient nation of cannibals north of Scythia (according to Herodotus).

Ants – (< Orianian 'krayane', the ethnocultural nucleus of Ukrainians) one of three basic groups of Slavs of ancient times and early Middle Ages. They are mentioned for the first time in *The Veles Book* during the return of Slavs from Indian Punjab at the beginning of the 1st millennium BCE.

Anu* – also **An**; (from Sumerian *An* = sky, heaven) a sky-god in Sumerian mythology, the god of heaven, lord of constellations, king of gods, spirits and demons, and dwelt in the highest heavenly regions. It was believed that he had the power to judge those who had committed crimes, and that he had created the stars as soldiers to destroy the wicked. His attribute was the royal tiara, mainly decorated with two pairs of bull horns. He was one of the oldest gods in the Sumerian pantheon, part of a triad including Enlil, god of the sky and Ea/Enki, god of water. He was called **Anu** by the Akkadians. By virtue of being the first figure in this triad, Anu came to be regarded as the father of Enlil & Ea/Enki, and king of the gods. Anu is prominently associated with the E-anna temple in the city of Uruk (biblical Erech) in southern Iraq. (Jordon, Michael (1993). *Encyclopedia of Gods: Over 2,500 Deities of the World*. New York: Facts on File, Inc.. ISBN 978-0816029099).

Apollo – the 13th Titan, son of Zeus and Lato, twin brother of Artemis. Originated in Hyperborea, from where he annually returned to Greece for a half year. The earliest manifestation – in the form of a human sacrifice with a set of specific features – is to be found in Aryan kurhan No. 1-II near Kairy, in burials of the Ingul archaeological culture of c.1800 BCE. The most widespread epithet – Targelia: meaning 'Triumphant (or Vanquished) Sun' of the summer solstice. Plutarch interpreted the name Apollo to mean something outside a city, i.e. a 'non-polis', 'a-polis', viz. not a place where people lived but a place they visited, e.g. a sanctuary-observatory maidan; the epithet Paion (< Aryan Parjani > Slavic Perun) is connected with the times of the supremacy of Taurus in the solar zodiac (4400-1700 BCE).

Aras* (also known as Araks, Arax) — one of the largest rivers of the Caucasus. Its source is in the uplands east of the Black Sea and it discharges into the western shore of the Caspian Sea, to the south of the mouth of the Volga.

Aratta – the earliest world power, which arose in 6200 ± 97 BCE in the Danube-Dnipro region based on pre-Aratta, the pre-State country of hunters of 20th – 7th millennium BCE. The blossoming of Aratta, between the mid-6th – 3rd millennium BCE, is now most widely known under the name of the "Cucuteni-Trypillia archaeological culture" or "Trypillian archaeological culture". The most developed centre of Aratta was found in the area of the present-day Talne district in the Cherkasy region of Ukraine. Here, probably in 9th – 11th centuries, Arsania was located with its capital Arta (which is known by several other names) – a principality and maybe even a State in the composition of Kyivan Rus. The memory of Aratta remains, in particular, in the name of Artaplot in the Poltava Region. Being the nucleus of the Indo-European association of peoples, the ethnoculture of Aratta radiated throughout the world by its migrants (Sumerians, Leleges, Ruthenians, Aryans and others); however, Ukrainians remain the direct descendants on its territory and land.

Arga – a Hyperborean pilgrim who travelled to the temples of Artemis and Apollo on Delos.

Argo – the vessel, on which the heroes of Hellas, on the eve of the Trojan War, sailed to Eya, where the sorceress Medea lived.

Aria* – name of a region in the eastern part of the Persian empire, often confused with *Ariana* in the classical sources. It is described in a very detailed manner by Ptolemy, 6.17; Strabo, 11.10.1.

Arián* – also **Ariana,** a name introduced by Eratosthenes; **Arianus,** a Latinised form of Greek **Arianē**. The Greek term is based on Old Persian **Āryana,** the name of the Aryans' mother country, whose location is disputed. *'It was a large region that included almost all countries east of Media and Persia and south of the great mountain ranges up to the deserts of Gedrosia and Carmania, Aria, the Paropamisadae.'* (Strabo's Geographica, Book XV – "Persia, Ariana, the Indian subcontinent". Strabo emphasised the name meant "as of a single nation."). Apollodorus called Bactria "the ornament of Ariana as a whole". (Encyclopaedia Iranica, by Rüdiger Schmitt)

Arkaim – steppe-hylile valley in the South Trans-Ural mountains, which in 1800-1600 BCE became perhaps the most important centre on part of the migratory route of the *Aryans* from Ukraine into India (at that time Oriana and Pendeb, respectively, according to *The Veles Book*). At Arkaim (an ancient Russian site) there are concentrated settlements, sanctuary-observatories and late burial grounds (relative to the Dnipro-Dniester region) of Aratto-Aryan type.

*It was a settlement of the Sintashta-Petrovka culture. The site was discovered in 1987 by a team of Chelyabinsk scientists who were preparing for the area to be flooded to create a reservoir, and was examined in rescue excavations led by Gennadii Zdanovich. (Zdanovich G 1999 Arkaim Archaeological park: A cultural-ecological reserve in Russia in Panel-Philippe, G.; Stone-Peter, G.(eds.) The Constructed Past: Experimental Archaeology, Education and the Public, Routledge Chapter 20 p283-291). At first their findings were ignored by Soviet authorities, who planned to flood the site as they had flooded Sarkel earlier but the media attention forced the Soviet government to revoke its plans for flooding the area. It was designated a cultural reservation in 1991.

Arminghall* – timber circle and henge monument at Arminghall village, county of Norfolk, England. The henge is orientated towards the mid-winter sunset.

Artemis – Connected with the lunar calendar and the struggle of the Olympian-gods against the Titans. The earliest image (up to the Trojan War at the end of the 2nd millennium BCE) is to be found in the 'Grotto of Artemis' at Stone Grave. Also closely connected with Taurida and human sacrifices (especially in the legend about Iphigeneia – the daughter of Agamemnon, god of the Trojan War). Her close relationship with Apollo points to the time of matriarchal Aratta and the emergence of areas (5th – 4th millennium BCE) that only from approximately 2300 BCE ended the dominance of lunar viziers in favour of those of the solar-zodiac. There is possible significance of the name: Arta-m-Ida – 'Ar(at)ti-m(other) Ida. Combining images of Artemis and Apollo could have occurred in Oriana (at the maidan near the village of Mayaky in the Bilhorod-Dniester district of the Odessa region), because there the transformation of female ceremonial figurines into male, phallic figurines took place.

Ashnan* – Sumerian goddess of grain, she was often shown with ears of corn sprouting from her shoulders. She and her brother Lahar, god of cattle, were created by Enlil to provide food for the gods. Because they had too much to drink one day and could not serve as they should, Enlil decided to create humans to serve the gods instead. (Samuel Noah Kramer (1964). *The Sumerians: their history, culture and character.* University of Chicago Press. pp. 220–. ISBN 9780226452388).

Ashurbanipal* — the son of Esarhaddon and the last great king of the Neo-Assyrian Empire (668 – c. 627 BCE). He established the first systematically organised library in the ancient Middle East, the Library of Ashurbanipal, which survives in part today at Nineveh.

Ashvamedha* – **"horse sacrifice"** was one of the most important royal rituals of Vedic religion, described in detail in the Yajurveda (Ralph Thomas Hotchkin Griffith, *The Texts of the White Yajuveda. Translated with a Popular Commentary* (1899), 1987: Munshiram Manoharlal, New Delhi.

Askold or **Oskold**– a Varangian, belated Kyiv usurper-prince (862-882); a character of *The Veles Book* and *The Tale of Bygone Years*.

Asparuh* or **Isperih** – ruler of a Bulgar tribe in the second half of the 7th century, credited with the establishment of the First Bulgarian Empire in 680/681. (Formation of the Bulgarian nation. Dimitar Angelov (Science and Art Publishing House, "Centuries", Sofia 1971) p. 203-204 (in Bulgarian)).

Assyria – a sub-Aryan State (close to the Hurrites), eventually semiticised tribes, separated during 2200-2100 BCE from the Sumero-Akkadian kingdom, and in 2000-1100 - from the kingdoms of Babylon and Mitanni. The rise and fall of Assyria during the 8th – 7th century BCE coincided with the settlement on its territory of Cimmerians, who came to the Middle East from the Northern Black Sea.

Asura – the primary embodiment and epithet of the Indo-Aryan, Vedic Varuna, who in the mythology of the Irano-Aryan *Avesta* becomes the sun-like bearer of the good Ahura-Mazda.

Atlant – Titan grandson of the god Uranus, son of Iapetus, nephew of progenitor Pelasg, brother of Prometheus. He originates, possibly, from the coastal region of Aratta that was flooded by the World Flood – or from Oriana, the threshold of subsequent floods between the 3rd – 2nd millennium BCE.

Atlantis – A legendary country, known from the ancient Greek testimonies of Plato and Diodorus. First records pursue a political objective which is far removed from the secondary folk legends recorded by authors. These traditions associated Atlantis with the shores of Lake Triton, which, after the formation of the Bosphorus Strait (probably in the 4th – 2nd millennia BCE), became the Sea of Marmara. In folk legends of its origin and destruction, as well as the connection of Atlantis with Troy, Herakles and the Argonauts, there are hints of its origin from Hyperborea – the Northern Black Sea area.

Avesta – the sacred book of the Persian branch of late Aryan ("Indo-Iranian") community of tribes. It is based on the general (Indo-)Aryan Vedas of the 5th – 2nd millennia BCE; the most ordered is Zarathustra at the beginning of the 1st millennium BCE, and ends just after the millennium. It is imbued with a polar dualism (the struggle between good and evil) much more than the Vedas, in which the Trinity predominates and the removal of contradictions [between life and death].

Babylon – the successor of pre-Indo-European Sumer, semiticised at the end of the 3rd millennium BCE by the Akkadian dynasty of proto-Arabic Sinai.

Balarama* – also named **Baladeva**, **Baldau**, **Balavir**, **Balabhadra** and **Halayudha**, is the elder brother of Krishna in Hinduism. Within Vaishnavism and a number of South Indian, Hindu traditions Balarama is worshipped as an avatar of Vishnu, and is listed as such in the Bhagavata Purana. (Bhag-P 1.3.23 "In the nineteenth and twentieth incarnations, the Lord advented Himself as Lord Balarama and Lord Krishna").

Balaton, Lake* – a freshwater lake in the Trans-Danubian region of Hungary. It is the largest lake in Central Europe. (Encyclopaedia Britannica). It is often called the "Hungarian Sea".

Bald mountain (Lysa Hora) – near the regional centre of Vasilivka of the Zaporizhia region; also other legendary places with tombs and human offerings of the earliest Aryans of the Dnipro-Donets archaeological culture, 5th – 4th millennium BCE. Similar treeless elevations were used for the building of maidans and calendar-astronomical observations, and also for rituals connected with them.

Belarus* – The name Belarus derives from the term White Rus. The Latin term for the area was *Alba Ruthenia.* In English, the country was referred to as White Ruthenia. Belarus was named Belorussia in the days of Imperial Russia, and the Russian Tsar was usually styled Tsar of All the Russias – Great, Little, and White. (Szporluk, Roman (2000). *Russia, Ukraine, and the Breakup of the Soviet Union.* Hoover Institution Press. ISBN 0-8179-9542-0). Belorussia was the Russian name of the country until 1991, when the Supreme Soviet of the Belorussian Soviet Socialist Republic decreed that the new independent republic should be called Belarus in Russian and in all other language transcriptions of its name.

Beloberezhie – Derived from Belovodie - the legendary country of wise men, who lived at first in the Borustan-Berezan area.

Berehynia – the Foremother heiress of Çatal Höyük temple 23/VII which in 6200 ± 97 BCE was decorated with a copy of the chronicle from Stone Grave. This copy heralded the beginning of Aratta and civilisation (statehood) in general, and since then Berehynia (the Foremother, "serpent-legged Goddess" of ancient times) has been annually painted on Ukrainian pysanky [Easter] eggs.

*Known as **Berehynia** in Ukrainian, or **Bereginia** in Russian, she is regarded as a "Slavic goddess" with a function of "hearth mother, protectress of the home". In the late 20th century Ukrainian romantic nationalism was centred on matriarchal myth (Rubchak, Marian J., (2001). *In Search of a Model: Evolution of a Feminist Consciousness in Ukraine and Russia.* The European Journal of Women's Studies (Valparaiso University, Indiana: SAGE Publications) 8 (2): 149). In 2001, a column with a statue of Berehynia on top, as protector of Kyiv, was erected at Maidan Nezalezhnosti (Independence Square) in the centre of the city, replacing the Lenin monument.

Berezan (<Aryan Borustan, 'High place') – the island is the remnant of a former cape in the Black Sea near the Dnipro-Buh estuary. This place is one of the most ancient colonies (7th century BCE) of immigrants from Greece to the Black Sea coast.

Bharata – the autonym of India, which comes from Aratta of the Ukrainian Dnipro area ("Old Syndica"), also of Indian Punjab and is connected with the legendary events of the *Mahabharata.*

*In the Hindu epic *Ramayana*, Bharata was the second brother of the main protagonist Lord Rama.

Bharatta* – a modern place situated in Naogaon Zl, Rajshahi Div, Bangladesh.

Boh (God) – the Slavic name of the highest, though blessed and humane force. (In the ancient times **Boh** was also equated with gladness).

Bohdan Khmelnytsky* – (c. 1595-1657) was a hetman (leader) of the Zaporozhian Cossacks who organised a rebellion against the Polish-Lithuanian Commonwealth (now Ukraine). This uprising (1648-1654) resulted in the creation of a Cossack state. In 1654, he concluded the Treaty of Pereyaslav with Muscovy (today Russia), that ultimately led to the transfer of the Ukrainian lands east of the Dnipro River from Polish to Muscovite control. (Encyclopaedia Britannica).

Bohomyr – the legendary Slavic progenitor, between the 2nd – 1st millennium BCE, a character of *The Veles Book* and of figurines of the Retra sanctuary. The most likely interpretation of his name: God-omir, 'Divine Omir' ('narrator', similar to Homer < Omir); the most reliable homeland – the North Adriatic.

*The name **Bohomyr** has a variety of spelling variants. In *The Veles Book* there are two forms: Bohomyr and Bohumir; the latter was found in the text that was probably revised in 7th century. In the English language, he is generally known as Bogumir or Bogomir. It must also be recognised that the Cyrillic letter 'г' in Russian is pronounced 'g' but in Ukrainian it is 'h', hence Богомир is respectively pronounced Bogomir (in Russian) and Bohomyr (in Ukrainian).

Boruses – one of the ancient Slavic tribes from the shores of the Borysthenes (i.e. the Dnipro river).

Borysthen* – the Ukrainian pink granite crystalline massif of the Dnipro southern steppelands was referred to by the ancient tribes as *borysthen,* 'the storehouse of vital forces' [V.N.Danylenko].

Borysthenes – (Aratto-Aryan Borusten); the ancient Greek name for the Dnipro River. Thought to be derived from the local name of the 'Northern river'.

Bosphorus – 'Bull crossing', (the modern Kerch strait), which in Cimmeria reflected the settling of the Aratto-Aryan or Indo-European tribes from the Northern Black Sea area.

Bosphorus kingdom – the largest grouping of Greek settlers of the Northern Black Sea area, emerged in 500 BCE. The mid-eastern migration site of the exhausted Cimmerians.

Boyan – legendary psaltery player, mentioned above in the *Tale of Igor's Campaign.* Academic tradition attributes him to between the 11th – 12th centuries. Meanwhile G. R. Derzhavin, N. M. Karamzin and other known researchers of Russian culture had at their disposal a copy of one of the old Boyan anthems, deciphered for the first time and published in 1995 - 2000 by A. I. Asov. *The anthem of dutiful Boyan to Sloven: the old, young, deceased and living, and Zlatohor – Magi of Svaroh* recalls Prince Bus (brother of the same name – by descent of surname? – Magi Zlatohor, who was crucified by the Goths) as father of Boyan and is dated, consistently (as well as with written language) to the 4th century – just like the text on the statue of Prince Sloven buried in 368 near *Piatihorsk.* "The unconditional authenticity of the runic inscription on the plinth of the dated memorial of the 4th century acknowledges the authenticity of the *Boyan Anthem.* And the authenticity of the *Boyan Anthem* once again confirms the authenticity of *The Veles Book*, – confirming the observation of A. I. Asov (by Oksentii Onopenko, Boyan also was Boian Prophetic - the title of acting hetman; 'boian' means *to prophesy* in the old English language).

Boyan Anthem – literary document of the 4th century, returned (just like *The Veles Book*) to Ukraine (or rather Russia) from France on boundary of the 18th – 19th century, where it had been taken to in the 11th century by Queen Anna, daughter of Yaroslav the Wise. The Anthem is devoted to the victory of Rus over Hermanaric's Goths.

Boyan (Boian) culture* – a Neolithic culture (4300-3500 BCE) centred in what is now southern Romania; it was characterised by terraced settlements, consisting at first of mud huts and later of fortified promontory settlements. The Boyan phase was marked by the introduction of copper axes, the extension of agriculture, and the breeding of domestic animals. The distinctive Boyan pottery was decorated by rippling, painting, and excised or incised linear designs. By spreading northward into Transylvania and north-eastward to Moldavia, the Boyan culture gradually assimilated earlier cultures of those areas. (Encyclopaedia Britannica).

Bozh (Bus, God Bus) – Magian or Antian prince (of Ruses), a character of *The Veles Book, The Tale of Igor's Campaign* and the book *Getica/Origin and Deeds of the Goths* by Jordanes. Crucified along with 70 elders 375 by the Goths of Hermanaric, this led to the rebellion of [Kyivan] Rus and the defeat of the Goths. He corresponds (according to A. I. Asov) with the Magi Zlatohor to whom is devoted *the Anthem* of Boyan.

Brahman – a representative of the superior Varna [caste] of Aratto-Aryan society; forerunner of the Ukrainian (b)rahman.

Budini* – an ancient people who lived in Scythia, in what is today Ukraine. Herodotus wrote in his *Histories* (iv. 21, 108, 109): "Above the Sauromatae (Sarmatians), possessing the second region, dwell the Budini, whose territory is thickly wooded with trees of every kind. The Budini are a large and powerful nation: they all have deep blue eyes, and bright red hair. The Budini, however, do not speak the same language as the Geloni, nor is their mode of life the same. They are the aboriginal people of the country, and are nomads." Also known as 'Shepherd Scythians'.

Buh – in English this river is named 'Bug', as also in west European countries but in Ukraine it is known as the Buh (in 1920 Russians changed the name to 'Bug', though the real, old, Ukrainian name is Boh). The name of this river of the southern Black Sea area is related to Boh, meaning *God* (Aryan. *Bhaga* - 'Happily betrothed DESTINY', was the name of one of the 6-12 sons of the Foremother, Aditi).

Buh-Dniester culture* – an early Neolithic precursor to the Cucuteni-Trypillian culture. (*Cucuteni-Trypillia. A Great Civilisation of Old Europe.* Palazzo Della Cancelleria, Rome, Vatican. 2008. Hers Consulting Group, p.31. ISBN 978-973-0-05830-7). Also known as the Bug-Dniester culture.

Bulan* – a Khazar king who led the conversion of the Khazars to Judaism. The date of his reign is unknown, as the date of the conversion is hotly disputed, though it is certain that Bulan reigned some time between the mid-700s and the mid-800s. The name **Sabriel** is given in the *Schechter Letter* for the Khazar king who led the conversion to Judaism. (Refs: Kevin Alan Brook. *The Jews of Khazaria.* 2nd ed. Rowman & Littlefield Publishers, Inc, 2006; Douglas M. Dunlop, *The History of the Jewish Khazars,* Princeton, N.J.: Princeton University Press, 1954; Norman Golb and Omeljan Pritsak, *Khazarian Hebrew Documents of the Tenth Century.* Ithaca: Cornell Univ. Press, 1982).

Burty – a grand maidan near the city of Chyhyryn in the Cherkasy region, which equated to the Indo-European "Rotunda" of Central and Western Europe, and to the Aryan sanctuary-observatories of Trans-Urals etc. Partially studied at the turn of the 19th and 20th centuries but destroyed at the end of the 20th century.

Bus Beloyar* – a fictional Slavic kniaz (Prince) described in the Book of Veles, who ruled the Ruskolan state in the 4th century CE from its capital Kiyar and fought against Huns in the East, Romans in the South and Germans in the West against the Goths' king Hermanarich. He was eventually crucified by the Goths. First mentioned in the 4th century in the Slavic writing - Boyans Anthem (A. Asov - The Runes of the Slavs; Runes of Slavs and "Boyan anthem. 2nd ed. / Runy slavyan i "Boyanov gimn". 2-e izd. by Asov Alexandr Igorevich (Hardcover - 2008). The name Bus is mentioned in The Tale of Igor's Campaign as [They] *Sing to the time of Bus*.

Calendar – according to Roman fables this was 'the gift of Kola [Svaroh]' from the Etruscans (Rusenes - Ruthenians).

Calendar-zodiac* – The name 'zodiac' normally dates from the first millennium BCE but here the term is used descriptively. The zodiac measured divisions of celestial longitude centred on the plane of the ecliptic [apparent path of the sun across the celestial sphere over course of a year.] The classical 'tropical zodiac', which divided the celestial sphere into 12 sectors of 30 degrees of arc, developed without awareness of precession of the equinoxes. Earlier the Vedic *naksatra* system used a 27-'division' 'sidereal zodiac' which divided the celestial sphere into vectors based on fixed stars, thus accounting for and accommodating the shift in the equinoxes.

Catacomb culture* – c. 2800-2200 BCE, an early Bronze Age culture occupying what is essentially present-day Ukraine. It was related to the Yamna culture, and would seem more to cover several related smaller archaeological cultures. The name comes from its burial practices, similar to the Yamna culture, but with a hollowed-out space off the main shaft, creating the 'catacomb'. Animal remains were incorporated into a small minority of graves. In certain graves there was the distinctive practice of what amounts to modelling a clay mask over the deceased's face, creating an obvious if not necessarily correct association with the famous gold funeral mask of Agamemnon. (Refs. V. Kulbaka, "Indo-European populations of Ukraine in the palaeometallic period", Mariupol 2000. Mallory, J. P. (1997), "Catacomb Culture", *Encyclopedia of Indo-European Culture*).

Çatal Höyük – a settlement in the south of Turkey, known from archaeological studies in 1960s to have been a proto-city, 7th – 6th millennium BCE with an area of 14 ha and with 40 temples. In the temple of 23/VII, dated by J. Mellaart at 6200 ± 97 BCE, was located a relief image of an Oranta-woman‡ in childbirth, covered with symbols. They were deciphered by A. G. Kifishin in 1994-1998 as representing a copy of the symbols found at the beginning of the world's earliest chronicle at Stone Grave, 12th – 7th – 3rd millennium BCE. Attention had been initially drawn to the inter-relationship between these monuments by V. Danylenko in 1965-1969.

‡**Oranta*** - The Praying Virgin of Eastern Orthodoxy.

Cecrops* – a mythical king of Athens. The name is not of Greek origin according to Strabo, it might mean 'face with a tail': it is said that, born from the earth itself, he had his top half shaped like a man and the bottom half in serpent or fish-tail form. (Smith, William; *Dictionary of Greek and Roman Biography and Mythology*, London (1873).

Chaush – the greatest Aryan kurhan at the Novoselska ferry across the Lower Danube, excavated in 1987. At the base it was identified the sacrificial remains of a rider embodying the Vedic Saviour Gandkharva.

Cherkasy – one of the oldest names of the Cossacks derived from the Polovetsian chirykisov (the 'peoples army' frontier-guards of Kyivan Rus) in the 11th – 13th century and Circassians, led from the Caucasus in the headstream of the Rapids by Prince Vytautas at the beginning of the 15th century.

Chernolis culture* – an Iron Age archaeological unit dating c. 1025-700 BCE. It was located in the forest-steppe between the Dniester and Dnipro Rivers, in what is now northern Ukraine. This location corresponds to where Herodotus later placed his Scythian ploughmen. From 200 BCE, the culture was overrun by the arrival of Germanic and Celtic settlers to the region. (James P. Mallory, "Chernoles Culture", *Encyclopedia of Indo-European Culture*, Fitzroy Dearborn, 1997).

Chernyakhov/Chernyakhiv culture* – a (2nd to 5th century) culture situated in what is today Ukraine, Romania, Moldova, and parts of Belarus (Matthews, John; Heather, Peter (1991), *The Goths in the fourth century*, Liverpool University Press, ISBN 0853234264). The culture probably corresponds to the Gothic kingdom of Oium as described by Jordanes in his work *Getica*. (The Cambridge Ancient History, Vol. 13: The Late Empire, p. 488 (1998).

Chongar — (Чонгар, pronounced Chonhar in Ukrainian and Chongar in Russian). The peninsula in the Sivash gulf of the Sea of Azov, through which runs a well-known road (especially in the history of the civil war of 1918-1920) to the Crimea. It is the location of the Garman kurhan and other kurhans and burial grounds of Aryans, Scythians and Polovets. Also unique for the Azov area of Aratta are two Cimmerian settlements (near the village of Chonhar/Chongar) and several camps of ancient and medieval times. The name corresponds to the Aryan tribe Changar, hitherto dwelling from Punjab to Tajikistan. There is probably a relationship between the words: Chanhar-Chingyan-Gipsies.

Churingas* – objects of wood or stone that are considered sacred by various aboriginal tribes of Central Australia. They bear incised designs are are believed to represent either the spiritual double of a living native or the spiritual embodiment of a totemic ancestor. Similar tile-tablets have been found at Stone Grave (See Table XIII, 16-19).

Cimmeria – the ancient-Slavic state on the coast of Bosphorus (the modern Kerch strait), which arose (according to *The Veles Book*, *Iliad* and archaeological data) in the 13th – 9th centuries BCE and became the basis of the formation of Surozh Rus from ancient times and the early Middle Ages.

Cimmerians* (or **Kimmerians)** – ancient people living north of the Caucasus and the Sea of Azov, driven by the Scythians out of south-eastern Ukraine, over the Caucasus, and into Anatolia toward the end of the 8th century BCE. Ancient writers sometimes confused them with the Scythians. Most scholars now believe that the Cimmerians assaulted Urartu (Armenia) about 714 BCE, but in 705, after being repulsed by Sargon II of Assyria, they turned aside into Anatolia and in 696-695 conquered Phrygia. In 652, after taking Sardis, the capital of Lydia, they reached the summit of their power. (Encyclopaedia Britannica). According to *The Veles Book* Cimmerians arose from Slavic tribes that returned from Punjab to the middle area of the left bank of the Dnipro river.

Circum-Pontic zone – 'Around the Black sea', the region of formation of Arián and other nations in the 7th – 1st millennium BCE.

Constantine VII* — *Porphyrogennetos* or *Porphyrogenitus*, "the Purple-born", (CE 905 – 959). Byzantine emperor from 913 to 959. His writings are one of the best sources of information on the Byzantine Empire and neighbouring areas. (Encyclopaedia Britannica).

Corded Ware culture* – also characterised as the **Battle Axe culture** or **Single Grave culture;** an enormous European archaeological horizon that begins in the late Neolithic (Stone Age), flourishes through the Copper Age and finally culminates in the early Bronze Age, developing in various areas from c. 3200-2900 BCE to ca. 230-1800 BCE. It represents the introduction of metal into Northern Europe. Corded Ware culture is commonly associated with the Indo-European family of languages. It encompassed most of continental northern Europe from the Rhine River on the west, to the Volga River in the east, including most of modern-day Germany, the Netherlands, Denmark, Poland, Lithuania, Latvia, Estonia, Belarus, the Czech Republic, Slovakia, northern Ukraine, western Russia, as well as coastal Norway and the southern portions of Sweden and Finland. The contemporary Beaker culture overlapped with the western extremity of this culture, west of the Elbe, and may have contributed to the pan-European spread of that culture, while Scandinavia and the North European Plain continued their local traditions. Although a similar social organisation and settlement pattern to the Beaker were adopted, the Corded Ware group lacked the new refinements made possible through trade and communication by sea and rivers. (Cunliffe, Barry (1994). *The Oxford Illustrated Prehistory of Europe*. Oxford University Press. pp. 250-254.)

Cossacks – the successors of the caste of Kshatriya (Rajania) of Dandaria, from the lower reaches of the Dnipro and Kuban. The name probably arises from the word 'kosa'-"oseledets" ['braid' or 'plait' in English] of the Brahman Vasistha and Siva Keshava (i.e. long hair with a number of thin braids): Kosaki > Cossacks (Ukr.). One Cossack means one braid of Siva. There are other explanations, which clearly do not correspond with the undoubtedly Aryan traditions of Ukrainian Cossacks (nor also the Persian, namely Indian type).

Cromlech – an annular stone enclosure of cultic designation.

Cucuteni-Trypillian culture* – also known as Cucuteni culture (Romania), Trypillian culture (Ukraine) or Tripolye culture (Russia), a late Neolithic archaeological culture that flourished between c. 5500 BCE and 2750 BCE, from the Carpathian Mountains to the Dniester and Dnieper regions in modern-day Romania, Moldova, and Ukraine, encompassing an area of more than 35,000 km^2 (Mantu, Cornelia-Magda (2000). At its peak the Cucuteni-Trypillian culture built the largest Neolithic settlements in Europe, some of which had populations of up to 10,000 -15,000 inhabitants. (Monah, Dan (2005), "Religie si arta in cultura Cucuteni", in Dumitroaia, Gheorghe (in Romanian), Bibliotheca memoriae antiquitatis XV, Piatra-Neamţ, Romania: Editura Foton, pp. 162–173, OCLC 319165024).

Daksha – 'Given' son of Foremother Aditi, her [alternate] male counterpart. The earliest embodiment is traced in the sacrifice and construction of the filling over grave No. 3 of High Grave, mid-3rd millennium BCE. A possible prototype of Dazhboh.

* The line in the *Rigveda*, "Daksha sprang from Aditi and Aditi from Daksha" (Mandala 10.72.4) references "the eternal cyclic re-birth of the same divine essence".

Dana (Aryan Dan (Celtic god) <proto-Arattan Divanna) – Slavic Goddess of rivers and waters in general.

Dandaka – **t**he forest of Dandaka was the largest forest in ancient India. It stretched from Vindhya ranges in central Indian to the banks of River Krishnavenna (now known as River Krishna) and Tughabhadra in the south. This sacred forest is mentioned in the Mahabharata (3-85). In Ukraine, **Dandaka** (meaning 'Mace-bearing', 'Cany' and such like) is a locality and ancient settlement near the Kamyshly tract (south-west

Crimea). Possibly this is the Dandaka in the Indo-Aryan poem *Ramayana*.

Dandarica – 'Mace-bearing Aria'; the ancestral homeland of Aryans mentioned by ancient authors in the 2nd century CE. (Also Dandaka in the 4th century). The principal territory in ancient times was the left bank of the Dnipro-Buh estuary (that is inherited in the name Tendry or Tendrivska scythe), however the tribe of Dandar and its homonymous ruler is also known near the mouth of the River Kuban. Aryan Dandaria semantically corresponds to the Scythian Palak and Slavic Kyiv (region).

Danylenko, Valentin (1913-1982) – the greatest Ukrainian archaeologist-historian of the 20th century, the main researcher of Stone Grave. He was the first person to show Yu. Shilov that the scenes from the *Rigveda* were incarnated in the base of Aryan kurhans.

Dardanus* – In Greek mythology, he was a son of Zeus and Electra (daughter of Atlas). Dardanus' original home was Arcadia – a mountainous region of the central Peloponnesus of ancient Greece – where he and his elder brother Iasus/Iasion ruled as kings after Atlas. After their land was visited by a great flood, they fled across the sea to the island of Samothrace. In some traditions, Samothrace was also visited by a flood, Dardanus and his people sailed for Phrygia, settling in the Troad, a region surrounding Troy in Asia Minor. He was ancestor of the Dardanians of the Troad; he founded the city of Dardania on Mount Ida.

Day of Brahma (Kalpa, Ritual) – the age 'of Prayers' spanning 4,320,000,000 years embodying the highest manifestation of God. Within that time the Universe is self-created from a Fiery Embryo and passes through 4 mahayuga – 'great generations'. Then the Almighty-serpent Shesha awakes and burns the Universe by its fiery breath; then begins the Night of Brahma of the same duration ... The sources of this doctrine are traced in the periodic self-burning of cities and villages of Aratta (because of the reduction of crops on worn-out fields, as well as of aged wooden buildings) that underwent development in the mythological rituals of Aryan kurhans, such as High Grave etc.

Dazh(d)boh – 'rain-giving God'; Taurus, according to *The Veles Book*. The sources of this tradition are presented in the «Grotto of the bull» at Stone Grave, where this dominating animal with water streaming from its mouth is twice depicted (more realistic images are inherent to Sumer); Here there are corresponding inscriptions about Taurus and the Water Court. Images that are dated at 4th – 3rd millennium BCE are consistent with the years when Taurus led the zodiac: 4440-1720 BCE (according to N. A. Chmykhov); the image of Dazh(d)boh-Taurus could only form at that time.

Deioces* – the first king of the Medes according to Herodotus (*Herodotus: The Histories*, tr. Aubrey De Sélincourt (Penguin Books, 1954), p. 54).

Delos – the sacred island in the Cyclades archipelago of the Aegean Sea. It was proclaimed in the ancient world, by the temples of Apollo and Artemis, that Lado/Leto (the Hyperborean) was born here and was esteemed by Hyperborean pilgrims.

Delphi – a city near the base of Mount Parnassus, celebrated as the site of the central temple of Apollo, who went there in summer after living in Hyperborea for the six months of winter.

Demeter* – in Greek mythology she is the daughter of the deities Cronus and Rhea, sister and consort of Zeus, and goddess of agriculture. Demeter is rarely mentioned by Homer, nor is she included among the Olympian gods, but the roots of her legend are probably ancient. The legend centred on the story of her daughter Persephone, who was carried off by Hades, the god of the underworld. (Encyclopaedia Britannica).

Derbent* – a city in the Republic of Dagestan, Russia, close to the Azerbaijani border. It is the southernmost city in Russia.

Dereivka – a village on the right-bank of the Dnipro opposite the mouth of the River Psel, near the upper reaches of Dnipro rapids. It is known for the settlement of the Seredny Stoh archaeological culture, 4th millennium BCE, horse breeding and other signs, which indicate connection with the earliest Aryans.

Dev(as) – Vedic 'radiant' gods of the Sky, netherworldly adversaries of the Asuras – 'without-waters', and 'vitality'. First headed by Dyaus and Indra, and secondly, by Varuna-

Asura and Vritra.

Didukh* – a sheaf of wheat which at Christmas celebrations is used to decorate the table, having been brought in by the head of the household. It represents the importance of the ancient and rich wheat crops of Ukraine, the staff of life through the centuries. Didukh means literally "grandfather spirit" so it symbolises the family's ancestors. (Ref. Canadian Institute of Ukrainian Studies, Encyclopedia of Ukraine).

Di(e)v(a) – 'Day', 'Sky' (explicitly) in male and female guises; the supreme Indo-European deity, epithet of Shiva and some other gods. It forms the root of the name for Devich-mountains and such like.

Dionysus – 'Our-God', surpassing his elder brother Apollo around 1700 BCE – after replacing the rule of Taurus with that of Aries. Embodied the dying and rising of Taurus. His appearance is traced in later monuments of the Ingul archaeological culture in the lower reaches of the River Dnipro.

Dioscuri* – in classical mythology, the twin heroes Castor and Pollux were called the Dioscuri.

Dir(os) – intermediary (between the Rusy dynasties of Kyan and Riuriks) protégé of Byzantium on the Kyivan throne beginning in 860 BCE.

Div(-)anna – possibly, the 'Celestial-Sky' in female and male guises. She was the earliest goddess of the Slavs, and perhaps of all Indo-Europeans – symbols of whom (as Celestial Deer, tree and water) reach back to Mesolithic times. She was the precursor of Dana of the Ruthenians (Etruscans) and Romans, as well as, evidently, Aratto-Sumerian Inanna.

Dniester* – this river is also known as the Dnistro (Ukrainian).

Dnipro* – The major Ukrainian river, flowing through Kyiv down to the Black Sea. Known as the Dnieper via Russian influence (in English, Italian, Polish and Portuguese) and as the Dnepr (in Russian, Czech, Estonian and Finnish).

Dnipro-Donets culture* – c. 5000-4000 BCE. A Neolithic culture in the Northern Black Sea/Azov area, between the Dnipro [Dnieper in Russian and English] and Donets Rivers. It was a hunter-gatherer culture that made the transition to early agriculture. The economic evidence from the earliest stages is almost exclusively from hunting and fishing. Inhumation was in grave pits, with the deceased being covered in ochre. Burial was sometimes individual, but larger groupings are more common, with burials being done sequentially in the same grave. The precise role of this culture and its language to the derivation of the Pontic-Caspian cultures such as Sredny Stog and Yamna culture, is open to debate, though the display of recurrent traits points either to long-standing mutual contacts or underlying genetic relations. (J.P.Mallory - In Search of the Indo-Europeans, 1989).

Dolmen* called *cromlech* in Brythonic Welsh – a single-chambered megalithic construction in the form of a box made from stone slabs and endowed with symbols of rebirth. Widespread in the Caucasus, as well as on the islands of Malta and Sicily, on the coast of Spain and in other *Aryan* countries which suggests maritime liaisons between their populations, 3000-2000 BCE.

Dorians* – a name applied by the Greeks to one of the principal groups of Hellenic peoples, in contradistinction to Ionians and Aeolians. In Hellenic times a small district known as Doris in north Greece, between Mount Parnassus and Mount Oeta, counted as "Dorian" in a special sense. Practically all Peloponnese, except Achaea and Elis, was "Dorian," together with Megara, Aegina, Crete, Melos, Thera, the Sporades Islands and the S.W. coast of Asia Minor, where Rhodes, Cos, Cnidus and (formerly) Halicarnassus formed a "Dorian" confederacy. The Dorian people are traditionally acknowledged as the conquerors of the Peloponnese, in the period 1100-1000 BCE. (Encyclopaedia Britannica).

Dravidian* – family of some 70 languages spoken primarily in South Asia. The Dravidian languages are spoken by more than 215 million people in India, Pakistan, and Sri Lanka. (Encyclopaedia Britannica).

Dulebs* — A tribe of Early Eastern Slavs between the 6th and the 10th centuries. They were among the twelve Eastern Slavic tribes mentioned in the Primary Chronicle.

Dumuzi – Sumerian "shepherd of the time before the Deluge"; beloved husband of the goddess Inanna, until he was banished to live in the netherworld for half of the year as her substitute; dying and reborn as a vegetation deity. Among the inscriptions of Stone Grave the name Dumuzi is traced from the 7th millennium BCE; it is possible that this Aratto-Sumerian deity became the prototype of the Aryan Daksha.

Dyaus Pitar (**Patare Dyaie** of *The Veles Book*) – the supreme Indo-European deity and corresponding mythological formation of the Indo-aryan *Rigveda*. From him are derived Div, Zeus and others.

*In the Vedic pantheon **Dyaus Pita** is the Sky Father, divine consort of the Prithvi and father of Agni, Indra (Rigveda 4.17.4) and Ushas, the daughter representing dawn.

Dziewona* (or **Devana**) – The Slavic equivalent of the Roman Diana.

Elam* – an ancient civilisation located in what is now south-west Iran, stretching from the lowlands of Khuzestan and Ilam Province, as well as a small part of southern Iraq. Situated just to the east of Mesopotamia, Elam was part of the early urbanisation during the Chalcolithic era [cf. Eneolithic]. The emergence of written records from around 3000 BCE also parallels Mesopotamian history. In the Old Elamite period (Middle Bronze Age), Elam consisted of kingdoms on the Persian plateau, centred in Anshan, and from the mid-2nd millennium BCE, it was centred in Susa in the Khuzestan lowlands. (Elam: surveys of political history and archaeology, Elizabeth Carter and Matthew W. Stolper, University of California Press, 1984, p. 4).

Elena – the beautiful Spartan queen, for whom the heroes of Hellas contested, became the motive for the Trojan War. In the ancient culture, there was an extended version about her escape to Taurida and an afterlife stay on the island of Levka(da) opposite the mouth of the Danube. The name Elena (Sun) is found in Ukrainian folklore, despite superiority of the national Olena ('Olenka'?).

Eneolithic* – (from the Latin *aeneus*, copper, and Greek *lithos*, stone), also known as the Chalcolithic period (from the Greek *chalcos*, copper).

Enlil– (Slavic *Lel*) – Aratto-Sumerian creator-god: 'Lord of the Winds', originated in the Worldwide mountain Kian, formed after the separation/division of the Earth-*Ki* and Sky-*An*; Sumer itself, was also called "Kur-gal" or "Great Land".

Enmerkar* – an ancient Sumerian ruler, according to the Sumerian king list, listed as having reigned for "420 years" (some copies read "900 years"). The Sumerian king list implies that Enmerkar inherited official kingship at E-ana after his father Mesh-ki-ang-gasher, son of Utu, had "entered the sea and disappeared." Enmerkar is also known from a few other Sumerian legends, most notably *Enmerkar and the Lord of Aratta*, where a previous confusion of the languages of mankind is mentioned. Here, Enmerkar is called 'the son of Utu', the Sumerian sun god. Besides founding Uruk, he is documented as having built a temple at Eridu, and is even credited with the invention of writing on clay tablets for the purposes of coercing Aratta into submission. (*Legends: The Genesis of Civilisation* (1998) and *The Lost Testament* (2002) by David Rohl).

Epos* – A body of poetry, not formally united, in which the tradition of a people is conveyed, especially a group of poems concerned with a common epic theme e.g origin of the Aryan peoples.

Esarhaddon* — King of Assyria who reigned 681 – 669 BCE. He was the youngest son of Sennacherib and the Aramean queen Naqi'a (Zakitu), Sennacherib's second wife.

Eshnunna* – (modern **Tell Asmar**, Iraq), an ancient Sumerian city and city-state in lower Mesopotamia. Occupied from the Jemdet Nasr period about 3000 BCE, Eshnunna was a major city during the Early Dynastic period. Starting with the rise of the Akkadian Empire, Eshnunna oscillated between times of independence and domination by empires such as the Third Dynasty of Ur and Isin. Because of its control over lucrative trade routes, Eshnunna did function somewhat as a gateway between Mesopotamian and Elamite culture. (City In the Sand (2nd Edition), Mary Chubb, Libri, 1999, ISBN 1-901965-02-3).

Etruscans* – They were called by a variety of names. The Romans knew them as Tusci or

Etrusci - from which the name of Etruria comes. Virgil refers to them as Lydians. The Greeks called them Tyrrhenoi, alluding to the migration across the sea led by Tyrrhenos, son of Athys, king of Lydia. The Greek historian Hellanicos identifies them with the nomadic Pelasgians. According to the ancient writers the Etruscans' own name for themselves was Rasena. The records of other peoples mention the existence in the Mediterranean basin of the Tyrrhenians, under the name of Tyrsenes or Tursa - from which no doubt the Latin "Tusci" is derived. An Egyptian inscription of the thirteenth century BCE speaks of the "Tursa of the sea", mercenaries in the service of the king of the Libyans. Thucydides mentions the Tyrsenes, sea pirates who were said to have occupied the islands of Lemnos and Lesbos. (Ref. *Etruscan Italy*. Contributors: James Hogarth - transltr., Henry Harrel-Courtes - author. Publisher: Orion Press. Place of Publication: New York. Publication Year: 1964.)

Eya (Eon, Oium et al.) – a former island, and with time a cape (the Taman peninsula) to the Black Sea prior to the Cimmerian Bosphorus (Kerch strait). Its name stems from the composition of the names Med*ea* and Kirk*ei* – sorceresses from Pelasgian-Greek poems of the journeys of the Argonauts and Odysseus; Eya was, thus, the final location of their aspirations.

Fatianov Culture* – one of two variants of the Global Amphora Culture in the Moscow area (the other being the Balanov Culture). It was located in the upper valley of the Volga, east of Moscow, and the Balanov Culture in the upper valley of the Volga south-east of the Fatianov. The Global Amphora Culture is contiguous with the Battle Axe Culture. (Ref. *Bronze Age in the USSR,* lecture by Professor Alexeev, 29 July 1991. www.drummingnet.com/alekseev/Lecture11.doc).

Fedorivka – a village in the Karlivka district of the Poltava region, known for its excavation of an *Aryan kurhan*-sanctuary with an outstanding stone idol from the early 2nd millennium BCE.

Feosta* – equated with Svaroh. An interesting passage about him is found in the Hypatian Codex, a 15th century compilation of several much older documents from the Ipatiev Monastery in Russia. The complete passage, reconstructed from several manuscripts, translates as follows: *(Then) began his reign, Feosta (Hephaestus), whom the Egyptians called Svarog... during his rule, from the heavens fell the smith's prongs and weapons were forged for the first time; before that, (people) fought with clubs and stones. Feosta also commanded the women that they should have only a single husband... and that is why Egyptians called him Svarog... After him ruled his son, his name was the Sun, and they called him Dažbog... Sun king, son of Svarog, this is Dažbog.*

Fribritz – a city in southern Austria. Known from the excavation of a "rotunda" (maidan) from the 5th – 4th millennium BCE, that contained sacrificed men and women.

Gandkharva – a character of the *Rigveda*; the later Vedas also mention Gandkharva. He corresponds to the Centaur and centaurs of Greek mythology, as well as to the Divine rider of *The Veles Book*, hero ancestor from Savur-grave, to Cossack Mamai, pilgrim knight and others. An image near the central altar of Stone Grave, corresponding finds of "horsehead sceptres" and the remains of sacrificial rider behind Chaush kurhan, as well as Indo-Aryan texts and customs, permit reconstruction of the image of ancient Gandkharva as the Saviour of the Aryans.

Garman – (pronounced 'Harman', in Ukraine) in the Chongar peninsula of the Sivash gulf of the Azov Sea, near the village of Chongar in the Heinichesk district of the Kherson region. It is one of the largest kurhans in the world: 0.5 km long. It was excavated in 1990. The upper filling personified the unique mythology of the Aratto-Aryan Day of Brahma involving the Almighty-Serpent Shesha and the Creator-God Vishnu.

Garuda* – a large mythical bird, the mount of Lord Vishnu.

Gatumdug – the Great mother and "Sacred cow" of Sumer [mother goddess in the city-state of Lagash], whose name is present at Stone Grave amongst the earliest inscriptions of the 12th – 7th millennium BCE.

Gelon – (Holun or Kolun - 'Assembly', 'Vault' of *The Veles Book*), a city-state near the present village of Belsk on the border of the Poltava and Kharkiv regions of Ukraine.

It reveals the lineage from Homeric Ilium (Troy), which perished in the 13th or 11th century BCE. The area of this greatest settlement of ancient European times amounts to the total area of Babylon, Carthage and Rome.

Gerros – the 'Crane' River in Scythia. Researchers identify it with the Konka or, more probably, with the Molochna.

Gilgamesh* – 5th ruler of Uruk, c. 2700 BCE, according to the Sumerian king list. The best known of all ancient Mesopotamian heroes. Numerous tales in the Akkadian language were told about Gilgamesh and the whole collection has been described as an odyssey–the odyssey of a king who did not want to die. The fullest extant text of the Gilgamesh epic is on 12 incomplete Akkadian-language tablets found at Nineveh in the library of the Assyrian king Ashurbanipal (reigned 668-627 BCE). (Encyclopaedia Britannica).

Glagolitic alphabet* – also known as *Glagolitsa,* is the oldest known Slavic alphabet. The name was not coined until many centuries after its creation, and comes from the Old Slavic *glagolъ* "utterance". Since *glagolati* also means *to speak*, the *glagolitsa* poetically referred to "the marks that speak". It has been conjectured that the name *glagolitsa* developed in Croatia around the 14th century and was derived from the word *glagolity*, applied to adherents of the liturgy in [Old] Slavonic. (Bernard Comrie and Greville G. Corbett, *The Slavic Languages,* Taylor & Francis, 2002, p. 29). Although popularly attributed to Saints Cyril and Methodius and the introduction of Christianity, the origin of the Glagolitic alphabet is obscure. (Florin Curta & Paul Stephenson, *Southeastern Europe in the Middle Ages, 500-1250,* Cambridge University Press, 2006, p 214: "At the emperor's request, Constantine and his brother started the translation of religious texts into Old Church Slavonic, a literary language most likely based on the Macedonian dialect allegedly used in the hinterland of their home-town, Thessalonica. Constantine devised a new alphabet, later called Glagolitic, to render the sounds of the new language and to adapt it to the new conditions in Moravia. The two brothers seem to have initially translated only texts for religious instruction, such as the excerpts from the Gospels that were used in liturgy").

Goths – Germanic tribes in the southern Baltic, captured the Northern Black Sea area in the 3rd – 4th century. After a crushing defeat in 375 CE from the Rusy and Huns some turned back, some went into Western Europe and dispersed, some resettled in Taurida. The Goths principality remained there until the Tatar-Mongol invasion of the 13th century.

Hacilar* – a site of early human settlement in south-western Turkey, dated from 7040 BCE. Archaeological remains indicate that the site was abandoned and reoccupied on more than one occasion in its history. What remained of Hacilar became a mound on the plain that was excavated for the first time, from 1957 - 1960, by James Mellaart. (Mellaart, James. «Hacilar: A Neolithic Village Site» – Scientific American, August 1961, p. 86).

Hades* – the ancient Greek god of the underworld whose name came to designate the abode of the dead.

Hamangia* – a Middle Neolithic culture in Dobruja (Romania and Bulgaria) on the right bank of the Danube in Muntenia and in the south. It is named after the site of Baia-Hamangia. (Dumitru Berciu, *Cultura Hamangia. Bucureşti: Editura Academiei Republicii Socialiste România* (1966).).

Heathens/Pagans – the 'communal believers' [i.e. in a single God], according to a modern translation from the old Rus language. Hostility to their ecclesiastical-state ideology is attributed to its claim of being international. Prior to the ecclesiastical reform of Patriarch Nikon in the 17th century, they were called Pravoslavne [i.e. Orthodox] – i.e. those 'carolling Prava', [i.e singing carols to divine Heaven.] They worshipped a single God in his various manifestations (each deity known by various names which are still inherent to Ukrainians, Russians and other Slavic nations. These [polynomials] may be compared with the Elohim-'Gods' of the supposedly monotheistic Bible, commemorating Eloi, Yahweh, the [Heavenly] Host, as well as

Christ). The manifestations of their single god included the Tri-unity (which is comparable to the Biblical Trinity) and the Saviour (rider in *The Veles Book*). The pagans had no religion since their beliefs originated with the dawn of science, philosophy, art, politics and cultures in general. This life-giving syncretism also persisted in Buddhism and was dangerously polarised by the beginning of the first world religion – Judaism.

Hellas – the primary name of Greece derived from legendary Hellen, son of Deucalion and the brother of Il/Ilus, founder of Ilium. The significance of the name is linked with the 'Sun'.

Hellespont – the 'Sun path'. The ancient name of the Dardanelles Strait; also sometimes called *Borisfen* (Borusphen, Dnipro).

Herakles – the son of Zeus and a mortal woman. '(Goddess) Hera', illustrious hero-'saviour'. Hera ('Год' ='God' means 'Year'), the treacherous wife of Zeus, forced Herakles to carry out 12 labours which – not by coincidence – accord with the number of months of the year. The journey of the Hellenic hero is like that of the Aryan rider Gandkharva who also had to journey over the course of a year and then perished by a frightful death (just like Herakles). Herakles, in his labours, falls into the cave of the Serpent-legged goddess Borysphen and became the progenitor of Agathirs, Gelon and Scyth. There is evidence that draws together Herakles with Dionysus and Krishna... The hero reflects the earliest Saviour of pre-state times during the supremacy of the hunting economy – not yet knowing the bow but relying on the club (i.e. in the late Palaeolithic epoch). There is even a possible link between Pre-Grecian Herakles and an image at Stone Grave (where the greatest tradition of Palaeolithic culture in Europe was esteemed; located in the creek of the River Gera (Molochna). This image of the Hero could have entered embryonic Greek ethnoculture from this site.

Hermanaric/Ermanaric* – (died between 370 and 376), king of the Ostrogoths, the ruler of a vast empire in Ukraine. Although the exact limits of his territory are obscure, it evidently stretched south of the Pripyat Marshes between the Don and Dniester rivers. The only certain facts about Ermanaric are that his great deeds caused him to be feared by neighbouring peoples and that he committed suicide because he despaired of successfully resisting the Huns, who invaded his territories in the 370s. His kingdom was thereupon destroyed and his people became subject to the Huns for about 75 years. (Encyclopaedia Britannica).

Herodotus (484-425? BCE) – an Ancient Greek historian, the first to employ a systematic approach to the writing of historical narrative in *The Histories,* for which he was exalted by the ancient Greeks as, "'Father of History". He left a unique description of Scythia, prioritising the role of Cimmerians and downgrading political ideas that had previously favoured Greece and the Bosphorus empire.

Hesperia* – The Hesperides had the task of tending Hera's orchard, where golden apples grew that gave immortality. They are variously listed as the daughters of Atlas by Hesperis (Diodorus Siculus, *The Library of History* 4.26.2), or by Zeus and other deities.

Hesychius* – of Alexandria, a grammarian who flourished probably in the 5th century CE. He compiled the richest lexicon of unusual and obscure Greek words that has survived (in a single 15th century manuscript). The work, titled "Alphabetical Collection of All Words", includes approximately 51,000 entries, a copious list of peculiar words, forms and phrases, with an explanation of their meaning, and often with a reference to the author who used them or to the district of Greece where they were current. Hence, the book is of great value to the student of the Greek dialects, while in the restoration of the text of the classical authors generally, and particularly of such writers as Aeschylus and Theocritus, who used many unusual words, its value can hardly be exaggerated. Hesychius is important, not only for Greek philology but also for studying lost languages and obscure dialects (such as Thracian and the ancient Macedonian language) and in reconstructing Proto-Indo-European. Hesychius' explanations of many epithets and phrases also reveal many important facts about the religion and social life of the ancients. (Refs. Harry Thurston Peck, *Harpers Dictionary of Classical Antiquities* 1898. Eleanor Dickey, *Ancient Greek Scholarship* (Oxford 2007) 88-90).

High Grave – near the village of Starosillia of Velyko Oleksandrovka district, excavated in 1972; 14 additional barrows in the region, within a radius of about 2 km, were excavated there in 1995. In conjunction with the materials of the Velyko Oleksandrivsk kurgan, the primary history of Aryans and the *Rigveda* of mid-4th – 2nd millennium BCE is clearly traced.

Hiranyagarbha* – literally the 'golden womb' or 'golden egg', (poetically rendered 'universal germ') is the source of the creation of the Universe or the manifested cosmos in Indian philosophy. In classical Puranic Hinduism, Hiranyagarbha is a name of Brahma, so called because he was born from a golden egg (Manusmrti 1.9), while the Mahabharata calls it the Manifest. (The Mahabharata, Book 12: Santi Parva. Kisari Mohan Ganguli, tr. Section CCCIII The Mahabharata).

Historical materialism* – a methodological approach to the study of society, economics, and history, first articulated by Karl Marx (1818-1883). Historical materialism looks for the causes of developments and changes in human society through the economic means used to produce the necessities of life. The non-economic features of a society (e.g. social classes, political structures, ideologies) are seen as being a product of its economic activity.

*"In the Soviet view, the most important object of study in history is the 'productive forces' or 'means of production', for it is upon these that 'social relationships' and thus the 'social system' depend. There are believed to be five systems which followed one another consecutively: the primitive social, slave-holding, feudal, capitalist, and socialist systems. The 'periodisation' of known history into these five stages is one of the main preoccupations of Soviet historians. The first and last systems are classless while classes are the main feature of the middle classifications. .... With regard to the first three stages, the words prehistoric, ancient and medieval can be substituted for the Marxist primitive, slave-holding, and feudal without much loss of meaning. .... The view that primitive society is classless has given archaeology a special interest in Soviet eyes. .... Engels using Marx's notes and making considerable additions of his own, published in 1884 *The Origin of the Family, Private Property, and the State.* From this book a system of periodisation was worked out in the 1930s. There are five stages: the primitive herd (lower palaeolithic), primitive community (upper palaeolithic), matriarchal clan society (neolithic), patriarchal clan society (Bronze Age), and the period of the break-up of tribal society (Iron Age)". (M. W. Thompson, translator's Foreword in *Archaeology in the USSR* by A. L. Mongait (1961), Penguin books, originally published in 1955 as *Arkheologiya v SSSR*).

Holodomor* – (Ukrainian: Голодомор; translation: murder by hunger) was a famine in the Ukrainian SSR from 1932-1933, during which millions of inhabitants died of starvation in a peacetime catastrophe unprecedented in the history of Ukraine. Estimates on the total number of casualties within Soviet Ukraine range mostly from 2.6 million to 10 million. Primarily as a result of economic and trade policies instituted by Joseph Stalin, millions of Ukrainians starved to death over the course of a single year. (Encyclopedia of Ukraine). The joint statement at the United Nations in 2003 has defined the famine as the result of cruel actions and policies of the totalitarian regime which caused the deaths of millions of Ukrainians, Russians, Kazakhs and other nationalities in the USSR (Joint Statement on the Great Famine of 1932-1933 in Ukraine (Holodomor) on Monday, November 10, 2003 at the United Nations in New York). As of March 2008, Ukraine and nineteen other governments have recognised the actions of the Soviet government as an act of genocide. On 23 October 2008 the European Parliament adopted a resolution that recognised the Holodomor as a crime against humanity. (European Parliament Press Release, 23-10-2008).

Homer – (Pelasgian Omir, 9th? century BCE) legendary author of the Trojan War epics, the

Iliad and *Odyssey*. Authorship of the *Geranomachia*, a poem about the mythical battle of cranes and pygmies, is also ascribed to him. The poem was initially considered a parody until sources of the Indo-Aryan *Mahabharata* were traced in *Geranomachia*, i.e. generic sources of Indo-European epics.

Huns – nomadic tribes of uncertain ethnocultural provenance. There is ambiguity attributed to the consonance of ethnonyms of several little-known tribes of Europe and Asia between the 1st millennium BCE to the 1st millennium CE. Thus, *The Veles Book* refers to Ehuns and other tribes of the Punjab, the lower reaches of the Volga and elsewhere. The Huns that appeared in the Northern Black Sea area in 375 CE, were, possibly, Mongolians.

Hurrians* (also known as **Khurrites**) – people of the Ancient Near East, who lived in northern Mesopotamia and areas to the immediate east and west, beginning approximately 2500 BC. The largest and most influential Hurrian nation was the kingdom of Mitanni. (Ref. Cambridge Encyclopaedia).

Hyksos – nomadic tribes of uncertain origin, governing Egypt between the end of the 18th – 16th centuries BCE where they initiated the pharaonic Khyan/Khian dynasty and also introduced the horse chariot. These and other signs point to the carriers of the Ingul archaeologic culture, successors of Oriana.

Hypatian Codex* – a compendium of three chronicles: the Primary Chronicle, the Kyiv Chronicle, and the Galician-Volhynian Chronicle. It is the most important source of historical data for southern Rus'. (Dimnik, Martin, 1994, *The Dynasty of Chernihiv 1054-1146*. Pontifical Institute of Mediaeval Studies. p. xii. ISBN 0888441169). The codex was rediscovered in 1617, in what is today Ukraine, and was then copied by monks in Kyiv in 1621. The codex is the second oldest surviving manuscript of the Primary Chronicle, after the Laurentian Codex. The Hypatian manuscript dates back to c.1425, (Velychenko, Stephen (1992). *National History as Cultural Process: A Survey of the Interpretations of Ukraine's Past in Polish, Russian, and Ukrainian Historical Writing from the Earliest Times to 1914* (illustrated ed.). CIUS Press. p. 142. ISBN 0920862756). It incorporates much precious information from the lost 12th-century Kyivan and 13th-century Galician chronicles. The codex was possibly compiled at the end of the 13th century. The Hypatian Codex was re-discovered again in the 18th century at the Hypatian Monastery of Kostroma by the Russian historian Nikolay Karamzin. Since 1810, the codex has been preserved in the Russian National Library, St Petersburg.

Hyperborea – the 'Extreme north' country, ancestral homeland of Pelasg, Atlant, Apollo, Achilles and other deities and heroes of Hellas. Corresponding Pelasgian and Greek myths indicate its location on the Black Sea coast. Later, ancient authors pushed the borders of legendary Hyperborea even to the Arctic but in doing so over-looked references to the extraordinary fertility of its lands and the happy prosperity of its agricultural population. In the opinion of Yu. Shilov, the location of Hyperborea coincided with the Donets Ridge.

Iasion – son of Zeus and brother of Dardanus at the time when Atlantis disappeared; beloved of Demeter, the goddess of agriculture, 'mother of gods'. He corresponds to the Slavic Iasi, Yasen and other similar gods. The name of Iasion is also linked to the leader of the Argonauts – Jason.

Ida – the Aryan, Pelasgian and Greek goddess of sacrifices and mountains. She is a possible forerunner of Artemis.

Ilium – a poetic name for the city of Ilion/Ilios located on the coast of the Dardanelles Strait, Asia Minor; principally known from Homer's epic *Iliad,* where the city was called Troy. It was allegedly founded by the ancestors of Ilus or Tros, whose father and grandfather (Deucalion and Dardan) were the contemporaries at the time of the World Flood. After Troy was destroyed by the Greeks, a new capital called Ilium was founded on the site in the reign of the Roman Emperor Augustus. Analysis of the *Iliad* and archaeological excavations at the end of the 19th century allowed H. Schliemann to identify Troy with remains under the hill at Hissarlik (Turkey). However, modern researchers find no definite correspondences between that epic and the material remnants in any of the 9 city ruins dated between 2920-500 BCE at this hill. The most appropriate description from the *Iliad* fits Troy-VI (1700-1250 BCE), which perished as a result of an earthquake, and the following Troy-VII (1250-1020 BCE) which was twice captured by enemies. The latter circumstance coincides with Greek legends which describe the destruction of the city in the first instance by Herakles, and then under the rule of Priam (son of Laomedon, who was slain by Herakles). In that case it is necessary to date the Trojan War to 1030-1020 BCE.

Ilmarinen* – the Eternal Hammerer, blacksmith and inventor in the Kalevala, is an archetypal artificer from Finnish mythology. Immortal, he is capable of creating practically anything, but is portrayed as unlucky in love. He is described as working the known metals of the time, including brass, copper, iron, gold and silver. The great works of Ilmarinen include the crafting of the dome of the sky and the forging of the Sampo. (Lönnrot, Elias (1999) *The Kalevala.* Bosley, Keith, translator. Oxford World's Classics. Oxford: Oxford University Press).

Ima(-ir) – First-man of the Indo-European people and of the *Veda Slovena*. The forerunner of Yama – God of the dead in the *Rigveda* and in *The Veles Book*.

Imdugud* – also known as **Zu**, and **Anzu**, in Persian and Sumerian, (from *An* "heaven" and *Zu* "to know", in the Sumerian language) a lesser divinity of Akkadian mythology, and the son of the bird goddess Siris. He is also said to be conceived by the pure waters of the Apsu-gods and the wide Earth. (*Greek Myths and Mesopotamia: Parallels and Influence in the Homeric Hymns and Hesiod,* by Charles Penglase, 1994, Pub. Routledge.).

Inanna – in Sumerian, Arattan and similar mythologies, she was the 'Dominion of Heaven', and embodiment of the planet Venus. At Stone Grave she appears from the beginning of the chronicle (12th – 7th millennium BCE).

Indo-European language community (Aryan nations, Indo-Europeans and others) – the provisional scientific name of the tentative pre-nation (or, vice versa, the union of peoples) which formed in the Circum-Pontic zone in 7th – 4th millennium BCE and eventually settled Europe, India and all continents. The basis and foundation of the Indo-European community, and even civilisation common to all mankind, was the world's earliest state of Aratta whose traditions were inherited more than anywhere else by Ukraine and India.

Indra – the main protagonist in the mythology of the *Rigveda*: victor over the serpent Vritra and deliverer of Vala. Behind this mythology stand the archetypes of conception, where Vala and Vritra represent the egg and sperm, and Indra embodies fertilisation (according to F. B. Ya. Kuiper, and findings at Tsehelnia and Kormylytsia).

Ingul archaeological culture* – according to S. Pustovalov, this was the highest tier of the 'Catacomb ethno-social' group and controlled the other two tiers of that complex, viz. the East Catacomb and Yamna groups [Ref. Pustovalov, S., 1994, Economy and Social Organisation of Northern Pontic Steppe - Forest- Steppe Pastoral Populations: 2750-2000 BC (Catacomb Culture), Baltic-Pontic Studies 2, 86-134]. In Pustovalov's opinion, the Ingul society owed its dominant position to the control and mining of diabase deposits (on the Inhulets River) [gold ore has been found in diabase deposits e.g. in modern day China, which raises the possibility that this may have been a contributory reason for such mining] and ochre (in the vicinity of the town of Krivyi Roh), and the redistribution of these goods. The argument in support of this latter theory is the presence of the two most important shrines, the temples at Molochna and Kamiennaya Mogila, in the territory controlled by the western group. Pustovalov is eager to assign to the temples the role of community-wide ceremonial centres (Ref. Katarzyna Slusarka (2006) "Funeral rites of the Catacomb community: 2800-1900 BC. Ritual, Thanatology and Geographic origins", Baltic-Pontic Studies, Vol. 13).

Inhul & **Inhulets** – Ukrainian rivers flowing into the right-bank of the lower Dnipro; the outstanding Aryan kurhans of Velyko-Olexandrivsk, Starosillia, Starohorozheno and others are built along its banks. These rivers give their name to the Ingul archaeological culture of the Hyperboreans (Pelasgians, Pre-Hellenes). The names of these rivers derive from the Aryan word 'Khingula' meaning 'red lead' colour, that

results from the iron and other ores of Kirovohrad from where they emerge.
*These rivers are often known as Ingul & Ingulets (from Russian translation).

Ishkur – the possible forerunner of Iasion. Visualised in the form of a mammoth/great bull and over time becoming the Thunder-god of Stone Grave and Sumer.

Isogloss* – a specific type of language border, being the geographical boundary or delineation of a certain linguistic feature (e.g., the pronunciation of a vowel), the meaning of a word, or use of some syntactic feature.

Ivan Kupala Day – The festival of St. John the Baptist (who is called Ivan Kupala in Ukraine) is celebrated in Orthodox countries on the day of summer solstice. The name of this festival combines the words Ivan (the Slavic name of John the Baptist), and "Kupala", a word derived from the Slavic word for bathing. Many rites of this festival are connected with water, fertility and purification. Alternatively, Ivan Kupala in Sanskrit is Yuval Gopala (i.e. young Gopala; Gopala is the second name of Krishna). The 'Hopak', famous Ukrainian folk dance, is derived from Gopala).

Ixion* – in Greek legend, the son of either the god Ares or of Phlegyas, king of the Lapiths in Thessaly. (Encyclopaedia Britannica).

Jason – leader of the crew of the Argo, the seafaring-heroes of Hellas who visited Eya (the modern Taman peninsula) on the eve of the Trojan War.

Jemdet Nasr* Jemdet Nasr is the type site of an Early Bronze Age culture of southern Mesopotamia, the **Jemdet Nasr period** (or **Uruk III period**), which dates to around 3000 BCE. During the Jemdet Nasr period, writing began in southern Mesopotamia. The earliest cylinder seals also came into use in the period. It also represents the urban revolution when the numerous small Mesopotamian settlements developed into major cities. The site of Jemdet Nasr was first explored in 1926 and 1928 by a team of British and American archaeologists headed by Stephen Langdon. The objects recovered were divided between the Ashmolean Museum at Oxford University and the Iraq Museum at Baghdad receiving the epigraphic objects and with most of the pottery ending up at the Field Museum in Chicago". (Matthews, Roger (2002), *Secrets of the dark mound: Jemdet Nasr 1926-1928*, Iraq Archaeological Reports, **6**, Warminster: BSAI, ISBN 0856687359).

Jericho – a city in Palestine, founded in the 9th millennium BCE by the carriers of the Afro-Asian language community (Natufian archaeological culture), considered the earliest city in the world. At the end of the 8th millennium BCE it was captured by carriers of the Eurasian community (Svidertian culture) and became one of the centres of germination for the proto-Indo-European community (Takhuny culture) – the largest of which, in the 7th millennium BCE, became five times larger (by area, 14 hectares) than the city of Jericho near the present Turkish town of Çatal Höyük.

Julius Caesar – the first Roman emperor in the 1st century BCE and author of *Commentaries on the Gallic War*, where he mentioned the Ants and the Veneti tribes (who, perhaps, destroyed his fleet).

Kabiri* – (or **Cabeiri)** were a group of enigmatic chthonic deities centred in the northern Aegean islands. [Peck, Harry Thurston (1898). "Cabeiria". *Harpers Dictionary of Classical Antiquities*] They were thought of as amphibious beings like the Telchines, also skilled in metallurgy.

Kairy — a village in the Hornostaivka district of the Kherson region. Aryan, Cimmerian and Scythian kurhans, and nearby Cimmerian tombs, were investigated there in 1989-1991. In kurhan No. 1-II a unique 18th century BCE complex was revealed, in which the deceased of burials No. 11 and No. 13 embodied the ancient forms of Zeus (Cretan Taleisky) and Apollo (Hyperborean Targelia). A burial in kurhan No. 12-I included a unique complex of figured ditches that personified the basic Vedic myth of the hero Indra's fight with the serpent Vritra for Vala – the embryonic new-year universe. In kurhans No. 2-I, No. 4-I and others, were traced the transformation of this mytho-ritual into the Greco-Scythian legend of marriage of Herakles with the serpent-leg goddess Borysthenes.

Kalach* (also known in Ukraine as **kolach**) — a traditional East Slavic bread, commonly served during various ritual meals. The name originates from the Old Slavonic word 'kolo' meaning "circle" as well as "wheel". In Ukraine, kalaches are a symbol of luck, prosperity, and good bounty, and are traditionally prepared for the Christmas Eve *Svyat Vechir (Holy Supper)* ritual, usually in the form of three round loaves stacked one atop the other with a candle in the middle.

Kamyana Mohyla* – see Stone Grave.

Kar Sevak* – A person who offers free services (i.e. a volunteer) to a religious cause. The name originates from the Sanskrit words *kar* (hand) and *sevak* (helper). (*Image journeys: audio-visual media and cultural change in India.* Sage Publications. 1999. p. 134. ISBN 9780761993254).

Kartvelian* – a language group, also called South Caucasian languages, or Iberian languages, including Georgian, Svan, Mingrelian, and Laz that are spoken south of the main range of the Caucasus. (Encyclopaedia Britannica).

Kashchey – the (Immortal) Tripetovich of the Slavs preserves the tradition of the Greek seedsman Triptolemus – the teacher of agriculture to mortals, having received from Demeter (in Aides) the grains of wheat and a golden chariot drawn by serpents.

Kemi Oba culture – c. 3700-2200 BCE. Named after an Aryan kurhan in Bilohorsk, in Crimea. A study in 1957 by A. A. Shchepinsky and others made it possible to distinguish the Kemi-Oba archaeological culture of brahmans.

*It was a component of the larger Yamna horizon. The economy was based on both stockbreeding and agriculture. It had its own distinctive pottery, which is suggested to be more refined that that of its neighbours. The inhumation practice was to lay the body on its side, with the knees flexed, in pits, stone lined cists or timber-framed graves topped with a kurhan. Of particular interest are carved stone stelae or menhirs that also show up in secondary use in Yamna culture burials. Metal objects were imported from the Maikop culture. Strong links have been suggested with the adjacent/overlapping Lower Mikhaylovka group. The Kemi Oba culture is contemporaneous and partly overlapping with the Catacomb culture. (Ref. J. P. Mallory, "Lower Mikhaylovka group", *Encyclopedia of Indo-European Culture*, Fitzroy Dearborn, 1997).

Kerch – the modern city over the Kerch Strait, on the site of Panticapaeum – the capital city of the Bosphorus Empire; then medieval Korchev The city was founded under the name of Rosia by Cimmerians around 3000 years ago (*The Veles Book*).

Kernosivka – a village in the Novomoskovsk district of the Dnipropetrovsk region. In 1973 L. P. Krylovoy found a most expressive Aryan idol in a nearby kurhan which probably personified Vishnu Prajapati.

Keshava* – In the *Bhagavad Gita* Arjuna uses the name Keshava as an epithet for Krishna a number of times, referring to him as the 'Killer of the Keshi demon'. (Maharishi Mahesh Yogi on the Bhagavad-Gita, a New Translation and Commentary, Chapter 1-6. Penguin Books, 1969, p 148-149 (v 54)). In Ukrainian Keshava is 'koshlaty,' i.e. hairy or shaggy.

Kharakternykes (< Rusenian/Ruthenian Kuretes, military priests) – Cossacks of highest rank preserving the traditional Varnas of the Brahmans and Rajans of Oriana and Dandaria of the Dnipro area.

Khmelnytsky, Bohdan* – (c. 1595-1657) was a hetman (leader) of the Zaporozhian Cossacks who organised a rebellion against the Polish-Lithuanian Commonwealth (now Ukraine). This uprising (1648-1654) resulted in the creation of a Cossack state. In 1654, he concluded the Treaty of Pereyaslav with Muscovy (today Russia), that ultimately led to the transfer of the Ukrainian lands east of the Dnipro River from Polish to Muscovite control. (Encyclopaedia Britannica).

Khortytsia – the largest European river island (26.5 km^2) in the lower reaches of the Dnipro rapids. The primary settlements and sanctuaries of the 5th – 4th millennium BCE were left by the carriers of the Dnipro-Donets and Seredny-Stoh archaeological cultures. Aryan kurhans of the 3rd – 2nd millennium BCE include sanctuary-observatories that reflect the main mytho-rituals of the *Rigveda*. The Krariyska passage ('Neck of Aryan') is mentioned in a 10th century Byzantine description of Khortytsia. In 1930, during the building of the Dniprelstan settlement on the mountain above Khortytsia, the burial of Prince Svyatoslav was found, who had been killed there in 972 in combat with the Pechenegs. Khortytsia is most widely known as the Cossack centre of the Zaporozhian Sich, which existed (with short interruptions) from 1556 until 1775. A mysterious Black Stone, which is locally reputed to have magical power, stands near the islands largest kurhan.

Khwarezm* – (also spelled Khorezm, Chorasmia), an historic region along the Amu Darya (ancient Oxus River) of Turkistan, in the territories of present-day Turkmenistan and Uzbekistan. Khwārezm formed part of the empire of Achaemenid Persia (6th – 4th century BCE). (Encyclopaedia Britannica).

Khyan, Khian or **Khayan*** – was reportedly the fourth Hyksos king of the 15th dynasty of Egypt who ruled approximately c.1610-1580 BCE (Kim SB Ryholt, *The Political Situation in Egypt during the Second Intermediate Period*, CNI Publications, (Museum Tusculanum Press: 1997), p.256).

Kibitka* – This word has two meanings: (1) a tent, like a Yurt, and (2) a covered vehicle, either a snow-sleigh or wheeled gypsy-wagon.

Kifishin, Anatoly Georgievich – the brilliant Sumerologist/linguist who deciphered the earliest written language in the world at Stone Grave, Ukraine, between 1994-2001, as well as the annals and sacred texts,

Kisek – one of the Russian princes who ruled in the Kiseisky mountains (see: Pyatigorsk) from the beginning of the New Era, the descendant of forefather Oriy.

Kish* – (modern **Tell al-Uhaymir**, Iraq), was an ancient city of Sumer, located some 12 km east of Babylon, and 80 km south of Baghdad. It was occupied from the Jemdet Nasr period, gaining prominence as one of the pre-eminent powers in the region during the early dynastic period. The Sumerian king list states that it was the first city to have kings following the Deluge, naming 40 kings of Kish spread over four dynasties. (Hall, John Whitney, ed. (2005) [1988]. "The Ancient Near East". *History of the World: Earliest Times to the Present Day*. John Grayson Kirk. 455 Somerset Avenue, North Dighton, MA 02764, USA: World Publications Group. p.30. ISBN 1572154217).

Kobyla* – in Czech and Slovak languages means a mare (female horse).

Kobzari — Ukrainian singers [who play the kobza, a Ukrainian folk music instrument of the lute family], successors of the Aryan Rishi^ [composers of hymns].

Koleda* (**Koliada, Kolyada)** – in Slavic mythology, Koleda is the most ancient God of the sky. According to *The Veda Slovena*, Koleda was known at least 5000 years ago; every year on December, 25 he was re-born giving rise to a new sun. Gradually Koleda was transformed to Koliada (compare the Greek *kalandai* and the Latin *calendae*). With the adoption of Orthodox Christianity in Ukraine the pagan feast of Koliada was unified with the festival of Christmas which takes place between January 6 and January 19 (see also Canadian Institute of Ukrainian Studies, Encyclopedia of Ukraine). Today, Koleda is the original Slavic word used for Christmas in modern Bulgaria, Macedonia, Serbia and Slovak Republic. In modern Ukrainian language (Koliada) in Russian, Czech, Croatian (Koleda) and Polish (Kolęda), the meaning has shifted from Christmas itself to the tradition of singing carols on Christmas Eve.

Kolo* – The Coles are recorded as one of the earliest races of India, prior to the legendary invasion of young Rama, prince of Oude who spread Brahminism with his conquests and won the hand of King Jannuk's daughter, Seeta, by bending her father's bow. The Coles dwelt in the mountains of Curruckpore in the Rajmahal and Paras-nath range and had no vocation but collecting iron from the soil which occurred abundantly in nodules. (Sir Joseph Dalton Hooker, *Himalayan Journals* pub 1854, Murray, London.)

Kolyada* – See Koleda, above.

Kolyadky* – the custom of house-to-house carol-singing (Koliadka, pl. Kolyadky) at the eve of the New Year. Kolyada, or Koleda, is the original Slavic festival. In modern Ukraine it is called Koliada – a cycle of winter rituals performed between Christmas Eve (6 January) and Epiphany (19th January).

Konka (< Aryan Kanka, 'Crane') – left-bank tributary of the Lower Dnipro whose valley constituted the Velyky Luh ('great meadow') and the Pleteno ('extensive') estuary below Khortytsia Island.

Kormylytsia – one of the ancient Aryan kurhans with the first stone stelas that embodied the main characters of Vedic mythology: the Creator-God Vishnu and the heroic serpent-warrior Indra. It is located at the village of Erystivka near the town of Komsomolsk in the Kremenchuk District of the Poltava Region. It was excavated in 1993.

Korovai* – a traditionally large, round, braided bread used in Ukrainian weddings. Symbolic figures such as birds and suns may adorn the bread, while herbs, nuts, flowers or coins might serve as decoration. In the Volyn region, korovai additionally has two high sticks coated with baked dough cones and decorated with coloured ribbons; note "korovai" could be derived from the word "korova" (i.e. cow), as a symbol of prosperity in ancient time (V. Krasnoholovets).

Koshchuns*, or Koshcheis – of Russian folklore were later interpreted as evil beings by Christians. (V. Krasnoholovets).

Kozarovychi – a village near Kyiv. The remnants of a Late-Trypillian *maidan* of Aratta was excavated there in 1960.

Krashanky* – Easter eggs that have been dyed a uniform colour.

Krishna – the Indian avatar-incarnation of Vishnu. In the *Rigveda* he is only mentioned as the archer Krishanu. His corresponding images exist in Stone Grave and in the grave of kurhan No. 28 near Novosvobodnoi.

Kshatriya* – (or **Kashtriya)** - meaning warrior, is one of the four varnas (social orders) in Hinduism. The earliest Vedic texts listed the Kshatriya (holders of *kshatra*, or authority) as first in rank, then the Brahmans (priests and teachers of law), next the Vaishya (merchant-traders), and finally the Sudra (artisans and labourers). (Encyclopaedia Britannica).

Kudurru* – a stone stela resembling the shape of a cocoon or headless anthropomorphous figure. They appeared in Stone Grave amongst other images and inscriptions of 6000-4000 BCE, after which they were personified in the stelae of Aratto-Aryan kurhans and entered into the culture of Sumer, where they were the most sacred object of Sumerian temples (Shilov). They were also used as a type of stone document, such as their use as boundary stones and as records of land grants to vassals by the Kassites in ancient Mesopotamia between the 16th and 12th centuries BCE. (Bahn, Paul G. (2000). *The Atlas of World Archaeology*. New York: Checkmark Books. p. 78. ISBN 0-8160-4051-6).

Kulla* – Mesopotamian god of builders. He was responsible for the creation of bricks and, as a Babylonian god, for the restoration of temples.

Kul-Oba* – Scythian burial tumulus (kurhan), located near Kerch in eastern Crimea, Ukraine. Kul-Oba was the first Scythian royal barrow to be excavated in modern times. Uncovered in 1830, the stone tomb yielded a wealth of precious artefacts which drew considerable public interest to the Scythian culture. (Ref. Michael Rostovtzeff. *Scythia and the Bosporus*. Leningrad, 1925).

Kupala – the Slavic form of Pelasgian-Greek Apollo, Indo-Aryan Gopala(na) (Krishna), Rusy-Etruscan Kupavon and others. The Ukrainian celebration of Ivan Kupala Day falls on the summer solstice [Ivan Kupala is the same as John the Baptist] .

Kura-Araxes culture* – (or **Early trans-Caucasian culture)** a civilisation that existed from 3400 BCE until about 2000 BCE. (The early Trans-Caucasian culture - I.M. Diakonoff, 1984). The earliest evidence for this culture is found on the Ararat plain; thence it spread to Georgia by 3000 BCE. During the next millennium it proceeded westward to the Erzurum plain, south-west to Cilicia, and to the south-east into an area below the Urmia basin and Lake Van, down to the borders of present day Syria. Altogether, the early Trans-Caucasian culture, at its greatest spread, enveloped a vast area approximately 1000 km by 500 km. The name of the culture is derived from the Kura and Araxes river valleys. Its territory corresponds to parts of modern Armenia, Georgia and the Caucasus. (Encyclopaedic Dictionary of Archaeology - Page 246 by Barbara Ann Kipfer).

Kur-gal – Sumerian 'great mountain' from which the word 'kurhan/kurgan' was probably derived.

Kurhan – (Aratta-Sumerian Kur-gal and Kur-An that respectively mean 'Great Mountain' and 'Sky Mountain', the epithets of the Creator-God *Enlil,* Slavic 'Lel'); the cult construction of a temple, observatory and funeral designation. They were conceived in the Dniester-Dnipro area of Aratta and Arián between the 5th – 4th millennium BCE; it is possible that Stone Grave became their prototype, followed by ziggurats of Sumer and pyramids of Egypt. Kurhans were traditionally selected by Slavs for the spring celebration of Red Hill, the main character of which was *Lel'.*
*The word kurhan (or kurgan in Russian) is of Turkic origin, for a tumulus, a type of burial mound or barrow, heaped over a burial chamber. They were built in the Eneolithic, Bronze, Iron, Antiquity and Middle Ages, with old traditions still extant in Southern Siberia and Central Asia.

Kurukshetra War* – a dynastic struggle between the sibling clans of the Kauravas and the Pandavas at Kurukshetra [Haryana in India. The war forms an essential component of the Hindu epic *Mahabharata* which states that it lasted eighteen days during which vast armies from all over the Indian Subcontinent fought alongside the two rivals. The chapters dealing with the war (chapters six to ten) are considered amongst the oldest in the entire *Mahabharata.* The Kurukshetra War is believed to date variously from 6000 BCE to 800 BCE, based on astronomical and literary information from the *Mahabharata.* (Yogananda, Paramahansa (2007). *God Talks With Arjuna.* Diamond Pocket Books (P) Ltd. p. xxi. ISBN 9788189535018).

Kvasura(-sir) – the legendary ancestor of the Slavs between the 2nd – 1st millennium BCE, a character of *The Veles Book*, the Nordic sagas and found at Retra on metal figurines in the Pagan temple of Radegast in the Slavic town in Rugen.

Kyaxares* — or Cyaxares, (died 585 BCE), king of Media, who reigned from 625 to 585 BCE. According to Herodotus the 5th century BCE Greek historian, Cyaxares renewed the war with the Assyrians after his father, Phraortes, had been slain in battle. While besieging Nineveh, he was attacked and defeated by a great army of Scythians, who then ruled Media (653–625) until their chiefs were slain by Cyaxares at a banquet. It was probably Cyaxares, not his father, as is maintained by Herodotus, who united the tribes of ancient Iran. (Encyclopaedia Britannica).

Kyi, Shchek, Khoryv – legendary brothers, the rulers of tribes and the patriarchs of nations. According to *The Veles Book* – they are the sons of ancestor Oriy with whom they founded the primary Sl(o)avic union of Orianian and Borusian kin [from those who wanted to return to the Dnipro area) from Indian Punjab, where their ancestors had taken part in the migration of Aryans (including Orianians and Borusians). Possibly the Kyi(van) dynasties were begun in the process of this pilgrimage into India, Khwarezm and Persia; their representatives and legends are clearly traced in Armenia and Gothia – not to mention Kyivan Rus.

Kyivan Rus* – First eastern Slavic state. Is first flicker of development began with the Varangian ruler, Oleg. Initially Oleg was the ruler of Novhorod from *c.* 879, he then seized Smolensk and Kyiv (882) where he settled. Extending his rule, Oleg united local Slavic and Finnish tribes, defeated the Khazars, and, in 911, arranged trade agreements with Constantinople. Kyivan Rus peaked in the 10th and 11th centuries under Vladimir I and Yaroslav, becoming eastern Europe's chief political and cultural centre. At Yaroslav's death in 1054, his sons divided the empire into warring factions. The 13th-century Khazakh-Tatar (by other studies, Mongol-Tatar) conquest decisively ended its power. The term "Kyivan Rus'" (*Ки́евская Русь* Kievskaya Rus') was coined in the 19th century in Russian historiography to refer to the period when the capital centre was located in Kyiv (Tolochko, A. P. (1999). *Khimera "Kievskoy Rusi.* Rodina (in Russian) (8): 29–33). In English, the term was introduced in the early 20th century, when it was found in the 1913 English translation of Vasily Klyuchevsky's *A History of Russia*, (vol. 3, pp. 98, 104).

Lad(a) (Pelasgian Rato; Aryan Rita) – female and male forms of that definition of the Zodiac as the 'Revolving Circle', highest embodiment of World order. The wife of Div

(Grandfather Springtime).

Ladon – serpent guardian of apples in the garden of the Hesperides in Atlantis, shot by Herakles.

Lad(t)on(a) *– Hellenic form of Lad(a). Slavic goddess of love and beauty; cognate with Freya, Isis, Venus/Aphrodite etc. Lada is sometimes represented with a wreath of wheat ears braided into her hair, which symbolise her function of fertility deity. Sun symbols, a mark of life-giving power, were sometimes placed on her breasts. As a fertility goddess, Lada had her annual cycles; she resides in the dwelling place of the dead until the vernal equinox. Proof that Lada's reign begins in spring is that *ladenj*, a Slavic name for the month of April is derived from this goddess. At the end of summer, Lada returns to Irij.

Laertes – one of the Argonauts who together, or almost simultaneously, with Herakles visited Atlantis. He was the father of Odysseus, the itinerant hero of the Trojan War.

Lagash* –- one of the most important cities in ancient Sumer, located midway between the Tigris and Euphrates rivers. The ancient name of the mound of Telloh was actually Girsu, while Lagash originally denoted a site south-east of Girsu, later becoming the name of the whole district and also of Girsu itself. The French excavated at Telloh between 1877 and 1933 and uncovered at least 50,000 cuneiform texts that have proved one of the major sources of knowledge of Sumer in the 3rd millennium BCE. (Encyclopaedia Britannica).

Lake Balaton* – a freshwater lake in the Trans-Danubian region of Hungary. It is the largest lake in Central Europe. (Encyclopaedia Britannica). It is often called the "Hungarian Sea".

Laomedon – Trojan King, killed by Herakles on the eve of the Trojan War. *In some accounts, he was a son of Herakles by Omphale Queen of Lydia. Etymological link to Omphalos, world axis.

Lato* – the equivalent of Leto (Greek) and Latona (Latin).

Lel* – the Slavic God of love, marriage and domestic happiness. He was possibly the son of Lada and brother of Po**l**el′ (Linda Ivanits, *Russian Folk Belief*, Armonk: M. E. Sharpe, 1989).

Leleges* – one of the aboriginal peoples of south-west Anatolia, already there when the Indo-European Hellenes emerged. According to Homer (*Iliad* 10.429) the Leleges were a distinct Anatolian tribe but according to the 4th century BCE historian Philippus of Theangela (*Fragmenta Graecorum Historicorum* 741) they also had connections in Messenia, in mainland Greece.

Lendel* – one of the cultures of the Dnipro basin originating from the early stages of the Eneolithic Period (4th century BCE). They represent the mid Trypillia culture (Trypillia, Shkarovka, Kolomyishchyna, Veremia, Hrebni, Myropillia, and others), the Lendel culture (Prypiat basin), the Stohiv culture (Khortytsia, Seredny Stoh, Zolota Balka), the Yamna-Hrebni culture (the Desna basin, Psla, Sula), and others. (Source: Thousand Years of Podniprovya (The Land Along the Dnipro)

Lepenski Vir* – an important Mesolithic archaeological site in Serbia in the central Balkan peninsula. It consists of one large settlement with around ten satellite villages. The evidence suggests the first human presence in the locality around 7000 BC with the culture reaching its peak between 5300 BC and 4800 BC. Numerous piscine sculptures and distinctive [trapezoid concrete] architecture are testimony to a rich social and religious life led by the inhabitants and the high cultural level of these early Europeans. (Dragoslav Srejovic *Europe's First Monumental Sculpture: New Discoveries at Lepenski Vir.* (1972) ISBN 0-500-390-096).

Levka(da) (Greek 'White cliff' at the entrance of the netherworld, Hades) – presently the Black Sea Snake Island near the mouth of the Danube. The abode of the souls of Achilles, Helen and certain other heroes of the Trojan War.
*This is not to be confused with **Lefkada,** an island on the west coast of Greece: postulated that several passages in the Odyssey point to Lefkada as a possible model for Homeric Ithaca.

Lithuania – formerly called Belorussia in the composition of the Grand Duchy of Lithuania in the 14th – 16th centuries which began to “gather the lands of [Kyivan] Rus” after their collapse due to the Tatar-Kazakh invasion in 1240 (by other studies, Tatar-Mongol). The longest maintained pagan ideology in Europe (until 1385-1391 CE).

Little Russia* – The terms Little Russia (*Malorossia*), Little Russian (*malorusskii*), and Little Russians (*malorossy*) were only used officially in the 19th century and at the beginning of the 20th century for Russian-ruled Ukraine and its inhabitants (Encyclopedia of Ukraine).

Lower Mikhaylovka culture* [Ukr. Lower Mykhaylivka] - 3600–3000 BC, a late copper age archaeological culture of the lower Dnieper River immediately underlying remains of the successor Yamna culture site named Mikhaylovka I, noted for its fortifications. It is related to the Kemi Oba culture and seems to have connections to the Maykop [Maikop] culture. (J. P. Mallory, "Lower Mikhaylovka group", *Encyclopedia of Indo-European Culture*, Fitzroy Dearborn, 1997).

Leukomorie – the north-western coast of the Blue Sea (presently the Azov), adjacent to Biloberezhia.

Lynceus* — King of the Scythians. Demeter turned him into a lynx because after Triptolemus had taught him the arts of agriculture, he refused to teach it to his people and then tried to kill Triptolemus.

Maeotae* — (Greek, Maiotai), the collective name for the ancient tribes that lived in the first millennium BCE on the eastern and southeastern coasts of the Sea of Azov and along the middle course of the Kuban River. The name “Maeotae” was mentioned by ancient Greek and Roman authors and in inscriptions of the Bosporan Kingdom. The best attested tribe amongst them was the Sindi. A Maeotian princess, wife of a Sindic king, was called Tirgatao, comparable to Tirgutawiya found on a tablet in Hurrian Alalakh. Karl Eichwald considered them a Hindu colony.

Mahabharata – an epic poem, ultimately established in India at the beginning of the 1st millennium CE; however, its content reaches back to the times of the Dnipro area, original homeland of Aryans, as well as local and Punjabian Aratta 4,000 BCE. In support of this assumption is the common root of the *Mahabharata* and the *Illiad* in the *Geranomachia* - 'Battle of the Cranes and Pygmies’ in the valley of Gera/Konka (Molochna).

Mahadevi* – "Great Goddess" In Hinduism, a term used to denote the Goddess or Devi that is the sum of all other Devis. (*Encountering The Goddess: A Translation of the Devi-Mahatmya and a Study of Its Interpretation* (ISBN 0-7914-0446-3) by Thomas B. Coburn).

Mahayuga* – a Hindu measure of time equalling 4,320,000 sidereal years. (Encyclopaedia Britannica).

Maidan – (Ukrainian ‘maidan’; Indus ‘maidan’; Persian ‘aidan’; Russian, ‘kurgan with “beard”; English ‘henge’; French ‘rotunda’). Maidans were sanctuary-observatories, which arose in the times of Aratta and resembled subsequent kurhans. The latest maidans were built before the Christendom of Kyivan Rus; in the Baltic States and Scandinavia they continued to be built until to the 13th century.

*In modern Ukrainian the name ‘maidan’ means a central square in a city, village, etc. – also a central place of the community.

Maikop – a city in the North Caucasus. In 1897, a nearby kurhan was excavated, dated to 2500-2400 BCE, built by descendants from Northern Syria who were the banished semitic founders of the Akkadian dynasty of Sumer (according to V. A. Safronov and N. A. Nikolaeva). These descendants of Hurrian origin (according to R. M. Munchaev and Yu. A. Shilov) began the Maikop and Starosillia archaeological cultures.

Makhno, Nestor (Ivanovich) (1888-1934) — A communist anarchist of (*Slavic*) orientation, the heroic protector of peasantry in the Civil War (waged by the Communists-Bolsheviks of Zionist sense); the last Ataman [General] of the *Zaporozhian Cossacks* who was the bearer of their living tradition.

Mamai – Cossack Mamai was the successor of the Aryan Deliverer Gandkharva, according to Yu. A. Shilov. Another Mamai was a rebellious General (Prince) of the Golden

Horde of Khan Tokhtamysh. After an unsuccessful attempt to depose the Khan, the crushing defeat on the Kulikov battlefield in 1380 CE and his the murder in Taurida, the son or nephew of the same name Mamai proved to be in the service of the Lithuanian Prince Vytautas, from whom he received the princely title and family name Glinski (for his rescue after an unfortunate battle with Tokhtamysh in 1399 CE in the upper reaches of the River Vorskla). This Mamai-Glinski became the grandfather of the Muscovite Tsar Ivan IV the Terrible; and according to L. N. Gumilev he became the prototype of Cossack Mamai of popular legends and pictures.

Marmara Sea* – Turkish inland sea, connected to the Black Sea and the Aegean Sea via the straits of the Bosphorus and the Dardanelles.

Manu(s) – Pre-human in the mythologies of Aryans and Pelasgians-Trojans; exhibited contrasting qualities to his brother Yama. His earliest image is found in paintings (mid-3rd millennium BCE) of tomb No. 4 from High Grave.

Manusmriti* – (also known as **Mānava-Dharmaśāstra**), is the most important and earliest metrical work of the Dharmaśāstra textual tradition of Hinduism. Generally known in English as the **Laws of Manu**. (Olivelle, Patrick (2005). *Manu's Code of Law: A Critical Edition and Translation of the Mānava-Dharmaśāstra*. O.U.P.

Mara (Marena) – female opposite of Kupala, deadly deity of Slavs and Indo-Aryans.

Mariupol culture* – a transitional culture from the Neolithic to Eneolithic (Copper Age) of the second half of the 5th millennium BCE at the Sea of Azov and neighbouring regions along rivers Dnieper, Don, Orel', Chir; Crimean peninsula, reaching as far as North Caucasus and Kuban Region as well as River Volga. In older works it is referred to as a part of the wider Dnieper-Donetsk culture or called *Mariupol type*. As noted by an expert on Neolithic and Eneolithic Eastern Europe, D. Ya. Telegin: The Mariupol-type cemeteries seem to have had their origins in the late Mesolithic and endured into the Copper Age, a period of more than two thousand years (c. 6500-4000 BCE). They were primarily fisher-hunter-gatherers familiar with livestock through exchange or pastoralism. It was superseded by Sredny Stog culture. (*Neolithic cultures of the Ukraine and adjacent areas and their chronology*, by D. Ya. Telegin; Journal of World Prehistory 1987, Volume 1, Number 3, 307-331).

Marr, N. Ya.* – Director of the Georgian Academy for the History of Material Culture from 1930 to the time of his death in 1934. Before the First World War he had been Professor of Armenian at St. Petersburg. After the Revolution he became a Marxist and grafted Marxism onto his own 'Japhetic' theory of language. Towards the end of his life his linguistic theories became absurd and were finally denounced as non-Marxist by Stalin in 1950. (M. W. Thompson, translator's Foreword in *Archaeology in the USSR* by A. L. Mongait (1961), Penguin books, originally published (in 1955) as *Arkheologiya v SSSR*).

Maruts (Mar-Moria of *The Veles Book*) – the sons of Rudra and companions of Indra; meaning 'Sea' storm, and possibly, 'Dead'.

Marzanna (Morana/Morena)* – Slavic goddess of death and winter.

Maslenytsia* – Shrovetide Festival.

Masliana* – a week-long holiday that takes place during the last week before Lent begins, the traditional period of abstinence that precedes Easter.

Massageteans* – Persian nomadic confederation in antiquity known primarily from the writings of Herodotus (*The Histories*, 1.215). "In their dress and mode of living the Massagetae resemble the Scythians. They fight both on horseback and on foot, neither method is strange to them: they use bows and lances, but their favourite weapon is the battle-axe. Their arms are all of either gold or brass. For their spear-points, arrow-heads and battle-axes, they make use of brass; for head-gear, belts, and girdles, of gold. So too with the caparison of their horses, they give them breastplates of brass, but employ gold about the reins, the bit, and the cheek-plates. They use neither iron nor silver, having none in their country; but they have brass and gold in abundance". (*The Histories*, 1.215).

Matarisvan – 'Pregnant mother(-Earth)', the deceased messenger of Vivasvat, who steals the netherworldly Agni-'Ogon' [fire] and conveys it to heaven – from where devas give it to people. He is the "Aryan Prometheus". The earliest embodiment of Matarisvan, at the end of the 3rd millennium BCE, is found in the Aryan burial No. 5 of kurhan No. 1 near the village Vasylivka in the Novotroitsk district of the Kherson region.

Matir-s(o)va-Slava [Mother-Owl-Glory] – the main female deity of *The Veles Book* and a possible forerunner of Matarisvan. In the myths of Indo-Europeans and Slavs her image bears distinctly alien, zoomorphic characteristics.

Mayaky – a village at the mouth of the Dniester. Known for its maidan and burial ground of Late Trypillian, Usativ archaeological culture. (Oriana, coastal area of Aratta).

Maydanets – village in the Talne District of the Cherkasy region, near to the location of the second largest city of Aratta (about 300 ha), at the end the 4th millennium BCE.
*Site of the Trypillian culture in Ukraine, it had up to 10,000 citizens in total and an area of approximately 250 ha. The settlement was oval in plan 1,5 km long and 1,1 km wide; there were 1575 houses.

Medes* – Medea, daughter of Aeëtes, king of Colchis, wife of Jason. Her son Medeus fled Athens for the Persian plateau and lived amongst the Aryans, who then changed their name to the Medes (Persians) [Herodotus]

Meotida – 'Mother' Sea (presently Azov), 'Kormylytsia' Meotians and other Aryan tribes.

Meskheti* – a former province of southwestern Georgia.

Meslamtea* – 'He who comes out of the Water Temple'; brother of Ninazu 'Water Sprinkler' and Ennugi 'God who Returns Not'; son of Enlil and Ninlil. He and his brothers were engendered to take the place of Enlil in the underworld, after Enlil's punishment for raping Ninlil, young Goddess of Grain. [Merriam-Webster's Enc. of World Religions]

Mesopotamia – the 'Interfluve' region between the Tigris and Euphrates, location of Sumer.

Mezhyrich* – a village in central Ukraine, in the Kanivskyi Raion (district) of the Cherkasy Region, near the point where the Rosava River flows into the Ros'. In 1965, a farmer in the process of expanding his cellar, unearthed the lower jawbone of a mammoth. Further excavations revealed the presence of 4 huts, made up of a total of 149 mammoth bones. These dwellings, dating from 15,000 years ago were determined as being some of the oldest shelters known to have been constructed by pre-historic man. Also found on the site were (1) a map inscribed onto a bone, presumably showing the area around the settlement; (2) remains of a "drum", made of a mammoth skull painted with a pattern of red ochre dots and lines; (3) amber ornaments and fossil shells. (Pidoplichko, I. H. (1998) *Upper Palaeolithic dwellings of mammoth bones in the Ukraine: Kyiv-Kirillovskii, Gontsy, Dobranichevka, Mezin and Mezhirich*, Oxford: J. and E. Hedges. ISBN 0-86054-949-6.)

Mitanni – the earliest state of the Aryans (after Aratto-Arián Oriana), founded in 2800-2600 BCE along with the Hurrians in northern Mesopotamia. The origin of Mitanni can be considered to be represented by a fortress near the village of Mykhaylivka, at the end of the 3rd millennium BCE.

Mithridates VI* — from Old Persian *Mithradatha*, "gift of Mithra"; 134 BC-63 BCE; also known as Mithradates the Great and Eupator Dionysius. He was king of Pontus and Armenia Minor in northern Anatolia (now Turkey) from about 120 - 63 BCE. He is remembered as one of the Roman Republic's most formidable and successful enemies, who engaged three of the prominent generals from the late Roman Republic in the Mithridatic Wars: Lucius Cornelius Sulla, Lucullus and Pompey.

Moesia* — A province of the Roman Empire, in the south-eastern Balkans in what is now Serbia, part of Macedonia, and part of Bulgaria. Its first recorded people were the Moesi, a Thracian tribe. (Encyclopaedia Britannica).

Mohenjo-daro and **Harappa** – Pre-Aryan cities in Punjab (North-west India, *Bharata*), possibly Aratta of the Indo-Aryan *Mahabharata*.
*The archaeological importance of Mohenjo-daro was first recognised in 1922, and subsequent excavations revealed that the mounds contain the remains of what was once the largest city of the Indus civilisation. Because of the city's size – about 3 miles (5 km) in circumference – and the comparative richness of its monuments and

their contents, it has been generally regarded as a capital of an extensive state. Mohenjo-daro was designated a UNESCO World Heritage site in 1980. (Encyclopaedia Britannica).

Mohyla – besides the primary meaning of a grave, it has the purely Ukrainian meaning of a 'kurhan' or kurhan-like hill.

Mokosh* – (or Makosh). A goddess of fertility, water, and women in old Ukrainian mythology. According to folk belief she shears sheep and spins thread. The name itself is derived from the word combination *maty kota* 'mother of the cat,' that is, 'mother of good fortune.' She is related to Hecate and Aphrodite in classical mythology and to Zhyva and Morena in western Slavic mythology. Mokosh is mentioned in the Primary Chronicle among the chief gods, which include Perun, Khors, Dazhboh, and Stryboh. Some scholars believe that Mokosh was Perun's wife. She is depicted with a cornucopia on the Zbruch idol. In the 14th to 16th centuries her cult was transformed into that of Saint Parasceve, and 10 November (28 October os) was assigned as her feast day. (Online Encyclopaedia of Ukraine).

Molochna – the steppe river on the left bank of the lower reaches of the river of the Dnipro, in the flood plain of which stands Stone Grave. Nun-Bird of Aratto-Sumerian times and Ger (-ra, -os) of ancient times.

*The Ukrainian name 'Molochna' translates as 'Milk'. In Hindu cosmology, the 'Ocean of Milk' (*kṣīroda, kṣīradhi* or *Kshira Sagar*) is the fifth from the centre of the seven oceans that surround loka (or directional space) and separate it from aloka (or non-directional space). It surrounds the continent known as Krauncha. (D. Dennis Hudson: The body of God: an emperor's palace for Krishna in eighth-century Kanchipuram, Oxford University Press US, 2008, ISBN 978-0-19-536922-9, pp. 164-168). In Hinduism, the devas, (gods) and asuras, (demons) worked together for a millennium to churn the ocean and release Amrita the nectar of immortal life.

Morana* – the goddess Morana/Morena was one of the major personages associated with Kupala – a Slavic celebration of ancient pagan origin with the solstice marking the end of the summer and the beginning of the harvest (mid-summer). Morana is a Slavic goddess of nature and death.

Mother Prithivi – (Earth Mother, of *The Veles Book*) – Vedic 'Expanse (Earth)' stratum of the Indo-European *Rigveda*.

Multi-Roller ceramic culture/Corded-Ware culture* – the name is connected with Indo-Iranian tribes who traditionally decorated ceramic ware with braided rollers [lengths of rolled clay braided together]. They had settled in the steppe and the forest-steppe zones between the Don and Prut Rivers by the 17th – 16th centuries BCE. (*Preserving the Dnipro River, harmony, history and rehabilitation,* by V. Ya. Shevchuk, G. O. Bilyavsky, V. M. Navrotsky and O. O. Mazurkevich; Mosaic Press, Canada, ISBN 0-88962-827-0). "....S. S. Berezanskaya's conclusions on the ethnic identity of the Timber-grave culture are of great importance. Having taken into account that according to linguists, Persian hydronyms are widespread in the Ukraine [...] and that these hydronyms are of pre-Scythian date (Grantovsky, 1970), she superimposed the map of the hydronyms onto the map of the Timber-grave culture. Their areas appeared to be the same. 'The toponymical data indicate that the Persian element was widespread over the Ukraine' (Berezanskaya 1982: 207)...[...]...in 1984, N.N. Cheredichenko suggested another way of solving the problem of origins of the Timber-grave culture without assuming a change of population." In the Ukraine this is the Multi-roller Ware culture that is connected with the Catacomb culture". [*The Origin of the Indo-Iranians* by Elena Efimovna Kuz'mina; page 355]

Muromets, Ilya – Old-Rusian hero from the village of Muromets in the Kyiv-Chernhiv region; buried in Kyiv-Pechersk Lavra. His other name (Ilya-Thunderer) in Slavic myths arises, perhaps, not from the biblical prophet [Elijah], but from the Pelasgian-Etruscan Iloya. In the same way, Ivan primarily signified the male hypostasis of the World Tree Willow (the Ukrainian White willow – from which is derived Verbio, the companion of Ruthenian-Etruscan Diana). Also the following word-derivation is possible: Ivan -Arattan-Aryan Ivan - Slavic Yunosha ('junior' in English).

Mykhaylivka – village in the Novo-Vorontsovky district of the Kherson Region, just above the Lower Dnipro ferry crossing. The oldest known remains in western Europe of a stone fortress were partially excavated in 1952-1956 by F. Lagodov, O. G. Shaposhnikov et al.

Myrmidons* or **Myrmidones** – a legendary tribe of ancient Greece, brave and skilled warriors as described in Homer's *Iliad* who were commanded by Achilles.

Nabsursar* / **Nabusar** — *The Veles Book*, Board 6-C of Part II, refers to Nabsursar or Nabusar, a major king in the Middle East. He is said to have oppressed the Rusy tribes. This king ruled before the Persians came to power; it was their victory which enabled the Rusy to depart, after long years of servitude, from the Middle East. The Rusy were evidently not on good terms with the Persians, since the scribes of *The Veles Book* mistrusted their intentions. King Nabusar made war against the Prince (or land) of Egypt. From this history we can identify Nabusar as Nebuchadnezzar, king of the Babylonian Empire. He came to the throne in 604 BCE, and ruled until 561 BCE. The Babylonian Empire was subsequently taken over by the Persian and Median armies in 539 BCE. Somewhere near this time, the Rusy had taken advantage of political upheavals in the Empire, and departed hurriedly from the Babylonian Empire to the north. (*The Trans-Caucasian Migration of the Rusi Tribes*, by Victor Kachur, Midwestern Epigraphic Society).

Natufian culture* – a Mesolithic Mediterranean culture, unusual in that it was sedentary, or semi-sedentary, before the introduction of agriculture. There is no evidence for cereals being cultivated although wild cereals were used and animals were hunted. (Moore, Andrew M. T.; Hillman, Gordon C.; Legge, Anthony J. (2000). *Village on the Euphrates: From Foraging to Farming at Abu Hureyra*. Oxford: Oxford University Press. ISBN 019510806X.)

Nava – the otherworldly, underground world of *The Veles Book* and others.
*In Slavic mythology Nava was land of the dead. The word *Nava* is cognate with 'boats' e.g. 'Navy', 'navigate'.[An implied connection with water.]

Navski* – During the Easter season in Ukraine the cult of the dead is observed. The dead are remembered on Maundy Thursday and also during the whole week after Easter (called the 'Week of the Nymphs' [navskyi tyzhden], especially on the first Sunday following Easter Sunday). For the commemoration of the dead (provody) the people gather in the cemetery by the church, bringing with them a dish containing some food and liquor or wine, which they consume, leaving the rest at the graves. (Encyclopedia of Ukraine).

Neman* – A major Eastern European river rising in Belarus and flowing through Lithuania before draining into Baltic Sea. It is the 14th largest river in Europe, the largest in Lithuania and the 3rd largest in Belarus. It is navigable for most of its 900km length.

Nestor* – the Chronicler (c. 1056 - c. 1114) was a monk from the Monastery of the Caves in Kyiv from 1073. His chronicle (also called the *Tale of Bygone Years* and *The Russian Primary Chronicle*), is a medieval Kyivan Rus historical work that gives a detailed account of the early history of the eastern Slavs to the second decade of the 12th century. It was compiled in Kyiv about 1113, based on materials taken from Byzantine chronicles, west and south Slavic literary sources, official documents, and oral sagas. (Encyclopaedia Britannica).

Neuri* – according to Herodotus (*The Histories*) the Neuri were a tribe living north of the Tyras, and the furthest nation beyond the Scythian farmers along the course of the River Hypanis (Southern Bug River), west of the Borysthenes (Dnipro River), roughly the area of modern Belarus and Eastern Poland. Anciently thought of as a race of Scythians, Greeks and Hebrews who accompanied the Budini or 'Shepherd Scythians'.

Ninazu* – 'Lord-Healer'. Agrarian deity linked to vegetation and agriculture, also 'lord who stretches the measuring line over the fields'. Later, a Sumerian deity of the netherworld. This narrative fragment pre-dates a later Sumerian myth involving Ninazu, called 'How grain came to Sumer' - the story relates to events before the dawn of civilisation. Anu issued grain/seed from heaven to Enlil [also god of agriculture, creator of the hoe] who gave the Innuha barley to the kur [the 'great below', or netherworld] and closed the passages so it became inaccessible but Ninazu wished to bring the barley to Sumer and appealed to Utu for help. Enlil confronted Ninazu but the barley eventually reached Sumer. The obvious point of the narrative was a story describing the beginning of agriculture but a second obvious point was that Ninazu was to act behind Enlil's back, changing his decision about the designation of that grain. Since Enlil had closed the passage to the Kur, Ninazu could not have been a netherworld deity at that time. These points suggest the narrative wasn't only about the beginning of agriculture but also about the divine character of Ninazu who has a chthonic aspect - he seems to have been one of the local incarnations of a young dying god. A puzzling passage describes his mother Ereshkigal as a mourning mother - it may hint at that role. Other sources say Enlil and Ninlil are his parents.

Nindara* – warrior god, deity of the lower abyss, also called Uras, Ninurta, Adar, Ninib. He was the nocturnal sun, the sun hidden in the lower world during half his course. One of the Seven Lords in Egypt, Sumer and India, responsible for creation in its earliest stages, dwelt in the Underworld where there was an exact replica of our solar system ['*Meaning of Sumerian Tablets of Destiny*' - Papers in the Attic by Asaru Clan]

Ningursu* – identified with **Ninurta** in Sumerian and Akkadian mythology who was the god of Nippur, with whom he may always have been identical. (Encyclopaedia Britannica).

NKVD* – Soviet secret police agency, a forerunner of the KGB. (Encyclopaedia Britannica).

Noricum – The area between the Upper Danube and the headwaters of the Dravy, populated in ancient times by Slavic-Venedi.
*It included a region of Europe north of what is now Italy, roughly comprising modern central Austria and parts of Bavaria, and originally it was a kingdom controlled by a Celtic confederacy that dominated an earlier Illyrian population. (Encyclopaedia Britannica). Noricum was incorporated into the Roman Empire in 16 BCE.

Nostratic* – a family of indigenous languages proposed by the Danish linguist Holger Pedersen in 1903 to encompass Indo-European, Uralic, Altaic, Afro-Asiatic, and possibly other language families under one broad category. They are based on an earlier, hypothetical ancestral language, called Proto-Nostratic, which would have been spoken at an earlier time than the language families descended from it, in the Epipaleolithic period, close to the end of the last glacial period. (Bomhard, Allan R. (2008). *Reconstructing Proto-Nostratic: Comparative Phonology, Morphology, and Vocabulary*, 2 volumes. Leiden: Brill. ISBN 978-9004168534).

Novhorod/Novgorod* – also called Velikiy Novgorod, city and administrative centre of Novgorod *oblast* (region), north-western Russia, on the Volkhov River. Novgorod is one of the oldest Russian cities, first mentioned in chronicles of 859. (Encyclopaedia Britannica). At its peak the city was one of the largest in Europe with a reported population of 400,000 in 1300 - 1400 AD. (Langer, W. L. (Editor), Encylopedia of World History. (Houghton Mifflin Co., Boston, 1952). In the 16th-17th centuries Novhorod's Slavic inhabitants were gradually killed by Muscovite Tsars and substituted for Muscovite inhabitants, i.e. Finno-Ugric tribes (known today as Russians).

Novoselska/Novosilske – a village in the Reni district of the Odessa Region standing besides the most convenient crossing of the Lower Danube. The basis of the crossing constitutes Cape Bujak, where a settlement, hillfort and burial ground of 5th millennium BCE – 4th century CE has been investigated.

Nun-birdu – This name was found by Kifishin carved in large letters on a boulder on the side of Stone Grave, overlooking the adjacent River Molochna. Whilst Kifishin defines 'nun' as meaning 'Empress' and that 'birdu' means 'steppe', he suggests that together 'Nun-birdu' was "obviously also the ancient name of the river" since in Sumerian legends a river of this name is where Enlil tempted the youthful maiden Ninlil. (Ref. Kifishin, A. G., *Ancient Sanctuary of Stone Grave. The experience of*

Decipherment of the Proto-Sumerian archive of XII-III millennia BCE, Aratta, Kyiv, 2001; 846 pages).

Oceanus – (Arattan-Sumerian *Akian*: A-Ki-An, 'Opposite the Earth and Sky') – the son of the most ancient gods: Uranus-Sky and Gaia-Earth. Later, a divine figure in classical antiquity, believed by the ancient Greeks and Romans to be the divine personification of the sea; an enormous river encircling the world. R.S.P.Beekes suggested a Pre-Greek proto-form *-kay-an-.

Odesa* – the administrative centre of the Odessa Oblast (i.e. province or region) located in southern Ukraine. The city is a major seaport on the Black Sea and it is the fourth largest city in Ukraine.

Odin – Aryan God of German tribes. He arises from the legendary leader the Aces and Vans in the Don region, whom he took into Scandinavia during Cimmerian or Scythian times.

Odoacer* – (435-493), a German warrior and probably a member of the Sciri tribe or Heruli. About 470 he entered Italy with the Sciri; he joined the Roman army and rose to a position of command. After the overthrow of the Western emperor Julius Nepos by the Roman general Orestes (475), Odoacer led his tribesmen in a revolt against Orestes, who had reneged on his promise to give the tribal leaders land in Italy. On Aug. 23, 476, Odoacer was proclaimed king of Italy by his troops. Orestes was captured and executed. The date on which Odoacer assumed power, 476, is traditionally considered to mark the end of the Western Roman Empire. (Encyclopaedia Britannica).

An alternative, more objective account states; (http://uk.wikipedia.org/wiki/Одоакр), Odoacer was a Slavic commander and tsar of the Veneti who was in the service of the Romans. After 476 he became the first Slavic ruler of Italy. He originated from the tribe of Rugii. In 476. Odoacer overthrew the last Western Roman Emperor Romulus Augustulus and declared himself the king. An inscribed plate found in the catacombs of the early Christians in the church of St. Peter in Salzburg says: "AD 477 Odoacer, King of Ruthenians ("Odoacer Rex Rhutenorum") and Gepids, Goths, Ungaris and Herules, rebelled against the church of God; pious Maxim with his 50 disciples, who prayed with him in this hillside cave, were thrown from the cliff for their confession of faith, and the province of Noricum was ravaged by sword and fire". This inscription was engraved on a marble slab laid in the "Monash Mountains" catacombs in the former city of Juvavum - fortress in the province Noricum whose wealth and majestic palaces caused it to be called "Northern Rome" (now Salzburg). (Chronicle Gottfried Winterberski XII. [240. 13-14]). Bohdan Khmelnytsky, Hetman of Ukraine, brought his family just from Odoacer (Dr. Yu. Shilov).

Oenotrius* – in Greek mythology he was youngest of the fifty sons of Lycaon from Arcadia. Together with his brother Peucetius, he migrated to the Italian peninsula, dissatisfied by the division of Peloponnesus amongst the fifty brothers by their father Lycaon. According to the Greek and Roman traditions, this was the first expedition dispatched from Greece to found a colony, long before the Trojan War. He was the eponym of Oenotria, giving his name to the Italian peninsula, especially the Southern Pass (modern Calabria). (Pausanias. *Description of Greece*, Arcadia, 8.3.5).

Ognichanin* / **Огнищáнин** — a Princely adviser of noble blood; permitted to perform the highest rank of service.During those times, consecration by fire was universal e.g. a Vedic animating fire ritual existed that could bring victory in all endeavours.

Oleh* / Oleg – (died c. 912), semi-legendary Viking (Varangian) leader who became prince of Kyiv and is considered to be the founder of the Kyivan Rus state. (All previous rulers were from the varna of priests; he became the first ruler of the varna of Kshatriyas, i.e. the warrior caste). Extending his authority east and west of the Volkhov–Dnipro waterway, he united the local Slavic tribes under his rule and became the undisputed ruler of the Kyivan–Novhorodian Rus.

Olympus – the highest mountain of Greece; the abode of the Hellenic gods.

Oranta* - The Praying Virgin of Eastern Orthodoxy.

Orbin, Mavro* – (also Mavro Orbini, Mauro Orbin, or Mauro Orbini) (mid-16th century -

1614) was a writer, ideologue and historian from the Republic of Dubrovnik. His work *The Realm of the Slavs* influenced Slavic ideology and historiography in the later centuries.

Oriana – the coastal region of Aratta, conventionally referred to as the *"Usativ* archaeological culture of ancient Trypillia". It appeared at the end of the 4th millennium BCE due to the "World Flood" and was under the influence of neighbouring Aryans. It was also known by another name: *Orissa* or *Odissa* (perhaps the ancestral homeland of the kin of Odysseus? – who returning from Troy, sailed along the coast of Oriana-Odissa). With almost the oldest fleet in the world, it took metals and other items from Asia Minor, where the overspill population of Oriana resettled from time to time. Probably one of the most recent and massive migrations took place around 2390 BCE, when after a 60-year break the rebuilt Troy (III, according to L. Townsend) was destroyed by a terrible fire. Migrations of Orianian sailers into Troad is shown by the spread of their specific stelas, figurines, ceramics, etc. Overland migrations from Oriana are traced principally eastward. Evidence of a campaign into India of some Orianians together with some Borusians and other Aryans exists in *The Veles Book*. From there some of the migrants returned to the land of Slavs.

Orissa* – a modern state of India, established in 1936, located on the east coast of India, near the Bay of Bengal. Orissa has a history spanning a period of over 3,000 years which in many ways is atypical from that of the northern plains, and many of the common generalisations that are made about Indian history do not seem to apply to the Oriya region. (http://www.infoofindia.com/orissa/history.htm).

Oriy (also **Ori, Or)** – mouthpiece of the Voice (Veche [= meeting]) of Aryans, forefather of Slavs and the father of Kyi, Shchek, Khoryv at the time of the earliest return of Slavs from India (according to *The Veles Book*).

Oseledets* (Ukrainian: оселедець, "herring") – a traditional Ukrainian Cossack haircut, featuring a lock of hair sprouting from the top or the front of an otherwise closely shaven head. [compare to Ancient Egyptian sidelock]

Ossetians* – "The Ossetians, calling themselves Iristi and their homeland Iryston are the most northerly Persian people. ... They are descended from a division of Sarmatians, the Alans who were pushed out of the Terek River lowlands and the Caucasus foothills by invading Huns in the fourth century A.D." (James Minahan, "One Europe, Many Nations", Published by Greenwood Publishing Group, 2000. p. 518).

Palak, the son of **Skilur** — Kings of the late Scythians. The name of the former is Irano-Scythian, tracing from Indo-Cimmerian or Aryan Dandaka and Slavic Kyi.
*Also known as Palakus and Skilurus.

Palestine – The country between the Mediterranean Sea and Dead Sea by the River Jordan. It was one of the territories of resettlement by Pelasgians (Peleset, Philistines, "people of sea") of late Aratta.

Palladium – a sacred wooden statue [a patron deity] on which the safety of a city depended.

Pannonia* – province of the Roman Empire, corresponding to present-day western Hungary and parts of eastern Austria, as well as portions of several Balkan states, primarily Slovenia, Croatia, and Serbia (Vojvodina). The Pannonians were mainly Illyrians, but there were some Celts in the western part of the province. (Encyclopaedia Britannica).

Paphlagonia* – ancient district of Anatolia adjoining the Black Sea, bounded by Bithynia in the west, Pontus in the east, and Galatia in the south. The Paphlagonians were one of the most ancient peoples of Anatolia. (Encyclopaedia Britannica).

Parashurama* – (Sanskrit: "Rama with the Ax") the sixth of the 10 avatars (incarnations) of the Hindu god Vishnu. The *Mahabharata* ("Epic of the Great Bharata Dynasty") and the Puranas ("Ancient Lore") record that Parashurama was born to the Brahman sage Jamadagni in order to deliver the world from the arrogant oppression of the baron or warrior caste, the Kshatriyas. (Encyclopaedia Britannica).

Pechenegs* or **Patzinaks** – A semi-nomadic, apparently Turkic people who occupied the steppes north of the Black Sea (8th – 12th centuries); by the 10th century they were in control of lands between the Don and lower Danube rivers (having driven out the Hungarians); they thus became a serious menace to Byzantium. (Enc. Britannica).

Pectoral* – jewellery suspended from the neck to lay upon the breast, with perhaps a thematic, iconographic function i.e. worn for more than just adornment.

Pelasgian – the primary name of the Hellenic Greeks from the time of their establishment of the cult of Zeus from Egypt (according to Herodotus: *The Histories* II, 55-56). Descendants of the ancestral Pelazg who was considered a Hyperborean, and the earliest (2800 BCE) embodiment of Zeus is identified in a kurhan near Kairy in the lower reaches of the Dnipro: it is here, perhaps, that Pelazgia originated. This ethnonym is translated into Ancient Greek language as an autonym of 'Leleges' (Ukrainian; Rusian 'cranes'). They were probably called Hellenic (after their autonym) Greeks (in Russian 'greki', which is similar to 'grachi' (Russian) and 'hraky' (Ukrainian) which mean 'rooks' - dark birds; their tribes probably had dark hair and swarthy skin).

Pelasgus* – in Greek mythology he was the eponymous ancestor of the Pelasgians. In his *Description of Greece*, Pausanias mentions the Arcadians who state that Pelasgus (along with his followers) was the first inhabitant of their land. (Pausanias. *Description of Greece*, 8.1.4). Upon becoming king, Pelasgus was responsible for inventing huts, sheep-skin coats, and a diet consisting of acorns. Moreover, the land he ruled was named "Pelasgia". (Pausanias. *Description of Greece*, 8.1.5 & 8.1.6).

Persephone* – in Greek mythology she was the daughter of Zeus and the harvest goddess Demeter, and queen of the underworld; she was abducted by her uncle, Hades, the king of the underworld. (Hesiod, Theogony, line 914).

Perun – God of thunder, warriors and netherworldly Yava.

Petrovka/Petrivka* – the name for the Orthodox festival of St. Peter in Ukrainian folklore.

Phaethon* – In Plato's *Timaeus*, Critias tells the story of Solon's visit to Egypt shortly after Solon was elected archon in 594 B.C. Solon was puzzled by the fact that the Greeks had no history prior to the Trojan War and told the Egyptians that history must begin with the first man (Phoroneus) and woman (Niobe) and, after the Deluge, with Deucalion and Pyrrha. To which the Neith priest identified by Plutarch as Sonchis the Saite said, "in mind you are all young; there is no old opinion handed down among you by ancient tradition, nor any science which is hoary with age. And I will tell you why. There have been, and will be again, many destructions of mankind arising out of many causes; the greatest have been brought about by the agencies of fire and water, and other lesser ones by innumerable other causes. There is a story, which even you have preserved, that once upon a time Phaethon, the son of Helios, having yoked the steeds in his father's chariot, because he was not able to drive them in the path of his father, burnt up all that was upon the earth, and was himself destroyed by a thunderbolt. Now this has the form of a myth, but really signifies a declination of the bodies moving in the heavens around the earth, and a great conflagration of things upon the earth, which recurs after long intervals." In Aristotle's *Meteorology*, Aristotle says, "...the stars...fell from heaven at the time of Phaethon's downfall." Aristotle is saying Phaethon caused a meteor shower. This has led many eminent scientists including Immanuel Velikovsky, to speculate that Phaethon was a comet. (*Worlds in Collision*, (1950), Abacus, London).

Phoebe – daughter of Uranus, sister and spouse of Titan Coeus, mother of Leto, grandmother of Apollo and Artemis. Just like the latter, she was involved in the lunar calendar – which gave way to the solar along with the assertion of the cult of Apollo (adopting, in this regard, the epithet Feb – ('Shining'), from Phoebe).

Photius* – or **Fotios**, also known as **St. Photios the Great** by the Eastern Orthodox Church, was Patriarch of Constantinople from 858 to 867 and from 877 to 886. He is widely regarded as the most powerful and influential Patriarch of Constantinople since John Chrysostom, and as the most important intellectual of his time, "the leading light of the ninth-century renaissance" (Louth 2007, Chapter Seven: "Renaissance of Learning: East and West", p. 159). He was a central figure in both the conversion of the Slavs to Christianity and the Photian schism (Treadgold, Warren T. (1983).

"Review: Patriarch Photios of Constantinople: *Speculum* (Medieval Academy of America) 58 (4): 1100–1102.

Piatigorsk (Ukr. Piatihorsk) – of Kiseisky mountains in Late Romanian times, where Prince Kisek ruled, one of the heroes of *The Veles Book*. The location of important archaeological memorials from the 3rd millennium BCE – 1st millennium CE, amongst which belongs the prominent statue of the Antian Prince Bus. Even now, the people of Adygea 'carol' the Hero and his effigy. These songs (on the "heroism of Baksan illuminating the Ants nation") are given in the manuscript of Sh. B. Nogmov *The history of the Adygeisk nation,* corrected by A. S. Pushkin. The statue of Bus (who is identified by A. I. Asov with the Magian Zlatohor from the Boyan's Anthem, who was crucified with his brother Bozh by the Goths) near the kurhan at the Etoko creek, began to be studied by Russian and German researchers from the mid 18th century. From the middle of the 19th century it was stored in Moscow, in the vaults of the State Historic Museum. There are 8 lines of writing on the statues, where the letters resemble the letters of *The Veles Book,* ending (in the translation by A. I. Asov) with the date: 5875, 31 Luten' (i.e. in modern style: 21 March 368 CE).

Pindar* – an Ancient Greek lyric poet. Of the canonical nine lyric poets of ancient Greece, Pindar is the one whose work is best preserved. Since the end of the 19th century the brilliance of Pindar's poetry began to be more widely appreciated by modern scholars and yet there are still peculiarities in his style that challenge the casual reader and he continues to be a largely unread, even if much admired poet. ('Some Aspects of Pindar's Style', Lawrence Henry Baker, *The Sewanee Review Vol 31 No. 1* January 1923, page 100).

Pokrova* – an important festival of Protection (14 October in the modern calendar), celebrating the Goddess who descended to cover/veil people against the Saracens. (V. Krasnoholovets).

Polians (<Orianian Pals – Roman Spalei) – the dominant tribe of Slavs of the times of Kyivan Rus, which inherited the ruling tradition from the Black Sea (steppe, "field") Aryan ("Indo-Iranian") tribes of Dandaria and Pals.

Polovtsy* – Related to the Pechenegs; they inhabited a shifting area north of the Black Sea known as Cumania along the Volga River. They eventually settled to the west of the Black Sea, influencing the politics of Kyivan Rus', Bulgaria, Serbia, Hungary, Moldavia, Georgia and Wallachia. The *Cuman* and Kipchak tribes joined in political alliance to create a confederacy known as the Cuman-Kipchak confederation. (István Vásáry (2005), *Cumans and Tatars*, Cambridge University Press).

Pomaks* – a Slavic Muslim population group native to some parts of Bulgaria, Turkey, Greece, Republic of Macedonia, Albania and Kosovo. They speak Bulgarian as their native language with some Turkish, Albanian and Greek as a second language. (Encyclopaedia Britannica).

The origin of the Pomaks has been debated (Olga Demetriou, "Prioritising 'ethnicities': The uncertainty of Pomak-ness in the urban Greek Rhodoppe, in Ethnic and Racial Studies, Vol. 27, No. 1, January 2004, pp.106-107) but today they are usually considered descendants of native Bulgarians who converted to Islam during the Ottoman rule of the Balkans. (The Balkans, Minorities and States in Conflict (1993), Minority Rights Publication, by Hugh Poulton).

Pomors* – (**Pomory**). Russian settlers and their descendants on the White Sea coast. In the 10th - 12th centuries, the term *Pomor* originally, meant "a person who lived near sea".

Pompeius Trogus* – 1st century BCE Roman historian whose work, though not completely preserved, is important for Hellenistic studies. Trogus was a Vocontian Gaul from Gallia Narbonensis whose grandfather gained Roman citizenship (and the name Pompeius) from Pompey and whose father was secretary to Julius Caesar. Trogus wrote a zoological work, *De animalibus,* in at least 10 books, which is quoted by the elder Pliny, and a history, *Historiae Philippicae,* ("Philippic Histories") in 44 books, so called because the Macedonian empire, founded by Philip II, is its central theme.

Potebnia, Olexander (1835- 1891)* – his theory of language and consciousness, in the field of comparative linguistics and historical syntax, has been compared to the importance of Darwin's theory of the origin of species.

Pozharna Balka – a tract and village below Poltava; famous for an archaeological excavation in 1953 of Slavic sanctuaries, 700-500 BCE, with a relic of the Kolodia the Deliverer.

Prava – the celestial, divine world of *The Veles Book* and others. Hence – Pravoslavne [Orthodoxy].*In Slavic mythology Prava was the bringer of order.

Pravoslavny* – those who praise Prava, i.e. God. This term was substituted in western Christianity for the term ***orthodox***, which then became associated with the notion of Christianity of eastern rite. (V. Krasnoholovets).

Pripyat River* – (also spelled Pripiat, or Pripets, Ukrainian Pryp'yat), in Ukraine and Belarus, a tributary of the Dnieper [Dnipro] River. It is 480 miles (775 km) long and drains an area of 44,150 square miles (114,300 square km). It rises in north-western Ukraine near the Polish border and flows eastward in Ukraine and then Belarus through a flat, forested, and swampy basin known as the Pripet Marshes to Mazyr; there it turns south-eastward, re-enters Ukraine, and joins the Dnieper in the Kyiv Reservoir. (Encyclopaedia Britannica).

Prithvi* – the Hindu earth and mother goddess. According to one tradition, she is the personification of the Earth, and to another its Mother. As Prithvi Devi, she is one of two wives of Lord Vishnu. As *Prithvi Mata* "Mother Earth" she contrasts with *Dyaus Pita* "father sky". In the *Rigveda*, Earth and Sky are frequently addressed in the dual, probably indicating the idea of two complementary half-shells. She is the wife of Dyaus Pita ('father Dyaus'). She is the mother of Indra and Agni; she is associated with the cow. (*Dictionary of Hindu Lore and Legend* (ISBN 0-500-51088-1) by Anna Dallapiccola, 2002).

Proboscidiform* – ['having a 'trunk']. Having the form or uses of a proboscis; such as, a proboscidiform mouth. Webster's Dictionary

Prometheus – 'Fore-Thinker' (as in foresight;seer) son of Titan Iapetus, brother of Atlant. His cousin Zeus punished him for giving fire to the feeble humans; he was freed by Herakles. He preserves the tradition of the local, pre-Grecian God of the aboriginal population of the Balkans. Grandfather of Ellen * progenitor of the Ellenes/Hellenes (also called "Myrmidones") led by Achilles.['Iliad']

Prussians – Slavified descendants of Estis of the 'East', who arrived in the Baltic lands in the 2nd century BCE where they were fully established by the mid 5th century CE. They later experienced Lithuanian influences and annihilation by the Germans.

Punjab (Pendeb of *The Veles Book*) – "Piatyrichia" (i.e. five rivers) in north-west India According to the *Mahabharata*, it was the location of Aratta.

Purusha –Aryan 'Male-Person'; first man, from [his] sacrificial dismemberment the gods created the universe (according to the *Hymn of Purusha* in the *Rigveda*). In kurhans from the Dnipro, original homeland of Aryans, the image of Purusha is represented by human sacrifice and stelas.

Pushan – 'Magnificent' core of Suria; the goat-like deity of male strength and well-being, conductor from the netherworld. Mythological complexes of Pushan (bones of a goat or ram in pots etc.) are widely represented in Yamna and Catacomb archaeological cultures of Aryan kurhans of the end of the 3rd millennium BCE.

* A Vedic solar deity, the god of meetings and journeys. Also responsible for marriages, feeding cattle and conducting souls to the netherworld.

Pyrgi Tablets* – found in an excavation of a sanctuary in 1964 of ancient Pyrgi on the Tyrrhenian coast of Italy (today the town of Santa Severa), there were three golden leaves that record a dedication made around 500 BC by Thefarie Velianas, king of Caere, to the Phoenician goddess 'Ashtaret'. Pyrgi was the port of the southern Etruscan town of Caere. Two of the tablets are inscribed in the Etruscan language, the third in Phoenician. (The specific dialect has been called "Mediterranean Phoenician" by Philip C. Schmitz, *The Phoenician Text from the Etruscan Sanctuary at Pyrgi*, Journal of the American Oriental Society **115**.4 (October - December 1995), pp. 559-575). These writings are important not only in providing a bilingual text that allows researchers to use knowledge of the Phoenician language to read Etruscan, but they also provide evidence of Phoenician/Punic influence in the Western Mediterranean. The tablets are held at the National Etruscan Museum, Villa Giulia, Rome.

Pysanka* (plural **Pysanky**) – Easter egg. *Pysanka* painting is a widely practiced form of decorative art in Ukraine. The practice originated in the prehistoric Trypillian culture. Ukrainian *pysanky* have a symbolic significance. They symbolise spring, renewed life, and resurrection and have thus become associated with the celebration of Easter. Today *pysanky* are also appreciated as works of art. (Encyclopedia of Ukraine).

Ra – pre-Indo-European name of the Sun which was preserved in the *Rigveda* within the name of the Sacred River Rasa (Dnipro and Ros River, then Volga).

Radegast* (also **Radigost, Redigast, Riedegost** or **Radogost)** – in *Gesta Hammaburgensis Ecclesiae Pontificum* by Adam of Bremen, he is recorded as the deity worshipped in the Lutician city of Retra/Rethra on the isle of Rugen. Likewise, Helmold in his *Chronica Slavorum* wrote of Radegast as a Lutician god. However, Thietmar of Merseburg wrote in his *Chronicon* that the pagan Luticians in their holy city of "Radegast" worshipped many gods, the most important of whom was called *Zuarasic*, identified as either Svarog or Svarožič. According to Adam of Bremen, *Johannes Scotus* [John the Scot, Bishop of Mecklenburg], was sacrificed to that deity on 10 November of 1066, during a Wendish pagan rebellion against Christianity. [The Lutici were part-descendants of the Veleti/Wilzi/Wiltsi tribe]

Radziwiłł Chronicle* — One of the Old Eastern Slavic manuscripts held by the Library of the Russian Academy of Sciences in Saint Petersburg. It is a 15th-century copy of a 13th-century original. Its name is derived from the Radziwiłł Princes of the Grand Duchy of Lithuania. This monumental work reveals the history of Kyivan Rus and its neighbours from the 5th to the early 13th century in pictorial form, representing events described in the manuscript with more than six hundred colour illustrations.

Rahman Great Day* (Rahmanski Velykden) – An ancient pagan celebration. In Ukraine, the celebration of Easter is called Great Day (Velykden), but unlike other festivals, this also has other associated celebrations. Rahman Great Day is dedicated to the mysterious Rahmans who, according to Ukrainian legend were wisdom keepers/ sorcerers of the highest social class. It probably originates from Arattan-Aryan teachings, traced to the Dnipro area, of the 'Day of Brahma', where according to Brahmanic doctrine the universe cyclically dies and is recreated. The essential difference from the conventional Great Day is its specific imitation of the allied celebration of Red Hill. Perhaps because of its pagan overtones, the celebration of Rahman Great Day is less widespread than that of the more conventional Great Day.

Rajania — Aryan Varna of warriors (Kshatriya); its ruling elite.
*Kshatriya – (or Kashtriya**)** - The earliest Vedic texts listed the Kshatriya (holders of *kshatra*, or authority) as first in rank, then the Brahmans (priests and teachers of law), next the Vaishya (merchant-traders), and finally the Sudra (artisans and labourers). (Encyclopaedia Britannica).

Rama* or **Ramachandra** – is the seventh avatar of Vishnu in Hinduism (Ganguly, S. (2003). "The Crisis of Indian Secularism". *Journal of Democracy* **14** (4): 11–25), and a legendary king of Ayodhya in ancient Indian Puranas. One of the many popular figures and deities in Hinduism.

Ramayana – an epic poem; although it ultimately became rooted in India in the second half of the 1st millennium BCE, the information within the text reaches back to the times of the Aryans in their original Dnipro homeland and is connected with Tauridian Dandaka. This assumption is supported in specific correspondences with Ukrainian folk-lore.

Rapids – the intersection with the Dnipro river of the residue of almost the earliest mountain range on Earth. Granite cliffs and island(s) between Kremenchuk and Zaporizhia (of Kichkas).

Red Hill* – An Easter celebration. Each day of the Easter Week has a name and certain traditions are observed. Many of these traditions are a mixture of pagan and Christian beliefs. Red Hill, which takes place on the Sunday after Easter, is the day for welcoming Spring. A straw doll is placed at the top of a hill where men and women meet to sit in a circle, to sing and dance. The day is thought of as a festival for virgins, because this is when matchmaking starts again and when weddings can take place (since weddings are not allowed during Lent). (Ref. http://www.passportmagazine.ru/article/211/).

Retra – the main city and the temple [to Radegast] of the Slavic Ratar tribe (neighbours of the Lutici/Liutyches and Obodrites) who populated the lower reaches of the River Laby (Elbe). In the temple stood the "idols of gods ... each carved with his name. Chief amongst them, who was particularly respected and revered by all *pagans* [i.e. believers in a single, common God and his aspects], was Svarozhich" as recorded at the beginning of the 11th century by the German bishop Titmar. The Emperor formed a Catholic alliance which was responsible for burning Retra in 1067-1068 CE. The priests of the temple gathered and buried the melted metal statues with runic inscriptions, similar to those of *The Veles Book* in shape and contents. After 600 years they were found by a German clergyman, and in 1771 CE were published by another priest A. M. Gottlieb in an illustrated book *Gods who served the ancient Obodrites*.

Rhyton* – a drinking vessel made of clay, metal or horn, in the shape of a horn of an animal. A rhyton was often 'terminated' with decorated sculpture and reliefs.

Rigveda – the earliest of the Indo-Aryan, and perhaps Indo-European, Vedas. Its origins are traced from the 4th millennium BCE in the first Aryan kurhans of Tsehelnia and Kormylytsia, and the primary composition of High Grave around the mid-2nd millennium BCE.

Rishi* – composers of Vedic hymns. However, according to post-Vedic tradition the *rishi* is a "seer" to whom the Vedas were "originally revealed" through states of higher consciousness. The rishis were prominent when Vedic Hinduism took shape, as far back as three thousand years ago. Some of the ancient rishis were in fact women. (Apte, Vaman Shivram (1965), *The Practical Sanskrit-English Dictionary* (Fourth Revised and Enlarged ed.), New Delhi: Motilal Banarsidass, ISBN 81-208-0567-4).

Roerich, Nicholas – also known as **Nikolai Konstantinovich Rerikh** (1874-1947), was a Russian painter, philosopher, scientist, writer, traveller, and public figure. (Russian philosophy: Dictionary / Edited by M. Maslin. / V. V. Sapov. – Moscow, "Respublika", 1995).

Ros' – a right-bank tributary of the Dnipro, the northern border of *Aratta* in its heyday.

Roxolani* – a Sarmatian people. Their first recorded homeland lay between the Don and Dnipro rivers; in the 1st century BCE they migrated towards the Danube, to what is now the Baragan steppes in Romania. The Greco-Roman historian Strabo (late 1st century BCE – early 1st century CE) described them as "wagon-dwellers" (i.e. nomads). (*Geographika,* Book VII). The Roxolani were conquered by the Huns in the mid-4th century.

Rudra – known as the 'Roaring' and 'Ancestral' God of Aryans, (father of the Maruts). *God of the storm, the wind, and the hunt, in the *Rigveda.*

Rurik – The leader of one of the detachments of Varangians who vainly tried to "nestle" in Kyiv (according to *The Veles Book*). According to *The Tale of Bygone Years,* in 862 CE Rurik, along with two brothers ("they took their kins, and all Rus with them"), was invited to rule by the people of Novhorod. However, the people eventually expelled him for outrages, as they had done in the past when they expelled similar detachments of employed "protectors" and usurpers. Nevertheless throughout 870-879 CE, until his death, Rurik again ruled in Novhorod Rus and again from 882 CE. After he treacherously killed Prince Askold in Kyiv, he settled Oleh in Kyiv – governor for Rurik and uncle of Rurik's infant son Ihor, founder of the Rurik dynasty in Kyivan Rus.

Recent studies by Oksenti Onopenko (a Ukrainian linguist) indicate that someone with the name 'Rurik' probably did not exist and 'rurik' was synonymous with 'peasant'. In the *Geographus Bavarus* (an anonymous document, dated to the first third of the 9th century) there is an account titled *Description of cities and lands north of the Danube* in which the land of modern Ukraine is described as having consisted of three parts: Zueriani (occupied the modern regions of Bukovyna, Halychyna and Volyn); Sittychi (occupied the land around Kyiv and especially to the north, up to modern Belarus) and Stadici (modern regions of Poltava, Kharkiv and to Zaporizhia). The word 'Sittychi' can easily be understood from the old German, Swedish, Gothic and Frankish lexeme "sitten" (satt), meaning to be seated or perched. In Latin this lexeme is translated as "rura" and "rus", i.e. field, land, countryside and only in Tacitus and Ovid was it additionally interpreted as a country. Thus, Sittychi (to the north of Kyiv) was settled by peasants and in the time of the *Geographus Bavarus,* when authors were required to write in the Latin language which was internationally recognised among Christians, the author used the Latin term 'ruris' regarding a peasant (from which the English word 'rural' is derived).

Hence, O. Onopenko came to the conclusion that Rurik (the predecessor of Oleh who become the ruler of Kyivian Rus) was a person from peasant kin and that towards the end of 9th century it was a peasant from the north who seized power in Kyiv, and the era of feudalism began. (O. Onopenko, Yu. Shilov, V. Krasnoholovets)

Rurik Dynasty* – the princes of Kyivan Rus and, later, of Muscovy (Moscowia), were descendants of the Varangian Prince Rurik, who had been invited by the people of Novhorod to rule that city (c. 862); the Rurik princes maintained their control over Kyivan Rus and, later, Muscovy, until 1598. (Encyclopaedia Britannica)

Beginning in the 16th century with the reign of Ivan IV (nicknamed 'The Terrible'), the Muscovite (Moscowian) branch of the Rurik dynasty ruled over the Tsardom of Muscovy. The death of Tsar Feodor I, in 1598, ended the rule of the Rurik dynasty in Muscovy. The titles 'Rossia' and 'Russia' were introduced to the Tsardom by Peter I in a special decree in 1721. (V. Krasnoholovets).

Rus – a public state of Slavs, led by the Varna of Kshatryias (warrior caste; Aryan 'rajania' > 'rasia' > rus). So, Rus was the name of the caste which, having subsequently been applied to the whole country and ethnicity, was founded on the totemic veneration of the bull (Indo-European Taurus > tur, Telets; hence Tauris), of the west and veneration of the colour white (according to S. I. Nalyvayko & O. N. Trubachev). Between 1300 BCE-500 CE, *The Veles Book* and other written sources certify the existence of Adriatic Ras of the Rusen-Etruscans (or Ruthenian-Etruscans) and Rosia of Tauris, and also the following countries: Carpathian Rus, Venetian (Baltic) Rus, Taurian Rus, Surozhian Rus (Black Sea), Novhorod Rus, and in the course of time, Kyivan Rus.

Rusalka* – In Slavic mythology a rusalka was a female ghost or nymph-like mermaid. (Canadian Institute of Ukrainian Studies, *Encyclopedia of Ukraine.* Toronto: University of Toronto Press, 1993).

Rusian Primary Chronicle* – "Tale of Bygone Years", also called Chronicle of Nestor of Kyiv, is a medieval Kyivan Rus historical work that gives a detailed account of the early history of the eastern Slavs to the second decade of the 12th century. The chronicle, compiled in Kyiv about 1113, was based on materials taken from Byzantine chronicles, west and south Slavic literary sources, official documents, and oral sagas. The earliest extant manuscript is dated 1377. While the authorship was traditionally ascribed to the monk Nestor, modern scholarship considers the chronicle a composite work. (Encyclopaedia Britannica).

Rusian Sea – The Baltic Gulf of the Neman along Rusy land of late Romanian times. During the times of Byzantium the Black Sea was also called the Rusian Sea.

Ruseni (Ruthenians) – the autonym of the Etruscans who were so-named after migrating from Troad and elsewhere into Italy and developing their territories between Rome and Florence.

Rusy – Rusychi (or Ruses, Rusians) is the autonym of those Slavic groups who particularly venerated the Taurus-Telets/Taurus totem based on the warrior caste (rajania -rasia-Rus). They can be traced to the emergence of Oriana and the period of the Trojan War; the public state appeared near the beginning of the 1st millennium BCE, Kyivan Rus formed during the 5th – 9th century CE.

*The term 'Rusy/Rusian' should not be confused with Russian, the latter only appearing around 1721, when the Moscowian Tsar Peter I issued a decree in which he stated that Moscowia became the Rossiya (Russian) Empire. Prior to that, the native names Rus, Rusia, Ruses, Rusenes belonged to the land and population of the territory of modern Ukraine. Peter I introduced the names Veliko-Rossy (Greater Russia) for his Moscowian realm and Malo-Rossy (Little Russia) for Rus/Ukraine. Peter I wanted to establish Muscovy, as the successor of Kyivan Rus. For this, he bribed the Patriarch of Constantinople who issued the relevant decree. As a consequence of such corrupt practice the Patriarch was impeached shortly afterwards. (V. Krasnoholovets).

Ruthenians/Rusyns/Rusenes – the autonym of the Etruscans who were so-named after migration from Troad into Italia where they developed territories between Rome and Florence.
*The name is a culturally loaded term and has different meanings according to the context in which it is used. Originally the term Rusyn (Rousyn) was an ethnonym applied to eastern Slavic-speaking ethnic groups who inhabited the cultural and ethnic region of Rus', often written through its Latin variant Ruthenia. Then, the terms "Ruthenians" or "Ruthenes" were the Latin terms referring to Slavic Orthodox people (they spoke the Ruthenian language) who lived in the Grand Duchy of Lithuania. They inhabited the area that is now Belarus, Ukraine and a part of Western Russia (the area around Belgorod, Bryansk, Kursk, Rostov, Voronezh, and also partly Smolensk, Velizh and Vyazma). It was also the ethnonym used by the Ukrainian kozaks[/Cossacks] to describe themselves. After the area of White Ruthenia (Belarus) became part of the Russian Empire, the people of the area were often seen as a sub-group of Russians, and they were often named White Russians due to a confusion of the terms "Russia" and "Ruthenia". (Refs. Encyclopaedia Britannica & Catholic Encyclopedia, New York: Robert Appleton Company. 1913.)

Ruyan (Ruegen) – the maritime island near the mouth of the River Oder; throughout the 5th century BCE – 12th century CE it was the sacred centre of the Slavic tribes of the Venedi, Ruges and Pomors.

Sabatynivka culture* – originated at what is now the village of Sabatynivka in central Ukraine, although it is more generally known to Russians as the Sabatinovka culture. It was a Late Bronze Age culture of the north-eastern Black Sea region and has been considered a sub-phase of the contemporary but independent neighbouring Srubna Culture. The Sabatinovka Culture belongs to the cultures of 'Knobbed Ware' pottery and originated in the period after the Catacomb Grave Culture, when different cultural components were fused together. When compared to the Srubna Culture in the north and east, the main difference is the climatic environment with its economic consequences. On the basis of palaeo-botanical investigations of daub and pottery the Sabatinovka Culture has been shown to have had an agricultural economy with the cultivation of wheat, barley and millet. Amongst the animal bones, cattle are dominant, followed by sheep, goats and horses. Fishing is attested by bones and tools. An increasingly dry and cold period in the late 2nd millennium, and a transition to a more mobile way of life with more horse keeping finally led to the decay of the Sabatinovka Culture. (Ref. "Studies of Late Bronze Age Sabatinovka Culture in the lower Dnieper Region and the west coast of the Azov Sea" by Jakov Petrovic Gerškovic, ISBN=978-3-89646-256-5).

Sanskrit – a planned or constructed language, consciously devised by an individual or group of high level priests instead of evolving naturally. It translates as '*constructed, put-together*', a language reserved, like a ritual enclosure, for sacred rites and discourse. [The language of the Vedas. *Arya* was a cultural quality venerated in Sanskrit texts]. In modern linguistics, it's a 'synthetic' language as opposed to an 'analytic' language.

Sarama – celestial dog of Indra, carrying amrita and soma ("dead and living water") to him on the eve of the battle with Vritra, and afterwards finding the stolen cows beyond the River Rasa. There is a possible connection with a dog's skull in one of earliest Aryan burials on the Zaramy bank. An undoubted connection to the Sarama dog in the embodiment of Indra was found in Cimmerian burial 25 in kurhan 12-I near the village of Kairy, Ukraine. It preceded Semargl [a winged dog] in Persian and Slavic mythologies.

Samarran culture – (c. 5500-4800 BCE) identified at the rich site of Tell Sawwan, where evidence of irrigation – including flax – establishes the presence of a prosperous settled culture with a highly organised social structure. The culture is primarily known by its finely-made pottery decorated against dark-fired backgrounds with stylised figures of animals and birds and geometric designs. The Samarran Culture was the precursor to the Mesopotamian culture of the Ubaid period. (Walid Yasin, Excavation at Tell es-Sawwan - the Sixth Season (1969), Sumer, vol. 26, pp. 3-20, 1970).

Sarmatians* – Iron Age Persians in Classical Antiquity, flourishing from about the 5th century BCE to the 4th century CE. (J. Harmatta: "Scythians" in UNESCO Collection of History of Humanity – Volume III: From the Seventh Century BC to the Seventh Century AD. Routledge/UNESCO. 1996. pg. 182). Their territory was known as **Sarmatia** to Greco-Roman ethnographers, corresponding to the western part of greater Scythia (modern Ukraine, Southern Russia, and the eastern Balkans). At their greatest reported extent, around 100 BCE, these tribes ranged from the Vistula River to the mouth of the Danube and eastward to the Volga, bordering the shores of the Black and Caspian seas as well as the Caucasus to the south. (Apollonius (*Argonautica*, iii)). The Sarmatians declined in the 4th century with the incursions connected to the Migration period (Huns, Goths). The Greek name *Sarmatai* sometimes appears as "Sauromatai", which is almost certainly no more than a variant of the same name. Nevertheless, historians often regard these as two separate peoples, while archaeologists habitually use the term 'Sauromatian' to identify the earliest phase of Sarmatian culture (Richard Brzezinski and Mariusz Mielczarek (2002). The Sarmatians 600 BC-AD 450 (Men-At-Arms nr. 373). Oxford: Osprey Publishing, p.6. ISBN 978-1-84176-485-6). The descendants of the Sarmatians became known as the Alans during the Early Middle Ages, and ultimately gave rise to the modern Ossetic ethnic group. (James Minahan, "One Europe, Many Nations", Published by Greenwood Publishing Group, 2000. p. 518).

Saster – an archive of ritual admonishments of Aryan origin which was used by the population of the Greek city-colony Chersonese of Taurida.

Sauvira – a kingdom mentioned in the epic *Mahabharata.*

Saviour – one who removes the contradiction between existence and non-existence. The earliest mythology and cult of the Saviour was formed between the 7th – 3rd millennium BCE, forming the foundation of the state traditions of Aratta created by Indo-Europeans. The Saviour is their foremost characteristic. The most developed cults of Saviours were: Aratto-Slavic Kolodia and Aryan-Indian Gandkharva. Their traditions still exist amongst Slavs (especially Ukrainians), providing them with the ecclesiastical cult of Christ-Saviour.

Savitr – abstracted theonymic agent who maintains the 'vivifying power of the Sun '(Voice/ Voz - proto-Slavic)', solar impeller of, and 'father' of [being actively bound to] Surya, the sun and his opposite, in the sense of the evening and nocturnal, 'netherworld' aspect between setting and rising.

Savur-grave – (Savuriuga <Aryan Suvar-south, the 'Golden Age') - the legendary kurhan over the River Konka, between the villages of Hrihorivka and Yulivka of the Zaporizhia region.

Scholia* – grammatical, critical, or explanatory comments, either original or extracted from pre-existing commentaries, which are inserted on the margin of the manuscript of an ancient author.

Scirii* (also **Sciri**, **Scirians**, **Skirii**, **Skiri** or **Skirians**) – an East Germanic tribe of Eastern Europe, attested in historical works between the 2nd century BCE and 5th century CE. The Scirii are believed to have first lived within the territory of modern Poland. They migrated southwards apparently around 200 BCE (some secondary works give a more precise date of 230 BCE), along with the Bastarnae. The Protogenes Inscription (3rd century BCE) mention the Sciri when they tried unsuccessfully to capture the

Greek city Olbia, north-west of the Black Sea. (Studies in the History and Language of the Sarmatians - János. Harmatta, Acta Universitatis de Attila József Nominatae. Acta antique et archaeologica Tomus XIII. Szeged 1970).

Scythia – the ancestral home of the Scythians to which the Aryan 'wanderers' returned in the 6th century BCE, having left it many generations before, around mid-2nd millennium BCE. Some forms of 'Scyth' can be ascribed to 'Skotychi' (according to *The Veles Book* and others) – descendants of the cattle owners, with totems of the Taurus-bull and Earth-cow.

* According to Herodotus, all the Scythian leaders descended from Scythes, the youngest of three sons born to Herakles by Borysthena, the serpent-legged goddess. *The Veles Book* speaks of Scyth and Slaven as 'sworn brothers'. Scyth is also mentioned in the *Boyan Anthem.*

Scythia Minor* — in the modern territory of Romania and Bulgaria; distinguished by the Greeks from Greater Scythia which extended eastwards from the Danube across the Northern Black Sea steppes to the lower Don basin.

Semiramis* – Greek name for the Assyrian queen **Sammu-ramat,** (9th century BCE), who became a legendary heroine. Sammu-ramat was the mother of the Assyrian king Adad-nirari III (reigned 810-783 BCE). (Encyclopaedia Britannica).

Seredny-Stoh – a rocky islet near Khortytsia, just below the River Dnipro. Known for one of the most ancient Aryan settlements, which gave its name to the Seredny-Stoh archaeological culture.

*Also generally known as Sredny Stog (the conventional Russian-language designation for the Ukrainian village of Seredny Stoh where it was first located). It dates from 4500-3500 BCE. One of the best known sites associated with this culture is Dereivka, located on the right bank of the Omelnik, a tributary of the Dnieper, and is the most impressive site within the Sredny Stog culture complex, being about 2,000 square meters in area. It seems to have had contact with the agricultural Trypillian culture in the west, and was a contemporary of the Khvalynsk culture. It was succeeded by the Yamna culture. Inhumation was in a ground level pit, not yet capped by a tumulus (kurgan). The deceased was placed on his back with the legs flexed. Ochre was used. Phase II also knew corded ware pottery, which it may have originated, and stone battle-axes of the type later associated with expanding Indo-European cultures to the West. Most notably, it has perhaps the earliest evidence of horse domestication (in phase II, ca. 4000-3500 BC) with finds suggestive of cheek-pieces (psalia). (J. P. Mallory, "Sredny Stog Culture", *Encyclopedia of Indo-European Culture*, Fitzroy Dearborn, 1997).

Serpent earthen-walls – immense constructions, which stretch from the Poltava region (but predominantly from the Dnipro right-bank of Trypillia, Kyiv Region) to the Danube, where they are called Trojans or Trojan walls ('Earth Walls' in Moldavian). According to Ukrainian legends – they had been ploughed up by a dragon, which had been harnessed by the Cossack-blacksmiths Kuzma and Demian (names derived from Old-Rusy for smithy and blast furnace, respectively). References to the construction of defensive earth walls exist in the chronicles of Kyivan Rus. The Cimmerian earth walls, mentioned by ancient authors on Taman, near Sudak and Perekop - extend the time when their construction began. Even more ancient are the elongated Aryan kurhans of the mid-2nd millennium BCE in the form of serpents, such as Garman (in Crimea). It is possible the beginning of their construction was Arattan; evidence for this assumption is found near Trypillia, and also Svitlovodsk, where an immense wall and lakes along it were created, according to legend, by the landowner Reva (perhaps by Reva and his son Revan from the Indo-Aryan epic of the *Mahabharata*?).

Sevan, Van – Lakes in the territory of Armenia (Transcaucasia), near which, in the mid-2nd – 1st millennium BCE, the important centres of Aryans were concentrated and, derived from them, the Cimmerians and Vans, whose settled at Asia Minor Troad and Scandinavian Svineld (Sweden).

Shaka Samvat* – the official, civil calendar of India (sometimes called **Saka calendar**). It derives its name from the rulers of Shaka dynasty of India. This calendar came into use in Nepal during the reign of King Mandev (386-428 Shaka Sambat, or 464-506 CE).

Shara – warrior god of the Moon in Sumerian mythology, son and/or lover of Inanna. He was put to death because he had human feet. He was first mentioned among inscriptions of 6th – 4th millennium BCE at Stone Grave. A funereal embodiment with Sumerian inscription on a sepulchral plate was found in a kurhan near Nadezhdino village in the lower reaches of the Molochna river.

Shesha – the Almighty-serpent who was the netherworldly bed of the creator-God Vishnu. He awakes at the end of every Day of Brahma, his breath burning and renewing the Universe. Expressive embodiments are found in the upper (mid-2nd millennium BCE) fillings of kurhan Garman and kurhan No. 6 near Mala [Lesser] Bilozirka.

Shevchenko, Taras (Hryhorovych) (1814-1861) — A talented artist and brilliant poet who absorbed and improved the skilful lyrics of the Ukrainian kobza-singers; a banner of the Ukrainian nation.
*His literary heritage is regarded to be the foundation of modern Ukrainian literature. His influence on Ukrainian culture has been so immense that after Ukraine gained its independence in the wake of the 1991 Soviet Collapse, some Ukrainian cities replaced their statues of Lenin with statues of Taras Shevchenko. (Catherine Wanner, *Burden of Dreams: History and Identity in Post-Soviet Ukraine*. Penn State Press: 1998). One of the main boulevards in Kyiv is named after him, on which stands St. Volodymyr's Cathedral, the National Academic Theatre, the Botanic Garden and many important civic buildings.

Shiva (Siva) – the 'Benefactor' from the Trinity (Trimurthy) of Indian gods, which includes Brahma and Vishnu. Considered the eternal deity of Indian Pre-Aryan origin. However such specific features of Shiva as the trident and Maiden-mountain (mountain of Diva-'god') had been widespread in the Aryan world since the times of Aratta. Undeniable epithets of Shiva were encountered amongst inscriptions of Dandarica (Odessa) of 200-300 BCE, and Si(e)va – son of legendary Bohomyr Progenitor of Slavs – mentioned in *The Veles Book*, and also amongst inscriptions at Retra from the beginning of the 1st millennium BCE. According to the range of attributes (pictorial canons and others), Shiva is allied to Cossack Mamai... The above data agrees with testimonies of *The Veles Book* describing the campaign of Orianians and Borusians along with other Aryans of the Dnipro area into India and their partial return from there.

Shruti (Aryan 'listen') – a complex of three altars, hitherto constructed in India for proclaiming the anthems of the *Rigveda*. The earliest of such complexes is found in the upper layering of High Grave from the period of the partial migration of the Aryans from Ukraine into India.

Shudra – representative of the lowest strata in the social system of the *Aryans*, not included in the three *varna* either because of their failure to pass the initiation or because they were deprived of social rights. Later, as in India, it was fourth (the lowest) in the social strata, "untouchable".

Shu-eden-na Ki-dug – 'Hand/Law of the Blessed Steppeland', autonym of a proto-city near Çatal Höyük.
*A strict translation of each term from Kifishin's Proto-Sumerian/Russian dictionary is "Hand/Law-Steppe-Stone Blessed-place". (Kifishin, A. G., *Ancient Sanctuary of Stone Grave. The experience of the decipherment of the Proto-Sumerian archive of XII-III millennia BCE*, Aratta, Kyiv, 2001; 846 pages.

Shu-Nun – the autonym of Stone Grave, 'Hand/Law of the Empress (a real person)' during Sumerian times, as well as the name of a Sumerian city in the north of Mesopotamia.
* The name 'Shu-Nun' in proto-Sumerian was found by Kifishin to have been carved onto one of the boulders of Stone Grave. He identified the proto-Sumerian word '**su**' ('Шу' [Shu] in Russian) which means 'hand' and 'law', together with '**nun**' which means 'empress'. (Ref. Kifishin, A. G., *Ancient Sanctuary of Stone Grave. The experience of the decipherment of the Proto-Sumerian archive of XII-III millennia*

BCE, Aratta, Kyiv, 2001; 846 pages).

Sich (< barricade) – fortified Cossack settlements, amongst which the most well known is the Zaporozhian Sich on the islands of Lesser and Greater Khortytsia. *Reconstruction of a reduced copy of the Zaporozhian Sich on Khortytsia began in 2004, enclosed by a moat, rampart and timbered palisade with several towers. It was officially opened for visitors in 2009 as the Historical-Cultural Complex "Zaporozhian Sich".

Si(e)va – brother of Rus and son of Bohomyr, the of Progenitor of Slavs (according to *The Veles Book* and statuette of Retra city).

Sikelia* – The Classical Greek name for Sicily.

Sina* – The Sumerian Moon God was Nanna, later known as Sin, or Su'en, in the Akkadian Empire (2334-2154 BCE).

Sind (Indus) – The Indo-Aryan river; the name by which the Dnipro and Don rivers were known during Aryan times.

Sindi* — an ancient people in the Taman Peninsula and the adjacent coast of the Pontus Euxinus (Black Sea), in the district called Sindica, which spread between the modern towns of Temryuk and Novorossiysk (Herodotus. iv. 28; *l. c.*). Strabo describes them as living along the Palus Maeotis, and among the Maeotae, Dandarii, Toreatae, Agri, Arrechi, Tarpetes, Obidiaceni, Sittaceni, Dosci, and Aspurgiani, among others. (Strab. xi. 2. 11). The Great Soviet Encyclopedia classes them as a tribe of the Maeotae. In the 5th century BCE, the Sindi were subjugated by the Bosporan Kingdom. They left multiple tumuli which, when excavated by Soviet archaeologists, revealed that their culture was heavily Hellenized. The Sindi were assimilated by the Sarmatians in the first centuries CE.

Sindic (Indica) – The land in the lower reaches of the River Sind-Dnipro, including the modern Taman peninsula in the Kuban delta. These names were transferred to Aryans in India.

Sintashta-Petrovka culture* – (or **Sintashta-Arkaim culture**), is a Bronze Age archaeological culture of the northern Eurasian steppe, dated to the period 2100-1800 BCE. The earliest chariots known have been found in Sintashta burials, and the culture is considered a strong candidate for the origin of the technology which spread throughout the Old World and played an important role in ancient warfare. Sintashta settlements are also remarkable for the intensity of copper mining and bronze metallurgy carried out there, which is unusual for a steppe culture. (Ref. Anthony, D. W. (2009). "The Sintashta Genesis: The Roles of Climate Change, Warfare, and Long-Distance Trade". In Hanks, B.; Linduff, K.. *Social Complexity in Prehistoric Eurasia: Monuments, Metals, and Mobility*. Cambridge University Press. pp. 47–73).

Sintili* – Sintians lived on Sinteis (old name for Lemnos) and Sintiki province, Greece mainland.

Sivash (Sea) – a shallow bay of the Azov Sea, the Aryan Meotid. It seems the name is related to God Siva.

Sklavini* — the Greek term for the Slav settlements which were initially independent and outside Byzantine control. The Byzantines broadly grouped the numerous Slav tribes living in proximity with the Eastern Roman Empire into two groups: the Sklavenoi and Antes. Apparently, the Sklavenoi group were based along the middle Danube (Western Balkans), whereas the Antes were at the lower Danube, in Scythia Minor. (Hupchick, Dennis P. *The Balkans: From Constantinople to Communism.* Palgrave Macmillan, 2004. ISBN 1403964173).

Skoloty – Slavs of the 16th – 5th centuries BCE, recorded as the earliest ancestors of the Scythians by some ancient authors (e.g. Herodotus).

Skvortsovka – a steppe village in the Kakhovsky district, Kherson region. In 1987, this unique Aryan mound of mid-2nd millennium BCE was excavated, displaying the mythological birth, growth, and ascension of the Creator-God Vishnu.

Slavs; Slaviane, Sloaviane, Sloviane – the autonym of the union of part of the kin of Orianians and Borusians, who were formed in the Indian Punjab before returning to their Dnipro area ancestral home; "Slavs are those that glorify the gods by Vedic words" (according to *The Veles Book*). Upon returning, the active Slavs eventually extended their ethnonym to related local tribes of Orianians, Borusians, and also Skolotians, Cimmerians etc., that composed the ethnoculturnal nucleus of Aratta from its beginning, and became a self-consciously separate nation in 2300-1700 BCE.

Smolovska Grave – a unique Aryan kurhan, excavated in 1983 near the village of Novo-Mykolaivka in the Novo-Troitsk district, Kherson region. It displayed the mytho-ritual struggle of the hero serpent-warrior Indra with Shesha, the demon of drought.

Soma (Persian Khaoma > Ukrainian Khoma, intoxication) – a divine drink (suritsa in *The Veles Book* of Slavs) for the Aryans and Hindus, as well as the god of this drink and the Moon.
*Soma is also astronomical in its sense of nakṣatra - something that perennially binds together the constellations, also a [gravitational] force which creates a cosmic 'bridge' between universal mind and human mind - Soma as a divine drink aids this cosmic communion.

Srubna culture* – (also Timber-grave culture), a Late Bronze Age culture (16th – 9th century BCE). It is a successor to the Yamna culture, the Catacomb culture and the Abashevo culture. It occupied the area along and above the north shore of the Black Sea from the Dnipro eastwards along the northern base of the Caucasus to the area abutting the north shore of the Caspian Sea, across the Volga to come up against the domain of the approximately contemporaneous and somewhat related Andronovo culture. The name comes from Russian 'сруб' (srub), "timber framework", from the way graves were constructed. Animal parts were buried with the body. The economy was mixed agriculture and livestock breeding. The historic Cimmerians have been suggested as descended from this culture. The Srubna culture was succeeded by Scythians and Sarmatians in the 1st millennium BCE, and by Khazars and Kipchaks in the 1st millennium CE. (Ref. J. P. Mallory, "Lower Mikhaylovka group", Encyclopedia of Indo-European Culture, Fitzroy Dearborn, 1997).

Starohorozheno – a village in the Bashtan district of Mykolaiv region, over the River Inhul/ Ingul. It is known for its expressive Aryan kurhans with stelae, embodying Indra, Vishnu, and others.

Starosillia – a village 8 km from the district centre of Velyko-Olexandrivsk, Kherson region. Distinguished by High Grave and the Starosillia archaeological culture (Starosillia type Alazan-Bedensk Caucasian culture).

Stone Grave – prehistoric *Shu-Nun*: '*Hand/Law of the Empress*' of Aratta and Sumer. A unique hill near a settlement in the Melitopol district of the Zaporizhia region. Since 1889, its 63 caves, grottoes and rock slabs/plaques with images and symbols dated from 12th millennium BCE to the 1st millennium CE have been investigated. The worldwide importance of this monument is attributable to its archive of proto-Sumerian ancient writing, deciphered in 1994-2001 by linguist A. G. Kifishin.

Stonehenge – The famous sanctuary-observatory (Aryan *maidan*; "henge" or "rotunda", as such constructions are conventionally named in the West), constructed in phases, roughly 3rd – 2nd millennium BCE. Situated on Salisbury Plain in England.

Stovbuvata Mohyla* – the largest kurhan in the Poltava region, near the city of Kremenchuk.

Stryboh* – (Stribog, Stribozh, Strzybog) in the Slavic pantheon, is the god and spirit of the winds, sky and air; he is said to be the ancestor (grandfather) of the winds of the eight directions. (Encyclopedia of Ukraine).

Sukhur ('Carp') – antediluvian first-being of Proto-Sumerian mythology, attested for the first time in the most ancient inscriptions of Stone Grave, Ukraine.

Sumer – a collection of related city-states in Mesopotamia dating from the end of the 4th – 3rd millennium BCE. The Sumerians derived themselves from Aratta from which they became physically separated (from the basin of the future Meotida?) as a result of "the Flood", the flooded settlement in the lower reaches of the rivers to the Black Sea. From the end of 2600 BCE, Sumer fell under the authority of the semitic dynasty of Akkad and was much later transformed into the Babylonian empire then modern Iraq.

Surabhi* – a divine bovine-goddess in Vedic mythology, mother of all cows (later incorporated into Hinduism). As an Earth goddess she symbolises 'plenty' but only if the earth's resources are properly developed, then the world is like an ever-yielding cow from which virtue, profit and pleasure may be milked.

Surashtra* – a region of western India, located on the Arabian Sea coast of Gujarat state.

Suria – supreme 'Sun' God of the Aryans, Slavs and Hindus. The earliest embodiment is traced in burial No. 8 of High Grave, Ukraine (2,300 BCE).

Surozh – the importance of the Surozh tribe and their region of Crimea is reflected in the old name for the Black Sea, called the Sea of Sourozh at that time. The city of Surozh was built by Cimmerians about 3000 years ago and became the centre of Surozhian Rus; today this is the city of Sudak in eastern Crimea.

Svaroh – the solar zodiac who embodied (according to *The Veles Book* and others) "single and multiple (manifestations)" of the God of Slavs. Known also to Indo-Aryans (as Svarga) and the Berbers. There is a belief that the biblical Hosts, formed by the descendants of Pelasgians of Palestine, were derived from Svaroh.

Svarozhych* – god of the sun, fire, and hearth in Slavic religion. In myth he may have been the son of Svaroh/Svarog and the brother of Dazhboh/Dazhbog, or he may have been identical to the latter. (Encyclopaedia Britannica).

Svayamvara (Indian folktale) – Arattan-Aryan. The selection of an eligible bachelor by a girl who does the wooing. This custom persisted in Ukraine until the 18th century and echoes remained in the word ***Svayba*** (a Ukrainian folktale). This custom is referred to in the song "Oh, ascend Moon" from the national collection of the popular kobzar [player of the Slavic kobza musical instrument], Vasily Nechepa.

Svetovid* – the Slavic deity of war, fertility and abundance, sometimes referred to as Beli (or Byali) Vid, He is also associated with divination and depicted as a four-headed god with two heads looking forward and two back. A statue portraying the god shows him with four heads, each one looking in a separate direction, a symbolic representation of the four directions of the compass, and also perhaps the four seasons of the year. Each face had a specific colour. The northern face was white (hence Byelorus, the White sea), the western - red (hence Chervona Rus'), the southern Black (hence the Black sea) and the eastern Green (hence Zeleny Klyn‡). (Ukrainian Soviet Encyclopedic dictionary, Kyiv, 1987).

Zaleny Klyn – is a historical Ukrainian name of the land in the Russian Far East area (between the Amur River and the Pacific Ocean), also known as the 'Green Ukraine'.

Sviata Vecheria* – (also known as *Svyaty Vechir*) or "Holy Supper" is the central tradition of the Christmas Eve celebrations in Ukrainian homes.

Svidertians – the name used by archaeologists for Eurasians generated in the glacial-adjacent areas between the Carpathians and the Baltic. They were the first to have invented the use of the bow and began to tame wild animals amongst which the dog became the first domestic animal.

Syria – (< Hurrian-Aryan-Slavic Suriya) the land between the Middle Euphrates and the Orontes, east coastal Phoenicia.

Syriac Chronicle* – a truncated and anonymously revised Syrian version (mid 6th century) of the *Ecclesiastical history* composed by the Greek historian Zachariah the Rhetor, of Mitylene. The *Syriac Chronicle, Known as that of Zachariah of Mitylene* was translated into English by F. J. Hamilton & E. W. Brooks, Methuen & Co., London, 1899.

Tale of Bygone Years – a chronicle of the church-state, begun in Rus in the 12th century by Nestor, a monk of the Kyiv-Pechersk Lavra. The beginning of the chronicle bears on the testimonies of pagan times – and on *The Veles Book*.

Tale of the Campaign of Ihor Svyatoslavlich – epic tale of the campaign of Novhorod-Siversky Prince Ihor (1151-1202) in 1185 CE against the Polovets. The unsuccessful campaign motivated the author (Olstyn Oleksych) to call for the union of Rus on the eve of the Tatar-Kazakh (by previous studies - Tatar-Mongol) invasion. The poem was found in 1795 CE amongst the works of an ancient collection and issued for the first time in 1800 CE. Prior to the divulgence of the *Veda Slovena*, in the second half of the 19th century and a further century for *The Veles Book*, *The Tale* presented a level of poetic skill and patriotic ideology of Rus of that time that seemed so improbable that scientists tried to declare this work (and eventually the two others) as fake. After also finding the *Boyan Anthem*, it is necessary to exclude doubts and affirm the idea that it is precisely from *The Tale* that an epoch of Renaissance (of ancient, pagan culture – in defiance of church dominance) should begin in Europe – an epoch during which the West was only involved in the process of Renaissance for just two centuries.

Talianky – village in the Talne district of the Cherkasy region, near to the largest Trypillian city of Aratta of late 4th millennium BCE.
*The remains of a prehistoric settlement near the village, belonging to the Cucuteni-Trypillian culture, are the largest known in Europe during the Neolithic period. (Videyko, M. Yu. (2011). "Trypillia Culture Proto-Cities: 40 Years of Investigations". *Trypillian Civilisation Journal*). Talianky covered an area of about 450 ha, 3.5km x 1.1km, and supported 15,000 citizens in 2700 houses. The largest buildings were truly immense, 300-600 meters long with many rooms, with the walls and ceilings decorated with black and red patterns. Situated between the villages of Legedzine and Talianky, the site was excavated from 1981 under V. Kruts.

Taman – the peninsula opposite the [Crimean] city of Kerch, behind the homonymous strait. Formerly Eya, Syndica, Tamarkha, Tmutarakan.

Tank* – or roll, a form of religious art, particularly of Tibetan Buddhism. Tanks usually depict Buddha, or the lives of saints and great teachers.

Targitai – Progenitor of the Skoloty, the earliest representative of the ethnogenesis of Slavs (according to ancient Scythian traditions).

Taurida – the name of Aryan Crimea in ancient Scythian and Byzantian times. It meant, possibly, Taur-*Ida* – the goddess of sacrifices to Taurus and bulls, related to Tauropola, i.e. 'Bull protectress' (Artemis). Such sacrifices in the form of burned bovine jaws-bones were characteristic for a sanctuary of the Maiden in the Gurzuf Anticline investigated in the last decades of the 20th century by N. G. and V. I. Novichenkov.

Taur(os) – the ancient name of the Dniester and the city in its lower reaches which preceded the modern city of Bilhorod-Dniestrovsk; the name originated from taur, or tour - a type of ancient bull which lived in the northern area of the Black Sea.

Telchines – In Greek mythology, they were the original inhabitants of Rhodes. According to one legend, there were nine Telchines, children of Thalassa and Pontus. They had flippers instead of hands and dogs' heads and were known as fish children [Eustathius on Homer, p.771]. They were regarded as excellent metallurgists and made a trident for Poseidon and a sickle for Cronos. It was believed they could assume any shape they pleased [Diodorus Siculus, *Library of History*, 5. 55.]

Theodoric the Great* – (born CE 454 – died Aug. 30, 526), king of the Ostrogoths (from 471), who invaded Italy in 488 and completed the conquest of virtually the entire peninsula and Sicily by 493, making himself king of Italy (493–526) and establishing his capital at Ravenna. (Encyclopaedia Britannica).

Tiras* – the ancient name of the Dniester River.

Titans – 'renowned' deities of the earliest (Pelasgian) formation of Greek mythology, the children of Gaia-[Earth] and Uranus [-Sky]. The names of the 6 (or 7, since some myths name Apollo) brothers embody the months of a half-year: Oceanus, Coeus (father of Leto), Crius, Hyperion, Iapetus (son of the Hyperborean Pelasga; biblical Japheth), Kronos (father of Zeus); the names of the 6 sisters were: Tethys, Phoebe (grandmother of Apollo), Mnemosyne, Theia, Themis, Rhea (mother of Zeus). The earliest (1,800 BCE) Titanic embodiment of Apollo and his father-rival Zeus are found in the Ingul burials No. 13 and No. 11 of kurhan No. 1-II near the village of Kairy.

Tocharians* – the Tocharian-speaking inhabitants of the Tarim Basin were the easternmost speakers of Indo-European languages in antiquity. (Watson, Burton. Trans. 1993.

Records of the Grand Historian of China: Han Dynasty II. Translated from the *Shiji* of Sima Qian. Chapter 123: "The Account of Dayuan," Columbia University Press. Revised Edition. ISBN 0-231-08166-9, p. 234). The term Tocharian or Tokharian has a complex history. It is based on the ethnonym *Tokharoi* used by Greek historians (e.g. Ptolemy VI, 11, 6). The Greeks first mentioned the Tocharians in the 1st century BCE, when Strabo presented them as a Scythian tribe and explained that the Tocharians – together with the Assianis, Passianis and Sakaraulis – took part in the destruction of the Greco-Bactrian kingdom in the second half of the 2nd century BCE. (Strabo, 11-8-1).

Trihlav — meaning 'three-headed', the co-essential embodiment of Svaroh, Perun and Svitovyd (according to *The Veles Book*); the embodiment of the Trinity and the tri-seasonal calendar of Aryan times.

Trajan — Roman emperor; in 101-106 CE he successfully fought with Dacia, allies of the *Slavs*. One consequence of these wars was the partial transfer of the name Trajan to the ancient, pre-existing Earth-walls (in some places built/repaired by the hands of Roman captives); venerated by *Slavs*.

Transcarpathian Region – The Zakarpatska Oblast (administrative Region) of SW Ukraine, on the south-western slopes of the Carpathian Mountains.

Trinity, trident and others – the highest principle of the universe. Arising from its three dimensions, or levels, were the seasons of the year (in the earliest calendars. Summer was later allocated to the division between spring and autumn).

Triptolemos* – a demi-god of the Eleusinian mysteries who presided over the sowing of grain-seed and the milling of wheat. In myth, Triptolemos was one of the Eleusinian princes who received Demeter kindly when she came mourning the loss of her daughter Persephone. In return, Demeter instructed Triptolemos in the art of agriculture and gave him a winged chariot drawn by serpents so that he might travel the world spreading her gift. When he came to teach the arts of agriculture to Lynceus, King of the Scythians, Lynceus refused to teach it to his people and, having tried to kill Triptolemus, Demeter turned him into a lynx. Triptolemus was equally associated with the bestowal of hope for the afterlife associated with the expansion of the Eleusinian Mysteries (Kerenyi, Karl, 1967. *"Eleusis: Archetypal Image of Mother and Daughter* (Princeton:Bollingen Series LXV.4).

Troad* – (or **Troas)** the land of Troy, ancient district formed mainly by the north-western projection of Asia Minor (modern Turkey) into the Aegean Sea. It extended from the Gulf of Edremit (ancient Adramyttion) on the south to the Sea of Marmara and the Dardanelles on the north and from the Ida mountain range and its northerly foothills on the east to the Aegean on the west. (Encyclopaedia Britannica).

Trojan earth-walls — Also called Serpent walls and, in Moldavian, 'Val' meaning earth wall, (see Fig. 86, example at Trypillia). There is no connection [of this name] with the Roman emperor Trajan.

Troy – the primary name of Ilion/Ilium (from between 900-800 BCE). The name is associated with the triple-stage city-wall, erected by three tribes of Pelasgians and others.

Trypillia – a village, now a town, near Kyiv. It stands under a Maiden-hill on the right bank of the Dnipro River, from which the three multi-kilometre long Serpent earth-walls diverge. From them, perhaps, the name Trypillia is derived (Arattan-Pelasgian, Three-polis, 'Thrice defended' place). Based on materials from the 1893 excavation there, the culture associated with this settlement was distinguished as the Trypillian archaeological culture («Trypillia»), which is a reflection of Aratta, the apotheosis of the most ancient state in the world (according to Kifishin – Shilov).

Trysuttya* – a famous Ukrainian symbol, representing the Tree of Life, combining the three mythological archetypes of Slavic wisdom - Java, Nava and Prava.

Tsehelnia – appears to be the earliest kurhan in the world, located above the floodplain of the mouth of the River Psel near the village of Podluzhe in the Kremenchuk district of the Poltava region. Excavations in 1992 showed that it was founded by the carriers of the early Seredny-Stoh and of the developed Dnipro-Donets archaeological cultures between the 5th – 4th millennium BCE. The kurhan reflected the origin of the main Vedic mythology and of yoga, and also the archetypes of conception, embryo, generation, resurrection and revival.

Tsnori – Georgian hamlet above the river Alazan. Known for the large kurhans of Alazan-Bedensk archaeological culture of the 3rd – 2nd millennium BCE excavated in 1970 by Sh. Sh. Dedabrishvili.

Tsyhancha – a kurhan near Chaush kurhan that is situated in the lower reaches of the Danube. Constructed by Aryans, it left a unique human sacrifice, which embodied Purusha. Later, the Scythians dug a chamber into the kurhan and arranged a unique sanctuary in it with a stone idol of the Primogenitor, which was later buried. Tsyhancha is named in a local legend, used by A. S. Pushkin in the creation of the poem *The Gypsies (the death of Zemfira).*

Tuva* – A Republic situated in the far south of Siberia.

Ubaid period* – a prehistoric period of Mesopotamia. The tell (mound) of **al-`Ubaid** west of nearby Ur in southern Iraq has given its name to the prehistoric Neolithic to Chalcolithic [cf. Eneolithic] culture, which represents the earliest settlement on the alluvial plain of southern Mesopotamia. The Ubaid culture had a long duration beginning before 5300 BCE and lasting until the beginning of the Uruk period, c. 4000 BCE. (Carter, Robert A. and Philip, Graham *Beyond the Ubaid: Transformation and Integration in the Late Prehistoric Societies of the Middle East (Studies in Ancient Oriental Civilisation, Number 63)* The Oriental Institute of the University of Chicago (2010) ISBN 978-1-885923-66-0).

Ugrians* – the ancestors of the present Magyars of Hungary. In the 12th-century Primary Chronicle (by Nestor), the ancestors of the Hungarians are called Ugry, or Ugrians.

Ukraine – the 'Sacred (heartwood) Country' of ancient Scythians, perhaps since Aratto-Aryan times, which began to be formed under the leadership of the caste of Ukrs, priests and others. By the 12th – 13th centuries its formation continued to be led by warriors and later it was identified by Muscovites as 'Okraina (borderland). From the mid 17th century, in the circumstance of the war of national liberation under the leadership of Hetman Bohdan Khmelnytsky, the name Ukraine replaced the former name of this territory as Rus, again fulfilling a prophecy of eternal significance.

Uliches (**Ugliches**)* — (Уличи (Угличи) in Russian, Уличі (Угличі) in Ukrainian) were a tribe of Early Eastern Slavs who, along with Tiverians and Bessarabians, inhabited the territories along the rivers Bug, Lower Dnipro and the Black Sea coast between the 8th - 10th centuries. The tribal name comes from their location in Bessarabia called Ugol (corner) in Slavic and Ογλος in Greek (Greek ογλος, "an angle or corner"). (Runciman, Steven (1930). *A History of the First Bulgarian Empire*. London: George Bell & Sons. OCLC 832687).

Unified whole* – conveys the complex meaning of a constant, indivisible singular whole, an immutable elementary or fundamental state.

Upanishads* – philosophical texts considered to be an early source of Hindu religion. More than 200 are known, of which the first dozen or so, the oldest and most important, are variously referred to as the principal, main (*mukhya*) or old Upanishads. The oldest of these, the *Brihadaranyaka*, Jaiminiya Upanisadbrahmana and the *Chandogya* Upanishads, were composed during the pre-Buddhist era of India. (Ref. Olivelle, Patrick (1998), *Upaniṣads*, Oxford University Press, ISBN 0192822926).

Uranus – Arattan-Sumerian *Urash* (sky god), the earliest god of Greek mythology, also well known to Slavs and Thracians. God of heaven, grandfather of Zeus. The story of how Uranus was castrated by his son Kronos ('Time') reflects the change of the calendar systems.

Usan* – the successor of Kavi Kavata was Kavi Usan (Persian Kai Kaus), whose name has been compared with that of an ancient seer who is known as Kavya Usanas in the Vedas, where he is renowned for his wisdom. There he is said to have driven the cows on the path of the sun and to have fashioned for Indra the thunderbolt with which the god slew Vritra. The identification is not quite certain, however, because the character of Usan was completely altered in Persia into that of an ordinary king, although a trace of his quality of driver of cows may perhaps survive in the legend of his wonderful ox, to whose judgement all disputes were referred with regard to the boundary between Persia and Turan. (Ref. Persian Mythology, by Albert J. Carnoy, Chapter V. Traditions of the Kings and Zoroaster. (http://rbedrosian.com/carn5.htm))

Usativ – a village near Odessa. Famed for its Aratto-Aryan (Orianian) kurhans and settlement, as well as a Cossack cemetery with stone crosses, respectively decorated with pagan symbolism.

Ushanas* – the name of a Vedic rishi (i.e. a "seer" to whom the Vedas were originally revealed) with the patronymic *Kāvya* (descendant of Kavi, Atharvaveda 4.29.6), who was later identified with Shukra. (Ref. http://encyclopedia.thefreedictionary.com/Ushanas).

Ushas – Goddess of the morning dawn (and New Year); daughter and spouse of Suria. "Most liked to Indra" (according to the *Rigveda*) owing to the involvement of both towards the mythological rituals of Aryan kurhans, [i.e. where Indra released the dawn goddess from imprisonment.]

Utu* – Sun god in Sumerian mythology. He was son of the Sumerian moon god Nanna and goddess Ningal. His brother was Ishkur and his sisters were Inanna and Erishkigal. He corresponds to the Akkadian god Shamash. Utu was not only the sun-god but in charge of justice and righteousness, but also the God of Music & Song, and is said to have invented the lyre and flute. (TMH NF, no.5 by Dina Katz, Leiden; Merriam-Webster's Enc. of World Religions.)

Vainamoinen* – a central character in Finnish folklore and the main character in the national epic Kalevala. Originally a Finnish god, he was described as an old and wise man, and he possessed a potent, magical voice.

Vaishya – commoners, a Varna (then a caste) which was subordinate to the Varna Brahmans and Rajania. Corresponds to the Indian vish(s)a and the Rusy vesi [villages] (recorded as "cities and villages" with the meaning of a 'rural district', of the peasantry).

Vajri (< Aryan vaja, 'seed') – the magical weapon of the god Rudra and Hero-serpent-warrior Indra. Principally imagined as phallus-like club-like, symbols of which (particularly allied to maces from Aryan burials) persisted in Ukraine and into Cossack time.

Vala – the egg-shaped embryo of the New Year (Spring equinox) universe, in compliance with the main mythology of the *Rigveda*.

Van, Sevan – Lakes in the territory of Armenia (Transcaucasia), near which, in the mid-2nd. millennium BCE, the important centres of Aryans were concentrated and, derived from them, the Cimmerians and Vans, whose settlements in Asia Minor Troad and Scandinavian Svineld (Sweden) related the Aryans with the Trojans and the Germans.

Vandals – and their successors, the Berbers are the Slavic tribe of Balts who earned fame by their final victory over Rome; their direct descendants are now living in the African Sahara.

Vara* – Sacred concept that an observed order in Nature exists which corresponds with the aspect of physical reality as expressed in buildings and sustainable designs of settlements. Vara symbolised man's alignment with, and acknowledged respect for, a sacred, harmonic 'order' in nature.

Varaha* – (Sanskrit: "Boar") the third of the 10 incarnations (avatars) of the Hindu god Vishnu. When a demon named Hiranyaksha dragged the earth to the bottom of the sea, Vishnu took the form of a boar in order to rescue it. (Encyclopaedia Britannica).

Varangians* – or Varyags, sometimes referred to as Variagians, were mainly Baltic Slavs living at the south coast of Baltic Sea. Varyags were warriors who acted as guards of trade caravans, mainly by sea and rivers. The Ukrainian word 'variazhyty' means to plough the sea. The word 'barge' is probably derived from 'variag', 'variazhity' (in Ukrainian, soft letters (like "v") sometimes may be substituted for a hard one (as "b"). Their Viking Norsemen went southwards and eastwards through what is now Belarus, Ukraine and Russia mainly in the 9th and 10th centuries. (Schultze, Sydney (2000). *Culture and Customs of Russia.* Greenwood Publishing Group. p. 5.

ISBN 0313311013).

Varna – Varna was different from subsequent caste systems because it was defined not by a person's lineage, but by their individual abilities.

Varuna (>Vparuna>Perun of *The Veles Book*) – the supreme deity of the underworld (night, celestial ocean, underworld), one of the principal sons of Foremother Aditi. Overseer of the implementation of Universal law; Asura, but also Dev. His image is traced for the first time, beside the image of his brother Mitra, in murals from High Grave (tomb No. 4, mid-3rd millennium BCE).

Varyags* – sometimes referred to as *Variagians*.

Vasistha – ancestor of one of the Brahmanic clans who authored the collection of sacred anthems of the *Rigveda*. From this Aryan Brahman, devotee of god Varuna, came the "oseledets" haircut, and perhaps the name Co(a)zach (< kosak < kosa [plait]), i.e. Cossack.

Veche* (or **Viche**) – a popular assembly that was a characteristic institution in Russia from the 10th to the 15th century. The *veche* probably originated as a deliberative body among early Slavic tribes. As the tribes settled in permanent trading centres, which later became cities, the *veche* remained as an element of democratic rule, sharing power with a prince and an aristocratic council. Although its power varied from city to city, the *veche* could generally accept or reject the prince who "inherited" the city and, by controlling the town's militia, could veto a prince's plans for a military campaign. (Encyclopaedia Britannica). The word is inherited from Proto-Slavic *větje*, meaning 'council' or 'talk' (which is also represented in the word "soviet", both ultimately deriving from a Proto-Slavic verbal stem of větiti 'to talk, speak'). (Max Vasmer's *Etymological dictionary of the Russian Language*, published as *Russisches Etymologisches Wörterbuch* in four volumes by Heidelberg University in 1950-58. The Russian translation of Vasmer's dictionary with extensive commentaries by Oleg N. Trubachev was printed in 1964-73). The semantic derivation that yields the meaning of the word veche is parallel to that of *parliament*.

Veda (< Slavic **Wise** > wizard and witch) – highest learned and written Knowledge, embodied in sacred texts of Aryan peoples. These texts include: the Indo-Aryan *Vedas* (Rigveda, Yajuveda, Samaveda and Atharvaveda), the *Veda Slovena* (Slavic Veda), the Irano-Aryan *Avesta*, and the Icelandic *Edda*.

Veda Slovena – the earliest of the Vedas, found and published (in Belgrade and St. Petersburg) by Serbian ethnologist S. I. Verkovich in the Rodope mountains (Bulgaria) in the second half of the 19th century. The third edition is presently being prepared in Moscow (*Science and religion*, 2001, No. 2 and following).

Veles – (<Volokh<Vola of *The Veles Book* < Aryan Vala< Vlas of the *Veda Slovena*) humane, favoured God of netherworld; patron of stock raising, animal husbandry and trade, as well as of the dead.

Veles Book – a sacred assemblage of legends, fables, doctrines and teachings of Slavs from the 1st millennium BCE – 879 CE. Historic memories recorded by priests on wooden boards, which came down to the 20th century perhaps from the library of Yaroslav the Wise. The recorded history begins c. 19th millennium BCE (corresponding with dates of the earliest myths at Stone Grave; a Kyiv Region myth recording 198 centuries of the Earth's existence; preserved references in Slavic folk-lore about ornamentation of mammoths, as well as the maximum glaciation of the 20th – 17th millennium BCE).

*The book was allegedly discovered in 1919 and lost in 1941 but opinions about the authenticity of the book are divided. Whilst Academic Science of Russia strongly advocated *The Veles Book* to be fake, Academic Science of Ukraine takes a softer stance with proponents of its authenticity among leaders of the academic research institutions. ("Ukrainian Studies: Textbook". Authors led by Professor P. Kononenko (Director of State Research Institute of Ukrainian Studies). – Kyiv, 1996 (§ 4. "Ukraine, nation, state". The goddess "Mother Glory")).

Velianas* – King of Caere, Italy, is mentioned in the Etruscan golden Pyrgi tablets having made a dedication to the Phoenician goddess Ashtaret. ('Velianas sal cluvenias' is his name in Etruscan.)

Velykden [Great Day, Easter in Ukraine] – It arises, perhaps, from the New Year of 'Veles day'. The presence of Ordinary Velykden, (B)Rahmanski, Mretski or Navski, and Babski reaches back to matriarchal Aratta and indicates changes at the turning-points of the zodiacal constellations, which were falling on the New Year Spring equinox. It can be assumed that these Velykden titles reflected the consecutively retrospective supremacy in the calendar of Pisces, Aries, Taurus and Gemini between our time and 5th – 7th millennium BCE. This assumption is confirmed by the presence of a Great Day (the obvious explanation of the name Velykden) at Sumer, as well as by dating the appearance of Ukrainian pysanky-art.

*In Ukraine there are several different forms of Velykden (Great Day). Babski is one of these but there is also a Rahmanski Velykden. This is not as widespread as the conventional Velykden but both involve baking cakes and decorating eggs "which are consecrated in the church (though not without complaints from some priests about paganism)". The essential difference from the conventional Velykden is the specific imitation of the allied Red Hill celebration. (Ref. Shilov, *Origins of Slavic Civilisation*, Part II: *The Vedantic Heritage of Ukraine*. 2008. Moscow. ISBN 978-98967-006-0).

Velyko-Olexandrivsk kurhan – excavated in 1981. Two cromlechs at the base of the kurhan contained burials of descendants from Sumer and Aratta, and also almost the earliest Aryan Brahmin whose varna arose as a result of the interrelations of Aratta and Sumer with the Aryans.

Venedi/Veneti/Enedi/Eneti and others – a Slavic tribe (that, according to the opinion of Roman-Byzantine historians, gave rise to the Ants and Sklavins) who came from the Northern Azov area into Asia Minor and Troad at the beginning of the 2nd millennium BCE and after the Trojan War in the 13th (or, rather, 11th) century BCE, went under the leadership of Aeneas and Antenor, to northern Italy and the Adriatic. According to the testimonies of *The Veles Book*, ancient authors and archaeological data, in the 9th – 7th – 5th centuries BCE, the Veneti migrated from there to the southern Baltic area, from where in the 3rd – 5th century CE they partially returned, during the corresponding migration of Goths, to the Slavic ancestral home – possibly having generated here the Ants of the Northern Black Sea area.

*These people were called *Veneti* by the Romans and *Enetoi* by the Greeks.

Venetic* – an extinct Indo-European language that was spoken in ancient times in the North-Italian Veneto and modern Slovenia, between the River Po delta and the southern fringe of the Alps. The language is attested by over 300 short inscriptions dating from the 6th to the 1st century BCE. Its speakers are identified with the ancient people called *Veneti* by the Romans and *Enetoi* by the Greeks. (Wallace, Rex (2004). *Venetic*, Roger D. Woodard (ed.), The Cambridge Encyclopedia of the World's Ancient Languages, University of Cambridge, pp. 840-856. ISBN 0-521-56256-2).

Verbivka – a village near the village of Burty (Cherkasy region), noted for its kurhan investigated by A. A. Bobrinsky in 1903. It is possible, this was one of the ancient, Arattan kurhans. On the plates of its cromlech was read (by Sumerologist A. G. Kifishin) the names of the Aratto-Sumerian goddesses Gatumdug and Inanna.

Vesnianky* – the ancient spring festival.

Vinča culture* – an early culture of Neolithic Europe between the 6th and 3rd millennium BCE, stretching around the course of the Danube in what today are Serbia, Hungary, Croatia, Bosnia and Herzegovina, Romania, Bulgaria, Macedonia, Montenegro and Greece. (Chapman, John (2000). *Fragmentation in Archaeology: People, Places, and Broken Objects*, p.239. London: Routledge. ISBN 978-0415158039). Vinča settlements were considerably larger than any other contemporary European culture, in some instances surpassing the cities of the Aegean and early Near Eastern Bronze Age a millennium later. The largest sites, more than 29 hectares, may have had populations of up to 2,500 individuals. (Chapman, John (1981). *The Vinča culture of south-east Europe: Studies in chronology, economy and society (2 vols)*. BAR International Series. **117**. Oxford: B.A.R. ISBN 0-86054-139-8).

Vishna* – a male god in the *Veda Slovena*. (V. Krasnoholovets).

Vishnu – 'All embracing' creator-God of Arattans, Slavs, Aryans, and Hindus; He helped the hero serpent-warrior Indra to implement his cosmogonic act – the main mythology of the *Rigveda*.

Voivode* – the commander of an army in medieval Russia; also in the Muscovite period, the governor of a town or province. (Oxford Russian Dictionary, 3rd edition, Oxford University Press, 2000).

Volhvs* (Volkhvy, Magi) – A pagan priest in pre-Christian Rus'. *Volkhvy* were believed to possess mystical powers, particularly the ability to predict the future. The first literary reference to a *volkhv* occurs in the Primary Chronicle under the year 912; there, the priest-soothsayer predicts Prince Oleh's death. (Canadian Institute of Ukrainian Studies, Encyclopedia of Ukraine).

Vritra – netherworld Serpent, the embodiment of negative qualities of Asura, the main adversary of Indra in development of the main mythology of the *Rigveda*. It relates to Vratar and the "Grief-Grief Mound" [burial kurhan of the ancestors] at the centre of Slavic Vesnianky (ancient spring festival) also Red Hill Day which can take place on a mound, hill or a burial kurhan.

Vytautas – the last great prince (1392-1430) of the Grand Duchy of Lithuania, who gathered together the lands of Kyivan Rus after its dissolution resulting from the Tatar-mongol invasion in the 13th century.

World Deluge – a legendary event of the 4th millennium (?) BCE recorded in the chronicle of Stone Grave and in the Sumerian *Epic of Gilgamesh*, the source for the flood described in the Bible. According to the latest geological data: the Bosphorus strait formed as a consequence of the level of the Black Sea (formerly not connected, rather like the current Caspian and Aral Seas) catastrophically rising by dozens of metres, inundating the northern coasts as far as 300 km and forming the Sea of Azov.

Yajurveda* – the third of the four Vedas, canonical texts of Hinduism. It contains liturgical texts used during various important Hindu rituals.

Yama – a deity of the netherworld in the Aryan Vedas and *The Veles Book* of Slavs. His successor is Aryan Ima from the *Veda Slovena* and others.

Yamna culture* – or "Pit [Grave] Culture", a Copper–Bronze Age culture of the late 3rd to early 2nd millennium BCE that existed along the Dnipro River, in the steppe region, in the Crimea, near the Danube River estuary, and in locations east of Ukraine (up to the Urals). Sites have been excavated since the mid-19th century, and the culture was classified by Vasilii Gorodtsov in the early 20th century. This culture took its name from pit graves used for burials in family or clan kurhans. Corpses were covered with red ochre and laid either in a supine position or on their sides with flexed legs. Grave goods included egg-shaped pottery containing food, stone, bone, and copper implements, weapons, and adornments. The culture's major economic occupation was animal husbandry, with agriculture, hunting, and fishing of secondary importance. Excavations at Pit-Grave sites also revealed primitive carts that were pulled by oxen and stelae bearing images of humans. The people of this culture usually lived in surface dwellings in fortified settlements. They had contacts with tribes in northern Caucasia and with Trypillian culture tribes in Ukraine. Significant culture sites include Mykhaylivka settlement and Storozhova Mohyla. (Encyclopedia of Ukraine, Vol. 4. 1993).

Yangshao culture* – a Neolithic culture that existed extensively along the central Yellow River in China. It is dated from around 5,000 to 3,000 BCE and named after the first excavated representative village of this culture, which was discovered in 1921 in the Henan Province by the Swedish archaeologist Johan Gunnar Andersson (1874-1960). Although early reports suggested a matriarchal culture, others argue that it was a society in transition from matriarchy to patriarchy, while still others believe it to have been patriarchal. The debate hinges around differing interpretations of burial practices. (Jiao, Tianlong (2001). *Gender Studies in Chinese Neolithic Archaeology*. In Arnold, Bettina; Wicker, Nancy L. *Gender and the Archaeology of Death*. AltaMira Press. pp. 53–55. ISBN 0-0759-0137-X). The archaeological site of Banpo village, near Xi'an, is one of the best-known ditch-enclosed settlements of the

Yangshao culture. Another major settlement called Jiangzhai was excavated out to its limits, and archaeologists found that it was completely surrounded by a ring-ditch. Both Banpo (4800-4200 BCE) and Jiangzhai also yielded controversial incised marks on pottery which a few have interpreted as numerals or perhaps precursors to the Chinese script. (Woon, Wee Lee (1987). *Chinese Writing: Its Origin and Evolution.* Joint Publishing, Hong Kong).

Yaroslav Mudryi (Yaroslav the Wise) – the greatest prince of Kyivan Rus (1034-1054), who expanded the frontiers of Rus as far as the Black and Baltic Seas, up to the Carpathians and the River Oka to the east. An outstanding warrior, diplomat, builder, the compiler of the archive of laws of Rusian Truth and the collector of a famous library – part of which became the dowry of his daughter Anna, Queen of France. Between the 18th – 19th century a part of his library was at last brought to Russia.

Yasha – reminiscent of the mammoth in Slavic folk-lore.

Yava – earthly, "white world" of Slavic-pagans.
* In Slavic mythology Yava was the land of the living.

Yoga – Indo-Aryan doctrine for the 'harness', 'ways' of improving a person.

Yuga – 'team' or 'generation', meaning an Epoch of the Vedas. Scientists connected it with the Day of Brahma, the origins of which are traced in Aratta, as well as in some Aryan kurhans (e.g. High Grave, Garman, Savur-grave and others).

Yuri Day* – April 23rd. In the calendar of many countries, first names are associated with particular days of the year, principally because particular saints were celebrated on those days. Since the name Yuri (Yuriy, or Jurij) is the Ukrainian and Russian variant of George, Yuri Day is St. George's Day.

Zarubyntsi culture* – a culture that from the 3rd century BCE until 1st century CE flourished in the area north of the Black Sea along the upper and middle Dnipro and Pripyat Rivers, stretching west towards the Boh River [in the communist time, the name was changed to Southern Bug]. Zarubintsy sites were particularly dense between the Rivers Desna and Ros as well as along the Pripyat River. It was identified around 1899 by the Czech-Ukrainian archaeologist V. V. Chvojka and is now attested by about 500 sites. The culture was named after finds of cremated remains in the village of Zarubyntsi, on the Dnipro. (J. P. Mallory, "Zarubintsy Culture", *Encyclopedia of Indo-European Culture*, Fitzroy Dearborn, 1997).

Zbruch Idol* – (see Fig. 136). A 9th - 10th century stone statue of an ancient Slavic god (commonly believed to be Sviatovyt/Svetovid, the god of war). It was discovered in 1848 in the Zbruch River near Horodnytsia, Ternopil region. Boris Rybakov (1987, *Paganism of Ancient Rus*, Moscow: Nauka), argued that four sides of the top tier represent four different Slavic gods, two female and two male, with their corresponding middle-tier entities always of the opposite gender. In Rybakov's hypothesis, the male deity with the horse and sword is Perun, the female with the horn of plenty is Mokosh, the female with the ring is Lada, and the male deity with the solar symbol, above the empty underworld, is Dažbog, (the God of sunlight for whom the sun was not an object but an attribute, thus the symbol's position on his clothing rather than in his hand). Further, Rybakov identifies the underworld deity as Veles. It is believed that the sculpture was disposed of in a pit some time after the baptism of Kyivan Rus, like the idols in Kyiv and Novgorod. In the 19th century, when the Zbruch River (Dniester's tributary) changed its bed, the area where the pillar was buried became submerged (Marta Zaitz, 2005, *Swiatowid - kamienny posag z IX wieku*, Museum's Website. Archaeological Museum of Kraków. Retrieved 2007-01-24). The statue is now on display in the Archaeological Museum in Kraków, Poland, with exact copies located in a number of museums, including the State Historical Museum in Moscow.

Zeus (Dii <Divas <Dyaus) – the supreme God of Pelasgians and Greeks; the head of Gods, living on Olympus.

Archaeological and traced records of Ukraine

Upper left : Aryan idol, 2nd millennium BCE.
Centre : Scythian idol, mid 1st millennium BCE.
Lower right : Old Rusian idol, end of 1st millennium CE.
Lower left : Proto-Sumerian inscription, 6th - 4th millennium BCE at Stone Grave (Zaporizhia region).
Upper right : Sanskrit-runic lines from *The Veles Book*, 1st millennium BCE - 9th century CE.

Made in the USA
Middletown, DE
14 May 2018